FROM
SIENA
TO
NUBIA

FROM
SIENA
TO
NUBIA

Alessandro Ricci in Egypt and Sudan, 1817–22

Translated and edited by
Daniele Salvoldi

The American University in Cairo Press
Cairo New York

This publication was made possible by the generous support of the American Research Center in Egypt.

First published in 2018 by
The American University in Cairo Press
113 Sharia Kasr el Aini, Cairo, Egypt
200 Park Avenue, Suite 1700, New York, NY 10166
www.aucpress.com

Dar el Kutub No. 10116/17
ISBN 978 977 416 854 3

Dar el Kutub Cataloging-in-Publication Data

Salvoldi, Daniele
    From Siena to Nubia: Alessandro Ricci in Egypt and Sudan, 1817–22 / Daniele Salvoldi.—Cairo: The American University in Cairo Press, 2018.
        p.   cm.
        ISBN: 978 977 416 854 3
        1. Ricci, Alessandro—ca 1795–1834—Travel
        2. Sinai (Egypt)—Description and travel
        3. Nubia (Egypt)—Description and travel
        916.2

1 2 3 4 5   22 21 20 19 18

Designed by Sally Boylan
Printed in China

To Maya, with love

Contents

Acknowledgments

A s can be expected in a work that has taken many years and many travels to be completed, the list of people that helped in numerous ways must be a long one. Back in 2008, Dr. Monica Hanna, whom later I had the luck to marry, directed me toward the National Archives of Egypt in search for new documents on early Egyptologists and deserves my first address of gratitude. My then-PhD supervisor at the University of Pisa, Prof. Maria Carmela Betrò, further directed my research toward the Ricci manuscript and encouraged me after its discovery up to a successful dissertation defense in 2011.

At the National Archives of Egypt, where I returned after the discovery for further research, I found a welcoming and stimulating environment which I owe to the open-mindedness of then-director Dr. Zain Abd al-Hadi and then–research director Dr. Emad Helal. In other archives and libraries I also found many people ready to help and make my research as pleasant as possible: special thanks go to Dr. Patricia Usick (Honorary Archivist, The British Museum) who constantly assisted me during my five months' Accademia dei Lincei grant in the United Kingdom in 2011 and afterward. I wish to remember with gratitude also the fruitful cooperation with Dr. James Grasby (Curator, Wessex Region, The National Trust), Maria Cristina Guidotti (Director, Egyptian Museum, Florence), Dr. Mark Forrest (Archive Service Officer, Dorset History Centre), Dr. Robert Gray (at the time, House and Collections Manager, Kingston Lacy, The National Trust), and the whole staff of the Dorset History Centre in Dorchester. The help of Prof. Dr. Karl-Joachim Seyfried (Field Director, Heidelberg Archaeological Mission), Dr. Sue Giles (Senior Collections Officer, World Cultures, Bristol Museum & Art Gallery), Dr. Joachim Karig (honorary member of staff, Neues Museum, Berlin), and Dr. Felicitas Weber (Ancient Egyptian Demonology Project, Swansea University) was also deeply appreciated. I am grateful to Mr. Fabrizio Finetti for showing me his letters of Alessandro Ricci and for his permission to use them in this study.

As the geographical, scientific, and historical frame covered by Ricci's work is really wide, many people helped me to find a way through it: Dr. Stefano Struffolino (Department of History, University of Milan) for Siwa and Dr. Eng. Ahmad Shams al-Din (Department of Archaeology, Durham University) for Sinai, in particular. I wish to thank also Prof. Gino Fornaciari (Full Professor of History of Medicine, University of Pisa), Dr. Bishoi Hanna (Biology Department, The University of New Mexico), and Mr. Matteo Donati (Veterinary Medicine Faculty, University of Milan). I am very grateful to Fr. Justin (Librarian, Holy Monastery of St. Catherine, South Sinai), who made accessible to me the entire Monastery of Saint Catherine and discussed with me some details of Ricci's account.

Because of the poor legibility of some of the drawings, especially those drawn in pencil on paper, due to the weak pencil marks and the spots of mold, ink, and dirt on the paper, a number of plates are published here as line tracings. These were all made by me, with the exception of plates 50.1, 51, 52, 53, 54, and 55.1–2, 5. These were made by Dr. Simon Delvaux, whom I warmly thank for his selfless help and sheer professionalism. Many thanks to Michael Hanna for helping with editing some of the maps.

Above all, I must thank the American Research Center in Egypt (ARCE), whose generous and patient support made this publication possible.

I am sure I have forgotten to mention many helpful colleagues and friends in this list, and I hope they will forgive me.

Sources of Plates

Plate 1[1]
Document 62, Ms. 300.4, Folder 17, Biblioteca Universitaria, Pisa[2]

Plate 2
No. 114 [1], Museo Egizio, Florence[3]

Plate 3
Number 1. No. 133 [1], Museo Egizio, Florence
Number 2. No. 133 [2], Museo Egizio, Florence
Number 3. No. 133 [3], Museo Egizio, Florence

Plate 4
No. 5, Museo Egizio, Florence

Plate 5
No. 109, Museo Egizio, Florence

Plate 6
(Left) No. 49, Museo Egizio, Florence; (Right) II.A.6, Deposit/Bankes of Kingston Lacy and Corfe Castle, Dorset History Centre, Dorchester[4]

Plate 7
Number 1. Document 22, Ms. 300.4, Folder 10, Fond Rosellini, Biblioteca Universitaria, Pisa
Number 2. II.A.12, Deposit/Bankes of Kingston Lacy and Corfe Castle, Dorset History Centre, Dorchester
Number 3. No. 36, Museo Egizio, Florence
Number 4. No. 135, Museo Egizio, Florence

Plate 8
II.A.17, Deposit/Bankes of Kingston Lacy and Corfe Castle, Dorset History Centre, Dorchester

Plate 9
Number 1. No. 117, Museo Egizio, Florence
Number 2. AES 1520, British Museum[5]
Number 4. No. 143, Museo Egizio, Florence

Plate 10
Number 1. No. 130, Museo Egizio, Florence
Number 2. No. 133 [4], Museo Egizio, Florence
Number 3. II.C.17, Deposit/Bankes of Kingston Lacy and Corfe Castle, Dorset History Centre, Dorchester
Number 4. No. 114 [2], Museo Egizio, Florence
Number 5. No. 114 [3], Museo Egizio, Florence

Plate 11
No. 133 [5], Museo Egizio, Florence

Plate 12
No. 119, Museo Egizio, Florence

Plate 13
No. 120, Museo Egizio, Florence

Plate 14
Number 1. No. 34, Museo Egizio, Florence
Number 2. XII.C.7, Deposit/Bankes of Kingston Lacy and Corfe Castle, Dorset History Centre, Dorchester
Number 3. XII.C.6, Deposit/Bankes of Kingston Lacy and Corfe Castle, Dorset History Centre, Dorchester
Number 4. No. 34, Museo Egizio, Florence
Numbers 5–6. XII.C.9, Deposit/Bankes of Kingston Lacy and Corfe Castle, Dorset History Centre, Dorchester
Numbers 7–8. XII.B.3, Deposit/Bankes of Kingston Lacy and Corfe Castle, Dorset History Centre, Dorchester

Plate 15
Number 1. XII.A.8, Deposit/Bankes of Kingston Lacy and Corfe Castle, Dorset History Centre, Dorchester

Plate 63
Number 1. XV.A.1, Deposit/Bankes of Kingston Lacy and Corfe Castle, Dorset History Centre, Dorchester
Number 2. XV.A.11, Deposit/Bankes of Kingston Lacy and Corfe Castle, Dorset History Centre, Dorchester
Numbers 3–5. No. 69, Museo Egizio, Florence
Numbers 6–7. No. 110, Museo Egizio, Florence
Plate 64
Number 1. XV.A.3, Deposit/Bankes of Kingston Lacy and Corfe Castle, Dorset History Centre, Dorchester
Number 2. XV.A.6, Deposit/Bankes of Kingston Lacy and Corfe Castle, Dorset History Centre, Dorchester
Plate 65
Number 1. (Left) XV.A.8a; (Right) XV.A.8, Deposit/Bankes of Kingston Lacy and Corfe Castle, Dorset History Centre, Dorchester
Numbers 2–3. XV.A.33, Deposit/Bankes of Kingston Lacy and Corfe Castle, Dorset History Centre, Dorchester
Plate 66
Number 1. XV.A.20, Deposit/Bankes of Kingston Lacy and Corfe Castle, Dorset History Centre, Dorchester
Number 2. XV.A.13, Deposit/Bankes of Kingston Lacy and Corfe Castle, Dorset History Centre, Dorchester
Number 3. XV.A.12, Deposit/Bankes of Kingston Lacy and Corfe Castle, Dorset History Centre, Dorchester
Number 4. XV.A.27, Deposit/Bankes of Kingston Lacy and Corfe Castle, Dorset History Centre, Dorchester
Number 5. XV.A.9, Deposit/Bankes of Kingston Lacy and Corfe Castle, Dorset History Centre, Dorchester
Plate 67
Numbers 1–2. XV.B.4, Deposit/Bankes of Kingston Lacy and Corfe Castle, Dorset History Centre, Dorchester
Number 4. XV.B.1, Deposit/Bankes of Kingston Lacy and Corfe Castle, Dorset History Centre, Dorchester
Plate 68
Numbers 1–2. No. 72, Museo Egizio, Florence

Plate 69
Numbers 1–2. No. 72, Museo Egizio, Florence
Numbers 3–4. XV.A.32, Deposit/Bankes of Kingston Lacy and Corfe Castle, Dorset History Centre, Dorchester
Plate 70
XVI.A.2, Deposit/Bankes of Kingston Lacy and Corfe Castle, Dorset History Centre, Dorchester
Plate 71
Number 1. No. 112, Museo Egizio, Florence
Number 4. No. 127, Museo Egizio, Florence
Number 7. No. 50, Museo Egizio, Florence
Plate 72
Number 2. No. 79, Museo Egizio, Florence
Number 4. No. 55, Museo Egizio, Florence
Number 5. No. 129, Museo Egizio, Florence
Number 6. No. 78, Museo Egizio, Florence
Number 8. No. 84, Museo Egizio, Florence
Plate 73
Number 1. No. 46, Museo Egizio, Florence
Number 10. No. 76, Museo Egizio, Florence
Plate 74
Numbers 1–5. No. 54, Museo Egizio, Florence
Plate 75
Number 1. II.B.2, Deposit/Bankes of Kingston Lacy and Corfe Castle, Dorset History Centre, Dorchester
Plate 76
Number 5. No. 47, Museo Egizio, Florence
Plate 77
Number 1. No. 53, Museo Egizio, Florence
Number 8. No. 43, Museo Egizio, Florence
Plate 78
Numbers 1–2. No. 52, Museo Egizio, Florence
Number 3. No. 44, Museo Egizio, Florence
Plate 79
No. 116, Museo Egizio, Florence
Plate 87
(Top) No. 121; (Bottom) No. 41, Museo Egizio, Florence
Plate 89
XXI.C.5, Deposit/Bankes of Kingston Lacy and Corfe Castle, Dorset History Centre, Dorchester
Plate 90
XXI.C.8–10, Deposit/Bankes of Kingston Lacy and Corfe Castle, Dorset History Centre, Dorchester

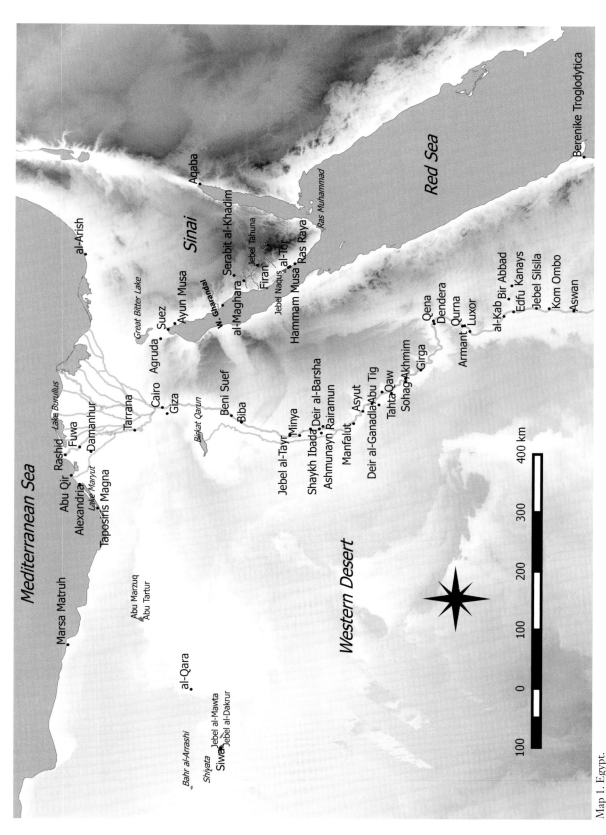

Map 1. Egypt.
Maps 1–10 © Daniele Salvoldi, 2017. Maps created with QGIS and Natural Earth Data.

Mediterranean Sea

Marsa Matruh

Abu Qir
Alexandria
Taposiris Magna

Rashid
Fuwa
Damanhur
Lake Maryut
Lake Burullus

Tarrana

al-Arish

Sinai

Aqaba

al-Qara

Bahr al-Arrashi
Shiyata
Jebel al-Mawta
Siwa Jebel al-Dakrur

Abu Marzuq
Abu Tartur

Cairo
Giza
Agruda
Suez

Great Bitter Lake

Ayun Musa
W. Gharandal
Serabit al-Khadim
al-Maghara
Firan
Jebel Tahuna
Jebel Naqus al-Tor
Hammam Musa Ras Raya

Ras Muhammad

Red Sea

Birkat Qarun

Beni Suef
Biba

Jebel al-Tayr
Minya
Shaykh Ibada Deir al-Barsha
Ashmunayn Rairamun
Manfalut
Asyut
Deir al-Ganadla Abu Tig
Tahta Qaw
Sohag Akhmim
Girga
Qena
Dendera
Armant Qurna
Luxor

al-Kab Bir Abbad
Edfu Kanays
Jebel Silsila
Kom Ombo
Aswan

Berenike Troglodytica

Western Desert

100   0   100   200   300   400 km

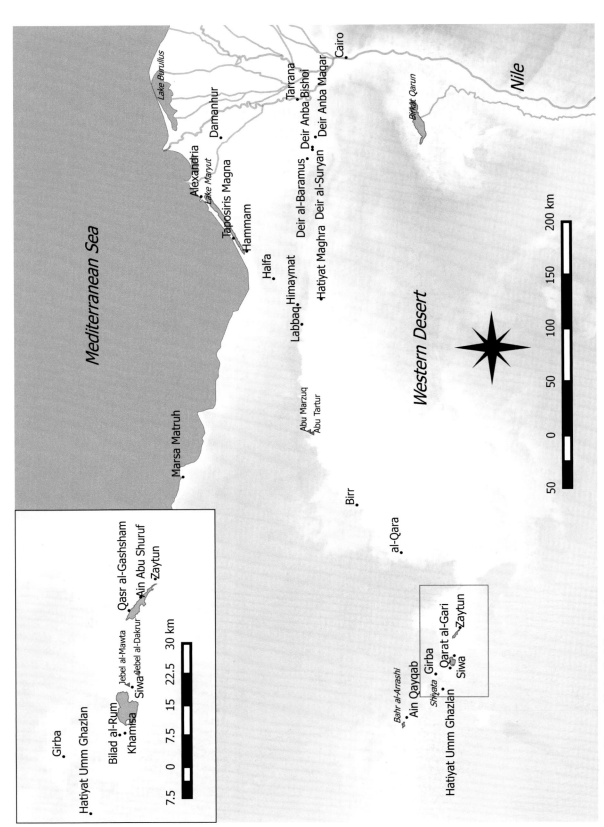

Map 2. Western Desert, with detail of Siwa Oasis.

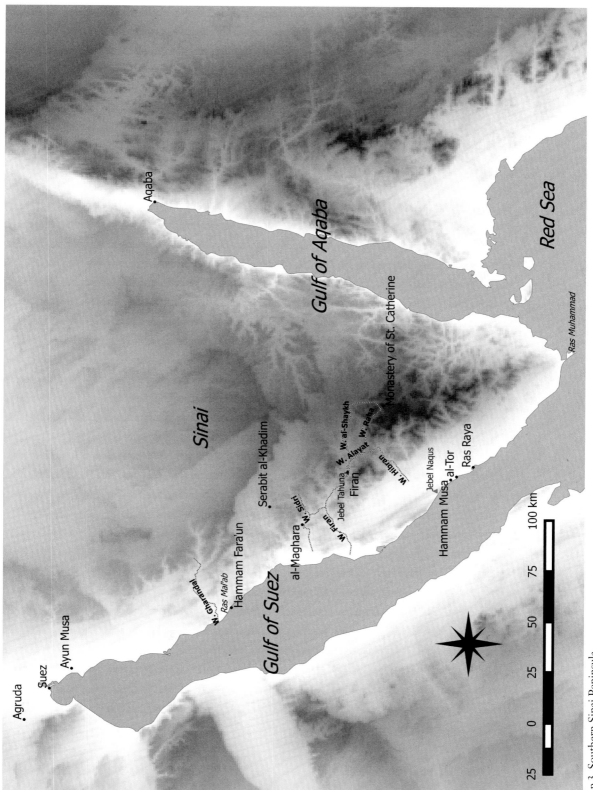

Map 3. Southern Sinai Peninsula.

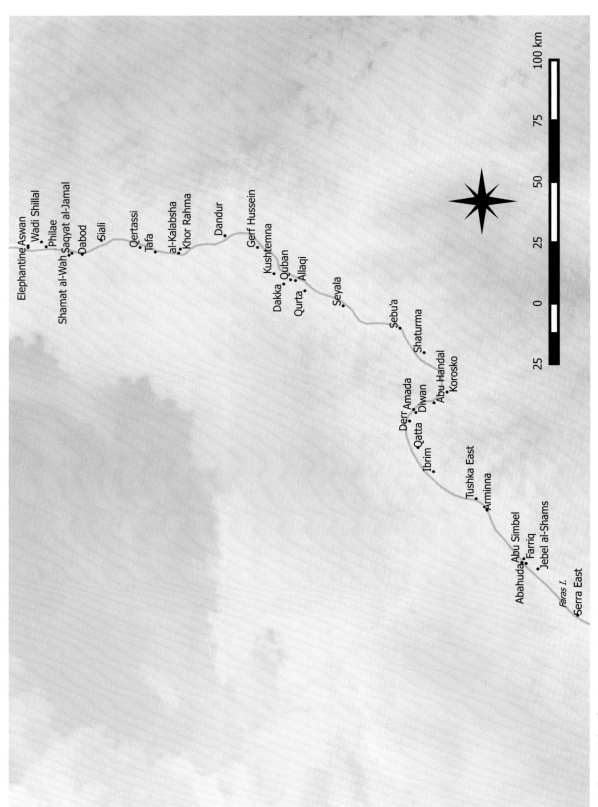

Map 4. Lower Nubia, from Aswan to Serra East.

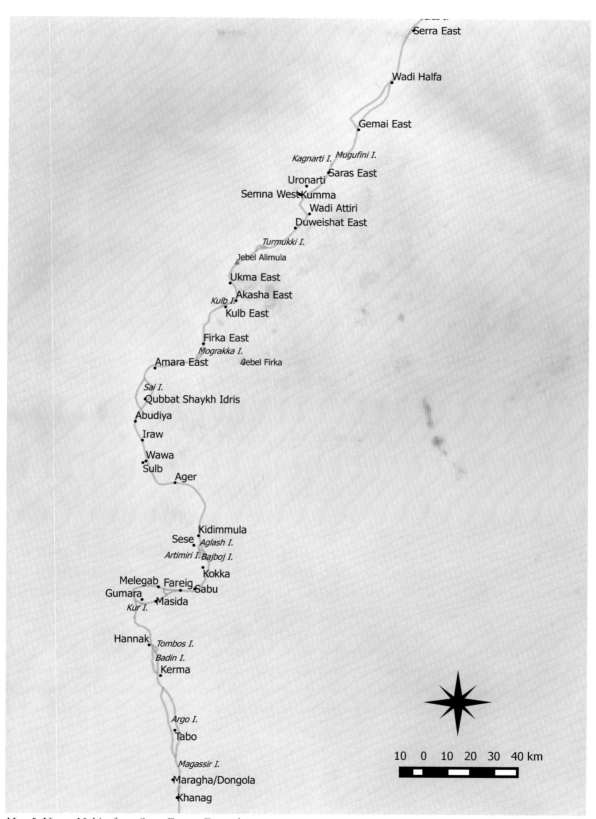

Serra East

Wadi Halfa

Gemai East

Kagnarti I. *Mugufini I.*
Saras East
Uronarti
Semna West Kumma
Wadi Attiri
Duweishat East

Turmukki I.
Jebel Alimula
Ukma East
Akasha East
Kulb I.
Kulb East

Firka East
Mograkka I.
Amara East   Jebel Firka

Sai I.
Qubbat Shaykh Idris
Abudiya
Iraw
Wawa
Sulb
Ager

Kidimmula
Sese *Aglash I.*
Artimiri I. Bajboj I.
Kokka
Melegab Fareig Sabu
Gumara Masida
Kur I.

Hannak
Tombos I.
Badin I.
Kerma

Argo I.
Tabo

Magassir I.
Maragha/Dongola
Khanag

10 0 10 20 30 40 km

Map 5. Upper Nubia, from Serra East to Dongola.

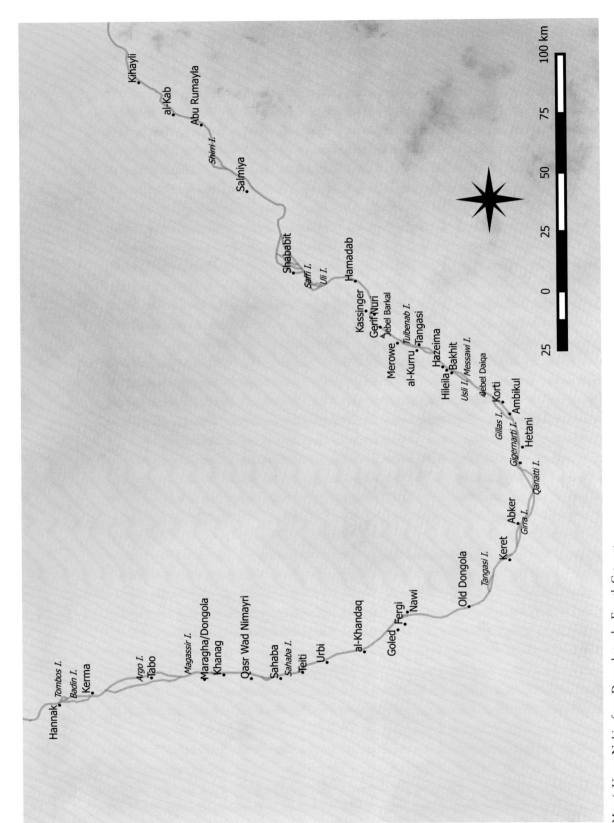

Map 6. Upper Nubia, from Dongola to the Fourth Cataract.

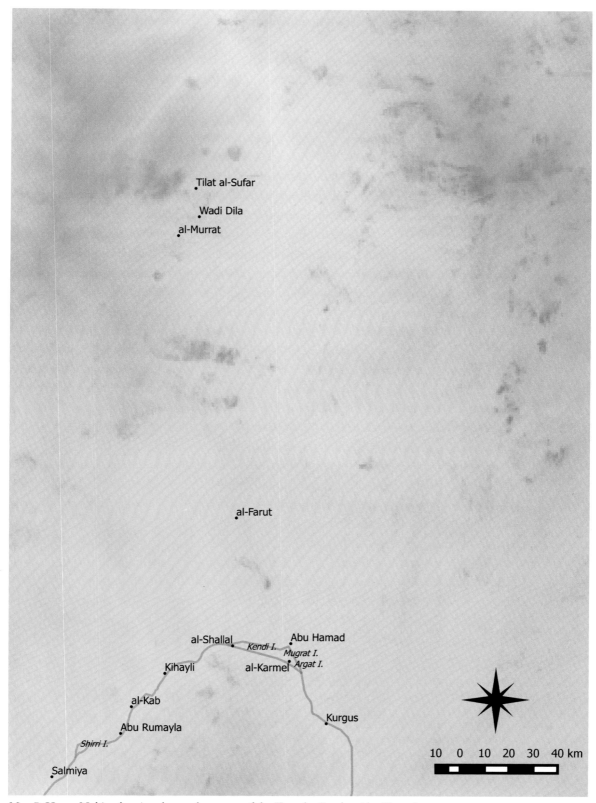

Tilat al-Sufar

Wadi Dila

al-Murrat

al-Farut

al-Shallal   Abu Hamad
          Kendi I.
                Mugrat I.
Kihayli   al-Karmel *Argat I.*

al-Kab

Abu Rumayla

Shirri I.   Kurgus

Salmiya

10 0 10 20 30 40 km

Map 7. Upper Nubia, showing the southern part of the Korosko Road to Abu Hamad.

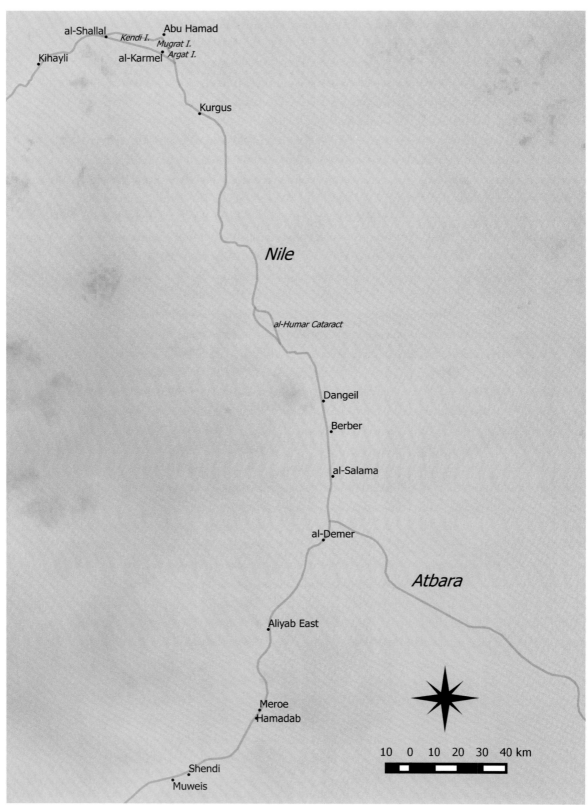

Map 8. Upper Nubia, from Mugrat Island to Shendi.

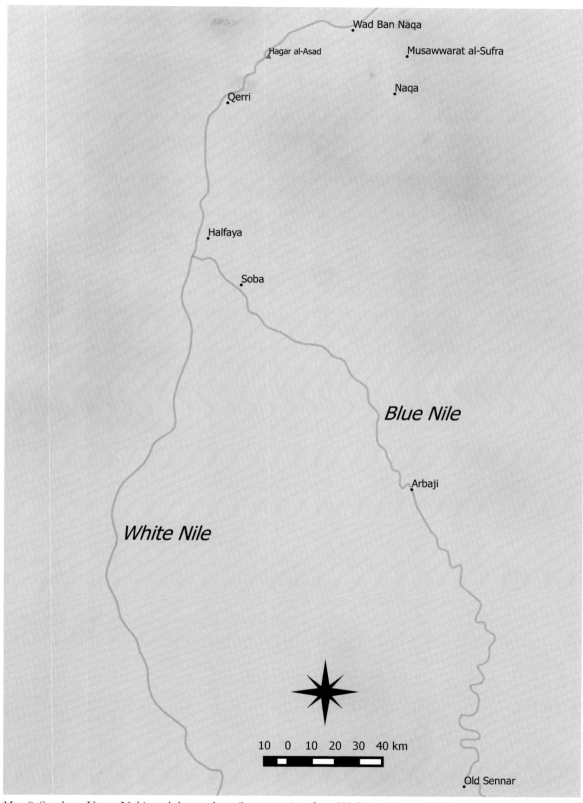

Wad Ban Naqa

Hagar al-Asad

Musawwarat al-Sufra

Naqa

Qerri

Halfaya

Soba

Blue Nile

White Nile

Arbaji

10 0 10 20 30 40 km

Old Sennar

Map 9. Southern Upper Nubia and the northern Sennar region, from Wad Ban Naqa to Old Sennar.

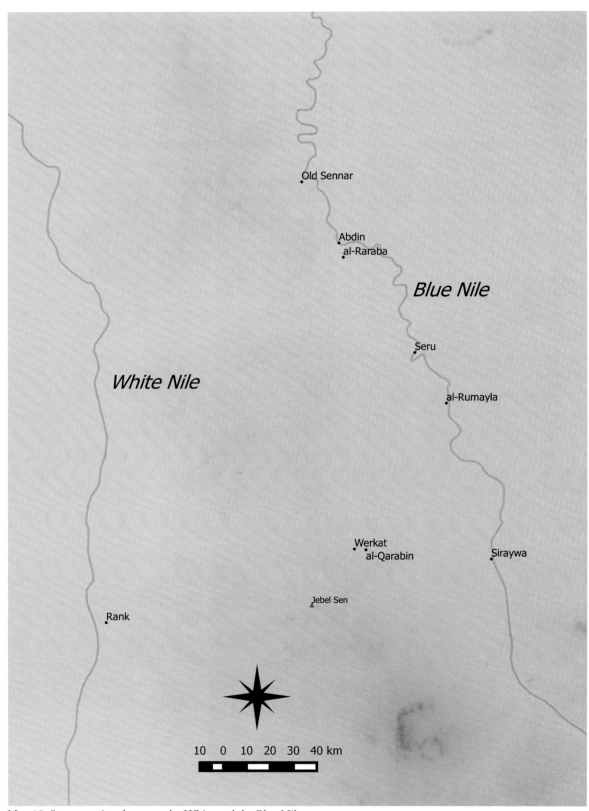

Old Sennar

Abdin
al-Raraba

Blue Nile

Seru

al-Rumayla

White Nile

Werkat
al-Qarabin

Siraywa

Jebel Sen

Rank

10 0 10 20 30 40 km

Map 10. Sennar region, between the White and the Blue Nile.

Alessandro Ricci and His Travels

1
Tuscany, Egypt, Ricci, and the First Steps of Egyptology

The Grand Duchy of Tuscany and Egypt

Alessandro Ricci was born in Siena at the end of the eighteenth century; he was therefore a subject of the Grand Duchy of Tuscany, a small country in central Italy that had enjoyed great prestige in the previous centuries as the birthplace of the Renaissance. At the turn of the nineteenth century, before and after the Napoleonic wars, Tuscany was still a dynamic state. Under Grand Duke Peter Leopold I, it was the first country in the world to abolish capital punishment (1786). The universities of Pisa and Siena were leading academies in Italy and were connected to a large network of European scholarship. The grand ducal government focused on domestic policy through land reclamation, improvement of infrastructures, and development of trade relations.[1] The diplomatic and commercial relationship between this small Italian state and Egypt, which at the time of Ricci's visit was still a province of the Ottoman Empire, was surprisingly intense.

The dock of Livorno was still one of the busiest ports in the Mediterranean, and its shipyards were particularly renowned. In the period 1825–28, through the mediation of the Livornese trader Dionisio Fernandez, the shipbuilder Luigi Mancini was able to sell various military ships to the viceroy of Egypt, Muhammad Ali.[2] In the same period, workers specializing in the manufacture of silk and cotton were sent from Livorno to the Egyptian factories of the pasha.[3]

In 1823, Félix Mengin published the complete year data on Egyptian imports and exports. Among the import records, eight are from Tuscany: all were luxury items, in particular fabrics (taffeta, brocade, and satin weave), but also paper, wine, and hats.[4] A checklist of the ships transiting through the harbor of Alexandria during the year 1826 reveals interesting data, too.[5] Tuscany held a respectable position; in that year, one can count no fewer than thirteen Tuscan vessels. It seems a small number compared to the 352 Austrian, 79

French, or 77 British ships, but they were still more than those belonging to Sweden–Norway, the Two Sicilies, the Netherlands, Denmark, Portugal, Prussia, and the United States of America.

Since Egypt was still formally a province of the Ottoman Empire, its ruler Muhammad Ali was a *wali*, a governor. For this reason, diplomats in Egypt had the rank of consul, not of ambassador, and Muhammad Ali had no right to appoint his own ambassadors abroad.[6] Other forms of diplomatic representation were nevertheless possible. A trade agent of the pasha, named Isma'il Gibraltar, is attested in Livorno in 1816. The following year he provided Ricci with a letter of recommendation for Boghos Yusufian, head interpreter of the pasha (p. 165).[7] In the period 1819–20, Othman Agha, a general in Muhammad Ali's army, is reported to be residing in Tuscany, too. It is noticeable that when Ricci left Italy an Egyptian frigate was anchored in the harbor of Livorno.

From 1747, the Grand Duchy of Tuscany had the faculty to appoint its own consuls in the East; nevertheless, it seems the right was never exercised permanently until 1826, though in 1764 a Tuscan consul named Giovan Francesco Agostini, acting also as Austrian vice-consul, is attested. The strict dynastic bond between Tuscany and Austria allowed the small Italian state to share some diplomatic benefits with the powerful Habsburg empire. When he left Italy in 1817, Ricci was carrying a letter of recommendation addressed to the Austrian general consul in Cairo, Carlo de Rossetti (1736–1820),[8] who had been in charge since 1784.

The warm relations between Muhammad Ali and Grand Duke Leopold II are well expressed in this dispatch by the governor of Livorno to the Tuscan Foreign Office in 1829: "Professor Rosellini . . . asked me to let Your Excellency know that in the farewell audience with the Viceroy, he expressed to him the most friendly feelings toward Tuscany, declaring to be much in debt to its Sovereign for the protection granted to the ships he had made in Livorno, of which he was very satisfied, and for the mutual kindness."[9]

A peculiar thermometer of diplomatic relations between Egypt and other countries is the gift of exotic animals by the pasha. For this period, we are aware of a giraffe for Sultan Mahmud II in 1824—Ricci had the chance to see it directly in Sennar (pp. 308)—an elephant for the king of Sardinia, Charles Felix, in 1826; a giraffe for the king of France, Charles X, in 1827; another giraffe for the Austrian emperor Francis II the following year; and a third giraffe sent to His Britannic Majesty shortly after. The grand duke of Tuscany, Leopold II, received a giraffe also, in 1835: "I reveal to you that His Highness the Pasha finally declared in a public *diwan*[10] that the first giraffe he will receive from inner Africa is destined for His Imperial and Royal Highness the Grand Duke our August Master to whom he professes profound friendship."[11]

The Napoleonic campaign in Egypt (1798–1801) had opened the road to travelers and professionals who wanted to try their luck in the newborn Turco-Egyptian regime of Muhammad Ali (r. 1805–48). The almost continuous state of war made a large number of military practitioners particularly in demand. A lot of Italians were already serving in the French army and decided to settle in Egypt once the war was over, as officers, trainers, physicians, and dragomans (translators). Other Italians were in Egypt as diplomats and traders.

In fact, in the 1820s Italian was still the lingua franca of the Near East,[12] to the extent that lessons at the public schools of Bulaq (1821) and Qasr al-Aini (1825)[13] were imparted in Italian and the first book published by the Bulaq Press was an Italian–Arabic dictionary (1822).[14] The impact of the Italian community was still visible at the end of the century: in 1882, there were 38,175 Greeks, 24,467 Italians, 19,557 British, 14,115 French, 7,117 Austro-Hungarians, 3,193 Russians, 1,277 Germans, and 4,625 people of other nationalities living in Egypt.[15] A quick statistic derived from a list of more than 150 famous Italians in Egypt at the time shows that people from Tuscany (Grand Duchy of Tuscany and Duchy of Lucca together) made up most of the Italians in Egypt. The same statistic for the occupation of these Italians in Egypt shows that the vast majority were physicians and pharmacists. Therefore, Ricci belonged to the most popular profile at the time for an Italian in Egypt: a Tuscan doctor.

In the period between 1805 and 1819, prior to the famous student missions sent by Muhammad Ali to France in 1826, around twenty-nine young Egyptians studied in Italy. Among them, the most distinguished were Othman Nur al-Din and Nikola Musabiki. Othman, later to become director of the schools of Bulaq and Qasr al-Aini, spent the years 1809–16 between Livorno, Milan, and Rome, where he studied engineering, typography, and military science. Musabiki became director of the Bulaq Press immediately after his return from Milan in 1819.[16] The 1826 student mission arrived in Paris, instead of an Italian city, only after the intervention of French consul Bernardino Drovetti. "If there was a Tuscan consul in Egypt, the young Turks and Arabs would not have gone to Paris, and Mr. Drovetti would not have succeeded in thwarting my project."[17] Both Muhammad Ali and Boghos Yusufian inclined toward Italy, but Drovetti had words of discouragement, describing the backwardness of Italian academia and the prevailing religious prejudice against Muslims.

Egyptian missions continued nonetheless to reach Italy, and in particular Tuscany, up to an official visit of Ibrahim Pasha, at the time the heir apparent, in 1845. A letter from the consulate chancellor to Ippolito Rosellini in 1830 states: "Othman Bey and Boghos, who send their greetings, assure me that the first student mission the pasha will send to Europe will be exclusively for Tuscany, and will be specifically recommended to Mr. Prof. Rosellini. It will leave next spring."[18] Ricci mentions one of these missions in his account, referring to a soldier of the pasha treated by him after a hunting accident and later met in the Tuscan city of Prato (chapter 10, note 'q').

The Napoleonic Campaign and the Rise of Muhammad Ali Pasha

European travel to Egypt never ceased, with the exception perhaps of the high Middle Ages, at least in the form of a pilgrimage. The holy places of Sinai, recording the deeds of Elijah, Moses, St. Catherine, and St. Helena, were reachable either via Jerusalem or via Alexandria–Cairo. Consequently, most travelogs before the nineteenth century were limited to these two main Egyptian cities and the route between them and Sinai. Only a handful of travelers ventured to the south of Cairo, such as the so-called Venetian Anonymous (1589), Protais and Charles-François d'Orléans (1670), Johann Michael Vansleb (1678), Paul Lucas (1704), Charles Perry (1743), and Frederik Ludvig Norden (1755).

The situation changed radically with two main episodes during the eighteenth and nineteenth centuries: the Napoleonic campaign in Egypt (1798–1801) and the consolidation of the power of Muhammad Ali (1807–11). These two events, together with the later decipherment of hieroglyphic script (1822), prompted the birth of scientific Egyptology.

Napoleon invaded Egypt in 1798, declaring war on the Ottoman Empire, with the intent of disrupting British Indian trade. Before the existence of the Suez Canal, most British ships leaving India would moor at Suez, where trade agents would unload them and transport the goods on camel to Alexandria. From here, they would ship them over to Britain. It was a long and costly procedure, but still preferable to the circumnavigation of the whole of Africa. The military occupation of Egypt was quick, thanks to the superior technical ability of the French army. Hoping to establish a durable colonial tenure of the region, Napoleon brought with him a large number of scholars, called *savants*, charged with the task of studying all aspects of the country: not only its antiquities, but also its modern social and economic features. Soon after, he founded the Institut d'Égypte (1798), a modern scientific academy provided with a printing house. During less than three years of research, the scholars of the Institut amassed an impressive amount of data: reports, descriptions, topographical maps, plans, landscape views, and archaeological items. Among the latter was the famous Rosetta Stone, a stela dating to the period of Ptolemy V (204–181 BC) and containing a priestly decree written in hieroglyphics, Demotic, and Greek. It was soon clear that the object had an extreme importance, for careful comparison between the Greek and the Egyptian versions of the text could (and actually did) lead to the ultimate decipherment of hieroglyphs.

It did not matter that the British eventually defeated the French in 1801 and that the stela was taken as a spoil of war to London, where it still resides. Newspapers had been informing Europe about the discoveries of the French scholars for years and new publications on them soon reached the libraries of the continent. The monumental work of the Institut d'Égypte was to be published under the auspices of the emperor in large folio volumes, lavishly illustrated with beautiful lithographs: the *Description de l'Égypte*. However, this enormous task took decades to be completed: the first volume appeared in 1809 and the last of the Imperial edition in 1822. Its impact was surely great in the long term, but most people in Europe referred to another publication by a member of the same expedition, Dominique Vivant Denon, who had already published his own illustrated account of the expedition in 1802.[19] The book was an immediate success and was very quickly translated into many languages.

Interest in ancient Egypt in Europe was now extremely high, but, still, the country was in a state of anarchy. In 1807, the British attempted to occupy it, but were defeated by an Albanian general, previously sent by the Ottoman sultan to fight the French: Muhammad Ali Pasha. He soon managed to replace the Ottoman governor of Egypt and gradually established himself as the ruler of the country. In 1811, he had all the Mamluk chiefs slaughtered in what is remembered as the 'Massacre of the Citadel': only a few escaped his fury, fleeing to Dongola, in Nubia. Muhammad Ali was a talented and ambitious ruler who controlled the country with a handful of loyal retainers and family members, monopolizing its economy and increasing political control within its borders. He also expanded these borders, occupying peripheral areas of his *pashalik* (province) by conquering the Sinai, the Western Oases, the Arabian Peninsula, and, finally, most of modern Sudan and South Sudan. The country, now firmly in his hands, was much safer than before. At the same time, he was desperate to improve the functionality of his province, both economically and militarily. He therefore hired a large number of European advisers for the various tasks: hydraulic engineering, factory management, higher education, mining surveyance, and military drilling. Lured by a desire for upward social mobility and economic gain, thousands of Europeans moved to Egypt.

The War of the Consuls and the Beginning of Egyptology

The energetic policies of Muhammad Ali required a good amount of diplomatic activity. As mentioned before, representatives of the pasha were sent around Europe, while European powers accredited their own consuls in Egypt. These were people recruited in a very different way from today. Most of the time they were not trained diplomats, but rather traders and businesspeople, often looking for chances to expand their own economic gain. The two factors previously highlighted—increased interest in ancient Egypt and the higher security of the country—converged in the businesslike minds of these consuls: they soon started to manage their own digs around the country in order to collect antiquities. This also fueled an interest among the natives, who started to dig in their villages to provide the foreigners with pieces for their growing collections. Prices rose and antiquities flooded the market: it was definitely a profitable business.[20] Most of the activities in this period were concentrated in the hands of the consuls of France, Bernardino Drovetti, and of Great Britain, Henry Salt, but not limited to them, as everyone in the diplomatic corps exploited this opportunity. Rivalry was fierce, sometimes violence broke out between the agents of Britain and France, and Egypt was divided into zones of control. For example, the French would excavate in eastern Thebes (Karnak and Luxor) and the British would work in the western part (Valley of the Kings, Tombs of the Nobles, Memnonium). In the time of Ricci, anyone could excavate, purchase, and remove any sort of antiquity, provided the local authorities did not prevent them. This obstacle could be easily removed in exchange for money and gifts. Shortly after, the trade was partially regulated: in 1828, the pasha ceased to grant excavation permits to anyone who was not his close acquaintance, and in 1835 he issued a law prohibiting the destruction of ancient buildings and the export of antiquities, and establishing an antiquities museum, the first such in Egypt.[21]

The birth of Egyptology as a scientific discipline is usually dated to 1822, when Jean-François Champollion published the results of his decipherment of hieroglyphs.[22] This was undoubtedly the most important scientific result in the field and enormously expanded knowledge of ancient Egypt. Still, this is an evaluation that exclusively highlights the philological side of the discipline, leaving out other earlier achievements in the study of ancient Egyptian art, architecture, and archaeology.

In the years between the Napoleonic campaign and 1822, and, more precisely, in the years between 1811 and 1822, there was an impressive amount of scholarly or semi-scholarly fieldwork in Egypt. It was not carried out by full-time academics, but by a variety of people with different backgrounds, sometimes academic, sometimes more technical or artistic, sometimes completely amateurish. This work had two primary focuses: the collection of new hieroglyphic texts and the study of monuments from an architectural and artistic point of view.

The search for a new Rosetta Stone was actually successful: the small obelisk at Philae, discovered in 1815, carried a hieroglyphic inscription with the cartouches of Ptolemy VIII, Cleopatra II, and Cleopatra III. The names were replicated in the Greek inscription on the base, which, unlike the Rosetta Stone, was not a translation of the hieroglyphic text. It was exactly by comparing the Greek names to their hieroglyphic rendering that William J. Bankes managed to isolate some phonetic signs of the hieroglyphic system. This famous small obelisk is now in the gardens of Kingston Lacy House, Dorset, and was brought to England by Bankes himself. He was a member of a very rich family and had notable interests in the classics (he was a Cambridge graduate), art, and architecture.

His contribution to the field of Egyptology was not limited to the discovery and the publication of the Philae obelisk. Between 1815 and 1822, he set up several scientific expeditions, composed of many talented artists, in order to study the Egyptian monuments in the Nile Valley, with a specific focus on Nubia. The number of drawings, maps, plans, epigraphic copies, and notes he amassed is just incredible. No fewer than 1,700 documents were authored by himself and the men in his employ: William H. Beechey, Louis M.A. Linant de Bellefonds, and Alessandro Ricci in particular. He had a special interest in architecture and Greek inscriptions, hundreds of which he copied throughout the Nile Valley. Despite not being able to understand hieroglyphs, the men in his service put their best efforts into copying the signs as accurately as possible. This was not the case during the Napoleonic campaign and before, when hieroglyphic inscriptions were sometimes left blank or serialized. Intelligent notes regarding Egyptian architectural styles in diachrony often accompany the many measured plans of the ancient buildings. Bankes never published his huge portfolio, but news of his deeds, and those of his men, reached Europe through newspaper articles, and the achievements of his research were discussed in academic circles. His man Linant de Bellefonds was the first European to visit the ruins of Meroe, Naqa, and Musawwarat al-Sufra, in 1822. Frédéric Cailliaud, who visited only a few weeks after, was nevertheless to take most of the credit because, unlike Linant and Bankes, he did publish his account and drawings.

Shortly after Bankes's men had left the Siwa Oasis in 1820, attached to an expedition formally headed by the French consul Drovetti, another expedition set off for the same oasis. It was headed by Baron Johann Heinrich Menu von Minutoli, and was an official scientific expedition funded by the Prussian government. The results of his explorations in the Western Desert were published as early as 1824.

Those were years of intense publication, in particular by the London-based publisher John Murray, who specialized in Egyptian travel accounts and published the most important travelogs, such as those of Swiss orientalist Johann Ludwig Burckhardt and Italian adventurer Giovanni Battista Belzoni. The latter, in the service of Henry Salt, had opened the second pyramid of Giza, discovered the tomb of Seti I in the Valley of the Kings, and cleared the entrance of the great temple of Abu Simbel. Alessandro Ricci is so far an elusive figure. Although he is mentioned everywhere in these early accounts and in modern scholarly literature, very little is known about him. Still, he was involved in many of the exciting developments of the age and played an important role in many of them.

2
Alessandro Ricci: Early Life, Personality, and Cultural Background

Early Life

No birth record for Alessandro Ricci survives in either the Florence or the Siena cathedral; both cities had a single baptistery so that all newborn Catholics would be registered in a single book. Since these registers are completely preserved, one must assume that Ricci was not born in Siena or Florence. Maybe he was born in some village in the countryside, probably in the adjoining territory of Siena, as he claims that this was his home city.

The death record of Alessandro Ricci survives in the civil register of Florence,[1] where he is described as a forty-two-year-old physician, unmarried at the time of his death on 29 January 1834. This puts Ricci's birth in 1792.

The *Raccolta biografica* by Ettore Romagnoli[2]—which is, however, often imprecise—describes Ricci as "not rich." Being the son of Angelo Ricci of Florence, specialized stonemason, and Rebecca Gabrielli of Siena, Alessandro did not come from a particularly wealthy family. He inherited his father's house in Florence, where after his return from Egypt he would open a small private museum of Egyptian antiquities. A strong desire to publish his travels emerges from his letters to Patrizio Rontani, Champollion, and Rosellini, and it is always and clearly in order to make profit. In a letter to Dr. Rontani, Ricci confesses: "I don't have much money, because I spent part of my savings traveling."[3] From papers in Florence and Berlin, it appears Ricci had at least two brothers, Giovanni and Luigi.

Despite coming from a working-class family, Ricci managed to get a degree in medicine. The aforementioned *Raccolta biografica*[4] claims that Ricci graduated from the University of Siena, but this is not possible for the following reasons. His arrival in Egypt in 1817 surely follows his degree in medicine. At that time, a medical degree was obtained after four years of theory classes and two of practice;[5] a student was allowed to begin his studies at seventeen.[6] But when the University of Siena was shut down by Napoleon in 1808 (only

11

to be reopened in 1815), Ricci was only sixteen. In addition, his name appears neither in the yearbook of that university nor in that of Pisa, the only two universities in the Grand Duchy of Tuscany at that time. Documents may have been lost, or one must assume that Ricci obtained his degree somewhere else. It is impossible that he only pretended to be a physician. He not only proves to be competent on more than one occasion, but also asks his friends in Italy to send him up-to-date books and tools.[7] Moreover, before being hired by Henry Salt as family doctor, he most likely had to show his recommendation letters and licenses to practice medicine.

The two portraits made during the Tuscan expedition of 1828–29 show him as an adult; at the time, he was thirty-seven. The portraits are quite different, except that in both he is balding and bearded. The painting by Giuseppe Angelelli, on display at the Egyptian Museum of Florence,[8] shows a man of strong constitution in a heroic pose. The Ricci sketched by Salvador Cherubini is thin, with unkempt hair and his eyeglasses slipping down a big nose.[9] The fact that he wore eyeglasses is confirmed by his own account of his first entrance into the temple of Abu Simbel (p. 187).

Personality

We have many accounts of the personality of Ricci. Romagnani's *Raccolta* calls him "resourceful and a free spirit." More interesting is the description made by Ippolito Rosellini in a letter dated 19 April 1830 and addressed to Neri Corsini (1771–1845), minister of foreign affairs of the Grand Duchy of Tuscany.[10] In a letter written two days earlier, the minister had asked Rosellini his opinion on who should be appointed as the new Tuscan consul in Egypt. Answering a precise question by the minister, Rosellini thought Ricci not suitable for the position.

> He is for sure a good and honest fellow, and this is also the reputation he has earned in Egypt, where, I think, he would go back willingly if there was a possibility to earn something. But, to tell the truth, I have to say that he lacks the dexterity and steadiness of character that is necessary to represent a foreign Government in a Turkish Country. Dr. Ricci is that kind of man of good faith who is easily deceived by the less cunning, and this is the reason he lost a large part of his fortune. His devotion [for Ibrahim Pasha], even if it comes from good will, and the weakness of the unwise character of Dr. Ricci are poorly suited for a person who is going to fill such an important position.

Louis Maurice Adolphe Linant de Bellefonds (1799–1883), the traveler who accompanied Ricci on many of his travels, describes Ricci as grumpy and touchy: the doctor cannot stand to be treated "as a servant." With what seems a childish attitude he sulks, refusing to set off because Linant's dragoman, Giovanni Finati, has taken the camel he intended to mount himself.[11]

The two profiles traced by Rosellini (honest but naive) and Linant (moody) converge in a single picture and are confirmed by the consistent difference of salary between Ricci and Linant.[12] As will be discussed later, Linant received a salary ten times greater than Ricci's. This is proof that Ricci could be hired for a low price, exploiting his enthusiasm for exploration, and, perhaps, his low self-confidence. On the other hand, the different social backgrounds of the two men should not be underestimated and probably contributed to a tense situation. At the time, a physician, even though cultured, was not considered to be on the same social level as a gentleman. While Salt and Bankes were both esquires, Beechey the son of an aristocrat, and Linant de Bellefonds a gentleman of old ancestry, Ricci was merely the son of a stonemason.

Another proof of this disparity of treatment is that Ricci never had direct correspondence with Salt and Bankes, while Linant did on a regular basis. Just a few years later, in the loneliness of a second African journey, Linant wrote to Salt bitter words about his fellow traveler: "I even miss the bad company of the redneck fellow Ricci,"[13] where the original French word *bourin*, based on the Italian vernacular *burino*, is a derogatory term with strong social characterization. In another letter to Bankes, Linant adds a postscript about certain disputes regarding benefits: "We have received all that you had the kindness to send us, but I dare beg you in case you are to send something else, please make the division yourself; we would avoid much discussion here."[14]

Ricci liked solitude; sometimes he would leave the caravan to walk alone on a different track and join the rest of the group later. He was constantly pushed by his love for exploration and did not waste any opportunity to visit sites reported to be of some interest. During the sickness of Linant in Sinai, after having provided the necessary medical care, he would roam around alone to complete his survey of the area. His scientific and geographic curiosity surpassed his interest in medicine and desire to pursue a career in the field, to the point that he would refuse the offer made by Ibrahim Pasha to become his personal physician (p. 303).

He did not withhold treatment from whoever needed it and apparently did so without charging money. In his letter to Marquess Antonio Canova from the Siwa Oasis, his fellow traveler Domenico Enegildo Frediani remembers how Ricci divided his time between "good humanitarian care" toward Hassan Bey's soldiers and his epigraphic work.[15] Likewise, Linant testifies to Ricci's diligence and, at the same time, his playful character: "The shaykh of the religion came to visit me: he was an old man and asked for a medicine for his eyes. As usual when dealing with the poor, the Doctor wanted to be begged and gave him the medicine only after the other told him he would give him all the money and diamonds he wanted; but in fact the Doctor has never taken anything for what medicine he has given away."[16] The *Travels* themselves are full of episodes where Ricci is seen offering medical assistance to the locals.

One of the letters Ricci wrote to his friend Patrizio Rontani expresses a certain titillating humor, perhaps a little gross but probably permitted by the intimacy of the two friends: "Tell me whether Beppa performs her duty (if you know what I mean)," continuing a few lines later, to take up the theme, "I possess two very beautiful slaves, a black and an Abyssinian; maybe one day you will see them in Livorno."[17] The problem of the sexual behavior of nineteenth-century travelers is an important issue. In Ricci's text, his own moral and sexual behavior is portrayed with great steadiness, an example of Christian ethics. References to "public women," expressed in a tone of disapproval, appear throughout the *Travel to Sennar* (pp. 253, 283, 293, 295, 322, 331). Ricci had also "the occasion to fully satisfy curiosity" about female genital mutilation, a practice he firmly condemns (p. 298). He shows the same attitude toward slavery and its dramatic implications (pp. 313–14). This is in stark contrast to what he had written to Rontani about his own two slaves. The possession of female slaves would not have been a matter of great scandal: Linant, too, would arrive in Britain in November 1824 to deliver his portfolio of drawings and travel diary accompanied by an African woman.[18]

Patricia Usick has been the first and only scholar to doubt the generally accepted cause of Ricci's death. Since their appearance in 1832, the dementia and paralysis that would eventually kill Ricci were attributed to a simple scorpion sting. The accident had happened in Qurna in 1829, three years earlier.[19] The British scholar thinks that the most probable cause of his progressive debilitation, paralysis, and finally death was syphilis.[20] In fact, the progression of syphilis includes, in the later stages, paralysis, dementia, and death, but then again, many other parasitic diseases affect the brain with similar symptoms, and equatorial Africa is definitely the place where such diseases can be caught.

The myth of the scorpion sting can be easily explained in two different ways, whether the syphilis theory is true or not. After the onset of paralysis, which made it impossible for Ricci to take care of himself, his trustee Marquess Gino Capponi (1792–1876) decided to sell Ricci's Egyptian collection to the grand duke of Tuscany. The details of this transaction will be discussed in chapter 4, but here it is important to notice the involvement of the Tuscan head of state. In his petition to the grand duke to grant Ricci a lifetime pension, Capponi pointed out the fact that Ricci was in the service of the nation when the accident occurred (May 1829), that is, during the Franco-Tuscan Expedition, which was in fact funded by the government. Capponi succeeded and obtained both the granting of his plea and the purchase of the collection. But if Ricci was really suffering from syphilis, then there would be a good reason to push for the circulation of the story of the scorpion sting: the necessity to hide that Ricci was dying of a venereal disease, caught because of his loose moral behavior. The censorship authority of the Ministry of the Interior would never have allowed the association of the grand duke with a 'bad' Christian. Possibly connected to this is a statement in the biography of Giuseppe Angelelli, official painter of the expedition: "Angelelli did not allow a friend and a fellow to end up so miserably; he agreed . . . to take him in his house, almost at his own expense, and assist him, even though from different sides and for different reasons this earned him bitter reproach."[21] Why? Maybe Usick's theory of syphilis is not completely amiss. An event that occurred during the journey to Sennar casts doubts on Ricci's moral integrity. Linant states that the doctor had been sulking since they left Berber: "I could not think of anything but of one thing only that could have turned him in a bad mood, which is that at Berber I spent the night with a woman of the *malak*[22] without sharing her with me."[23]

Cultural Background

Besides his degree in medicine, there is not much information about Ricci's cultural training. The best source to understand his level of culture is of course the *Travels* itself, filled with observations relating to the classics, mineralogy, and biology, especially ornithology and botany. On different occasions, Ricci proves to be competent in chemistry, too. It should be noted that these are all subjects included in the medical curriculum of the time. In one of his footnotes, Ricci quotes Ottaviano Targioni Tozzetti (1755–1826), a Tuscan physician and botanist, professor of botany at Pisa University since 1802 and author of many books; whether Ricci was one of his students is an open possibility. Ricci's mineralogical interests were noticed and respected, as John Hyde writes, observing "a sort of stone like petrified wood & another species which the Dr. [Ricci] believes bones."[24]

His antiquarian, archaeological, and epigraphic interests were solid. His observations on cultural anthropology were very detailed, far beyond the simple and superficial utterances of mere travelers. During his travels, Ricci succeeded in amassing several collections as well. Unfortunately, only part of the archaeological collection survived, while the rest was lost during the adventurous return to Cairo in 1821.

Ricci had a real passion for bird hunting and more than once in the *Travels* he mentions his trophies. His observations on fauna and flora are frequent. Crocodiles, monkeys, lions, giraffes, hippopotamuses, Dongola horses, geckos, chameleons, elephants, and other animals are encountered and described, sometimes in detail. Ricci mentions over twenty different flora species, often by their scientific names.

Ricci spoke and wrote English (p. 167) and probably French, too. It is possible that he knew some Arabic, but he could not read it fluently (p. 311). In a passage of the *Travels*, Ricci clearly understands Arabic and behaves accordingly (p. 314). A dragoman was in any event necessary to speak with officers in Turkish or Albanian, and with the locals. The latter in particular spoke an increasingly corrupted Arabic in proportion to their distance from Cairo. Communication between Europeans was not a problem, as Italian was the bridging language. William John Bankes was fluent in Italian[25] and Henry Salt could understand both French and Italian.[26]

Belzoni expresses his deep appreciation for Ricci's artistic talent: "Signor Ricci . . . was very clever at drawing, and . . . with a little practice became perfect in his imitations of the hieroglyphics."[27] Henry Salt, too, and later Ippolito Rosellini—who would describe him as "the most skilled of my draftsmen"[28]—expressed their appreciation for Ricci's epigraphic talent.

Ricci also seems to be familiar with classical historiography on Egypt. It is possible that these notions were passed on to him through frequenting men of higher culture, such as Bankes, who was a Cambridge graduate. Anyway, medical curricula at the time would comprise some humanities, too. In his first letter to Patrizio Rontani, Ricci mentions the legend of the singing Memnon colossi.[29] In his second letter, he alludes to the destruction of Cambyses's army on its way to Siwa (Herodotus, *Historiae* III 26, 3; Plutarch, *Alexander* XXVI 6) and to the luckier expedition of Alexander the Great.[30] The same information is displayed at the beginning of the *Travel to the Oasis of Jupiter-Amun* (p. 194). In this part of the *Travels*, Ricci makes frequent comparisons between the archaeological ruins and the classical sources. Nevertheless, when he writes about the Temple of the Oracle (p. 216), he confuses Diodorus Siculus (*Bibliotheca Historica* XVII 50) with Herodotus. Later on, he also refers to Strabo, *Geographica* I 3, 4 (p. 217). At the end of his *Travel in Nubia*, commenting on Bankes's desire to visit Fayoum, Ricci explains that the English gentleman was moved by passages from the works of Herodotus and Pliny (p. 194). Finally, the story of the foundation of St. Catherine's Monastery in Sinai follows the version in the *Annales* of Eutychius of Alexandria (877–940), which was first published in the seventeenth century, but which Ricci could hardly have been aware of; he is quite certainly quoting what the monks told him. This, anyway, proves that Ricci did not know the more widespread version provided in the *De Aedificiis* by Procopius of Caesarea. The description of the scenes copied on Philae Island at the end of the first Nubian journey seems to draw from Plutarch's work on the myth of Osiris.

He is aware of the work of the French *savants* of the Napoleonic expedition because, when close to Suez, he searches for a certain Persian monument (p. 225) discussed by De Rozière in the *Description de l'Égypte*.[31] The same monument is quoted in the correspondence between Linant and Bankes, so it is possible that Ricci learned about it through the Frenchman or the English gentleman.[32] The quest for this monument was doomed to fail: as there was no agreement among the French *savants* on its location, it was not marked in the maps. Ricci was not aware of this detail and, while he seems to know the essay by de Rozière, he proves to be ignorant of the corrective essay by Devilliers.[33]

While traveling in Sinai, Ricci proves to know the biblical tradition of the Exodus and at many sites he refers to the scriptures, but without quoting them directly. He also discusses the identification of biblical sites such as Wadi Amura (p. 226), Hammam Fara'un (p. 228), and Wadi al-Arba'in (p. 241) related to, in order, Exodus 15:22–24, Exodus 14:15–31, and Exodus 17:1–7. The extreme caution in his biblical commentary is absolutely in line with the period and with Ricci's desire to publish the book, to do which he must please a wide audience. Ricci had clearly in mind the hostility of the Catholic Church in Tuscany to his friend Girolamo Segato, caused by the latter's connection with the circles of occultism.[34] After all, even Champollion's decipherment of the hieroglyphs was largely opposed by the Catholic Church as a threat to biblical chronology.[35]

Ricci's medical knowledge is fully consistent with the training imparted in the universities at the time, and all in all quite primitive. Medicine was still following centuries-old miasmatic theories, while treatments were limited to symptomatic therapies, aimed at stopping the symptoms rather than acting on causes, such as bloodletting (purges), anti-diarrheal treatments, emetics, blisters, and expectorants. Only with the advent of microbiology eighty years later would these theories be outdated. Ricci, whom contemporary sources call a 'surgeon,' was able to amputate (p. 218).

3
Travels in Egypt and Sennar (1817–22)

Organization and Funding

In his *Travels*, Ricci never openly mentions who is funding his explorations and drawings, thus giving a partial view of reality. In fact, the reader gets the idea that Ricci is traveling at his own expense, with peers, and that he is drawing simply to enrich his account with some illustrations. Nevertheless, some passages in the text give hints to the reality of facts confirmed by other sources.

At the beginning of his long Egyptian stay, Ricci writes: "I must remember with gratitude the family of Mr. Salt, British consul general . . . for the constant proofs of friendship and protection received under every circumstance during my stay in Egypt" (p. 167). Salt is also quoted in the farewell, on p. 320: "I bid farewell to Mr. Salt and my other acquaintances." Even though always mentioned with respect ("Mr. Bankes") and words of admiration, William John Bankes only appears as a travel companion.

It is probable that upon his arrival in Egypt, Ricci actually had his first contact with Salt: in this early phase Ricci probably made the drawings that are now kept at the British Museum under the label 'Salt Watercolours.'[1] In a letter to Dr. Rontani dated 13 November 1819, Ricci states clearly that he was performing the duty of physician of the consul, a position that he held until the end of his stay in Egypt. In the same letter, Ricci asks for books and tools: "All these orders you will entrust to Mr. Mansueto Pensa, who will give you the money and who will ship them to me as soon as possible."[2] Mansueto Pensa was the father-in-law of Henry Salt, who had married his daughter just a few days earlier, around the end of October 1819.[3] It is possible that Ricci had just entered the service of Salt, who was probably in need of a physician for the foreseeable pregnancy of his wife. In documents from Dresden, Ricci is defined as "Family Doctor of the English consul Salt in Alexandria."[4]

In spring 1818, Ricci is at Thebes, busy with a copy of the reliefs from the tomb of Seti I discovered by Belzoni just a few months earlier. The physician describes in polemical tones his collaboration with Belzoni, who was also in the service of Salt, giving a version of events that is in sharp contrast with what was stated by Belzoni himself.[5] According to Yanni D'Athanasi, the expedition to Berenike Troglodytica, organized by Belzoni and abandoned by Ricci after a few days in September 1818, was also funded by Salt's purse.[6]

In October 1818, the British traveler William John Bankes gathered in Luxor a number of explorers and was about to set off for Nubia: Ricci was also part of the group, probably recommended by Salt. Giovanni Finati states that Ricci was in the service of Bankes.[7] The information is confirmed by Charles Barry, who met the group in January 1819 and wrote the following note: "Mr. Bankes' drawings . . . are executed by himself and an Italian doctor in his employ."[8]

At the end of the journey, in May 1819, Ricci was again hired by Bankes to copy the tombs of Beni Hasan: "I have always looked upon these tombs as the most curious in Egypt as to their details, and left it in charge with Dr. Ricci, of Sienna, to complete the drawings of them, which he begun under my eye—a task which he however never thought fit to resume."[9] The same is repeated later in the book: "To Dr. Ricci it was left in charge to make accurate and detailed drawings of every figure to be found in the grottoes at Benyhassan . . . a task which, I know not for what reason, was never performed."[10] Another proof of this engagement is a highly fragmentary letter by Bankes written to an unknown recipient at an unknown date:

Should the Dr. choose to undertake the grottoes at Beny Hasan establishing himself there till the work is finished I have proposed to renew his salary to him of 500 p(iast) res monthly from the day on which he shall quit Cairo, and should he not find an opportunity of going up with you. . . . Mr. Lee his boat hire both in going and returning . . . be at my charge and the candles which he may use . . . his operations, but not his living . . . paper and pencils and all implements also are at [his charge?]. Should he agree on this, he may go up . . . can spare him, and he shall receive the [payment?] may be due for him so soon as I am in . . . Florence.[11]

A salary of 500 piasters was not bad: this was the amount the pasha paid for his physicians and, if Belzoni was paid as double as much,[12] Nathaniel Pearce in the service of Salt received a salary of only 200 piasters.[13]

When Bankes left Egypt, the supervision of men and resources passed to Salt, who actually organized the expeditions and managed payments. After their first trip together, the contacts between Ricci and Bankes were not frequent. In Bankes's archive there are some annotations by Ricci addressed to Bankes, but these are just technical details about the drawings.[14]

The following journey had the Siwa Oasis as its goal. Finati writes: "To Monsieur Linant an ample salary was assigned [by Bankes] for the purpose of visiting the Oasis of Siwah, and there copying all hieroglyphics and inscriptions; with a charge also of ascertaining particularly whether there is a triple inclosure [sic] about the ruin,"[15] referring to the triple enclosure wall of the Temple of Amun described by Diodorus. Linant was offered the sum of 2,000 piasters for the trip: 1,838 were spent on logistics and the remaining 162 were kept by the Frenchman as payment.[16] No mention of remuneration for Ricci is made in Bankes's or Salt's papers. Probably Salt or even Drovetti, who maintained a cordial relationship with the doctor, paid for Ricci's participation.

After the visit to Siwa, Ricci and Linant moved on to explore the southwest side of the Sinai Peninsula, with the intention to reach Aqaba and Petra via St. Catherine. Bankes, on his part, was strongly against this expedition, "which I have always been utterly unable to comprehend . . . was, so far as my views were concerned, so much time lost," he wrote.[17] In a letter to Patrizio Rontani "from the Monastery of Mount Sinai," Ricci writes: "I don't have much money, because I spent part of my savings traveling, even though the British consul provides the necessary means."[18] Nevertheless, there is no doubt that the funder was Bankes, as clearly pointed out by Linant's expense report.

The travel cost Bankes a considerable sum: Linant declared to have taken 6,920 piasters, to have spent 5,014 and have kept 1,906. Ricci was given 2,160 piasters: "Bill of Mr. Ritchi [sic]. I gave him five hundred piasters leaving to Mount Sinai, or better he just gave me five hundreds of an assignment of a thousand on my account: 500. I gave him at Suez 150, at Cairo 10, plus for his expenses 1,500. Total 2,160."[19] Ricci's position was actually different from that of Linant, as it emerges in a letter from Salt to Bankes:

> I enclose you an exact list (No. 1) of Mr. Linant expenses since your departure. There is one article for Ricci for the voyage to Mount Sinai 2,106[20] (Mr. Linant will explain to you that 500 of them were returned by Ricci without any knowledge) piasters for which I am answerable but as I think you may like to have the work complete, I have sent you the drawings made by him when on this expedition as a counterpart. That is if you think they are worth it or otherwise it can be partly balanced by the sums I advanced to Ricci on account of and in settlement of the voyage to Meroe.[21]

The last journey, to Sennar, was also funded entirely by Bankes. So writes Salt: "There are two young men of great talents Mr. Linant and Mr. Ricci gone up at Mr. Bankes' expense from whom we may expect most accurate views of everything in the way of antiquity."[22] Henry Salt insisted Ricci should go with Linant; Bankes, and Linant himself, did not agree. In the description of their fight in November 1821, Linant states: "He [Ricci] did neither have a firman[23] nor a letter of recommendation, . . . because neither the letters of Salt nor the firman mentioned him."[24] Later on, Linant quotes what he said directly to Ricci: "You perfectly know, Doctor, that if you came with me it is only because of Mr. Salt, who absolutely wanted it against my will, because I was not authorized in any way by Mr. Bankes to take you with me."[25] A long passage of a letter from Salt to Bankes explains the reason Ricci was sent along with Linant:

I am sorry that you continue to regret that Ricci was sent in to Nubia but I think if you will consider the matter you will be satisfied that all was for the best. When Linant left us, his health was in such a weak state that I felt afraid to trust him alone as a relapse would probably have proved fatal, and the Doctor's presence on that account was very desirable. Besides it had come to my knowledge that very advantageous proposals had been made by Baron von Minutoli to Ricci to undertake this voyage on his account & though Ricci said nothing of this to me I saw such a resolution on his part to make the voyage that I felt assured if I did not let him go with Linant he would go on his own. Besides, to tell you the truth, as Linant has already become somewhat extravagant in his expenses, according to my way of thinking, I judged that Ricci, from the instructions I gave him, would be rather a check upon him than an additional expense, as was in fact the case. The money I advanced to the Doctor for this trip was little and I made no engagement for his salary, explaining to him most clearly that I had no authority from you to send him up. Thus at little expenses in fact to you, I insured all he could do in this voyage for you. . . . Before he went [back to Europe] he gave up to me, for you, all his sketches made in Nubia which were very interesting as they express very correctly the different character of the sculpture found there from any existing in Egypt which with all Linant's talents he was not so capable of doing. These sketches I shall make up in a small case and send them by the first safe conveyance.[26]

The costs incurred by Bankes for the Sennar expedition, carefully registered by Linant, were particularly high, summing up to a total of 26,625 piasters. Of those, Linant kept 4,460 as salary. Much less, perhaps because he left earlier, was the sum received by Ricci: a copy of the receipt made by Salt reports the total at only 1,700 piasters.

For the travels to Siwa, Sinai, and Sennar, including the removal and shipment of the granite base of the Philae obelisk—which had already been removed by Belzoni in 1819—and large blocks of granite from Maharraqa to be used as a pedestal for the obelisk, Bankes invested the enormous sum of 52,195 piasters.[27] Of these, 37,017 piasters covered Linant's travel expenses and 11,318 were kept by the Frenchman as salary. Only 3,860 piasters was paid to Ricci, who had to use them to cover his own travel expenses.[28]

Tools

Nothing is known about the drawing instruments used by Ricci; he does not mention them. The accuracy of some of the drawings, sometimes copies of Egyptian reliefs of large size, implies the use of some sort of perspectival machines, such as the camera lucida or the camera obscura. One of the drawings made by Bankes in 1815, a view of the temple of Hathor at Deir al-Medina (DHC, D/BKL VII.A.35), shows a clear round distortion due to the use of an optical instrument. Similarly, a view of Luxor temple from the west bank, made by Linant (DHC, D/BKL II.C.19), shows the temple much smaller than it is normally seen from that distance and also implies the use of an optical instrument.

Nevertheless, most drawings seem to disrespect the proportions of wall reliefs and must have been done freehand.

As for the rest of the equipment, Giovanni Finati writes: "The traveller [Linant] was furnished by his employer [Bankes] with instruments of every description, and when all other requisites were provided, (the quantity of which was proportionably increased by engaging Dr. Ricci in the company, and two common servants) we all took our departure together for Assouan."[29] Among the scientific instruments, there was a telescope, mentioned several times (pages 199, 206, 208, 209, 312). A thermometer was certainly at their disposal, as Ricci could precisely measure temperature variations of both atmosphere and water (pp. 223, 227, 251). Astronomical instruments, probably used for orientation and mapping, were part of the equipment as well. A portable pharmacy was among the personal belongings of the doctor.[30] It probably contained the medicines often mentioned in the *Travels* such as quinine, mercuric chloride, tonics, poultices, enemas, sedatives, camphorated spirit of wine, and sweet almond oil. Other plants used for decoctions were probably collected on the spot: camphor, chamomile, lemon, tamarind, and cherries. He probably carried some arsenic to embalm the birds he was hunting and collecting.

As for clothing, it seems that Ricci always traveled dressed as a European, except on the journey to Sennar, as he himself writes (p. 251). On their first trip to Nubia, according to D'Athanasi, all members of the group wore oriental dress, except for Bankes and Hyde.[31]

All sources agree that Ricci was skillful in the use of firearms, both rifles and pistols. He himself mentions this ability more than once when he describes new acquisitions for his ornithological collection (pp. 270, 290), but also for personal defense (p. 199). Baroness von Minutoli mentions that Ricci was armed while traveling in her company between 1820 and 1821.[32]

Arrival in Egypt: 1815, 1817, or 1818?

Incertitude reigned for a long time over Ricci's date of arrival in Egypt, and the *Travels* add problematic information in this respect. Some scholars believed that Ricci was already in Egypt in 1815,[33] according to what is written in Finati's memoirs. Finati describes his first trip to Upper Egypt in that year: at the mention of Beni Hasan, Bankes added a footnote to express his disappointment that Ricci never accomplished the task of copying the reliefs.[34] In particular the sentence "He begun [*sic*] under my eye" made scholars think that Ricci was assigned the task in 1815. A second footnote in the section of the 1819 Nubian trip makes it clear that Bankes asked Ricci to copy the scenes in that year and not earlier.[35]

Ricci's first discoverer, Angelo Sammarco, had different opinions regarding Ricci's date of arrival in Egypt; in 1929 he thought that Ricci had arrived in February 1817.[36] In 1930, on the contrary, he wrote: "Alessandro Ricci . . . with explorations that lasted five years, from 1818 to 1822, went across Egypt."[37] In 1949, he wrote: "With explorations which lasted six years, from 1817 to 1822, Ricci traveled across Egypt."

The uncertainty between 1817 and 1818 is caused by a narrative anomaly in the account. At the very beginning, Ricci states: "I left Siena, my homeland, in January 1817 and reached Livorno in order to embark" (p. 165). A little later on the same page, he continues: "I embarked on 2 February 1817." Ricci landed at Alexandria on 21 February and arrived in Cairo on 5 March. Here, writing without a break of any sort: "There was much talking in Cairo in those days about the enterprise of the Italian Giovanni Battista Belzoni, who . . . had recently opened many tombs at Thebes," referring then more explicitly to the tomb of Seti I. This tomb was discovered by Belzoni only in October 1817. The chronology resumes a few pages later. At page 171, Ricci states: "I kept working without interruption until the seventh month"—which means at the end of the summer. After this period, Ricci joined Belzoni in his expedition to Berenike: "On 16 September 1818, we embarked at Qurna" (p. 171). It cannot be a mere copying mistake by Sammarco or a confusion between 1817 and 1818 by Ricci. To match the dates, one needs to imagine a period of silence that lasted exactly a year, even if the narration progresses fluidly without any sort of interruption.

All doubts are cast away by other sources. Champollion reckons the first stay of Ricci as six years.[38] Similarly, in 1828, Ricci wrote to Girolamo Bardi that he had six years of previous experience in Egypt.[39] If the interpretation of "R-c-i" (an abbreviation used by Rev. Joliffe in his book to designate the doctor who treated an injury to his foot in Cairo in September 1817) proves to be correct, then there is another proof of Ricci being in Egypt as early as 1817.[40]

By one of those strokes of luck that happen only very rarely, I was contacted in 2013 by a private collector of postal specimens, offering me the scanned images of two documents by Alessandro Ricci. They turned out to be two unpublished letters to Governor Spann-occhi-Piccolomini, both sent from Cairo and dated 2 August 1817 and 10 January 1818 respectively. The former is definitely the first letter written by Ricci from Egypt: he states his disappointment at the lack of medical jobs, but announces that he accepted a position as clerk at Antonacchi's, a trade firm based in Cairo. He also expresses his gratitude to the governor, calling him "patron and father," for a loan he had granted him upon his departure to Egypt.

In fact, in a letter to his friend Rontani, Ricci wrote: "I take advantage of the occasion . . . to give you my news, which I imagined you did not receive for a long time, as I spent the last two years traveling with no chance to write; so here I am. Tired of practicing medicine for the reasons I many times told you, I decided to go up to Thebes to see the Egyptian antiquities." This letter has always been interpreted as a first narration of his experience in Egypt: Ricci was tired of being a doctor and decided to leave Italy for Egypt. Observing the text at a closer distance, however, the letter does not look like a "first letter from Egypt," because it does not mention his crossing the Mediterranean and his first steps in Africa. Above all, Ricci did not write "I decided to go to Egypt" but "to go up to Thebes," which means he had already spent some time in Lower Egypt. In the same letter, he also stated that he entered the service of Henry Salt, probably marking a career step forward. Since he wrote at the end of 1819, the two years of travel he mentioned must be the same 1819 and 1818, during which he could not write as much as he probably had done before in 1817 upon his arrival in Egypt.

Alexandria to Cairo (February–March 1817)

Thanks to the aforementioned letters, there is no doubt that Ricci landed in Alexandria in 1817—more precisely, according to the *Travels*, on 21 February. Crossing the Mediterranean could take an extremely variable length of time, depending on wind and sea conditions: one could reach Egypt from Italy either in less than two weeks or in more than a month.[41] Ricci managed a quite smooth crossing of only nineteen days.

After a stop of a few days at Alexandria, Ricci set off to Cairo, visiting Abu Qir (25 February), Rosetta (26 February), Fuwa, and Tarrana. He arrived in Cairo a week after he had left Rosetta, so probably around 5 March. Here, Ricci showed his credentials and started searching for an employer. In his second letter to Governor Spannocchi, Ricci complains about the lack of assistance: "It seems that fate does not want to be particularly favorable in this stay, but I do not give up. The people to whom I was especially recommended by Your Excellency did not spend but little in my favor, and until now, despite daily promises, flatteries and kind welcomes, I am jobless."

Travel to Upper Egypt, Epigraphic Copy of the Tomb of Seti I, and Expedition to Berenike (February–September 1818)

Ricci's narrative resumes from a non-specified month, which should be January 1818. Belzoni reports that Ricci was sent up the Nile to Thebes with the British consular boat, carrying a letter from Belzoni himself to Henry Salt. No mention of the task is made by Ricci, who lists the stops on his way south: Giza, Beni Suef, Deir al-Barsha, Ashmunayn, Asyut, Qaw al-Kabir, Akhmim, Girga, Qena, and Dendera. At Girga, Ricci met the famous Fr. Ladislao, a Roman Catholic priest quite famous among travelers who also worked as an antiquities agent for Drovetti.[42]

According to the *Travels*, Ricci stopped to make some drawings; the trip was probably very fast, because once he received the letter from Belzoni, Salt left for Cairo, where he arrived already in early April. D'Athanasi is definitely mistaken when he writes that Ricci and Belzoni made the trip up the Nile together.[43]

That Ricci was responsible for the epigraphic copy of the tomb of Seti I has always been known. As Belzoni wrote in his account: "I had engaged Signor Ricci, a young man from Italy, who was very clever at drawing, and who with a little practice became quite perfect in his imitations of the hieroglyphics. He was to begin the drawings of the tomb on his arrival in Thebes."[44] Henry Salt, too, in his letters, alludes to the story: "Belzoni's models will be found interesting, and so will the sketches and outlines he takes home, done for him by a young Italian named Ricci—he himself does not draw so well."[45] And again: "I may mention that, during the whole of this year, while engaged in the drawings and models of the tomb, (in which he received every assistance and encouragement we could afford him,) both he and his artist, Mr. Ricci, lived entirely at my expenses, a table for all being kept at my desire by Mr. Beechey, and put down to my charge, to which I was by no means obliged by our contract."[46]

The *Travels* do not describe the methodology that Ricci adopted in his seven-month work, nor define how the wax models were prepared; it seems that Ricci worked alone for most of the time (p. 170). Ricci then left for Berenike on 16 September: this means that he had started the work around mid-February 1818. On 25 June 1818, nevertheless, Belzoni wrote to Bankes: "I am now taking the model of the new discovered toomb in Theebs and mean to have it imitated in Ingland. It is above six month we have begane this tidious work, the desin is two thards taken, the figures and erogliphiks are takaing in moles of wax,"[47] placing the start of the work directly at the beginning of 1818.

While working in the Valley of the Kings, Ricci offered medical assistance to anyone who needed it. Belzoni wrote about one of the miners belonging to Cailliaud's expedition: "It happened, that near the end of September, one of the miners, who was sent from the mountain to the Nile for provisions, had to come down from Edfu to Esne, and was returning to the desert, when he fell sick. Hearing from some of the Arabs that a Christian physician was at Beban el Malook, he came to beg the doctor would prescribe something to cure him."[48]

Baroness von Minutoli, who would later visit Upper Egypt in the company of her husband and Ricci, wrote a few details about the Theban period of Ricci:

Doctor Ricci, who spent nine months[49] at Thebes, told me that, once, taking his lunch close to the catacombs, saw a dozen of these animals [i.e., serpents], four to five feet long and pink colored, getting closer and slipping around vases filled with milk, which were on the ground, in order to drink. Their bodies, in the most gracious position, looked as being part of the vase itself to form a handle. And it is clearly in this way that these animals have given the ancients the idea of such gracious vases, whose elegant shapes we still try to imitate.[50]

Visiting the tomb of Seti I, the baroness added: "The two side walls flanking the entrance are covered in a great number of hieroglyphs; Mr. Ricci, who had copied them some time ago for Mr. Bankes, reckoned twenty thousand of them."[51] Indeed, there are within the Bankes manuscripts a few life-size drawings from the tomb of Seti I made by Ricci on transparent paper (DHC, D/BKL II.B.6–26, II.B.28–35).

Instead of giving clearer information on the work relationship between Belzoni and Ricci, the *Travels* provides contradictory details.[52] Ricci presents his interest in the tomb as a matter of private curiosity, completely autonomous from any paid engagement (p. 167). In another passage, Ricci directly accuses Belzoni of the theft of his drawings, which he had left in the tomb before the Berenike expedition and could not find at his return. Only the mediation of Henry Salt allowed Ricci to get paid for the drawings and receive Belzoni's public apologies (p. 176). He speaks again about it in his letter to Bernardino Drovetti, dated 28 August 1819 and written almost a year after the events. The letter can now be interpreted in its true meaning: "Since his arrival at Thebes Mr. Salt spent himself to settle the issue, finally, at the island of Philae, we reached an agreement that was not much disadvantageous to me, and Belzoni apologized in front of Mr. Bankes and Mr. Salt."[53]

What is written by Ricci is in sharp contrast with Belzoni's version. It is probably true that Belzoni took the drawings without Ricci knowing it, but there is evidence that Belzoni had already given Ricci a down payment, and therefore that there was an agreement between the two. In a letter by Belzoni to Bankes, the giant of Padua writes: "I shall take it as a favor if you would request the Doctor Ricci to send me a recept of the sume he resived [sic] in payment for his occupations for me, as well as medical assistance."[54] A note written by Sarah Belzoni in a small diary miraculously survives in the Bristol City Museum & Art Gallery: "Doctor Ricci received in Cairo previous to his departure 300, received at destination 356, received from Mr. S[alt] 2,000 total 2,656. Drawing is 1,400 professional 256."[55] The first sum mentioned looks like a down payment to reach Thebes with the consular boat and thus start the work. Then a second installment is received upon arrival. A third sum is given by Henry Salt and could be the payment for some drawings (possibly the 'Salt Watercolours' at the British Museum) and for medical assistance. Finally, the note specifies which expenses were for the drawings and which for medical treatment. To add to the confusion, in his second letter to Spannocchi-Piccolomini, dated January 1818, Ricci announces that he has been engaged to draw the tombs of Luxor for Henry Salt and never mentions Belzoni.

The *Travels* gives additional information on the Berenike expedition, which was undertaken by Belzoni, D'Athanasi, Beechey, and Ricci himself. Belzoni recalls in his memoirs: "At this place [i.e., Wadi Bayza] Mr. Ricci, the doctor, was attacked with a violent disorder, and it was decided, that he should return the next morning, as it would increase if he advanced farther in the desert."[56] Ricci, referring to this very passage, reveals: "Belzoni wrote in his travel account to Berenike that from this point on I was forced to go back because I was sick. Even though this was the pretext I used not to continue the journey, I must in fact declare that a quarrel arisen between us because of his rudeness was the real cause of our separation" (p. 172). Later on, he adds: "I was forced to give up my journey to Berenike, because of the rudeness and arrogance of Belzoni" (p. 317). The words Ricci uses to describe the beginning of the same expedition are quite indicative too: "He proposed that I join him, or, better, he forced me" (p. 171).

Travel to Nubia (November 1818–May 1819)

Waiting for Belzoni to come back and thus retrieve his drawings, Ricci made some further explorations in the Theban necropolis and copied reliefs and objects. Once he resolved the dispute with Belzoni, Ricci joined Bankes, Salt, Baron von Sack, Linant, Finati, and D'Athanasi to explore the region between the First and the Second Cataracts.

The narration of Ricci is once more troublesome at this point, as he dates the departure to 1 January 1819 (p. 176). The date mentioned here is undoubtedly wrong, as it is contradicted by other records and Ricci's own notebook. In this short diary, published by Usick in 1999, the doctor states that the party left Qurna on 16 November 1818, and that on 1 January 1819 it was stationary at Gerf Hussein. So, Salt on the same topic: "Such were our occupations from October to February . . . about the middle of February, however, from some accidental cause, my health began to fail, and early in March I was obliged to quit the party and return to Cairo."[57]

The *Travels* lacks a description of the activities carried out in winter 1818–19. A reconstruction can be attempted through Ricci's notebook and other sources such as the accounts of Finati, Salt, Barry, Hyde, Linant, and D'Athanasi. During this long period, the large party visited the most important sites and produced a massive amount of plans, views, and epigraphic copies. Salt describes the group and its working routine:

> The party consisting only of very pleasant and agreeable people . . . the secondary planets were content to shine in their respective spheres, and looked up with all due deference to the more brilliant luminaries [i.e., Bankes, von Sack, and Salt himself]. All . . . were enthusiastically fond of the arts, and really vied with each other who should produce the best sketches; being generally occupied hard at it . . . from nine o'clock in the morning till dark.[58]

Despite the strong social differences (the party was made up of diplomats, aristocrats, gentlemen, and members of the middle class), all shared the efforts of the job, often working in teams.[59] The epigraphic copies made during those months are now extremely relevant, because many of the monuments recorded have since been lost: the portico and the inscribed shrine of the temple of Dabod, the South Temple at Tafa, the temple of Isis at Qurta, and the temples of Buhen, to mention just a few.

At Philae, Belzoni was asked by Bankes to remove the small obelisk (now at Kingston Lacy House, Dorset). The operations went on with some difficulties, both logistic—the obelisk fell into the Nile, but was successfully recovered by Belzoni—and diplomatic: Drovetti and Bankes were disputing the ownership of the monument. On this occasion, the hostility between Belzoni and Ricci burst out again: the former accused the latter of being a spy in the service of Drovetti.[60]

Besides working as draftsman, Ricci obviously served as physician, too. Under the date of 22 November 1818, he writes: "Two days ago Mr. Bankes was threatened by ophthalmia, caused by sand that had entered the globe of his eye; fortunately the application of a lead solution completely stopped the inflammation, and today he is able to proceed with his work."[61] On 15 December, he was even sent back from Dabod to the First Cataract to treat Huyot, who would later become his friend, probably for this reason.[62] Jean-Nicolas Huyot was a French traveler who followed Bankes on this trip by just a few days, recording almost the same archaeological sites.

On 13 December, leaving Philae, the party met with the travelers Baillie, Godfrey, Wyse, and Barry.[63] They would meet again exactly a month later.[64] Barry writes:

> Mr. Salt showed me the whole of the sketches that have been made since leaving Philae. They were all in pencil and very numerous. They are the work of himself, Mr. Beechey (whom he calls his Secretary) and a French artist named Linant. I looked over Mr. Bankes' drawings, which, on account of their great number, he kept in a basket. They principally relate to detail such as hieroglyphs, ornaments, etc.[65]

At the end of five months of feverish work, the group split into two parts. Ricci writes: "Mr. Salt and the rest of the party went back to Cairo, and I stayed with Mr. Bankes, determined to reach Dongola via land" (p. 176). Sources do not agree on the numbers making up this second group, as it seems that Salt, Linant, and von Sack had abandoned the trip only at Wadi Halfa and not earlier.[66] Still, Ricci insists that on 26 February, "Mr. Beechey and Mr. Hyde, who suddenly decided to make the journey with us, had left Mr. Salt and joined us at Wadi Halfa" (p. 177). The presence of Hyde at Wadi Halfa, even though confirmed by Finati ("Their number was augmented by two additional persons quite at last, who were a Mr. Hyde [an English gentleman not previously known to Mr. Bankes] and his Greek servant"),[67] is in contrast with the version given by Hyde himself, who dates his joining the group at Abu Simbel on 14 February 1819.[68]

The journey was not an easy one from the beginning. Without the mediation of Henry Salt, the only one with real political influence, the party met with problems in getting the necessary permissions granted. Hassan Kashif[69] warned them of the hazard of the journey and only after long insistence gave them a sealed letter for his son Ahmad Kashif, based at Mograkka (p. 177).[70]

The group left Wadi Halfa on 26 February, reached Semna East on 1 March, and entered the district of Mograkka a week later. Here something unpredictable happened: while our travelers were taking a bath, the guides fled with all the camels. The episode is also narrated by Finati and D'Athanasi in a similar fashion.[71]

The party had to find a way to cross the river, since Ahmad Kashif was at Amara, on the east bank. The description of the crossing has opposite tones in the two versions of Ricci and Finati. The latter states that, after they caught the attention of the inhabitants of a Nile island, they were assisted in the crossing and even "well fed and kindly received upon the little island, especially by the women."[72] Worried they would be asked to pay a high price, the members of the group crossed the other branch of the river alone overnight. On the other hand, Ricci states that the *kabir*, the head of the caravan, jumped into the Nile and swam to the small island, whence he came back with a raft. This way, divided into pairs, they could reach the island.[73] Ricci continues by describing the hostility of the natives (p. 180). According to him, they spent the night on the island and then crossed the second branch of the river to get to the east bank only early the following morning.

The treatment they received from the *kashif* was not friendly and, even though they had a letter from his father, he refused to let them proceed, granting them only one camel to carry their luggage. He gave them a few hours to make some drawings at Amara and to see, at a distance, Sai Island. The expedition had thus failed; there was nothing left to do other than head back to Egypt. Nevertheless, more adventures were waiting for the group. Finati narrates how through robbery they succeeded in securing more camels for themselves. Ricci fails to report a funny episode that can be found in Finati's pages:

We were already within about two days of Wadi Halfa, when all at once we recognized the Ababde chief of those who had thrown us into all our difficulties, coming towards us upon his camel in a narrow defile. . . . Such of our number as were then mounted sprung from their saddles, those on foot forgot all their weariness, and ran up, and the unconscious drivers of the beasts that we had waylaid stood in stupid astonishment to see the great Ababde surrounded in an instant, and dragged by the leg to the ground, where he lay at the mercy of all, and was most severely drubbed with whatsoever came first to hand, even the sick man, Mr. Hyde, sliding off from his tall beast, to take his full share in this administration of summary justice.[74]

The following encounter with Hassan Kashif is described by Ricci as a cold audience full of resentment and tension (p. 182). Completely different once again is the account of Finati, in which the old man reproves the behavior of his son and treats the party to a generous meal accompanied by music.[75] Of a similar tone is D'Athanasi's account.[76]

The group rested at Wadi Halfa for a week (18–23 March 1819), documenting the site of Buhen and particularly the discoveries made in their absence by the Portuguese Antonio da Costa.[77] At Wadi Halfa the party also met with John Fuller, accompanied by Henry Foskett and Nathaniel Pearce, who described Bankes's party in the following terms: "A little flotilla of boats belonging to Mr. Bankes, Mr. Beechey, and Mr. Hyde, who had just returned from an unsuccessful attempt to penetrate . . . above the Second Cataract."[78]

Finati's account, which until now was the only source for this part of the journey, records only two stops, at Maharraqa and Philae, on the way back to Cairo. On the contrary, Ricci describes in detail (even if no date is given) the period March to May 1819, spent in fruitful digging and epigraphic copy at Faras, Jebel al-Shams, Jebel Adda, Abu Simbel, Derr, Amada, Abu Handal, Wadi al-Sebu'a, Qurta, Dakka, Gerf Hussein, Dandur, Kalabsha, Tafa, Qertassi, and Dabod. At the end of the journey, back in Beni Suef on 18 May, Bankes proposes to his fellow travelers a trip to Fayoum to search for the famous Labyrinth, but nobody accepts and he ventures alone with the dragoman (p. 194). The trip to Fayoum is briefly mentioned in D'Athanasi's account[79] and Bankes must have accomplished it very quickly, since he was already back in Luxor before the end of May 1819.[80]

Work for William John Bankes (May 1819–February 1820)

Nothing is said in the *Travels* about Ricci's activity in Egypt between the end of the Nubian journey and the Siwa trip, which occurred nine months later. Little information can be gleaned from other sources, either. As stated before, Finati notes that Ricci was charged by Bankes to copy the reliefs in the tombs of Beni Hasan and that the doctor never accomplished the task.[81] In the letter to Drovetti written in Cairo on 28 August 1819, Ricci admits to being "forced to travel continuously to finish and arrange his drawings, since Mr. Bankes intends to leave the country at the first occasion."[82]

In a second letter, written from Cairo on 13 November 1819 and addressed to Patrizio Rontani, Ricci announces to his friend that he has become Salt's physician, but also that he is thinking about leaving for Upper Egypt in two to three months' time to finish his drawings there.[83] In the same letter, Ricci tells his friend about his decision to publish the *Travel in Nubia* with plates showing plans and reliefs. It is possible that Ricci spent this time taking personal copies of the drawings that he had made for Bankes and that he was due to hand over before the latter's departure.

Travel to Siwa (March–April 1820)

Due to its position far into the Western Desert, Siwa Oasis had until then maintained polit-ical autonomy and a certain degree of economic prosperity. At Siwa, the trade route coming from Cyrenaica and Fezzan divided in two, one reaching Cairo and one going south toward Asyut and thence Selima Oasis.[84] Obtaining control of these trade routes was the reason why Muhammad Ali decided to send a military force to conquer Siwa.

According to Edme-François Jomard, it was Drovetti who pushed the pasha to finally undertake the conquest.[85] Also according to the French consul Pillavoine,[86] Drovetti was involved in this expedition from the beginning. In his dispatch to the French minister of foreign affairs from Alexandria on 6 May 1820, he notes:

> Mr. Drovetti persuaded Ibrahim Pasha . . . to undertake an expedition against the nomadic Arabs who have taken over Siwa. . . . This idea of Mr. Drovetti was met with favor and he was entrusted with its execution under the orders of a Turk, at the head of some thousand men; the cannon made the Arabs flee and the army conquered an island where they found nothing but ruins.[87]

The protection of the Turco-Egyptian army was a great incentive for anyone who wanted to visit the remote oasis, not only because of the hazard of the long journey, but mainly due to the hostility of the inhabitants. The French explorer Frédéric Cailliaud had visited only a few months earlier (December 1819) with Pierre-Constant Letorzec, but could not work very profitably because of the continuous harassment of the inhabitants. Before him, other travelers had visited the oasis: Poncet in 1698, Browne in 1793, Hornemann in 1798, and Boutin also in 1819. Nevertheless, a systematic and updated description of the archaeolog-ical remains of the site was still missing.

The sources for the reconstruction of this journey are Jomard's book published in 1823, which is based on the notes taken by Drovetti together with the drawings made by the other members of the party; a long letter of Frediani to Marquess Canova, dated 30 March 1820; Frediani's newspaper report in the *Gazzetta di Milano*;[88] and a couple of unpublished note-books written by Linant and now kept at the Bibliothèque Centrale des Musées Nationaux in Paris (Mss. 267.4–5).

The members of the new expedition gathered around Drovetti, who had received the official appointment directly from Muhammad Ali. Frediani, who, as official dragoman, received permission to join the group directly from Boghos Yusufian, writes: "We were joined by Mr. Linan [*sic*] and Dr. Ricci, who were made part of the group through the attention of Mr. Salt, General Consul of Britain."[89] On his side, Linant states that he had to ask permission of the viceroy, who granted it on condition that Drovetti himself agreed upon the matter. Drovetti accepted, imposing his own condition: that all drawings would be handed to him at the end of the journey. He nevertheless promised to keep them for personal use only. He failed to keep this promise when he gave the drawings to Jomard, who published them in 1823.[90] It is not clear whether Ricci himself had to sign an agreement of the same kind, but it is probable because his drawings were also eventually published by Jomard.[91] Some of the drawings made by Linant and Ricci are preserved in the Bankes records,[92] with copies of the plates published by Jomard.[93] As seen previously, Ricci was already acquainted with Drovetti, to the point that in the letter dated 28 August 1819 he had written: "Since my return from Nubia I should have performed my duty towards your precious person." It is possible that Ricci had met Drovetti in Luxor during his work in the tomb of Seti I, but what was "his duty" remains unclear.

At the beginning, the group decided to follow the army, which had a few days' advantage. Hassan Bey Shamashurgi, leading a force of one thousand or two thousand men consisting of irregular bashi-bazouk, Bedouins, and some pieces of artillery,[94] was proceeding with forced marches, hoping to outrun an epidemic of plague that had spread in his encampment. Fearing the pestilence and worried that they would find all wells empty, the party decided to take a different route. They avoided the coastal road to Marsa Matruh and advanced into the desert at al-Hammam. Here, Ricci states that he copied three inscriptions. The place was at that season covered in lilies and anemones, while under the soil they even found white truffles.

The party proceeded into the middle of the desert, reaching Alam al-Halfa and al-Himaymat. Thence they followed the line formed by the northern border of the Qattara Depression, reaching Labbaq (9 March), Abu Marzuq, and Abu Tartur (10 March). Finally, on 14 March, they reached the oasis of al-Qara, in the territory of Siwa. Here they met with the army of Hassan Bey, while the inhabitants of al-Qara had already abandoned the village.

Following the army at a short distance, Ricci and the others could see the military maneuvers in detail and record interesting particulars about the war. Near Birkat Zaytun, thirty kilometers east of Siwa, the soldiers of Hassan Bey were ambushed by the Siwans. The short battle was easily won by the Turco-Egyptians. After the fight, Drovetti and his men visited and recorded the monuments of the area (Abu al-Awaf, Zaytun).

On 18 March, not far from the city of Siwa, the Turco-Egyptian army was attacked again by the locals, who were easily routed by canister shot and took refuge inside the walled city. Siwa was immediately put under siege from the south side. Negotiations for the surrender started on 19 March, but by 24 March the city was still unable to fulfil the conditions dictated by the bey. Therefore, Ricci and the others started exploring the environs.

Al-Khamissa, Deir al-Rumi, and Jebel al-Mawta were the closest sites to the city, but since the negotiations were prolonged further, the party also decided to visit al-Arrashi Oasis, nowadays in Libya. Ricci (p. 207), Frediani, and Jomard report fabulous stories told by the natives about this place.[95] The group returned to the encampment on 29 March and was informed that the city had in the meantime fully surrendered.

The comprehensive description of the oasis made by Ricci deals with almost all aspects of the republic: customs, laws, agriculture, social organization, diet, and demography. It is fully comparable with contemporary and previous descriptions, at the same time enriching the sources at our disposal on the subject. It is rather peculiar that none of these travelers mentions a social custom quite widespread in Siwa until at least after the Second World War and denounced as scandalous only in 1917:[96] institutionalized homosexual weddings. Ricci and the others do, however, notice an important fact related to this practice: that the city had two quarters, one for married people and one for unmarried young men (p. 211). These were the *zaggala*s (lit. 'club-bearers'), part of the military class that was in charge of the defense of the oasis and that entertained open homosexual relationships.[97]

After the city had surrendered, Drovetti, Ricci, Linant, and Frediani dedicated their time to the study of what they thought was the Temple of the Oracle, consulted by Alexander the Great. Following the interpretation provided by those who preceded them, they concentrated their efforts on the ruins of Umm al-Ubayda, a small temple built by Nakhthorheb (Nectanebo II, 360–343 BC). They copied reliefs and dug around, discovering two enclosure walls. The Temple of the Oracle is now believed to be in the village of Aghurmi, a few hundred meters north of Umm al-Ubayda. It is a temple built during the Twenty-sixth Dynasty (664–525 BC) and altered during the Ptolemaic period (305–30 BC). The building is incorporated into the village, where houses used to be five floors high. In fact, the group visited Aghurmi—referred to as Shargiya by Ricci: Drovetti reports on the village and Linant made a drawing of the main square with its well and the mosque;[98] it seems that the inhabitants kept the temple secret, so that nobody was actually able to see it.

After they finished their work on the monuments, the group left the oasis, which greatly displeased the bey, who recognized the usefulness of the presence of a European doctor in the camp. After they had visited the ruins of Qasr al-Gashsham and Abu Shuruf, on 4 April the group was already back at al-Qara and immediately proceeded along the Qattara Depression. On 10 April they arrived at Labbaq: from this point onward they cut through the desert toward the east in the direction of Hatiyat Maghra. Thence on the morning of 14 April they entered Wadi al-Natrun (also known as Scetis), with the purpose of visiting the Coptic monasteries and refilling water and food provisions.

Ricci's descriptions of the monasteries are vague. It seems that he is mixing information related to at least three of the four monasteries of Scetis: Deir al-Suryan, Deir Anba Maqar (St. Macarius), and Deir al-Baramus—Deir Anba Bishoi (St. Bishoi) is the fourth. Ricci states that the name of the first monastery was "Sidi Suryan" in Arabic and "St. Macarius" according to the monks, while in reality the two names identify two different monasteries. The mention of a church without paintings suggests Deir al-Baramus, the rich library with Coptic-only manuscripts seems to exclude Deir al-Suryan, while the legend of St. Ephraim's stick points back to Deir al-Suryan. Despite all these inaccuracies, Ricci is an important source, being the only westerner to leave a description of the monasteries between 1799 (visit of Andréossy) and 1837 (visit of Lord Curzon). Baron von Minutoli, even though he mentions them, and not in a very flattering way (the monks according to him are "very rough and without culture"),[99] does not actually visit them in his 1820 travel. The same can be said for Lord Prudhoe in his 1828 journey.

The party reached Cairo on 17 April 1820 (p. 222). We do not know what Ricci did between this date and the following journey to Sinai. He was probably still busy finishing drawings for Bankes and accordingly was often out of Cairo. On 4 May 1820, Salt wrote to Nathaniel Pearce, who was now his house manager, that "Mr. Bokty's family are to have the chambers below, the great hall above, and Mr. Ricci's chamber."[100]

Travel to Sinai (September–November 1820)

After Muhammad Ali had consolidated his power in Egypt, Sinai became more accessible to adventurers and pilgrims. In fact, the Bedouins had signed some agreements with the pasha, exchanging military exemption for the duty of patrolling the borders and protecting caravan routes.[101]

Many travelers had visited the peninsula in the years before Ricci: even William John Bankes himself in 1815. Unfortunately, the English gentleman did not leave much information about his journey.[102] William Turner also visited Sinai in the same year, while Burckhardt did in 1816 and John Hyde in 1819. The latter went on behalf of Bankes, searching for certain manuscripts and to return others,[103] and was preceded by only a few weeks by Frediani with two other unidentified Italians.[104] In 1820, Sir Frederick Henniker visited the peninsula as well.[105]

The journey to Sinai was undertaken four and a half months after the return from Siwa and started on 1 September 1820. According to Ricci, it was on his own initiative and Linant was involved only later (p. 222). Whether the initiative was in fact Ricci's, or whether it was Linant's, is not clear. It is nevertheless certain that Bankes, at the time already in England, strongly opposed the idea, convinced as he was that this trip was just a waste of time and that Linant should already have been on his way to Meroe. Linant wrote to Bankes in April 1821:

> I am very sorry that I still do not know your opinion on . . . [my] journey to Sinai. . . . You will receive, Sir, via the same ship that has come to take Mr. Salt's antiquities another travel [account],[106] which even though has not the same interesting subject as that of Siwa, it does not lack to record things that might attract your attention. It is a journey to Mount Sinai that I undertook in mid September because a certain Mr. Stink, who had gone that way searching for mines, told Mr. Salt that he had seen a number of caves covered in hieroglyphs, many inscriptions and other antiquities. . . . In fact we found many caves, but these were nothing else than mines and this Mr. Stink had mistaken the chisel marks on the stone for hieroglyphs. However, we found on the nearby stones many very interesting hieroglyphic stelae. The most remarkable thing that we have seen is an Egyptian monument particularly interesting; I presume that you will see in my report that this could reasonably be nothing else but a cemetery.[107] It's the monument we were told about by Mr. Hyde and that Niebhur had visited long before him.[108]

Since Linant's travelog seems to have been lost on its way to Britain, Ricci's account is the only narrative source for this travel.

The two men visited the most important sites on the southwestern side of the peninsula and stopped for some time at the Holy Monastery of St. Catherine, even if their original goal was to reach Aqaba and Petra, already visited by Bankes five years before. This further exploration had to be abandoned when the monks of St. Catherine strongly advised against it and the Bedouins refused to guide them since Aqaba was regarded as a very dangerous place (p. 244). The same advice had been given the previous year to John Hyde, who wrote to Bankes in the following terms: "The Greek who accompanied Sheikh Ibr(ahi)m [i.e., Burckhardt] on his excursion to Akaba . . . strongly dissuaded me from attempting to visit that place from the hostile temper the Arabs in that part of the desert had recently manifested."[109]

Ricci and Linant left Cairo traveling toward Suez along the traditional route of the Islamic pilgrimage, the Darb al-Hagg, reaching the city only after three days' march and a short stop at the castle of Agruda. At Suez, the stay was prolonged for twelve days. The city hosted a British consular agent who had charge of the shipment of trade goods—especially coffee—toward the Mediterranean. This same agent welcomed the two travelers and gave them the money necessary to continue the trip, because, lamented Linant, Salt "left for Alexandria and I stayed in Cairo without knowing what to do."[110]

Since the Bedouin guide promised by the local *kashif* was out of town on other business, Linant and Ricci decided to leave alone. The two men visited Ayun Musa (13 September), a little palm oasis traditionally identified with one of the stops of the biblical Exodus. Ricci noted the ruins of a village, excavated by Supreme Council of Antiquities officials only in the 1990s and discovered to have pottery kilns of the Coptic and Islamic periods and a tomb dated to the Coptic period.[111]

Following the coastline, Ricci and Linant crossed Wadi Amura and Wadi Gharandal, and reached Hammam Fara'un, another site traditionally connected to the Exodus. Ricci described the caves with hot springs and recorded the temperature, which was not different from the one measured by the French commission and remains unchanged until now (around 70°C).

From this point onward, the route followed by the two travelers is not completely clear, since the only toponym quoted by Ricci, "Jebel al-Kabrit," cannot be exactly located, even though it suggests the presence of sulfur deposits. The route is tracked on an unpublished map drawn by Linant and kept in Dorchester (see plate 89).[112] The road taken seems to be as follows: from Hammam Fara'un, the two men entered Wadi Wasayit to the east, went around the mountain of Hammam Fara'un in order to go back to the coast at the sulfur mines (Ricci's Jebel al-Kabrit), and finally took to the east again along Wadi Sidri, and thence to al-Maghara.

Along the way, Linant was attacked by fever and Ricci provided him the necessary assistance. Waiting for Linant's health to improve, Ricci visited Wadi Mukattab, where he copied seven inscriptions (p. 230). The wadi is famous for its many Arabic, Greek, Nabataean, and even Armenian[113] inscriptions dated to the second century AD and later. Waiting for Linant to recover, Ricci visited the turquoise mines of al-Maghara and copied fifteen more inscriptions. In 1825, Champollion was shown these drawings and he made a personal copy of five inscriptions, which were later published by his brother in the *Notice descriptive*. These texts were also copied by other travelers, but were destroyed at the beginning of the nineteenth century when a British mining company resumed the exploitation of the mines, using dynamite and causing the collapse of the caves.[114]

On 23 September, the caravan moved toward Wadi Firan, which represents the main access to the Monastery of St. Catherine from the west. The site, which still nowadays represents the largest oasis in South Sinai, was already an archbishopric in the fourth century, when a bishop named Nectarios appears to be in charge.[115] The ruins were imposing even before the recent excavations directed by Peter Grossmann uncovered most of the town.[116] Here, Ricci says they were received with much hospitality by the local shaykh, Salah. Ricci inquires about habits, customs, and food, and gathers ethnographic information about the Bedouins of Sinai. He also describes a sword given by General Kléber to a Bedouin shaykh during the French expedition. Taking advantage of Linant's sickness, Ricci visited the nearby Jebel Tahuna, a legendary mountain with many monastic ruins, already described by the pilgrim Egeria at the end of the fourth century.[117]

From Firan, through Wadi Aliyat and Wadi Raha, the two men finally reached the Monastery of St. Catherine on 28 September. Here they were greeted with cordiality by the monks. During the whole stay, which lasted twenty-two days, Linant was convalescent and Ricci visited alone the vast area of Jebel Musa, Jebel Safsafa (Horeb), and Wadi al-Arba'in. A couple of very fine views of the monastery are the only drawings of the location made by Linant and the proof that he was confined sick.[118]

Since Ricci's visit, the monastery has changed a lot, especially in order to adapt to mass tourism in the last forty years. Two more gates have been added to the only two available at the time (the Justinian Gate and the so-called Patriarch's Gate): a western entrance in 1861 and a northern gate in the 1990s. The bell tower was erected only around 1871 to host a concert of nine bells donated by Czar Alexander II (1818–81). The entire south wing was demolished and rebuilt between 1930 and 1951 to host the new library building donated by King Faruq of Egypt. Many cult chapels and the so-called Patriarchal Apartment were also demolished. A great number of Greek inscriptions copied by Ricci in the monastery are now lost: one on a copper plate hanging on the kitchen door, another on the door leading to the monks' quarters, a third in the "subterranean storerooms," another on the so-called Tower of Empress Helena, and the monumental inscription of Emperor Justinian. Unfortunately, none of Ricci's copies survives in Dorchester. They were shipped by Salt along with Linant's journal and must have been lost on their way. Salt writes: "At the same time . . . I forwarded you two Greek inscriptions copied by Dr. Ricci, one in comparatively modern Greek and the other placed by Justinian over the gateway. . . . You have never acknowledged the receipt of these so that I fear they have also miscarried."[119]

Also quite interesting is the mention of a series of portraits of the archbishops of Sinai (p. 236). Nowadays, only one of those visible at the time survives: the portrait of Archbishop Ananias (r. 1660–70). Another painting, portraying Archbishop Constantius II (r. 1804–59), who was reigning during Ricci's visit, was painted after 1833, because it displays a badge of the Greek Order of the Redeemer, established only in that year.

Ricci visited the holy spots around the monastery with a local guide. Either an unprepared guide or Ricci's fallacious memory is responsible for the many inaccuracies at this point of the *Travels*: the compass orientation is completely inverted; the description of Jebel Katrina is mixed with that of Jebel Safsafa; the Chapel of the Oikonomissa becomes the House of Prophet Elisha; the Fatimid mosque atop Jebel Musa is described as a Christian chapel. Despite these mistakes, Ricci's description is quite important, since it records sites most times neglected by other travelers, such as the series of chapels on Jebel Safsafa. Ricci mentions only those of St. Gregory of Mount Sinai and two others without specifying the names, but possibly St. Anne and the Holy Girdle. Many of these chapels are now in ruins.[120] Ricci also visited the monastery, the garden, and the chapel of Wadi al-Arba'in.

After they paid the monks for their hospitality, Ricci and Linant headed toward the coast, following Wadi al-Shaykh, then crossed the mountain chain of Agrat Safha and Wadi Hibran, and entered the plains in view of the Red Sea and the coastal town of al-Tor (22 October). Ricci describes the town in detail, unlike most of the travelers of his period. A beautiful drawing by Linant records how the town looked two hundred years ago; now the historic city center is completely falling into decay.[121] The Greek cultural heritage of al-Tor is suffering most: the flourishing community witnessed by Ricci in 1820 (p. 245) is reduced today to a scant ten families. Ricci describes also a *kathisma* (a small hermitage) in the oasis of Hammam Musa, to the north of the town. Here in 1988, the Egyptian authorities expropriated the monks, confining them to a corner of the oasis, and built a spa of doubtful success, cementing the warm-water spring and erecting more buildings in the palm grove.[122] One of the few images representing the building as it was two hundred years ago is again a drawing by Linant.[123] The Greek community of al-Tor also suffered from the Israeli occupation in 1967: the monks report that the entire Greek population of the town was forcibly deported by the authorities. The inhabitants, leaving on government buses, gave the monks custody of their belongings.[124]

After failing to hire Bedouin guides to reach Aqaba, Ricci and Linant set off to Ras Muhammad, the southern edge of the peninsula (24 October). They immediately turned back and bypassed al-Tor to observe the phenomenon of the booming sand near Jebel Naqus (p. 247).[125]

Crossing Wadi Hibran again, and thence to Wadi Firan and Wadi Mukattab, the two men reached the foot of the mountain of Serabit al-Khadim on 29 October 1820 (p. 247). Leaving the rest of the caravan behind, Linant and Ricci climbed up along the al-Khassif route to the shrine of Hathor. In a short span of time, they copied as many inscriptions as possible, both in the shrine and in the mines. Linant even drew a quick plan.[126] In particular, Ricci made a copy of the inscription carved by Sobekherheb, which Champollion would see and copy in Florence in 1825.[127] Five more inscriptions, including one of Thutmose IV and another of Seti I, were copied by Ricci and were later published in the *Lettres à M. le Duc de Blacas*, also by Champollion.[128]

The ancient Egyptian sanctuary of Serabit al-Khadim was the last site visited by the two men in Sinai. After two days of rest at Suez, Ricci and Linant proceeded to Cairo. Trying to break the record of the fastest ride between the two cities, Linant arrived after thirteen hours, but fell sick and was confined to bed for four months. Ricci arrived in fourteen hours and a half. So Linant writes to Bankes:

> I doubt I would have survived without the cares of Dr. Ricci; I recovered ten days before reaching Cairo, but the day after my arrival, I fell sick again with an obstruction of the liver, one of the bladder, and a strong dysentery. I stayed in bed from November until February and it has been only fifteen to twenty days that I am now completely well. Many people say that my illness comes because of traveling from Suez in thirteen hours and the movement of the dromedary disturbed my intestines. In my opinion, it is because of the bad waters I drank.[129]

At the end of this journey, according to Ricci, he was received in an audience by the viceroy, where he presented the prince with a large rough turquoise stone in order to encourage him to resume the exploitation of the mines of Serabit al-Khadim (p. 249).

Second Voyage to Upper Egypt with Baron von Minutoli (December 1820–February 1821)

Baron Johann Heinrich Menu von Minutoli (1772–1846), a former general of the Prussian army, was assigned by the King of Prussia Friedrich Wilhelm III (r. 1797–1840) the task of undertaking a scientific expedition in Egypt, and especially to explore the Libyan Desert and the Siwa Oasis. The expedition set off from Cairo on 5 October 1820, and, after some days of exploration, left Siwa on 12 November: unlike Drovetti, the baron followed the coastal road to Marsa Matruh and then headed south. Coming back, he followed the same road Drovetti had taken, along the Qattara Depression, across Wadi al-Natrun, and finally reaching the Nile.

In 1824, the baron published the results of his exploration, enriched by many plates. Some of the plates were authored by Ricci, who must have provided him with copies of the drawings previously done for Drovetti, since he did not take part in the expedition. Minutoli's wife, Countess von Schulenburg (a very prestigious house of Saxony-Anhalt), also wrote a quite interesting memoir, published in French in 1826. The book is a detailed source on a second journey undertaken by the couple in Upper Egypt. She writes: "We rented for the purpose a large boat, with two comfortable rooms and an antechamber for our servants. Doctor Ricci, a young man full of talents, accompanied us as physician and draftsman."[130]

The journey started around mid-December 1820[131] and followed, by roughly a month, the return of Ricci from Sinai. The main stops were sites well known to Ricci, such as Beni Hasan, Hermopolis, Girga, Abydos, Qena, and Dendera. The party stayed in the Theban area for eight full days (17–24 January 1821). The group proceeded south to Isna, al-Kab, Edfu, Jebel al-Silsila, Kom Ombo, Aswan, and Elephantine. Baroness von Minutoli records an interesting anecdote about Ricci that is not found in any other source. It is almost the whole chapter 11 of the first volume of her memoir. It refers to the ancient Coptic monastery of Jebel al-Tayr, in the Minya region. Because of its rarity and importance, it is copied here in its entirety:

Our boat passing very quickly at this point, I fixed my eyes upon the rocks, diving into one of those dreams the soul cannot measure, when Doctor Ricci, approaching me, told me that this mountain chain hid a Coptic monastery, whence the monks would ordinarily come down to ask for alms from the travelers. It is in this monastery—he added—that I made a very interesting encounter the first time I traveled to Upper Egypt; it sounds like a fantasy story, but it really happened. These few words aroused my curiosity and I begged him to satisfy it, which he did, telling me what follows, roughly in these terms: "I wanted to visit Upper Egypt and I accepted, some years ago, the proposition made by an Englishman to accompany him. I was struck just like you by the strange shape of these rocks, when a different sight captured my attention. I saw, at the top, a man descending by the means of a rope, with incredible dexterity. Soon the man disappeared; he then jumped in the water and approached our boat, asking for alms for his convent. He was one of those Coptic monks who came to implore the charity of the passers-by. The extreme agility with which this man came down and some questions we addressed to him regarding his monastery, awoke our curiosity and we had the *ma'ash* approach the bank. We then followed our guide, who had taken the same narrow path cut in the rock he had used to descend; with some effort, we reached the top, where our eyes discovered an immense horizon. . . . Having satisfied our curiosity, we were about to leave this place so little agreeable, when we suddenly heard some harmonious words of the beautiful language of Petrarch and Tasso. Turning toward the voice, we saw a very old man, whose imposing build could not be bent by age and who, introducing himself as the abbot of the monastery, invited us, in the choicest words, to join him for some rest. Extremely surprised to find under the rough tunic of a Coptic monk a man familiar with the languages and the customs of Europe, we accepted his invitation. We sat on a stone bench with our host and three other monks, the only inhabitants of the monastery, who hastened to serve us dates and hot bread. . . . In the meanwhile, I was casting curious glances at the singular and surprising person we had met so unexpectedly in this wild place. . . . Unable to resist any longer my interest, or, better, the feeling of curiosity that dominated me, I dared with some embarrassment ask some questions on his condition and on the reasons that brought him to embrace it, adding that certainly Egypt could not be his fatherland. A shade of melancholy soon spread across his forehead and, feeling my indiscretion, I asked him to forgive my curiosity for the interest he inspired in me. He then answered, undoubtedly to reassure me, that his fate was nothing particular to deserve to inspire interest in anyone whatsoever; that he was a Roman by birth and that he was destined, as a younger son, to the ecclesiastical career, for which he had a strong aversion; that, fleeing his father's authority, he spent most of his life among the Infidels, whose faith he even embraced; that the death of a loved person made him feel the enormity of his sins and his mistakes and that, having decided to spend the rest of his life in penitence, he chose this wild and isolated place to end his days. . . . Moved by these words and by the expression that accompanied them, we bid farewell to the august old man, who gave us his blessing. Nine months later, coming back from Upper Egypt, wishing to see again the Coptic abbot, I proceeded to the convent; while approaching, one of the monks recognized me and showed me a freshly covered grave. He had ceased to suffer.[132]

The journey was pleasurable and probably did not involve many obligations for Ricci. The daily routine, described by the baroness, revolved around food provisioning: "After breakfast . . . my husband and Doctor Ricci, with their rifles, and I, followed by my little negro, descended to the river, and while these gentlemen were busy hunting, I enjoyed collecting plants and walking in the countryside."[133]

The party was back in Cairo on 28 February 1821. From there the German couple returned to Europe via Livorno. They had previously tried visiting Syria with Drovetti, but had failed to do so.[134] Ricci was getting ready for new adventures; but the relationship with Minutoli was not severed, as in the latter's book there are many references to incidents involving Ricci during his Sennar trip which followed.

In the letter of Henry Salt to William John Bankes, dated December 1822 and mentioned previously, the British consul shows he knows about the strong relationship between Ricci and Minutoli.[135] It seems that Ricci had earned the respect and the trust of the baron, and that he was negotiating a further collaboration.

Travel to Sennar (June 1821–February 1822)

The military expedition sent by Muhammad Ali against the regions of the Upper Nile in 1820 has aroused great interest among historians. The invasion of Dongola, Sennar, Kordofan, and Darfur has been explained in different ways, from the acquisition of gold mines to the desire to get rid of the Mamluk remnants who had taken refuge in Dongola after the 1811 massacre.[136] Even though the complete destruction of the Mamluks was the official reason the viceroy offered to Constantinople, the real motivation was the capture of black slaves to be enrolled in the army that Muhammad Ali was in such desperate need to recruit. Ricci seems to be aware of the real reasons behind the war (pp. 176–77). In a letter addressed to his son Isma'il Pasha, head of the expedition, the viceroy wrote: "The value of slaves who prove to be suitable for our services is more precious than jewels . . . hence I am ordering you to collect 5,000 of these slaves."[137] The viceroy also asked his son not to get distracted by searching for gold mines or collecting taxes.

The small Turco-Egyptian army, under the command of Isma'il Pasha, assisted by Abdin Bey, Bimbashi Haggi Ahmed, and Bimbashi Omar Agha, had set off in August 1820. Subsequently, Muhammad Defterdar Bey, son-in-law of the viceroy, had left Egypt in 1821 to conquer Darfur with men and artillery pieces hived off from the first army at Aswan. The border city had become the base for all operations.[138] Toward the middle of the same year, 1821, a third support expedition, with a supply of ammunition, uniforms, weapons, and fresh men, had left under the command of Ibrahim Pasha (1789–1848), adopted son of Muhammad Ali.[139]

In a letter to Patrizio Rontani dated 1 October 1820, Ricci quantifies the strength of the Turco-Egyptian army at Sennar as ten thousand men.[140] Quite different is Khaled Fahmy's estimation: "The total force of the two expeditions of Isma'il and Muhammad Defterdar was 4,000 soldiers, with Albanians, mamluks, Maghribis and Egyptian Bedouins."[141] McGregor agrees.[142]

Even though the army succeeded in the conquest of Sennar and the establishment of an administrative and fiscal control system, from the casualties' point of view the conquest was a disaster for both sides. One year after the departure, in September 1821, the dead in Isma'il's encampment had already reached six hundred, only to double within the short space of a month. The young son of the viceroy proved to be inadequate to conduct such a complex military campaign. In the words of Khaled Fahmy: "Isma'il was inexperienced, indecisive, stubborn, and failed to inspire the troops, who deserted him in a steady stream. His brutality, rashness, and impetuous nature eventually cost him his life. Moreover, owing to the haphazard way in which the campaign was conducted, there was a heavy toll on Sudanese civilians."[143] News of the atrocities committed on the natives by Isma'il Pasha and the Defterdar Bey reached Cairo, upsetting the 'Franks'[144] and Muhammad Ali himself. As for the slaves so ardently desired, thousands died even before reaching Egypt. The approximately twenty thousand who were lucky enough to get to Aswan to be drilled, suffered much and by 1824 were reduced to only three thousand.[145] Cornevin estimates that the number of Nubians killed or enslaved surpassed fifty thousand people.[146] The complete failure to achieve the objectives of the campaign forced Muhammad Ali to radically reform his army, levying Egyptian peasants for the first time.

For the reconstruction of the long and perilous journey to Sennar, many sources are available: Linant's own diary, in two different copies published fragmentarily by three different scholars;[147] the short account by Giovanni Finati;[148] the account of Cailliaud,[149] who preceded Linant and Ricci by a few months; the letters of Salt and Bankes; and the accounts of English[150] and Waddington and Hanbury.[151]

Bankes assigned the task of searching for the ruins of Meroe, which was, ideally, to continue the previous journey interrupted by the hostility of Ahmad Kashif at Mograkka, to Linant immediately after the failure of that expedition in 1819. So writes Finati on the matter:

> I have already mentioned Monsieur Linant, the young Frenchman whom Mr. Bankes on his final departure from Egypt had left there with a salary, upon condition of his taking the very earliest opportunity of following up the discoveries upon the Nile to the southward, with a view especially to fixing the site and examining the remains of Meroe. . . . Full twelve months had elapsed before I heard of any preparation at all for the journey.[152]

Bankes adds a note, full of resentment: "I am as much at a loss upon this point as the author can be, since the departure of the Egyptian army . . . for the expedition which was to open the upper country, took place in the autumn of 1820, and Monsieur Cailliaud and Monsieur Jomard[153] seem to have gone up with it at that time on the part of the French government."[154] Bankes was also upset about the presence of Ricci, whom he had to maintain. Salt had successfully distracted the doctor from Minutoli's attentions and succeeded in engaging him for a trivial amount of money. Salt presented the deal to Bankes as convenient in many respects, not least the advantage to Linant of traveling in the company of a physician.[155] In the same letter Salt reassures his friend about the (bad) quality of the competitors. Bankes was especially worried about competition because Sennar was at the time quite crowded with westerners.

> The persons now up the Country, I mean beyond Wadi Halfa, are Calliaud [sic] who draws so indifferently, and a Mons. Constant, a young astronomer,[156] but who is fit for nothing else; Mons. Le Chevalier Frediani, who is now employed as historiographer to the pasha and who writes a farrago of nonsense that nobody can understand; and besides these, two Prussian Naturalists who are wise in simples [medicinal herbs] and such like, but cannot draw.[157]

He adds: "It gives me great delight that this is likely to be so satisfactorily accomplished. Linant is wonderfully improved in his drawing and writes totally well and there is no person nor has been anyone above who can pretend to compete with him."[158]

According to Ricci's account, the travel had a personal dimension, too: "The departure of Ibrahim to Sennar aroused in me the desire to follow him, in order to visit the region." Linant and Ricci planned to leave on 5 June, five days after Ibrahim Pasha had set sail. Obtaining a firman was nevertheless not easy.

> You must know I had a great battle with the pasha about Linant's firmans. There had been an intrusion above by which Isma'il Pasha had been persuaded to write to his father not to let any travellers come up but especially English ones, and the pasha for some time absolutely refused to grant the one I demanded for Linant. I had three conferences with him on the subject and at last drove him to grant it by declaring that if he did not, it would put an end to all friendly communication between us and that I was sure it would be taken very ill by our Minister at home etc. This at last induced him to comply.[159]

A little south of Cairo, the boat of Ricci and Linant met with that of Le Lorrain, who was transferring the famous Dendera Zodiac, now in the Louvre (Inv. D 38), a masterpiece dating back to the time of Cleopatra VII (69–30 BC).[160] The massive reliefs, part of the roof of the temple, are one meter thick and weigh sixty tons. The Frenchman used dynamite to open cracks in order to facilitate the use of saws to extract it. In just three weeks, helped by a small group of locals, he succeeded in detaching the zodiac and loading it on his boat.[161] This ruthless operation greatly upset the European community in Egypt, perhaps hypocritically.[162]

A stop in the Theban area allowed Ricci to see again the Valley of the Kings, devastated that same year by a violent flash flood.[163] During this period, Linant and Ricci saw and copied the paintings detached from the tomb of Nebamun and temporarily stored in Yanni D'Athanasi's house, waiting to be shipped to the British Museum, where they are now held (No. 37984).[164] Linant's drawings are among the Bankes Mss. (NT/BKL II.A.1 and 2), while another copy of the dance scene, split into two drawings, is at the University Library of Pisa (Fonds Rosellini, Ms. 300.4, f. 62, c. 250 and Ms. 300.1, f. 61, c. 250).[165] There is no doubt that the author of the Pisan drawings is Ricci. The dance scene had so much captured the imagination of the travelers that Bankes, once he heard of it, asked for the immediate shipment of a copy.[166]

On 11 July, they had a quick stop at Jebel Silsila, then at Kom Ombo the day after, and finally Aswan and Elephantine (p. 255). Here they also arranged with the local authorities to remove the pedestal of the Philae obelisk, according to the instruction received by Bankes. It seems the agreements did not have any effect, as Salt was forced months later to arrange it again himself. Ricci and Linant spent a few days between Elephantine and Aswan working on the chapels of Amenhotep III and Ramesses II. Their drawings, in particular Ricci's epigraphic copies, are very valuable records because both chapels were demolished the following year.[167]

Ibrahim Pasha crossed the First Cataract on 24 July, while the two men found enough camels to proceed and set off on 15 August 1821. Linant observed that Ricci was in a bad mood, "which is very common for him," and refused to talk, apparently because his camel was uncomfortable.[168] Baron von Minutoli quotes an incident that happened to Ricci during this time:

> About half an hour south of Aswan there is a holy shrine called Fataha, a place for pilgrimage by both the inhabitants of the village and those of the surrounding country, who go there in order to check, by the following experiment, whether they are sinless or not. To determine this, the inquirer must first make a prayer, and he is stripped bare except for the shirt or petticoat. Then he sits down cross-legged, his hands resting against the head. Afterward, one of the bystanders hits him roughly on the shoulders. If he is thereby set in a circular motion, this is a proof of his sinlessness, and then he makes room for others, jubilant with joy; in the opposite case, he withdraws ashamed. Dr. Ricci also tried his luck, and succeeded in turning against expectations of all those present, so this circumstance contributed not a little to recommend him in their eyes as a true believer. Infertile women go to that place, in order to bear children by this procedure; while visibly pregnant women to facilitate childbirth.[169]

In the following days Linant and Ricci passed, without stopping, al-Kalabsha (16 August), Gerf Hussein, Dandur (18 August), Quban (19 August), Wadi al-Sebu'a (20 August), Amada

(22 August), Derr (23 August), Qasr Ibrim (25 August), Abu Simbel (27 August), and Wadi Halfa (28 August). Here, they showed their safe-conduct to the agha and successfully passed the Second Cataract on 29 August.

The caravan arrived at Kumma on 31 August and stayed for a couple of days to copy the reliefs and draw a map of the site. Ricci often proceeded alone, walking along different tracks and making his own explorations. On 5 September, they reached Mograkka, the limit of the unfortunate journey undertaken two and a half years before with Bankes (p. 268).

On 11 September, they finally crossed the border between Mahas and Dongola, not far from Tombos Island. Shortly after, they visited the ruins of Kerma, which unfortunately is described in only a few lines by both Ricci and Linant. On 14 September, they reached Maragha, or New Dongola, the eponymous capital of the kingdom, which they left on 22 September on a small boat.

The following day, they passed Qasr Wad Nimayri and on 25 September, Nawi Island. According to the boat crew, the inhabitants of this haunted island turned into crocodiles during the night (p. 277). On the evening of the same day, the group docked at Old Dongola to explore some of the ruins. On 4 October they met *malak* Sibayr of Hannakab, one of the local kings recently defeated by Isma'il Pasha, and hosted him on their boat (p. 282). Ricci describes also an unusual encounter, not noted by Linant, with the ruling queen of a small village (p. 283). This piece of information, which apparently is not to be found in other sources, might have a base of truth. According to Spaulding, in fact, "the status of nobility among the Funj apparently descended from mother to son, for as part of the coronation ritual a new Funj sultan was given a wife from the royal clan capable of bearing noble heirs. . . . For the royal wives were 'spies upon their husbands, and keep up the consequence of their birth in their husband's house, even after they are married.'"[170]

On 6 October the two men dismissed the boat in order to spend some days working on the ruins of Napata, Nuri, and Jebel Barkal. A map of the site was traced and the Meroitic pyramids were thoroughly explored. Linant and Ricci were only able to leave on 17 October, after they finally found camels for hire. They then crossed the Fourth Cataract and arrived at Abu Rumayla on 22 October. At this point, the head of the cameleers fled, apparently because he did not want to lead them into the district of Berber. On 24 October, the turmoil among the cameleers reached alarming proportions. Ricci remembered with apprehension what had happened during his first Nubian trip with Bankes and was afraid the incident would repeat itself. Finally, the arrival of some boats allowed the dismissal of the camels. The journey continued on the Nile without any particular difficulties, except for the passage of many strong cataracts (p. 293).

On 5 November they reached Berber, not before they were amazed at an encounter with a hippopotamus. Ricci marks the departure from the city three days after their arrival, so on 8 November, while Linant states that they immediately left Berber the morning of the same day and that they arrived at al-Demer in the evening. It is difficult to understand how such a discrepancy could have arisen. It is in any case noteworthy that Linant's own two accounts do not often agree on dates: the separation between Ricci and Linant dates to 7 November in the Kingston Lacy version and to 8 November in the version of the Bibliothèque Centrale des Musées Nationaux. The sudden separation of the two fellows is depicted by Ricci with a few simple words (p. 296). According to the doctor, it was simply a matter of logistics. Linant's version is much more accurate, and unpleasant. In the Kingston Lacy version of the diary Linant writes:

> At midday I ordered to start loading and I was not expecting what was about to come. The doctor had been sulking since Berber and it was impossible for me to guess the cause of his mood. Seeing that he would not talk, appearing hard-nosed, I would not talk to him, and this lasted until al-Demer. Being annoyed by his mood and always happy when he would come to talk, this time I also acted sulky, but only because I saw him being so. . . . As we were loading and he had his belongings loaded on a camel, I entered the place where we were and he said to me these words: "See, your dragoman took the camel that I wanted to ride; it does not suit me." I told him that my dragoman had ridden it the previous day and that I myself would have taken it if he had not; that if he had said so, my dragoman would have certainly given it to him; and moreover that he got what he deserved—since he had been sulking and not speaking we could not guess his wishes—and that I, for my part, did not care whether this had happened or even whether he sulked. Then I went out and he had his camel unloaded, saying that he would not leave. I did not want to talk with him about this madness because I would have become upset and this would have given a scandal to all the people of the country, which was not convenient, and they had already seen enough. Many *jalaba* and my dragoman tried to bring him to reason, but in vain; I thought that if I were to leave, he would have followed me, because I would not believe he would stay there without provisions. I set off and I left him two camels to carry him, but I sent word to the *kashif* not to give him any camel to go back and I said the same to the shaykh; I then left, telling him that he was a fool and that he alone would answer for this inconsiderate move. On my way, I thought that he would not return, because I knew his character. In addition, I recommended him to many *jalaba* and told them that they would be accountable for whatever happened to him.[171]

Finati simply writes: "At Damer, in consequence of some dispute, Dr. Ricci separated from Mr. Linant, and left us, and we heard no more of him for the present, nor did we even know in what direction he was gone, till we reaped the benefit of some good offices that he had done us at head-quarters before we arrived there."[172]

At this point, the two travelers separated. On 15 November, Ricci reached Shendi via the Nile, bypassing the ruins of Meroe that Linant would discover only on his way back. In the African city, Ricci visited the marketplace—one of the most important of the region—and gathered information on female genital mutilation, describing the procedures in detail.

Under the date of 17 November, Ricci notes a last meeting with Linant. Dating the incident to 13 November, Linant writes:

In the morning my dragoman had gone to the *kashif* and I was very surprised to see him come back followed by the doctor. My first impulse was to reach out to the doctor, unable to sulk and believing that he came to continue the journey with me. But I was wrong, because when my dragoman said: "I knew that the doctor would not go back," he answered: "How could I go back? If I had the money and the provisions, I would not have returned." These words showed me his black heart and touched me very deeply; I swore to myself I would not take him back with me and I behaved very coldly with him. Shortly after, he talked to me in particular and told me that when I left he went to the *kashif* and that he had asked for camels to come to Shendi, that they were given to him, and that the following day, when he was getting ready to set off, he saw a boat coming and, thinking that it was the one carrying the belongings of the doctor of Ibrahim Pasha, he went to embark in it with the intendant of the doctor, a Greek called Walnas. . . . I clearly saw from the way he spoke that he wanted to come back with me, but since he was undoubtedly waiting for some word from me to persuade him to stay, I was very careful to avoid it. On the contrary, I told him that everything he did was good and that I had no orders to give him, and that only Mr. Salt and Mr. Bankes would judge his actions and to them he would account for all that might come from this inconsiderate move. He told me that he did not want to be treated like a servant and that my men regarded him as such. This is false; it is known that he was my friend and he was considered like me, but this has always been his idea; I did not answer his words. Then, when he told me that he intended to go to Sennar, where he would certainly find some boats, I told him that the pasha would not give him any, because he had neither a firman nor a letter of recommendation, and that maybe he would be received badly because neither the letters of Salt nor the firman mentioned him. He told me that he would manage this. He asked me for some provisions, but this was impossible, and I told him that if I were to give him some, this could prevent me from undertaking my journey and that I did not want to run this risk, having to account for my conduct to Mr. Bankes. I went to the market with him and I left him when he was about to embark, telling him that at Sennar I would do all that I could for him.[173]

The separation was definitive, even if afterward the two men would exchange warm messages through couriers. Some time later, Linant had words of praise for his old companion: "I am very sorry of not having the doctor here any more, but I console myself knowing that he is running his luck. I am happy that I contributed a little to the fortune of my friend, because I can say that the main cause of his luck was our little quarrels and my small faults, and also his; I would be glad to see him in Cairo swimming in prosperity, because he deserves it, for more than one reason."[174] And, again: "I learned the sad news of the tragic death of Mr. Brine, I assure you, Sir, that it is the greatest sorrow I had during my journey, even greater than my separation from Ricci, so you can judge my grief."[175]

An interesting question is whether Ricci was just lucky to enter Ibrahim Pasha's encampment a few hours before the chief physician Antonio Scotto died, or whether he knew about the severe condition of his health, maybe through his "intendant," who gave him a lift on the boat to the encampment (p. 297). Ricci just mentions "a Greek who was on board," but does not reveal his identity, possibly to create a suspense effect. Without money and a firman, therefore lacking any sort of protection, Ricci would have probably not ventured alone had he not known about the illness of Scotto and the proximity of Ibrahim. Moreover, Ibrahim Pasha was suffering from severe dysentery and urgently needed a replacement for his chief physician, Scotto. Ricci was an ideal candidate in the eyes of the pasha, being already in the service of the British consul.

Ricci continued his trip south and passed by the sites of Musawwarat and Naqa, where the captain of the boat did not allow a stop. All intentions of a visit during the return would be frustrated by Ibrahim Pasha's sickness. On 24 November, Ricci reached the confluence of the White and the Blue Niles, at the spot where Muhammad Ali would soon build the city of Khartoum. Ricci reached Sennar city in just six days. He passed it, heading directly to Ibrahim Pasha's camp. Here, on 30 November, the welcome was extremely warm. Ricci refused the position of chief physician, but assured the pasha he would assist him until his full recovery. Antonio Scotto died the morning after, on 1 December 1821. Ricci arranged a Christian burial, assisted by the Copts in the army. Salt writes to Bankes about the issue:

The wretched medical man young Bosari and his tribe with Isma'il Pasha were held in so much contempt by Ibrahim Pasha that he would not employ them, but on hearing of Ricci's arrival he instantly sent for him, and pro tempore made him his first physician, at the same time writing down in the handsomest terms to me and assuring me that it should be no detriment to the mission, but on the contrary that he would send up for Linant and take him also in his company—on the expedition he had planned up the Nile and the Bahr el Abiad. This in fact he did and the *chaous*[176] and camels sent down for Linant were of great service in getting him up to Sennaar.[177]

A short time later, Linant received a letter from Ricci. As he describes it:

I saw a dromedary coming to us. It was an Ababda courier of Ibrahim Pasha. He told me that he had been searching for me for six days and that Ibrahim Pasha had sent him to deliver a letter that he gave me—it was from the doctor. He sent me a letter in which he wrote that he was worried for me and was afraid, since rumors were circulating about many assassinations, that something could have happened to me; that Ibrahim Pasha had sent two dromedaries on two different routes in order to find news about me. He also told me that His Highness wished me to join him quickly at Sennar and that the pasha would wait for me two or three days. At the end, he announced to me that Doctor Scotto had died and that the pasha had taken him in his place. This news pleased me a lot, and even more seeing that the doctor had no rancor.[178]

Linant answered immediately, announcing his arrival at Sennar in six days.[179] The men exchanged other letters during those weeks, traveling separated but not very far from one another. In the meanwhile, Linant wrote back to Salt to inform him about the recent developments.

> You know from the letter that I wrote you from Shendi that the doctor had left me and that he went to Sennar ahead of me. Seeing that I would not come to Sennar and fearing for me that they had killed me or that I was sick, he begged Ibrahim Pasha to send two dromedaries to find news about me. I found them at Halfaya, where they gave me two letters from the doctor, who let me know about his concerns. . . . He has now left with the pasha, while I am waiting for a man that the governor of Sennar has sent to the pasha in order to know his orders.[180]

Waiting for Ibrahim Pasha to get better, Ricci received permission to visit the city of Sennar. There he met his old travel companion Frediani, now mad and secluded in a subterranean room. Ricci also writes that he took advantage of his familiarity with the pasha to propose the organization of an expedition to find the sources of the Nile. The pasha seemed enthusiastic and granted Ricci full support. In reality, it is quite improbable that Ricci was the only promoter of the idea. The rumor of a geographical expedition had been circulating in Cairo for some time, as a passage of a letter by Samuel Briggs to Bankes points out: "His Highness does not however intend to pursue his conquest further into the interior of Africa, excepting a small expedition which he has ordered to reconnoitre the source of the Bahr el Abiat, the result of which must prove interesting for the development of the African Geography."[181] In a letter to William Hamilton on 10 October 1821, Salt had already written: "Ibrahim Pasha, who has lately gone up, is to send an expedition to examine the course of the Bahr el-Abiad, which will be accompanied by several European travellers."[182]

Despite Ricci's advice against it, Ibrahim Pasha moved the camp on 12 December 1821. They camped at al-Raraba, about thirty-five kilometers south of Sennar, where the pasha received two local kings. They refused to help him by convincing other kings to submit without further fight. On 15 December, they continued by boat as far as a place Ricci calls "Servi," about ninety kilometers south of al-Raraba along the Nile. Here, since the boat did not have enough draft, they were compelled to proceed by land, forcing the army to open a road in the forest. The following day they reached al-Daramayla, thirty-five kilometers to the south. The last stop was at Werkat, in the hinterland of Sennar Island, almost halfway between the White and the Blue Nile. Taking advantage of a moment of rest, Ricci went to a mountain called San. Having climbed it, he was able to see with a telescope al-Rank, a mountain that flanks the White Nile. With this image of a vast unexplored land in his mind, Ricci went back to Werkat to find Ibrahim Pasha prostrated by dysentery (p. 314). In the words of Salt: "The Pasha had another most violent attack that induced Ricci very wisely to recommend an instant return to Cairo as the only means of saving his life."[183] Having reached the twelfth degree of latitude, Ricci started his journey back to Egypt: it was 24 December 1821.

On 28 December, the pasha was already at Sennar; on 11 January 1822 at Shendi; on 16 January at Berber;[184] two days later at Abu Hamad. Here, because Ibrahim Pasha was eager to reach Cairo, he preferred to take the land route, crossing the desert for almost four hundred kilometers up to Wadi al-Sebu'a and therefore cutting out the broad bend of the Nile, which would have meant about 1,100 kilometers of navigation. The crossing, which in fact followed a known trail, is presented by Ricci as very perilous (p. 315). On 23 January, they were already running short of water. Their hopes were pinned on a well near Murrat. "What a surprise when we found that instead of the drinkable fresh water that we hoped could fill our goatskins, we found bitter water" (p. 316). They tested the water on a camel: "this died swollen before dawn." Nothing else was left to do other than to ration the little water left and leave immediately, hoping to reach Wadi al-Sebu'a as soon as possible. On 27 January, the party was so tormented by hunger and thirst that there was little hope for survival. Unexpectedly, a caravan sent from Wadi al-Sebu'a managed to reach them that night with water and food. On 28 January, they finally reached Wadi al-Sebu'a, and the day after they were already at Aswan, where they stayed until 4 February. They were in Cairo only five days later. Salt informs Bankes with words of wonder: "They made a forced march down in six and thirty days—a thing almost incredible, to Cairo, during which Ricci was constantly in his *canja*[185] . . . and succeeded in restoring him to health."[186]

The scientific results of the enterprise were significant and would have been the foundation of Nubian studies if only Bankes had published the many drawings made by the two travelers. Salt, who collected and shipped them to Britain, writes about this material with the utmost praise: "When you receive the beautiful drawings made by the latter [i.e., Ricci] of all the hieroglyphic monuments they met with, which I have in hand, you will not be sorry that I sent him up as it will make your work very complete. . . . He [Linant] has been a little extravagant in dress and female slaves etc. but when the whole comes to be laid before you, you will have a great reason to be satisfied."[187] It was not only Salt who was enthusiastic about the drawings: "Ibrahim Pasha speaks very highly of what he [i.e., Linant] has done, and says that his map is better than that of Cailliaud, though he also said that Constant,[188] who was with Cailliaud, was a clever young man. The voyage of Linant is likely to be of great interest; he has visited and taken drawings of every piece of antiquity between the cataracts and Sennaar."[189]

Last Works in Egypt

In the capital, Ricci was received by the viceroy and obtained great honors (p. 319). A few pages on, however, Ricci specifies that in fact it was Ibrahim Pasha who honored him on the spot with saber, fur, and horses. The gift of fur was a high honor in Turkish society at the time: Consul Salt received a fur and a horse only when taking office, still describing them as "an honour never before bestowed on a Consul here."[190] In fact, fur and a horse were also the gift Muhammad Ali gave to the French consul Roussel.[191] The trader Omar Baffi, saltpeter manufacturer for the pasha, whom Ricci met at Tarrana (p. 167), received the same gift,[192] as did Tusson Pasha, son of the viceroy, after the massacre of the Mamluks in 1811.[193] As for the sum granted, Ricci speaks of a capital able to profit six hundred thalers a year. The *Diario Senese* by Anton Francesco Bandini states that the viceroy "granted him a present of more than a hundred thousand piasters of that country, and many gifts, including the fur of Grand Vizier."[194] Ettore Romagnoli writes about six thousand scudi,[195] Félix Mengin about ten thousand thalers,[196] while Henry Salt informs Bankes that the agreed sum was eight thousand thalers,[197] adding that "both the Great Pasha and Ibrahim Pasha profess their gratitude for this to me which they consider almost miraculous, and have promised to make Ricci's fortune and I do believe something handsome will be done for him though as usual it is protracted from day to day."[198] The sum did not make him rich, but it was enough to make him write to his friend Rontani: "For one of those extraordinary accidents that rarely happen in life, I obtained if not a splendid, at least a good, fortune, enough to live in my country without the help of Asclepius."[199] In the same letter, as in the passage of the *Travels* mentioned before, Ricci alludes to court intrigues that damaged him:

In this case I used with great advantage a treatment previously used by me in only two desperate circumstances, also with great success. This treatment divided the opinion of the court physicians: some admired it and some approached the pasha calling it hazardous in order to damage me. Despite all the shameful intrigues I triumphed and received the highest honors by His Highness, and I would have become court physician, if the love for Europe had not called me back to spend there the rest of my days.[200]

Among the court physicians of Muhammad Ali there were Yanni Botsaris (Giovanni Bozaris), chief physician, and Giovanni Martini from Pisa: these were sent by the viceroy to meet Ibrahim Pasha at Aswan on his way to Cairo, as Ricci himself specifies in the *Medical Memoir*. In other passages of the *Travels* other polemical allusions are to be found: "In fact Ibrahim did for me, on his side, what he could: and if the reward did not correspond to his promises, I believe the reason is not his ingratitude, but something too common at court, where competition is always dangerous."[201]

The large number of European physicians in Egypt at the time, employed both at the court and in the army, indeed made competition and rivalry very tough, and violence and subterfuge were not spared. Regarding Frediani's mental illness, Linant writes: "I think he owes this madness to the other Europeans who are in Sennar with him."[202] Cailliaud was suspicious of the brother of the chief physician Yanni Botsaris, Demetrios, and thought he had in fact poisoned Frediani.[203] The same Demetrios, physician of Isma'il Pasha, had reportedly poisoned the Italian doctor Andrea Gentili in Sennar.[204] An interesting anecdote is also narrated by Ricci himself.

It is appropriate here to remember the answer given by Ibrahim to an Armenian physician attached to this army, who went to visit him late in the evening, when I was resting in my tent: an officer witnessing the meeting reported it to me. This one, after asking him about his health and after he gathered information on his improvements and relapses, suggested he should fire me, pointing out that European doctors make a practice of prolonging illnesses for the double goal of interest and glory, and that in his current condition, he himself would take the responsibility to heal him completely in fifteen days, under the threat of having his head cut off. Ibrahim, who did not miss the reason behind this extravagant and malicious speech, answered laughing: "I care for my life more than your head, which I can have at any time."

There is no doubt Ricci is here referring to Demetrios, a schemer hated by many, who would be slain by the natives in October 1822. The natives also had reason to dislike him, because they saw him actively engaged in the bloody hunt for the ears of enemies, sometimes cut from living people, a hunt that was promoted by Isma'il Pasha in exchange for a reward.[205]

After two months of rest (presumably February and March 1822), Ricci seems to have made up his mind about returning to Europe, but not before finishing some works in the Giza necropolis (p. 319). From the rebukes of Linant in Sennar ("I was not authorized in any way to take you with me by Mr. Bankes, moreover that you have other works to do for him"[206]), it is probable that Ricci was still finishing some drawings for Bankes. Nevertheless, in the Bankes Mss. there are no drawings from the Giza necropolis. It seems Ricci was for the first time copying reliefs for his own sake, in order to publish them as plates of the *Travels*. As Sir Gardner Wilkinson mentions, Ricci was still the personal physician of Henry Salt at the time. Coming back from Thebes in mid-August 1822, the British aristocrat proceeded to Alexandria, in order to take Ricci to Cairo and treat his fellow traveler Wiggett.[207] It is not clear whether Ricci actually reached Cairo, because in September he was reported back again in Alexandria. Ricci had at the time acquired a certain reputation, "for [he] was known to have cured Muhammad Ali's son of a similar affliction." Apparently Linant was also in the city,[208] so that both travelers could report to Salt on the expedition to Meroe:

> The doctor with Linant has behaved so ill . . . I hope you will be assured that I have done everything for the best—these young men have since you left Egypt given me much trouble and cost me no inconsiderable sum but I am really fond of both of them and especially Linant and should have been truly sorry not to have obtained for you the completion of this voyage, which you have so much at heart.[209]

In the aforementioned letter to Rontani, Ricci declares himself to be waiting for the payment of his reward and announces his intention to make another short journey:

In this span of time it is highly probable I will undertake another trip, short enough to allow me to be back in Cairo when a possibility to leave would show up. So I will have a complete journal, and the glory of being the only among the modern Italian travelers to have traveled deep into a part of Africa where few belonging to other nations had taken many risks.[210]

No further mention of this last travel is made and it is possible that it was never undertaken.

By mid-November 1822, Ricci declared his epigraphic work at Giza finished. At this point, he thought his experience in Egypt had ended. He boarded a ship on 28 November 1822 and landed at Livorno on Christmas Eve with his archaeological collection, a bunch of diaries, and over a hundred drawings.

4
With Champollion and Rosellini between Europe and Egypt

Work on the Manuscript, Research for a Publisher, and Acquaintance with Champollion

Ricci arrived back in Italy on 24 December 1822 and spent the quarantine at the lazaretto of St. Leopold in Livorno. He was likely alone and did not take with him the two slaves he had boasted about in a letter to Rontani back in 1819. Once out of the lazaretto, he learned about the death of his patron, the governor of Livorno (p. 320). In his letters to Rontani, Ricci often mentions his correspondence with Spannocchi-Piccolomini, who like him was a native of Siena. His death represented as well the loss of a possible sponsor for the publication of the *Travels*. No trace of these letters remains in the correspondence of the governor, now at the State Archive of Siena, except for the two letters mentioned in the previous chapter, belonging to a private collector.

After the quarantine, Ricci moved to Florence, where he dictated the *Travels* using his notes (p. 320). The work on the manuscript took quite some time. Many indications such as reference to future episodes in the life of Ricci and scientific and bibliographical updates show that the *Travels* is not a diary, but rather a thoroughly revised work. In note [q] (chapter 10) Ricci mentions a Mamluk he later found in the Italian city of Pistoia. When he refers to part of the Salt collection being at Thebes in 1818, he also states that the items were bought on behalf of the Louvre by Champollion, which happened only in February 1826 (p. 170).

There are quite a few scientific and bibliographical updates, too. In note [c], for example, while describing the events of 1818, Ricci refers to Belzoni's *Narrative of the Operations*, published in London in 1820. He points to the same work on page 172. Ricci also quotes the works of Hanbury and Waddington (1822),[1] Denham, Clapperton, and Oudnay (1826),[2] and Cailliaud (1826).[3]

The *Travels* also presents a good many Egyptological updates. On page 167, speaking about the royal tombs of Thebes discovered by Belzoni, Ricci clarifies: "Among them, the very famous one of Biban al-Muluk, believed by him to be the tomb of Psamme-tichus [Psamtik], but recognized with certainty by Champollion to be that of Pharaoh Usirei-Akenkheres I, twelfth king of the Eighteenth Diospolitan Dynasty."[4] On page 187, referring to Abu Simbel, Ricci writes: "We are indebted to the triumphant system of Mr. Champollion the Younger if we now know that the king portrayed everywhere in this temple is Sesostris." He later hints at the worthiness of his collection of cartouches in the last two plates of the *Travels*, "useful and fruitful to those who would like to deal with the interpretation of those names according to the principles established by Mr. Champollion the Younger on reading hieroglyphs." Champollion officially announced his translation system in 1822 with his *Lettre à M. Dacier*. The Italian translation appeared in the Florentine journal *Antologia* in 1823, and in 1824 the scientific debate was already heated.[5]

While working on the *Travels*, Ricci put on show, and possibly on sale, his collection of Egyptian antiquities in his Florence house. During the summer of 1823, he was back to his native Siena for the holidays. So the *Diario Senese* of Anton Francesco Bandini notes on the subject: "We have here in Siena that Dr. Ricci who happened to heal the Prince of Egypt. . . . He has a beautiful Arabian horse given to him by the aforementioned. . . . He came to see his friends and to enjoy the feasts, since the air of Siena is healthier in this season than that of Florence."[6]

In 1825, Champollion finally decided to visit Italy in search of hieroglyphic inscriptions in the many Egyptian collections of the peninsula. The decipherer had several reasons to consider Tuscany for a stop: Egyptian antiquities for sale filled the dockside warehouses of Livorno; in the Gardens of Boboli, Florence, he could admire the obelisk of Ramesses II; while in the grand ducal galleries there were many Egyptian antiquities, including the newly acquired first Nizzoli collection. In Florence, Champollion could also meet many travelers who had been in Egypt, such as Girolamo Segato, Giovanni Battista Caviglia, and, of course, Alessandro Ricci. The French scholar writes to his brother in the follow-ing terms (Turin, 17 February 1825): "As for his [i.e., Huyot's] friend, Alessandro Ricci, of Florence, he has very important drawings that I will see at my passage. . . . He desires my coming very much and insists I go to his place, otherwise I will not see anything."[7] About ten days later, he writes to Huyot himself: "Be persuaded that my first visit in Florence . . . will be for Mr. Ricci, your friend; he already had the kindness to offer me a bed at his place and I am extremely grateful for this invitation that I attribute for the most part to your friendship. I will do all that is in my power to please him."[8] Jean-Nicolas Huyot, who had followed Bankes and his party in their first Nubian journey, had become a friend of Ricci and probably encouraged the two men to meet. Champollion was extremely intrigued by Ricci's collection, but more by the drawings than the objects themselves: "There are . . . inscriptions of temples bearing dates. . . . They tell me there is also the copy of a hundred names of kings and queens (cartouches) copied from different buildings."[9]

Champollion finally arrived in Florence for the first time in summer 1825; he was received in an audience by Grand Duke Leopold II, who assigned him the task of compiling a catalog of the Nizzoli collection. According to Hermine Hartleben, Ricci would later express the dissatisfaction of the prince with the delay in the accomplishment of the job.[10] In the Tuscan capital, Champollion met with Ricci, who, according to the French scholar, "put all his papers at my disposal."[11] In a letter to his brother, Champollion described the activities in which he was engaged in Florence, adding:

> Moreover, I was looked after by Doctor Ricci, friend of Huyot, who has spent six years across Egypt and Ethiopia, where he has drawn a lot and very well. I extracted from his large collection of cartouches some new names and very valuable and comprehensive information on the date of the erection of many temples. I also copied from his collection a dozen royal stelae dating to the kings of the Seventeenth and Eighteenth Dynasties. Most of these very interesting bas-reliefs come from Arabia— Serabit al-Khadim and Maghara—where the ancient pharaohs exploited the copper mines. This is valuable for the kings of the Seventeenth Dynasty who, confined in Upper Egypt, could communicate via sea with Serabit despite the Shepherds,[12] who had no fleet.[13]

Back in Florence in 1826, Champollion met and became friends with the Pisan professor Ippolito Rosellini, in whose company he visited the entire Italian peninsula looking for Egyptian monuments. They also visited the Salt collection of Egyptian antiquities, at that time deposited in a warehouse at the dock of Livorno; Champollion in fact negotiated its purchase on behalf of the Louvre Museum. In Tuscany, he also met with Giovanni Battista Caviglia, who apparently was sent to Italy by the British consul himself to invite the decipherer to Egypt. Champollion also made the acquaintance of Girolamo Segato, who was part of Minutoli's party in 1820.

In a letter from Ippolito Rosellini to Neri Corsini, there is mention of a journey made by Ricci to Paris in 1827 in order to meet Champollion again:

> I want to notify Your Excellency . . . being absolutely true that the late Dr. Alessandro Ricci, being in Paris in 1827, left in the hands of Mr. Champollion-Figeac a manuscript of about two hundred pages with word between them to publish it and share the profit. I was a witness of this myself. Ricci did not leave the manuscript in the hands of Champollion the Younger, as thought by his brothers. After our journey, the papers were left to Mr. Champollion-Figeac and Dr. Ricci agreed to the proposal made by Champollion the Younger to use some of the drawings in his future publication and to pay him accordingly.[14]

It seems that even Rosellini promised Ricci some help to get the *Travels* published. In a letter from Ricci to Rosellini dated 16 October 1827, we can read: "At the moment I have not made a decision about the publication of my *Travels*, and I cannot decide anything, being left in the incertitude of your silence regarding what you promised to write for me."[15]

The notes taken by Rosellini while attending Champollion's classes in Paris in 1827 prove that the French scholar was successfully using Ricci's *Travels* and drawings: three Ptolemaic hieroglyphic inscriptions copied by Ricci at Dakka are in fact explicitly mentioned.[16]

The Franco-Tuscan Expedition to Egypt (1828–29)

As early as 1826, Champollion and Rosellini were discussing a plan for a joint scientific expedition to Egypt. The proposal was sent to the grand duke of Tuscany in July 1827 and was firmly approved. At the end of November,[17] Champollion wrote Leopold II about the necessity to postpone the departure due to the tensions that had arisen after the European powers had entered the Greek War of Independence (1821–32). France and Britain were in fact fighting against the Ottoman Empire and its Egyptian province.

Being in contact with both directors, Ricci was easily recruited among the members of the expedition. He was almost essential: six years' experience in Egypt and Nubia—a thorough knowledge of places, customs, local officers, and European diplomats;[18] an exceptional ability in epigraphic drawing long practiced on Egyptian monuments; medical experience in those specific areas, and the fame of being Ibrahim Pasha's savior; and finally the respect and the favor he had presumably gained at the court of Muhammad Ali. At the beginning of October 1827, Ricci was received in an audience by the grand duke himself and wrote about it to Rosellini.

> Last week I went to thank His Imperial and Royal Highness our grand duke, for the honor he gave me to be part of the Tuscan expedition to Egypt. I cannot express with how much interest he talked about it and how encouraging he was with me; be assured that from my side I will second with all my strength and in all possible manners the desires of the prince and the activity of the government. He asked me many questions about Egypt, and then we started talking about the various illnesses typical of the climate. I answered everything systematically and I reached the conclusion that the members of the expedition would better preserve their health by leaving for Cairo either at the first of autumn or at the end of January, or in February. My arguments and the reasons I expressed persuaded the Sovereign, and he asked me to write you about it.[19]

The position of Ricci as physician was actually decided by the government in Florence, as specified in the letter of participation addressed to Rosellini by the minister of interior Neri Corsini. At point 2, the minister writes: "You are authorized to take with you three Tuscan draftsmen, among them Dr. Alessandro Ricci, from Siena, who will also be responsible for the medical and surgical assistance to the members of the expedition."[20] In the regulations prepared by Champollion and Rosellini at Alexandria in September 1828, there is a similar stipulation for Ricci: "Art. 15. The head of the health service is especially in charge of setting the dietary regime to be followed either on board or ashore. Every morning the cook has to submit to him the menu of the daily meals. All food provisions are submitted to his control and are expressly handed over to him."[21] Furthermore, it was stated that "the architect of the expedition is in charge with the head of the health service of choosing a suitable place either for the encampment or the lodgings."[22] Ricci's engagement was regulated by a specific contract, since he was both a draftsman and a physician; point 10 of his regulations states: "[He will not be allowed] to work on his own or for others without the permission of the Head of the Expedition."[23]

In the meanwhile, Ricci superintended the epigraphic education of Giuseppe Angelelli, a talented young artist of the Fine Arts Academy of Florence, also part of the Tuscan Expedition: "Young Angelelli is assiduous in copying the monuments you assigned him, and he is progressing."[24] Ricci was also in contact with Girolamo Segato, whom, even if never mentioned in the *Travels*, he probably met in Egypt in 1820 when both were in the service of Baron von Minutoli.

The details of the Tuscan expedition will not be discussed here as they are both well known and much studied, even recently;[25] Ricci will be the focus of this outline, where new documents are discussed.

The expedition left Europe in July 1828 and reached Egypt on 18 August. Despite appearances, the mission was not particularly welcome in Egypt because of the Greek War of Independence. An unpublished report by Riccardo Fantozzi, general consul of the Kingdom of the Two Sicilies, in September 1828 states:

Similarly, a scientific party of Franco-Italians made up of fifteen people under the direction of Mr. Champollion the Younger and Mr. Ippolito Rosellini, professors of ancient oriental languages, arrived here from Toulon on 18 [August], on the sloop-of-war of His Most Christian Majesty *L'Aigle*. The mission was announced over a year ago to His Highness by the general consul of France Chevalier Drovetti, and the prince promised to welcome it and give it protection and help, but also asked for it to be postponed until a more favorable time because of the ongoing war. For this reason, its untimely arrival did not please His Highness: when the members of the two expeditions were presented by the consuls of France and Tuscany, he made them feel it, by telling them that the period was not favorable. Nevertheless, he gave them the necessary firmans to allow them to travel freely in Upper Egypt and Nubia, and they left immediately. It seems that the consul's advice to postpone the expedition did not reach France on time. Anyway, according to my experience, and not only here but generally all over the Levant, these large groups of travelers are not welcome, as they are not welcome by the Ottoman Government in its own territory.[26]

It was previously known that the expedition had been delayed by a year in 1827, but it was not known that its arrival in 1828 did not please Muhammad Ali. A letter by Bernardino Drovetti addressed to Ippolito Rosellini and dated 3 May 1828 was in fact quite clear on the subject.

The circumstances are now not favorable for the literary expedition that you have in mind to undertake toward the end of the summer; it is still possible that they develop in a way to bring peaceful arrangements, which would be necessary to ensure the purity and the tranquillity of your journey in Egypt. He who governs will provide the protection you need, but there are cases when the authority itself might not prevail on criminals. Be then patient, *quod differtur non aufertur*,[27] and if you cannot satisfy by the end of this year the noble ambition to explore the beautiful remains of the cradle of sciences and arts, you will find a compensation thinking that later you will not risk interruption.[28]

A similar letter, dated the same day, was sent by Drovetti to Jean-François Champollion.[29] On 22 August 1828, Champollion wrote to his brother that he had just discovered that Drovetti had actually written to him suggesting delaying the expedition.[30]

Other problems arose when the pasha opposed granting a permission of excavation to the two groups.

The concession of the two firmans was no easy task. The pasha answered that he had not granted this favor except to his very good friends and, had he given it to us, he could not refuse it later to others, basically with no limits, to the extent that the country would be emptied of its antiquities and become unattractive for the travelers. Mr. Drovetti, consul of France, proposed to cede to the French commission his own firman; the pasha answered he could not allow it, unless the Tuscans had one too, and, almost joking, asked Mr. D'Anastasy, consul of Sweden, if he would yield his firman to the Tuscan commission. Mr. D'Anastasy answered he would do it with pleasure, and so this is how we got it.[31]

The same incident is described in Champollion's letters and in the unpublished correspondence of the Tuscan consul De Rossetti. In a letter written by De Rossetti to Count Vittorio Fossombroni, minister of foreign affairs, he writes:

I met many difficulties to obtain the permission to dig for the expedition, because people of influence intrigued at court not to have it granted to the two groups, probably being afraid it would damage their business, since they are antiquity traders. I hope I succeeded in solving the issue and I assure Your Excellency that nothing will be spared from my side in order to fulfill the Sovereign's wishes.[32]

We know nothing about Ricci's behavior during the audience with the pasha, who years before had rewarded him so well. Ibrahim Pasha was at that moment returning from the Morea campaign and did not meet with the members of the expedition until their own return from Nubia. In a letter to Neri Corsini, Rosellini states: "It does not seem that the viceroy showed any particular consideration for Ricci. Ibrahim himself did not present him with any gift, as he had hoped and as it is always the case in these countries."[33]

The journey along the Nile, from Alexandria to Cairo and thence further south to Wadi Halfa, comprising a long stay at Thebes, is rich in episodes involving Ricci. Champollion called him an "old regular of the country."[34] Being in charge of the supply logistics, Ricci was often sent around in search of food. This is the context of a funny episode recalled by Champollion near the ancient Sais: "Waiting for the wind to rise, I went with Rosellini to have a walk in the village, where we found Doctor Ricci, who had gone to make provisions, surrounded by a crowd of half-naked women."[35] At Contra Latopolis, another misadventure is recalled by Rosellini, also with humoristic tone:

> We found Dr. Ricci and the *rais* all laboring and panting to empty the water out of the *ma'ash*. The very same hole that in this kind of boat is made to sink when needed, was plugged at Akhmim with flax tow and tallow. Big mice, which live on the boat in a prodigious quantity, gnawed the flax tow and opened the hole wide, so that water entered freely. Luckily, the depth was very shallow, and water entered only enough to put the boat on the sand at the same level of the river.[36]

Ricci's experience must have influenced the choice of places to visit, even if this is never explicitly acknowledged in the sources. The doctor knew very well the site of Beni Hasan, which aroused great astonishment in the members of the expedition, not least Rosellini himself, who blamed the Napoleonic commission for not documenting such a wonderful place: "The *Description de l'Égypte* mentions these grottoes, but in such an imperfect way that the first visit filled us with amazement and satisfaction for the many interesting things we could see."[37] They stayed for two entire weeks and the party produced no less than four hundred drawings.

Since Ricci knew places, people, and customs, he was very useful in tasks where he had to manage alone. For example, as soon as the expedition arrived at Bulaq on 19 September, Ricci was sent to Cairo with a letter from Champollion to the French vice-consul Derché[38] and a letter from Rosellini to the Tuscan vice-consul MacArdle.[39] Again, Ricci was sent from Mit Rahina to Saqqara in order to decide where to camp and how to organize the excavations.[40] On 28 February, Ricci was sent from al-Kab on a dromedary to take possession of the belongings of the expedition, which were in Qurna in the hands of Piccinini, who was about to leave the country.[41] It is Ricci again who is sent on a (boring) diplomatic mission to the *mamur*[42] of Qena, Hassan Bey, who was then camped at Qurna, with a present of forty bottles of wine. His familiarity with the place and his independent spirit made him settle separately from the other members of the expedition, staying in a house in Qurna instead of in one of the tombs in the Valley of the Kings.[43]

At Abu Simbel, Ricci, Rosellini, and Champollion were the first of the party to enter the great temple of Ramesses II.[44] At the same site, on 16 January 1829, Ricci proved once again to be a skilled shooter by firing at a crocodile that was attacking Champollion's boat.[45] At Derr, Ricci again shot at some crocodiles in the (vain) hope of catching one: hunting must definitely have been one of his passions.[46]

At Buhen, the doctor was to take a decision that would in the future fuel a dispute between Rosellini and Champollion-Figeac. The stela of Senwosret I in the sanctuary was at first assigned to Champollion together with the other stela, of Ramesses I. It was only thanks to Ricci's instructions that the half-buried stela was found by the Franco-Tuscan expedition: he had in fact already copied it for Bankes in 1819.[47] A copy of this drawing was in the hands of Champollion as early as 1825 and the stela was also meant to feature on a plate of Ricci's *Travels*. Champollion noted that the stela was damaged and that some of the hieroglyphs copied by Ricci had already gone.[48] Ricci had the stela loaded on Rosellini's boat. Champollion and Rosellini were at the time busy and did not realize what was going on; anyway, nobody protested. According to Hartleben, this "theft" was considered unforgivable by Champollion-Figeac, who since then had grown more and more hostile toward Rosellini.[49] The Pisan professor never mentions the stela, while it seems that Champollion-Figeac's enmity was more related to competition in the publication of the results of the expedition. This task was entrusted by Champollion the Younger to his brother on his deathbed. Jacques-Joseph mentioned the incident in a note on the stela in the *Notice descriptive*: "The far more valuable stela of Osortasen I, of the Sixteenth Dynasty, was carried away, we know how, by the Tuscan commission and deposited at the Museum of Florence (Note of the Editor J.J.C.F.)."[50]

The most famous event related to Ricci during the Franco-Tuscan expedition is the scorpion sting that later would be held responsible for his infirmity and eventual death. The episode is narrated in detail by Rosellini.

> We went back at night to the house of Qurna . . . Gaetano Rosellini and Ricci accompanied me. At a certain point, the latter shouted: "Was I stung by a scorpion? A serpent?" I had a candle in my hands and looking on the ground I saw a large scorpion running away, which I immediately crushed with my foot. In the meanwhile, fright and severe pain agitated Ricci in the injured part. We went up to the room: the sting was on his left heel, which was bare since he was wearing an open slipper without socks. We got the lancet and made an incision, we then strewed sal ammoniac on the spot, but the position of the wound was not clear. Ricci started to have convulsions and what looked like an unbearable spasm. In less than fifteen minutes, his face became deformed: his frightened eyes were almost popping out of his face; he was deadly pale and dripping all over cold sweat. To be sincere, I do not know how much fright was adding to the effects of the poison, but he became furious, he wanted to flee away and, out of his mind, was shouting ramblings. Two of our Arabs could barely hold him. . . . We asked for one of those Arabs who claim to have received by saints the power of healing from the bites of serpents and scorpions. . . . When the Arab arrived, he started to rub the leg down from top to bottom, solemnly reciting long pieces of the Quran. Then, when he finished lowering the poisoned blood through the rubbing, he applied to the heel a suction cup, with which he alternately sucked and paused for some time. . . . Only after three hours of agitation did Ricci start to calm down.[51]

Besides this episode where Ricci was patient rather than doctor, he always tried to help the locals as he used to do in his first stay ten years before. So writes Rosellini in his travel journal about Saqqara: "At sunset and at dawn, large was always the crowd of Arabs who came to sell antiquities or to be treated by Dr. Ricci for monstrous eye diseases."[52] Rosellini notes another incident: "Today the *kashif* who lives in Beni Hasan sent servants and two horses to the boats asking for our doctor. The dragoman answered he would not be back until the evening; at dusk he came back with the *qaymaqam*[53] and Dr. Ricci visited him. He suffered from venereal disease."[54]

The documents of the Tuscan diplomatic correspondence reveal that Ricci sent and received letters during the whole expedition, even though it is impossible to determine who were the recipients and senders. The content of the letters is unknown as well, because they are all lost. One of the nine or so letters Ricci received in Egypt was transmitted to the Tuscan consulate via the British consulate and was sent by Lord Burghersh (1784–1859), British envoy accredited to the court of Florence between 1814 and 1830.[55] Other letters reached Ricci between December 1828 and August 1829.[56] Upon his arrival in Alexandria, Ricci wrote to Count Girolamo Bardi, director of the Museum of Natural Science. Bardi passed the letter to Gian Pietro Vieusseux, who in turn published it in *Antologia*.[57] It is a letter full of verve, written in the good style of Ricci, rich in observations and comments, especially of medical subjects. A letter by Giuseppe Raddi, a member of the expedition who most of the time traveled alone in other parts of the country, was addressed to Rosellini and contained questions Grand Duke Leopold II had for Ricci:

His Grand Ducal and Royal Highness[58] our master orders me to ask Dr. Ricci, physician of the expedition, as an expert of the country: 1. Whether the areas close to the Mareotis Lake, Eddkomm, Abuqir, Boures, and Mengaleh[59] are unhealthy because of the fevers, and whether malaria is stronger in the branch that connects these lakes to the sea or in the part where the Nile enters the lakes themselves. 2. Whether an epidemic of malaria comes before the plague or there is no connection between the two. Please forward these questions to Dr. Ricci in my name inviting him to answer as quickly as possible with all the information he can give on the subject raised by His Royal and Grand Ducal Highness, and send him my warmest greetings.[60]

The Tuscan prince was evidently interested in health issues related to swamp land, which was common in many parts of his principality and would soon be the object of reclamation through the help of the engineer Gaetano Rosellini, uncle of Ippolito and member of the same expedition.[61] On 28 July, Raddi replied to another letter of Rosellini: "Dearest Professor, I received two days ago your precious letter dated 3 July, along with Ricci's own letter. Please forward him my thanks for the information he had sent and let him know that I will personally forward his report to the grand duke as soon as I am in Alexandria."[62]

Ricci maintained a cordial relationship with Drovetti, too. The diplomat had honored the doctor with a box of wine bottles, "most part of which was drunk toasting the donor.

This reminded me of the pleasure I had in traveling with you."[63] Ricci attentively addresses suggestions for Drovetti's health and invites him to return to Italy with him at the end of the expedition, which Ricci forecasts for September. The party had to wait a long time for the availability of a vessel. Even if it was not his field of expertise, while waiting for the ship Ricci apparently painted an oil portrait of Champollion.[64] Finally, the expedition was able to leave on 17 October 1829 and reached Livorno on 28 November, after forty-two days at sea.[65]

Sales Promotion of Rosellini's Book in Europe (1831)

After the expedition, Ricci and Rosellini maintained a strong relationship. The latter, pressed by the Tuscan government, was about to start the publication of his discoveries in Egypt and Nubia. It is clear from Rosellini's correspondence that a first publication notice was issued in January 1831 and advertised a Tuscan-only book.[66] The grand duke had only granted Rosellini a loan; he needed to fund the expensive publication by himself. The professor asked permission of the minister of the interior to send Ricci to different European courts, academies, and libraries in order to promote the subscription of potential supporters. So he writes to Neri Corsini on 26 January 1831:

> I begged the clemency of His Imperial and Royal Highness the Grand Duke to have a letter of recommendation addressed to Tuscan ministers and envoys in the various cities of Germany and England issued. His Highness condescended and I am now asking Your Excellency to comply, and also to protect Dr. Ricci's mission with a favorable note on his passport and any other sort of recommendation that could help dignify a mission run under the auspices of His Highness.[67]

A second letter sent only two days afterward explained the contractual conditions for Ricci's engagement: "We agreed I should assign him a daily allowance of 10 groschen for five or six months, such being the duration of his journey; he has to provide for all expenses out of his own pocket. As a reward he will get 10 percent out of the subscriptions he collects."[68] Minister Corsini answered on 8 February; the letter is lost, but its content can be understood from Rosellini's reply on 14 February. The minister probably objected that the agreements signed with Ricci were too generous and asked for a renegotiation. Rosellini answered that he had previously gathered information on the topic and that he understood that sending an agent was far more profitable than using the usual network of librarians. He also pointed out that the average charge for an agent was 15 percent instead of the 10 percent asked by Ricci: "Your Excellency will agree that I cannot write to Dr. Ricci in order to propose to him a different agreement."[69]

Ricci probably left shortly after, but the stops of his journey are not known in detail. On 18 May 1831 he left the capital of the Kingdom of Saxony, Dresden, where he was able to sell some pieces of his collection of Egyptian antiquities.[70] During the summer he was in Berlin, as a letter by Rosellini to the government dated 26 August testifies. The Prussian Secret Archive in Berlin also holds proof of the visit made by Ricci in 1831, surprisingly in order to sell a collection of Renaissance miniature paintings to the Egyptian Museum.[71] From a letter by Consul Acerbi to Rosellini it is known that Ricci also visited Austria: "Since I left Vienna, where I left Dr. Ricci, I know nothing about your enterprise. A slow pace in accomplishing it will be detrimental."[72] The original itinerary apparently included English stops, but nothing is known about them. A letter to Giuseppe Passalacqua, director of the Egyptian Museum in Berlin, dated 12 July 1831, had been sent by Ricci from Florence.[73] He writes about the subscriptions he collected in Germany and the others to be collected in the future in France, England, and Italy. At the same time, he takes himself off the job ("my appointment ended the moment I arrived"). The general tone of the letter is depressed: Ricci seems frustrated by something (maybe the publication of his travels) and worried about his financial position.

Sickness, Death, and Inheritance (1832–34)

When Ricci came back from his European tour he fell severely ill: there is no precise information on this, but it must have been around autumn 1831. On 20 February 1832, Rosellini wrote to Giuseppe Acerbi about the matter, prompted by the Austrian consul, who had asked for news of the members of the expedition he had met in Egypt: "Our other companions are well, except for Dr. Ricci who, back from Germany, was paralyzed in the left part of his body, affecting his brain and leaving him an imbecile. The Government took care of him and entrusted me with his guardianship."[74] In a later letter, Acerbi asked Rosellini to greet all members of the expedition, including poor Ricci "if he is in the condition of remembering me."[75] Rosellini's answer gives no hope: "Poor Ricci lives without mind and without being able to move."[76]

Ricci had two brothers, Luigi and Giovanni, living in Rome—at that time, part of the Papal States—but they "could not move to Florence, being poor artisans."[77] Once Ricci was paralyzed, the government appointed Marquess Gino Capponi (1792–1876) as his trustee.[78] According to the biographer of Angelelli, "since he did not have a family, the government thought of putting him in a private room in San Bonifacio Hospital," but Angelelli would not allow it and he took him into his own house.[79] It is probable that the term "family" here means specifically a wife or children, since we know Ricci had two brothers. It is possible that Ricci's brothers were minor in age and could not handle legal matters by themselves. If they were hypothetically born right before or after the death of their father, perhaps around 1816, they would be only sixteen years old in 1832.

The trustee petitioned the grand duke on 19 June 1832, directly linking the 1829 scorpion accident to Ricci's current infirmity. It was a smart move, as the misfortune of Ricci appeared to have occurred in the service of the state. The petition offered an exchange rather advantageous to the crown, since Ricci was believed to be unable to recover and very close to death. The collection of Egyptian antiquities amassed by Ricci was valued at 6,146 lire, 13 soldi, and 4 denari: Marquess Capponi proposed that the government buy the entire collection in exchange for a payment of 1,500 lire to pay off Ricci's debts and provide a pension for life at the discretion of the government.[80] The president of the Academy of Fine

Arts, Antonio Ramirez di Montalvo, sponsoring Capponi's petition, proposed to the secretary of the royal finances a life pension of less than 140 lire per month and the government granted 100 lire.[81] As expected, the sickness lasted a few more months and Ricci died on 29 January 1834.[82]

Many months after Ricci's death, on September 20, 1834, the testamentary trustee Francesco Pacini asked the government's permission for the heirs and the creditors to cash the difference between the value of the collection and the life pension paid to Ricci, about 2,813 lire 6 soldi and 8 denari.[83] Despite the fact that the agreement did not bind him to do so, the grand duke, "willing to show a benign regard toward creditors and the heirs of Dr. Alessandro Ricci, for a special trait of his sovereign mercy," granted the payment of the remaining money.[84]

5

The Archaeological, Anthropological, and Natural History Collections

The Dresden Collection (1831)

It was mentioned in the previous chapter that Ricci took advantage of his advertising tour around Europe to sell part of his archaeological collection in Dresden in May 1831. There is not much documentation on the presence of Ricci in the Saxon capital. At the time, Saxony was undergoing a period of political turmoil that was spreading across Europe after the July Revolution in France (1830), causing the fall of Charles X (r. 1824–30) and the ascent of Louis Philippe of Orleans (r. 1830–48). In September 1830, Frederick Augustus of Saxony was nominated prince coregent to assist his uncle, King Anton Clemens, and a new constitution was granted in 1831. Ricci was traveling across Europe with the publication notices for Rosellini and could likely not carry with him the entire collection, which comprised hundreds of pieces including coffins, mummies, stone stelae, and stone and pottery vessels. A few boxes, possibly only one, were on the contrary enough to move amulets, scarabs, rings, bronze statuettes, and papyri; the rest of the collection was possibly described in a catalog.

It seems that at the beginning Ricci approached Heinrich Hase, inspector of the Royal Collection of Antiquities, who was in favor of the acquisition of the collection—a "small treasure"—and forwarded the proposal to the prime minister, Bernhard August von Lindenau (1779–1854). Hase underlines the quality of Ricci's pieces, a collection "that is characterized more by the selection of the pieces than by the amount."[1]

Egyptian antiquities were not new in the Saxon capital. Augustus II the Strong (r. 1697–1733) had already acquired some pieces in 1728. Ricci's collection, composed of small objects and papyri, was particularly interesting because the royal collection was mainly formed of mummies and statues. Ricci asked for the sum of 800 thalers, "but he said that he would lower the prices, if you seriously intend to buy it." According to Hase, who warmly supported the purchase, "even amateurs can see that the price is not high."[2]

The lot purchased from Ricci was over time subjected to substantial modifications.[3] Six pieces were donated in 1925 to the Royal House of Wettin, after the monarchy was abolished; twenty-six objects were lost during the Second World War, when collections from Russian-occupied Germany were transferred to the Soviet Union. They were later returned in a disorderly fashion to the German Democratic Republic. Other pieces are now impossible to identify because of the incompleteness or destruction of the catalogs. Of the three hundred original pieces sold by Ricci to the King of Saxony, only 195 are today undoubtedly recognizable at the Albertinum.[4]

Most of the surviving pieces are amulets of different types: Wedjat Eye, Isis Knot, headrest, palm tree, pomegranate, heart, *nefer* sign, set square, and various scaraboids. They are almost all Late Period objects, easy to find on the antiquities market at the time. Some of them are nevertheless Middle Kingdom, Second and Third Intermediate Periods, New Kingdom, and Ptolemaic. There are also a small Ramesside cartouche in faience (No. 155) and a golden amulet with a sphinx of clearly Levantine artisanship (No. 250).

The collection comprised New Kingdom faience rings, one with the cartouche of Tutankhamun (Nebkheperure) (No. 205) and another with the cartouche of Amenhotep III (Nebmaatre) (No. 165), a golden ring with lapis lazuli (No. 156), and a gold and amethyst ring (No. 167), both also dating to the New Kingdom. There are also nine small bronze statues of the Late Period and a faience game token. The collection has many scarabs made of stone, faience, and carnelian, dated to the Second Intermediate Period, New Kingdom, and Late Period. There is an ivory scarab with a cartouche of Taharqa (No. 021), a set of five "Menkheperra scarabs" (Nos. 024–027, 060), and a glazed stone wedding scarab of Amenhotep III (No. 091). There is also a series of black scarabs in the same style and mold (No. 092).

The Dresden collection comprises many anonymous ushabtis in stone and faience dating to the New Kingdom. Other ushabtis do bear the name of the deceased: a wooden one for a certain Meryre who lived in the Nineteenth Dynasty (No. 399), a faience ushabti for a certain Amenemipet dating to the Eighteenth–Nineteenth Dynasty (No. 397), another one crafted for a certain Asetreshet of the Twenty-sixth Dynasty (No. 428), two ushabtis belonging to a General Heribamun of the Late Period (Nos. 426–27), and a faience ushabti made for a certain Heru of the Thirtieth Dynasty (No. 425).

Two fragments of male statues in marble and faience probably date back to the last phase of the Egyptian civilization. A limestone relief fragment with a male figure wearing a wig (No. 739) belongs to the Old Kingdom and possibly comes from Giza, a site much frequented by Ricci.

Finally, the collection comprises a fine wooden scribe palette with its two reeds, dating to the New Kingdom (No. 735), and three papyri: a *Book of the Dead* written in the Twenty-first Dynasty for a certain Ankhefenamun (No. 775);[5] another illustrated funerary text written for a certain Paiufmut in the same dynasty (No. 776); and a Demotic letter possibly dating to the Roman period (No. 828).

On the origin of the pieces, unfortunately not much can be said: among the very few mentions of objects in the *Travels*, none of the pieces in Dresden can be recognized. The existence of a set of objects (black stone scarabs, Heribamun's ushabtis) could imply intact archaeological contexts. While the ivory scarab of Taharqa might have been found by Ricci during his Nubian travels, he never mentions digs made for himself or for others: his main task was in fact epigraphy. The *Travels* often give a partial view of the events, but it is likely that Ricci bought the pieces on the antiquarian market, with which he was surely acquainted, having dealt with the most active traders, diggers, agents, and buyers of the time and having spent much time in 'hot' areas such as the Theban west bank. He actually explicitly hints at the antiquities trade in one passage of his travelog (pp. 253–54).

The small collection amassed by Ricci aroused much interest among Saxon scholars, an echo of which can be found in a letter sent in 1834 by Carl Falkenstein, royal librarian in Dresden, to Bernardino Drovetti. The German scholar thanks the French consul for the gift of a Greek papyrus and asks him to send over whatever documents he might donate of his correspondence, "especially of travelers who have illustrated Egypt under your protection so rightfully renowned: for example of Burckhardt, Seetzen, Hornemann, Salt, Cailliaud, Lord Valentia, Lyon, Waddington, Hanbury, Röntgen, Pacho, Rifaud, Denon, Champollion, Rosellini, Raddi, Ricci, Belzoni, Caviglia, etc."[6]

The Florence Collection (1832)

The Egyptian collection acquired by the Tuscan government in 1832 was of a completely different kind. Only four years earlier, the grand duke had refused to buy the second Nizzoli collection, despite positive recommendations by Ippolito Rosellini himself. Antonio Ramirez di Montalvo, writing to the sovereign about the collection of Ricci, states:

> I examined the catalog made by Professor Migliarini and asked him for clarification about the importance of the pieces in themselves and how they compare to the collection already owned by Your Imperial and Royal Highness. I am convinced that, despite the fact that the Ricci collection as a whole is not of the highest importance because it has many pieces now common in Europe, it still has many objects very valuable for rarity, state of preservation, or other particularities. The Ricci collection would not add useless duplicates either to the Nizzoli collection of the Royal Gallery or to the collection acquired by the Tuscan expedition to Egypt. On the contrary, it would add value to the other pieces, filling some gaps, adding better objects or interesting variations.[7]

The catalog Ramirez di Montalvo was referring to in his letter is a detailed inventory made by Arcangelo Michele Migliarini in May 1832. The list comprised 180 entries, some of those including dozens of objects, for an overall total of more than 1,200 pieces.

Migliarini's catalog is a list of nineteenth-century fashion, with categories that would not be used nowadays: "Wood" (coffins with their mummies, boxes, statues, a chair, stelae, headrests, ushabtis); "Stone" (stelae, sculptures, and ostraca); "Stone vessels" (canopic jars, alabaster, limestone, and sandstone vases); "Vases" (pottery); "Bronzes" (mirrors, statuettes, inlaid works, 240 Roman imperial coins); "Collection of figurines representing stone mummies" (alabaster, dark stone, limestone, and painted limestone ushabtis); "Wooden mummy figurines"; "Varnished porcelain mummy figurines"; "Pottery mummy figurines"; "Collection of small monuments of different material" (scarabs, amulets, beads, small rings, scaraboids, cameos); "Papyri" (actually, just a few thorn fragments); "Reed, palm leaves, and other fiber products" (sandals, baskets, bread loaves, dates, seeds and other fruits, a mummified human hand, and mummy hair).

For most of the objects in Florence, provenance (archaeological site) and origin (dig or antiquarian market) are also unknown. Nevertheless, there are a few helpful hints in the *Travels*. On page 173, describing the scenes copied in the tomb of Ramesses III in the Valley of the Kings, Ricci states: "The frame around this figure has the exact shape of a portable shrine, where family idols used to be placed. I have one in my collection very similar to this." It is an ushabti box, specifically No. 4 of Migliarini's catalog (corresponding to No. 2190 of the modern inventory): "A box made of white painted wood, with four legs. Its shape is that of an ark with tympanum. It has a line of black hieroglyphs."[8] On page 175, Ricci writes: "I possess a loaf of bread found in a tomb at Qurna, which has exactly the same five holes." This is the "fragment of barley loaf," No. 162 of Migliarini's catalog.[9] In the description of one of the reliefs copied in the temple of Abu Simbel, Ricci states: "The same god is portrayed on No. 2 of the same plate, where the king with a knife is about to knock down or has already knocked down four urns, each topped with two feathers. . . . I have in my collection one of these urns, four times higher than the ones represented in this scene" (pp. 185–86). This can be easily identified with the canopic box No. 3 in Migliarini's catalog (No. 2184).[10] The box belonged to a Nineteenth Dynasty woman called Takharu, who was buried at Deir al-Medina.[11] Belonging to the same burial is an ushabti box (No. 2191), probably bought by Ricci along with the canopic box and marked No. 14 in Migliarini's catalog. In his *Travel to the Oasis of Jupiter-Amun*, Ricci writes regarding the baskets carried by the women of Siwa: "I bought one of these baskets and I still have it in my collection" (p. 212). It is possible that this is No. 160 of Migliarini's catalog: "A basket used to sow in the fields."[12] If the identification is correct, then it is not an ancient object. Another item that could be in the Florentine collection, since it belongs to a typology not found in the Dresden collection, is described in another manuscript of Ricci's: "I have in my collection a symbolic faience hoe." The last mention of an object of his collection in the *Travels* is on page 312: "At Werkat and in other parts of Sennar the inhabitants are used to resting their head on a sort of stand, made of one piece of very hard wood, half a foot high and with a large base. . . . The use of these headrests is very old. I have two of them in my collection: one is modern and the other was found in a tomb of Qurna." Actually, in the catalog written by Migliarini there are three headrests, plus another modern one ("N.B. Another smaller specimen is modern, and was used by Dr. Ricci in his travels"): they are Nos. 28, 29, and 30 (Nos. 2340, 2342, 2343).[13]

The Ricci collection in the Egyptian Museum of Florence is still awaiting a thorough study as a group, and it is a pity that the *Travels* can contribute so little to the identification of the pieces. In addition to the two objects coming from Deir al-Medina, textual evidence assigns some stelae to the Theban necropolis and others to Abydos (Nos. 2496, 2585). It is noteworthy that Ricci does not mention Abydos at all in his account.

Natural History and Anthropology Collections

Ricci's interest in natural history and anthropology has been previously mentioned. When the doctor fell ill, all his collections were grouped together. With the collection of Egyptian antiquities there were "some pieces of natural history and modern art also collected in Egypt."[14] The purchase of the archaeological collection was finalized in 1832 and the compensation was paid to heirs and creditors two years later. At that time, the Egyptian collection was still lying in the Academy of Arts and Crafts of St. Catherine, with the pieces of the Tuscan expedition and other objects belonging to Ricci. The latter were specifically "some objects of natural history, a portable pharmacy, and other things of lesser importance . . . they are not to be considered as part of the purchase made by the royal government."[15] More information is to be found in a letter by Migliarini to Antonio Ramirez di Montalvo: "At the same time I would like to remind you to notify the director of the Imperial and Royal Cabinet in order to have the minerals and the shells checked. I do not think these things would be useful, but maybe you would like to purchase the pieces of petrified wood, because they are now objects of much study in Germany and elsewhere."[16]

More information can be found in the *Travels*. Ironically, there are more details on these pieces than on the archaeological items. They can be grouped into two categories: minerals and birds. In the first category we can list some "pieces of porphyry, corals, petrified wood, and other stones" (p. 197) collected in the Libyan Desert near Qarat al-Himaymat; fragments "of porous rock, perfectly red . . . pure iron oxide" (p. 228) found at Hammam Fara'un in Sinai; a "hard green stone" (p. 245) collected in Wadi al-Shaykh in Sinai; and some "little globes . . . pure copper" and "fragments of real turquoise" (p. 249) found at Serabit al-Khadim.

The ornithological passion of Ricci is also mentioned many times in the *Travels* (pp. 270, 290, 297). A letter written by the naturalist and explorer Wilhelm Friedrich Hemprich (1796–1825) and addressed to the French consul Drovetti states with admiration: "The sight of a small collection of birds assembled by Dr. Ricci gives us hope that we will find in Sennar and Kordofan what we are looking for."[17]

The collections of specimens of natural history and anthropology that made it to Florence were just a part of what Ricci had collected during his travels. The whole collection formed during the Sennar journey, in fact, was lost: "I also abandoned my ornithological collection, an assortment of seeds, and many other objects acquired during my journey or received by the pasha as a present, such as clothes, agricultural tools, musical instruments, and furniture" (p. 314). Among the everyday ethnic objects amassed by Ricci, there were a lyre and a horse bard (a type of armor), gifts received from a local chief after the successful treatment of his wife (p. 302).

6
The *Travels:*
Topics and Problems

Story of an Account Lost and Found Several Times

It was mentioned in the previous chapters that in 1827 Ricci had left the manuscript of the *Travels* in the hands of Champollion-Figeac with an agreement to publish it and share the profit. It was also mentioned that Champollion the Younger apparently encouraged Ricci to publish, but at the same time kept the manuscript and the drawings for his studies.

In June 1836, Rosellini asked the Tuscan minister of the interior to retrieve from France some of the drawings made during the Franco-Tuscan expedition he had sent to Champollion for the planned joint publication. The Pisan professor also urged the minister to ask for the restitution of Ricci's manuscript and drawings. One could argue that Ricci had willingly left the manuscript to Champollion-Figeac for publication and that therefore the Tuscan government had no rights to it. In fact, with the 1834 deal between the government and Ricci's heirs, the grand duke agreed to pay the rest of the sum due for the collection, provided the heirs handed over all documents relating to Egypt made by Ricci. In a letter from Ansano Baroni to Giuseppe Passalacqua, dated 20 March 1837, we have the last mention of the manuscript. According to Baroni: "Since for the same reason, which is for sale, the same Dr. Ricci had left in the hands of Mr. Champollion-Figeac in Paris some manuscripts, the Ricci brothers pleaded HIRH the grand duke of Tuscany for the restitution of these objects via his minister in Paris Mr. Berlinghieri; the sovereign graciously accepted the petition and the result was that Mr. Champollion promptly returned everything."[1] If this claim is true, then the manuscript of the *Travels* was last seen in Rome in 1836–37.

Despite claims that the manuscript had been returned to the Ricci brothers in Rome in 1837 or earlier, in 1928 it was rediscovered in Cairo, where it had come from Paris. The discoverer was Ernesto Verrucci Bey (1874–1947), quite a famous Italian architect at the Egyptian court. Angelo Sammarco (1883–1948), translator and censor in the service of

Sultan (later King) Fu'ad I (r. 1917–36), describes the discovery in these words: "The manuscript was presented to us by the Great Officer Ernesto Verrucci Bey, Chief Architect of the Royal Palaces of Egypt, who, sensing its importance, bought it on behalf of HM Fuad I from the Moscato Bookshop in Cairo, where the manuscript had arrived from an antiquarian bookshop of Paris."[2] Sammarco wrote also that "on the occasion of the centennial of Rosellini's death [1943], Ricci will be published with an introduction, notes, rare or unpublished documents, and plates, under the auspices of the Ministry of Italian Africa." When this article was actually published, Sammarco had been dead for a year and the publication of the *Travels* was not yet ready: Rosellini celebrations were planned for 1943 and then delayed to 1949 because of the war. The span of time between the discovery of the manuscript and Sammarco's death (1928–48) was filled with dozens of publications of the royal translator, especially the four volumes of the series *Il regno di Muhammad Ali nei documenti diplomatici italiani inediti*. Ricci's publication, too, was planned in a series of two volumes: the former, comprising the edition of the *Travels*, was never published, while the latter, printed in 1930, collected many interesting documents about Ricci. The incompleteness of this two-volume series led to the misunderstanding that the travel account was actually published.[3]

In the preface of a volume in memory of Ippolito Rosellini (1949), editor Evaristo Breccia wrote that the original typescript of Sammarco's *Ricci* was returned to the heirs by the Ministry of Italian Africa, which was about to publish it in 1943. Breccia thought the original manuscript was in Cairo, where Sammarco had lived until the end of the Second World War, and that nobody had done any research to track it down, to the point that it was lost again. In the meanwhile, Georges Douin used it for his book on the Egyptian conquest of Sennar, where parts of the manuscript regarding Ibrahim Pasha's expedition are published in French translation.[4]

In 2009, the present author was doing research in the Dar al-Watha'iq al-Qawmiya (National Archives of Egypt) in Cairo. The entire documentation collected in years of research by Angelo Sammarco was amassed in a fonds labeled "Italian." It comprised mainly typewritten copies of documents from different Italian archives, such as the State Archives of Florence and Naples, the City Historical Archive of Livorno, and other institutions in Rome, Mantua, Turin, Venice, and Vienna. Much of the diplomatic correspondence of the Grand Duchy of Tuscany, which is now absent from the State Archive of Florence, possibly destroyed by the Arno flood in 1966, is also now in Cairo. Among the Sammarco papers, there was a typescript of 303 pages: Ricci's *Travels*.[5] A second typewritten sheaf of only twelve pages contained the beginning of the *Travels* with comment notes by Sammarco himself.

Unfortunately, there is no trace of Ricci's original manuscript: research was done both in other fonds of the National Archives and at the Kutub Khan (Arabic Manuscripts Archive) in Cairo. Since Verrucci Bey purchased it on behalf of the crown, the manuscript should now be part of the Royal Library in Abdin Palace, seat of the royal court at the time, where Sammarco also had his office. After the 1952 coup, the palace became a presidential residence and its library was divided into two lots: one was kept at Abdin, the other was donated to Asyut University. Part of the latter was later donated to Aswan University.

The importance of Ricci's *Travels* did not allow waiting for the discovery of the original manuscript for its publication. The typescript which is the base for the current edition undoubtedly preserves a faithful copy of the original manuscript; pencil corrections in fact confirm that the copy was carefully revised. The typewritten copy is translated and reproduced here with only a few small omissions (see p. 163).

The Plates:
Sources and Descriptions

7
Identifying the Drawings for the Intended Plates

The Importance of Ricci's Drawings

Alessandro Ricci was a fine draftsman. His artistic ability was universally acknowledged by his contemporaries: Belzoni, Salt, Champollion, and Rosellini all had words of praise for his ability to catch the style of Egyptian reliefs of different periods. Contrary to his companions, possibly because he had studied science rather than art or drafting, Ricci's production does not comprise landscapes and portraits: his plates were mostly epigraphic copies.

Comparison with eighteenth-century drawings down to the Napoleonic campaign proves the striking superiority of Ricci's production: there, the representation of Egypt is grotesque, awkward, and so imbued with classicism as to betray completely the ancient Egyptian spirit. The other draftsmen who worked with Ricci were almost all, except Belzoni, highly skilled as well; many of the works by Salt, Bankes, Beechey, and Linant are faithful reproductions of reliefs and inscriptions or beautiful general views of the archaeological sites. The overall production of all these artists is stunning for epigraphic faithfulness and artistic quality, and its quality was attained only by the following Franco-Tuscan expedition in 1828–29 and a few other artists. Epigraphic faithfulness has its main limit in the lack of knowledge of the hieroglyphs, which caused many misunderstandings. Where later copies are available, in general these are better.

Published Plates and Dispersion of the Originals

Ricci intended to accompany the *Travels* with ninety numbered plates, some of them comprising more than one figure: up to 324 drawings. Only a few originals survive with their plate numbers, while most of the drawings that were conceived to be part of the *Travels* are scattered on different sheets or have a different numbering system. Many drawings in his possession were just sketches, quick copies of much more refined works handed over to Bankes or Salt.

It seems that some of the original drawings were with the manuscript when Ricci gave it to Champollion-Figeac, as stated by Rosellini: "The manuscript and the drawings of Ricci were kept by Mr. Champollion-Figeac; a recent proof is that last year a first batch of the drawings of *Les Monuments de l'Égypte et de la Nubie* has come out. . . . there is a drawing I am absolutely sure was among those left by Dr. Ricci."[1]

Some other papers of Ricci's were in Florence when he fell sick in 1832 and still other papers were in Berlin, among them the parchments left in the hands of Giuseppe Passalacqua for sale in 1831 and possibly the drawings handed over to Minutoli back in 1820. A letter by Arcangelo Michele Migliarini to Antonio Ramirez di Montalvo is quite explicit on the matter:

> Dr. Ricci had many drawings, made during his first journey, of monuments that had already disappeared in his second, and many written notes. It is also true that his drawings were moved or lost, but I suggest that what is left should be examined. If Your Most Illustrious Excellency will approve the proposal, it would be appropriate for the trustee to get back the portfolio in Paris and other belongings left in Berlin. The first has the drawings of the stelae of Serabit el-Khadim and Maghara. If the Chevalier Champollion[2] had decided to publish them as an appendix to the *Travels*, they must be valuable. I perfectly remember that I saw them: most are votive stelae.[3]

In 1835, after Ricci's death, Ramirez di Montalvo followed Migliarini's suggestions and instructed him to visit the lawyer Francesco Pacini, testamentary trustee of Ricci, "to see the manuscripts and drawings related to the Egyptian antiquities."[4] All the papers were handed over to the Academy on 27 January 1835[5] and, after Migliarini had examined them, were partly kept and partly given back to the heirs on 30 March.[6]

To sum up, when Ricci died, his papers were already divided into at least four different lots: a portfolio of Sinai drawings (and maybe something more) in Paris; some drawings at the Academy of Fine Arts in Florence; a batch in Berlin; other papers given back to the heirs because they were not directly connected with Egypt or the antiquities.

Some of Ricci's drawings were published in the nineteenth century, a few even during his lifetime:

- twelve drawings of Siwa Oasis, published in 1823 by Jomard;[7]
- ten Sinai inscriptions, published by the Champollions in 1826 and 1844–89;[8]
- seven drawings of different Egyptian and Nubian monuments, published by Baron von Minutoli in 1824;[9]
- four drawings of Egyptian monuments, published by Rosellini in 1832–44;[10]
- eight drawings from the tomb of Seti I, published by Belzoni in 1820.[11]

Florence Egyptian Museum

Since its acquisition made by Migliarini in 1835 on behalf of the Academy of Fine Arts, and for more than 160 years, nobody had catalogued or studied the portfolio of drawings made by Ricci. This serious gap was finally filled in 1997 by the important study of Patricia Usick.[12] Only in 2011 was a complete photographic record of the drawings made, at the expense of the PhD program in Oriental studies of the University of Pisa.

Patricia Usick listed 144 drawings, but possibly not all were made by Ricci. Nevertheless, the Florence portfolio represents the core of the drawings Ricci intended to publish with the *Travels*. It comprises maps and plans, copies of hieroglyphic inscriptions, stelae, and reliefs of many sites of Egypt and Nubia. Most sites are represented by one or two drawings only, such as Ashmunayn, Amara, Tombos, Jebel Silsila, Semna, Kumma, Beni Hasan, Luxor, Wadi al-Sebu'a, Buhen, and Ellesiya. Other sites received more attention: Kanays (three drawings), Abu Simbel (four drawings), Kom Ombo (five drawings), Jebel Barkal and Nuri (seven drawings), Philae (six drawings), Serabit al-Khadim and al-Maghara (twelve drawings each, all stelae), the Theban necropolis and the Valley of the Kings (fifteen drawings), Giza (twenty drawings of the mastabas of Khafre-ankh, Debhen, Iymery, Seshemnefer, and Nebemakhet), and Elephantine (fifteen drawings).

This last group is extremely important because it records with plenty of details the bark-chapels of Amenhotep III and Ramesses II, destroyed in 1822. Quite surprisingly, a drawing definitely belonging to this series is kept in the Wilkinson collection of the Griffith Institute, Oxford (MS. Wilkinson dep.a.21 Draw. No. 345). How the drawing ended up in the Wilkinson collection is not clear, but, as pointed out in the previous chapters, Ricci and Wilkinson had in fact met at least once, in 1822.

Pisa University Library

Many drawings by Ricci are kept in the University Library of Pisa, but were made during the 1828–29 Franco-Tuscan expedition. Among this collection, there are nevertheless four drawings certainly made by Ricci during his previous journey in 1817–22. Two of them were surely intended to illustrate the *Travels* because they retain the original numbering system as indicated in the text. These are:

- "Pl. I Sceyh-Abade." A copy of the famous scene in the tomb of Djehutyhotep at Deir al-Barsha, showing the transportation of a colossal statue, but without hieroglyphic text.[13]
- "Pl. VII Gurnah." Despite the caption, this drawing is the copy of a scene representing weavers from the tomb of Khety at Beni Hasan. This drawing, cut in the shape of a stripe, does not form the entire Plate 7, which according to Ricci had three more figures, but only two others are now preserved in Florence.[14]

Two other drawings,[15] not signed, are copies of two scenes detached from the tomb of Nebamun by Yanni D'Athanasi on behalf of Henry Salt and now kept at the British Museum

(EA 37984). The fragments were stored in the house of D'Athanasi in July 1821 when Ricci and Linant stopped at Qurna on their way to Sennar and had effectively a chance to copy them. The two Pisan drawings are similar to another copy made by Linant and now kept in Dorchester. Despite the drawing not being signed, the style differences and the fact that it ended up in Rosellini's collection in Pisa push for an identification of the author as Ricci. The two drawings were not intended to appear in the *Travels*.

In the Rosellini Fonds of the Pisa University Library there are many other drawings by Alessandro Ricci that correspond to the descriptions made in the *Travels*; however, in absence of a clear sign, such as the original numbering, they must be dated to 1828–29.

Mss. Bankes

Properties and collections belonging to the Bankes family were bequeathed to the National Trust in 1981. The rich documentation amassed by William John Bankes during his journeys is now deposited at the Dorset History Centre in Dorchester, Dorset, United Kingdom.[16] Only twelve documents, two by Ricci, are displayed at Kingston Lacy, Bankes's family house.

Even though the Bankes manuscripts are quoted by Bertha Porter and Rosalind Moss in the *Topographical Bibliography*, who also made a partial list of the collection, a complete catalog was not available until 2011.[17]

Besides William John Bankes himself, the other main contributors to the archive are Ricci, Linant, and Beechey, as shown in the following table (notes and low-quality sketches are not counted): it might be surprising to discover that Ricci appears to be the main author.

Artist	Quantity	Percentage
Alessandro Ricci	359	29
William John Bankes	331	27
Adolphe Maurice Linant de Bellefonds	288	23
William Henry Beechey	124	10
Uncertain or unidentified author and other authors	134	11
Total	**1,236**	

Epigraphic copies make up most of the collection and were the main task assigned to Ricci, as shown in the following table about the doctor's work.

Subject	Quantity	Percentage
Non-hieroglyphic inscriptions	1	0.25
Plans and measured sections	16	4.5
Landscape and monument views	1	0.25
Egyptian epigraphy	332	92.5
Maps	0	0
Architectural details of monuments	9	2.5
Anthropology, fauna, and flora	0	0
Objects, statues	0	0
Total	**359**	

The relationship between the drawings by Ricci in Dorchester and those in Florence is not clear. It seems that some of the Florence drawings are copies, sometimes just sketched, of the British originals. Possibly Ricci intended to refine the drawings at a second stage. There are nevertheless important exceptions where the Florence drawings are of a better quality. In fact, the two collections are not exactly superimposable: at Dorchester there are no drawings made by Ricci at Giza, Kanays, and Elephantine, a total of thirty-eight. It seems that the drawings of Giza were made by Ricci at the end of his Egyptian stay and so possibly for his own sake. The Kanays drawings, too, were made on his way to Berenike, so Bankes had no right to them. The valuable drawings of Elephantine are a different case.

Bristol City Museum & Art Gallery
The large collection of drawings made in 1818 by Ricci and Belzoni in the tomb of Seti I is held at the Bristol City Museum & Art Gallery. The fonds comprises around 350 drawings, but only a few are signed. It is not completely published, but research was done by the curators to find out the origin of the material and to identify the authors.[18]

In autumn 2011, I made a rapid survey of the drawings, coming to the following conclusions. The material is clearly divided into different series, but their authorship is possibly different from what was previously believed. First, there is the series of original drawings made by Ricci inside the tomb. These are mounted on a strong canvas support and are of a very good epigraphic quality. The paper is worn, dusty, and full of ink, soil, and wax spots: a circumstance that perfectly agrees with the working conditions described by Ricci. There is only a mistake in the color palette: the *nemes* headdress of Seti I in this series is painted green-blue, instead of yellow as in the other series and in reality. Then there is a second series, possibly used for the exhibition at the Egyptian Hall in London in 1821. These drawings are clearly an inept copy of Ricci's own drawings: hieroglyphic signs are simplified, proportions are not respected, and bodylines are deformed and inelegant. These are the same drawings published by Belzoni in his 1820 book. A last series comprises pencil key notes for the reconstruction of the tomb; plates with coloring instructions for details such as bracelets, belts, wigs, and crowns; and a few drawings only partially painted, possibly a model for typographers.

The archive holds as well a small notebook and a sketchbook by Belzoni and his wife, but nothing else by Ricci. Some of Belzoni's papers are also held at the City Library of Padua, Italy, but were not checked for this study.

Salt Watercolours

The so-called 'Salt Watercolours' at the British Museum were published (without photographs) by Morris L. Bierbrier in 1983. It is a collection of fifteen fine watercolors by Salt, Beechey, and Ricci.

Eight drawings are annotated by Salt as work done by Ricci: five Theban stelae in the Salt collection (now BM 8461, 8462, 8504, 8450; one is lost); a Theban stela in the Bankes collection (now at Kingston Lacy House, National Trust Inventory Number 1257709);[19] the garden scene from the Theban tomb of Sennefer;[20] the colossus scene from the tomb of Djehutyhotep at Deir al-Barsha.[21]

According to Bierbrier, the drawings were possibly made between 1817 and 1818, or late in 1818. Because Ricci worked for Salt from 1818 to 1822, the drawings could have been done any time between the two dates, even though an early date is in fact more likely. As mentioned before, Belzoni states that Ricci practiced on hieroglyphics for some time before starting to copy the reliefs in the tomb of Seti I: it is possible that the doctor copied the stelae in the Salt collection, which at the time were likely already stored in the British consulate in Cairo.

Three drawings in the British Museum portfolio are surely connected with the *Travels*: the garden of Sennefer, the colossus of Djehutyhotep, and the stela of Nestjerenmaat, chantress of Montu. The latter drawing is a very fine copy of a Theban stela (BM 8450), possibly the model for the drawing Florence No. 88, and featured on Plate 9, Number 2.

Mss. Minutoli

The Mss. Minutoli are, in fact, lost. The name here refers to those drawings made by Ricci for Minutoli that appear in his 1824 publication. The papers belonging to Baron von Minutoli were probably merged with the family archive of the Grafen von Pfeil, now in Poland. At the end of the Second World War, the Polish administration confiscated all valuables and transferred them to a secret location.

Some subjects were shared between the collections listed previously and Minutoli's publication, but substantial differences signal that we are dealing with different drawings, rather than different copies of the same drawing. A comparison between the subjects of Plates 2, 4, and 5 in the two different versions easily proves this.

8
List of Plates

Each listing includes, when available: description of the item; location of the original item; historical period when it was created; bibliographical references to the original item; location(s) of Ricci's drawing and any known copies; or related drawings, such as drawings made by Bankes or Linant that Ricci might have intended to copy; any additional information.

The abbreviation D/BKL in the plate descriptions stands for the collection Deposit/ Bankes of Kingston Lacy and Corfe Castle, Dorset History Centre, Dorchester.

Travel in Nubia
Plate 1

Transportation of a colossal statue on a sledge pulled by four rows of men under the supervision of officers.

Deir al-Barsha, tomb of Djehutyhotep II, inner chamber, left wall (middle-upper register).

Twelfth Dynasty, reigns of Amenemhat II (1932–1896 BC), Senwosret II (1900–1880 BC), and Senwosret III (1881–1840 BC).

Porter and Moss, *Topographical Bibliography* 4:180 (14–15).

Document 62, Ms. 300.4, Folder 17, Biblioteca Universitaria, Pisa, watercolor and ink on paper.

Bibliography: Rosellini, *Monumenti Civili*, pl. XLVIII [1].

Other copies: (a) I.I.7–8, D/BKL (Ricci); (b) Mss. Minutoli (*Reise*, pl. XIII).

Subsequently, the relief was severely damaged in the left and upper parts as early as 1893; the head of the statue, the row of men on the left, and the crowded row of men in the first register in particular are now missing. The value of the plate is diminished by the fact that Ricci did not copy the hieroglyphic inscriptions. Ricci's drawing must be one of the first copies, if not the first, because the tomb of Djehutyhotep was discovered by Irby and Mangles in 1817.

Plate 2

Reliefs in the temple portico and column with image of Thoth.

    Ashmunayn, temple of Thoth.

    Dynasty of Macedonia, reigns of Alexander III (332–323 BC) and Philip III Arrhidaeus (323–317 BC).

    Porter and Moss, *Topographical Bibliography* IV, 165–67.

    No. 114 [1], Museo Egizio, Florence[1] (only the column), watercolor and ink on paper; unpublished.

    Other copies: Mss. Minutoli (*Reise*, pl. XIV [5]–[6]).

The drawing is a valuable record of the temple that was destroyed in 1822, shortly after Ricci's visit. The temple is portrayed in the *Description de l'Égypte* (Paris: Imprimerie Impériale, 1822), A., IV, pls. 51–52, with a general view, a reconstruction, a plan, and some details. Ricci's copy adds reliefs and inscriptions not copied by the *savants*. Ricci in the *Travels* states that the color of the columns was in some areas well preserved, so the plate is probably reproducing the original colors. The temple reliefs copied by Ricci show scenes of adoration of the gods by the pharaoh and the decoration of the cavetto cornice.

Plate 3

Number 1

Plan of the temple

    Kanays, rock temple.

    Nineteenth–Twentieth Dynasty, reigns of Seti I (1296–1279 BC), Ramesses II (1279–1212 BC), and Ramesses VI (1141–1133 BC).

    Porter and Moss, *Topographical Bibliography* 7:322.

    No. 133 [1], Museo Egizio, Florence, ink on paper; unpublished.

It is a very accurate plan, even if of small dimensions. A similar plan was published by both Belzoni and Cailliaud.

Number 2

Bowing Seti I in *shendyt* and wig offers a representation of Maat.

    Kanays, rock temple.

    Nineteenth Dynasty, reign of Seti I (1296–1279 BC).

    Porter and Moss, *Topographical Bibliography* 7:324 (19)–(20).

    No. 133 [2], Museo Egizio, Florence, ink on paper; unpublished.

Number 3

Dedicatory inscription of Seti I.

    Kanays, rock temple.

    Nineteenth Dynasty, reign of Seti I (1296–1279 BC).

    No. 133 [3], Museo Egizio, Florence, ink on paper; unpublished.

The site was described and recorded by Nestor l'Hôte and Cailliaud. The inscription, with focus on the ankh sign, was probably engraved on a lintel.

Plate 4

Three gods with crocodile, tortoise, and bull head seated on a podium; hieroglyphic inscription in a column on the right.

> Valley of the Kings, tomb of Ramesses III (KV 11), chamber H.
> Twentieth Dynasty, reign of Ramesses III (1185–1153 BC).
> Porter and Moss, *Topographical Bibliography* 1, Part 2:525 (46) III.
> No. 5, Museo Egizio, Florence, watercolor and ink on paper.
> Bibliography: Bresciani, "Il richiamo della piramide," 156.
> Other copies: (a) Mss. Minutoli (*Reise*, pl. XXI [2]); (b) II.B.1, D/BKL (Ricci).

The detail copied by Ricci was taken from one of the side chambers of the second corridor of the tomb. The colors of the hieroglyphic inscription were copied faithfully. In Minutoli's publication, the upper part and the frame are missing.

Plate 5

God portrayed with frontal face, holding an ankh sign and a *was* sceptre, standing inside a naos in front of an offering table.

> Valley of the Kings, tomb of Ramesses III (KV 11), precise location unknown.
> Twentieth Dynasty, reign of Ramesses III (1185–1153 BC).
> Porter and Moss, *Topographical Bibliography* 1, Part 2:525 (46) III.
> No. 109, Museo Egizio, Florence, watercolor and ink on paper.
> Bibliography: Guidotti, "Dall'Egitto a Firenze via Pisa," 157.
> Other copies: Mss. Minutoli (*Reise*, pl. XXI [3]).

Plate 6

Neferhotep and Parennefer granted the golden collar.

> Theban West Bank, Shaykh Abd al-Qurna, tomb of Neferhotep (TT 50), vestibule, south wall.
> Eighteenth Dynasty, reign of Horemheb (1328–1298 BC).
> Porter and Moss, *Topographical Bibliography* 1, Part 1:95 (2).
> No. 49, Museo Egizio, Florence, pencil on paper (left); II.A.6, D/BKL, watercolor on paper (right); unpublished.

The subject of this plate is split into two different sheets, one in Dorchester and the other in Florence. The latter is extremely detailed and, even though it does not reproduce the hieroglyphic text, it shows details not present in Hari's publication of the tomb. Ricci describes one of the figures as "wearing gloves." It must not be forgotten that Ricci's interpretations are made in a pre-Egyptological context. The gloves could be the fruit of Ricci's imagination, as they do not appear in Hari's book. It could otherwise be the line of the sleeves of a tight tunic.

Plate 7

Number 1

Two net makers working one in front of the other, and a weaver at the loom.

Beni Hasan, tomb of Khety (No. 17).

    Eleventh Dynasty (2160–1994 BC).

    Porter and Moss, *Topographical Bibliography* 4:155 (2)–(3).

    Document 22, Ms. 300.4, Folder 10, Fonds Rosellini, Biblioteca Universitaria, Pisa, watercolor and ink on paper.

    Bibliography: Rosellini, *Monumenti Civili*, pl. LXXVI [2]; Champollion, *Monuments de l'Égypte et de la Nubie*, pl. CCCLXVI.

    Other copies: (a) Mss. Minutoli (*Reise*, pl. XXIV [1]–[2]); (b) I.B.11, D/BKL (Ricci).

Ricci is mistaken both in the caption of this plate and in the *Travels*, identifying this scene as coming from a Theban tomb. Nevertheless, Ricci's drawing is valuable since it represents a detail of a much larger scene, reproduced in Newberry's publication only in an approximate manner.

Number 2

The deceased comes back from hunting with his bow, a gazelle tied with a rope, a goat in his right hand, and a hare in his left.

    Theban West Bank, tombs of the nobles, unidentified tomb.

    Eighteenth Dynasty (1549–1298 BC).

    Original not found.[2]

    Other copies: II.A.12, D/BKL (Ricci?).

Number 3

Relief with female deceased facing west, holding sistrum and lotus flowers.

    Theban West Bank, tombs of the nobles, unidentified tomb, right door jamb.

    Nineteenth–Twentieth Dynasty (1298–1069 BC).

    No. 36, Museo Egizio, Florence, pencil on paper; unpublished.

    The same relief was copied by the *savants* and published in the *Description de l'Égypte*, A. II, pl. XLV [15]. The original watercolor, made by H.J. Redouté and kept at the Bibliothèque Nationale de Paris, bears the following caption: "Figure cimbolique [*sic*] placée sour l'embrasure de la porte d'entrée d'une grotto vis-à-vis le Memnonium."[3]

Number 4

Personified *djed* pillar holding crook and flail, and bearing the *atef* crown, raised in the arms of Nebsumenu.

    Theban West Bank, Khokha, tomb of Nebsumenu (TT 183), transverse hall, west wall.

    Nineteenth Dynasty, reign of Ramesses II (1279–1212 BC).

    No. 135, Museo Egizio, Florence, ink on paper; unpublished.

    Bibliography: Porter and Moss, *Topographical Bibliography* 1, Part 1:289 (10). Further publication by Karl Joachim Seyfried, Jan Assmann, and Mohamed Saleh, in preparation.

Plate 8

Garden of the temple of Amun, with vineyards, palm trees, lakes, and buildings.

Theban West Bank, Shaykh Abd al-Qurna, tomb of Sennefer (TT 96), south wing, transverse hall, west wall.

Eighteenth Dynasty, reign of Amenhotep II (1424–1398 BC).

Porter and Moss, *Topographical Bibliography* 1, Part 1:198 (4).

Original not found.

Other copies: (a) II.A.17, D/BKL (Ricci); (b) Document 137, Ms. 300.4, Folder 34, Fonds Rosellini, Biblioteca Universitaria, Pisa (Ricci) (*Monumenti Civili*, pl. LXIX) (c) AES 1524, British Museum (Ricci).

The three existing copies of this drawing show some differences. In particular, the drawing in Dorchester is hasty in treating some details such as palm branches, lakes, and the bedding around them. It seems that this copy also integrates some figures now missing. The original wall painting is badly preserved, with cracks, color fadings, and dirt. Ricci's copy is therefore of some importance.

Plate 9

Number 1

Wooden coffin lid with stretched figure of Nut.

Theban West Bank, tombs of the nobles, unidentified tomb.

Twenty-fifth–Twenty-sixth Dynasty (752–525 BC).

No. 117, Museo Egizio, Florence, pencil on paper; unpublished.

Ricci copied a coffin lid seen "at an Arab's of Qurna, who lived in a tomb" (p. 174). It seems the piece is not to be found in the Ricci Florence collection or in Dresden. As he describes it, it was a piece of wood painted black with the figure of Nut in yellow: the goddess is naked, her body filled with stars, and the sun disk between her stretched hands, at her mouth, and at her pubis. The drawing shows in detail the shape of the broken lid. A short inscription runs over the head of the goddess: *ṯꜢw nḏm ꜥnḫ r ḥꜥw* (?)[4]=*k*, 'The sweet breath of life for your limbs (?).' Although black and yellow coffins are typical of the Eighteenth Dynasty, only royal sarcophagi of the period (with very few exceptions) were decorated inside, and even more rarely with an image of Nut. This subject becomes more frequent during the Third Intermediate Period, but at the bottom of the sarcophagus and with a different iconography. Iconographic and stylistic details (stars on the body, hairstyle) date the piece to the Twenty-fifth–Twenty-sixth Dynasty, approximately.[5]

Number 2

Wooden stela of Nestjerenmaat, chantress of Montu, offering loaves, geese, and flowers to Re-Horakhty, with a short dedicatory inscription.

Probably Theban West Bank, tombs of the nobles, unidentified tomb.

Twenty-second Dynasty (948–715 BC).

No. 88, Museo Egizio, Florence, pencil on paper; unpublished.

Other copies: AES 1520, British Museum (Ricci).

Bibliography: Bierbrier, "The Salt Watercolours," 11.

The drawing in Florence is a rough copy of an original made for Henry Salt and now in London. The stela, made of sycamore wood, is also at the British Museum (AES 8450) and was part of Salt's collection.

Number 3

Wooden stela with king (?) offering to Khonsu, followed by a soldier with standards.

Probably Theban West Bank, tombs of the nobles, unidentified tomb.

No example of this drawing was found.

Number 4

List of offerings.

Luxor, temple of Amun, unidentified location.

Eighteenth–Nineteenth Dynasty (1549–1187 BC).

No. 143, Museo Egizio, Florence, pencil on paper; unpublished.

Described by Ricci as a "tally," according to Patricia Usick it could be a "Festival Calendar";[6] the text appears to be an offering text listing aromatic oils, cosmetics, and wine.[7] Offering lists in the Luxor temple are numerous: Porter and Moss, *Topographical Bibliography* 2:323 (124), 324 (138) and (140), 327 (153), 328 (157)–(158), 329 (161)–(162). Nevertheless, after a survey carried out in January 2012, none of these lists seems to be the one copied by Ricci.

Plate 10
Number 1

Relief with name of gods and offering list.

Luxor, temple of Amun, second antechamber (room VIII).

Eighteenth Dynasty, reign of Amenhotep III (1388–1348 BC).

Porter and Moss, *Topographical Bibliography* 2:321 (125).

No. 130, Museo Egizio, Florence (caption "Bas-relief in a room of Luxor temple. X. No. 1"), ink on paper; unpublished.

No. 118, Museo Egizio, Florence, is a preliminary sketch of this polished drawing.

Number 2

Relief with head of king wearing an elaborate crown.

Luxor, temple of Amun, unidentified location.

Eighteenth–Nineteenth Dynasty (1549–1187 BC).

Porter and Moss, *Topographical Bibliography* 2:301–35.

No. 133 [4], Museo Egizio, Florence, ink on paper; unpublished.

Number 3

Bas-relief with Hekau and Hapi presenting the *ka*s of child Amenhotep III and Horus presenting the same to Amun.

> Luxor, temple of Amun, birth room.
> Eighteenth Dynasty, reign of Amenhotep III (1388–1348 BC).
> Porter and Moss, *Topographical Bibliography* 2:326 (152) I 2–3.
> Original not found.
> Other copies: (a) Mss. Minutoli (*Reise*, pl. XXIII [1]); (b) II.C.17, D/BKL (Ricci).

In the *Travels* Ricci describes with curiosity the two gods Hekau and Hapi, who, because of the apparent contradiction between their feminine breasts and the beard, intrigued him. Another drawing at the Egyptian Museum of Florence (No. 123) represents Nile geniuses from the tomb of Ramesses III (KV 11) [Porter and Moss, *Topographical Bibliography*, 1 Part 1:520 (14) I], but for this plate Ricci clearly specifies that the relief was copied in the temple of Amun at Luxor.

Number 4

Rekhyt bird on a *neb* sign with wings and arms raised in worship.

> Luxor, temple of Amun, unidentified location.
> Eighteenth–Nineteenth Dynasty (1549–1187 BC).
> No. 114 [2], Museo Egizio, Florence, ink on paper; unpublished.
> Other copies: Mss. Minutoli (*Reise*, pl. XX [6]).

This is a small detail extracted from a larger scene.

Number 5

Ibis (hieroglyphic sign or relief).

> Luxor, temple of Amun, unidentified location.
> Eighteenth–Nineteenth Dynasty (1549–1187 BC).
> No. 114 [3], Museo Egizio, Florence, ink on paper; unpublished.
> Other copies: Mss. Minutoli (*Reise*, pl. XXI [13]).

Plate 11

Relief partly covered in sand: Thutmose III introduced by Dedwen to Khnum and the same king consecrating offerings to Khnum; temple door with Thutmose II and Seni, mayor of the Southern City, overseer of the South Lands.

> Semna East (Kumma), temple of Khnum, Hall II, north wall.
> Eighteenth Dynasty, reigns of Thutmose II (1491–1479 BC), Thutmose III (1479–1424 BC), and Amenhotep II (1424–1398 BC).
> Porter and Moss, *Topographical Bibliography* 7:152–53 (5)–(6), (8).
> No. 133 [5] and 131, Museo Egizio, Florence, ink on paper.
> Bibliography: Bresciani, "Il richiamo della piramide," 155.
> Other copies: XIII.B.2, D/BKL (Ricci).

The entire relief was later copied by Lepsius, after the sand that covered half of its scenes had been removed. Cf. Lepsius, *Denkmäler aus Aegypten und Aethiopien* 3:pl. 58.

Plate 12

Temple plan.

    Amara.

    Meroitic period (300 BC–AD 350).

    Porter and Moss, *Topographical Bibliography* 7:157.

    No. 119, Museo Egizio, Florence, ink on paper; unpublished.

    The temple is now destroyed, but Ricci was not the only person to document its plan.

Plate 13

Carved column with four registers of scenes and text.

    Amara, temple.

    Meroitic period (300 BC–AD 350).

    No. 120, Museo Egizio, Florence, ink on paper; unpublished.

    The scenes on the columns of Amara were also copied by Pococke, Cailliaud, and Prudhoe.

Plate 14

Number 1

Plan of the temple.

    Buhen, temple of the Horus of Buhen ("South Temple").

    Eighteenth Dynasty, reigns of Hatshepsut (1472–1457 BC) and Thutmose III (1479–1424 BC).

    Porter and Moss, *Topographical Bibliography* 7:131–38.

    Nos. 33 and 34r, Museo Egizio, Florence, pencil and ink on paper; unpublished.

    The two copies are very different. No. 34 is a plan of the hypostyle hall, while No. 33 is a sketch of the same hall with accurate measurements. The two plans are schematic sketches with no formal accuracy and undoubtedly were preparatory material in need of working up. As is clear from Bankes's own plan of the building, now in Dorchester, the temple was partly buried under the sand: the only visible parts were the forecourt and the row of columns on the south side of the sanctuary. Ricci's map is therefore a (wrong) hypothetical reconstruction.

Number 2

Plan of the temple.

    Buhen, temple of Isis ("North Temple").

    Eighteenth Dynasty, reign of Amenhotep III (1388–1348 BC).

    Porter and Moss, *Topographical Bibliography* 7:129–31.

    Nos. 31 and 32, Museo Egizio, Florence, pencil and ink on paper; unpublished.

No. 32 is a map with accurate measurements; No. 31 is a reduced-scale map with a long note in English by Bankes, almost illegible. These two plans are, like the previous, schematic sketches with no formal accuracy.

Number 3

Stela of General Montuhotep in its wall niche; Senwosret I receiving life from Montu holding ten captives, with hieroglyphic text.

> Buhen, temple of Isis ("North Temple"), today at the Egyptian Museum of Florence, No. 2540A+B.
>
> Twelfth Dynasty, year 18 of Senwosret I (1956 BC).
>
> Porter and Moss, *Topographical Bibliography* 7:130 (9).
>
> No. 107, Museo Egizio, Florence, pencil on paper; unpublished.
>
> Other copies: XII.C.6, D/BKL (Ricci).

Another rougher copy in Florence is marked No. 108 and bears technical annotations on colors. The stela, in the meanwhile heavily damaged, was copied a second time by Ricci in 1829, when it was taken by the Tuscan expedition. The comparison with the first copy shows many large lacunae. A second fragment of the same stela was recovered in 1893 by Capt. H.G. Lyons and put back with the first piece in Florence. The two Florentine drawings reproduce only two lines of the six lines and sixteen columns of the stela. The Dorchester copy of this drawing shows the complete text. On the other side, the two drawings in Florence mark lacunae arbitrarily integrated in the Dorchester copy.

Number 4

Plan of a ruin, east of the "North Temple."

> Buhen.
>
> No. 34, Museo Egizio, Florence.
>
> Other copies: XII.C.9, D/BKL (Bankes).

Number 5

Plan of a ruin, east of the "North Temple."

> Buhen.
>
> Original not found.
>
> Other copies: XII.C.9, D/BKL (Bankes).

Number 6

Plan of a ruin, east of the "North Temple."

> Buhen.
>
> Original not found.
>
> Other copies: XII.C.9, D/BKL (Bankes).

Numbers 7 and 8
Plan of two rock niches.

> Faras Island.

> Original not found.

> Other copies: XII.B.3, D/BKL (Bankes); No. 8, Ms. Linant 265, Bibliothèque Centrale des Musées Nationaux, Paris.

Plate 15
Number 1
Rock stela of Hor, deputy of Wawat, worshiping Anuket of Amenheri, followed by his son.

> Jebel al-Shams ("Mashaket"), north of the niche of Pesiur.

> Probably Eighteenth Dynasty, reign of Horemheb (1328–1298 BC).

> Porter and Moss, *Topographical Bibliography* 7:122.

> Original not found.

> Other copies: XII.A.8, D/BKL (Ricci).

Number 2
Plan of the temple.

> Jebel Adda, rock temple of Amun-Re and Thoth.

> Eighteenth Dynasty, reign of Horemheb (1328–1298 BC).

> Porter and Moss, *Topographical Bibliography* 7:119–21.

> Original not found.

> Other copies: No. 7, Ms. Linant 265, Bibliothèque Centrale des Musées Nationaux, Paris.

> A map of the temple by Gaetano Rosellini is published in Rosellini, *Monumenti del Culto*,

pl. III [2], and in other nineteenth-century publications.

Number 3
Column of the first hall.

> Jebel Adda, rock temple of Amun-Re and Thoth.

> Eighteenth Dynasty, reign of Horemheb (1328–1298 BC).

> Porter and Moss, *Topographical Bibliography* 7:119–21.

> Original not found.

Number 4
Relief showing Anuket suckling the young pharaoh before Khnum.

> Jebel Adda, rock temple of Amun-Re and Thoth.

> Eighteenth Dynasty, reign of Horemheb (1328–1298 BC).

> Porter and Moss, *Topographical Bibliography* 7:121 (2)–(3).

> Original not found.

> Other copies: (a) XII.A.12, D/BKL (Ricci); (b) Nos. 4 and 5, Ms. 300.3, Folder 2, Fonds Rosellini, Biblioteca Universitaria, Pisa (Ricci).

Number 5

Plan of the temple.

    Abu Simbel, temple of Re-Horakhty ("Large Temple").

    Nineteenth Dynasty, reign of Ramesses II (1279–1212 BC).

    Porter and Moss, *Topographical Bibliography* 7:96.

    Original not found.

    Other copies: No. 3, Ms. Linant 265, Bibliothèque Centrale des Musées Nationaux, Paris.

Number 6

Plan of the temple.

    Abu Simbel, temple of Hathor of Abeshek and Nefertari ("Small Temple").

    Nineteenth Dynasty, reign of Ramesses II (1279–1212 BC).

    Porter and Moss, *Topographical Bibliography* 7:112.

    Original not found.

    Other copies: No. 4, Ms. Linant 265, Bibliothèque Centrale des Musées Nationaux, Paris.

Number 7

Pillar with Hathor head and inscription.

    Abu Simbel, temple of Hathor of Abeshek and Nefertari ("Small Temple"), first hall.

    Nineteenth Dynasty, reign of Ramesses II (1279–1212 BC).

    Porter and Moss, *Topographical Bibliography* 7:114–15.

    Original not found.

    Other copies: XI.B.29–30, D/BKL (Ricci).

Plate 16
Numbers 1 and 2

Lateral and front views of an Osiris pillar.

    Abu Simbel, temple of Re-Horakhty ("Large Temple"), first hall.

    Nineteenth Dynasty, reign of Ramesses II (1279–1212 BC).

    Porter and Moss, *Topographical Bibliography* 7:104–106.

    Original not found.

    Other copies: XI.A.20, D/BKL (Ricci).

Plate 17
Number 1

Series of reliefs: 1. Ramesses II offering incense and libating in front of ram-headed Mery-mutef and a lion-headed goddess; 2. Ramesses II followed by Thoth kneeling in front of the sacred tree and Re-Horakhty; 3. Ramesses II offering incense to Amun-Re of Jebel Barkal with large uraeus.

Abu Simbel, temple of Re-Horakhty ("Large Temple"), great hall, south wall.

Nineteenth Dynasty, reign of Ramesses II (1279–1212 BC).

Porter and Moss, *Topographical Bibliography* 7:102 (39)–(40), upper register.

No. 113, Museo Egizio, Florence, pencil, red and black ink, grayscale watercolor on paper; unpublished.

Bibliography: Usick, *Adventures in Egypt and Nubia*, 93–94.

Other copies: XI.A.2–3, XI.A.5, D/BKL (Ricci).

Number 2

Relief with Ramesses II offering four cloth boxes in front of Amun-Re.

Abu Simbel, temple of Re-Horakhty ("Large Temple"), great hall, south wall.

Nineteenth Dynasty, reign of Ramesses II (1279–1212 BC).

Porter and Moss, *Topographical Bibliography* 7:102 (39)–(40), upper register.

Original not found.

Other copies: XI.A.3, D/BKL (Ricci).

Number 3

Relief with Ramesses II in front of his deified self.

Abu Simbel, temple of Re-Horakhty ("Large Temple"), second hall, pillar XII.

Nineteenth Dynasty, reign of Ramesses II (1279–1212 BC).

Porter and Moss, *Topographical Bibliography* 7:109.

Original not found.

Other copies: XI.A.26, D/BKL (Ricci).

Number 4

Relief with Ramesses II offering an emblem of Maat to Thoth.

Abu Simbel, temple of Re-Horakhty ("Large Temple"), vestibule, north wall.

Nineteenth Dynasty, reign of Ramesses II (1279–1212 BC).

Porter and Moss, *Topographical Bibliography* 7:110 (107).

Original not found.

Other copies: XI.A.27, D/BKL (Ricci).

Plate 18

Number 1

Relief with Ramesses II offering two rows of prisoners (only one row copied by Ricci) in front of Re-Horakhty, his deified self, and Iusas.

Abu Simbel, temple of Re-Horakhty ("Large Temple"), great hall, west wall, north side.

Nineteenth Dynasty, reign of Ramesses II (1279–1212 BC).

Porter and Moss, *Topographical Bibliography* 7:104 (44).

Original not found.

Other copies: XI.A.16–17, D/BKL (Ricci).

Describing this scene, Ricci mentions Ramesses II with a quiver in the presence of the god Re, allowing an identification of this plate with the scene portraying Hittite prisoners, and not the parallel scene with Nubian prisoners where Ramesses II holds a bow. Ricci mistakenly mentions "prisoners of different appearances."

Number 2

Detail of the Nubian and Hittite prisoners' faces.

> Abu Simbel, temple of Re-Horakhty ("Large Temple"), great hall, east and west walls.
> Nineteenth Dynasty, reign of Ramesses II (1279–1212 BC).
> Porter and Moss, *Topographical Bibliography* 7:104 (43)–(44).
> No. 136, Museo Egizio, Florence, ink on paper.
> Bibliography: Bresciani, "Il richiamo della piramide," 155.

Number 3

Relief with feather-bearing prince.

> Abu Simbel, temple of Re-Horakhty ("Large Temple").
> Nineteenth Dynasty, reign of Ramesses II (1279–1212 BC).
> Original not found.
> Other copies: XXI.H.11, D/BKL (Ricci?).

Number 4

> Statue of feather-bearing prince.
> Abu Simbel, temple of Hathor of Abeshek and Nefertari ("Small Temple"), façade.
> Nineteenth Dynasty, reign of Ramesses II (1279–1212 BC).
> Porter and Moss, *Topographical Bibliography* 7:111 (1)–(6).
> No example of this drawing was found.

At the Egyptian Museum in Florence there is a rough ink sketch (No. 138; copy of another sketch by W.H. Beechey, XI.B.35, D/BKL) representing the façade of the Small Temple of Abu Simbel; the sketch features the colossi of Ramesses II and Nefertari only, while the statues of the princes are omitted.

Plate 19

Number 1

Relief with Ramesses II offering to Horus of Miam.

> Abu Simbel, temple of Re-Horakhty ("Large Temple"), second hall, pillar XII, west side.
> Nineteenth Dynasty, reign of Ramesses II (1279–1212 BC).
> Porter and Moss, *Topographical Bibliography* 7:109.
> Original not found.

Ricci gathered in this plate the east and west sides of pillar XII. Unfortunately in Florence and Dorchester there are only the drawings of the south sides of pillars XI and XII and the north sides of pillars IX and X, published here as a replacement for the missing ones.

Number 2

Relief with Ramesses II welcomed by Amun-Re.

Abu Simbel, temple of Re-Horakhty ("Large Temple"), second hall, pillar XII, east side.

Nineteenth Dynasty, reign of Ramesses II (1279–1212 BC).

Porter and Moss, *Topographical Bibliography* 7:109.

Original not found.

Plate 20

Relief with Ramesses II offering lettuce to Min-Amun, Isis, and his deified self.

Abu Simbel, temple of Re-Horakhty ("Large Temple"), vestibule, west wall.

Nineteenth Dynasty, reign of Ramesses II (1279–1212 BC).

Porter and Moss, *Topographical Bibliography* 7:109 (97).

Original not found.

Other copies: XI.A.21, D/BKL (Ricci).

Ricci correctly observes that the figure of deified Ramesses II was added later, but wrongly identifies the offering as corncobs. Lettuces mistaken for corncobs are a gross historical anachronism.

Plate 21

Number 1

Relief with Queen Nefertari playing the sistrum.

Abu Simbel, temple of Hathor of Abeshek and Nefertari ("Small Temple"), first hall, pillar IV.

Nineteenth Dynasty, reign of Ramesses II (1279–1212 BC).

Porter and Moss, *Topographical Bibliography* 7:114–15; Desroches-Noblecourt and Kuentz, *Le petit temple*, pls. LXXV–LXXVI.

Original not found.

Other copies: (a) Mss. Minutoli (*Reise*, pl. XXIV [5] left); (b) XI.B.38, D/BKL (Ricci).

Number 2

Relief with Queen Nefertari crowned by Hathor of Abeshek and Isis.

Abu Simbel, temple of Hathor of Abeshek and Nefertari ("Small Temple"), vestibule, south wall.

Nineteenth Dynasty, reign of Ramesses II (1279–1212 BC).

Porter and Moss, *Topographical Bibliography* 7:116 (34).

Original not found.

Other copies: (a) Mss. Minutoli; (b) XI.B.6, D/BKL (Ricci).

Plate 22

Relief with Ramesses II offering flowers to anthropomorphic Taweret, followed by Queen Nefertari playing the sistrum.

Abu Simbel, temple of Hathor of Abeshek and Nefertari ("Small Temple"), vestibule,
   south wall.
Nineteenth Dynasty, reign of Ramesses II (1279–1212 BC).
Porter and Moss, *Topographical Bibliography* 7:115 (30).
No. 125, Museo Egizio, Florence, ink on paper; unpublished.
Other copies: XI.B.4, D/BKL (Ricci).

A comparison with the actual scene shows how Ricci left out of the text the third column from
the left (*nṯr nfr nb t3.wy*) and other details from the queen's figure (second braid, crown elements).

Plate 23
Number 1
Plan of the temple.
   Wadi al-Sebuʿa, temple of Amun and Re-Horakhty.
   Nineteenth Dynasty, reign of Ramesses II (1279–1212 BC).
   Porter and Moss, *Topographical Bibliography* 7:53.
   Original not found.
   Other copies: IX.A.21, D/BKL (Ricci); No. 10, Ms. Linant 265, Bibliothèque Centrale
      des Musées Nationaux, Paris.

Number 2
Plan of the temple.
   Maharraqa, temple of Serapis.
   Roman period (30 BC–AD 284).
   Porter and Moss, *Topographical Bibliography* 7:51.
   Original not found.
   Other copies: VIII.E.6, D/BKL (Ricci).

Number 3
Plan of the temple.
   Maharraqa, small temple.
   Roman period (30 BC–AD 284).
   Porter and Moss, *Topographical Bibliography* 7:51–52.
   Original not found.
   Other copies: VIII.E.6, D/BKL (Ricci).

Number 4
"Red granite block, with lines on its surfaces forming squares."
   Maharraqa, small temple.
   Roman period (30 BC–AD 284).
   Porter and Moss, *Topographical Bibliography* 7:52.
   Original not found.
   Other copies: VIII.E.5, D/BKL (Linant).

Number 5

Plan of the temple.

> Qurta, temple of Isis.
>
> Roman period (30 BC–AD 284).
>
> Porter and Moss, *Topographical Bibliography* 7:50.
>
> No example of this drawing was found.

Number 6

Plan of the temple.

> Dakka, temple of Thoth of Pnubis.
>
> Greco-Roman period (332 BC–AD 284).
>
> Porter and Moss, *Topographical Bibliography* 7:40–50.
>
> Original not found.
>
> Other copies: No. 45, Ms. Linant 268, Bibliothèque Centrale des Musées Nationaux, Paris.

Plate 24

Relief with Ramesses II censing the bark of Amun-Re.

> Wadi al-Sebu'a, temple of Amun and Re-Horakhty, sanctuary, southwest wall.
>
> Nineteenth Dynasty, reign of Ramesses II (1279–1212 BC).
>
> Porter and Moss, *Topographical Bibliography* 7:62 (118).
>
> No. 128, Museo Egizio, Florence, pencil on paper; unpublished.
>
> Other copies: IX.A.15, D/BKL (Ricci)

The scene was copied by Nestor l'Hôte, Hay, and Lepsius. A comparison with the latter shows that Ricci left out a good deal of text above the scene, a row in front of the king, and a module (*ir n=f*) in the row under the scene. In general, nevertheless, Ricci's copy is more plastic and closer to the original style than Lepsius's rigid drawing.

Plate 25

Number 1

Plan of the temple.

> Gerf Hussein, temple of Ptah.
>
> Nineteenth Dynasty, reign of Ramesses II (1279–1212 BC).
>
> Porter and Moss, *Topographical Bibliography* 7:32–37.
>
> Original not found.
>
> Other copies: VIII.B.25, D/BKL (Bankes); No. 42, Ms. Linant 268, Bibliothèque Centrale des Musées Nationaux, Paris.

Number 2

Plan of the temple.

> Dandur, temple of Peteisi and Padihor.

Roman period, reign of Augustus (30 BC–AD 14).

Porter and Moss, *Topographical Bibliography* 7:27–33.

Original not found.

Other copies: VIII.A.8, D/BKL (Bankes); No. 15, Ms. Linant 265, No. 40, Ms. Linant 268, Bibliothèque Centrale des Musées Nationaux, Paris.

Number 3

Plan and front view of the temple.

Dabod, temple of Isis.

Meroitic (300 BC–AD 350) and Greco-Roman period (332 BC–AD 284).

Porter and Moss, *Topographical Bibliography* 7:1.

Original not found.

Other copies: VI.A.19verso, D/BKL (Bankes); No. 29, Ms. Linant 268, Bibliothèque Centrale des Musées Nationaux, Paris.

Plate 26

Number 1

Relief with offerings to Osiris and three lines of hieroglyphs.

Philae, temple of Isis.

Greco-Roman period (332 BC–AD 284).

No example of this drawing was found.

Number 2

Relief with standing Isis suckling Horus.

Philae, temple of Isis.

Ptolemaic period, reign of Ptolemy II Philadelphus (285–246 BC).

Possibly Room I or Room X.

Porter and Moss, *Topographical Bibliography* 6:238 (295), 243 (354)–(355) or (356)–(357).

No example of this drawing was found.

Number 3

Relief with offerings to Osiris, offerer holding ankh sign.

Philae, temple of Isis.

Greco-Roman period (332 BC–AD 284).

No example of this drawing was found.

Number 4

Relief with the *abaton* of Osiris.

Philae, temple of Isis.

Gate of Hadrian and Marcus Aurelius, south side.

Roman period, reigns of Hadrian (AD 117–38) and Marcus Aurelius (AD 161–80).

Porter and Moss, *Topographical Bibliography* 6:254–55 (6)–(7).

No. 83, Museo Egizio, Florence, pencil on paper; unpublished.

Other copies: (a) V.C.3, D/BKL (Ricci?); (b) No. 43, Ms. 300.3, Folder 16, Fonds Rosellini, Biblioteca Universitaria, Pisa (Ricci).

The relief was copied by different artists, and had appeared (not very accurately) already in the *Description de l'Égypte*, A., I, pl. 19. The Florence copy lacks part of the hieroglyphic inscription and the figure of Thoth.

Number 5

Relief with sacred bark.

Philae, temple of Isis.

Possibly room VI.

Ptolemaic period, reign of Ptolemy II Philadelphus (285–246 BC).

Porter and Moss, *Topographical Bibliography* 6:241 (318).

No example of this drawing was found.

Plate 27

Detail of a cult scene of Osiris; female figures playing the harp and the cymbal.

Philae, temple of Isis, unidentified location.

Greco–Roman period (332 BC–AD 284).

Original not found.

Other copies: XXI.G.6verso, D/BKL (Ricci).

Plate 28

Relief with scene of worship of the emblems of Osiris's dismembered body and funerary scenes of Osiris.

Philae, temple of Isis, upper floor, "room of Osiris," south wall.

Ptolemaic period? (332–30 BC).

Porter and Moss, *Topographical Bibliography* 6:249 (401).

No. 73, Museo Egizio, Florence, ink on paper; unpublished.

Other copies: (a) V.B.69, D/BKL (Beechey); Nos. 67, 68, 70, 71, Ms. 300.3, Folder 23, Fonds Rosellini, Biblioteca Universitaria, Pisa (Ricci).

The Florence drawing is very clear; nevertheless, some details have been omitted, such as the star and the scorpion over the heads of the two goddesses in the first register, and the feathers and horns on the head of the personified *djed* pillar, also in the first register. Ricci did not copy the inscriptions.

Plate 29

Series of different reliefs: 1. Osiris crowned by Isis and Nephthys in the presence of other gods; king in front of Min; 2. Sokar bark with four Sons of Horus; 3. Khnum and Anubis with priests pouring water on a tree.

Philae, temple of Isis, upper floor, "room of Osiris," north wall.

Ptolemaic period? (332–30 BC).

Porter and Moss, *Topographical Bibliography* 6:249 (398)–(399).

No. 74, Museo Egizio, Florence, ink on paper; unpublished.

Other copies: (a) V.B.70, D/BKL (Beechey); (b) Nos. 72–75, Ms. 300.3, Folder 24, Fonds Rosellini, Biblioteca Universitaria, Pisa (Ricci).

Plate 30

Series of reliefs: 1. king offering incense and pouring a libation to Amun-Re, the Hermopolitan Ogdoad, Atum, Thoth, and Nehemawat; 2. king offering food to Ptah as potter, Hapi, and other gods with nome standards.

Philae, temple of Isis, upper floor, "room of Osiris," east wall.

Ptolemaic period? (332–30 BC).

Porter and Moss, *Topographical Bibliography* 6:249 (400).

No. 82, Museo Egizio, Florence, ink on paper; unpublished.

Other copies: (a) V.B.74–76, D/BKL (Beechey); (b) Nos. 58–61, Ms. 300.3, Folder 21, Fonds Rosellini, Biblioteca Universitaria, Pisa (Ricci).

Plate 31

Series of reliefs: king offering incense and pouring a libation to a row of seated gods; king offering food to Khnum as potter, Hapi, and a row of gods with nome standards.

Philae, temple of Isis, upper floor, "room of Osiris," east wall.

Ptolemaic period? (332–30 BC).

Porter and Moss, *Topographical Bibliography* 6:249 (402).

Nos. 75 and 80, Museo Egizio, Florence, pencil and ink on paper; unpublished.

Other copies: (a) V.B.71–73, D/BKL (Beechey); (b) Nos. 62–66, Ms. 300.2, Folder 22, Fonds Rosellini, Biblioteca Universitaria, Pisa (Ricci).

Travel to the Temple of Jupiter-Amun
Plate 32
Numbers 1 and 2

Architectural detail (cornice of the gate).

Bilad al-Rum, west of Siwa, "Doric temple," second room.

Greco-Roman period (332 BC–AD 284).

Bibliography: Fakhry, *Siwa Oasis*, 70–71.

No examples of these drawings were found.

Number 3

View of the temple.

Qasr al-Gashsham, east of Siwa.

Fakhry, *Siwa Oasis*, 79–81.

Original not found.

Other copies: No. 18, Ms. Linant 268, Bibliothèque Centrale des Musées Nationaux, Paris (Jomard, *Voyage*, pl. VIII).

Number 4

View and/or plan of the temple.

Qasr al-Gashsham, east of Siwa.

Fakhry, *Siwa Oasis*, 79–81.

No example of this drawing was found.

Numbers 5 and 6

View and/or plan of the temple.

Abu Shuruf, east of Siwa.

Fakhry, *Siwa Oasis*, 73–79.

No examples of these drawings were found.

Number 7

Relief (painting?) of the ceiling.

Jebel al-Mawta, tomb of Padjehuty.

New Kingdom (1549–1069 BC) or Twenty-sixth Dynasty (664–525 BC).

Porter and Moss, *Topographical Bibliography* 6:314.

No example of this drawing was found.

The plan of the monument as described by Ricci clearly corresponds to the tomb of Padjehuty. This tomb was first documented only in 1897, and later published by Steindorff in 1926 and Fakhry in 1944. There are significant details in Ricci's description: "At the bottom of the first room there are two statues in bas-relief, seated, representing a man and a woman with some badly damaged hieroglyphs around them. There are also other bas-reliefs: I copied the best preserved, which is also colored and makes the ornamentation of the ceiling" (p. 203). It seems that in 1820 the tomb was much better preserved than when documented by Silva White in 1897: at that time there was no trace of the statue or of the ceiling decoration mentioned by Ricci—unless Ricci is largely inaccurate.

Number 8

Greek inscription.

Jebel al-Dakrur, southeast of Siwa, necropolis.

Ptolemaic period? (332–30 BC).

Fakhry, *Siwa Oasis*, 66.

No example of this drawing was found.

Of the four Greek inscriptions mentioned by Ricci at this site and that make up numbers

8 to 11 of this plate, only two (CIG III 494958b; 4958c) were published in Jomard, *Voyage*, pl. VII [12] (drawings by Cailliaud). These are: 1. Φίλων, Λύσις σ<ύ>νσιτοι ('Phylon, Lysis brethren'); 2. Παιδέας τέκτων, | Φίλων Ἕρμων[ος], | ἐνκαυτής ('Paideas builder, Philon, son of Hermon, decorator'). There is also a third inscription: Ἀκοσίλας Γλωχία Ἐλυεθρναος ('Glochia, son of Acosilas, from Eleutherna'). The three are also published in Fakhry, *Siwa Oasis*, 66; in Letronne, *Recueil des inscriptions grecques et latines*, DLX and DLXI; and in Kuhlmann, *Das Ammoneion*.

Numbers 9 to 11
Greek inscriptions.
> Jebel al-Dakrur, southeast of Siwa, necropolis.
> Ptolemaic period? (332–30 BC).
> Fakhry, *Siwa Oasis*, 66.
> No examples of these drawings were found.

Numbers 12 and 13
View of plan of the ruins.
> "al-Mallah," between Maryut and Burg al-Arab.
> No examples of these drawings were found.

Numbers 14 and 15
Hieroglyphic inscriptions.
> Al-Hammam.
> No examples of these drawings were found.

Number 16
Non-hieroglyphic inscription.
> Al-Hammam.
> No example of this drawing was found.

Plate 33
Number 1
Frieze of the doorway, with crowned uraeus, row of cartouches, and hawk wearing the red crown.
> Siwa, Umm al-Ubayda, temple of Amun, south side of doorway.
> Thirtieth Dynasty, reign of Nakhthorheb (Nectanebo II) (360–342 BC).
> Porter and Moss, *Topographical Bibliography* 7:312.
> Original not found.
> Other copies: XIX.A.2, D/BKL (Ricci) (Jomard, *Voyage*, pl. XVII [1]; Minutoli, *Reise*, pl. X).
> The doorway was destroyed and Ricci's drawing is the only record.

Number 2

Pillars with Seth or Bes on each face.

  Siwa, Umm al-Ubayda, temple of Amun, southern side of doorway.

  Thirtieth Dynasty, reign of Nakhthorheb (Nectanebo II) (360–342 BC).

  No example of this drawing was found.

Numbers 3 and 4

Cartouches between protective hawks.

  Siwa, Umm al-Ubayda, temple of Amun, east wall, detail of the upper register.

  Thirtieth Dynasty, reign of Nakhthorheb (Nectanebo II)(360–342 BC).

  Porter and Moss, *Topographical Bibliography* 7:312.

  No examples of these drawings were found.

Number 5

Doorway of funerary chapel.

  Abu al-Awaf, east of Siwa, necropolis.

  Ptolemaic period (332–30 BC).

  Porter and Moss, *Topographical Bibliography* 7:316.

  No example of this drawing was found.

Numbers 6 and 7

Plan of rock tomb.

  Jebel al-Dakrur, southeast of Siwa, necropolis.

  Fakhry, *Siwa Oasis*, 66.

  No examples of these drawings were found.

Number 8

View of the necropolis.

  Abu al-Awaf, east of Siwa, necropolis.

  Ptolemaic period (332–30 BC).

  Porter and Moss, *Topographical Bibliography* 7:316.

  Original not found.

  Other copies: (a) XIX.B.5, D/BKL (Linant); (b) No. 15, Ms. Linant 268, Bibliothèque
    Centrale des Musées Nationaux, Paris (Jomard, *Voyage*, pl. IV).

Number 9

View of a funerary chapel.

Abu al-Awaf, east of Siwa, necropolis.

  Ptolemaic period (332–30 BC).

  Porter and Moss, *Topographical Bibliography* 7:316.

Original not found.

Other copies: (a) XIX.B.6, D/BKL (Linant); (b) No. 16, Ms. Linant 268, Bibliothèque Centrale des Musées Nationaux, Paris (Jomard, *Voyage*, pl. V).

Plate 34

Relief on six different registers: 1. frieze of cartouches and hawks; 2. offering bearers; 3. columns of hieroglyphic text; 4. Amun-Re on his throne worshiped by Wenamun, Great Chief of the Foreign Lands, followed by thirteen gods; 5. ten gods and two shrines with a crocodile and an ichneumon (or mongoose); 6. five gods, Wenamun with *djed* pillar in front of a god under a canopy; geometric frieze.

> Siwa, Umm al-Ubayda, temple of Amun, west wall.

> Thirtieth Dynasty, reign of Nakhthorheb (Nectanebo II) (360–342 BC).

> Porter and Moss, *Topographical Bibliography* 7:312.

> Original not found.

> Other copies: XIX.A.3, D/BKL (Ricci) (Jomard, *Voyage*, pl. XIV; Minutoli, *Reise*, pl. VIII).

This drawing is very important because it is possibly the only record of this wall of the temple, completely destroyed between 1893 and 1898. As often happens, Ricci did not copy the hieroglyphic texts, leaving only empty columns.

Plate 35

Number 1

Relief with a king offering bread to ram-headed Amun-Re and Mut; sphinx, sun disk, hawk, and another offering king.

> Siwa, Umm al-Ubayda, temple of Amun, north side of the doorway and part of the façade.

> Thirtieth Dynasty, reign of Nakhthorheb (Nectanebo II) (360–342 BC).

> Porter and Moss, *Topographical Bibliography* 7:312.

> Original not found.

> Other copies: XIX.A.1, D/BKL (Ricci) (Jomard, *Voyage*, pl. XVI; Minutoli, *Reise*, pl. X [2]).

Number 2

Block of stone with relief showing a procession of seven different gods.

> Thirtieth Dynasty, reign of Nakhthorheb (Nectanebo II) (360–342 BC).

> Porter and Moss, *Topographical Bibliography* 7:313.

> Original not found.

> Other copies: XIX.A.7, D/BKL (Ricci) (Jomard, *Voyage*, pl. XVIII; Minutoli, *Reise*, pl. X [3]).

Number 3

Relief with six vultures divided by lines and stars, carrying feathers.

 Siwa, Umm al-Ubayda, temple of Amun, ceiling.

 Thirtieth Dynasty, reign of Nakhthorheb (Nectanebo II) (360–342 BC).

 Porter and Moss, *Topographical Bibliography* 7:313.

 Original not found.

 Other copies: XIX.A.8, D/BKL (Ricci) (Jomard, *Voyage*, pl. XVII [2]; Minutoli, *Reise*, pls. VIII, IX).

Travel to Mount Sinai

Plate 36

Number 1

Dedicatory Greek inscription of Emperor Justinian.

 Monastery of St. Catherine, monumental northwest gate.

 Byzantine period, reign of Justinian I (AD 527–65).

 No example of this drawing was found.

Number 2

Greek inscription commemorating St. Gregory of Mt. Sinai.

 Jebel Safsafa, Chapel of St. Gregory of Mt. Sinai.

 Medieval–modern period.

 No example of this drawing was found.

Numbers 3 to 7

Nabataean inscriptions.

 Wadi Mukattab.

 Original not found.

 Other copies: XX.C.1, D/BKL (Linant).

Numbers 8 to 19

Greek, Arabic, and Nabataean inscriptions.

 Wadi Mukattab.

 No examples of these drawings were found.

Numbers 20 to 22

Nabataean inscriptions.

 Wadi Hibran.

 Originals not found.

 Other copies: XX.C.2, D/BKL (Linant).

Numbers 23 to 25

Ricci gives no description for these numbers.

Numbers 26 and 27

Greek or Nabataean inscriptions.

Wadi Alayat.

No examples of these drawings were found.

Plate 37

Numbers 1 and 2

Ricci gives no description for these numbers.

Number 3

Graffito of Sabi, Inspector of Administrators.

al-Maghara, Inscription Sinai No. 20.

Old Kingdom (2584–2117 BC).

Porter and Moss, *Topographical Bibliography* 7:342.

No. 67, Museo Egizio, Florence (left), pencil on paper; unpublished.

Other copies: XX.A.8, D/BKL (Ricci).

The graffito is now lost. On the side of this short framed inscription, Ricci copied three cartouches out of context: those of Menkauhor (Sinai No. 12, now at Cairo Museum, No. 57106), Djedkare Isesi (Sinai No. 15, now possibly dispersed), and Sahure (Sinai No. 9, now at Brussels Museum, No. E. 7545).

Numbers 4 to 8

Ricci gives no description for these numbers.

Number 9

Polished stones with holes.

al-Maghara.

No example of this drawing was found.

Plate 38

Number 1

Rock stela with double representation of Niuserre: 1. king (missing) in front of a god; 2. king smiting a Syrian; hieroglyphic inscription with *hes* vase.

Originally al-Maghara, currently at Cairo Museum, No. 57105 (Inscription Sinai No. 10).

Fifth Dynasty, reign of Niuserre (2359–2348 BC).

Porter and Moss, *Topographical Bibliography* 7:341.

No. 58, Museo Egizio, Florence, pencil on paper; unpublished.

Other copies: XX.A.5, D/BKL (Ricci).

The inscription is copied by Ricci in an accurate manner, even if the standard edition (Gardiner et al.) of 1952 is clearer. Ricci's drawing shows that the god behind Niuserre smiting the Syrian had a human head. The copy later made by Lepsius (*Denkmäler aus Aegypten und Aethiopien* 2:pl. 152 [a]) is of much poorer quality.

Number 2
Hieroglyphic inscription with date; possibly the stela of Ameny, Great Overseer of the Cabinet of the treasury, with invocation to Seneferu.
    al-Maghara, Inscription Sinai No. 28.
    Twelfth Dynasty, year 42 of the reign of Amenemhat III (1800 BC).
    Porter and Moss, *Topographical Bibliography* 7:343.
    No. 10, Museo Egizio, Florence, pencil on paper.
    Bibliography: Champollion, *Notice descriptive* 2:689 [2]–[3], 690.
    Other copies: XX.A.11, D/BKL (Ricci).

Numbers 3 to 6
Ricci gives no description for these numbers.

Number 7
Hieroglyphic inscription; possibly the rock stela of Dedusobek-Renefseneb.
    al-Maghara, Inscription Sinai No. 27.
    Twelfth Dynasty, year 41 of the reign of Amenemhat III (1801 BC).
    Porter and Moss, *Topographical Bibliography* 7:343.
    No. 7, Museo Egizio, Florence, pencil on paper; unpublished.
    Other copies: XX.A.15, D/BKL (Ricci).

Number 8
Hieroglyphic inscription; possibly from the stela of Khufu (Cheops) smiting an enemy in front of Thoth.
    al-Maghara, Inscription Sinai No. 7.
    Fourth Dynasty, reign of Khufu (Cheops) (2470–2447 BC).
    Porter and Moss, *Topographical Bibliography* 7:340–41.
    No. 16, Museo Egizio, Florence, pencil on paper; unpublished.
    Other copies: XX.A.3, D/BKL (Ricci).
    The inscription is now lost.

Plate 39
Number 1
Rock stela of Khufu (Cheops) smiting an enemy in front of Thoth.
    al-Maghara, Inscription Sinai No. 7.
    Fourth Dynasty, reign of Khufu (Cheops) (2470–2447 BC).

Porter and Moss, *Topographical Bibliography* 7:340–41.

No. 13, Museo Egizio, Florence, pencil on paper; unpublished.

Other copies: XX.A.3, D/BKL (Ricci).

Ricci's copy gives a small hint on how to integrate the inscription behind Khufu (Cheops). This copy also allows us to notice that Thoth's *was* sceptre was enriched by a *djed* sign exactly where there is a lacuna in the modern edition (Gardiner 1952); the god also holds an ankh sign in his left hand. This stela is now lost.

Number 2

Rock stela with Sanakht and standards.

al-Maghara, Inscription Sinai 3.

Third Dynasty, reign of Sanakht (2565–2556 BC).

Porter and Moss, *Topographical Bibliography* 7:340.

No. 15, Museo Egizio, Florence, pencil on paper; unpublished.

Other copies: XX.A.1, D/BKL (Ricci).

Number 3

Graffiti of emblems (arms, boomerang, ibex, bow) and hieroglyphic inscription with cartouche of Niuserre.

al-Maghara, Inscription Sinai No. 11.

Fifth Dynasty, reign of Niuserre (2359–2348 BC).

Porter and Moss, *Topographical Bibliography* 7:341.

No. 11, Museo Egizio, Florence, pencil on paper; unpublished.

Other copies: XX.A.14, D/BKL (Ricci).

Number 4

Hieroglyphic inscription of Khuy, Servant of the Great House, and Nabataean inscription.

al-Maghara, Inscription Sinai No. 33.

Twelfth Dynasty, year 6 of Amenemhat IV (1792 BC).

Porter and Moss, *Topographical Bibliography* 7:343.

No. 8, Museo Egizio, Florence, pencil on paper.

Bibliography: Champollion, *Notice descriptive* 2:692 [2].

Other copies: XX.A.12, D/BKL (Ricci).

The standard edition (Gardiner 1952) does not show the Nabataean inscription and the elegant architectural frame around the hieroglyphic inscription, which on the contrary are in Champollion's publication. The text copied by Ricci allows the integration of two signs at the bottom of the last column. The original inscription is now lost.

Number 5

Hieroglyphic inscription with date; possibly the stela of Senaib, Overseer of the Treasury, with invocation to Seneferu.

    al-Maghara, Inscription Sinai No. 35.

    Twelfth Dynasty, year 6 of Amenemhat IV (1792 BC).

    Porter and Moss, *Topographical Bibliography* 7:343.

    No. 9, Museo Egizio, Florence, pencil on paper.

    Bibliography: Champollion, *Notice descriptive* 2:692 [1].

    Other copies: XX.A.16, D/BKL (Ricci).

    Ricci's copy shows the frame around the inscription, not included in the standard edition (Gardiner 1952). This inscription too is now considered lost.

Plate 40

Number 1

View of Ras Raya fortress.

    al-Tor, South Sinai.

    Byzantine period, reign of Anastasius I (AD 491–518).

    Original not found.

    Other copies: XX.D.17, D/BKL (Linant).

Number 2

View of the Chapel of Our Lady of the Storehouse.

    Ascent to Jebel Musa.

    Medieval period.

    No example of this drawing was found.

Number 3

View of the Chapel of Prophets Elijah and Elisha.

    Ascent to Jebel Musa, Basin of Elijah.

    Byzantine–medieval period.

    No example of this drawing was found.

Number 4

View of the Basilica of the Theotokos.

    Jebel Musa, top.

    Byzantine period, reign of Justinian I (AD 527–65).

    No example of this drawing was found.

Number 5

View of the Peak of the Theophany.

    Jebel Musa, top.

    No example of this drawing was found.

Number 6

View of the arch where traditionally Moses is held to have received the Tablets of the Law.

Jebel Musa, top.

No example of this drawing was found.

Number 7

View of the Fatimid mosque.

Jebel Musa, top.

Fatimid period (AD 969–1171).

No example of this drawing was found.

Number 8

View of the Chapel of the Holy Girdle of the Virgin Mary.

Jebel Safsafa.

No example of this drawing was found.

Number 9

View of the Chapel of St. Anne.

Jebel Safsafa.

No example of this drawing was found.

Number 10

Ruins of monastic settlements.

Wadi Firan, Jebel Tahuna.

Grossmann, "Early Christian Ruins," 80.

Original not found.

Other copies: XX.D.15, D/BKL (Linant).

Number 11

View of the Chapel of St. Gregory of Mt. Sinai.

Jebel Safsafa.

No example of this drawing was found.

Number 12

Greek inscription.

Monastery of St. Catherine, door of the "monks' quarters."

No example of this drawing was found.

Number 13

Greek inscription.

Monastery of St. Catherine, crypt (?).

No example of this drawing was found.

Number 14

Greek inscription on a copper plate.

  Monastery of St. Catherine, door of the monks' kitchen.

  No example of this drawing was found.

Number 15

Greek inscription.

  Monastery of St. Catherine, door of St. Helena's Tower.

  No example of this drawing was found.

Plate 41

Number 1

Relief showing Seti II with high officers; traces of a palimpsest with Thutmose III in front of Hathor followed by Sennefer, Overseer of the Treasury, and Kanunu.

  Serabit al-Khadim, sanctuary of Hathor, outer side of the southern pylon, Inscription Sinai No. 194.

  Eighteenth–Nineteenth Dynasty, reigns of Thutmose III (1479–1424 BC) and Seti II (1201–1195 BC).

  Porter and Moss, *Topographical Bibliography* 7:351.

  No. 142, Museo Egizio, Florence, pencil on paper; unpublished.

  The inscription behind Hathor, with titulary of Thutmose III, does not appear in the standard edition (Gardiner 1952).

Number 2

Rock stela with a row of overseers; possibly Inscription Sinai No. 125 or Inscription Sinai No. 183.

Serabit al-Khadim, mines.

Porter and Moss, *Topographical Bibliography* 7:349, 354.

No example of this drawing was found.

Numbers 3 and 4

Rock stelae.

  Serabit al-Khadim, mines.

  Without further indications in the *Travels*, it is impossible to identify these two figures. The Egyptian Museum in Florence has two copies of stelae from Serabit al-Khadim that could fit:

1. Rock stela of Thutmose IV in front of Hathor, followed by Neby, mayor of Tjaru, with a graffito of the sculptor Igref. Inscriptions Sinai Nos. 58 and 58bis; Eighteenth Dynasty, year 4 of Thutmose IV (1394 BC).

   Porter and Moss, *Topographical Bibliography* 7:345. Original drawing is No. 87, Museo Egizio, Florence, pencil on paper. The line under the scene was published in

Champollion, *Lettres écrites d'Égypte et de Nubie*, pl. VIIIbis [F]. The texts copied by Ricci are not very accurate; on the other hand, Ricci's drawing is of a much higher quality than the one published in Gardiner 1952.

2. Rock stela of Saneferet, overseer of the Cabinet, Overseer of Lower Egypt, and of General Iuki, with Amenemhat III in front of Hathor. Inscription Sinai No. 56; Twelfth Dynasty, reign of Amenemhat III (1842–1797 BC).

Porter and Moss, *Topographical Bibliography* 7:345. Original drawing is No. 65, Museo Egizio, Florence, pencil on paper; unpublished. Another copy is XX.B.1, D/BKL (Ricci).

A third possible candidate is the drawing of a rock stela, labeled by Ricci as from Serabit al-Khadim, but actually from al-Maghara. It shows Thutmose III in front of Hathor and Hatshepsut in front of Sopdu. Inscription Sinai No. 44, now at the Cairo Egyptian Museum, No. 45493; Eighteenth Dynasty, year 16 of Thutmose III (1463 BC).

Porter and Moss, *Topographical Bibliography* 7:343. Original drawing is No. 63, Museo Egizio, Florence, pencil on paper; unpublished. Another copy is XX.A.17, D/BKL (Ricci).

Plate 42

Stela with king in front of Hathor and Ptah under a canopy.

Serabit al-Khadim, sanctuary of Hathor, Inscription Sinai No. 432.

Middle Kingdom (according to Gardiner 1952, Peet, and Černý) or Eighteenth Dynasty (according to Porter and Moss).

Porter and Moss, *Topographical Bibliography* 7:362.

No. 141, Museo Egizio, Florence, pencil on paper; unpublished.

Other copies: XX.B.13, D/BKL (Ricci).

Plate 43

Stela with Thutmose III in front of Hathor, followed by Tey, Chancellor of the King of Lower Egypt, Overseer of the Treasury, with hieroglyphic text, and Samontu, Subordinate of the King's Envoy.

Serabit al-Khadim, sanctuary of Hathor, room N, Inscription Sinai No. 196.

Eighteenth Dynasty, year 25 of Thutmose III (1454 BC).

Porter and Moss, *Topographical Bibliography* 7:351.

No. 59, Museo Egizio, Florence, pencil on paper; unpublished.

Other copies: XX.B.6, D/BKL (Ricci).

Plate 44

Number 1

South side of the stela of Djefi, Great Overseer of the Cabinet of the Treasury, with Khentekhtai in front of Hathor.

    Serabit al-Khadim, sanctuary of Hathor, Inscription Sinai No. 120.

    Twelfth Dynasty, year 6 of Amenemhat IV (1792 BC).

    Porter and Moss, *Topographical Bibliography* 7:356.

    No. 61, Museo Egizio, Florence; pencil on paper; No. 62, Museo Egizio, Florence, pencil on paper; unpublished.

    Other copies: XX.B.9–10, D/BKL (Ricci).

    The drawing in Florence shows the scene and only one line of text.

Number 2

East side of the stela of Djefi, Great Overseer of the Cabinet of the Treasury, with Amenemhat IV offering to Khentekhtai and Seneferu offering to Sopdu.

    Serabit al-Khadim, sanctuary of Hathor, Inscription Sinai No. 122.

    Twelfth Dynasty, year 9 of Amenemhat IV (1789 BC).

    Porter and Moss, *Topographical Bibliography* 7:356.

    No. 66, Museo Egizio, Florence, pencil on paper; unpublished.

    Other copies: XX.B.8, D/BKL (Ricci).

Plate 45

Number 1

East side of stela with Seti I in front of Re-Horakhty and hieroglyphic text; Ashahebused, Ambassador in All Lands, worshiping the sovereign's cartouches.

    Serabit al-Khadim, sanctuary of Hathor, Inscription Sinai No. 247.

    Nineteenth Dynasty, years 7 and 8 of Seti I (1289–1288 BC).

    Porter and Moss, *Topographical Bibliography* 7:348.

    No. 85, Museo Egizio, Florence, pencil on paper.

    Bibliography: Champollion, *Lettres à Monsieur le Duc de Blacas*, pl. VIIIbis [G].

    Other copies: XX.B.2, D/BKL (Ricci).

It seems problematic that Champollion could have actually copied the inscription from this very same drawing, since in his publication there are parts that are here missing or badly copied. Champollion was probably using a more accurate copy made by Ricci and possibly later kept by Champollion-Figeac.

Number 2

Stela of Saneferet, Overseer of the Cabinet, Overseer of Lower Egypt.

    Serabit al-Khadim, sanctuary of Hathor, porch, Inscription Sinai No.112.

    Twelfth Dynasty, reign of Amenemhat III (1842–1797 BC).

    Porter and Moss, *Topographical Bibliography* 7:355.

No. 86, Museo Egizio, Florence, pencil on paper; unpublished.

Other copies: XX.B.7, D/BKL (Ricci).

Number 3

Fragment of stela.

Serabit al-Khadim, sanctuary of Hathor.

No example of this drawing was found.

Number 4

Rock stela.

Serabit al-Khadim, mines.

No example of this drawing was found.

Plate 46

Rock stela of Sobekherheb, Overseer of the Cabinet of the Treasury.

Serabit al-Khadim, mines, Inscription Sinai No. 53.

Twelfth Dynasty, year 44 of Amenemhat III (1798 BC).

Porter and Moss, *Topographical Bibliography* 7:345.

No. 60, Museo Egizio, Florence, pencil on paper.

Bibliography: Champollion, *Notice descriptive* 2:691; Champollion, *Lettres à Monsieur le Duc de Blacas*, pl. VIIIbis [E]. Champollion published only the dating protocol of this hieroglyphic inscription, and not the whole inscription.

Travel to Sennar

Plate 47

Relief with Seti I welcomed by Hathor.

Valley of the Kings, tomb of Seti I (KV 17), hall E, pillar C.

Nineteenth Dynasty, reign of Seti I (1296–1279 BC).

Porter and Moss, *Topographical Bibliography* 1, Part 2:538, C (b).

Original not found.

Other copies: No. H4414.d, Bristol City Museum & Art Gallery (Ricci).

Plate 48

Relief with Seti I libating or censing in front of Maat, Sokar-Osiris, Hathor, and Osiris.

Valley of the Kings, tomb of Seti I (KV 17), room F, pillar B (all four faces).

Nineteenth Dynasty, reign of Seti I (1296–1279 BC).

Porter and Moss, *Topographical Bibliography* 1, Part 2:539, B.

No. 48, Museo Egizio, Florence, red and black ink on paper; unpublished.

Other copies: No. H4426.a, Bristol City Museum & Art Gallery, showing only scene (a) (Ricci).

Plate 49

Relief with Queen Nefertari playing the sistrum in front of Taweret as a human-headed hippopotamus, followed by Thoth and Nut.

   Jebel Silsila, shrine of Ramesses II.

   Nineteenth Dynasty, reign of Ramesses II (1279–1212 BC).

   Porter and Moss, *Topographical Bibliography* 5:217.

   No. 114 [4], Museo Egizio, Florence, ink and watercolor on paper; unpublished.

   Other copies: (a) No. 97, Ms. 300.3, Folder 31, Fonds Rosellini, Biblioteca Universitaria, Pisa (Ricci, copy from Duchêsne); (b) Mss. Minutoli (*Reise*, pl. XXII [1]); (c) IV.A.10, D/BKL (Ricci?).

The relief had already been copied at the time of the French expedition and published in the *Description de l'Égypte*, A., I, pl. 45 [14]; it was later copied by Lepsius (*Denkmäler aus Aegypten und Aethiopien* 3:pl. 175 [c]). The drawing in Florence lacks the eleven columns of hieroglyphic text and oddly portrays Nut with a lion head. It is not clear whether the mistake was due to unfavorable light conditions or whether Ricci personally reworked the scene from memory.

Plate 50

Number 1

Relief with goddess of the fields carrying offerings, with lotus flowers and flying birds.

   Kom Ombo, temple of the triads of Harwer and Sobek, gate of the first pylon.

   Ptolemaic period, reign of Ptolemy XII Neos Dionysos (117–51 BC).

   Porter and Moss, *Topographical Bibliography* 6:181 (6)–(7).

   No. 90, Museo Egizio, Florence, ink on paper; unpublished.

   Other copies: IV.B.3, D/BKL (Ricci).

The relief, now partially destroyed, was not copied by any other Egyptologist, even though there are photographs made by the Preußische Akademie der Wissenschaften.

Numbers 2 and 3

Decorative detail of the cornice: cobra-headed vulture and hawk-headed sphinx.

   Kom Ombo, temple of the triads of Harwer and Sobek, hypostyle hall.

   Ptolemaic period, reign of Ptolemy VIII Euergetes II (182–116 BC).

   Porter and Moss, *Topographical Bibliography* 6:189.

   No. 89, Museo Egizio, Florence, ink on paper; unpublished.

   Other copies: IV.B.16, D/BKL (Ricci).

Plate 51

Number 1

Plan of the island with general legend.

   Elephantine.

   Porter and Moss, *Topographical Bibliography* 5:224.

No. 98 [1], Museo Egizio, Florence, ink on paper; unpublished.

It seems (p. 256]) that the inspiration for this map was *Description de l'Égypte*, A., I, pl. 31. The differences between the two maps are nevertheless so many that either Ricci copied from another French map or he intended to copy from the *Description*, but then did not follow through. The map places the temples of Ramesses II and Amenhotep III, the gate of Nectanebo II, and the Roman graffiti at the Nilometer, but the orientation is faulty.

Number 2
Plan of the northern bark chapel ("Small Temple" or "North Temple").
> Elephantine.
> Nineteenth Dynasty, reign of Ramesses II (1279–1212 BC).
> Porter and Moss, *Topographical Bibliography* 5:229.
> No. 103 [2], Museo Egizio, Florence, ink on paper; unpublished.

Number 3
Plan of the southern bark chapel ("Large Temple" or "South Temple").
> Elephantine.
> Eighteenth–Nineteenth Dynasty, reigns of Amenhotep III (1388–1348 BC), Seti I (1296–1279 BC), and Ramesses IV (1155–1149 BC).
> Porter and Moss, *Topographical Bibliography* 5:230.
> No. 103 [1], Museo Egizio, Florence, ink on paper; unpublished.
> Other copies: IV.C.4, D/BKL (Ricci or Linant).

Number 4
Nilometer with six Greek inscriptions.
> Elephantine.
> New Kingdom (1549–1069 BC)–Roman period (30 BC–AD 284).
> Porter and Moss, *Topographical Bibliography* 5:225–26.
> No. 98 [2], Museo Egizio, Florence, ink on paper; unpublished.

Plate 52
Elephantine, southern bark chapel.
> Eighteenth–Nineteenth Dynasty, reigns of Amenhotep III (1388–1348 BC), Seti I (1296–1279 BC), and Ramesses IV (1155–1149 BC).
> Porter and Moss, *Topographical Bibliography* 5:227–28.

Number 1
East front (façade).
> No. 100 [1], Museo Egizio, Florence, ink on paper; unpublished.

This drawing proposes a reconstruction of the northern part of the façade, at the time already collapsed.

Number 2

Inscription of the west front.

    No. 100 [2], Museo Egizio, Florence, ink on paper; unpublished.

Plate 53

North front.

    Elephantine, southern bark chapel.

    Eighteenth–Nineteenth Dynasty, reigns of Amenhotep III (1388–1348 BC), Seti I
        (1296–1279 BC), and Ramesses IV (1155–1149 BC).

    Porter and Moss, *Topographical Bibliography* 5:227–28.

    No. 94, Museo Egizio, Florence, pencil and ink on paper; unpublished.

    In this front view of the chapel, two of the five pillars are reconstructed by Ricci. Drawing No. 64, Museo Egizio, Florence, is a preliminary version of this plate. Inscriptions on the pillars, with the name of Amenhotep III, are worship formulas addressed to Amun-Re, Neith, Anuket, and Khnum.

Plate 54

East front of the shrine.

    Elephantine, southern bark chapel.

    Eighteenth–Nineteenth Dynasty, reigns of Amenhotep III (1388–1348 BC), Seti I (1296–
        1279 BC), and Ramesses IV (1155–1149 BC).

    Porter and Moss, *Topographical Bibliography* 5:227–28.

    No. 101, Museo Egizio, Florence, pencil on paper; unpublished.

Plate 55

Elephantine, southern bark chapel.

    Eighteenth–Nineteenth Dynasty, reigns of Amenhotep III (1388–1348 BC), Seti I
        (1296–1279 BC), and Ramesses IV (1155–1149 BC).

Number 1

Reliefs: 1. Amenhotep III crowned by Khnum and Anuket in front of Mut; 2. Amenhotep III offering flowers to Anuket; 3. Amenhotep III offering sacrifice to Khnum and Satet; 4. Amenhotep III offering four calves to Amun-Re ithyphallic.

    Northern wall of the sanctuary, north face.

    Porter and Moss, *Topographical Bibliography* 5:228 (2)–(3).

    No. 81 [1]–[4], Museo Egizio, Florence, pencil on paper; unpublished.

Number 2

Relief with Amenhotep III purified by two hawk-headed gods.

    Southern wall of the sanctuary, south face.

    Porter and Moss, *Topographical Bibliography* 5:228 (5).

    No. 81 [5], Museo Egizio, Florence, ink on paper; unpublished.

Numbers 3 and 4

Relief with Satet holding an elaborate staff.

    Southern wall of the sanctuary, south face.

    Porter and Moss, *Topographical Bibliography* 5:228 (4).

    No. 96, Museo Egizio, Florence, ink on paper; unpublished.

    Other copies: Mss. Minutoli (*Reise*, pl. XXIII [3]).

    Minutoli seems to be the only scholar who published this relief, surely from a copy made by Ricci now lost. The drawing at the Florence Egyptian Museum shows only a detail with Satet holding a staff and another staff out of context.

Number 5

Reliefs with Amenhotep III embraced by Khnum and the same king receiving life from Amun-Re.

    Northwest and southwest corner pillars.

    Not mentioned in Porter and Moss, *Topographical Bibliography* 5.

    No. 95, Museo Egizio, Florence; ink and pencil on paper, unpublished.

Plate 56

Reliefs with: 1. Amenhotep III followed by Queen Tiye in front of the sacred bark of Khnum; 2. Amenhotep III introduced by Satet to Khnum on his throne.

    Elephantine, southern bark chapel, southern wall of the sanctuary, north face.

    Eighteenth Dynasty, reign of Amenhotep III (1388–1348 BC).

    Porter and Moss, *Topographical Bibliography* 5:228 (7)–(8).

    No. 17, Museo Egizio, Florence, ink on paper.

    Bibliography: Bresciani, "Il richiamo della piramide," 158.

    No. 93, Museo Egizio, Florence, is a very fine detail of the scene with Queen Tiye holding a sistrum and a bunch of flowers; published in Minutoli, *Reise*, pl. XXIII [5].

Plate 57

Relief with a procession of priests bearing offerings and a group of princesses playing the sistrum.

    Elephantine, northern bark chapel, south wall of the sanctuary, south face.

    Nineteenth Dynasty, reign of Ramesses II (1279–1212 BC).

    Porter and Moss, *Topographical Bibliography* 5:229.

    No. 12, Museo Egizio, Florence, pencil on paper; unpublished.

    Other copies: IV.C.2–3, D/BKL (Ricci).

    The copies made by Ricci are, along with those of Denon and Barry, the only record left of this temple. Another scene from the same wall (which is not the façade, as in Porter and Moss) is published in Minutoli, *Reise*, pl. XXIII [2]. The original drawing for this plate published by Minutoli is not in Florence. Ricci also marked a Greek graffito made up of a few letters, unfortunately illegible. Ricci probably intended to collate the two sketches into one single drawing, since they both belong to the same scene.

Plate 58

Series of reliefs: 1. Thutmose III offering incense to Sopdu; 2. Thutmose III embraced by Dedwen; 3. Thutmose III in front of deified Senwosret III; 4. Thutmose II embraced by Satet; 5. Thutmose III offering to Horus of Miam; 6. Thutmose III in front of Horus; 7. Thutmose III offering milk to Horus of Miam; 8. Thutmose III offering bread to Thoth; plan of the temple.

> Ellesiya, rock temple, shrine (now in Turin Egyptian Museum, S. 18016).
> Eighteenth Dynasty, reign of Thutmose III (1479–1424 BC).
> Porter and Moss, *Topographical Bibliography* 7:90–91 (6) (8) (10).
> No. 71, Museo Egizio, Florence, ink and pencil on paper; unpublished.
> Other copies: X.E.1–3, D/BKL (Ricci).

Of the three scenes copied, two are also in Lepsius, *Denkmäler aus Aegypten und Aethiopien* 3:pls. 45d, 46b. The other was copied by Ricci only (in the two versions: Florence and Dorchester, X.E.2). The Florence drawing is, nevertheless, very inaccurate, even if his copy shows more text than the standard edition (Desroches-Noblecourt, Donadoni, and Moukhtar). In the scene marked "d" Ricci drew four calves instead of the four offering tables (Desroches-Noblecourt, Donadoni, and Moukhtar, *Le speos*, pl. XVIII). In the scene marked "5," Ricci shows Thutmose III between a hawk-headed god and an anthropomorphic god wearing the double crown: in reality the scene shows Thutmose III embracing Satet and Anuket (Desroches-Noblecourt, Donadoni, and Moukhtar, *Le speos*, pl. IX).

Plate 59

Numbers 1 and 2

Plan of the temple.

> Semna East (Kumma), temple of Khnum.
> Eighteenth Dynasty, reigns of Thutmose II (1491–1479 BC), Thutmose III (1479–1424 BC), and Amenhotep II (1424–1398 BC).
> Porter and Moss, *Topographical Bibliography* 7:152.
> No. 115, Museo Egizio, Florence, ink on paper; unpublished.
> Other copies: XIII.B.9 (Bankes), XIII.A.12 (Linant), D/BKL.

Number 3

Upper half of a relief with Khnum and Thoth; empty space once occupied by Hatshepsut, hammered out by Thutmose III.

> Semna East (Kumma), temple of Khnum.
> Eighteenth Dynasty, reigns of Thutmose II (1491–1479 BC), Thutmose III (1479–1424 BC), and Amenhotep II (1424–1398 BC).
> Porter and Moss, *Topographical Bibliography* 7:152 (7).
> No. 132, Museo Egizio, Florence, ink on paper; unpublished.
> Other copies: XIII.B.2–3, D/BKL (Ricci).

Plate 60

Rock stela of Thutmose I.

> Tombos.
>
> Eighteenth Dynasty, year 2 of Thutmose I (1501 BC).
>
> Porter and Moss, *Topographical Bibliography* 7:174.
>
> No. 139, Museo Egizio, Florence, pencil and ink on paper, and No. 126 (less accurate version); unpublished.
>
> Other copies: XIV.E.2, D/BKL (Ricci).
>
> In both Florence versions Ricci copied only the first eighteen lines.

Plate 61

Number 1

Plan of the site of Jebel Barkal, with the temples and the northeast and southeast necropoleis. Porter and Moss, *Topographical Bibliography* 7: 204.

> No. 38, Museo Egizio, Florence, pencil on transparent paper; unpublished.

It is a very rough map. Ricci would have needed to rework it heavily in order to publish it. The location of the monuments is nevertheless correct and allows identification with the buildings described in the *Travels*. While in the text the pyramids are numbered with a double series of alphabet letters ("a" to "h" for the northeast necropolis, "a" to "d" for the southeast necropolis), on the map the pyramids are marked with one series only, from "a" to "n." In this map only seven pyramids are drawn in the northeast necropolis, while in the *Travels* Ricci describes eight monuments. In Dorchester there are very accurate plans of the individual pyramids, but not a general map of the site.

Number 2

Ricci gives no description for this number.

Number 3

Plan of the rock-cut monuments of Jebel Barkal between temple B 300 (Temple of Mut of Napata) and temple B 700.

> No example of this drawing was found.

Plate 62

Number 1

Plan of pyramid No. 3.

> Jebel Barkal, northeast necropolis.
>
> Meroitic period (300 BC–AD 350), anonymous queen.
>
> Porter and Moss, *Topographical Bibliography* 7:205.
>
> Original not found.
>
> Other copies: XV.B.11, D/BKL (Linant).[8]

Number 2

Front view of pyramid No. 3.

    Jebel Barkal, northeast necropolis.

    Meroitic period (300 BC–AD 350), anonymous queen.

    Porter and Moss, *Topographical Bibliography* 7:205.

    Original not found.

    Other copies: XV.B.12, D/BKL (Linant).

Number 3

Plan of a pyramid.

    Jebel Barkal, northeast necropolis.

    Porter and Moss, *Topographical Bibliography* 7:207.

    No example of this drawing was found.

Number 4

Plan of the temple.

    Jebel Barkal, Temple of Hathor, Tefnut, and a third unknown goddess (Fisher, Lacovara, Ikram, and D'Auria, *Ancient Nubia*, 287).

    Twenty-fifth Dynasty, reign of Taharqa (690–664 BC).

    Porter and Moss, *Topographical Bibliography* 7:208.

    Original not found.

    Other copies: XV.B.3, D/BKL (Linant).

Number 5

Plan of the temple.

    Jebel Barkal, Temple of Mut of Napata (Fisher, Lacovara, Ikram, and D'Auria, *Ancient Nubia*, 287).

    Twenty-fifth Dynasty, reign of Taharqa (690–664 BC).

    Porter and Moss, *Topographical Bibliography* 7:208–11.

    Original not found.

    Other copies: XV.B.2, D/BKL (Linant); No. 10, Ms. Linant 269, Bibliothèque Centrale des Musées Nationaux, Paris.

Plate 63

Number 1

Relief with procession of male figures dressed in long tunics, led by a priest censing and a man holding (perhaps) flowers, standing in front of a seated queen or a princess.

    Jebel Barkal, northeast necropolis, pyramid No. 3, chapel, south wall.

    Meroitic period (300 BC–AD 350), anonymous queen.

    Porter and Moss, *Topographical Bibliography* 7:205.

    Original not found.

    Other copies: XV.A.1, D/BKL (Linant).

Number 2

Relief representing Prince Yetaretey with censer, followed by a god and offering-bearers in front of Queen Nawidemak and a winged goddess.

Jebel Barkal, northeast necropolis, pyramid No. 6, chapel, north wall.

Meroitic period, reign of Nawidemak (90–50 BC).

Porter and Moss, *Topographical Bibliography* 7:206.

No. 68, Museo Egizio, Florence, pencil on paper; unpublished.

Other copies: XV.A.11, D/BKL (Ricci).

Ricci's version, despite being schematic, incomplete, and partly disturbed by the annotation on the colors, shows more details than Lepsius's own copy, such as the queen's feet.

Numbers 3 to 5

Inscriptions on the pedestal of the 'Prudhoe lions.'

Jebel Barkal, temple B 1100, entrance.

Eighteenth Dynasty, reign of Amenhotep III (1388–1348 BC).

Porter and Moss, *Topographical Bibliography* 7:212, 1 and 2.

No. 69, Museo Egizio, Florence, pencil on paper; unpublished.

Numbers 6 and 7

Upper and side view of a granite pedestal.

Jebel Barkal, unknown location.

Meroitic period (300 BC–AD 350).

Porter and Moss, *Topographical Bibliography* 7:222.

No. 110, Museo Egizio, Florence, pencil on paper; unpublished.

Other copies: XV.A.33, D/BKL (Ricci).

Number 8

Hieroglyphs carved on the pedestal of a lion statue.

Jebel Barkal, temple B 700.

Napatan period, reigns of Atlanersa (653–643 BC) and Senkamanisken (643–623 BC).

No example of this drawing was found.

Plate 64

Number 1

False door.

Jebel Barkal, northeast necropolis, pyramid No. 3, chapel, west wall.

Meroitic period (300 BC–AD 350), anonymous queen.

Porter and Moss, *Topographical Bibliography* 7:205.

Original not found.

Other copies: XV.A.3, D/BKL (Ricci).

Number 2

False door.

> Jebel Barkal, northeast necropolis, pyramid No. 5, chapel, west wall.
>
> Meroitic period (300 BC–AD 350), anonymous prince.
>
> Porter and Moss, *Topographical Bibliography* 7:206.
>
> Original not found.
>
> Other copies: XV.A.6, D/BKL (Ricci).

Plate 65

Number 1

Relief representing a prince with censer in front of a seated king, followed by standing winged Isis and Osiris; behind the prince, three registers with gods and offerings, scene of judgment of the dead, and men with palm tree branches.

> Jebel Barkal, northeast necropolis, pyramid No. 5, chapel, south wall.
>
> Meroitic period (300 BC–AD 350), anonymous prince.
>
> Porter and Moss, *Topographical Bibliography* 7:206.
>
> No. 134, Museo Egizio, Florence, pencil on paper; unpublished.
>
> Other copies: XV.A.8 and XV.A.8a, D/BKL (Ricci).

Numbers 2 and 3

Granite pedestal with tied prisoners held by a vulture.

> Jebel Barkal, unknown location.
>
> Meroitic period (300 BC–AD 350).
>
> Porter and Moss, *Topographical Bibliography* 7:222.
>
> No. 110, Museo Egizio, Florence, pencil on paper; unpublished.
>
> Other copies: XV.A.33, D/BKL (Ricci).

Plate 66

Number 1

Reliefs representing Onuris and Nefertem with hieroglyphic inscription.

> Jebel Barkal, Temple of Mut of Napata (B 300, called 'Typhonium'), central shrine, south wall.
>
> Twenty-fifth Dynasty, reign of Taharqa (690–664 BC).
>
> Porter and Moss, *Topographical Bibliography* 7:211 (9)–(10).
>
> Original not found.
>
> Other copies: XV.A.20, D/BKL (Ricci).

Number 2

Bes-pillars.

> Jebel Barkal, Temple of Mut of Napata (B 300, called 'Typhonium').
>
> Twenty-fifth Dynasty, reign of Taharqa (690–664 BC).

Porter and Moss, *Topographical Bibliography* 7:211.
Original not found.
Other copies: XV.A.13, D/BKL (Ricci).

Number 3

Hathor column.

Jebel Barkal, Temple of Mut of Napata (B 300, called 'Typhonium'), second hall.
Twenty-fifth Dynasty, reign of Taharqa (690–664 BC).
Porter and Moss, *Topographical Bibliography* 7:209 (1).
Original not found.
Other copies: XV.A.12 [1], D/BKL (Ricci).

Number 4

Relief on three registers with priests, royal princesses of Atlanersa, and faces of two women with sistrum.

Jebel Barkal, temple B 700, pylon, west tower.
Napatan period, reigns of Atlanersa (653–643 BC) and Senkamanisken (643–623 BC).
Porter and Moss, *Topographical Bibliography* 7:214.
Original not found.
Other copies: XV.A.27, D/BKL (Ricci).

Number 5

Relief representing three registers of priests or offering-bearers, with a prince censing a seated king and a winged goddess.

Jebel Barkal, northeast necropolis, pyramid No. 5, chapel, north wall.
Meroitic period (300 BC–AD 350), anonymous prince.
Porter and Moss, *Topographical Bibliography* 7:206.
Original not found.
Other copies: XV.A.9, D/BKL (Ricci).

Plate 67
Number 1

Plan of the temple.

Jebel Barkal, temple B 600.
Meroitic period (300 BC–AD 350).
Porter and Moss, *Topographical Bibliography* 7:215.
Original not found.
Other copies: XV.B.4, D/BKL (Linant); No. 11, Ms. Linant 269, Bibliothèque Centrale des Musées Nationaux, Paris.

Number 2

Plan of the temple.

Jebel Barkal, temple B 700.

Napatan period, reigns of Atlanersa (653–643 BC) and Senkamanisken (643–623 BC).

Porter and Moss, *Topographical Bibliography* 7:213–15.

Original not found.

Other copies: XV.B.4, D/BKL (Linant); No. 11, Ms. Linant 269, Bibliothèque Centrale des Musées Nationaux, Paris.

Number 3

Ricci gives no description for this number.

Number 4

Plan of the temple.

Jebel Barkal, Great Temple of Amun (B 500).

Eighteenth–Nineteenth Dynasty, with Twenty-fifth Dynasty and Meroitic modifications.

Porter and Moss, *Topographical Bibliography* 7:210.

No. 42 [2], Museo Egizio, Florence, pencil on paper; unpublished.

Other copies: XV.B.1, D/BKL (Linant); No. 8, Ms. Linant 269, Bibliothèque Centrale des Musées Nationaux, Paris.

Plate 68

Numbers 1 and 2

The two fronts of a granite altar with Nile geniuses performing the *sema-tawi*.

Jebel Barkal, Great Temple of Amun (B 500).

Twenty-fifth Dynasty, reign of Taharqa (690–664 BC).

Porter and Moss, *Topographical Bibliography* 7:220 (43).

No. 72, Museo Egizio, Florence, pencil on paper; unpublished.

Other copies: XV.A.30, D/BKL (Ricci).

The altar is shown in its original context in a beautiful plate by Linant, unfortunately unpublished (No. 19, Ms. Linant 269, Bibliothèque Centrale des Musées Nationaux, Paris).

Plate 69

Numbers 1 and 2

The two fronts of a granite altar with four images of Taharqa upholding the sky.

Jebel Barkal, Great Temple of Amun (B 500).

Twenty-fifth Dynasty, reign of Taharqa (690–664 BC).

Porter and Moss, *Topographical Bibliography* 7:220 (43).

No. 72, Museo Egizio, Florence, pencil on paper; unpublished.

Other copies: XV.A.30 (Ricci), XV.A.31 (Linant), D/BKL.

Numbers 3 and 4

Black granite pedestal with figures of Taharqa upholding the sky.

    Jebel Barkal, Great Temple of Amun (B 500).

    Twenty-fifth Dynasty, reign of Taharqa (690–664 BC).

    Porter and Moss, *Topographical Bibliography* 7:220 (40).

    Original not found.

    Other copies: XV.A.32, D/BKL (Ricci).

Plate 70

View of the necropolis, with the pyramid of Taharqa.

    Nuri.

    Porter and Moss, *Topographical Bibliography* 7:223.

    Original not found.

    Other copies: XVI.A.2, D/BKL (Linant).

Plate 71

Number 1

Relief representing two men hoeing and six men holding whips and leading a herd of rams into the fields.

    Giza, mastaba of Iymery (G 6020), room II.

    Fifth Dynasty, reign of Niuserre (2359–2348 BC) or later.

    Porter and Moss, *Topographical Bibliography* 3, Part 1:173 (10) V.

    No. 112, Museo Egizio, Florence, pencil on paper; unpublished.

    Other copies: No. 249, Ms. 272, Folder 51, Fonds Rosellini, Biblioteca Universitaria, Pisa (Ricci?).

    Compared with Lepsius's drawing (*Denkmäler aus Aegypten und Aethiopien* 2:pl. 51), this plate looks clearer and closer to the Old Kingdom style. The texts are copied with remarkable precision.

Number 2

"A man carries a cage of chickens on his head and a bunch of garlic on his shoulder, probably to sell them. He is preceded by a dancer."

    Giza.

    No example of this drawing was found.

Number 3

Relief representing a plowing scene with hieroglyphic inscription.

    Giza, possibly mastaba of Iymery (G 6020), room II.

    Fifth Dynasty, reign of Niuserre (2359–2348 BC) or later.

    Porter and Moss, *Topographical Bibliography* 3, Part 1:173 (10) IV.

    No example of this drawing was found.

Number 4

Relief representing reaping scenes, scribes recording the harvest, and donkeys ready to be loaded with wheat.

Giza, mastaba of Iymery (G 6020), room II.

Fifth Dynasty, reign of Niuserre (2359–2348 BC) or later.

Porter and Moss, *Topographical Bibliography* 3, Part 1:173 (10) II–III.

No. 127, Museo Egizio, Florence, pencil on paper.

Number 5

"Animals that look like bulls, but with different horns: they seem to be employed in agriculture, because among the hieroglyphs there is a sickle, its most common symbol."

Giza.

No example of this drawing was found.

Number 6

A row of men hunting birds with the use of a net trap.

Giza.

No example of this drawing was found.

Number 7

"Fishing. Small metal globes are hanging from the net to drag it down more quickly. The fishermen are standing on a raft."

Giza, mastaba of Khafre-ankh (G 7948), chapel.

Fifth Dynasty (2392–2282 BC) or later.

Porter and Moss, *Topographical Bibliography* 3, Part 1:207 (2) V–VI.

No. 50, Museo Egizio, Florence, pencil on paper; unpublished.

Number 8

"Bargaining over a bird, which is being sold."

Giza, possibly mastaba of Nebemakhet (LG 86), room I.

Fourth Dynasty, reign of Khafre (Chephren) (2437–2414 BC) or Menkaure (Mycerinus) (2414–2396 BC).

Porter and Moss, *Topographical Bibliography* 3, Part 1:230 (3) I.

No example of this drawing was found.

It is possibly the detail of a much larger scene; see Lepsius, *Denkmäler aus Aegypten und Aethiopien* 2:pl. 12a, third register, right scene.

Number 9

"Harvest of fruits that look like figs or pomegranates and their storage in vases or baskets."

Giza, possibly mastaba of Iymery (G 6020), room II.

Fifth Dynasty, reign of Niuserre (2359–2348 BC) or later.
Porter and Moss, *Topographical Bibliography* 3, Part 1:172 (9) II.
No example of this drawing was found.

Number 10
"Woman clapping her hands, followed by a monstrous figure, in front of a sort of idol."
Giza.
No example of this drawing was found.

Number 11
"Table with many objects, a bunch of garlic among them."
Giza, unknown location.
No example of this drawing was found.

Number 12.
"Way of carrying weights, used up to the present day, especially in Sennar."
Giza.
No example of this drawing was found.

Number 13
"A man carrying a bunch of lotus flowers."
Giza, possibly mastaba of Nebemakhet (LG 86), room II.
Fourth Dynasty, reign of Khafre (Chephren) (2437–2414 BC) or Menkaure (2414–2396 BC).
Porter and Moss, *Topographical Bibliography* 3, Part 1:231 (4) III.
No example of this drawing was found.

Number 14
Relief with a stork warden holding a stick.
Giza, possibly mastaba of Iymery (G 6020), room I.
Fifth Dynasty, reign of Niuserre (2359–2348 BC) or later.
Porter and Moss, *Topographical Bibliography* 3, Part 1:171 (4).
No example of this drawing was found.

Plate 72
Number 1
Relief with three carpenters and a scribe writing an inventory.
Giza, mastaba of Iymery (G 6020), room I.
Fifth Dynasty, reign of Niuserre (2359–2348 BC) or later.
Porter and Moss, *Topographical Bibliography* 3, Part 1:171 (5) III.
No example of this drawing was found.

Number 2

Relief with registration of cereal quantities, and punishment of a thief.

    Giza, mastaba of Iymery (G 6020), room II.

    Fifth Dynasty, reign of Niuserre (2359–2348 BC) or later.

    Porter and Moss, *Topographical Bibliography* 3, Part 1:173 (10).

    No. 79, Museo Egizio, Florence, pencil on paper; unpublished.

    Other copies: Nos. 366 and 367, Ms. 300.4, Folder 86, Fonds Rosellini, Biblioteca Universitaria, Pisa.

Number 3

Relief with offering bearers of both genders, hieroglyphic texts.

    Giza.

    No example of this drawing was found.

Number 4

Relief with two donkeys carrying goods to a warehouse, two men unloading, and a scribe recording.

    Giza, mastaba of Iymery (G 6020), room II.

    Fifth Dynasty, reign of Niuserre (2359–2348 BC) or later.

    Porter and Moss, *Topographical Bibliography* 7:173 (10) III.

    No. 55, Museo Egizio, Florence, pencil on paper; unpublished.

    Part of the scene was already published in *Description de l'Égypte*, A., V, pl. 17 [13].

Number 5

Two registers with a row of standing scribes, two men carrying geese, and a man pulling a bull, with hieroglyphic inscriptions.

    Giza, mastaba of Iymery (G 6020), room I.

    Fifth Dynasty, reign of Niuserre (2359–2348 BC) or later.

    Porter and Moss, *Topographical Bibliography* 3, Part 1:171 (2) II–IV.

    No. 129, Museo Egizio, Florence, pencil on paper; unpublished.

Number 6

Three offering-bearers and a man driving three bulls, with hieroglyphic inscriptions.

    Giza, mastaba of Iymery (G 6020), room I.

    Fifth Dynasty, reign of Niuserre (2359–2348 BC) or later.

    Porter and Moss, *Topographical Bibliography* 3, Part 1:171 (4).

    No. 78, Museo Egizio, Florence, pencil on paper; unpublished.

Number 7

Row of offering-bearers and animals.

    Giza.

    No example of this drawing was found.

Number 8

Three seated scribes writing, with hieroglyphic inscription.

    Giza, mastaba of Khafre-ankh (G 7948), chapel.

    Fifth Dynasty (2392–2282 BC) or later.

    Porter and Moss, *Topographical Bibliography* 3, Part 1:208 (4)–(5).

    No. 84, Museo Egizio, Florence, ink on paper; unpublished.

Number 9

"Scribal and art schools."

    Giza.

    No example of this drawing was found.

Numbers 10 and 11

Painting or relief with dancers of both genders.

    Theban West Bank.

    No example of this drawing was found.

Number 12

Painting or relief with harp player.

    Theban West Bank.

    No example of this drawing was found.

Numbers 13 and 14

Relief with harp players.

    Giza.

    No example of this drawing was found.

Plate 73

Number 1

"Fabrication of pottery vases."

    Giza, mastaba of Nebemakhet (LG 86), room II.

    Fourth Dynasty, reign of Khafre (Chephren) (2437–2414 BC) or Menkaure (2414–2396 BC).

    Porter and Moss, *Topographical Bibliography* 3, Part 1:231 (6) V.

    No. 46, Museo Egizio, Florence, pencil on paper; unpublished.

It is a draft drawing, with some arbitrary additions of missing parts in the relief; Lepsius's copy (*Denkmäler aus Aegypten und Aethiopien* 2:pl. 13) has, more accurately, some lacunae, although it is possible that Ricci saw the relief in a better condition. The scene depicts the fabrication of metal, and not pottery as Ricci believed.

Number 2

Relief with men working metal.

> Giza, possibly (a) mastaba of Iymery (G 6020), room I; or (b) mastaba of Nebemakhet (LG 86), room II.
>
> (a) Fifth Dynasty, reign of Niuserre (2359–2348 BC) or later; (b) Fourth Dynasty, reigns of Khafre (Chephren) (2437–2414 BC) or Menkaure (2414–2396 BC).
>
> (a) Porter and Moss, *Topographical Bibliography* 3, Part 1:171 (3); (b) Porter and Moss, *Topographical Bibliography* 3, Part 1:231 (6) III.
>
> No example of this drawing was found.

Since the men in the scenes are blowing into tubes, Ricci mistakenly interpreted the scene as glass production.

Numbers 3 and 4

"Tanning of some leather strips."

> Giza.
>
> No example of this drawing was found.

Number 5

"A mummy bed or a chair is being cleaned."

> Giza, possibly mastaba of Nebemakhet (LG 86), room II.
>
> Fourth Dynasty, reign of Khafre (Chephren) (2437–2414 BC) or Menkaure (2414–2396 BC).
>
> Porter and Moss, *Topographical Bibliography* 3, Part 1:231 (5) f I; Lepsius, *Denkmäler aus Aegypten und Aethiopien* 2:pl. 14a.
>
> No example of this drawing was found.

Number 6

"A servant, who with a very elegant attitude offers in a cup the liquid poured from two ampoules, which he holds in his left hand."

> Giza.
>
> No example of this drawing was found.

Number 7

Relief with scene of meat cooking.

> Giza.
>
> No example of this drawing was found.

Numbers 8 and 9

Relief showing a banquet, dancers, flute players, and four women clapping their hands.

> Giza, mastaba of Iymery (G 6020), room II.
>
> Fifth Dynasty, reign of Niuserre (2359–2348 BC) or later.
>
> Porter and Moss, *Topographical Bibliography* 3, Part 1:172 (8) V.
>
> No example of this drawing was found.

Number 10

Relief showing a scene of baking, and spit-roasting of a duck.

   Giza, mastaba of Iymery (G 6020), room II.

   Fifth Dynasty, reign of Niuserre (2359–2348 BC) or later.

   Porter and Moss, *Topographical Bibliography* 3, Part 1:172 (7).

   No. 76, Museo Egizio, Florence, pencil on paper; unpublished.

Plate 74

Numbers 1 and 2

Relief on two registers with carpenters.

   Giza, mastaba of Iymery (G 6020), room I.

   Fifth Dynasty, reign of Niuserre (2359–2348 BC) or later.

   Porter and Moss, *Topographical Bibliography* 3, Part 1:171 (3).

   No. 54, Museo Egizio, Florence, pencil, ink, and watercolor on paper; unpublished.

Number 3

Earthenware and glass production.

   Giza.

   No example of this drawing was found.

Number 4

Leather tanning.

   Giza.

   No example of this drawing was found.

Number 5

List of unguents; pressing and sale of oil, which is poured into jars.

   Giza, mastaba of Iymery (G 6020), room I.

   Fifth Dynasty, reign of Niuserre (2359–2348 BC) or later.

   Porter and Moss, *Topographical Bibliography* 3, Part 1:171 (3).

   No. 54, Museo Egizio, Florence, pencil, ink, and watercolor on paper; unpublished.

   Ricci thought that the scene represented wine production; the procedure was very similar, and actually only the ability to read hieroglyphs would have spared him the misunderstanding.

Plate 75

Number 1

"Sailing boat."

   Valley of the Kings, tomb of Ramesses III (KV 11), side room D.

   Twentieth Dynasty, reign of Ramesses III (1185–1153 BC).

   Porter and Moss, *Topographical Bibliography* 1, Part 2:519 (9).

   Original not found.

   Other copies: II.B.2, D/BKL (Ricci).

Number 2

"Cruising boat in the shape of a gondola, with folded sail."

    Theban West Bank, tombs of the nobles.

    No example of this drawing was found.

Number 3

Relief or painting with wine production scenes: vintage, pounding the grapes, squeezing the canvas, decanting wine into other jars.

    Theban West Bank, tombs of the nobles.

    No example of this drawing was found.

Plate 76

Number 1

Relief with rowing boat.

    Giza.

    No example of this drawing was found.

Number 2

Boat moored with three ropes.

    Giza.

    No example of this drawing was found.

Number 3

Relief representing a "naval show."

    Giza, mastaba of Iymery (G 6020), room II.

    Fifth Dynasty, reign of Niuserre (2359–2348 BC) or later.

    Porter and Moss, *Topographical Bibliography* 3, Part 1:173 (10) IV.

    No example of this drawing was found.

Number 4

"Various birds with two pelicans."

    Giza.

    No example of this drawing was found.

Number 5

Relief with sailing boat; three sailors attend the sails, a fourth is seated below deck, while the owner is seated on a chair.

    Giza, mastaba of Seshemnefer (G 4940), chapel.

    Fifth Dynasty, reigns of Sahure (2385–2373 BC) and Neferirkare (2373–2363 BC).

    Porter and Moss, *Topographical Bibliography* 3, Part 1:142 (2) I.

    No. 47, Museo Egizio, Florence, pencil on paper; unpublished.

Number 6

"Another boat sailing along the banks, in the vicinity of a lotus plantation."

Giza.

No example of this drawing was found.

Number 7

"Three fish, two open to dry."

Giza.

No example of this drawing was found.

Plate 77

Number 1

"Sailboat with oars."

Giza, mastaba of Seshemnefer (G 4940), chapel.

Fifth Dynasty, reigns of Sahure (2385–2373 BC) and Neferirkare (2373–2363 BC).

Porter and Moss, *Topographical Bibliography* 3, Part 1:142 (2) I.

No. 53, Museo Egizio, Florence, ink on paper; unpublished.

Number 2

Relief with "a cow giving birth with the help of a man."

Giza, mastaba of Iymery (G 6020), room II.

Fifth Dynasty, reign of Niuserre (2359–2348 BC) or later.

Porter and Moss, *Topographical Bibliography* 3, Part 1:172 (7) V.

No example of this drawing was found.

Number 3

"The same cow suckling the bullock."

Giza, mastaba of Iymery (G 6020), room II.

Fifth Dynasty, reign of Niuserre (2359–2348 BC) or later.

Porter and Moss, *Topographical Bibliography* 3, Part 1:172 (7) V.

No example of this drawing was found.

Numbers 4 and 5

"Various monkeys."

Giza.

No example of this drawing was found.

Number 6

"Men driving cattle."

Giza.

No example of this drawing was found.

Number 7

"A variety of Egyptian vases."

Giza.

No example of this drawing was found.

Number 8

Relief showing "an offering."

Giza.

No. 43, Museo Egizio, Florence, pencil on paper; unpublished.

The drawing represents an offering scene: the main figure, headless due to a large lacuna, is seated on a chair in front of an offering table with bread loaves. In front of the deceased, a man is kneeling, followed by two standing men, one bearing a censer and the other a vase. No hieroglyphic text was copied by Ricci. Comparisons with Lepsius's copies of the Giza mastabas did not give any result and the scene still awaits an identification.

Number 9

"A hippopotamus."

Giza, possibly mastaba of Debhen (LG 90), room II.

Fourth Dynasty, reign of Menkaure (2414–2396 BC).

Porter and Moss, *Topographical Bibliography* 3, Part 1:236 (8).

No example of this drawing was found.

Number 10

"A suckling gazelle."

Giza.

No example of this drawing was found.

Number 11

"Birds of various kinds."

Giza.

No example of this drawing was found.

Plate 78

Numbers 1 and 2

Officer carried on a palanquin, followed by family members and servants.

Giza, mastaba of Iymery (G 6020), room I.

Fifth Dynasty, reign of Niuserre (2359–2348 BC) or later.

Porter and Moss, *Topographical Bibliography* 3, Part 1:171 (5) I–II.

No. 52, Museo Egizio, Florence, watercolor on paper; unpublished.

Number 3

Relief showing a "temple, or other place, where people go to present offerings."

Giza, mastaba of Debhen (LG 90), room II.

Fourth Dynasty, reign of Menkaure (2414–2396 BC).

Porter and Moss, *Topographical Bibliography* 3, Part 1:236 (5) VII.

No. 44, Museo Egizio, Florence, pencil on paper; unpublished.

Number 4

"Greyhound."

No example of this drawing was found.

A drawing of a greyhound by Linant is No. 34ter, Ms. Linant 269, Bibliothèque Centrale des Musées Nationaux, Paris.

Number 5

"Young gazelles carried on the shoulders by a man."

Giza.

No example of this drawing was found.

Number 6

"Typhon playing a sort of harp, accompanied on the sistrum by a monkey."

Giza.

No example of this drawing was found.

Number 7

"Two fish."

Giza.

No example of this drawing was found.

Plates 79–86

Cartouches of Khafre (Chephren) from Giza, of Senwosret I from the Heliopolis obelisk, of Amenhotep III from Luxor, and of Horemheb.

No. 116, Museo Egizio, Florence, pencil on paper; unpublished.

This series of plates originally comprised a list of royal cartouches. Plates 80–86 could not be located. In the Florence portfolio only one drawing could fit this description. Another drawing with many cartouches is No. 50, Ms. Linant 268, Bibliothèque Centrale des Musées Nationaux, Paris.

Plate 87

Selection of hieroglyphs from different inscriptions.

No. 121, Museo Egizio, Florence (signs marked 1 to 97), pencil, ink, and watercolor on paper; No. 41, Museo Egizio, Florence, ink on paper; unpublished.

Plate 88

Partial map of the travel to Siwa.

No example of this drawing was found.

Plate 89

Partial map of the travel to Sinai.

Original not found.

Other copies: XXI.C.5, D/BKL (Linant); unpublished.

It is the first relatively precise map of the southwest part of the peninsula. It also marks the borders of the areas controlled by different tribes, indicated by twelve subdivisions of the Awlad Sa'id. The map tracks clearly the path followed by Ricci and Linant in 1820.

Plate 90

General map of the travel to Sennar.

Original not found.

Other copies: XXI.C.8–10, D/BKL (Linant); unpublished.

These three large color maps cover the entire area of Nubia and Sennar. The first map includes the Nile Valley from Philae to Wadi Halfa (XXI.C.8); the second map from Wadi Halfa to Halfaya (XXI.C.10); the third map from Halfaya to Siraywa on the Blue Nile (XXI.C.9). The map is enriched by a large display of toponyms and the specification of the borders of the different kingdoms within the Funj Sultanate.

Notes
to Sources of Plates and Chapters 1–8

Notes to Sources of Plates

1   When a copy of the original drawing, rather than the original itself, appears in the Plates section of this book, the source cited here is that of the copy.
2   All images identified as "Biblioteca Universitaria, Pisa" are © Biblioteca Universitaria, Pisa, courtesy of the Ministero dei Beni e delle Attività Culturali e del Turismo, and may not be further reproduced.
3   All images identified as "Museo Egizio, Florence" are © Museo Egizio di Firenze, courtesy of the Ministero dei Beni e delle Attività Culturali e del Turismo.
4   All images identified as "Dorset History Centre, Dorchester" are © The National Trust.
5   All images identified as "British Museum" are © The Trustees of the British Museum.
6   All images identified as "Bristol Museum & Art Gallery" are © Bristol City Council.

Notes to chapter 1

1   Elena Fasano Guarini, Giuseppe Petralia, and Paolo Pezzino, *Storia della Toscana*, vol. 2, *Dal Settecento ad oggi* (Rome–Bari: Laterza, 2004), 20.
2   Folder 15, Italian Fonds, National Archives of Egypt.
3   Édouard Driault, *La formation de l'empire de Mohamed Aly de l'Arabie au Soudan (1814–1823): correspondance des consuls de France en Égypte* (Cairo: Société Royale de Géographie d'Égypte, 1927), 99.
4   Félix Mengin, *Histoire de l'Égypte sous le gouvernement de Mohammed-Aly: ou, Récit des événemens politiques et militaires qui ont eu lieu depuis le départ des Français jusqu'en 1823* (Paris: A. Bertrand, 1823), pl. 13.
5   "Return of the British and foreign vessels that entered and sailed from the port of Alexandria during the year ending 31 December 1826 with those that remained in the harbor on 1 January 1827," Folder 25, Foreign Office, National Archives of Egypt.
6   Khaled Fahmy, *All the Pasha's Men: Mehmet Ali, His Army and the Making of Modern Egypt* (Cairo: American University in Cairo Press, 2002), 2–3.
7   Page numbers in brackets in chapters 1 through 5 refer to page numbers in chapter 10 of this volume—Ricci's account of his travels.

8   Warren R. Dawson, Morris L. Bierbrier, and Eric P. Uphill, *Who Was Who in Egyptology* (London: Egypt Exploration Society, 1995), 364.

9   Paolo Garzoni Venturi to Vittorio Fossombroni, 1 December 1829, Folder 21, Italian Fonds, National Archives of Egypt.

10 'Council' or 'public audience.'

11 Andrea Antonelli to the secretary [of the grand duke of Tuscany?], 1830?, Folder 10, Italian Fonds, National Archives of Egypt; same information in: Annibale de Rossetti to Paolo Garzoni Venturi, 28 August 1835, Folder 10, Italian Fonds, National Archives of Egypt.

12 "Italian is the current medium of conversation in this country"; Frederick Henniker, *Notes during a visit to Egypt, Nubia, the Oasis, Mount Sinai, and Jerusalem* (London: John Murray, 1823), 17.

13 Alain Silvera, "The First Egyptian Student Mission to France under Muhammad Ali," *Middle Eastern Studies* 16 (1980): 7.

14 Richard N. Verdery, "The Publications of the Bulaq Press under Muhammad 'Ali of Egypt," *Journal of the American Oriental Society* 91 (1971): 129.

15 Luigi Antonio Balboni, *Gl'italiani nella civiltà egiziana del sec. XIX* (Alexandria: Stabilimento Tipo-Litografico V. Penasson, 1906), 487.

16 Silvera, "The First Egyptian Student Mission," 7.

17 Giovanni Martini to Giuseppe Paver, 8 February 1827, Folder 10, Italian Fonds, National Archives of Egypt.

18 Andrea Antonelli to Ippolito Rosellini, 9 January 1830, Folder 23, Italian Fonds, National Archives of Egypt.

19 Dominique Vivant Denon, *Voyage dans la Basse et Haute-Égypte pendant les campagnes du général Bonaparte* (Paris: P. Didot, 1802).

20 Daniele Salvoldi, "Per una stima in termini di valuta contemporanea delle spese sostenute dai pionieri dell'Egittologia britannica," in *Sotto l'ala di Thot: Un contributo alla diffusione della cultura dell'antico Egitto*, ed. Gilberto Modonesi (Milan: Museo di Storia Naturale, 2012), 96.

21 Donald Malcolm Reid, *Whose Pharaohs? Archaeology, Museums, and Egyptian National Identity from Napoleon to World War I* (Berkeley and Los Angeles: University of California Press, 1997), 21.

22 Jean-François Champollion, *Lettre à M. Dacier relative à l'alphabet des hiéroglyphes phonétiques* (Paris: Firmin Didot, 1822).

Notes to chapter 2

1   Archivio di Stato di Firenze, Stato civile della restaurazione (1816–1860), Firenze, Morti, 1834, No. 170.

2   "Raccolta biografica di illustri Senesi che a seguito alle Pompe Senesi del P. Ugurgieri, informe-mente in parte accozzata da E.R." The part dedicated to Ricci is published in Angelo Sammarco, *Alessandro Ricci e il suo giornale dei viaggi*, vol. 2, *Documenti inediti o rari* (Cairo: Société Royale de Géographie d'Égypte, 1930).

3   Sammarco, *Alessandro Ricci*, 157.

4   Sammarco, *Alessandro Ricci*, 3–4.

5   Annalucia Forti Messina, "Studenti e laureati in medicina a Pavia nell'Ottocento preunitario," *Mélanges de l'École Française de Rome, Moyen-Age, Temps modernes* 97, no. 1 (1985): 494.

6   Giuseppe Gabrieli, *Ippolito Rosellini e il suo Giornale della Spedizione Letteraria Toscana in Egitto negli anni 1828–1829* (Rome: Reale Società Geografica Italiana, 1925), 6.

7   Alessandro Ricci to Patrizio Rontani, 13 November 1819, published in Sammarco, *Alessandro Ricci*, 152.

8   Maria Carmela Betrò, ed., *Lungo il Nilo: Ippolito Rosellini e la Spedizione Franco-Toscana in Egitto (1828–1829)* (Florence: Giunti, 2010), 18–19.

9   Patricia Usick, *Adventures in Egypt and Nubia: The Travels of William John Bankes (1786–1855)* (London: The British Museum Press, 2002), 141n79.

10 "Copialettere riguardante la Spedizione letteraria di Toscana in Egitto 1827–1829," 65–66, Ms. 379, Fonds Rosellini, Biblioteca Universitaria di Pisa; Gabrieli, *Ippolito Rosellini*, 282–83.

11 Sammarco, *Alessandro Ricci*, 18–21.

12 Daniele Salvoldi, "Per una stima in termini di valuta contemporanea delle spese sostenute dai pionieri dell'Egittologia britannica," in *Sotto l'ala di Thot: Un contributo alla diffusione della cultura dell'antico Egitto*, ed. Gilberto Modonesi (Milan: Museo di Storia Naturale, 2012), 93–104.

13 Louis Maurice Adolphe Linant de Bellefonds to Henry Salt, 7 March 1826, HJ 1/269, Deposit/Bankes of Kingston Lacy and Corfe Castle, Dorset History Centre, Dorchester.

14 Louis Maurice Adolphe Linant de Bellefonds to William John Bankes, 15 April 1821, HJ 1/147, Deposit/Bankes of Kingston Lacy and Corfe Castle, Dorset History Centre, Dorchester.

15 Sammarco, *Alessandro Ricci*, 131.

16 Sammarco, *Alessandro Ricci*, 18.

17 Sammarco, *Alessandro Ricci*, 152–53.

18 William J. Bankes, *Narrative of the Life and Adventures of Giovanni Finati, Translated from the Italian and Edited by W. John Bankes* (London: John Murray, 1830), 2:427–28.

19 Gabrieli, *Ippolito Rosellini*, 177.

20 Usick, *Adventures in Egypt and Nubia*, 199 and n. 35.

21 Guglielmo Enrico Saltini, *Giuseppe Angelelli pittore toscano, ricordo biografico* (Florence: F. Bencini, 1866), quoted in Sammarco, *Alessandro Ricci*, 148.

22 Arabic 'king,' a title used by upper Nile chieftains.

23 Sammarco, *Alessandro Ricci*, 18.

24 Usick, *Adventures in Egypt and Nubia*, 122.

25 Usick, *Adventures in Egypt and Nubia*, 15.

26 John J. Halls, *The Life and Correspondence of Henry Salt Esq. FRS* (London: Richard Bentley, 1834), 1:410.

27 Giovanni Battista Belzoni, *Narrative of the Operations and Recent Discoveries within Pyramids, Temples, Tombs and Excavations in Egypt and Nubia* (London: John Murray, 1820), 251.

28 Ippolito Rosellini, *Monumenti dell'Egitto e della Nubia: Monumenti del Culto* (Pisa: Niccolò Capurro, 1844), 144.

29 Sammarco, *Alessandro Ricci*, 151.

30 Sammarco, *Alessandro Ricci*, 154; Plutarch, *Alexander* XXVII 1–2.

31 François-Michel de Rozière, "Notice sur les ruines d'un monument persépolitain découvert dans l'isthme de Suez par M. de Rozière, ingénieur en chef des mines," in *Description de l'Égypte, Antiquités, Mémoires* (Paris: Imprimerie Impériale, 1809), 1:265–76.

32 Louis Maurice Adolphe Linant de Bellefonds to William John Bankes, 15 April 1821, HJ 1/139, Deposit/Bankes of Kingston Lacy and Corfe Castle, Dorset History Centre, Dorchester.

33 Édouard Devilliers, "Description des antiquités situées dans l'Isthme de Suez par M. Devilliers ingénieur en chef des ponts et chaussées," in *Description de l'Égypte, Antiquités, Descriptions* (Paris: Imprimerie Impériale, 1818), 2:8–10.

34 Edda Bresciani, "Il richiamo della piramide: J.-F. Champollion e I. Rosellini in Egitto," in *La Piramide e la Torre: Duecento anni di archeologia egiziana*, ed. Edda Bresciani (Pisa: Cassa di Risparmio di Pisa, 2000), 27.

35 Bresciani, "Il richiamo della piramide," 22.

Notes to chapter 3

1 Morris L. Bierbrier, "The Salt Watercolours," *Göttinger Miszellen* 61 (1983): 9–12.

2 Alessandro Ricci to Patrizio Rontani, 13 November 1819, published in Angelo Sammarco, *Alessandro Ricci e il suo giornale dei viaggi*, vol. 2, *Documenti inediti o rari* (Cairo: Société Royale de Géographie d'Égypte, 1930), 152.

3 John J. Halls, *The Life and Correspondence of Henry Salt Esq. FRS* (London: Richard Bentley, 1834), 2:147.

4 Heinrich Hase to Bernhard August von Lindenau, 14 May 1831, Akten der Königlichen Antiken-Sammlung (1830–1842), Staatliche Kunstsammlungen zu Dresden.

5 Cf. Daniele Salvoldi, "Ricci, Belzoni, Salt and the Works in the Valley of the Kings: New Light from the Ricci Travel Account," in *L'Egitto in Età Ramesside: Atti del Convegno, Chianciano Terme, 17–18 Dicembre 2009*, ed. Daniela Picchi (Cinisello Balsamo: Silvana Editoriale, 2011), 33–41.

6 Giovanni D'Athanasi, *A Brief Account of the Researches and Discoveries in Upper Egypt, Made under the Direction of Henry Salt Esq.* (London: John Hearne, 1836), 26–27.

7 D'Athanasi, *A Brief Account*, 301.

8 Unpublished manuscript quoted in Peter Clayton, *The Rediscovery of Ancient Egypt: Artists and Travellers in the Nineteenth Century* (London: Thames and Hudson, 1984), 45.

9 William J. Bankes, *Narrative of the Life and Adventures of Giovanni Finati, Translated from the Italian and Edited by W. John Bankes* (London: John Murray, 1830), 104 (footnote).

10 Bankes, *Narrative*, 344.

11 William John Bankes to unknown recipient, unknown date, HJ 1/80, Deposit/Bankes of Kingston Lacy and Corfe Castle, Dorset History Centre, Dorchester.

12 Halls, *The Life and Correspondence*, 2:15.

13 Halls, *The Life and Correspondence*, 2:144.

14 List of drawings made at Siwa, XXI.B.28; payment receipt, HJ 1/198; list of measures for the large drawing of the garden scene in the tomb of Sennefer, II.A.15; Deposit/Bankes of Kingston Lacy and Corfe Castle, Dorset History Centre, Dorchester.

15 Bankes, *Narrative*, 344–45.

16 Expense report, HJ 1/197, Deposit/Bankes of Kingston Lacy and Corfe Castle, Dorset History Centre, Dorchester.

17 Henry Salt to William John Bankes, 6 January 1822, HJ 1/169, Bankes of Kingston Lacy and Corfe Castle, Dorset History Centre, Dorchester.

18 Sammarco, *Alessandro Ricci*, 157.

19 Expense report, HJ 1/197, Deposit/Bankes of Kingston Lacy and Corfe Castle, Dorset History Centre, Dorchester.

20 To be corrected to "2,160."

21 Henry Salt to William John Bankes, 7 February 1823, HJ 1/196, Deposit/Bankes of Kingston Lacy and Corfe Castle, Dorset History Centre, Dorchester.

22 Extract from a letter of Henry Salt to William Hamilton, 10 October 1821, HJ 1/160, Deposit/Bankes of Kingston Lacy and Corfe Castle, Dorset History Centre, Dorchester.

23 Persian and Turkish 'decree,' 'permission,' but in this case 'safe-conduct.'

24 Sammarco, *Alessandro Ricci*, 21.

25 Margaret Shinnie, *Linant de Bellefonds, Journal d'un Voyage à Meroe dans les années 1821–1822* (Khartoum: Antiquities Service Occasional Papers, 1958), 77.

26 Henry Salt to William John Bankes, 14 December 1822, in Patricia Usick, *Adventures in Egypt and Nubia: The Travels of William John Bankes (1786–1855)* (London: The British Museum Press, 2002), 165.

27 Expense report, HJ 1/197, Deposit/Bankes of Kingston Lacy and Corfe Castle, Dorset History Centre, Dorchester.

28 Daniele Salvoldi, "Per una stima in termini di valuta contemporanea delle spese sostenute dai pionieri dell'Egittologia britannica," in *Sotto l'ala di Thot: Un contributo alla diffusione della cultura dell'antico Egitto*, ed. Gilberto Modonesi (Milan: Museo di Storia Naturale, 2012), 98–99.

29 Bankes, *Narrative*, 356–57.

30 Giovanni Mapelli to Francesco Pacini, 30 March 1835; published in Sammarco, *Alessandro Ricci*, 95.

31 D'Athanasi, *A Brief Account*, 43.

32 "Another minute and the barbarians would have crowned their brutality with blood, if my husband and Mr. Ricci, guns in hand, had not intervened to prevent the unfortunate consequences of this brawl," Wolfradine A.L. Schulenburg-Minutoli, *Mes souvenirs d'Égypte* (Paris: Nepveu, 1826), 2:47.

33 Edda Bresciani, "Il richiamo della piramide: J.-F. Champollion e I. Rosellini in Egitto," in *La Piramide e la Torre: Duecento anni di archeologia egiziana*, ed. Edda Bresciani (Pisa: Cassa di Risparmio di Pisa, 2000), 17; Raymond Weill, *Recueil des inscriptions égyptiennes du Sinaï* (Paris: Société nouvelle de librairie et d'édition, 1904), 64n1.

34 Bankes, *Narrative*, 104.

35 Bankes, *Narrative*, 344.

36 Angelo Sammarco, "Alessandro Ricci da Siena e il suo giornale dei viaggi recentemente scoperto," *Bulletin de la Société Royale de Géographie d'Égype* 17 (1929): 300–301.

37 Sammarco, *Alessandro Ricci*, iv.

38 Jean-François Champollion to Jacques-Joseph Champollion, 2 July 1825; published in Sammarco, *Alessandro Ricci*, 146.

39 Alessandro Ricci to Girolamo Bardi, 26 August 1828, published in *Antologia* 32 (1828): 141; republished in Sammarco, *Alessandro Ricci*, 162–63.

40   Usick, *Adventures in Egypt and Nubia*, 115.

41   From Alexandria to Trieste, Chancellor Nizzoli took forty-two days in 1822; the return journey in 1824 took only twelve days; Sergio Daris, *Giuseppe Nizzoli: Un impiegato consolare austriaco nel levante agli albori dell'Egittologia* (Naples: Graus Editore, 2005).

42   Silvio Curto and Laura Donatelli, eds., *Bernardino Drovetti Epistolario* (Milan: Cisalpino Goliardica, 1985), 252–59, 598–99.

43   D'Athanasi, *A Brief Account*, 25.

44   Giovanni Battista Belzoni, *Narrative of the Operations and Recent Discoveries within Pyramids, Temples, Tombs and Excavations in Egypt and Nubia* (London: John Murray, 1820), 251.

45   Halls, *The Life and Correspondence*, 2:501.

46   Halls, *The Life and Correspondence*, 2:22.

47   Giovanni Battista Belzoni to William John Bankes, 25 June 1818, HJ 1/88, Deposit/Bankes of Kingston Lacy and Corfe Castle, Dorset History Centre, Dorchester. No attempt to correct Belzoni's English is made here.

48   Belzoni, *Narrative*, 276–77.

49   This detail seems exaggerated if compared with what Ricci and Belzoni state.

50   Schulenburg-Minutoli, *Mes souvenirs*, 2:18.

51   Schulenburg-Minutoli, *Mes souvenirs*, 2:5–6.

52   Cf. Salvoldi, "Ricci, Belzoni, Salt."

53   Curto and Donatelli, *Bernardino Drovetti*, 138.

54   Giovanni Battista Belzoni to William John Bankes, 22 August 1819, HJ 1/100, Deposit/Bankes of Kingston Lacy and Corfe Castle, Dorset History Centre, Dorchester.

55   Diary of Sarah Belzoni, Bristol City Museum & Art Gallery. The sums here are incorrect; either "1,400" must be corrected to "2,400," or "256" to "1,256."

56   Belzoni, *Narrative*, 285.

57   Halls, *The Life and Correspondence*, 2:135.

58   Halls, *The Life and Correspondence*, 2:134.

59   Patricia Usick, "Not the Travel Journal of Alessandro Ricci," in *Studies in Egyptian Antiquities: A Tribute to T.G.H. James*, ed. Vivian W. Davies (London: The British Museum Press, 1999), 118.

60   "The suspicion Belzoni had cast in the minds of those gentlemen, i.e., that I was reporting their plans, made me wait, as I feared the letter would have been stopped. But since he invented all this, they did me justice by not believing him"; Curto and Donatelli, *Bernardino Drovetti*, 138.

61   Usick, "Not the Travel Journal," 117.

62   Usick, "Not the Travel Journal," 118.

63   Usick, "Not the Travel Journal," 118.

64   Usick, "Not the Travel Journal," 118.

65   Unpublished manuscript quoted in Clayton, *The Rediscovery of Ancient Egypt*, 44–45.

66   Bankes, *Narrative*, 320; Ms. 267, 1821–22, Louis Adolphe Linant de Bellefonds, Bibliothèque Centrale des Musées Nationaux, Paris; D'Athanasi, *A Brief Account*, 41.

67 Bankes, *Narrative*, 320.

68 John Hyde Ms. 42102, c. 82, quoted in Usick, *Adventures in Egypt and Nubia*, 119.

69 *Kashif* is a Mamluk military rank; Peter M. Holt, *A Modern History of the Sudan, from the Funj Sultanate to the Present Day* (London: Weidenfeld and Nicolson, 1961), 24.

70 According to D'Athanasi the letters were addressed to his brother, Muhammad Kashif; D'Athanasi, *A Brief Account*, 41.

71 Bankes, *Narrative*, 325; D'Athanasi, *A Brief Account*, 44.

72 Bankes, *Narrative*, 327.

73 A version very close to that of D'Athanasi, *A Brief Account*, 44–45.

74 Bankes, *Narrative*, 337–38.

75 D'Athanasi, *A Brief Account*, 339.

76 D'Athanasi, *A Brief Account*, 48.

77 Bankes, *Narrative*, 340; Patricia Usick, "The First Excavation of Wadi Halfa (Buhen)," in *Studies on Ancient Egypt in Honour of H.S. Smith*, ed. Anthony Leahy and John Tait (London: Egypt Exploration Society, 1999), 331–36.

78 John Fuller, *Narrative of a Tour through Some Parts of the Turkish Empire* (London: Richard Taylor, 1829), 211.

79 D'Athanasi, *A Brief Account*, 49.

80 Halls, *The Life and Correspondence*, 2:139.

81 Bankes, *Narrative*, 104, 344.

82 Curto and Donatelli, *Bernardino Drovetti*, 138.

83 Sammarco, *Alessandro Ricci*, 151–52.

84 Robert Cornevin, *Histoire de l'Afrique*, vol. 2, *L'Afrique précoloniale du tournant du XVIe au tournant du XXe siècle* (Paris: Payot, 1966), map 17.

85 Edme-François Jomard, *Voyage à l'Oasis de Syouah, rédigé et publié par M. Jomard* (Paris: De Rignoux, 1823), 5.

86 Drovetti was removed from the position of general consul of France with the fall of Napoleon and the restoration of the Bourbon dynasty (1814).

87 Édouard Driault, *La formation de l'empire de Mohamed Aly de l'Arabie au Soudan (1814–1823): correspondance des consuls de France en Égypte* (Cairo: Société Royale de Géographie d'Égypte, 1927), 195.

88 *Gazzetta di Milano* 185 (3 July 1820), 943.

89 Domenico Enegildo Frediani to Antonio Canova, 30 March 1820, in Sammarco, *Alessandro Ricci*, 123.

90 Jean Mazuel, L'*Oeuvre Géographique de Linant de Bellefonds: Étude de Géographie Historique* (Cairo: Société Royale de Géographie d'Égypte, 1937), 12; drawings by Linant published in Jomard, *Voyage*, pls. II, III [1], [5]–[6], IV, V, VII [1]–[5], VIII, IX [1], X, XII, XIII, XIX, XX [1]–[2].

91 Jomard, *Voyage*, pls. III [2]–[4], VII [9]–[10], XIV, XV, XVI, XVII, XVIIbis, XVIII.

92 The entire Folder XIX, and a view of the Oasis of Shiyata, XXI.B.15. There is also a list of drawings copied by Ricci for Bankes: "Travel to Siwa. Details of the Ombeda Temple. 1. Front part of the gate. 2. Rear part of the same. 3. Right side. 4. Left side. 6. [*sic*]. Piece on the ground. Drawings made by Dr. Ricci," XXI.B.28. All items in Deposit/Bankes of Kingston Lacy and Corfe Castle, Dorset History Centre, Dorchester.

93   XIX.B.14–18, Deposit/Bankes of Kingston Lacy and Corfe Castle, Dorset History Centre, Dorchester.

94   Andrew J. McGregor, *A Military History of Modern Egypt: From the Ottoman Conquest to the Ramadan War* (Westport: Praeger Security International, 2006), 64.

95   Sammarco, *Alessandro Ricci*, 127; Jomard, *Voyage*, 2.

96   Mahmud M. Abd Allah, "Siwan Customs," *Harvard African Studies* 1 (1917): 1–28. More reticent were previous descriptions: "The morals of the Siwans have always been a byword and a reproach amongst those who come in contact with them, and there is no doubt that they are sadly lacking in this respect," C.V.B. Stanley, "The Oasis of Siwa," *Journal of the Royal African Society* 11, no. 43 (1912): 307. On the issue, cf. Walter B. Cline, *Notes of the People of Siwah and el Garah in the Libyan Desert* (Menasha: G. Banta Pub. Co., 1936).

97   Ahmed Fakhry, *Siwa Oasis: Its History and Antiquities* (Cairo: Government Press, 1944), 9–10.

98   "N. 12. Vue de l'intérieur de la Ville d'Agarmi ou Cherquié," XIX.B.2, Deposit/Bankes of Kingston Lacy and Corfe Castle, Dorset History Centre, Dorchester.

99   Hugh G. Evelyn-White and Walter Hauser, *The Monasteries of Wâdi 'n Natrûn*, part 2, *The History of the Monasteries of Nitria and of Scetis* (New York: The Metropolitan Museum of Art, 1932), 431.

100   Halls, *The Life and Correspondence*, 2:155.

101   George W. Murray, *Sons of Ishmael: A Study of the Egyptian Bedouin* (Cairo: Farid Atiya Press, 2012) [original edition London: Routledge, 1935], 41.

102   Usick, *Adventures in Egypt and Nubia*, 29–30.

103   John Hyde to William John Bankes, 7 October 1819, HJ 1/103, Deposit/Bankes of Kingston Lacy and Corfe Castle, Dorset History Centre, Dorchester.

104   John Hyde to William John Bankes, 7 October 1819, HJ 1/103, Deposit/Bankes of Kingston Lacy and Corfe Castle, Dorset History Centre, Dorchester.

105   Frederick Henniker, *Notes during a Visit to Egypt, Nubia, the Oasis, Mount Sinai, and Jerusalem* (London: John Murray, 1823), 197–247.

106   This manuscript could not be traced in the Bankes Archive; it is mentioned in another letter by Salt to Bankes; Henry Salt to William John Bankes, 10 October 1821, HJ 1/159, Deposit/Bankes of Kingston Lacy and Corfe Castle, Dorset History Centre, Dorchester. In a third letter, written more than a year later, the manuscript is mentioned again in relation to a group of drawings by Ricci also missing from the collection; Henry Salt to William John Bankes, 14 December 1822, HJ 1/187, Deposit/Bankes of Kingston Lacy and Corfe Castle, Dorset History Centre, Dorchester.

107   He is referring to the stelae in the sanctuary of Serabit al-Khadim.

108   Louis Maurice Adolphe Linant de Bellefonds to William John Bankes, 15 April 1821, HJ 1/147, Deposit/Bankes of Kingston Lacy and Corfe Castle, Dorset History Centre, Dorchester.

109   John Hyde to William John Bankes, 7 October 1819, HJ 1/103, Deposit/Bankes of Kingston Lacy and Corfe Castle, Dorset History Centre, Dorchester.

110   Louis Maurice Adolphe Linant de Bellefonds to William John Bankes, 15 April 1821, HJ 1/147, Deposit/Bankes of Kingston Lacy and Corfe Castle, Dorset History Centre, Dorchester.

111 Said Gohary and Jocelyn Gohary, "Report on Cultural Heritage Sites in South Sinai," http://st-katherine.net/en/downloads/Cultural%20Heritage%20Sites.pdf

112 Map of the Sinai Peninsula, [1820], XXI.C.5, Deposit/Bankes of Kingston Lacy and Corfe Castle, Dorset History Centre, Dorchester.

113 Michael E. Stone, "Sinai Armenian Inscriptions," *The Biblical Archaeologist* 45 (1982): 28.

114 Of all the inscriptions copied by Ricci at al-Maghara, inscriptions Sinai 10, 12, and 44 are currently at the Cairo Egyptian Museum; inscriptions Sinai 7 and 35 were destroyed; and inscriptions Sinai 11, 15, 20, 27, 28, and 33 are now lost or probably destroyed. Cf. also Georges A. Barrois, "The Mines of Sinai," *The Harvard Theological Review* 25 (1932): 101.

115 René-Georges Coquin, "Pharan," in *The Coptic Encyclopedia*, vol. 6, http://ccdl.libraries.claremont.edu/cdm/singleitem/collection/cce/id/1573/rec/1

116 Peter Grossmann, "Early Christian Ruins in Wadi Fayran (Sinai): An Archaeological Survey," *Annales du Service des Antiquités de l'Égypte* 70 (1985): 75–81; Peter Grossmann, "Excavations in Firan–Sinai (February 1998)," *Annales du Service des Antiquités de l'Égypte* 76 (2001): 135–41; Peter Grossmann, "Report on the Season in Firan–Sinai (February–March 1992)," *Byzantinische Zeitschrift* 89 (1996): 11–36; Peter Grossmann, "Wadi Fayran/Sinai: Report on the Seasons in March and April 1985 and 1986 with an Appendix on the Church at Mount Sinai," *Annales du Service des Antiquités de l'Égypte* 75 (1999–2000): 153–65.

117 Grossmann, "Early Christian Ruins," 78–80.

118 View of the Holy Monastery of St. Catherine, XX.D.19; Panoramic view of the Holy Monastery of St. Catherine, XX.D.20; Deposit/Bankes of Kingston Lacy and Corfe Castle, Dorset History Centre, Dorchester.

119 Henry Salt to William John Bankes, 14 December 1822, HJ 1/187, Deposit/Bankes of Kingston Lacy and Corfe Castle, Dorset History Centre, Dorchester.

120 The Byzantine archaeological heritage of Jabel Safsafa is noteworthy; compare Israel Finkelstein and Asher Ovadiah, "Byzantine Monastic Remains in the Southern Sinai," *Dumbarton Oaks Papers* 39 (1985): 42.

121 View of the port of al-Tor, 1820, XX.D.7, Deposit/Bankes of Kingston Lacy and Corfe Castle, Dorset History Centre, Dorchester.

122 Joseph J. Hobbs, *Mount Sinai* (Austin: University of Texas Press, 1995), 86–88.

123 View of the Greek Orthodox *kathisma* of Hammam Musa, 1820, XX.D.13, Deposit/Bankes of Kingston Lacy and Corfe Castle, Dorset History Centre, Dorchester.

124 Oral witnesses obtained from Fr. Nilos, Monastery of St. Catherine, and from Fr. Dionysios, Monastery of St. George (al-Tor), collected in August–September 2010.

125 Nathalie M. Vriend, Melany L. Hunt, Robert W. Clayton, Christopher E. Brennen, Catherine S. Brantley, and Angel Ruiz-Angulo, "Solving the Mystery of Booming Sand Dunes," *Geophysical Research Letters* 34 (2007), doi: 10.1029/2007GL030276; Frank Kühnemann, "Physics of the Sand" (presentation, Physics Department, German University in Cairo, 3 March 2008), http://physics.guc.edu.eg/pdfs/BoomingSand.pdf

126 Measured annotated groundplan of the temple of Serabit al-Khadim, 1820, XX.D.1, Deposit/Bankes of Kingston Lacy and Corfe Castle, Dorset History Centre, Dorchester.

127 Jean-François Champollion, *Notice descriptive* (Paris: Firmin Didot, 1844–89), 2:691.

128 Jean-François Champollion, *Lettres à M. le Duc de Blacas d'Aulps* (Paris: Firmin Didot, 1826), pl. VIIIbis, [F], [G].

129 Louis Maurice Adolphe Linant de Bellefonds to William John Bankes, 15 April 1821, HJ 1/147, Deposit/Bankes of Kingston Lacy and Corfe Castle, Dorset History Centre, Dorchester.

130 Schulenburg-Minutoli, *Mes souvenirs*, 1:111–12.

131 "1821" corrected; Schulenburg-Minutoli, *Mes souvenirs*, 1:111–12.

132 Schulenburg-Minutoli, *Mes souvenirs*, 1:114–22.

133 Schulenburg-Minutoli, *Mes souvenirs*, 1:136–37.

134 "Mr. Drovetti lately set out for Syria with General Minutolo, who is travelling on account of the Government of Prussia; but their journey seems to have been suddenly interrupted"; Robert Thurburn to William John Bankes, 9 May 1821, Deposit/Bankes of Kingston Lacy and Corfe Castle, Dorset History Centre, Dorchester.

135 Henry Salt to William John Bankes, 14 December 1822, in Usick, *Adventures in Egypt and Nubia*, 165.

136 Holt lists the final destruction of the Mamluks, the revival of trade with Nubia, the capture of slaves, and the exploitation of natural resources such as gold; Holt, *A Modern History of the Sudan*, 35–37.

137 Khaled Fahmy, "The Era of Muhammad 'Ali Pasha, 1805–1848," in *The Cambridge History of Egypt*, vol. 2, *Modern Egypt from 1517 to the End of the Twentieth Century*, ed. Martin W. Daly (Cambridge: Cambridge University Press, 1998), 153.

138 McGregor, *A Military History*, 74; Arthur E. Robinson, "The Conquest of the Sudan by the Wali of Egypt, Muhammad Ali Pasha, 1820–1824," [Part I], *Journal of the Royal African Society* 25, no. 97 (1925): 48–49.

139 Mohamed Rifaat Pasha, *The Awakening of Modern Egypt* (Cairo: The Palm Press, 2005), 30–31.

140 Sammarco, *Alessandro Ricci*, 157.

141 Fahmy, "The Era of Muhammad 'Ali Pasha," 153.

142 McGregor, *A Military History*, 68.

143 Fahmy, "The Era of Muhammad 'Ali Pasha," 153.

144 "There is a general outcry against the cruelty of the Deftardar Bey, who is committing all sorts of horrors. It is better, however, to say nothing, or else it will only the more confirm his erroneous notion that we go up to spy the land," Halls, *The Life and Correspondence*, 2:187.

145 Halls, *The Life and Correspondence*, 2:154.

146 Cornevin, *Histoire de l'Afrique*, 261.

147 Shinnie, *Linant de Bellefonds*, publishes the copy kept at Kingston Lacy, limited to the parts of the journey between 27 August 1821 and 14 June 1822; the copy kept at the Bibliothèque Centrale des Musées Nationaux for the periods 15 June to 30 August 1821 and 11 June to 24 July 1822 is published in Jean Vercoutter, "Journal d'un voyage en Basse Nubie de Linant de Bellefonds," *Bulletin de la Société Française d'Égyptologie* 37–38 (1963): 39–64, and Jean Vercoutter, "Journal d'un voyage en Basse Nubie de Linant de Bellefonds (suite)," *Bulletin de la Société Française d'Égyptologie* 41 (1964): 23–32; Sammarco, *Alessandro Ricci*, 17–32, publishes fragments of the same manuscript.

148 Bankes, *Narrative*, 354–424.

149 Frédéric Cailliaud, *Voyage à Méroé, au Fleuve Blanc, au-delà de Fâzoql dans le midi du royaume de Sennâr, à Syouah et dans cinq autres oasis: fait dans les années 1819, 1820, 1821 et 1822: accompagné de Cartes géographiques, de Planches représentant les monuments de ces contrées, avec des détails relatifs à l'état moderne et à l'histoire naturelle* (Paris: Imprimerie Royale, 1826).

150 George B. English, *A Narrative of the Expedition to Dongola and Sennaar, under the Command of His Excellence Ismael Pasha, Undertaken by Orders of His Highness Mehemmed Ali Pasha, Viceroy of Egypt* (London: John Murray, 1822).

151 George Waddington and Barnard Hanbury, *Journal of a Visit to Some Parts of Ethiopia* (London: John Murray, 1822).

152 Bankes, *Narrative*, 2:354.

153 Not Jomard, but Pierre-Constant Letorzec.

154 Bankes, *Narrative*, 2:355–56.

155 Henry Salt to William John Bankes, 10 October 1821, HJ 1/159, Deposit/Bankes of Kingston Lacy and Corfe Castle, Dorset History Centre, Dorchester.

156 Again, Letorzec.

157 "A party of Prussian naturalists who understand well the drying of plants and skinning of frogs, but nothing more." Henry Salt to William John Bankes, 6 January 1822, HJ 1/169, Deposit/Bankes of Kingston Lacy and Corfe Castle, Dorset History Centre, Dorchester.

158 Henry Salt to William John Bankes, 6 January 1822, HJ 1/169, Deposit/Bankes of Kingston Lacy and Corfe Castle, Dorset History Centre, Dorchester.

159 Henry Salt to William John Bankes, 6 January 1822, HJ 1/169, Deposit/Bankes of Kingston Lacy and Corfe Castle, Dorset History Centre, Dorchester.

160 Sylvie Cauville, *Le Zodiaque d'Osiris* (Leuven: Peeters, 1997).

161 Clayton, *The Rediscovery of Ancient Egypt*, 101.

162 Curto and Donatelli, *Bernardino Drovetti*, 190; "You have doubtless learned from the French papers the robbery of the circular hemisphere at Dendera," Henry Salt to William John Bankes, 2 May 1821, HJ 1/153, Deposit/Bankes of Kingston Lacy and Corfe Castle, Dorset History Centre, Dorchester.

163 "A terrible rain which fell at this place in 1819 injured every thing; the water penetrated into the tomb, and ever since the stone has suffered greatly from the damp," D'Athanasi, *A Brief Account*, 14.

164 Richard B. Parkinson and Patricia Usick, "The History of the Nebamun Wall Paintings: An Archival Investigation," in *The Nebamun Wall Paintings: Conservation, Scientific Analysis and Display at the British Museum*, ed. Andrew Middleton and Ken Uprichard (London: Archetype Publications, 2008), 5–15.

165 Usick, *Adventures in Egypt and Nubia*, 40n14; Maria Carmela Betrò, ed., *Ippolito Rosellini and the Dawn of Egyptology: Original Drawings and Manuscripts of the Franco-Tuscan Expedition to Egypt (1828–29) from the Biblioteca Universitaria di Pisa* (London: Golden House Publications, 2010), 120–27; Maria Carmela Betrò, ed., *Lungo il Nilo: Ippolito Rosellini e la Spedizione Franco-Toscana in Egitto (1828–1829)* (Florence: Giunti, 2010), 184–87.

166 "I will not forget to send you the coloured sketch you desire of the dancing girls," Henry Salt to William John Bankes, 14 December 1822, HJ 1/187, Deposit/Bankes of Kingston Lacy and Corfe Castle, Dorset History Centre, Dorchester.

167 Daniele Salvoldi and Simon Delvaux, "The Lost Chapels of Elephantine: Preliminary Results of a Reconstruction Study through Archival Documents," in *Proceedings of the XI International Congress of Egyptologists, Florence, Italy, 23–30 August 2015*, ed. Gloria Rosati and Maria Cristina Guidotti (Oxford: Archaeopress, 2017), 552–58.

168 Shinnie, *Linant de Bellefonds*, 1.

169 Johann H.K.M. von Minutoli, *Reise zum Tempel des Jupiter Ammon in der Libyschen Wüste und nach Ober-Aegypten in den Jahren 1820 und 1821, nach den Tagebüchern Sr. Excellenz herausgegeben und mit Beilagen begleitet von Dr. E.H. Toelken* (Berlin: Rücker, 1824), 141–42.

170 Jay Spaulding, "The Government of Sinnar," *The International Journal of African Historical Studies* 6 (1973): 23–24.

171 Sammarco, *Alessandro Ricci*, 18–19.

172 Bankes, *Narrative*, 382–83.

173 Sammarco, *Alessandro Ricci*, 20–21.

174 Louis Maurice Adolphe Linant de Bellefonds to Henry Salt, 15(?) January 1822, HJ 1/162, Deposit/Bankes of Kingston Lacy and Corfe Castle, Dorset History Centre, Dorchester.

175 Louis Maurice Adolphe Linant de Bellefonds to Henry Salt, 20 March 1822, HJ 1/162, Deposit/Bankes of Kingston Lacy and Corfe Castle, Dorset History Centre, Dorchester.

176 Arabic شاويش *(shawish)*, 'sergeant.'

177 Henry Salt to William John Bankes, 2 May 1821, HJ 1/153, Deposit/Bankes of Kingston Lacy and Corfe Castle, Dorset History Centre, Dorchester.

178 Shinnie, *Linant de Bellefonds*, 86.

179 Shinnie, *Linant de Bellefonds*, 86–87.

180 Louis Maurice Adolphe Linant de Bellefonds to Henry Salt, 17 December 1821, HJ 1/162, Deposit/Bankes of Kingston Lacy and Corfe Castle, Dorset History Centre, Dorchester.

181 Samuel Briggs to William John Bankes(?), 22 November 1821, HJ 1/161, Deposit/Bankes of Kingston Lacy and Corfe Castle, Dorset History Centre, Dorchester.

182 Henry Salt to William Hamilton, 10 October 1821, HJ 1/160, Deposit/Bankes of Kingston Lacy and Corfe Castle, Dorset History Centre, Dorchester.

183 Henry Salt to William John Bankes, 2 May 1821, HJ 1/153, Deposit/Bankes of Kingston Lacy and Corfe Castle, Dorset History Centre, Dorchester.

184 Ricci actually mixes these two stops, placing Berber to the south of Shendi.

185 A common type of boat; see Ricci's own note [a] in chapter 10.

186 Henry Salt to William John Bankes, 2 May 1821, HJ 1/153, Deposit/Bankes of Kingston Lacy and Corfe Castle, Dorset History Centre, Dorchester.

187 Henry Salt to William John Bankes, 22 September 1822, HJ 1/183, Deposit/Bankes of Kingston Lacy and Corfe Castle, Dorset History Centre, Dorchester.

188 Pierre-Constant Letorzec.

189 Halls, *The Life and Correspondence*, 2:185.

190 Deborah Manley and Peta Rée, *Henry Salt: Artist, Traveller, Diplomat, Egyptologist* (London: Libri, 2001), 70.

191 Driault, *La formation*, **90**.

192 Curto and Donatelli, *Bernardino Drovetti*, 136.

193 Manley and Rée, *Henry Salt*, 277–78.

194 Quoting the *Gazzetta Fiorentina*, 9 October 1822; Sammarco, *Alessandro Ricci*, 4.

195 Sammarco, *Alessandro Ricci*, 3.

196 Félix Mengin, *Histoire de l'Égypte sous le gouvernement de Mohammed-Aly: ou, Récit des événemens politiques et militaires qui ont eu lieu depuis le départ des Français jusqu'en 1823* (Paris: A. Bertrand, 1823), 192n1.

197 Usick, *Adventures in Egypt and Nubia*, 165.

198 Henry Salt to William John Bankes, 2 May 1821, HJ 1/153, Deposit/Bankes of Kingston Lacy and Corfe Castle, Dorset History Centre, Dorchester.

199 Alessandro Ricci to Patrizio Rontani, 12 September 1822, quoted in Sammarco, *Alessandro Ricci*, 158.

200 Sammarco, *Alessandro Ricci*, 159.

201 Ernesto Verrucci Bey and Angelo Sammarco, *Il contributo degl'Italiani ai progressi scientifici e pratici della medicina in Egitto sotto il regno di Mohammed Ali: Ricerche e documenti inediti a cura di E. Verrucci Bey e A. Sammarco* (Cairo: Tip. A. Lencioni & Co., 1928). The "note [s]" referred to here is part of the "Medical Memoir," which is not included in this volume.

202 Shinnie, *Linant de Bellefonds*, 80.

203 Ludwig Keimer, "Glanures II: Les deux Botzaris," *Cahiers d'histoire égyptienne* 7, no. 3 (1955): n. 3, 196; Richard L. Hill, *A Biographical Dictionary of the Anglo-Egyptian Sudan* (Oxford: Clarendon Press, 1951), 133.

204 Keimer, "Glanures II," 202. According to Robinson, "The Conquest of the Sudan," 52, Gentili was wounded at the battle of Jebel Daiqa on 4 December and died four days later.

205 McGregor, *A Military History*, 77.

206 McGregor, *A Military History*, 77.

207 Jason Thompson, *Sir Gardner Wilkinson and His Circle* (Austin: University of Texas Press, 1992), 41.

208 Manley and Rée, *Henry Salt*, 204.

209 Henry Salt to William John Bankes, 6 January 1822, HJ 1/169, Deposit/Bankes of Kingston Lacy and Corfe Castle, Dorset History Centre, Dorchester.

210 Sammarco, *Alessandro Ricci*, 159.

Notes to chapter 4

1 George Waddington and Barnard Hanbury, *Journal of a Visit to Some Parts of Ethiopia* (London: John Murray, 1822).

2 Dixon Denham, Hugh Clapperton, and Walter Oudnay, *Narrative of Travels and Discoveries in Northern and Central Africa in the Years 1822, 1823 and 1824* (Boston: Cummings, Hilliard & Co., 1826).

3 Frédéric Cailliaud, *Voyage à Méroé, au Fleuve Blanc, au-delà de Fâzoql dans le midi du royaume de Sennâr, à Syouah et dans cinq autres oasis: fait dans les années 1819, 1820, 1821 et 1822: accompagné de Cartes géographiques, de Planches représentant les monuments de ces contrées, avec des détails relatifs à l'état moderne et à l'histoire naturelle* (Paris: Imprimerie Royale, 1826).

4   "Usirei-Akenkheres" is a defective spelling adopted by early Egyptologists (Champollion and Rosellini); Ricci here means Seti (I) Menmaatra.

5   Edda Bresciani, "Il richiamo della piramide: J.-F. Champollion e I. Rosellini in Egitto," in *La Piramide e la Torre: Duecento anni di archeologia egiziana*, ed. Edda Bresciani (Pisa: Cassa di Risparmio di Pisa, 2000), 24.

6   Ms. quoted in Angelo Sammarco, *Alessandro Ricci e il suo giornale dei viaggi*, vol. 2, *Documenti inediti o rari* (Cairo: Société Royale de Géographie d'Égypte, 1930), 5.

7   Jean-François Champollion to Jacques-Joseph Champollion-Figeac, 17 February 1825; published in Sammarco, *Alessandro Ricci*, 142.

8   Jean-François Champollion to Jean-Nicolas Huyot, 26 February 1825; published in Sammarco, *Alessandro Ricci*, 143.

9   Jean-François Champollion to Jacques-Joseph Champollion-Figeac, 17 February 1825; published in Sammarco, *Alessandro Ricci*, 141.

10 Quoted in Sammarco, *Alessandro Ricci*, 146.

11 Jean-François Champollion to Costanzo Gazzera, 29 June 1825; published in Sammarco, *Alessandro Ricci*, 144.

12 Champollion, who here follows Manetho's terminology, is referring to the Hyksos.

13 Jean-François Champollion to Jacques-Joseph Champollion-Figeac, 2 July 1825; published in Sammarco, *Alessandro Ricci*, 146.

14 Ippolito Rosellini to Neri Corsini, 6 June 1836; published in Sammarco, *Alessandro Ricci*, 42–43.

15 Alessandro Ricci to Ippolito Rosellini, 16 October 1827; published in Sammarco, *Alessandro Ricci*, 161.

16 Studi egiziani, Ms. 297a, 12 recto–verso, Fonds Rosellini, Biblioteca Universitaria, Pisa.

17 Edda Bresciani, "I Lorena e l'Egitto svelato," in *Sovrani nel Giardino d'Europa: Pisa e i Lorena*, ed. Romano Paolo Coppini and Alessandro Tosi (Pisa: Pacini Editore, 2008), 162.

18 Henry Salt would unfortunately die in October 1827.

19 Alessandro Ricci to Ippolito Rosellini, 16 October 1827; published in Sammarco, *Alessandro Ricci*, 160–61.

20 Giuseppe Gabrieli, *Ippolito Rosellini e il suo Giornale della Spedizione Letteraria Toscana in Egitto negli anni 1828–1829* (Rome: Reale Società Geografica Italiana, 1925), 190.

21 Gabrieli, *Ippolito Rosellini*, 22.

22 Gabrieli, *Ippolito Rosellini*, 22.

23 Ms. 948, c. 6, Fonds Rosellini, Biblioteca Universitaria, Pisa.

24 Ms. 948, c. 6, Fonds Rosellini, Biblioteca Universitaria, Pisa.

25 Maria Carmela Betrò, ed., *Ippolito Rosellini and the Dawn of Egyptology: Original Drawings and Manuscripts of the Franco-Tuscan Expedition to Egypt (1828–29) from the Biblioteca Universitaria di Pisa* (London: Golden House Publications, 2010); Maria Carmela Betrò, ed., *Lungo il Nilo: Ippolito Rosellini e la Spedizione Franco-Toscana in Egitto (1828–1829)* (Florence: Giunti, 2010).

26 Folder 21, Italian Fonds, National Archives of Egypt, Cairo.

27 Latin, 'What is delayed is not lost,' apparently a quotation of a distich by John Owen (1564–1622).

28 This second letter is not to be found in Drovetti's epistolary edited by Curto and Donatelli (1985) nor in the older edition by Marro (1940), and therefore must be considered unpublished; Folder 23, Italian Fonds, National Archives of Egypt, Cairo.

29 Silvio Curto and Laura Donatelli, eds., *Bernardino Drovetti Epistolario* (Milan: Cisalpino Goliardica, 1985), 551–52.

30 Christiane Ziegler, Hervé Champollion, and Diane Harlé, *L'Égypte de Jean-François Champollion: Lettres et journaux de voyage (1828–1829)* (Paris: Jean-Paul Mangès, 1989), 48.

31 Gabrieli, *Ippolito Rosellini*, 18–19.

32 Carlo de Rossetti to Vittorio Fossombroni, 11 September 1828, Folder 19, Italian Fonds, National Archives of Egypt, Cairo. Same subject in a letter to the governor of Livorno; Carlo de Rossetti to Paolo Garzoni Venturi, 10 September 1828, Folder 18, Italian Fonds, National Archives of Egypt, Cairo.

33 Ippolito Rosellini to Neri Corsini, 19 April 1830; published in Sammarco, *Alessandro Ricci*, 37.

34 Ziegler, Champollion, and Harlé, *L'Égypte*, 86.

35 Ziegler, Champollion, and Harlé, *L'Égypte*, 61.

36 Gabrieli, *Ippolito Rosellini*, 112.

37 Ippolito Rosellini to Leopold II of Tuscany, 24 November 1828, Ms. 379, 24r, Fonds Rosellini, Biblioteca Universitaria, Pisa.

38 Ziegler, Champollion, and Harlé, *L'Égypte*, 70.

39 Gabrieli, *Ippolito Rosellini*, 32.

40 Ziegler, Champollion, and Harlé, *L'Égypte*, 94.

41 Gabrieli, *Ippolito Rosellini*, 154–55. Piccinini (given name unknown) was an Italian excavator in the service of Ioannis Anastasi, merchant and consul general of Sweden-Norway to Egypt. He lived in the Theban West Bank. Warren R. Dawson, Morris L. Bierbrier, and Eric P. Uphill, *Who Was Who in Egyptology* (London: Egypt Exploration Society, 1995), 33–34.

42 A military or administrative title.

43 Gabrieli, *Ippolito Rosellini*, 170.

44 Ziegler, Champollion, and Harlé, *L'Égypte*, 152; Gabrieli, *Ippolito Rosellini*, 132.

45 Ziegler, Champollion, and Harlé, *L'Égypte*, 172.

46 Jean-François Champollion, *Lettres écrites d'Égypte et de Nubie, en 1828 et 1829* (Paris: Firmin Didot, 1833), 2:203.

47 XII.C.6, Deposit/Bankes of Kingston Lacy and Corfe Castle, Dorset History Centre, Dorchester; Nos. 107 and 108, Museo Egizio, Florence.

48 Jean-François Champollion, *Notice descriptive* (Paris: Firmin Didot, 1844–89), 1:35.

49 Champollion, *Lettres écrites d'Égypte et de Nubie*, 2:187.

50 Champollion, *Notice descriptive*, 1:35.

51 Gabrieli, *Ippolito Rosellini*, 177–78.

52 Gabrieli, *Ippolito Rosellini*, 54.

53 Arabic قائم مقام, 'colonel.'

54 Gabrieli, *Ippolito Rosellini*, 78.

55 Giacomo MacArdle to Ippolito Rosellini, 10 December 1829, Folder 23, Italian Fonds, National Archives of Egypt, Cairo. In the published correspondence of Lord Burghersh there is no mention of Ricci; cf. Rachel Weigall, *Correspondence of Lord Burghersh Afterwards Eleventh Earl of Westmorland, 1808–1840* (London: John Murray, 1912).

56 Carlo de Rossetti to Ippolito Rosellini, 22 December 1828 (he attaches more than one letter for Ricci); Giacomo MacArdle to Ippolito Rosellini, 14 April 1829 (one letter); Giacomo MacArdle to Ippolito Rosellini, 22 May 1829 (two letters); Carlo de Rossetti to Ippolito Rosellini, 29 May 1829 (one letter); Giacomo MacArdle to Ippolito Rosellini, 25 August 1829 (one letter), Folder 23, Italian Fonds, National Archives of Egypt, Cairo.

57 Alessandro Ricci to Girolamo Bardi, 26 August 1828, published in *Antologia* 32 (1828): 141; republished in Sammarco, *Alessandro Ricci*, 162–63.

58 Here Raddi clumsily uses a reference style of his own invention. The standard way to refer to the grand duke of Tuscany was "Imperial and Royal Highness"—"Imperial Highness" because he was an archduke of Austria, and "Royal Highness" since the time of Grand Duke Cosimo III (1691).

59 Eddkomm stands for Idku, Boures for Burullus, and Mengaleh for Manzala, all Delta lakes very close to the Mediterranean coast.

60 Giuseppe Raddi to Ippolito Rosellini, 7 May 1829, Folder 23, Italian Fonds, National Archives of Egypt, Cairo.

61 Flora Silvano, "Memorie d'Egitto a Pisa," in *La Piramide e la Torre: Duecento anni di archeologia egiziana*, ed. Edda Bresciani (Pisa: Cassa di Risparmio di Pisa, 2000), 181.

62 Giuseppe Raddi to Ippolito Rosellini, 28 July 1829, Folder 23, Italian Fonds, National Archives of Egypt, Cairo.

63 Alessandro Ricci to Bernardino Drovetti, 16 January 1829; published in Sammarco, *Alessandro Ricci*, 164 and in Curto and Donatelli, *Bernardino Drovetti*, 583.

64 Edda Bresciani, "De Jean-François Champollion à Angelica, le 6 décembre 1827: la lettre retrouvée. Un nouveau portrait de Champollion à Pise," *Bulletin de la Société Française d'Égyptologie* 119 (1990): 21–24; Flora Silvano, *La Collezione Picozzi* (Pisa: ETS, 1996), 42–43.

65 Gino Benvenuti and Gianfranco Benvenuti, *Vita di Ippolito Rosellini, padre dell'Egittologia italiana* (Pisa: Giardini, 1987), 72, 74.

66 Ippolito Rosellini to Giuseppe Acerbi, 20 February 1832, Folder 17, Italian Fonds, National Archives of Egypt, Cairo.

67 Ippolito Rosellini to Neri Corsini, 26 January 1831, published in Sammarco, *Alessandro Ricci*, 39.

68 Ippolito Rosellini to Neri Corsini, 28 January 1831, published in Sammarco, *Alessandro Ricci*, 42; original (examined to correct a date mistake) is Ms. 379, c. 70v, Fonds Rosellini, Biblioteca Universitaria, Pisa.

69 Ippolito Rosellini to Neri Corsini, 14 February 1831, Ms. 379, c. 72v, Fonds Rosellini, Biblioteca Universitaria, Pisa.

70 Heinrich Hase to Bernhard August von Lindenau, 14 May 1831, Akten der Königlichen Antiken-Sammlung (1830–1842), Staatliche Kunstsammlungen, Dresden.

71 Acquisition of a collection of miniatures of Ricci from Florence to enrich the collection of Karl Ferdinand Friedrich von Naglers, 1831, I. HA Rep. 137, I Nr. 19: Erwerbung von Holzschnittsammlungen und Kupferstichen durch die Artistische Kommission; Sale of a collection of miniature paintings of

Dr. Alessandro Ricci from Siena to the Egyptian Museum in Berlin, 1838(?), I. HA Rep. 81 Florenz/T nach 1807, Nr. 43: Forderungen und Unterstützungen, Geheimes Staatsarchiv Preußischer Kulturbesitz, Berlin. It was a collection of 121 fragments of parchment, apparently cut-out drop caps from large religious manuscripts, mainly choral books. Despite Ricci's claim that they were "from the School of Giotto," the presence of St. Bernardino of Siena in one of the illuminations dates the lot to the Renaissance, since this saint was canonized only in 1450. I am thankful to Dr. Paolo Bertelli and Prof. Massimiliano Bassetti, University of Verona, for their invaluable comments on the issue.

72 Giuseppe Acerbi to Ippolito Rosellini, 8 January 1832, Folder 17, Italian Fonds, National Archives of Egypt, Cairo.

73 Alessandro Ricci to Giuseppe Passalacqua, 12 July 1831, Sale of a collection of miniature paintings of Dr. Alessandro Ricci from Siena to the Egyptian Museum in Berlin, 1838(?), I. HA Rep. 81 Florenz/T nach 1807, Nr. 43: Forderungen und Unterstützungen, Geheimes Staatsarchiv Preußischer Kulturbesitz, Berlin.

74 Giuseppe Acerbi to Ippolito Rosellini, 8 January 1832, Folder 17, Italian Fonds, National Archives of Egypt, Cairo.

75 Giuseppe Acerbi to Ippolito Rosellini, 31 May 1833, Folder 23, Italian Fonds, National Archives of Egypt, Cairo.

76 Ippolito Rosellini to Giuseppe Acerbi, 15 July 1833, Folder 25, Italian Fonds, National Archives of Egypt, Cairo.

77 Ansano Baroni to Giuseppe Passalacqua, 20 March 1837, Sale of a collection of miniature paintings of Dr. Alessandro Ricci from Siena to the Egyptian Museum in Berlin, 1838(?), I. HA Rep. 81 Florenz/T nach 1807, Nr. 43: Forderungen und Unterstützungen, Geheimes Staatsarchiv Preußischer Kulturbesitz, Berlin.

78 A very cultured writer and politician, in 1823 he presented a project for a Tuscan constitution. In 1848, he became at first a member of the constituent assembly and then president of a short-lived cabinet. He cofounded the journal *Antologia* with Vieussex in 1821, and then became a member of the Tuscan Senate in 1848 and senator of the Kingdom of Italy in 1860; Elena Fasano Guarini, Giuseppe Petralia, and Paolo Pezzino, *Storia della Toscana*, vol. 2, *Dal Settecento ad oggi* (Rome and Bari: Laterza, 2004), 25, 28, 30–31.

79 Guglielmo Enrico Saltini, *Giuseppe Angelelli pittore toscano, ricordo biografico* (Florence: F. Bencini, 1866), 148.

80 Petition of Gino Capponi to Leopold II of Tuscany, June 1832, published in Sammarco, *Alessandro Ricci*, 53–55.

81 Francesco Baldasseroni to Antonio Ramirez di Montalvo, 20 July 1832, published in Sammarco, *Alessandro Ricci*, 49–50.

82 Archivio di Stato di Firenze, Stato civile della restaurazione (1816–1860), Firenze, Morti, 1834, No. 170.

83 Petition of Francesco Pacini to Leopold II of Tuscany, 20 September 1834, published in Sammarco, *Alessandro Ricci*, 88–90.

84 Antonio Ramirez di Montalvo to Luigi Pratellesi, 10 December 1834, published in Sammarco, *Alessandro Ricci*, 84–88.

Notes to chapter 5

1 Heinrich Hase to Bernhard August von Lindenau, 14 May 1831, Akten der Königlichen Antiken-Sammlung (1830–1842), Staatliche Kunstsammlungen, Dresden.

2 Heinrich Hase to Bernhard August von Lindenau, 14 May 1831, Akten der Königlichen Antiken-Sammlung (1830–1842), Staatliche Kunstsammlungen, Dresden.

3 Gudrun Elsner, *Ägyptische Altertümer der Skulpturensammlung: Ausstellung im Albertinum zu Dresden, 30. Juli 1993–24. Juli 1994* (Dresden: Staatliche Kunstsammlungen, 1993), 6–11.

4 Francesco Marchetti, "Alessandro Ricci da Siena e la sua collezione a Dresda" (MA thesis, University of Pisa, 2004), 47.

5 Felicitas Weber, "Der Totenbuchpapyrus des Anch-ef-en-Amun aus Dresden (Aeg. 775)" (MA thesis, Rheinische Friedrich-Wilhelms-Universität Bonn, 2012), 181, pl. II.c.

6 Silvio Curto and Laura Donatelli, eds., *Bernardino Drovetti Epistolario* (Milan: Cisalpino Goliardica, 1985), 647.

7 Antonio Ramirez di Montalvo to Francesco Baldasseroni, 14 July 1832, published in Angelo Sammarco, *Alessandro Ricci e il suo giornale dei viaggi*, vol. 2, *Documenti inediti o rari* (Cairo: Société Royale de Géographie d'Égypte, 1930), 51–52.

8 Sammarco, *Alessandro Ricci*, 57.

9 Sammarco, *Alessandro Ricci*, 74.

10 Sammarco, *Alessandro Ricci*, 57.

11 Maria Cristina Guidotti, "A proposito di Deir el Medina prima della scoperta: un pezzo della collezione Ricci nel Museo Egizio di Firenze," in *L'Egitto fuori dell'Egitto: Dalla riscoperta all'egittologia. Atti del Convegno Internazionale, Bologna 26–29 marzo*, ed. Cristiana Morigi Govi, Silvio Curto, and Sergio Pernigotti (Bologna: CLUEB, 1991), 209–19; Maria Cristina Guidotti, "Dall'Egitto a Firenze via Pisa," in *La Piramide e la Torre: Duecento anni di archeologia egiziana*, ed. Edda Bresciani (Pisa: Cassa di Risparmio di Pisa, 2000), 154.

12 Sammarco, *Alessandro Ricci*, 74.

13 Sammarco, *Alessandro Ricci*, 59–60.

14 Antonio Ramirez di Montalvo to Francesco Baldasseroni, 14 July 1832, published in Sammarco, *Alessandro Ricci*, 51.

15 Giovanni Mapelli to Francesco Pacini, 30 March 1835, published in Sammarco, *Alessandro Ricci*, 95.

16 Arcangelo Michele Migliarini to Antonio Ramirez di Montalvo, 19 November 1832, published in Sammarco, *Alessandro Ricci*, 82.

17 Curto and Donatelli, *Bernardino Drovetti*, 203.

Notes to chapter 6

1 Ansano Baroni to Giuseppe Passalacqua, 20 March 1837, Sale of a collection of miniature paintings of Dr. Alessandro Ricci from Siena to the Egyptian Museum in Berlin, 1838(?), I. HA Rep. 81 Florenz/T nach 1807, Nr. 43: Forderungen und Unterstützungen, Geheimes Staatsarchiv Preußischer Kulturbesitz, Berlin.

2 Angelo Sammarco, *Alessandro Ricci e il suo giornale dei viaggi*, vol. 2, *Documenti inediti o rari* (Cairo: Société Royale de Géographie d'Égypte, 1930), vi.

3   Gloria Rosati, "Alessandro Ricci," in *Il Nilo sui Lungarni: Ippolito Rosellini, egittologo dell'Ottocento*, ed. Maria Cristina Guidotti (Pisa: Nistri-Lischi and Pacini Editori, 1982), 39; Warren R. Dawson, Morris L. Bierbrier, and Eric P. Uphill, *Who Was Who in Egyptology* (London: Egypt Exploration Society, 1995), 356.

4   Georges Douin, *Histoire du Soudan Égyptien*, vol. 1, *La pénétration, 1820–22* (Cairo: Société Royale de Géographie d'Égypte, 1944), 182–88, 211–38.

5   Daniele Salvoldi, "Alessandro Ricci's Travel Account: Story and Content of His Journal Lost and Found," *Egitto e Vicino Oriente* 32 (2009): 113–19.

Notes to chapter 7

1   Ippolito Rosellini to Neri Corsini, 6 June 1836, published in Angelo Sammarco, *Alessandro Ricci e il suo giornale dei viaggi*, vol. 2, *Documenti inediti o rari* (Cairo: Société Royale de Géographie d'Égypte, 1930), 43.

2   Jean-François Champollion was Knight of the Order of Saint Joseph, honor of the Imperial and Royal House of Habsburg-Lorraine, Grand Duchy of Tuscany.

3   Arcangelo Michele Migliarini to Antonio Ramirez di Montalvo, 19 November 1832, published in Sammarco, *Alessandro Ricci*, 81–82.

4   Antonio Ramirez di Montalvo to Francesco Pacini, 21 January 1835, published in Sammarco, *Alessandro Ricci*, 93.

5   Receipt of the papers belonging to the late Dr. Ricci, 27 January 1835, published in Sammarco, *Alessandro Ricci*, 93.

6   Giovanni Mapelli to Francesco Pacini, 30 March 1835, published in Sammarco, *Alessandro Ricci*, 95–96.

7   Edme-François Jomard, *Voyage à l'Oasis de Syouah, rédigé et publié par M. Jomard* (Paris: De Rignoux, 1823), pls III [2]–[4], VII [9]–[10], XIV, XV, XVI, XVII [1]–[3], XVIII [1].

8   Jean-François Champollion, *Lettres à M. le Duc de Blacas d'Aulps* (Paris: Firmin Didot, 1826), pls. VIIIbis, letters E, F, G; Jean-François Champollion, *Notice descriptive* (Paris: Firmin Didot, 1844–89), 2:689–92.

9   Johann H.K.M. von Minutoli, *Reise zum Tempel des Jupiter Ammon in der Libyschen Wüste und nach Ober-Aegypten in den Jahren 1820 und 1821, nach den Tagebüchern Sr. Excellenz herausgegeben und mit Beilagen begleitet von Dr. E.H. Toelken* (Berlin: Rücker, 1824), pls. X, XIII, XIV, XX, XXI, XXIII, XXIV.

10   Ippolito Rosellini, *Monumenti dell'Egitto e della Nubia: Monumenti Civili* (Pisa: Niccolò Capurro, 1836), pls. XLI [5], XLVIII [1], XCVIII [4], XCIX [1].

11   Giovanni Battista Belzoni, *Narrative of the Operations and Recent Discoveries within Pyramids, Temples, Tombs and Excavations in Egypt and Nubia; and of a Journey to the Coast of the Red Sea, in search of the Ancient Berenice; and another to the Oasis of Jupiter Ammon* (London: John Murray, 1820), pls. II, III, VI, VII, VIII, XIII, XV, XVII.

12   Patricia Usick, "The Egyptian Drawings of Alessandro Ricci in Florence: A List of Drawings from a Portfolio in the Museo Egizio di Firenze," *Göttinger Miszellen* 162 (1998): 73–92.

13   Document 62, Ms. 300.4, Folder 17, Fonds Rosellini, Biblioteca Universitaria, Pisa.

14 Document 22, Ms. 300.4, Folder 10, Fonds Rosellini, Biblioteca Universitaria, Pisa.

15 Document 250, Ms. 300.1 'piccolo,' Folder 61, and Document 250, Ms. 300.4, Folder 62, Fonds Rosellini, Biblioteca Universitaria, Pisa.

16 Daniele Salvoldi, *Catalogue of William John Bankes (1786–1855): Egyptian Drawings* (Dorchester: Dorset History Centre, 2011), https://www.dorsetforyou.gov.uk/dorsethistorycentre

17 Daniele Salvoldi, "A Treasure House of Egyptology: The Catalogue of William John Bankes' Egyptian Portfolio (1815–1822)," *National Trust Arts, Buildings, Collections Bulletin* (Summer 2012): 11–12; Daniele Salvoldi, "The Catalogue of William John Bankes' Egyptian Portfolio (1815–1822)," *Bulletin of the Association for the Study of Travel in Egypt and the Near East* 51 (2012): 20.

18 Susan M. Pearce, "Giovanni Battista Belzoni's Exhibition of the Reconstructed Tomb of Pharaoh Seti I in 1821," *Journal of the History of Collections* 12, no. 1 (2000): 109–25; Sue Giles, "The Belzoni Collection of Paintings of the Tomb of Sety I in the Collections of Bristol Museums, Galleries & Archives," in *L'Egitto in Età Ramesside: Atti del Convegno, Chianciano Terme, 17–18 Dicembre 2009*, ed. Daniela Picchi (Cinisello Balsamo: Silvana Editoriale, 2011), 19–26.

19 "Stele. National Trust Inventory Number 1257709," National Trust Collections, http://www.nationaltrustcollections.org.uk/object/1257709

20 Bertha Porter and Rosalind L.B. Moss, *Topographical Bibliography of Ancient Egyptian Hieroglyphic Texts, Reliefs, and Paintings*, vol. 1, *The Theban Necropolis*, part 1, *Private Tombs* (Oxford: Clarendon Press, 1960), 198 (4).

21 Bertha Porter and Rosalind L.B. Moss, *Topographical Bibliography of Ancient Egyptian Hieroglyphic Texts, Reliefs, and Paintings*, vol. 4, *Lower and Middle Egypt* (Oxford: Oxford University Press, 1934), 180 (14)–(15).

Notes to chapter 8

1   The numbering is the one used in Usick, "The Egyptian Drawings of Alessandro Ricci in Florence: A List of Drawings from a Portfolio in the Museo Egizio di Firenze," *Göttinger Miszellen* 162 (1998): 73–92.

2   Here and in all other instances where the original drawing was not the one published, or where the original was not found, this is because a later, more polished version was published.

3   Fernand Beaucour, Ynes Laissus, and Chantal Orgozo, *The Discovery of Egypt* (Paris: Flammarion, 1990), 176.

4   The signs transcribed by Ricci are unclear: it might be *fnd*, or another name for 'nose,' 'nostrils,' or a late spelling of sign Gardiner D 26 (profile view of the mouth spilling water) as a variation of Gardiner D 21.

5   John H. Taylor, *Egyptian Coffins* (Princes Risborough: Shire Publications Ltd., 1989) and John H. Taylor, *Death and the Afterlife in Ancient Egypt* (London: The British Museum Press, 2001).

6   Usick, "The Egyptian Drawings," 92.

7   Peter Pamminger, "Amun und Luxor: Der Widder und das Kultbild," *Beiträge zur Sudanforschung* 5 (1992): 93–138.

8   In this and similar instances where Ricci's originals are missing, Linant's drawings from the Dorchester collection, which are probably very similar, have been used.

The Manuscript of the *Travels*

9

Note on the Original Manuscript, the Typewritten Copy, and the Present Edition

The present edition of the *Travels* of Alessandro Ricci is based on the typescript housed at the National Archives of Egypt, Italian Fonds, Folder 61. It was entirely retyped by the author in 2009 and checked again for mistakes in 2014. Ricci's notes are placed at the end of the text and indicated with letters. Completion of gaps is marked in square brackets. Whenever toponyms have been identified, they are given in the current English spelling. The typescript is here reproduced in its entirety, with only the omission of small parts at the end: the list of plates and the short discussion of a theory on the purpose of the pyramids.

As Sammarco describes it, the original manuscript was quite large (30 × 21 cm), made up of 160 sheets written on both sides "with a clear, accurate, dense handwriting, not Ricci's own, though,"[1] amounting to 317 pages.[2] The text written by the copyist was revised and corrected by Ricci himself "in the text and in the margins."[3] Unfortunately, these revisions were copied in the typescript with no distinction and are now indistinguishable.

The *Travel to Nubia* occupied pages 1 to 52; the *Travel to the Temple of Jupiter-Amun*, pages 53 to 106; the *Travel to Mount Sinai*, pages 107 to 156; the *Travel to Sennar*, with the *Medical Memoir*, pages 157 to 317.

There are a few cases of parts missed by the copyist in the typescript and that were not corrected later: the present edition tries to reconstruct the missing parts through comparisons. There is also a missing line on page 45 of the original typescript.

Notes

1 Angelo Sammarco, "Ippolito Rosellini e Alessandro Ricci da Siena," in *Studi in Memoria di Ippolito Rosellini nel primo centenario della morte*, ed. Evaristo Breccia (Pisa: V. Lischi, 1949), 111.

2 "A manuscript of around 200 pages," Ippolito Rosellini to Neri Corsini, 6 June 1836, published in Angelo Sammarco, *Alessandro Ricci e il suo giornale dei viaggi*, vol. 2, *Documenti inediti o rari* (Cairo: Société Royale de Géographie d'Égypte, 1930), 43.

3 Sammarco, *Alessandro Ricci*.

10
Travels of Doctor Alessandro Ricci of Siena

Made in the Years 1818, 1819, 1820, 1821, 1822 in Nubia, to the Temple of Jupiter-Amun, Mount Sinai, and Sennar

Travel to Nubia

Rising from the degradation in which it had lain for a long time under the iron fist of the Mamluks, Egypt attracted the attention of many European travelers during the reign of the viceroy Muhammad Ali. The purpose of my travel in those regions was to copy hieroglyphs and describe the places I intended to visit, as much as my little knowledge of such things and time would allow. I would have probably succeeded in the first aim if extraordinary circumstances had not happened to me, as the reader will discover reading the account of my travels.

I left Siena, my home, in January 1817 and reached Livorno in order to embark. There, I had the opportunity to meet Isma'il Gibraltar, great admiral of the viceroy of Egypt,[1] who, when he heard my intention, wanted to grant me a recommendation letter for Yusif Boghos,[2] chief interpreter of the Egyptian pasha. With this letter and another obtained

---

1   Isma'il Gibraltar, agent of the viceroy Muhammad Ali, is attested in Livorno as early as March 1816 and in Malta back in 1814; Marco Zatterin, *Il gigante del Nilo: Storia e avventure del Grande Belzoni* (Bologna: Il Mulino, 2008), 45.

2   Boghos Yusufian (1775–1844), known also as Boghos Bey, was an Armenian from Smyrna belonging to a merchant family. He worked as translator for the British in the Egyptian Campaign. In 1807, after the evacuation of the British, he was appointed governor of Alexandria instead of an Ottoman officer. From 1823, he was first secretary of Muhammad Ali and in 1826 he was promoted to minister of trade. In the administrative restructuring of 1837, Boghos Bey became minister of trade and foreign affairs. He could speak Italian quite well. Cf. Rouben Adalian, "The Armenian Colony of Egypt during the Reign of Muhammad Ali, 1805–1848," *Armenian Review* 33, no. 2 (1980): 115–44; Robert Hunter, *Egypt under the Khedives, 1805–1879: From Household Government to Modern Bureaucracy* (Pittsburgh: University of Pittsburgh Press, 1984), 24; Warren R. Dawson, Morris L. Bierbrier, and Eric P. Uphill, *Who Was Who in Egyptology* (London: Egypt Exploration Society, 1995), 456; Giovanni Marro, *Il corpo epistolare di Bernardino Drovetti ordinato ed illustrato* (Rome: Reale Società di Geografia d'Egitto, 1940), 393; Khaled Fahmy, "The Era of Muhammad 'Ali Pasha, 1805–1848," in *The Cambridge History of Egypt*, vol. 2, *Modern Egypt from 1517 to the End of the Twentieth Century*, ed. Martin W. Daly (Cambridge: Cambridge University Press, 1998), 146.

by General Spannocchi,[3] at that time governor of Livorno, and addressed to the Austrian consul general in Cairo, I embarked on 2 February 1817 on the Egyptian frigate *Asia*, due to sail to Alexandria, and so I left Europe.

Short and very happy was my journey and on the 21st of the same month I landed in Alexandria. The first thing that one sees approaching the city is the famous column, which is a reminder of the unhappy fate of Pompey and the luck of Caesar.[4] Even though Mr. Savary proved with wise observations that it was erected to honor Septimus Severus, a long habit, and possibly the deep impression of that great event, account for the column keeping its traditional name.[5] Anyway, this monument reminds the traveler that he is about to step onto a land of ancient memories. His spirit is nevertheless affected by involuntary sadness when he enters into the streets of Alexandria. Built not far from the ruins of the ancient city of Alexander, which can be seen for some distance on the plain, it retains nothing of its past magnificence. The lighthouse, once so famous, collapsed, the streets are narrow and irregular, most of the inhabitants live covered in filthy rags. The countryside is deserted and bare, while buildings are built irregularly and without architecture. Only the *masharabieh*,[6] or balcony windows, are a most beautiful ornament of houses: they stretch out onto the streets and are closed on all sides by wooden grates, carved with much craftsmanship and painted in many colors, especially those of the rich. Altogether they produce a pleasant effect and are used by the inhabitants, particularly the women, as relaxation spots: lying languidly on the comfortable sofas, they enjoy the fresh air and amuse themselves watching unseen all that happens in the streets.

On the fourth day after my arrival in Alexandria I moved toward Cairo, walking among the many and bleak ruins of the ancient city: in six hours I reached Abu Qir, famous for the memorable victory of Lord Nelson;[7] here, a few wooden huts built on the beach are used by travelers as a restplace. In one of them I spent the night, lying on a bad bench and tormented

---

3   Baron Francesco Spannocchi-Piccolomini (1750–1822) held the office of civil and military governor of Livorno between 1796 and 1799 and then between 1814 and 1822; Massimo Sanacore, *Francesco Spannocchi governatore di Livorno tra Sette e Ottocento* (Livorno: Debatte, 2007).

4   Bertha Porter and Rosalind L.B. Moss, *Topographical Bibliography of Ancient Egyptian Hieroglyphic Texts, Reliefs, and Paintings*, vol. 4, *Lower and Middle Egypt* (Oxford: Oxford University Press, 1934), 3.

5   François Savary de Brèves (1560–1628), French ambassador to the Sublime Porte and orientalist, visited Egypt in 1605; cf. *Relation des voyages de Monsieur de Brèves, tant en Grèce, Terre Saincte et Aegypte qu'aux royaumes de Tunis et Arger, ensemble un traicté faict l'an 1604 entre le roy Henry le Grand et l'empereur des Turcs, et trois discours dudit sieur, le tout recueilly par le S.D.C.* [Jacques Du Castel] (Paris: N. Gasse, 1628); Jean Leclant, "De l'égyptophilie à l'égyptologie: érudits, voyageurs, collectionneurs et mécènes," *Comptes-rendus des séances de l'année—Académie des inscriptions et belles-lettres* 4 (1985): 640. Pompey's Pillar was in fact erected for Emperor Diocletian (244–311) after the victory over the usurpers Lucius Domitius Domitianus and Aurelius Achilleus (297–98).

6   Arabic مشربية (*mashrabiya*), lit. 'the place of drinking.' These are balconies enclosed by wooden screens and decorated with geometrical motifs.

7   The naval battle of Abu Qir was fought in the first two days of August 1798 by the British fleet under the command of Sir Horatio Nelson (1758–1805) and the French fleet commanded by François-Paul Brueys d'Aigalliers (1753–98). The British victory was total and the French admiral died in the fight. Francesco Frasca, "La vittoria della Royal Navy nella battaglia d'Abukir," *Informazioni della Difesa* 2 (2003): 49–58.

by mosquitoes. The fort, which is built in an advantageous position, was at that time about to be enlarged, and many engineers had already arrived for the task, also entrusted to fortify the whole coast.

I left Abu Qir the following day and walking on sandy soil, marked now and then by large stones to guide the travelers, I arrived in the evening at Rashid, or Rosetta. It is a city to the west of the Nile, populous, pleasant for the variety of the colored bricks employed to build its houses. The territory is fertile and the green countryside that surrounds the city delights the sight and contrasts with the desert crossed to reach it. There is much game meat, banana trees, and all sorts of products. Here, I rented a *canja*[a] to proceed in my journey and I shortly arrived at Fuwa, to the east. After the opening of the famous Mahmudiya Canal, distinguished and grandiose work undertaken by Muhammad Ali, viceroy of Egypt,[8] the city has now become a rival of Rosetta. In fact, while the trade of Rosetta is decaying by the day, that of Fuwa is growing and the flow of merchants is large and continuous. I stayed at Tarrana, to the west, for a short rest. Here a certain Mr. Baffi, Italian, established a nitre factory, which was very prosperous at the time I saw it.[9]

I continued my journey and I reached Cairo on the seventh day after I left Rosetta. I must confess that it was very painful for me during this journey to drink the water of the Nile, which I found repulsive because of its reddish color. I tried to make it up by adding lemon and sugar, thereby insulting the lightest and healthiest water in the world.

When I arrived in Cairo[10] I presented my recommendation letters and was introduced to foremost European families settled there. Among them I must remember with gratitude the family of Mr. Salt, British consul general, whose language I spoke, for the constant proofs of friendship and protection received under every circumstance during my stay in Egypt.

There was much talking in Cairo in those days about the enterprise of the Italian Giovanni Battista Belzoni, who, under the auspices and by the means of the same Mr. Salt, had recently opened many tombs at Thebes.[11] Among them, the very famous one of Biban al-Muluk,[12] believed by him to be the tomb of Psammetichus [Psamtik], but recognized with certainty by Champollion to be that of Pharaoh Usirei-Akenkheres I, twelfth king of the Eighteenth Diospolitan Dynasty. My first thought was to move there in order to draw all the most remarkable scenes in the tomb, and without further hesitation I set off for Thebes. On my way, I visited the pyramids of Giza. Because of the beautiful and interesting sculptures, I decided to stop there on my return in order to draw them, a thing that I actually

---

8   Works at the canal started in 1817 and ended only three years later thanks to a work force estimated at 300,000; Fahmy, "The Era of Muhammad 'Ali Pasha," 152.

9   Omar Baffi, pharmacist and businessperson in the service of Muhammad Ali; Luigi A. Balboni, *Gl'italiani nella civiltà egiziana del sec. XIX* (Alexandria: Stabilimento Tipo-Litografico V. Penasson, 1906), 249–50.

10   Around 5 March 1817. Between this date and what is narrated in the following paragraph around ten months elapsed, unrecorded. Ricci leaves for Thebes at the beginning of 1818.

11   The tomb of Ay (KV 23) in October 1816, the anonymous KV 25, and the tombs of Montuherkopshef (KV 19), Ramesses I (KV 21), and Seti I (KV 17) in October 1817; Zatterin, *Il gigante del Nilo*, 364–65.

12   Arabic بيبان الملوك (*biban al-muluk*), lit. 'the kings' gates,' the Valley of the Kings.

did, as I will explain further on. I passed Beni Suef, to the west, where the road that leads to Fayoum starts. Beyond Shaykh ʿIbada,[13] where there are the ruins of the ancient Antinoopolis, there are many rock tombs, all more or less sculpted and painted. In one of them I copied a scene that clearly explains how the ancient Egyptians used to transport their colossal statues.[14] The statue is carved in delicate bas-relief, the rest is painted; cf. plate 1. The immense number of columns, statues, and obelisks observed among the ruins made people believe that the Egyptians used large and complicated machineries in order to move them, but even the superficial examination of this scene demonstrates that, taking advantage of the flat and clayey Egyptian soil, and making it more slippery by continuously adding water during the transport, they could easily move large monuments without risk by the sole power of men. This scene shows how they placed the statue on a sort of sledge and secured it with many ropes. It was then pulled with large ropes by a great number of men arranged in many rows. Two officers, one standing on the statue with a metal instrument in his hands, give the signal to pull the sledge at the same time. Another man on the base of the statue waters the soil, so as to ease the movement of the sledge. Behind there are the heads of the workers, painted in larger size and better dressed, as customary in Egyptian art, other men assigned to carry the water, and others with a sort of lever on their shoulders in case of need. They all follow alongside of the convoy. Groups of celebrating people follow from the other side.

Not far from Shaykh ʿIbada, on the west bank on the Nile, there are the ruins of the very old temple of Ashmunayn: a superb portico with twelve columns stands out among the ruins of that famed example of Egyptian architecture.[15] The elegant style of the columns convinced me to draw them; plate 2. In some, the color is still well preserved. The ibis-headed figure on the columns, also repeated on the molding of the portico, gives rise to the belief that Thoth was worshiped in this temple. This is a god corresponding to the Hermes of the Greeks.

I visited the large rum factory and the sugar refinery recently established by Mr. Brine,[16] an Englishman very hospitable with all travelers, at al-Rairamun, a village to the west, not far from Ashmunayn. I then arrived in the evening at Asyut, capital of Upper Egypt, a large and populous city that keeps an active caravan trade with Sennar, Shendi, Berber, and other

---

13   Actually Deir al-Barsha.
14   The tomb of Djehutyhotep II at Deir al-Barsha; Porter and Moss, *Topographical Bibliography* 4:179–81 (Tomb No. 2). It was discovered in 1817 by the two English captains Charles Irby (1789–1845) and James Mangles (1786–1867). They state that drawings of this tomb were made also by Beechey; Charles L. Irby and James Mangles, *Travels in Egypt and Nubia, Syria, and Asia Minor; during the years 1817 & 1818* (London: T. White and Co. Printers, 1823), 164; Percy E. Newberry, *El-Bersha, Part I, (The tomb of Tehuti-hetep)* (London: Egypt Exploration Fund, 1895), pls. XII, XV.
15   The temple of Thoth-Hermes Trismegistus, built by Alexander the Great and Philip Arrhidaeus and destroyed in 1822; Porter and Moss, *Topographical Bibliography* 4:165–67.
16   M.D. Brine, an English trader who established, on behalf of the viceroy, a sugar refinery and a rum factory in Upper Egypt. He wrote letters (in Italian) to Drovetti; Marro, *Il corpo epistolare*, 397; Gasparo Menconi, *Notizie compendiate di Egitto di Gasparo Menconi di Lucca* (Lucca: Benedini e Rocchi, 1820), 29–30. Cf. also page 252.

places. Here I met Mr. Marucchi,[17] Italian physician of the Defterdar Bey,[18] governor of the city, who was later forced to follow the same bey in his expedition against Kordofan.

The village of Deir al-Ganadla, near Abu Tig, is famous as the place where boys are operated upon to become eunuchs.[19] Southward there is Qaw, to the east. The Arts will soon deplore the complete destruction of its beautiful ruins:[20] exposed to the first surge of the current, there is no inundation that does not take with it some of its beautiful columns, which for their beauty should be carefully moved elsewhere, in order to avoid their complete loss. It is convenient to believe that in ancient times the river bank was at this point much higher or that the Nile had a different course, because it is not possible that the ancient Egyptians built a temple in a place so much exposed to the inundations as it is now.

After Qaw I arrived at Tahta, to the west, and then reached Akhmim, to the east. The islands, or better sand banks, which are in the Nile between these two cities, are much frequented by crocodiles. I could reckon up to twenty all together in one place. These amphibians are not to be seen to the north of this spot, and much less in the vicinity of Cairo, for the reason—at least according to the common opinion—that they are afraid of continuous noise, especially the firing of cannons and other guns.

In Girga, which follows to the west, lives a European priest called Ladislao,[21] profound in the knowledge of oriental languages and especially Arabic, who has the habit of searching for and welcoming all the foreigners passing by: I am grateful to this philanthropist for his attention during my short stay in that city.

The best vases to filter Nile water are fabricated at Qena, a large and populous city to the east. These are made of clay and retain their color even after the firing: they are called

---

17   Corrected from "Marzucchi" in the original. He was the uncle of Amalia Nizzoli, wife of the Austrian consulate chancellor Giuseppe, and was an amateur antiquities collector.

18   Muhammad Bey Khusraw al-Daramali was sent by the viceroy at the head of an army of five thousand men to conquer Kordofan in 1821; Margaret Shinnie, *Linant de Bellefonds, Journal d'un Voyage à Meroe dans les années 1821–1822* (Khartoum: Antiquities Service Occasional Papers, 1958), 30; Édouard Driault, *La formation de l'empire de Mohamed Aly de l'Arabie au Soudan (1814–1823): correspondance des consuls de France en Égypte* (Cairo: Société Royale de Géographie d'Égypte, 1927), xxxvii.

19   Gabriel Baer, "Slavery in Nineteenth Century Egypt," *The Journal of African History* 8 (1967): 419; Ehud R. Toledano, "The Imperial Eunuchs of Istanbul: From Africa to the Heart of Islam," *Middle Eastern Studies* 20, no. 3 (1984): 383; Daniele Salvoldi, "Representations of Copts in Early Nineteenth-century Italian Travel Accounts," in *Studies in Coptic Culture: Transmission and Interaction*, ed. Mariam Ayad (Cairo: American University in Cairo Press, 2016), 132–33.

20   Bertha Porter and Rosalind L.B. Moss, *Topographical Bibliography of Ancient Egyptian Hieroglyphic Texts, Reliefs, and Paintings*, vol. 5, *Upper Egypt: Sites* (Oxford: Griffith Institute, Ashmolean Museum, 1962), 15–16. Ptolemaic temple (cartouche of Ptolemy IV and Arsinoë III) and colonnade building to the west of the temple destroyed by the Nile in 1821. The forecast of Ricci was possibly added after the fact. Destructions were already recorded by Bankes in 1815: "At 'Gau' nine columns of the temple still remained standing, but by their next visit only one remained and that fell soon after," Patricia Usick, *Adventures in Egypt and Nubia: The Travels of William John Bankes (1786–1855)* (London: The British Museum Press, 2002), 51.

21   A Catholic missionary of the Sacred Congregation for the Propagation of the Faith, occasionally working as an excavation agent for Drovetti and in epistolary contact with him.

by the Arabs *qulla*. Two types exist: large, used excusively to filter water; small and very thin, used to cool water by exposing the vases, which are particularly porous, to the current or the wind.

Dendera, the ancient Tentyra, is famous for its temple, which is the best preserved of Egypt.[22] It lies three miles inland and was possibly founded by Ptolemy I. It is also famous for its zodiac.[23] During my journey to Sennar, I met Mr. Le Lorrain while transferring this beautiful monument to Europe.[24]

From Dendera to Thebes, all the villages to the east of the Nile are built directly on the banks, while to the west they are in a higher position and far from the river, in order not to be exposed to the inundations.

I finally arrived at Thebes: the majestic ruins of the large City of the Hundred Gates fill the traveler with admiration. I naively confess that, finding myself among this imposing mass of wonders, I was totally in awe. These ruins extend to a considerable surface on both banks of the Nile: Karnak and Luxor to the east, Qurna, the Memnonium, and Madinat Habu to the west. Even though I later visited all the ruins and explored almost all the caves, which used to be the tombs of the ancient Thebans, I consider it superfluous to describe them here, to avoid repetition of what has been narrated by many others on this subject. After I admired the wonderful remains of the Egyptian grandeur, I went to Biban al-Muluk, a league distant from the Nile, in the valley formed by a chain of mountains where there are the royal tombs explored by Belzoni. Here, there had been for some time Mr. Beechey,[25] secretary of the British General Consulate, to supervise the excavations ordered by Mr. Salt and to gather all the antiquities, which would form the valuable collection recently acquired[26] by the French government through Mr. Champollion. I chose to settle in a tomb close to Usirei's and planned to start my drawings, but the first time I penetrated the large, silent subterranean spaces, considering the immensity of the work I was about to start in such a heavy air, I was—I confess—about to give up. Finally, I overcame all aversion and began the work. For seven full months I used to spend eight, and frequently even twelve hours, every day in that gloomy abode, some hundred feet under the ground. I was almost buried among the ancient Egyptians, using wax candles, which, even though in large numbers, gave a gloomy light and contributed to making the air even impurer. Many times I was forced to go out to breathe. I was usually alone, because no Arab would accompany me since one of them had once fainted.

---

22 Bertha Porter and Rosalind L.B. Moss, *Topographical Bibliography of Ancient Egyptian Hieroglyphic Texts, Reliefs, and Paintings*, vol. 6, *Upper Egypt: Chief Temples* (Oxford: Griffith Institute, Ashmolean Museum, 1991), 41–110.

23 Porter and Moss, *Topographical Bibliography* 6:49–50.

24 Cf. "Travel to Sennar," 251.

25 Henry William Beechey (1789–1862), British artist and traveler, was secretary to Salt from 1815 to 1820; Dawson, Bierbrier, and Uphill, *Who Was Who*, 37; Patricia Usick, "Berth under the Highest Stars: Henry William Beechey in Egypt 1816–1819," in *Egypt through the Eyes of Travellers*, ed. Paul G. Starkey and Nadia El Kholy (Cambridge: ASTENE, 2002), 13–24.

26 The Salt Collection was acquired by Champollion on behalf of the Louvre Museum in February 1826.

Only two months after my arrival at Thebes, Belzoni also arrived. He examined my drawings and expressed his desire to purchase them. I showed interest in his proposal, but pointed out to him that, since the work was long, it was preferable to delay any engagement until I had finished, and I assured him that we would easily find an agreement. He was satisfied with my proposal and I kept working without interruption until the seventh month. Then, Belzoni shared with me his project of traveling to the Red Sea to discover the lost Berenike and explore the ancient desert road between that city and Egypt. He proposed that I join him, or, better, he forced me. I thought that since little was left to do in the tomb, I could delay the completion of the drawings until our return and I therefore prepared to set off. Mr. Beechey was also in the party.

On 16 September 1818, we embarked at Qurna, in the same spot where the terrain starts to become unequal and forms little hills, which gradually join the mountain chain, in the middle of which the ancient Egyptian monarchs placed their resting place. An extraordinary inundation of the Nile had raised the water three feet more than usual, so that during our navigation we witnessed the tearful consequences of this disaster. From our starting point to Edfu, to the west, we saw animals of every kind floating and even some human bodies. The palms and other trees uprooted by the stream floated in the river, mixed with scraps of houses destroyed by the waves, and for a long distance, all that we could see was a general devastation.

We landed on the east bank, half an hour beyond Edfu, in the small village seat of an Ababda shaykh.[27] He provided us with camels, food, and guides to continue the journey. It was our intention to visit also the emerald mines, already explored by Mr. Cailliaud.[28] This idea, imprudently expressed, excited the curiosity of an agha who had arrived the same day. He insisted on coming with us in this exploration and did not allow us to leave until we solemnly promised to wait for him at the first well in the desert, to proceed thence to the mines in his company. We left on the 23rd at dawn and after three hours we reached the well,[29] where we found a large number of Ababda Arabs who had descended from the nearby mountains to make their livestock drink. We waited the whole day in vain for the agha, who had promised to join us before the evening. On the morning of the 24th, since he did not show up, we continued our journey, and after almost four hours of forced march we came across two ruined enclosure walls, thirty-five feet apart from each other. The largest of the two measured fifty square feet. The walls, built with large stones in dry-wall technique,

---

27 Arabic شيخ (shaykh), 'elder,' the term also applies to a tribal chief. Ababda, "an arabized Beja tribe, who controlled camel transportation between Abu Hammad and Korosko by the desert route. Many became wealthy and settled at Dongola until the Mameluks drove them out," Shinnie, *Linant de Bellefonds*, 9.

28 This is a reference to Cailliaud's expedition undertaken in November the previous year and then published in two volumes, one posthumous: Frédéric Cailliaud, *Voyage à l'oasis de Thèbes et dans les déserts situés à l'orient et à l'occident de la Thébaïde fait pendant les années 1815, 1816, 1817 et 1818* (Paris: Imprimerie Royale, 1821–62).

29 Bir Abbad; Bertha Porter and Rosalind L.B. Moss, *Topographical Bibliography of Ancient Egyptian Hieroglyphic Texts, Reliefs, and Paintings*, vol. 7, *Nubia, the Deserts, and Outside Egypt* (Oxford: Griffith Institute, Ashmolean Museum, 1995), 321.

were five feet wide and even though sufficiently high, they must have been even higher in the past, judging from the large amount of ruined stones that can be found both inside and outside. The internal distribution demonstrates that these walls were originally divided into many rooms, no doubt to host the caravans that from Egypt transited to the Red Sea, and I guess that this was the first station of their journey.

After three more hours we reached Kanays,[30] where there is an Egyptian temple partly rock-cut and partly built. I drew its plan to the best I could due to the lack of time. Cf. plate 3, nos. 1–3.

The architecture of this temple is in good style and perfect craftsmanship, and looks to be very old. The portico is supported by four granite columns, while the vault of the temple is supported by four pillars cut in the rock. On the two sides of the main door there are statues of Isis and Osiris. To the rear of the sanctuary, and in each of the side rooms, there are three statues cut in the rock with the middle figure being a female. These statues are all more or less mutilated and their heads are damaged (cf. plan, no. 1). On the walls there are painted life-size figures, bowing in the act of presenting an offering. The color is still visible on some of them (no. 2). The hieroglyphs are superbly executed (no. 3). It is possible the two gods placed at the entrance of the main hall were worshiped in this temple.

We continued our journey on the 25th and at a certain distance from the temple we found more ruins of the same kind as those explored on the previous day. We all universally agreed they were the ruins of a second caravan station. The sandstone rocks covering the terrain made our path very difficult and the desert looked more horrible than usual, because the stone had blackened and it looked like we were walking on a black carpet. After nine continuous hours of march we reached Wadi Bayza,[31] to the north of which, on a granite rock, we saw some very well-preserved hieroglyphs. I intended to copy them before setting off, but since that very same day I decided not to proceed any further in the journey, I totally abandoned my intention. Belzoni wrote in his travel account of Berenike that from this point on I was forced to go back because I was sick.[32] Even though this was the pretext I used not to continue the journey, I must in fact declare that a quarrel that had arisen between us because of his rudeness was the real cause of our separation.

As a consequence of my decision, Mr. Beechey and Belzoni continued the journey on 26 September, and I took the road back to Thebes. Forcing the march extraordinarily, I reached the Nile on the second day and I spent a few days at the same Ababda shaykh's who had provided us with camels for the journey. Here I witnessed the humanity of this pious man who offered assistance to the poor inhabitants of some villages, gathering alternately

---

30 Kanays; Porter and Moss, *Topographical Bibliography* 7:321. Temple of Seti I, with later additions by Ramesses II and Ramesses VI.

31 Porter and Moss, *Topographical Bibliography* 7:326. Middle Kingdom graffiti.

32 "At this place Mr. Ricci, the doctor, was attacked with a violent disorder, and it was decided, that he should return the next morning, as it would increase if he advanced farther in the desert," Giovanni Battista Belzoni, *Narrative of the Operations and Recent Discoveries within Pyramids, Temples, Tombs and Excavations in Egypt and Nubia; and of a Journey to the Coast of the Red Sea, in search of the Ancient Berenice; and another to the Oasis of Jupiter Ammon* (London: John Murray, 1820), 307.

twice a week the poorest and serving them himself a soup and boiled mutton. The lunch was served in the open air, where those poor men, seated on the sand, would satiate themselves and sing the praises of their benefactor.

Back in Thebes with the intention of completing my work, I was surprised not to find my drawings, which I had left in the tomb. I asked the warden and he told me that the night before our departure Belzoni, accompanied by an Arab, had descended the tomb and come out with a bundle of sheets. I did not doubt any further that he had taken them despite our first agreement. I immediately understood it was unlikely I could get them back: I would have to suffer the arrogance of that overbearing man, as had happened with all who dealt with him. However, thinking that he could not have taken with him all the drawings, in order not to risk losing them in the desert, I deluded myself that I could find them; I carefully explored more than once all the tombs and caves around Biban al-Muluk. My search was vain and I decided to wait for him there. In the meantime, I settled in Qurna and explored the main ruins, making many drawings.

The scene copied in plate 4 exists in a tomb of Biban al-Muluk, not far from the one opened by Belzoni.[33] The subject is peculiar and if its meaning is not expressed in the line of hieroglyphs beside it, I do not think it will be easy to find out. Nevertheless, I think that the three seated figures represent the Nile, symbolized in different ways. It is well known that this river was worshiped as a god by the ancient Egyptians. First, I observe that all three are masculine, because very rarely women were painted in red in Egyptian art and also because there is no trace of the breasts, a feature never left out when depicting a female. These reasons, and especially the second one, exclude the possibility that the bull-head figure could be the Egyptian Venus, Hathor, who is often represented with this feature. Considering that the two figures with crocodile and tortoise heads perfectly suit the Nile, where they usually live, the last thing to be verified in order to validate my opinion is why the river is represented here also with a bull head. In ancient Greek, the term κέραια means at the same time 'horns' and 'branches of a river,' while another term, ταῦρος, means at the same time 'bull' and 'river.' This double meaning is the reason why rivers are mythologically portrayed under the appearance of bulls.[b] It does not matter that this used to happen among the Greeks and not the Egyptians because it would not be the first example of where the two mythologies mixed together and became one, common between the two civilizations. This is my opinion on this scene, an opinion that I do not claim to prove, but that, for the stated reasons, does not look completely unfounded.

Plate 5, copied in the same tomb, represents one of the few full-face figures in Egyptian art. No doubt this is a god since he is holding in his hands the key and the sceptre, ordinary symbols of divine life. The frame around this figure has the exact shape of a portable shrine, where family idols used to be placed. I have one in my collection very similar to this.[34]

---

33 Tomb KV 11, belonging to Ramesses III; Bertha Porter and Rosalind L.B. Moss, *Topographical Bibliography of Ancient Egyptian Hieroglyphic Texts, Reliefs, and Paintings*, vol. 1, *The Theban Necropolis*, part 2, *Royal Tombs and Smaller Cemeteries* (Oxford: Griffith Institute, Ashmolean Museum, 1999), 518–27.

34 An ushabti box.

Plate 6 is a painted bas-relief scene copied in a tomb of Qurna. The subject seems to be the initiation of the king into holy mysteries. One can clearly distinguish in this scene the priests from the monarch's servants. These are the two following him and the one in front with a feather and a ribbon, and maybe the two other bowing behind this. A noticeable thing in this scene is the gloves worn by the priests, something I have never seen in any other painting or sculpture. The limestone where this scene is carved is fine-grained and well polished. The figures are carved in outline and look embedded in the stone, which has everywhere the same smooth surface. This demonstrates that the wall was perfectly polished before carving the figures. In all bas-relief sculptures the same technique is used.

Plate 7 contains many paintings and sculptures copied in the tombs of Qurna. No. 1 is a fresco painting representing the jobs of weaver and net maker. No. 2 is another painting featuring a hunter. No. 3 is a woman sculpted on the doorjamb of another tomb. The magnificent dress of this figure, the sistrum, the ivy, and the lotus she holds with her right hand, which are all priestly symbols, indicate that this tomb possibly belonged to a priestess, and that this is her portrait, or that of another priestess going to her tomb for the anniversary celebrated yearly by the Egyptians in memory of their dead. This was not really celebrated by playing mournful music, generally with the sistrum, but more likely by offering lotus flowers. Women represented in tombs are generally more comfortably dressed than the ones represented elsewhere, whose clothing is so tight and close-fitting that it appears impossible for them to move. No. 4 is an image of the god Ptah with a Nilometer as head, an elaborated crown, sceptre, and flail: the hieroglyphs are perfectly preserved.

Plate 8 is an exact copy of a scene eight arms long and seven and a half tall, painted in another tomb of Qurna. The subject is extremely interesting since it provides a clear depiction of ancient Egyptian gardens.[35] The different parts of the garden are marked in the plate so I avoid repeating them here. The blue stripe that runs in front of the main gate of the garden might be the Nile or a water reservoir, connected to the garden through subterranean ducts. One can observe that the lack of perspective—a fault common to all Egyptian paintings—causes the entrance gate and the other inner gates to be drawn edgeways. A closer examination is enough to understand what their position should be. For the same reason, the trees planted outside the façade wall, on both sides of the entrance door, cover the path that leads to it, which at a first glance looks like part of the same garden. This scene is certainly worth full attention and I have no information about it being published by any other traveler until now.

At an Arab's of Qurna, who lived in a tomb, I observed a coffin lid painted in black with a delicate female figure in yellow. From the diadem, the disk that is raised between her hands and that is repeated at her chin and pudenda, and finally from the stars scattered everywhere on her body, it can be easily guessed that this is Nut, the Urania of the ancient Greeks, and that the mummy once in this coffin probably belonged to an astronomer or someone serving

---

35 Reference to the representation of the garden of the temple of Amun in the tomb of Sennefer (TT 96), mayor of Thebes during the reign of Amenhotep II; Bertha Porter and Rosalind L.B. Moss, *Topographical Bibliography of Ancient Egyptian Hieroglyphic Texts, Reliefs, and Paintings*, vol. 1, *The Theban Necropolis*, part 1, *Private Tombs* (Oxford: Clarendon Press, 1960), 198 (4).

the cult of this goddess.[36] I made a drawing of it, which is no. 1 of plate 9. Nos. 2 and 3 of the same plate are two wooden funerary stelae: in the first, there is the figure of a deceased woman offering bread, geese, and flowers to the god Re, the sun, who has a disk surrounded by a uraeus over his head, a symbol of his supreme power. The loaves of bread, which are part of the offering, are recognized thanks to the five holes on the surface, which are rendered in painting with dots. I possess a loaf of bread found in a tomb at Qurna, which has exactly the same five holes. In the other stela there is a king offering to the god Khonsu, or Moon. The servant who follows the monarch holds one of those military standards also represented all together in a room of the temple of Philae, about which I shall write further on. No. 4 of the same plate is a reckoner, represented in bas-relief in a room of Luxor temple. From the same temple I drew the content of plate 10: no. 1 is a bas-relief with the names of many gods; no. 2 is the head of a king with a crown, the richest I have ever seen in all the monuments of Egypt. No. 3 is a bas-relief whose meaning I would not be able to explain without reading the hieroglyphs beside it. It is doubtless that the two figures are female because of the body shape of the one painted red, similar to the one painted blue, though in a different position. It is peculiar here that these two colors were chosen instead of yellow, which is usually preferred for women in all Egyptian monuments. On the other hand, the beard that they have makes me think they belong to the priestly order. In fact, I observed in many temples that the lower frieze of sculptures or paintings on the walls is composed of a line of these bearded women, holding in their hands offerings of flowers and other objects. I think that they cannot be anyone else than people consecrated to the cult of the gods and employed in the service of the temples.

No. 4 is a bird carved in bas-relief, possibly representing the symbolic phoenix. No. 5 is an ibis, a bird highly revered by the ancient Egyptians, to the point of making it the image of the god Thoth, who often is represented with the head of this bird.

I was busy with these drawings when many travelers arrived at Thebes: Mr. Bankes returning from Syria and Mr. Salt coming from Cairo were getting ready to proceed up to the Second Cataract in the company of Baron von Sack[37] and Messrs. Huyot,[38] Gau,[39]

---

36   Ricci calls this goddess Tpé, following the reading used by Champollion and Rosellini of the hieroglyph for 'sky,' *pt*.

37   Baron Albert von Sack (1757–1829) was chamberlain of the King of Prussia and a famous naturalist. He had already traveled in French Guyana when he landed in Egypt, coming from Rome in August 1818, aiming at the First Cataract of the Nile, and then was interested in pursuing his trip by heading to Jerusalem, Constantinople, and Greece; Driault, *La formation*, 118; Usick, *Adventures in Egypt and Nubia*, 77; Mario Kramp, "Ägypten für Entschlossene: Die abenteuerliche Expedition des Kölners Franz Christian Gau 1818/1819," in *Ägypten, Nubien und die Cyrenaika: Die imaginäre Reise des Norbert Bittner (1786–1851)*, ed. Lisa Schwarzmeier, Ernst Czerny, and Mario Kramp (Ruhpolding: Verlag Franz Philipp Rutzen, 2012), 33, 41.

38   Jean-Nicolas Huyot (1780–1840), French architect and draftsman, a friend of Champollion and Ricci; Dawson, Bierbrier, and Uphill, *Who Was Who*, 213; Pierre Pinon, "L'Orient de Jean Nicolas Huyot: le voyage en Asie-Mineure, en Égypte et en Grèce (1817–1821)," *Revue du monde musulman et de la Méditerranée* 73–74 (1994): 35–55.

39   Franz Christian Gau (1790–1853) was a German-born naturalized French architect. He went to Egypt with Baron von Sack, but soon parted company with him after a disagreement. According to Champollion he was an inaccurate draftsman; Dawson, Bierbrier, and Uphill, *Who Was Who*, 164; Kramp, "Ägypten für Entschlossene."

Hyde,[40] and Linant.[41] Almost at the same time Messrs. Beechey and Belzoni also arrived from Berenike.[42]

The gathering of so many distinguished people was very timely for me in order to call Belzoni to account for the arbitrary way he had taken my drawings without my knowledge. I immediately consulted with Mr. Salt, who, knowing his character, made it clear to me that any attempt to get the drawings back would be useless. He suggested I try to get the best out of them, offering to be mediator of the negotiations and of our reconciliation.

My respect for Mr. Salt pushed me to agree on everything and, even though the offer Belzoni made was very low, I accepted in order to end this distasteful dispute and avoid disturbing the spirit and the good harmony reigning in the party by our private dissension.[c]

Once the issue was settled, everybody arranged to set off: I also joined the party to make the journey. Belzoni stayed at Thebes, entrusted by Mr. Bankes to move to Cairo the Philae obelisk. The deed was carried out with full success, but much difficulty.[43]

On 1 January 1819[44] we embarked: this was possibly the first time so many travelers sailed together up the Nile. The main goal was to visit all the ancient sites between the First and the Second Cataracts in order to compare them with those published in the great work compiled by order of Napoleon. The result of this operation will be published by Messrs. Salt and Bankes. Once this job was over,[45] Mr. Salt and the rest of the party went back to Cairo, while I stayed with Mr. Bankes, determined to advance to Dongola by land. This journey was at the time extremely risky and all our courage and steadfastness were necessary to undertake it.

Egypt was at that period preparing an expedition, at the beginning thought to be against Abyssinia, but that had no other aim, as it was later found out, than to conquer Sennar.

---

40 John Hyde (?–1825), English traveler. After spending some time in Egypt and Nubia, he proceeded to Palestine, Syria, Mesopotamia, and India, where he died; Dawson, Bierbrier, and Uphill, *Who Was Who*, 213.

41 Louis Maurice Adolphe Linant de Bellefonds (1799–1883) was a French geographer, explorer, artist, and engineer of noble descent. After a period in a naval career, Linant went to Egypt in 1817 in the company of the Count de Forbin. He soon entered the service of Muhammad Ali and William J. Bankes. In 1869, he was created minister of public works by Khedive Isma'il; Dawson, Bierbrier, and Uphill, *Who Was Who*, 256–57; Jean Mazuel, *L'Oeuvre Géographique de Linant de Bellefonds: Étude de Géographie Historique* (Cairo: Société Royale de Géographie d'Égypte, 1937); Marcel Kurz, "Un homme d'action dans l'Égypte du XIXe siècle," in *Voyage aux mines d'or du Pharaon*, ed. Marcel Kurz (Saint Clément de Rivière: Fata Morgana, 2002), 17–101.

42 During the night of 25 October 1818; Belzoni, *Narrative*, 347.

43 It seems that Belzoni actually traveled with them to Philae; Belzoni, *Narrative*, 351: "Accordingly, on the 16th of November, we left Thebes for the first cataract of the Nile. The party was numerous—Mr. Bankes, Mr. Salt, Baron Sack, a Prussian traveller and a celebrated naturalist, Mr. Beechey, Mr. Linon, a draftman, Doctor Ricci, and myself."

44 The short diary of Ricci found by Patricia Usick among the Bankes papers marks the departure from Qurna on 16 November, as confirmed by Belzoni (cf. previous note). On 1 January 1819, Bankes's party was at Gerf Hussein. They had left the First Cataract on 3 December 1818; Patricia Usick, "Not the Travel Journal of Alessandro Ricci," in *Studies in Egyptian Antiquities: A Tribute to T.G.H. James*, ed. Vivian W. Davies (London: The British Museum Press, 1999), 117–18. It is not conceivable that Ricci here means the departure from the Second Cataract, because a few lines afterward (p. 177) we find him at Wadi Halfa (26 February 1819).

45 End of February 1819.

The objective was to capture slaves among the idolatrous peoples of that kingdom and to seize the gold mines of Fazogli. These movements did not pass unnoticed by the Mamluks, who, defeated and almost destroyed in Egypt, had taken refuge in the Kingdom of Dongola. Since they perfectly knew the character and the politics of their enemy, they were extremely wary, fearing that under this pretext he secretly wanted to exterminate them in their last asylum. In this state of mistrust and fear, whoever entered their territory would be regarded with suspicion and could not expect to be treated with humanity by the remnants of a people cruel by nature and forced to become even more so by the most excusable of all reasons: their own survival. On the other hand, the Egyptian governors of Nubia knew that the viceroy seldom granted permission to penetrate beyond the Second Cataract and sent away travelers and foreigners of all nations. The reason, they adduced, was that, being close to the Mamluks, they wanted to avoid all possible cause of friction.

Despite these difficulties, Mr. Bankes persisted in his plan and we introduced ourselves at Wadi Halfa to Hassan Kashif, supreme commander of Nubia, in order to obtain permission to reach Dongola. After many refusals, we were authorized to proceed only to the district of Mograkka, under the command of Hamid Kashif, his son, to whom he also directed a sealed letter. He assured us that he had written about our desire to visit Dongola and let us hope that we would not find opposition from his son. In this hope, we left on 26 February, marching on the west bank of the Nile. Five camels for us and for the provisions, at a daily price each of two and a half piasters of Cairo, all included to Mograkka, five Ababda Arabs, and a *kabir*[d] were part of our caravan. Mr. Beechey and Mr. Hyde, who suddenly decided to make the journey with us, had left Mr. Salt and joined us at Wadi Halfa, so that, with our dragoman, we were a total of eleven people. Because we left at four in the afternoon, we did not cover much distance that day and after three hours we camped in a sandy plain not far from the Nile, where we spent the night.

On the 27th we visited the ruins of Dull,[46] on a high black granite cliff. These look like a fortress, but almost completely destroyed: its walls, as those of the houses that were still standing, are made of sun-dried bricks.

On the 28th we met the ruins of many churches: the most noteworthy are those of Shargandi and Sabre. In the latter there are many fresco paintings of Christian themes, including a very well-preserved *Nativity*.

On 1 March we reached Semna,[47] a small and elegant temple, almost completely covered in sand: an enclosure wall of baked bricks, which surrounded and protected the temple, is still standing nearly complete.[48] Plate 11 shows a bas-relief in excellent style carved on the outer façade of the temple: the irregular line that cuts the drawing in its lower part marks the level of the sands. This temple seems to have been dedicated to Khnum, a modification of Amun, who is portrayed in bas-relief with his name made up of three ram's heads.

---

46   If he means the cataract of Dall, then Ricci is confused, since it is far south of Semna, which
       he had not yet reached. The area between Wadi Halfa and Semna East is dotted with Egyptian
       forts: Gabnarti, Mirgissa, Gemai, Shalfak, Uronarti, just to mention a few.
47   In fact Semna East, or Kumma.
48   Temple of Khnum built by Thutmose II, Thutmose III, and Amenhotep II; Porter and Moss,
       Topographical Bibliography 7:152–55.

Three falls, one after the other, form in this place a strong cataract. Toward the evening a small caravan coming from Dongola appeared, informing us that everything was calm in the kingdom.

On 2 March, continuing our journey, we visited the tomb of Shaykh Umar, an Arab saint much revered by the Muslims: it is remarkable for its round shape and extraordinary size. We overtook a low island, with some ruins of little interest, and encountered the remains of a fort (a building from a later period), placed in an elevated position and built with very large bricks,[49] the largest I have ever seen in my travels, even bigger than those of the famous walls of Eileithyia.[50] Shortly before the sunset we admired the beautiful Slave Island, mostly made of granite and of a really picturesque shape. In the evening, we reached a small village made up of only five houses. The miserable villagers willingly offered us milk and *kasherangegah* (so the Nubians call cooked beans), which we accepted with pleasure, rewarding them for their attentions.

The excessive heat and the roughness of the stretch of road covered during this day made us very tired. We then decided to stay another day with our hosts, who renewed their offers of food with the same cordiality.

On 4 March we met only two villages made up of a few houses, built with small shapeless pieces of granite, assembled with mortar and placed in so harsh and steep a spot that there was enough farmland to sustain only the small number of their inhabitants. We also saw three islands of average size, which we thought uninhabited due to the complete lack of houses and the apparent sterility of the surface. Three small falls at a short distance from one to the other are met near Turmukki, where we spent the night.

In the morning of the 5th, two hours after dawn, we reached Scaterendiff Island, rich in ruins, some of which are recognizable for modern fortifications, apt for the defense of the whole island. On the west side of the island, beyond the fortifications, the whole hill is terraced, and houses, now ruined, were built on its steep slope. What makes this part of Nubia particularly pleasant are the amenity of the Nile banks in front of the island and the bright green of the thick forest. We stopped a moment to contemplate such a beautiful landscape. We then continued the journey and reached the borders of the Kingdom of Sukkot, not different at its entrance from the Wadi Haggar, and similarly deserted and mountainous. After two hours' journey, the mountain chain becomes imperceptibly farther away, and a vast and well-cultivated plain replaces the monotonous, narrow, and steep terrain. Three quite large and populous villages are on the same line along this valley, whose fertility provides abundantly for all their needs. We spent the night in the last of these villages.

On the 6th the rising sun found us already walking. The valley was getting narrower and in a while we found ourselves between the mountains and the Nile, on uneven terrain covered with granite fragments, which makes it very difficult for travelers. Opposite Kumbo

---

49   The Middle Kingdom fort of Semna South; John Baines and Jaromír Málek, *Atlas of Ancient Egypt* (Oxford: Andromeda, 1995), 186.

50   al-Kab; Porter and Moss, *Topographical Bibliography* 5:171–75.

Island,[51] all well cultivated, we met the shaykh of the village, who was about to have his breakfast. After considering us for a long time, he approached us and invited us with courtesy to stay in his company. He was surprised by our European dress and asked what we were seeking in that country. We answered that we had no other object than to travel, but our answer did not satisfy him, and seeing that he was uneasy we thought it wise to thank him for his invitation and leave in order to avoid more questions.

During the night we were visited by a hyena, which was readily driven away by our Ababdas, who were taking shifts to watch our camp.

In the morning of the 7th while folding our tents a *jalaba*[e] of more than two hundred camels coming from Dongola passed by. It had a load of gum, ostrich feathers, elephant tusks, tamarind, and many other goods. There were also two hundred young female slaves, who looked very sorrowful for their fate. Three Mamluk officials were part of the caravan. They told us that, tired of living as fugitives, they had decided to go to Cairo to submit to the viceroy.

At around ten, we entered the Mograkka district, which was the limit established for us by Hassan Kashif, commander of the Kingdom of Sukkot. Here we were to present to the governor the letter written by the same Hassan, but we received the unpleasant news that the previous day he had left for another house he had at Amara, on the other side of the Nile. We decided to cross the river to find him and get permission to continue our journey, but the plan was more difficult than it appeared, due to the complete lack of boats. Mr. Bankes thought to cross on camels, but the Ababda refused firmly, observing that the rapidity of the current was an insurmountable obstacle. They also added that, in any case, they would not accompany us in a district inhabited by a large number of Arnauts,[52] against whom their tribe had a feud with mutual bloodshed. We did not insist and we deferred any decision to the next day, in the hope we could persuade our Ababda with money. They anticipated us and at late evening, under the pretext of taking the beasts to drink, at a certain distance from the camp they mounted the camels and speedily fled, leaving behind the saddles and giving up eight days of due salary. We had delayed payments on purpose to make sure of their loyalty. Considering the insatiable greed of these people for money, we understood they had very valid reasons not to follow us. We were displeased about the incident as well as uncertain about what to do, and spent the night on the same spot where we had been so barbarically abandoned. It is impossible to describe how critical our position was. We were opposite the southern edge of Mograkka Island, which we were to cross anyway in order to reach the other side of the Nile. The inhabitants of the island were those Arnauts so dreadful for our Ababda and whom as a consequence we were also to fear. On the other hand, the shortage of our provisions pushed us to make a decision. Without camels, and with heavy equipment we could not load on our own shoulders, we could not find a way out. Mr. Bankes, usually very firm, was in dismay, as were all of us. Then, our *kabir*, who was the son of a Bosnian of Aswan and a vigorous, determined young man, proposed voluntarily to swim to the island to find a *ramus*, or raft. He took off his *zabut*, a dark wool shirt which was

---

51   Unidentified toponym, unless Ricci means Kulb Island; Baines and Málek, *Atlas*, 186.
52   In Turkish it means 'Albanians,' but here it refers specifically to Albanian mercenary troops.

all of his clothing, hung a swollen goatskin to his neck, and jumped in the Nile. We stayed on the bank watching his efforts and making prayers for his safety, which is to say our own safety. We saw him bravely resist the current, avoid the rocks, and finally reach Mograkka Island in half a hour. He then left from there on board a *ramus*, which he had found on the banks of the island: this was made of eight palm-tree trunks, tied together with ropes made of palm fibers. On this boat, two at a time with our equipment, we safely crossed. At sunset we were all on the island. The *kabir* was handsomely rewarded by all of us. We intended to buy a ram for our dinner, but the inhabitants, having nothing of the human about them except the name, refused to sell us one at any price, and calling us "Christian dogs," laughed at our situation. If it were not so late at night, the better solution would have been to immediately cross the river, but we were afraid of hitting the rocks in the darkness of the night. We therefore decided to spend the most anguishing night among those unfriendly people. We all gathered in the most secluded area and kept watching our equipment while we collected some wood to light a fire. After a quick dinner, we rested fitfully, waiting with anxiety for the next day to come.

As soon as dawn of the 9th appeared, we prepared to leave. We were afraid that the owner of the *ramus* would come to claim it back, so, ignoring the danger, we decided to cross the Nile in two groups only. The passage was successful, but took much effort because the first group had to go upstream to pass the edge of the island. The ones of us left for the second journey—and I was among them—moved and waited for the boat on the other side of the island, so avoiding the same long circuit and speeding up the whole process, which was done in two hours.

Our first thought was to send our dragoman to Hamid Kashif in order to show him the letter of recommendation and ask on our behalf for permission to go pay him homage. Instead, he did not take notice of the letter of Hassan and chased away the dragoman, surprised that some Christians dared to place foot in his territory. It was already late in the evening when the dragoman gave us this bleak answer. Far from being discouraged, we decided to go see him the day after, hoping to render him more amenable by our submission.

On the 10th, at nine in the morning we set off, each of us loaded with the part of equipment he was able to carry, while the rest was put on the camel belonging to the *kabir*, the only one left behind by the Ababda. We had him cross the Nile swimming, tied to the *ramus*.

We did not suffer much as long as we walked in the shadow of the thick palm woods, but when we entered the sandy plain the heat became unbearable and we were forced to stop from time to time in order to refresh our feet. Although our shoes had double soles, they were not enough to protect us from the ardor of the sand. For this reason, we arrived very late at the *kashif*'s house, which was beside a palm forest, not far from Egyptian ruins called Amara.

We found him seated on a carpet, surrounded by around twenty Arnauts, smoking the *narghile*[f]. On the walls, a large number of weapons, both edged and guns, were hanging. As soon as we entered, without giving us a chance to explain the reason of our visit, he abruptly asked what we wanted from him. Once we had asked him to read the letter of Hassan Kashif, which informed him about our project to proceed to Dongola, he answered he could not and did not want to let us advance even by only one step beyond his territory. Prayers and presents, which were offered and usually help to smooth out any difficulty among the Turks, were on this occasion useless and we only obtained permission to go the following day to Sai Island, three hours from Amara. He assigned us an escort, ordering them not to lose sight of us for a moment and to bring us back to him before sunset. We could only visit a small part of the island[53] and observe some ruins from a distance, but we could not understand their kind or extent. When we returned, we tried again to obtain permission from the *kashif* to proceed, but in vain. We then lost hope and begged him only to give us camels for our return, offering to pay any price he asked, but even in this he was inexorable. As an act of grace, he only granted one camel in order to relieve us from the load we were forced to carry on our shoulders. We then abandoned all caution and reached the point of insulting him, threatening to report to the pasha the way he treated foreigners. As a response, he laughed at us. This proud man is, as I said, one of the many sons of Hassan Kashif, supreme chief of Nubia. He is of gigantic stature like his father, thin, and has an austere and expressive appearance. He was dressed in a long blue shirt with large sleeves, closed at the neck like those of the Ababda, a cashmere turban, and yellow shoes. A long curved saber, hanging from a large red silk rope on his shoulders, and a *kangiar*,[54] or dagger, were part of his weaponry.

Before setting off for the return, I wanted to take some drawings of the ruins of the temple of Amara, which is placed atop a sandy hill and surrounded by a mudbrick fence wall, for the most part destroyed.[55] The portico, the only part of this temple that somehow survives, is not large: it counts eight columns, five still standing, even though all except one are damaged: plate 12. The rest of the ruins and most of the floor, which was made of cemented stones on a layer of bricks, were removed by the Arabs probably to obtain lime. Bricks and pottery shards, scattered inside the enclosure wall, show, in my opinion, that once there were houses, too. The best-preserved column is in rough bas-relief and badly executed. Plate 13 shows the details of its four registers, divided by a line of hieroglyphs. I could copy only one of them with great effort, since the others had completely faded away. Many gods were possibly worshiped in this temple because a number of them are portrayed in the aforementioned column. The female figure, which can be observed in the second slot of the third register, carries on her head a crown that I have never seen in any other monument of Egypt (but I saw it in Nubia). By the enclosure wall there are many stones, some squared, some irregular, which look like petrified wood, but are not.

Continuously harassed by Hamid Kashif, who was impatient to see us go away from Amara, on 12 March at midday we set off, heading back to Mograkka Island, where we arrived in the late evening.

On the 13th, beyond Mount Meme, which forms a sort of island in the middle of the sands, we came across the ruins of two Christian churches reduced to a pile of stones. We

---

53   A town and fort dated between the reign of Senwosret III and the Eighteenth Dynasty; Porter and Moss, *Topographical Bibliography* 7:164–66.

54   Arabic خنجر *(khanjar)*, 'dagger.'

55   Probably the Meroitic temple (later destroyed); Porter and Moss, *Topographical Bibliography* 7:157.

recognized them as belonging to our religion by a cross carved on a broken stone between the ruins.

In this part of the Nile, the mountains are made of black rock, with shades of dark red in layers, completely different from the beautiful granite that is the principal element of all mountains on the west bank.

We arrived in the evening at Kolul after ten hours of uninterrupted march. It was extremely hard for us, not yet used to walking on the sands. Fortunately in the late afternoon we had found another camel, which we mounted in turns, and this was a great relief.

On the 14th, half an hour after we left, we had to cross a mountain almost completely covered in sand: we ascended in two hours of painful march and we descended in forty-five minutes only. In the evening, we took our rest at the borders with Sukkot, easy to recognize for the many heaps of stones raised here and there by Muslim travelers, who used to add a stone due to a longstanding religious superstition.

During the 15th and the 16th we traveled continuously on a stony and desert soil until we reached Contra Semene, a small village whose name derives from being in front of Semene on the opposite bank of the Nile. Here we were kindly welcomed by the inhabitants, who also provided us all with camels at a fair price. We could then send back to the rude Hamid Kashif the one he had rented us so reluctantly.

On the 17th we passed Aqabat al-Banat and camped in the evening three hours distant from Saras. Two Arabs, who by chance were passing by while we were pitching the tents, told us that Hassan Kashif, suddenly falling out of the viceroy's favor, had left Wadi Halfa and was camped in the neighborhood with a large number of soldiers. We immediately went to visit him and after the preliminary salutations we informed him of the ill treatment of his son Hamid, but only a few broken and meaningless words were his answer. We began to suspect, in my opinion very validly, that in the letter he had instructed Hamid on how he should behave toward us. We left very unsatisfied and on the following day, determined to sleep in our *canjiah* which we had left moored at Wadi Halfa, we walked continuously for fifteen hours, not caring about the discomfort and the heat, until we arrived around midnight at the starting point of this so ill-fated journey.

We stayed in Wadi Halfa for six full days because we needed rest and provisions. We therefore visited the many ruins and I drew all that could be recognized among the general devastation. The visible monuments are five, but the stones they are made of diminish by the day because the Arabs, here as well as in many other places, come for supplies to produce lime. It is possible that other monuments exist here, covered by the sand, because in this part of Nubia violent and whirling winds carry it in abundance.

The first monument to the south,[56] which is the most interesting, is the ruins of a large temple, completely built in stone. Nothing remains but the foundations of many columns and pillars: plate 14, no. 1. The part standing out of the sands is marked here with thin black lines, to differentiate them from the other foundations, barely visible, and so marked with dotted lines.

---

56 Temple of Horus of Buhen, built by Hatshepsut and modified by Thutmose III; Porter and Moss, *Topographical Bibliography* 7:131–38.

At the distance of 193 feet from this ruin there is a second,[57] much better preserved, even though everything, except the door frames, was made in mud bricks (no. 2). The interior of the temple is plastered with mortar, whitened and painted with much-damaged hieroglyphs. The color black, seldom used in other monuments, prevails here over all other colors. It took us three days to open a path through the sands to the sanctuary, in the middle of which there is an altar, possibly in its original position. In the bottom wall of the sanctuary there is a stucco bas-relief[58] with figures and hieroglyphs, whose colors are still well preserved. The subject must be interesting as it represents some events of Egyptian history: I deduce this from the representation of the god Amun-Re, or the sun god, with a number of prisoners, whom he himself drives, each of them with his name marked (no. 3). Only two pillars are left of the third ruin, at a distance of 102 feet from the second (no. 4). The foundations of two large rooms, built in mud bricks, are all that is left of the fourth ruin, which is 216 feet distant from the second (no. 5). And finally the fifth ruin[59] is made up of a few long mudbrick walls. No details can be ascertained, nor its purpose (no. 6).

The day before our departure from Wadi Halfa the Barabra[g] caught a male crocodile, four arms long, tangled by accident in a hook thrown in the Nile to hunt for tortoises. It had been a long time that I had wanted to dissect one of those amphibians in order to figure out from which part of its body comes the smell of musk, there being many opinions on this matter. I took advantage of the chance and I bought it for few piasters, with the obligation of giving back the male organ to the seller because the Nubians consider it very important and believe it is a strong aphrodisiac when, dried under the sun and reduced to powder, it is drunk. After the most accurate observations, I believe that only the testicles and the nearby small glands emanate the musk odor: this is for sure the reason why this smell is in the females much less than in the males. The conformation of the reproductive organs in this amphibian is ambiguous, because in both genders nothing appears but a fleshy cavity, somehow serving as a protection to the organs, which are hidden two inches deep.

The crocodile hunt is made in two different ways here: the first method is to openly attack the animal with gunfire as it comes out of the Nile, aiming at its chest when, climbing the bank, this part of the body is more exposed. Only then the shot is deadly, otherwise the scales that cover it everywhere strongly protect it and the bullet cannot penetrate. The second way is to surprise the animal during the mating season, which is usually spring. It is necessary to prepare an ambush in the places the crocodile usually goes, easy to recognize by its traces on the sand. When the male crocodile is mating, he

---

57 North Temple, dedicated to Isis and built by Amenhotep II; Porter and Moss, *Topographical Bibliography* 7:129–31.

58 A stone stela portraying Senwosret I in front of Montu holding tied prisoners. The text refers to the Nubian campaign undertaken by the pharaoh in his eighteenth regnal year. The stela is now in the Egyptian Museum of Florence (No. 2540), where it arrived as a result of the Franco-Tuscan expedition, taken by Rosellini on the advice of Ricci; Porter and Moss, *Topographical Bibliography* 7:130–31.

59 Possibly part of the massive northeast fortifications of the Middle Kingdom fort; Porter and Moss, *Topographical Bibliography* 7:129. The other ruins cannot be identified with certainty.

instinctively turns the female supine and in this position he lies on her. After the intercourse, he comes down and helps her to turn back on her feet. The hunters surprise the
animal either during intercourse, firing simultaneously at both—and in this case they
might kill both—or appearing when the male detaches himself from the female after the
intercourse. In this case they do not give him a chance to turn the female back: the male
flees away scared and leaves the female, which is unable to turn herself into position,
struggling in vain and easily killed (and sometimes even captured alive). The Arabs are
greedy for crocodile meat: we also ate it roasted, and it seemed to taste like eel, but was
very indigestible for all of us.

We gave up the idea of proceeding beyond Wadi Halfa and set sail on the 24th toward
Egypt. We soon stopped at the Island of Faras. The ruins[60] are a couple of miles distant
from the Nile, to the west, and were visited by us the following day. These are two
rock-cut caves: one of them has the shape of a Greek cross and bears some inscription in
different characters, mostly Coptic; the other is completely bare. Plate 14, nos. 7 and 8.

From Faras we arrived at Mashakit,[61] to the east, a medium-high sandstone cliff
directly perpendicular to the Nile. There is a cave of almost eight square feet.[62] In the
back wall there is a much-damaged statue, while on the side walls there are some hieroglyphs, also in bad shape. Outside there is a scene carved on the rock with three figures
and some hieroglyphs;[63] plate 15, no. 1. This scene seems to represent a priest kneeling
in adoration in front of the goddess Tpé. A figure carved in smaller size follows the
priest, and since these figures always follow kings and high-ranking officers in all monuments, I think they must be regarded as servants. Their attitude, usually respectful and
humble, confirms my opinion on the subject.

We continued our journey and reached the temple of Adde,[64] to the east, also cut in
the rock directly on the Nile like Mashakit. The plan of this temple is roughly a cross;
same plate, no. 2. The vault of the entrance hall is supported by four columns, one of
those I drew myself, no. 3. At the entrance of the sanctuary there is a shaft where we
found human bones and the remains of mummy wrappings. What remains of poorly executed paintings of Christian saints proves that the temple was converted into a church:
for this reason hieroglyphs were covered in stucco. Outside, to the left of the door, there
is a carved Isis suckling Horus. She is followed by five human figures, one of them with
an ibis head, and the other four with the head of Anubis. Since these are the gods presid-
ing over mummification, according to Egyptian mythology, it is possible that the temple
was in fact used for this religious ceremony. No. 4 shows the outer façade of the grotto.

---

60   Porter and Moss, *Topographical Bibliography* 7:124–27. Ricci is possibly referring to the Ancho-
     rite Grotto and the New Kingdom tombs.
61   Also called Jebel al-Shams, on the east bank.
62   Rock shrine of Pesiur I, viceroy of Kush under Ay and Horemheb; Porter and Moss, *Topo-
     graphical Bibliography* 7:122.
63   Rock stela of Hor, deputy of Wawat, adoring Anuket of Amenheri; Porter and Moss, *Topo-
     graphical Bibliography* 7:122. Ricci calls Anuket "Tpé."
64   Jebel Adda: the rock temple, dedicated to Amun-Re and Thoth, was erected by Horemheb;
     Porter and Moss, *Topographical Bibliography* 7:119–21.

From Adde we reached Abu Simbel: this magnificent monument of Egyptian grandeur is placed to the west, almost at the mouth of a small valley, at the sloping end of a mountain chain that extends to the northwest. The sands had so much assaulted it that of the four colossal statues in the façade, only the uppermost part of the crown of one was visible. More than two-thirds of the temple was buried underneath. Its clearance is due to the tireless activity of Messrs. Beechey and Belzoni, who, in their first Nubian trip, overcoming with invincible constancy all difficulties opposing their plan, finally succeeded in removing the huge amount of sand and entering the majestic temple.[65] Twenty-six seated monkeys in a row, most of them damaged by time, make the upper decoration of the façade. Fourteen ovals, each flanked by two serpents with a seated human figure and a feather, make up the lower decoration. Underneath there is a niche with a hawk-headed standing human figure, surmounted by a globe, symbol of the god Re, or sun, flanked by two offering figures. Under it there is a line of hieroglyphs and then the entrance gate of the temple. The four seated colossi are sixty-six feet tall and are cut in the rock: it seems impossible that the sculptor could, in their immense proportions, give such an expressive and interesting appearance to the statues. We could access the temple with much difficulty only after we opened a gallery through the sands, with the result that the two colossi beside the gate are only half cleared. This narrow passage will be soon reoccupied if walls able to hold the sand are not placed on both sides. The internal distribution of the rooms is noble and imposing (cf. plan, plate 15, no. 5). In the first hall there are eight pillars, each with a painted colossal statue: on the arm they bear in hieroglyphs the name of Pharaoh Ramesses, more commonly known under the name of Sesostris;[66] plate 16, nos. 1 and 2.

The walls are all carved in bas-reliefs that represent very interesting war scenes and religious ceremonies. Scenes no. 1 and 2 in plate 17 are on top of the wall marked (a) in the plan. In the first register of no. 1 the king is making an offering to Amun and Khnum, or Khnouphis. In the second, the same king, kneeling on a round carpet between two figures of Thoth—the Trismegistus and the ibis-headed—presents to the latter a cup with an offering. In the third register, the king holds a knife and a cup with fruits. He is portrayed while offering bread, wine, and geese to the goddess Satet, symbolically represented as a uraeus coming out of a cave, adorned with many little serpents. Inside the cave there is a seated Amun-Re, the Egyptian demiurge, the creator of the world, in human guise. The same god is portrayed on no. 2 of the same plate, where the king with a knife is about to knock down or has already knocked down four urns, each topped with two feathers. As for dimension and shape, these urns look like those used by the ancient Egyptians to store, after the death of some important person, the four funerary vases containing the embalmed organs of the deceased. Their covers represent the four gods of the Amenti.[67] I have in my collection one

---

65   The temple was 'discovered' by Burckhardt in March 1813; a first mission by Belzoni was undertaken in September 1816, but only in July 1817 did he succeed in opening the temple, the façade of which was covered in sand; Belzoni, *Narrative*, 101, 211.

66   The mistake is common in early Egyptology: according to Champollion and Rosellini, the reading of the cartouche of Ramesses II Usermaatre Setepenre was Sesostris.

67   Ricci means here the canopic jars, even though the scene represents Ramesses II offering colored cloths to Amun-Re.

of these urns,[68] four times higher than the ones represented in this scene. Because these objects are very rare, I suppose that they were used only for people of rank. The scene might therefore point out that King Ramesses won and killed four mighty warriors.

No. 3 of the same plate is the drawing of a bas-relief existing on one of the four pillars of the second hall of the temple.[69]

No. 4 is taken from the right wall of the third room and represents another offering made by the same king to an ibis-headed Thoth.[70]

In Plate 18, no. 1, the king is introduced in front of Re and two other seated gods. With his left hand he is holding a quiver and many ropes tied to war prisoners of different races:[71] I marked them no. 2 of the same plate. One can easily detect the negro, while the other has the appearance of the ancient shepherd rulers of Egypt. Beside their facial features, these men are also dressed in a different way, leaving no doubt that they belong to two different peoples conquered by Ramesses. No. 3 represents one of those figures always standing on Egyptian monuments behind important characters: they are usually represented in smaller size, possibly to mark their inferiority. In my opinion, they are servants, busy refreshing their masters by moving a feather like a fan. At the feet of a colossal statue on the façade of the small temple there is one very similar figure, except that it is represented full face and standing. I put it in the same plate at no. 4 to compare it with the other one described above.

I already mentioned that the vault in the second hall is supported by four pillars: one is represented on plate 17, no. 3. These pillars are rectangular in shape. The beauty of their colors and the daintiness of the sculpture induced me to draw two parts of another pillar, which are the subject of plate 19, no. 1 and 2. The first represents Ramesses welcomed and patted by the goddess Neith, who, according to Egyptian beliefs, presided over science and war, and possibly refers to the wisdom and the valor of the king himself. In the second one, the same monarch presents an offering to the god Atum, the Egyptian Hercules.

From one of the walls in the same hall, which is the most magnificent as for colors, I took the drawing of a bas-relief represented on plate 20. Here the king presents Amun "Who-gives-birth" with a large offering of food and a couple of corn cobs.[72] In this scene, figure (a) is particularly noteworthy as it seems to have been added later.[73]

---

68 This is the canopic box no. 3 in the catalog of Migliarini (Nos. 2184 and 2191); Sammarco, *Alessandro Ricci e il suo giornale dei viaggi*, vol. 2, *Documenti inediti o rari* (Cairo: Société Royale de Géographie d'Égypte, 1930), 57. The object comes from Deir al-Medina and belonged to a woman called Takharu, who lived during the Nineteenth Dynasty; Maria Cristina Guidotti, "A proposito di Deir el Medina prima della scoperta: un pezzo della collezione Ricci nel Museo Egizio di Firenze," in *L'Egitto fuori dell'Egitto: Dalla riscoperta all'egittologia. Atti del Convegno Internazionale, Bologna 26–29 marzo*, ed. Cristiana Morigi Govi, Silvio Curto, and Sergio Pernigotti (Bologna: CLUEB, 1991); Maria Cristina Guidotti, "Dall'Egitto a Firenze via Pisa," in *La Piramide e la Torre: Duecento anni di archeologia egiziana*, ed. Edda Bresciani (Pisa: Cassa di Risparmio di Pisa, 2000), 154.
69 Porter and Moss, *Topographical Bibliography* 7:109.
70 Porter and Moss, *Topographical Bibliography* 7:110 (107).
71 Porter and Moss, *Topographical Bibliography* 7:104 (44).
72 Porter and Moss, *Topographical Bibliography* 7:109 (97); not corn, of course, but lettuce.
73 The figure of deified Ramesses II, indeed added later.

In the sanctuary there are four seated statues carved in the rock: three have a human head and the fourth the head of a hawk. Colors are perfectly preserved.[74]

The side rooms are not at the same artistic level as the others: yellow is the only color to be found. One of these rooms is unfinished and the decoration is only outlined in black. Inside the temple there are many life-size broken statues scattered on the ground.[75]

When Messrs. Beechey and Belzoni entered this temple for the first time the thermometer marked 84 degrees Fahrenheit. This temperature is constant inside the temple and one feels it as soon as he puts his head inside the building. When I entered, my eyeglasses fogged up and I felt oppression in my lungs similar to what happens when entering a very hot bath. Then, I began sweating violently and stopped only once I was outside the temple. It took me twenty days to copy and paint all the drawings. While I was busy with this operation, Mr. Bankes tried to free from the sands one of the two statues beside the entrance gate. Because this operation required much time and effort, he thought to dig a sort of well, upholding the sand around with water. With the workforce of our crew only, he was able to clear the base of one of the two colossi and to find, two arms under the knee, a short Greek inscription, in rough and bad writing, with the name of Psamtik. He copied it.[76]

Considering the position and solidity of this large rock-cut temple, the magnificent and peculiar order of its architecture, and the mythological and military representations that make up the decoration of the inner chambers, one cannot hesitate to regard it as the most interesting and glorious ancient Egyptian monument so far known. The representation of the civil and military deeds of the hero, carved with so much care and craftsmanship on the walls of the temple, makes me believe that it was excavated to perpetuate his memory. This tribute of gratitude was righteously due to the great Sesostris, nor could the Egyptians imagine anything more durable and grandiose.

We are indebted to the triumphant system of Mr. Champollion le Jeune if we now know that the king portrayed everywhere in this temple is Sesostris. Champollion finally lifted the mysterious veil that lay over hieroglyphs and for centuries had hidden their meaning to human comprehension. This piece of information exempts us from enquiring about the time of foundation of this temple since it probably dates back to the glorious reign of that powerful monarch. It is inconceivable how Egyptians decided to make such an extensive excavation in a place so exposed to the sands: maybe they did not foresee such a catastrophe. The extreme slowness of this invincible enemy in occupying the valley and the buildings of Abu Simbel justifies them. To have a better idea about the issue, it might be useful to know that from the bank of the Nile heading northwest, which is the part whence more sand comes, it takes forty-five minutes to reach the top of the mountain. It is part of a chain and surrounds and protects much of the valley. On top of it there is a vast plain of stony soil. After five hours' walk in the same direction, the mountain starts to slope down toward a sea of sand, down to the same level of the Nile. The

---

74   Porter and Moss, *Topographical Bibliography* 7:110, scene (115).
75   Porter and Moss, *Topographical Bibliography* 7:110–11.
76   This is an inscription carved by Greek mercenaries serving Pharaoh Psamtik in the seventh
       century BC. It served as an important dating element in Egyptian chronology; Usick, *Adventures
       in Egypt and Nubia*, 119.

sand has been lifted and transported by the winds all the way to the valley of Abu Simbel. If the obstruction of the valley did not occur all at once as a result of an extraordinary phenomenon, it is doubtless that it must have taken centuries before the sand could fill the valley to the top of the colossi (which are, as I said, sixty-six feet high).

I will now describe a phenomenon that I observed in the plain atop the mountain, but that I am unable to explain. I already mentioned that the soil is stony. It is composed of small blackish siliceous stones and other pebbles mostly round in shape, three inches in diameter. Shaking them one can easily feel a rattle: I broke some and found inside sometimes normal and sometimes clogged sand. Naturalists only can explain the cause of this singularity which overcomes the narrow limits of my intellect. I much regret that I lost the stones I took home to Europe for examination.

To the north of Abu Simbel there is another small temple,[77] whose entrance is to the south (cf. plan, plate 15, no. 6). The façade is covered with rock-cut bas-relief, six colossal statues thirty-four feet high, and rich hieroglyphic inscriptions. It is thirty-nine feet high in total. The first hall is supported by six pillars. In the front part, marked (a), there is the bas-relief copied at no. 7 of the same plate. On the other sides there are female figures;[78] plate 21, no. 1. No. 2 is a bas-relief on the wall marked (b). These reliefs are related to the mysteries of the goddess Hathor, who is nobody else than Isis, to whom the temple seems to have once been dedicated.

The bas-relief on plate 22 is taken from wall (c) and shows a king followed by a priestess offering two bunches of lotus flowers to Hathor, who is seated on her throne. The lotus flower is the plant most often associated with this goddess.[79] If there was any doubt about women serving as priestesses in ancient Egyptian sanctuaries, the small temple of Abu Simbel would cast away any incertitude on the matter. The color yellow is here predominant over any other: no wonder, since the sanctuary is dedicated to a female goddess and yellow is the more appropriate color for females, even in the hieroglyphs related to them.

These are until now the monuments discovered at Abu Simbel, but it is possible that on clearing the immense quantity of sand one might find other valuable and interesting things.

Until we stayed at Abu Simbel a strong and cold northeast wind blew. Mr. Bankes was close to losing his life because he had come out of the temple dripping with sweat and without precautions. The suppressed perspiration all at once caused him typhus, but he luckily recovered.

When he felt better, we resumed the journey and in two days we arrived at Derr, the capital of Nubia, after having visited on our way the small city of Ibrim, which lies on a granite rock. Here there is a Christian church,[80] on whose walls, in a place where the mortar had fallen, there were traces of ancient hieroglyphs. From this detail we inferred that it used to be an Egyptian temple later converted to a church.

At Derr we observed a peculiar phenomenon: a man, who came to us asking for alms, had very white pupils, hair, and skin, with black spots one inch wide. We asked him if he was born

---

77 Temple of Hathor of Abeshek and Nefertari; Porter and Moss, *Topographical Bibliography* 7:111–17.
78 Porter and Moss, *Topographical Bibliography* 7:114–15.
79 Porter and Moss, *Topographical Bibliography* 7:115 (30).
80 Porter and Moss, *Topographical Bibliography* 7:94.

like that or if it was the result of any sickness: he replied that once he was completely black, but then he was bitten by a small animal called *burts*[81] and a few days later he became as we saw him. He added that this change did not cause him any inconvenience and did not affect his sight. I had later the opportunity at Quban to see another example of this singularity, with the difference that the man, black by birth, had become completely white on the left side of his body only; he also considered the bite of the gecko as the cause of his mutation. This reptile has the shape of a little lizard, but is of a much brighter color, and has a subtle membrane between the fingers of its four legs. It hides behind the furniture or in the holes of the walls and makes a very light cry, or hiss, by which the people of the house recognize it. If an Arab sees it touching any food, he will instantly throw it away, because they strongly believe that the saliva of this reptile transmits a powerful poison. As for me, I think that the cause of the alteration of the skin color of the two men is completely different, since in Cairo, where this animal is common, nothing similar ever happened nor does this superstition exist. Anyway, in Nubia it is greatly feared and as soon as a Nubian discovers it in his house, he hunts it down, even during the night, and is restless and thinks he is unsafe until he kills it.

From Derr we reached Amada on the west bank of the Nile, where there are the ruins of an Egyptian temple[82] built in sandstone and of an ancient Christian monastery.

The former is very well preserved and is divided into two squares, one serving as a portico. There are many deeply carved hieroglyphs of good execution. The inner part of the temple is all covered in bas-reliefs: the side walls of the central hall bear many scenes with offerings of animals, fruits, and provisions. In one we also found a bark, almost completely covered in stucco. This place is in general much exposed to the sands, but the temple itself is built on a hill, so as not to be subjected to them.

From Amada we reached in one hour Araba Abuhanda,[83] to the west. This is an old town, regularly built, almost completely in stone, and dating back to the time of the Greeks or the Romans. The walls that surround it are remarkable for their thickness. Noteworthy are also the two beautiful or rather magnificent gates of the city, still intact.

Proceeding on our journey we reached Sebu'a, to the west, at some distance from the Nile.[84] This Egyptian monument is partly rock-cut and partly free-standing, built with small

---

81 Arabic برص (*burs*), 'gecko,' which, on the contrary, is a harmless animal. The reason for such hostility resides in Islamic beliefs.

82 Temple of Amun-Re and Re-Horakhty, built by Thutmose III, Amenhotep II, and Thutmose IV; Porter and Moss, *Topographical Bibliography* 7:65–73.

83 Ricci refers here to the name of the entire district of Abu Handal, on the east bank of the Nile, and maybe also to the district of al-Riqa on the west bank, though it is less likely to include the district of Wadi al-Arab, to the north. The site could be Shablul; Porter and Moss, *Topographical Bibliography* 7:64–65; Army Map Service, Corps of Engineers, U.S. Army. Al-Dîwân, North Africa [map]. 1:250.000. Series P502, Sheet NH 36–6. Washington D.C.: AMPV, 1954. Perry-Castañeda Library Map Collection, University of Texas at Austin. http://www.lib.utexas. edu/maps/ams/north_africa/txu-oclc-6949452-nf36-6.jpg. According to Patricia Usick the site, called by Bankes "Abou Hamdau," was on the east bank, to the south of Amada, and could be identified with Korosko; Usick, *Adventures in Egypt and Nubia*, 115.

84 Wadi al-Sebu'a, with the temple of Amun and Re-Horakhty built by Ramesses II; Porter and Moss, *Topographical Bibliography* 7:53–64.

sandstone blocks and mortar. We found it almost completely buried in sand and since we could not access it, we were forced to open a passage in the ceiling at the point marked (a) in the plan of the temple; cf. plate 23, no. 1. It took us three entire days of hard labor. This temple, as many others, was reduced to a Christian church and was almost completely plastered and painted over.[85] In the middle of the sanctuary there was an altar, on which we found a black pottery chalice, very thin and similar to the *bucchero*, and four lamps, also made of clay, but of a much rougher fabric. In two of them there still was a wick. On the other edge of the altar, on the left side, there was a stone cup with some grains of incense of a reddish color. We at first failed to recognize it, but then we ground it with a stone and to our surprise it not only burned, but also retained its natural scent. These objects will be featured in Mr. Bankes' collection. In the central wall of the sanctuary there is an image of St. Peter holding a large key and many other smaller keys hanging from his garment. The style is barbarous and the color even worse.

In front of the main gate, which looks toward the east, at the distance of 165 feet there are two standing statues, which used to be at the head of a double row of sphinxes, forming an avenue to the temple. Four of these sphinxes are still visible.[86]

In order to find the original hieroglyphs on the inner walls, we chipped off the plaster. This was an easy operation because it lay on the naked stone and was almost everywhere already gone. The most interesting subject is shown in plate 24. It is a bas-relief representing a sacred bark, very different from the many others I have seen before. The color yellow is almost exclusively used in the other bas-reliefs of this temple.

From Sebu'a, where we stayed for three days, we passed to Maharraqa, also on the west bank. Here there are the remains of a temple[87] built on a regular base of very hard limestone, which also forms the foundation of the building itself. The distribution of the inner rooms has nothing of the Egyptian and there are no hieroglyphs; cf. plate 23, no. 2. Its access is to the east, but it also has two doors to the north and to the west. In the point marked (a) there is a ditch two feet deep, but we could not imagine its purpose. No. 3 of the same plate points to the remains of a building,[88] which used to be adjacent to the temple and which probably served Christian worship. No. 4 is a red granite block with lines on its surface forming squares:[89] it lay close to the temple, so it might have been used as an altar, and then removed.

On the same line of Maharraqa, at a distance of two hours, there is Cassi, or Qurta,[90] a small Egyptian temple known interchangeably by these two names, cf. no. 5. The few hieroglyphs that can be found are carved partly in the first and partly in the second room, beside

---

85 A church dating back to the seventh–eighth century; Donatella Andriolo and Silvio Curto, *Catalogo delle chiese della Nubia* (Torino: Accademia delle Scienze, 2000), 53–54.

86 Porter and Moss, *Topographical Bibliography* 7:55.

87 Temple of Serapis, built in the Roman period; Porter and Moss, *Topographical Bibliography* 7:51.

88 Another small temple in ruins; Porter and Moss, *Topographical Bibliography* 7:51–52.

89 Maybe an offering table with Meroitic text, as shown on the drawing VIII.E.5, Deposit/ Bankes of Kingston Lacy and Corfe Castle, Egyptian Drawings, Dorset History Centre, Dorchester.

90 Temple of Isis, Roman period but built on a preexisting New Kingdom building, now destroyed; Porter and Moss, *Topographical Bibliography* 7:50; Usick, *Adventures in Egypt and Nubia*, 87.

the two entrance doors. A wall used to fence in the temple and opposite it there are the ruins of a large square structure.

Not far from Qurta lies Dakka:[91] its plan is very elegant and the propylaeum magnificent. From what is left of the walls it is still clear that this temple was surrounded by a double enclosure, cf. no. 6. The bas-reliefs that are inside look like they have been made in different periods and by different craftsmen. The hieroglyphic inscriptions are poorly made, but some small bas-relief figures on the door frames are to be considered masterpieces.

The ruins of the temple of Allaqi,[92] almost in front of Dakka to the east, consist of long walls, mostly destroyed. Only two bas-reliefs are preserved: one representing a battle and a sacrifice, but so much damaged to the extent that it was impossible for me to make a copy. Not far there is a large square building, which looks like a fortress built [in ancient times. Evidence that it must have suffered][93] invasions are many stone fragments with hieroglyphs scattered on the ground.

We left Allaqi at sunrise and in one hour we reached Kushtemna, to the west, and then after two hours Gerf Hussein.[94] In the former place everything is in ruin except the gate of the temple, supported on both sides by a piece of wall. On the lintel there is a hawk with a disk on its head.[95]

The beautiful temple of Gerf Hussein is all rock-cut, except for its vast propylaeum, built in sandstone. Cf. plate 25, no. 1. Six colossal statues eight feet tall, standing on high squared pedestals, serve as ornament and support to the first hall. Although in good style, the sculpture is shabby. On each side of the walls there are four niches, each with three seated figures. The second hall, much smaller, is supported by two pillars only. At the end of the sanctuary there are four more statues, also seated. The sculptures are of very old style. Two long rows of statues and sphinxes, difficult to say exactly how many, adorned the entrance of this temple.

Dandur, also to the west, is a small temple built in sandstone.[96] It has many hieroglyphs, cf. same plate, no. 2. A large enclosure wall ninety-six feet long and forty-nine feet wide was erected in front of the temple, but I cannot see the reason.

From Dandur we moved to Kalabsha,[97] to the west, a large temple built also in sandstone with a nice plan. The hieroglyphs that greatly enrich this temple are all in bas-relief and of refined work: the colors are well preserved and the most used is violet.[98] The rear wall is

---

91 Temple dedicated to Thoth of Pnubis, built in the Greco-Roman period; Porter and Moss, *Topographical Bibliography* 7:40–50.
92 Quban, the ancient Contra Pselchis; Porter and Moss, *Topographical Bibliography* 7:82–84.
93 A line is missing; conjecture is by the editor.
94 Rock temple built by Ramesses II; Porter and Moss, *Topographical Bibliography* 7:32–37.
95 Probably the fortress of Kori (Ikkur), dating back to the Old Kingdom with Twelfth Dynasty modifications; Porter and Moss, *Topographical Bibliography* 7:37.
96 Temple built by Emperor Augustus to the deified brothers Peteisi and Padihor; *Topographical Bibliography* 7:27–33.
97 Augustus erected a large temple dedicated to Mandulis; *Topographical Bibliography* 7:10–19.
98 A color in fact not used by the ancient Egyptians: it must have originally been blue or black; Alfred Lucas, *Ancient Egyptian Materials and Industries* (London: Edward Arnold & Co., 2003), 441; Lorna Lee and Stephen Quirke, "Painting Materials," in *Ancient Egyptian Materials and Technology*, ed. Paul T. Nicholson and Ian Shaw (Cambridge: Cambridge University Press, 2000), 113.

decorated with colossal bas-reliefs in beautiful style and perfect execution. The whole build-ing is surrounded by many enclosure walls.

Unlike the other places we visited, where the inhabitants are docile and well-mannered, in this part of Nubia we found them arrogant and nasty. More than once they came with weapons in large numbers asking for money, and by paying we always managed to calm them down. But in this place particularly, not happy with what we offered, they became so insolent and threatened to force us to leave. We were lucky enough to reach the Nile and board our boat in safety. We did not waste time and immediately set off.

After two hours of navigation we reached Tafa, a small temple to the west, with no hiero-glyphic inscriptions, except for a winged sun-disk on the main gate lintel. On a small hill close to the temple we found the lintel and the doorjambs of a small door, perfectly preserved and of skilled craftmanship, but not Egyptian: Mr. Bankes judged them Roman and fell so much in love with them that he absolutely wanted to take them with him. The transportation of these stones to the Nile occupied the rest of that day. We observed here the ruins of twenty-one buildings, covering an area of two hundred square feet. Their state of preservation did not allow us to determine what their purpose was, but they were likely fortifications.

The following day, we arrived early at the long wall of Qertassi,[99] built with large squared stones and quite concave in the middle. In the nearby quarries, where the materials were extracted, there are some Greek and Latin inscriptions and some outlined sculptures of a hybrid style. Mr. Bankes copied many inscriptions. The temple is a few steps from the wall, but nothing is left standing of the entire building with the exception of six columns, beau-tiful in style and well worked.

It is very likely that this wall dates back to the Roman period, since this place is the gateway to Nubia. The Romans possibly built it to defend the frontier or to establish an encampment. If this idea is right, the ruins of Tafa and those from Dandur onward are all castles that formed a defense line.

From Qertassi, heading to Dabod, we suffered from a strong north wind, preceded by a column of sand, which forced us to land to find shelter. This storm came three times during the day and then around midnight changed into a heavy shower, with frequent thunder, definitely an uncommon phenomenon in this region. At dawn, the storm had ceased, but the air was still filled with very thick fog, which disappeared with the sun. We moved toward Dabod,[100] where we arrived in little time. The plan of this temple is on plate 25, no. 3. The distribution of the inner rooms is nice and regular: three propylaea precede it, one after the other, and possibly this is the first example of such a feature. Hieroglyphs are in bas-relief and of good style, but in general the sculptures are unfinished and many walls are com-pletely empty. The existing reliefs are very well preserved.

From Dabod we reached the island of Philae, belonging to Nubia and called by the Arabs Bilaq, and also Anas al-Vodjud, for a remote tradition that this was the name of the

99   Qertassi; Porter and Moss, *Topographical Bibliography* 7:6–8.
100   Temple dedicated to Isis during the Greco-Roman or Meroitic period; Porter and Moss, *Topo-graphical Bibliography* 7:1–5.

king who erected the temples. This island, once very prosperous, is now deserted and uncultivated. Here we not only made many drawings, but also excavated around the large temple and found two subterranean chambers, where unfortunately nothing of interest was found.

The remains of many monuments on this island are all remarkable as for architecture and the many mythological scenes. Plate 26 gathers some, taken in different places. No. 1 seems to be an offering or a sacrifice to Osiris, with the prayers of the offerer expressed in three lines of hieroglyphs. No. 2 represents the goddess Isis suckling Horus. Usually this goddess is represented seated when suckling her son on her knees; it seemed therefore relevant here that Horus is standing next to his mother. In the temple of Adda there is a similar representation, though. No. 3 seems to show the same figure of no. 1, with the difference that here the offerer holds in his hand the key of life, symbol of divinity.

No. 4 is a bas-relief on the door of the small temple on the bank of the Nile,[101] and shows a crocodile, symbol for Typhon, between lotus plants next to the cataract, marked with the letter (a), carrying a mummy on its back. In the above register there is a sarcophagus. Also Osiris and Horus are represented seated, while Isis seems to walk away from the sorrowful tomb, looking back at it for the last time. All this makes me believe that this scene represents the death of Osiris by the hands of Typhon, who is then hiding the corpse in a steep place, symbolized by the cataract.

No. 5 is a sacred bark carved in one of the walls next to the sanctuary entrance, in the large temple.[102] The hawk, fish, and gazelle seem here to represent the three elements of air, water, and earth. Since fire, the attribute of Osiris, is missing, I think that the bark itself is carrying the corpse of the god, after he was found.

Plate 27 shows the copy of two bas-reliefs existing in the two walls of a corridor in the large temple, leading to the Typhonium. Harp, sistrum, and cymbal, held by many female figures, indicate that a celebration with a sacrifice is being held. A mummy raises its head, surmounted by the disk, and a hawk stands in similar attitude. Both are placed under some hieroglyphic text. This is undoubtedly Osiris, and the discovery of his body is possibly the subject of the scene.

Plate 28 is another bas-relief in the back wall of a room in the upper floor of the large temple, which can be reached through a staircase.[103] The whole composition seems to be about the death of Osiris, the mutilation of his body, and the dispersion of his limbs by Typhon. It is true that in this scene the god Horus is represented lying on a funerary bed, mourned by two female figures and a kneeling man, and this seems to me to be out of theme here, but who knows which rites were performed in the religious ceremonies at the death of a great man or a god by the ancient Egyptians?

Plate 29 also shows a bas-relief existing on the right wall of the same room. The sacred bark where the mummy lies is very similar to the one portrayed on plate 26 and strengthens

---

101 Gate of Hadrian and Marcus Aurelius; Porter and Moss, *Topographical Bibliography* 6:254–55 (6)–(7).

102 Possibly Room VI; Ptolemaic period, reign of Ptolemy II Philadelphus; Porter and Moss, *Topographical Bibliography* 6:241 (318).

103 The so-called 'Osiris Room'; Porter and Moss, *Topographical Bibliography* 6:249.

in me the opinion that both reliefs represent the transportation of the body of Osiris after its discovery.

All these scenes concerning the same subject and a large number of others in the great temple and in other monuments of Philae Island cast away all doubts that in this temple the main god was Osiris. He was the creative intelligence, which, according to Egyptian mythology, was used by Khnum, or the supreme intelligence, to create the universe.

The subjects on plates 30 and 31 are also reliefs in the same room. They show all the gods of ancient Egypt, represented with their attributes and symbols. This gathering, which is not to be observed in any other Egyptian monument as far as I remember, makes these two plates very interesting. The last register of each seems to show either different heraldic symbols or military insignia used by the Egyptians as well as items and animals considered sacred or symbolic, and objects of worship. In this last aspect, the importance of the two plates would be even greater, since all the Egyptian mythology would be represented here at once.

Fatigued by the journey and more by the discomfort and deprivation that are part of it, when we finished our work at Philae we decided to suspend all other research and go directly back to Cairo, to enjoy the rest that we all extremely needed. We set sail on 18 May and without stopping at all during the day we reached Beni Suef. Here Mr. Bankes, always active and tireless, noticed that we were in the place where the road leading to Fayoum begins. Already forgetting our proposition, he could not curb his curiosity and decided to make a trip to Lake Moeris. He wanted to search for the famous Labyrinth, described by Herodotus as one of the most magnificent monuments of Egypt[104] and that, according to Pliny, was to the west of the lake.[105] He proposed the trip to the whole party, but none of us had the strength to follow him. Since he wanted to do it at all costs, he decided to undertake the journey alone with the dragoman and stayed at Beni Suef to arrange all things and find guides. We left him and continued our journey toward Cairo, where we arrived in good health on 30 May 1819.

Travel to the Temple of Jupiter-Amun

The very old Republic of Siwa was a small country of Libya famous for the Temple of Jupiter-Amun. It retained its independence until very recently, not because its army could repulse foreign invasions, but because it was naturally defended by its geographical position. Anybody who wanted to take an army through the deserts that separate Siwa from Egypt would have to overcome many known dangers and discomforts. Cambyses, in fact, lost most of his soldiers.[106] If Alexander could consult the oracle of Amun, guided—as the myth says—by two crows[h] and helped by a miraculous rain,[107] it was only because of his constant luck, rather than his foresight.

---

104 Herodotus, *Historiae* II 148.
105 Pliny the Elder, *Naturalis Historia* XXXVI 19, where there is no specific information on the position of the monument with respect to the lake.
106 A reference to Herodotus, *Historiae* III 26, 3 and Plutarch, *Alexander* XXVI 6.
107 Plutarch, *Alexander* XXVII 1.

These difficulties did not dismay the enterprising Muhammad Ali, who absolutely wanted to subjugate the republic. In February 1820 he ordered a military expedition under the command of Hassan Bey, governor of Damanhur, to set off to Siwa.

No occasion could be more favorable to visit the famous temple, so I agreed with Mr. Drovetti, general consul of France,[108] Mr. Linant, and Mr. Frediani to follow the Egyptian army. We met at Tarrana, a small town on the banks of the Nile two days north of Cairo, whence we left on 1 March 1820 with the necessary firmans.[109] Our caravan was guided by two Arabs of the Awlad Ali tribe and was made up of fifteen camels, two interpreters, and four more Arab servants.

In the first four days we followed the Nile until Maryut, hoping to reach Hassan Bey. The commander headed an army of three thousand men,[110] between Mamluks and Arabs of different tribes, on foot and on horseback, and two pieces of field artillery. He had two days' advantage on us and because a plague had started to spread in his encampment, he was proceeding very fast. He hoped to defeat the disease by moving to a different climate, as in fact happened. It was very difficult to reach him without forcing the march extraordinarily and this was very dangerous for our health. Moreover, following his steps could expose us to thirst, because surely the wells would have been dried out serving such a large number of people. These thoughts and the certainty that the bey was marching along the Mediterranean coast made us decide to head directly to Siwa. This diversion did not separate us much from the army, because the bey turned south before reaching Paraetonium,[111] after he had marched along the coast for two days.

As a consequence of this decision, we left Maryut on 5 March heading to the west and entered the desert: the day was extremely hot and the northeast wind blew violently. The abundant rains, which had uncharacteristically fallen during the autumn and in the previous February, had embellished the large plain: a beautiful carpet of flowers of every kind covered its surface. Red and yellow anemones were the most abundant flowers and a sweet fragrance delighted our noses. The more we walked away from the sea, the less beautiful were the flowers, and the color less bright. I took advantage of the blossoming to gather a collection, which I called *Flora Libyca* and which I presented to Mr. Drovetti. It is believed that the plain I am describing used to be part of Lake Maryut and that the sands, filling it little by little, changed it into a desert. Many tribes of Bedouin have been living here for a long time.

After two continuous hours' march in this plain, we met with some ruins: the most noticeable is named al-Mallah. Here a large number of small square rooms are built around a tower, close to an abandoned well. There are also fragments of stones with some inscriptions. See plate 32, nos. 12 and 13. The strong winds that constantly blow in these regions

---

108 In fact at the time of this journey Drovetti was yet to be reappointed to this position (20 June 1821).
109 On 2 March according to Frediani; Sammarco, *Alessandro Ricci*, 123.
110 Only seven hundred soldiers, according to Ahmed Fakhry, *Siwa Oasis: Its History and Antiquities* (Cairo: Government Press, 1944), 105.
111 Marsa Matruh.

raised here four sand dunes at the same distance one from the other, shaping the slope as a rampart in defense of a fortification. We spent the night among these ruins.

On the 6th we continued our journey heading in the same direction and around midday we reached the remains of the ancient Abusir, known today by the same name and also called 'Tower of the Arabs':[112] not far from these ruins there is a round stone well, nicely built in the middle of the sands. On its edges one can still see the grooves produced by the ropes, proof that once it served both caravans and inhabitants of Abusir. We could not estimate its depth, since it is abandoned and filled with rubbish. The Arabs call it *hut*.[113] In the evening we reached Hammam, where we camped for the night. This is a nice, narrow valley with four very deep wells. Only one of them has water, but brackish: when closed in bottles, once reopened it releases hydrogen sulfide. All the caravans and the Arab tribes come here to make provision of it. The place where we camped was full of an amazing quantity of mallows, of different species and colors, and they made a nice view. Some Bedouin women came after a while and offered us white truffles, which we found excellent. Simple and amiable as they were, they accepted with much joy some small necklaces of colored glass and promised to come back early the day after with fresh milk. They surely kept their word, but, since we left before dawn, we did not see them again. Among the few ruins that are in this place, I copied three fragments of inscriptions, two in hieroglyphs and the other in the characters of al-Mallah. Plate 32, nos. 14, 15, and 16.

On 17 March, a cloudy and chilly day, we proceeded heading south: we found the road very stony and the anemones were not as beautiful as before, but lilies of different colors were thriving. Here we observed, scattered on the ground, a large quantity of snails, mostly empty shells in which bees had deposited violet-scented honey. Not all had honey, but it was easy to recognize which had it from the dirt left by the bees outside the shell. On the way, our Arabs found some truffles. They did so by carefully examining the soil: every time they saw a slot in a small hump, they opened it and there with no exception was the fruit. This is white, smaller than ours, but as fragrant and tasty. We collected a large number of truffles and we sent them back to our friends in Alexandria, giving them at the same time news about us. In the evening, we camped at Halfa and even though we were quite far, we heard during all the night the ripple of the sea, agitated by the north wind, which was blowing strongly.

The Arabs who live in small tribes in the desert between Maryut and Halfa stay here as long as there is water and the soil provides grazing for their livestock. When these resources are exhausted—usually two months after the rains—they leave and move to less arid places where they can subsist more easily.

We traveled for eight days through a pleasant plain, breathing pure air, and we did not realize we were in a desert, except when we had to use goatskins to drink. At Halfa

---

112   Burg al-Arab: the modern city is not far from the ruins of Abusir, the ancient Taposiris Magna. While Ricci focuses on the well, he forgets to mention the imposing enclosure of the temple of Osiris, built by Ptolemy V, and the tower itself, a Hellenistic lighthouse or a tomb. Both monuments are visible from Lake Maryut.

113   Possibly "Garm Houd," Edme-François Jomard, *Voyage à l'Oasis de Syouah, rédigé et publié par M. Jomard* (Paris: De Rignoux, 1823), pl. I (map).

this illusion begins to vanish: the green and blossomed soil changes little by little into an immense extension of sand, interrupted here and there by small limestone hills. The vegetation ends and the spirit is assaulted by all the horror inspired by an uninhabitable and truly desert country.

We left on the 8th and after five hours of boring march we reached the slopes of two mountains, shaped as pyramids and known by the name of Himaymat. They are made of limestone and the top is covered with a layer of fossils several feet deep. The rest of the surface is scattered with pieces of porphyry, corals, petrified wood, and other stones. I collected many and still have them in my collection. The largest pieces of petrified wood are placed by the Arabs in visible, high spots to mark the road. Who could ever say why these stones are in so large a number on these mountains, while no sign of them is in the plain beneath?

In the evening, we pitched the tents, but they were overturned twice by the north wind, which was blowing impetuously, accompanied by very fine rain. Since we could not find shelter, we decided to set off three hours before dawn. The markers were covered by the sand and we soon took a wrong path: instead of heading south, we moved southwest for three hours. Eventually our guides saw a mountain chain called Abu Tartur, realized the mistake, and corrected our direction. We soon reached the slopes of those mountains. Here the desert takes a completely different appearance: no more fossils, while there is a very high mountain chain to the right and a vast plain to the left, devastated by the current of many streams flowing from the mountains. In some places the terrain is covered in pure magnesia, possibly produced by the fossils. From Hammam to this point the road is dangerous because strong winds move large quantities of sand. When the sand lands, it covers the markers in all directions and puts travelers at risk of getting lost and dying. This would have happened to us, if we had not realized our mistake in time, because we had no water left. In the evening we reached Labbaq and nearby the Arabs found a small well of brackish water, which, nevertheless, looked delicious to us.

The dawn of the 10th seemed to announce a better day, but in the morning our hopes disappeared as the north wind started blowing violently like the previous day. To shelter ourselves we were forced to meander along the slopes of the mountains, strictly following the many curves. The plain on the left, which stretches to Abu Marzuq, is all made of natron and the camels are in certain spots at risk of sinking.[114] Our guides warned us about the dangers of such an insidious terrain, which, being shorter and looking beautiful and even, invites the traveler. I wanted to ascertain whether the information was true or just one of the usual children's stories of the Arabs. I dismounted and headed with a long stick toward the plain. As I was advancing, the soil became soft and soggy, and I soon reached the point where I could easily immerse the whole stick: after this experiment, I went back and observed on the surface a large quantity of muriate of soda. This phenomenon contributes to making this region the most horrendous and the scariest I have ever crossed. We camped in the evening in a bend of the mountain chain, called Abu Tartur, on the slope of which we observed many fossils, possibly dragged down from the top by the rains.

---

114 The Qattara Depression, whose depth can reach down to eighty meters below sea level.

From Maryut to this point our camels drank only once, on the second day, because the wells that we met on our way had enough water only for us. On the following day, 11 March, two hours after our departure, the camels started to speed up all together, showing so much impatience that we could barely contain them. From this we gathered that water was not far, since these animals have the peculiar property of being able to detect the proximity of this element. In fact, after midday we reached a water reservoir, which had enough water to quench their thirst. They became almost furious and wanted to throw themselves all together into the water. With much effort we succeeded in turning them away; we then tied their feet and made them lie down, distributing afterward the same quantity of water to each one of them until the reservoir was empty. After sunset we stopped at a place called Bi'r,[115] next to some palm trees at the slope of the same mountain chain that we had been following for two days.

On the 12th, while heading southwest, we came across many wild palm trees, which, although unattended, bring their fruit to perfect ripeness. This is smaller than the domestic date, but tastier and less sweet. Eating them was a great solace for us and we almost made a party, more so having found a well of less brackish water, where we filled our goatskins. In the evening we reached Abu Marzuq,[116] which is a bend almost at the end of the same mountain chain, and there we camped.

This long mountain chain, known by the Arabs under the name of Adera, goes from the east to the west, but shortly before reaching al-Qara opens to the northwest. It is easy to recognize by its sharp pyramidal peaks.

On the morning of the 13th, in the hope of sighting soon the mountain of Qara, which the guides had announced as close, we set off very early in the morning. At ten, the Adera chain was already far from us, and also far was the dangerous natron plain. The terrain we were now crossing was sandy and scattered with very small limestone and flintstone fragments. Finally, the longed-for mountains appeared.

On the 14th, an hour before dawn, we set off in the same direction and started climbing the hills around Qara Oasis at two in the afternoon. We were now in the territory of Siwa. Before proceeding to the small city, we halted in order to inquire whether the bey had already captured it or whether it was still in the hands of the Siwans. This inquiry was very dangerous because if the Egyptian army was still marching, the inhabitants, surely aware of the threat, would treat us as spies and possibly even our own guides would report us as Christians so as to have their own lives spared. In both hypotheses, our doom could not be but unhappy. It is true that the bey had two days' advantage on us, but he could have taken a longer road and unexpected difficulties could have delayed his march. For these reasons we were confused and did not know how to find out the truth. Gunshots at a certain distance suddenly drew our attention. Looking in the direction of the shots, we saw men coming

---

115 Marked under the French word *puits* in Jomard, *Voyage*, pl. I (map).

116 Ricci must be confused because, coming from the east, Abu Marzuq is reached before Abu Tartur and Bi'r. Furthermore, to be able to arrive at al-Qara only two days later, he could not be at Abu Marzuq on the evening of 12 March.

toward us and, even though we were using telescopes, we could not discern if they were friends or enemies. There was no more time for discussion; we were discovered and the best thing to do was to advance openly. We left behind the camels, took up our rifles, and advanced in a line toward the Arabs. When we reached a distance from where we could be heard, we stopped and, aiming at them, we asked them to declare, without moving a further step, to whom they belonged. "Hassan Bey!" they answered without hesitation, a bit surprised. Upon hearing this name, all suspicions vanished: we advanced fearless and explained to them the reason for our behavior. Our explanation satisfied them and they told us they had left the camp in order to hunt for gazelles. They also informed us that the army had arrived two days earlier and was getting ready to leave for Siwa the following day. Most of the inhabitants of al-Qara had fled to the capital, abandoning all that they could not carry with them. The bey captured the city without a single gunshot. We then set off to al-Qara and, one hour before sunset, we reached the bey's camp by the city, in the nearby plain. We immediately went to pay our respects. As soon as we entered, and one of us had offered greetings, he presented us with a goatskin of fresh water, the best available, foreseeing that this would be our first request. He was not wrong, because all along our journey we had found only bitter and brackish water to drink. He showed us his regret that we had not joined him from the beginning, assuring us that he always found soft, or at least bearable, water, enough for the whole army. His men had only suffered the death of a few from the plague in the first days' march, and a few horses and camels as well.

Even though sunset was close, we were very curious to see the town. We greeted the bey and we ventured there, but in less than half an hour we had explored it all. It is built on one of the many rocky hills in the valley and is made up of almost eighty houses. These are built here and there without order, all very low and erected with shapeless pieces of stone, badly connected, and covered with palm branches. The largest houses have two floors: the ground floor for humans and animals, and the first floor as a storeroom for the harvest and other provisions. The whole town is surrounded by weak walls with two gates. In the hills near the city there are some tombs, all of the same shape and size. The city was at that time almost deserted and we met only a few miserable people walking around the abandoned houses with an expression of pain impressed on their faces.

The oasis is small, possibly with a circumference of five to six miles. There are many springs, but few of fresh water. There are also woods of incredibly tall palm trees, which provide the main source of income for the inhabitants. They sell part of the dates to the desert Arabs and exchange what exceeds their own consumption for wheat, cotton cloths, and other goods in the markets of Alexandria.

On 15 March, an hour before dawn, the bey's army was deployed in the plain and shortly after moved toward Siwa. As for us, after a visit to the surroundings of the town, which offered nothing of interest, we proceeded beside them on a hill. It was nice to see the soldiers deployed in the huge plain, followed by more than four thousand camels for the transport of families and belongings of the different tribes that were part of the expedition. The cavalry and the infantry were marching mixed together, though still retaining a certain order, and not a few among the Arabs were mounted on their own camels, always staying close to their own tribe. It is a very old custom among the Arabs to put at the head of the tribe a virgin seated in a big basket secured to a camel, where she can comfortably lie sleeping.[117] The animal is adorned as richly as possible and a tent is mounted on the basket by means of four poles. The girl can open or shut the curtains as she prefers. For this occasion she wears her best clothes and jewels. She also has a small drum, made of a pottery or copper vase without a bottom and with animal skin stretched on the top. By playing this instrument she emboldens the men of her tribe and encourages them during the battle, singing warlike songs. The response of the soldiers is cries and the clapping of hands. The Arabs all die rather than abandon her and it would be an extremely bad omen if she were to die naturally before the start of the action or while marching against the enemy. To sum up, this virgin is like the flag of the tribe, defended by all to the last drop of blood.

The Arabs do not go to war without taking with them their families and belongings, which always follow the advancing column.

The bey continued his march and, while we descended the hills whence we had all day observed him, camped in a large plain of dried natron, where there was nothing else but a few palm trees and almost no vegetation. We stopped at the slope of the mountain and followed the army on the 16th. The soldiers reached the banks of a large lake, bordered here and there with palm trees, which could not be crossed except by a narrow path. Here, the army was attacked by the Siwans, who were waiting in ambush. For a few minutes they fired their muskets, but as the bey ordered one of his cannons to fire canister shot, the banks of the lake were rapidly cleared and the enemy hastily rushed back, abandoning their position. This small action caused few wounded and six casualties to the Egyptians, while the Siwans lost around forty of their men, some of whom, wounded, were collected and looked after by the bey. Once in control of such a dangerous passage with so little sacrifice, the bey ordered cavalry and cannons to cross quickly and pursue the enemies, who, favored by the night and more experienced with the terrain, managed to escape. Infantry and camels passed later on and it was already night when the operation finished. Not much later we also joined the army provisions and camped in the valley of Siwa.

The bey, who proceeded further with the cavalry, had immediately sent an envoy to the city, informing the heads of the government about his imminent arrival and intimating surrender. Nevertheless the envoy came back to the camp the following morning bearing no result because the citizens had refused to bend to any negotiation. The bey wanted to capture the city with no further bloodshed and sent a second envoy, who, less lucky than the first, was kept hostage.

While we were waiting for his return, we decided to visit the many monuments existing in that place,[118] which are four temples and a large number of tombs. The bey himself

---

117 George Waddington and Barnard Hanbury, *Journal of a Visit to Some Parts of Ethiopia* (London: John Murray, 1822), 96, n. [1].
118 Ptolemaic necropolis of Abu al-Awaf; Porter and Moss, *Topographical Bibliography* 7:316; Fakhry, *Siwa Oasis*, 76–79.

wanted to accompany us, satisfied to see us busy with the plans of the buildings. The better preserved monuments are those on plate 33, nos. 8 and 9. They are of Greco-Roman style, built with large stones without mortar and on a foundation of rough stone blocks, similar to those of most Nubian monuments, which also share almost the same plan. I drew one of the gates for its beautiful and peculiar architecture (no. 5 of same plate). The inside is simple, without decoration or hieroglyphs: it seems there never had been any. As for the nearby tombs, some are three to four feet under the ground, other are at ground level, built with stones or bricks, a vaulted ceiling, and inner walls plastered with natron, which had infiltrated in the form of stalactites. Not far from these ruins there is a spring whose waters are warm at night and cool during the day: they start warming up at sunset and they cool down at dawn. The water is soft and extraordinarily limpid.[119] The vegetation around the spring is very thick and the place is frequented by many birds. I observed the same phenomenon in other sandy places, where wells and springs almost always have these characteristics. Their waters look cool during the day, because bodies exposed to the heat are much hotter than them. For the opposite reason, they seem warmer at night: because the sands transmit part of the heat accumulated during the day, while the air cools down the bodies and disperses the heat. This difference is not particularly high, and, every time we measured, it never surpassed three degrees. Therefore the Fountain of the Sun[120] does not exclusively hold this attribute, otherwise all desert springs would be as many Fountains of the Sun and all nearby buildings many temples of Jupiter-Amun.

When in the evening the bey saw that the envoy did not come back, he understood what had actually happened. The point in the valley where the camp was, was eight hours distant from Siwa: since the man was riding a very fast camel, he should have gone and come back in less than four hours.

Outraged by this violation of international right, the bey ordered the march for the following day, the 18th. One hour before dawn the entire army was already moving, proceeding at forced marches because the bey wanted to attack the city on the same day. His plan could not be implemented as we found on our way natron, lakes, palm-tree woods, and thick and high weeds, all things that delayed the march. Furthermore, when he reached the wood, he was once again attacked by the enemy, who launched an ambush there. This second attack had the same result as the first: the Siwans, struck by the canister shots, fled and sheltered inside the city, carrying with them the dead and around twenty-five wounded. At sunset, the army arrived in front of Siwa and the bey gave orders to camp on a small hill to the south of the city. Many fires were lit in the camp and in the nearby plain to deceive the enemy as to the number of aggressors, while, for more than two hours, the cannons shot fireballs, which scared the inhabitants the most and forced them to capitulate. If the Egyptians had no artillery, they would have never surrendered because they are as skilled as any soldier in the use of rifles. We followed the army at a short distance and we camped

---

119 "Near Zaytun there is good water, quite warm and populated by snails," Frediani in Sammarco, *Alessandro Ricci*, 125.

120 The Fountain of the Sun described in Herodotus, *Historiae* IV 181, 3–4.

with it. We were so close to the city that we could hear all night the continuous cries of the besieged. At a certain point, we thought they were about to try a sortie: the alarm was given throughout the camp and the bey ordered a detachment of cavalry to advance to the walls in order to find out whether the suspicion was well founded or not. Although he was reassured that all was calm outside, he wanted most of the troops to spend the night armed.

At dawn on the 19th, a third envoy entered Siwa to order the inhabitants to release the hostage and send to the camp their own envoys to negotiate their submission with the threat, in case they refused, to burn the city and kill whoever was to be found carrying weapons. This second threat was very effective and the two envoys came back reporting that the citizens were ready to negotiate, but since the shaykhs were of a different opinion on the subject, it was necessary to summon a public *diwan*, after which they would submit their decision to the bey.[121] This was likely only a way to gain time, so the bey ordered horses and camels to be sent into the sown fields in order to accelerate negotiations through this very violent action.

Around midday a northerly whirlwind started blowing, so strong that it plucked up most tents and forced us to lie on the ground with our faces toward the south. A mass of very fine sand filled the air and it was not possible to see anything beyond a distance of ten feet. Luckily the storm did not last long, but many soldiers had injuries to their faces caused by stones and sand.

In the evening an envoy from Siwa came to announce to the bey that the city was ready to surrender and that the following morning they would send two shaykhs to negotiate the conditions. In fact, the day after, two men armed with a saber and dressed in a very simple way, without retinue, appeared at the outposts, asking to be introduced to the presence of the bey. He ordered them in, while the soldiers of his guard surrounded the tent in good order. As soon as they appeared, the bey asked them who they were and why they came. When he heard that one of them was called shaykh *hagg* Mahmud, he immediately made him sit.[122] With few words they said that the city would capitulate on the conditions the bey would like to impose, provided they were not too burdensome. The bey cut short the conversation, demanding that they recognize the sovereignty of Muhammad Ali, viceroy of Egypt, to be bound to an annual tribute, and to pay the war expenses, estimating them at ten thousand thalers. Hagg Mahmoud answered, barely holding back his tears: "We were hoping that the poverty of our country, where we have always lived in peace and freedom for so long, without committing any aggression against anyone whomsoever, would insure us against an occurrence as much unexpected as not provoked by us. But since God chose differently, I bend my forehead to His decrees. I must only tell you that the sum you ask

---

121 Siwa was governed by a *diwan* (council) composed of a variable number of shaykhs (twenty-two according to Cailliaud, only twelve per Drovetti). The eldest was chosen as head. Members of the *diwan* were changed every six years; Jomard, *Voyage*, 9; Johann H.K.M von Minutoli, *Reise zum Tempel des Jupiter Ammon in der Libyschen Wüste und nach Ober-Aegypten in den Jahren 1820 und 1821, nach den Tagebüchern Sr. Excellenz herausgegeben und mit Beilagen begleitet von Dr. E.H. Toelken* (Berlin: Rücker, 1824), 83.

122 A sign of respect toward a pilgrim *(hagg)* who had been to Mecca.

exceeds our possibilities: nevertheless, I will inform my fellow citizens about your requests and tomorrow you will know their opinion." The bey then consoled them and presented both of them with rich clothes, inviting them to wear them in his presence. When they left the tent, they found two horses with rich trappings; they mounted them and went back to the city, at least apparently very satisfied.

New envoys came the following day, better dressed than the previous ones and escorted by a number of soldiers with rifles. Among them there was the head of the republic, who more than anyone else contributed to the acceptance of the bey's conditions. They were welcomed with much pomp, and received presents like the others, but even more generous. Asked to declare the final decision of the citizens, they answered that they recognized the sovereignty of Muhammad Ali and were happy to pay for the annual tribute whatever he would ask, trusting his moderation, but that the sum of ten thousand thalers was too high and therefore pleaded for it to be reduced. On this point the bey was unrelenting, but in order not to send them away unhappy, he told them that, in the hope of seeing the payment readily made, he would order the devastation of their fields to cease. This he did immediately in their presence, also adding that he would soon send one of his aghas to collect the contribution.

While the army was idle, we decided to visit the environs of the city. Siwa is placed on the slope of a high mountain standing to the north. A salty lake defends it from the west and thick palm woods cover it from the east; only the south side is unprotected and therefore is the only spot from which one could successfully attack the city. Its walls, quite strong, were on this occasion reinforced from the outside with platforms and scaffolding, on which they had amassed baskets full of sand, capable of absorbing the impact of the cannonballs. Unable to penetrate the city for the moment, we started our observations in the north sector. Passing through many gardens, we got close to the village of Manshiyat, abandoned by its inhabitants, who sought refuge inside Siwa. We could not reach the village itself because we found the bridge by which one could get there across the lake to be broken. We moved to the northwest and after three-quarters of an hour we reached the mountain of the tombs, called al-Mawta, which is quite high. Its slopes have many scattered tombs, the most noticeable of which are at the top: among them, the largest and most beautiful at the same time is made up of three rooms, which one reaches through a comfortable staircase.[123] At the bottom of the first room there are two statues in bas-relief, seated, representing a man and a woman with some badly damaged hieroglyphs around them. There are also other bas-reliefs: I copied the best preserved, which is also colored and makes the ornamentation of the ceiling. Plate 32, no. 7. In the other rooms there are niches along the walls, intended to host the mummies, whose remains mixed with bones are still scattered on the ground. The tombs that are on the slope of the mountain are much smaller and do not offer anything remarkable.

---

123 Perhaps the tomb of Padjehuty; Jomard, *Voyage*, pl. VII [4]; Porter and Moss, *Topographical Bibliography* 7:314; Fakhry, *Siwa Oasis*, 127–31. None of the tombs of Jebel al-Mawta has statues in a niche. Moreover, the ceiling of the tomb of Padjehuty is not decorated.

From the top of this mountain Mr. Linant outlined the topographical map of the Siwa Oasis, it being impossible to find a better position to unite in one sight all that is noteworthy.

From here we passed to the village of Shargiya,[124] built on the top of a hill and weakly fortified with small palisades. While we were passing, many armed people appeared on the walls, but they did not molest us in any way.

At the distance of around ten minutes' walking from this village, there are the ruins of a temple, called by the Arabs Berbe, or Oumbeda.[125] The travelers who had preceded us in this oasis unanimously identified it with the Temple of Jupiter-Amun.[126] Because this was the only reason for our journey, before dealing with it, we decided to walk the oasis in all directions to be sure no other ruins could claim to be the Temple of the Oracle, either for their position or architecture. After a quick look at the ruins, we continued our explorations.

After two more hours, we reached another mountain to the northeast, which we found was the place whence the material for the aforementioned temple was quarried.[127] At about halfway up to the summit there are two caves in the rock,[128] both in Egyptian style: one, regular and finished, looks like a temple; the other, roughly worked and open to the west, looks like a shelter for workers, having also a niche in the back wall possibly to host lamps. These two monuments are marked on plate 33, nos. 6 and 7. On the top of this mountain there are the ruins of ancient buildings, but although we surveyed the nearby rocks in search for inscriptions, we did not find any except only a few at the slopes, in Greek. These are copied on plate 32, nos. 8–11. It is likely that these inscriptions date back to the visit of Alexander to the oasis, a thing that could be verified by comparing them with others of that period. I believe that also on the mountain there used to be inscriptions, as there usually are in places frequented by workers employed in public monuments, such as the valley of Biban al-Muluk at Thebes, Mukattab, and other places. Here the inscriptions were possibly destroyed or corroded by the air impregnated with salts, as often happens near the sea.

Upon our return to the camp, we were informed by the bey that the Siwans had brought 1,364 thalers which he refused to accept, threatening to attack them without further hesitation if the day after they did not bring the entire sum.

At dusk, the unexpected appearance of a large division of troops made the alarm resound in the camp. It did not take much time to recognize them to be three hundred Arabs of an allied tribe, which had come to reinforce the Egyptian army.

---

124 This is Aghurmi, the actual site of the Temple of the Oracle, hidden among the mud houses and thus invisible to Ricci and the other travelers.
125 Umm al-Ubayda.
126 Temple of Amun erected by Nakhthorheb (Nectanebo II); Porter and Moss, *Topographical Bibliography* 7:311–13.
127 The description of the site seems to fit Jebel al-Dakrur (sometimes Takrur), a high hill to the southeast of Siwa (and not to the northeast as stated here). The presence of two uninscribed tombs, one with a western access, of various Greek inscriptions, and of quarries all point to Jebel al-Dakrur, even though the distance from Umm al-Ubayda to Jebel al-Dakrur is in fact far less than two hours; Fakhry, *Siwa Oasis*, 66–67.
128 Fakhry, *Siwa Oasis*, 66.

On 24 March, we continued our observations, directing our research from the west to the north. After almost two hours' march we reached some ruins worthy of attention. They were in Egyptian style, built with large mud bricks and paneled with stone slabs measuring two feet by one, assembled with mortar, and well polished. Two large and thick parallel walls, fifty feet long, made us think that this was also a place intended for workers and that the annexed buildings were used as shelters. Between the two walls, in fact, we found scattered many stones, partly shaped and partly still rough. Those ruins were so badly preserved that it was impossible to make a plan. In vain we searched for inscriptions.

It took us half an hour to climb a little hill, on top of which we could see all the best and most fertile cultivated areas in this oasis. The gardens are here surrounded by walls, irrigated by many small streams, and bear abundant fruit. The more common tree is the olive, which produces extraordinarily large fruit: the Arabs get little oil and prefer to leave it to wither on the tree and then eat it with salt or to trade it for other goods. There is also a large number of pomegranates, bigger and tastier than the European. The quantity of apricots is also prodigious, but they are of small size. The inhabitants let them wither and then send them to Egypt, where they can be found in bazaars under the name of *mishmish*.[129] Sometimes they remove the kernel and make a sort of paste, similar in size and color to leather, called *qamaraddin*,[130] which they put in palm-leaf baskets, cut in square pieces. In both cases this fruit is very useful during desert travels, because the acidity of the apricot decreases thirst. Nevertheless, one must make moderate use of it in order not to get dysentery. Many vine bowers, well distributed, produce exquisite grapes and increase the beauty of the gardens. There are also plum trees, but the Arabs do not eat much of it and, anyway, do so with repugnance because they consider plums the cause of the fevers that usually strike the oasis when they ripen. For this reason most of the harvest of this fruit is, like the apricots, stored in baskets and shipped to Egypt. Wheat, barley, clover, cotton, a small-grained and reddish variety of rice, and many herbs grow in the lower grounds, all of a lesser quality than those of Egypt. All this production is proportionate to the availability of fertile soil, which is little and insufficient for the necessities of the population. No doubt this is the most beautiful and fertile spot of the entire territory of Siwa, a place where the industry of the inhabitants conquers even the sands, which cannot damage the fields, which are sheltered by the nearby rocks. In the middle of these gardens there are the ruins of a small village which used to be solidly built, since the debris is made up of large, regularly cut stones, well assembled with mortar. The few rooms that are still visible are oblong, but without the least ornament. Among so many beauties, made even brighter by the contrast with the nearby desert, we were horrendously molested by an immense quantity of mosquitoes, which soon forced us to abandon this place, called by the inhabitants Gari.[131]

---

129 Arabic مشمش *(mishmish)*, 'apricot.'
130 Arabic قمر الدين *(qamar al-din)*, 'moon of the faith'; still used to manufacture an apricot drink, used during the month of Ramadan or after the birth of a child.
131 Qarat al-Gari, on the west bank of Birkat Siwa.

In one hour we approached a temple, walking on natronous soil. Because of its mixed style of architecture, we recognized it as the one seen by Brown, called by him "Doric temple." The nearby inhabitants call it al-Khamisa and it is to the southwest of the oasis.[132] Of this large building only three rooms are still standing; the innermost of them has a Greek-style gate. The gate of the second room differs from the Egyptian style only in the molding, which is usually round while here it is triangular. Plate 32, no. 1. The two side windows are in Egyptian style. The whole building is 120 feet long and is badly damaged. This temple is built on a natron base with stones a foot and a half large, assembled with strong mortar. The blocks of the ceiling are in one piece and stretch from one side of the wall to the other. They are well polished, but corroded by the natron and without hieroglyphs. Only a few ornaments in Greek style can be seen on some pieces of stone scattered on the ground; same plate, no. 2.

After one more hour of march to the northeast, we encountered a few other insignificant ruins and observed on the nearby mountains a number of tombs, all made up of only one room. In some there still were bones. In this place, called by our guides Deir Rumi, there probably was in ancient times a city, of which these ruins are all that is left. At a little distance to the south there is another isolated mountain, beyond which there is Siwa. A salty lake lies in front of this mountain and wets its slopes, preventing us from climbing to the top of the mountain itself. We nevertheless succeeded in ascending to a point whence we could reckon the many tombs, lying in two levels on its slope, almost all with their entrance to the southwest. We observed them with telescopes and they looked of the same style as the previous ones. As far as we could see, they were without decoration or paintings.

Coming back toward the camp, we saw many ruined villages and empty houses. We crossed the salty lake that is to the west of Siwa, where there are paths, flanked by palm trunks in the manner of fences, large enough to allow two loaded animals to pass at the same time. In this lake there are some little islands, where an extraordinarily white salt is deposited, as happens on the banks of the lake itself. The path we took crosses the lake in all its width and then it divides into two, both leading to the gardens around the lake itself. Here there are many swamp birds of every kind.

We reached the camp before evening: we had crossed the entire oasis in only two days. We reckoned that we covered a daily distance of fifteen miles and deduced that its extent is not more than thirty to thirty-five miles. Half of the surface is farmland, almost all from the east to the west because the strong winds usually blow less in that direction than from the north to the south, and therefore it is less prone to sand invasion.

The Siwans went back to the camp on the 24th with 5,000 thalers, which the bey also refused, insisting that the peace could not be concluded until they paid the entire contribution. We would have liked to visit the city, but the bey judged it incautious to dare doing it at that time and asked us to be patient a few more days, with the promise to accommodate us after the settlement of all the difficulties delaying the peace.

---

132 Khamisah, where there is a temple. The description of the building and its identification with Brown's "Doric temple" by Ricci make clear that in fact he is describing a Greco-Roman monumental building at Bilad al-Rum, a site mentioned shortly after; Fakhry, *Siwa Oasis*, 68–71.

We did not meet during our explorations any ruins that could attract our further attention and we were about to move to Umm al-Ubayda in order to start our observations. We were then informed that at two days' march from the camp there was a salty lake called Birkat al-Arrashi,[133] close to a palm wood. The Arabs spoke of this place as enchanted and told us wonderful things about it: they said, for example, that the lake could be seen only during the day and that at night it disappeared, that in the woods horrendous howls were heard, that ghosts appeared, and similar things. Despite not believing a word of what was told us, we decided to try a new excursion there, a thing no traveler had ever done before.[134] In particular, we wanted to verify whether there were ruins of any sort. We told the bey about our intentions and he not only looked extremely satisfied, but also granted us an escort of an agha and two soldiers. We summoned our guides from Siwa and set off in the morning of the 25th heading northwest. We were quite worried about our guides seeming uneasy about accompanying us. We traveled half an hour in a cultivated plain and then started climbing a high mountain, one of those forming the valley of Siwa. Beyond it we found ourselves in a small valley, with drinkable water, where we took some rest. In the evening we reached a place called by our guides Germa Amun, which is 'House of Amun.' All our doubts disappeared and it was clear that the Siwa Oasis was the true Oasis of Jupiter-Amun and that the Umm al-Ubayda was the famous Temple of the Oracle. In fact, we had crossed the entire oasis in all directions, without finding among the many ruins a larger and more decorated building than the one described and imbued with mystery by the inhabitants. They call it Oumbeda, corresponding in their language to 'Palace of Wonders.' Despite this certainty, not willing to neglect any inquiry that could confirm it, we continued our journey toward the lake on the 26th, heading in the same direction. After a while we reached a small oasis of lovely appearance, where we observed, on a mountain on our left, some very simple Egyptian tombs without anything to offer.[135] The top of the mountain was flat and covered in silica stones. We followed the same direction for around three hours. On the way we asked our guides the reason for their uneasiness. From their answer, which also mentioned many wonders about the lake, we could understand that, if those were children's stories, true and real was the danger of being assaulted and massacred in the neighborhoods of the lake. Among the palm-tree woods by the lake, in fact, hordes of Arab bandits used to wait in ambush. For the same reason, the Siwans rarely went to this spot and only to hunt for wild buffaloes, but always well armed and in large numbers. They often had to defend themselves from fierce aggressors, who are enemies to everybody and live only from thefts and robberies. I must confess that this information much frightened us. We considered our small number and the little trust we had in our guides, and were almost at the point of turning back. On the other hand, in two or three hours' march we could reach the lake: luck had helped us until then, why should we despair of its favor for the future? We regained our courage, continued to advance, and arrived at night at Birkat al-Arrashi. There we pitched

---

133 Bahr al-Arrashi, now a Libyan oasis; Jomard, *Voyage*, 22–23, pl. XX.
134 In fact Cailliaud did it, just a few months earlier; Jomard, *Voyage*, 4.
135 Girba Oasis.

our tents among the rocks that surround the lake, all covered by salt. As we settled, we took a bath in the lake. Like the Dead Sea, the water of this lake has the property of keeping bodies afloat, without the necessity of moving. I had heard about the latter, but since I had never tried it in person, I was as much amazed as my fellow travelers. Our guides were waiting for the lake to disappear at any time, but this wonder did not happen, nor the howls nor the much-feared ghosts, so on this part their fears ceased. The next morning we bathed again, and just these two dips caused such a sour sweat for four days that our shirts crumbled.

In the event we needed to cross the lake—to reach an island or for any other reason— we took the precaution of bringing with us a small raft from the camp in Siwa, loaded on the back of a camel. It is called by the Arabs *ramus*,[i] is made of palm-tree trunks, and can carry two men in safety and comfort. We had it built in Tarrana before our departure. We observed with our telescope that the three islands in the lake were devoid of any vegetation and ruins, so we thought it useless to adventure on that weak raft and decided to walk all around the banks of the lake. We had to walk on hardened and crystallized natron, so sharp that the camels could not advance any further and we were forced to leave them behind while we wore very strong shoes and continued walking. It took us five hours to make the complete tour. When we arrived back at the camels, our shoes were already broken and we felt pain in our soles, similar to the pain one feels finally walking after a long sickness. This lake must have a circumference of seven to eight miles, and its banks are completely devoid of vegetation and no traces of houses can be observed anywhere. There are many fish and the banks are covered with shells. The woods of wild palm trees reach the shores in some places and are inhabited by hyenas and wild buffaloes, which have very long horns.

There was nothing left to see in this place, where we were luckily not molested by anyone. We therefore decided to go back, taking another route in order to see different things. We set off heading east and walked until the evening in a sandy plain, reaching Gega.[136] Here, sure that we did not need our *ramus* any more and willing to relieve our camels of a useless weight, we burned it. We completely ran out of water because we did not find any drinkable during the day. It was dangerous to go search for it late at night in an unknown desert, so, pressured by necessity, we began to dig a well on the spot. After two hours of hard work, especially for tired people like we were, some water appeared from the sand, at a depth of six feet. After a while more water appeared, enough to quench our thirst. It was whitish and bitter, but given the extreme need in which we were, it looked delicious. A few moments later we were all assaulted by strong belly pains, caused no doubt by the pernicious quality of the water. I resorted to my provision of tincture of cinchona,[137] which I always carry with me in the deserts: a good dose of this medication, taken twice, freed us from the pains. Nevertheless, burning thirst kept annoying us and there was never a time during the journey when we more desired the night to pass.

---

136 Perhaps Ayn Qayqab; "Ghaghab" in Jomard, *Voyage*, pl. I (map).
137 Extract of the cinchona (L. 1742), which has antimalarial, analgesic, and antipyretic properties due to the alkaloids of its bark.

Finally the dawn of the 28th came and we rapidly set off. After one hour, we left the oasis of Arrashi and entered a plain flanked by a chain of small sandy hills. We kept as far as possible from them because the guides had warned us that when strong winds blow, a huge quantity of sand is raised and, when it falls, can bury even large caravans, as had happened many times before. Here are the "mobile mountains" described by the ancient writers and mentioned in the *Travel of Alexander to the Temple of Jupiter-Amun*: their position corresponds perfectly with the route taken by the hero. It is believed he proceeded along the Mediterranean coast until Paraetonium, then entered the desert toward the temple; therefore he must have met them. I can give assurance, because I was an eyewitness that day, that even the slightest blow of wind can raise high columns of sand which, after whirling in the sky, fall here and there. Another thing I observed on this occasion is that in this place more than anywhere else the sands perfectly imitate sea waves by rippling with a weak blow of wind.

For eight hours we continued walking in the dangerous plain and at two in the afternoon we entered a little oasis called Shiyata, where there is a salted lake populated by an immense quantity of birds. A few reeds and wild palm trees overshadow its banks. Here and there are ruined houses and on the nearby mountains even some tombs. We also found a little quantity of drinkable water, which was a great refreshment for us. We accelerated our march, wishing to reach the camp as soon as possible in order to get rid of the thirst that was tormenting us, despite the little refreshment enjoyed. We would have continued the journey two more hours after sunset, were we not forced to stop by the sudden appearance of a group of armed men coming toward us from a certain distance. Encounters like this in the desert are almost always calamitous because it is unlikely that both caravans have water. If they do, each continues its journey. But if only one has water, the other will attack it without mercy and the fierce fight continues until one of the two parties conquers the water. If, because of weakness or to avoid the fight, one prefers to surrender the water voluntarily, then thirst is a second and more terrible enemy: if one is not lucky enough to find a well of water, he will die in the desert. It often happens that two caravans, both lacking water, attack each other in the hope of finding some: therefore, as I said, these encounters ordinarily are the cause of bloodshed and one becomes an assassin in order to preserve one's own existence.

The appearance of these armed men greatly worried us and we judged it wise to hide deep inside a bend of the mountains:[138] here, gathered in the smallest space possible, we waited for the result of the encounter, preparing ourselves for the defense. While we were speculating about the issue, I climbed the mountain with a telescope and I saw that the other caravan was calmly moving to the right. Despite this, we spent all the night in vigil, but in vain, since by dawn we had not seen anybody else. It is possible that they did not see us or that, having water, they wanted to avoid the encounter, fearing an attack on our part.

We continued our journey on the 29th and after an hour and a half we reached Germa Amun. Here, too, there is a salty lake: many plots of land are cultivated with wheat, rice,

---

138 At Hatiyat Umm Ghazlan, according to Frediani in Sammarco, *Alessandro Ricci*, 128.

and barley. They are irrigated by a spring of drinkable water. Here we took our rest and drank as much as we wanted. In this oasis there are four ruined villages and the remains of a small Greek temple. In the nearby mountain there is a large number of tombs, all consisting of one room only. We took the same path we had taken going: after midday, we reached Brown's temple and before sunset the camp. We took a more southerly route, in order to make a complete tour of the oasis. In this part, the land is uncultivated because the winds blow too strongly. As happens in Nubia, small hills are naturally formed by the roots of tamarisk trees, or other trees, covered by sand mixed with natron. The wind accumulates more sand and natron, which are hardened by water.

Upon our arrival, we heard from the bey that a peace deal had been reached with Siwa. The war contribution was lowered to six thousand thalers plus a year of tribute in advance, estimated at two hundred camel loads of dates and thirty slaves.[139] Among the slaves there were two who were married and the bey set them free, presenting them with money as well. Such a generous action aroused the admiration of the Siwans and had a positive effect of establishing good harmony between the inhabitants and the soldiers. These were finally allowed to enter the city, with the obligation of returning back to the camp in the evening. It was also strictly forbidden to molest anybody or to steal anything both in the city and in the countryside. Soldiers who disobeyed were beaten mercilessly with a stick under the walls of Siwa, in order to give the offended full satisfaction.

On the morning of the 30th we were invited to lunch by the bey. A Siwan cook prepared two dishes only: one made of bread with a sort of pasta; the other made also of pasta, with butter and sugar. All seemed delicious to us because for many days we had had nothing to eat but biscuit, dates, and a little rice. What we enjoyed most was a sort of dough made of honey and pepper, and we named it honey bun. Their bread is acidic because it is made without yeast and is cooked only a little, on two slabs of hot iron according to the custom of the Bedouins, which now seems a common feature even among the sedentary Arabs. The bey was in a very good mood about the steady and happy result of his expedition, and especially because he had been able to conquer Siwa with little bloodshed.

Communications with the city were by then established and the bey allowed us to visit it with the escort of a soldier. We crossed some streams of drinkable water via a series of small wooden bridges, which had been restored. These streams come from the nearby mountains and then flow into the plain. We entered Siwa by the south gate.

The houses are partly made of stone, partly of mud bricks. There are a few built with very hard natron stone, made of sand and natron. The houses are grouped together and so close to each other that some streets are absolutely dark even during the day. Those built on the rocky slope facing north are the highest, up to four floors. The first floor begins at almost half of the entire height and the windows are small and many, so that instead of homes they look like pigeon towers. The walls are plastered outside with clay mortar, which

---

139 Different surrender conditions are recorded by the general consul of the Kingdom of the Two Sicilies: "He forced the poor citizens to pay a contribution of ten thousand thalers and a yearly tribute of 2,400 loads of dates," Sammarco, *Alessandro Ricci*, 9.

covers cracks and irregularities and makes them look nice, but they are dark and uncomfortable inside. The houses built on the rock are much lower.

As we could understand it, Siwa has two different quarters: an upper and a lower, which is city and citadel. The latter can be reached through a narrow street, dark because of the many buildings on both sides. There is one gate only, which is always closed, as the acropolis is accessible only to married men and forbidden to the unmarried. We wanted to visit this part, too, but we were not allowed. In the lower city there is a large square for the market, with storehouses and stables.

In the rocky slopes where the city is built there are caves with a small antechamber, leading to two holes six feet deep in the rock. The inhabitants state that once upon a time those were all houses and I believe that these are the grottoes of the cavemen. I observed in one of the caves a sort of step, possibly cut to rest one's head. In this case, the antechamber could have served as home to two people and the holes as a place to sleep in.

After we visited the lower city, we tried again to get permission to visit the citadel, but the shaykhs opposed it, assuring us that no stranger and no unmarried man had ever entered before. They added that they would in any case discuss the matter and let us know the decision of the inhabitants before sunset.

We went back to the camp early in order to accompany the bey to the village of Shargiya, which he had not yet seen. This is built on a rock, like Siwa, but is much smaller than the capital. The houses are not particularly high and are all built with the natron rock I wrote about. It is surrounded by double walls and has two gates only. In the middle, there is a square where there is an old, very deep, perennial well, which provides the best water of the entire oasis. Here around a thousand inhabitants had found refuge. We then visited the village of Manshiyat, to the northeast of Siwa, which has nothing noteworthy but the tomb of a saint built in the shape of a pyramid. Its inhabitants had all fled to Siwa when the Egyptian army approached because the defense system of the village was too weak to offer any resistance. Anyway, after the peace was signed, they steadily returned. The population of this village was about a hundred people, while that of Siwa is more than three thousand. The entire district does not encompass six thousand inhabitants, approximately.[140]

In general, the men are not handsome, but are well built: thin and of average height. The color of their skin is as that of the people in Cairo. Many of them are emaciated because during the harvest season tertian fevers rage and are usually deadly for travelers and for many of the inhabitants as well.[141] Some of them cannot see very well, affected by ophthalmia caused by the quality of the air, impregnated with salt exhalations.

They wear a simple long white or blue tunic and a white and turquoise striped cloak, which they call *melajah*. Some do not cover their head, but most use a white wool cap, except the shaykhs and the rich who wear it red, almost all without turban. The latter use red or

---

140 "As an aproximate evaluation, it is believed that the oasis population reaches 5,000 inhabitants at the maximum, of which 2,000 in the city only," Jomard, *Voyage*, 9, and, again, Jomard, *Voyage*, 14: "The population . . . is of 2,000 to 2,500 people." So Frediani: "The number of the inhabitants is around 6,000," Sammarco, *Alessandro Ricci*, 129.
141 Ricci is referring here to malaria.

yellow slippers like the Egyptians, but the populace uses simple leather soles tied with laces to the foot instep.

Women, with few exceptions, are not beautiful, but much whiter than men. They also wear a long turquoise robe, rarely cover their face, and in any case never with the *kabar*[j] like in Egypt, but with a silk or cotton handkerchief that they put on their head and then leave loose behind. They also wear a *melajah* similar to that worn by men: they fix it on top of their heads and then cover the rest of their bodies. They divide their hair in three braids, one under the other, inserting in the lowest glass, amber, false coral,[142] or silver ornaments, according to their means. They also interwine the braids with black leather strips, which hang on their shoulders with little rattles. Many of the women have their nose perforated and bear in it a large silver or copper bell. They also, like the Egyptians, mark their forehead and chin with indelible blue ornaments, similar to the ones most of our sailors have printed on their arms and chest. They wear two large metal rings in their ears, shaped like a chain. Women belonging to the upper class wear on their neck large and solid silver rings, bearing a hanging plaque decorated with letters.[143] These rings also adorn their wrists and ankles, and the more numerous they are, the more distinguished is the lady who wears them.

Women rarely appear in public, being mainly busy with home affairs, such as weaving mats or small baskets. These are made of reeds or palm leaves: the colors are well distributed and the baskets are so well crafted that they can carry for some time even liquids without wasting a drop. I bought one of these baskets and I still have it in my collection.

Also among the Siwans, as generally in the whole of Arabia, there are slaves. Some of them settled with their families after being granted feedom by their owners and kept their own customs without being troubled.

We must acknowledge their humanity toward the poor, who are allowed to enter the fields of the rich and eat all that is inside, with the only condition that they do not take anything outside.

They can handle firearms quite well and are as good at their maintenance as the Europeans. Their manners are rough, their demeanor grave and dignified, the way they carry a conversation lively and almost dramatic, always speaking loudly and fast.

Their main occupation is agriculture. The richest possess many orchards, almost all fenced and irrigated by one or more streams of water. These are directed across the cultivated land by the landlords with much industry, without wasting water or letting them become too large. Dates are the most interesting product of this land and are of two species: one small and light-colored, which is the most valuable; the other is red and much larger, known under the name of *ghazali*. The Siwans eat the former and use less of the latter because they consider it an aphrodisiac. This is the reason they forbid women to eat

---

142 Women of Siwa believed that coral protected from the evil eye; Giovanni C. Bonotto, *Egitto magico: Monili e amuleti del deserto e delle oasi* (Turin: Celid, 2007), 182. Contrary to a common assumption at the time, the Siwan women did use real coral.

143 These jewels are well attested in Siwan tradition. The silver braid jewels are called *tashabat* and the rattles *galagil*; the ring is called *aghrow*, and this last jewel has a strong fertility symbolism; Bonotto, *Egitto magico*, 177–79.

it. Dates are kept in public storehouses, the keys of which are held by one of the shaykhs. They are stored in baskets or in goat-leather bags; in the latter case, they take off the kernel and turn the fruit into a paste, called *agua*.[144] The storehouses have a register recording the deposit of dates and the names of the owners, stating also if they are stored in bags or baskets, so that each one can easily find his own property.

As for their legislation and their customs, I will report what I could gather from one of the shaykhs, who used to come often to the camp.

The whole population of the oasis is divided into two tribes. The government is entrusted to many shaykhs from both, who meet daily. The populace, too, has voice to fix prices of food supplies and to administer justice. When in an affair opinions are in opposition, the decision is for the eldest of the shaykhs to make. Issues of public interest are discussed in general assemblies, summoned in the main square, where one of the shaykhs takes the office of speaker in order to persuade the audience of his opinion, which usually coincides with the other shaykhs'. It happened sometimes, even though rarely, that, having different opinions, the parties came to blows as in the ancient Roman assemblies. In order to avoid trouble, the shaykhs use all possible means of conciliation. Occasions to gather the general assemblies are in any case quite rare, as must be among people separated by many deserts from the rest of the universe, and are limited to the ordinary selection of a new shaykh on occasion of the death of one. Assassins are punished by death and are executed with a stick. Jealous of their freedom, they punish in the same way whoever dares to undermine it. In fact, one of the shaykhs, who at the arrival of the Egyptian army suggested surrender from the start and too insistently, was almost massacred by the populace. A shaykh is delegated to visit and question all the caravans passing by and to discover any suspicious people among its members: in cases where there are and the suspicion becomes a certainty, the culprit is killed on the spot. Outside the city walls there is a cave with a large basin, where tradition says traitors were slaughtered. Thieves are beaten with the whip on their shoulders, with their hands and feet tied. The number of lashes is proportionate to the gravity of the offense. Other offenses to public order are punished with date fines, which are paid to the needy. A man, for example, who hits another pays between fifteen and twenty-five baskets of dates.

Their wedding ceremonies are celebrated with much pomp and consist of dances and banquets. During funerals they cry and clap their hands for three consecutive days at the burial site. The whole ceremony ends with a banquet on the third day, attended by all the relatives of the deceased.

The most common illnesses reigning in the oasis are tertian fevers, dysentery, and ophthalmia. They treat the former with the bitter juice of a plant whose leaves are similar to those of the *Digitalis purpurea*. I could not verify it because the leaves I saw were dried, and I could not examine the plant itself since it was not the right season. Against dysentery, they have no other remedy than rice flour, and against ophthalmia they make many scarifications on different parts of the body and wash their eyes with mallow water.

---

144 Arabic عجوة (*agwa*).

Their language is completely different from Arabic, except for numbers and a few other terms introduced later because of lack of corresponding names in the native language or as a consequence of commercial relations between the republic and Egypt. Among the many opinions on this language, most scholars think it could be a remnant or a derivation from the ancient Punic language.[145]

Except aquatic birds, which populate the lakes in large numbers, and some sparrows and swallows, there are few other birds in the oasis, most of which just pass by. Rare also are poultry and pigeons. There are no horses or camels, while donkeys, sheep, and goats are the only domestic animals of Siwa. Dogs can be added to the number, but they are so few that one barely feels their presence. Gazelles, jackals, some hares, and a kind of very big mouse, which lives in large families and has a remarkably colored fur, are the wild species of the oasis. Sometimes hyenas appear, too, especially in winter. Wild buffaloes never leave the thick palm woods near Lake Arrashi.

Waters are in general very heavy and become foul easily when closed in a goatskin or a vase. Also abundant is a kind of fossil salt in small square crystals, so clear and transparent that it could be the most polished crystal. The inhabitants value it a lot and use it continuously.

I have gathered here all that relates to the Siwa Oasis, its form of government, products, manners, and customs, in order not to stop the flow of the narration, which it is now time to resume.

It was nine in the morning of 31 March and we were still waiting to know whether we were allowed to visit the citadel or not, despite their promise to let us know the evening before. The bey, too, was sorry for the delay and since he wanted to please us at all cost, he assigned us a very large escort, authorizing us with it to go back to the city and order the shaykhs in his name to open the gates of the citadel. We did as the bey suggested, assuring the elders that we would respect their women. At this intimation all difficulties disappeared: we left the escort at the gate and were ushered in by one of the shaykhs, who ran quickly to have all the women retired inside their houses. We went up a wooden staircase leading to a rock-cut staircase to the top of the citadel, where there is a square. Here lives the older shaykh, in a house that serves also as observatory whence the entire oasis can be seen. This open space is forty square meters wide and has four very deep wells cut in the rock. Two provide drinkable water and two salty water; all supply water to the entire citadel. There are also storehouses for provisions in case of need. The houses on both sides of the stairs we climbed are low and have very small doors. We found absolutely nothing of interest in that place and went back to the lower city through the same staircase. The shaykhs assured us we were the first ever to visit that part of the city, which had always been forbidden as an

---

145 So Jomard, *Voyage*, 13; Linant thought that the language was very old, a mix of Arabic and Barabra or Darfur dialects; Mazuel, *L'Oeuvre Géographique*, 14. As late as 1944 Fakhry wrote: "Most of the men understand Arabic as a foreign language and not without difficulty, many of the old men do not understand it at all, the small children speak Siwan only. The women understand their mother tongue only, for the seclusion has not given them the same opportunity, as their husbands and sons, of learning Arabic," Fakhry, *Siwa Oasis*, 2.

impenetrable harem for married men. They also told us that one year earlier, a short European had visited their city and, even though he was also curious to see the citadel, he failed to get permission. No doubt this European was Mr. Cailliaud.

We bid farewell and were all happy: they because of our modest behavior and we because we had obtained what we wanted. Nevertheless, a number of citizens followed us to the gates of the city, shouting insults. Concerning this, it is dangerous to frontally attack the prejudices and customs of men, especially among rough and almost savage people, who in their deep ignorance consider sacred the most incoherent and bizarre traditions.

As soon as we came back from Siwa, we moved to Umm al-Ubayda. The first two days of April were spent in the observation of the site and here are the results.

As I mentioned before, this building is ten minutes' walk from the village of Shargiya, half an hour north of Siwa, and sits on a natural platform, five or six arm lengths higher than the surrounding land. The natives call it Umm al-Ubayda, which means 'House' or 'Palace of Wonders.'

It is difficult to detect its original plan, all being devastated and ruined by the Arabs, who have overturned stones and soil in search of treasures, as much as by the salty air that permeates the entire oasis and corroded the hieroglyphs on the walls. The few walls still standing are those of the sanctuary, while all the rest has fallen into ruin and is so shattered that all that is left is a large pile of rubble.

The entrance to the sanctuary looks precisely to the north. The building sits on a limestone rock that is higher than the rest of the platform. This is either because the architect wanted it so or because he was forced to place large blocks in order to level the surface of the platform itself, as can be observed in many Nubian temples.[146] The southern wall has collapsed and not even the materials can be found. The other walls, which also suffered much, are six feet wide. The east wall is still in good shape, but only twenty-three feet are left over a total length of thirty-four. The sanctuary was fifteen and a half feet wide and twenty-one and a half feet tall. The materials used to build the temple were quarried, as I said, from the nearby mountains: it is limestone containing many fossil shells. The ceiling of the sanctuary was made of six large slabs of stone: five of them are still standing in the original place. The stone is nicely smoothed and the blocks are assembled with mortar as in the rest of the building. The decoration of the inner part of the eastern wall (plate 34, no. 1) is divided into many registers, of different height and subject: the upper one (a) has ovals with names alternated with a hawk with open wings. None of these ovals is intact; the better preserved are shown on plate 33, nos. 3 and 4. A row of figures in adoration and making offerings make up the second register (b). The third (c) was made up of perpendicular lines of hieroglyphs, now completely corroded. In the fourth (d), there is a representation of the god Amun with the disk on his head, seated on the throne. In front of him there is a kneeling figure in worship attitude. In the same register there is a procession of many male and female gods, which continues in the last two registers (e, f). The bottom part of the wall is decorated with

---

146   It is not clear even in the Italian version what Ricci means here.

a meander, which survives only to the left, while the rest is completely corroded. One can rarely observe such a motif on Egyptian monuments.

The molding of the outer part of the northern wall (plate 35, no. 1) is decorated with a series of names (a). Immediately underneath there is a sphinx holding a vase surmounted by the head of Amun and the disk. Then there is a hawk, symbol of the god Re, or the sun, and the fragment of another figure underneath. On the left side there is a goddess and then Amun, in front of whom there is a hero offering a sacrifice on an altar with fire; all the rest is lost. The inner part of the northern wall (plate 33, no. 1) little differs from the outer here described. On the gate there were two pillars with four sides, on each of which there was a Typhon in bas-relief (no. 2), exactly as in the small temple of Philae. The hollows that used to host the pillars are still visible.

The ceiling is also carved in bas-relief: each stone bears two open-winged vultures and two large feathers between their claws. A long line of hieroglyphs separates one from another (plate 35, no. 3).

All the reliefs on the outer part of the other walls are corroded and I could copy only a fragment on a stone lying on the ground, from which it appears that the outer reliefs were larger than the inner (same plate, no. 2).

The background color was green inside the sanctuary and turquoise outside. In some figures, such as no. 1 of the same plate, there are traces of other colors too, which I marked in the drawing.

From what is left of this temple it is clear that it was not particularly large, as many thought.

In order to cast away any doubt about this sanctuary not being the Temple of Jupiter-Amun, the three enclosure walls mentioned by Herodotus[147] remained to be discovered. To this purpose, no enquiry was left behind and we surveyed the nearby hills with much care. I would not be able to express our surprise and satisfaction when after many attempts we found the foundations of a wall parallel to the temple, in a place fifty steps from the sanctuary, where we dug because it caught our attention. Encouraged by this first success, we renewed the excavation at a similar distance and similarly found the remains of another wall with the same orientation. We searched in vain for the third wall, but we did not doubt for a moment that the Oumbeda was the real temple of Amun. Too many circumstances, in fact, contribute to confirm this opinion, besides the possibility that the third enclosure wall was at a smaller or greater distance, so that we could not find it. The existence of a palm-tree wood nearby the temple and of a fountain warm at night and cool during the day, which flows in large bubbles from a stalactite bottom, almost in the middle of the same wood, are also proofs. Not least, the many representations of Amun in the sanctuary would alone be enough to cast away any doubt. To this incontestable evidence, one needs to add all the others resulting from the exact correspondence between ancient descriptions of this oasis and this famous monument and their current situation. In fact, nowhere else can be

---

147 In fact Herodotus does not describe the Temple of the Oracle; Ricci is probably referring here to a passage of the *Bibliotheca Historica* by Diodorus Siculus (XVII 50).

the Oasis of Amun, no other temple can be his own, and no other fountain can be the Fountain of the Sun. The large number of tombs scattered on the mountains surrounding the territory of Siwa proves that its population was once very large. The marine fossils in the area confirm what Strabo wrote on this matter when he speaks about the land of Amun.[148] Finally, the name of Germa Amun used by the inhabitants to call the oasis seems to me the most triumphant point to prove our opinion.

Next to the Fountain of the Sun there is an oval-shaped ruin, but we could not track its plan because it was too badly damaged. Would it not be possible that this was the burial place of Alexander? The idea is not really so unlikely, if one considers in the first instance that the oval shape suits a tomb more than any other monument. Secondly, the fact that this ruin is so close to the Fountain of the Sun, which the Libyans worshiped under the name of Amun (alleged father of the hero), seems to suggest it, too. The priests remembered the generosity of Alexander toward their sanctuary and themselves when they gratified him with a pompous title, and chose out of gratitude this place instead of any other to lay his mortal remains. The beauty of the palm woods and the continuous noise of the waves must have been considered pleasant for the shade of the hero. On the other hand, since it was not customary at the time to bury inside temples, it is likely that they erected next to the sanctuary a special and magnificent tomb to the man who had filled the earth with his extraordinary deeds and who had been transferred after his death to the temple of Amun with so much pomp. Of such a tomb, among the general devastation, there should be some remains, still visible, as in fact happens with many other monuments of the same kind, which although destroyed and devastated by the avidity and ignorance of the barbarians, still preserve at least the foundations, to the point that one can say without mistake: this is the place! Now, neither close to the temple nor in the surrounding mountains, among the huge number of tombs, there is one outstandingly decorated to suggest it might be the tomb of Alexander. Therefore, I repeat again, it is not unlikely that the ruin next to the Fountain of the Sun is the monument where the remains of the Macedonian conqueror were laid.

I was and still am sorrowful that this idea popped into my mind only too late, when we were already close to Cairo, coming back from this journey. I therefore did not share it with my fellow travelers: had this idea come to my mind when we were on the spot, we probably would not have left the place so quickly. Who knows, maybe with more accurate research and excavations we could have succeeded in making a certainty out of what I describe now only as a mere possibility.

There is nothing else that I can add on the famous temple of Amun, except that all the travelers who visited before us neglected or failed to find the enclosure walls, the discovery of which is to our exclusive credit.

On 2 April, in the evening, we reached the camp of the bey and we announced to him our discoveries. We then showed him gratitude for the protection he granted us and we added that, since the goal of such a difficult journey was now achieved, we intended to leave on the

---

148 Strabo, *Geographica* I 3, 4.

next day. He was sorry about our decision and, referring to me in particular, proposed that we stay a few more days with him in order to assist the wounded that I had treated before—especially an Arab whose arm I had amputated: he did not want to undergo the surgery until the bey ordered him to. The Muslims in general are adverse to mutilation, to the point that most would prefer without hesitation to die.

I disengaged myself from the duty, assuring the bey that the Arab was absolutely out of danger, which was true, and showing the barber, who in the camp served as a surgeon, how to treat this patient and the other few wounded who were still convalescent.

We bid farewell to the bey and retired to our tent. While busy packing our belongings, the bey sent in biscuits, flour, and dates as a reward for my service in the camp. This present could not be more timely since we were almost running out of provisions, because what we had requested from Tarrana did not arrive.

On 3 April, we set off, heading north, where the road is better. After three hours of march we met a large salt lake,[149] full of weeds and very close to a small Greek temple completely ruined and made up of one room only[150] (plate 32, nos. 3 and 4). On the mountains to the right there are tombs, but they offer nothing of interest.

We then met another Greek temple, of the same style of the previous[151] (same plate, no. 5 and 6). After we left it, since our guides were not particularly practiced in the area, we found ourselves again in front of the lake, which we could not cross, but had to make a large detour. We then considered the dangers we could face if we went deep into the desert and we did not hesitate to go back to the first temple in order to take the right route. In the evening, we reached the aforementioned mountains.

Three hours before dawn we set off with the intention of reaching Qara in the evening, in order to make provision of water, because the water we were carrying from Siwa had already gone bad. We climbed the mountain to a height of three hundred feet and we felt very cold because of the strong north wind. Even though we dismounted the camels to walk and we drank a good deal of rum, we could not warm up until midday. At sunset we reached Qara, to where the inhabitants were returning after the peace was signed. Here we made provision of acceptable water from a reservoir in the middle of the village.

We set off early on the 5th and in the evening we reached Abu Marzuq, which marks the beginning of the Adera chain, taking the same road as when we came. We were a bit worried as we had not yet received the provisions from Tarrana, and all the more so because we had sent, on the same morning, an Arab mounted on the best camel of the caravan to search for them. According to our reckoning, they should not have been far off, but he came back at midnight without having met with anyone.

We continued on the 6th, and on the 7th after midday we reached the brackish spring of al-Hagg,[152] which means 'the holy place,' so called for the help it provides to travelers in

---

149 Birkat Zaytun, approched this time from the west, probably at its northern edge.
150 Perhaps Qasr al-Gashsham; Fakhry, *Siwa Oasis*, 73–74.
151 Likely to be Abu Shuruf; Fakhry, *Siwa Oasis*, 74–75.
152 "El-Hegyah," Jomard, *Voyage*, pl. I (map).

those remote lands.[153] In fact, around the spring grows much saltwort, which the camels eat with greed and which, on this occasion, refreshed us as well. There are many wild plants producing a sour fruit, quite refreshing though. When a camel falls sick or is not able to carry its load any more, it is abandoned in this place and often water, rest, and vegetation give it back life. The place is scattered with animal bones; some look calcined. Hyenas, lions, and crows devour the flesh of their corpses. Here we spent the whole day, hoping to see our provisions arrive. It was not to happen because the Arabs who carried them did not see us and passed beyond us at night. We took advantage of the stop to climb the Adera chain: we found that the mountains are made of limestone. When we reached the peak, with quite some effort, we found it plain and observed camel dung, proof that caravans pass by here, too, going up along paths viable for camels and unknown to our guides. This plain is as wide as the chain itself; it is covered with pebbles and silica stones. There are fossils of all kinds. I picked up a piece of shinbone, possibly belonging to a gazelle, and Mr. Drovetti found a petrified horn of the same animal. We then saw on the sand the footprints of a lion; this put an immediate end to our explorations and quickly sent us back to the well of al-Hagg.

On the morning of the 8th, two Arabs of Qara came and told us that the provisions we were longing for had already arrived there, so we immediately sent one of our guides to reach the caravan and force it to turn back, walking even during the night because we were left with little biscuit. Such was the anxiety to see the Nile again that two hours after the man left we thought that, before receiving the provisions, we would wait no less than five days. We then unanimously decided to continue the journey. We divided the food left into equal shares, so that each of us could manage at will his own share. We set off at dawn and, marching fast, we camped in the evening in one of the many bends of the mountain chain. On the 10th we marched without stopping until we reached Labbaq, where we slept by its brackish water well. The next day we abandoned the route we had taken before and, keeping east, we headed toward the natron lake in order to visit the monasteries and see the Bahr Bila Ma'.[154] An hour after midday, we reached al-Maghra,[155] where we found a spring of very fresh water, which, despite the hunger we started to feel, invited us to spend the night there. This is a small oasis with a salt lake three miles wide: its shores are adorned with thick bunches of reeds, which the Arabs of Tarrana come to collect in the proper season. They make nice mats which are easily sold in Cairo. This lake is populated by aquatic birds of all species and one can even see many flamingos and large serpents.

On the 12th before dawn, we moved the camp and reached in the evening the Bahr Bila Ma', where the camels ate the thorny bushes that blossom there. On the 13th, nothing was left to eat but three pieces of biscuit and a bottle of water already sour. Trusting in divine

---

153 This trail connecting Siwa to Egypt was traditionally used by Berber pilgrims heading to Mecca; Jomard, *Voyage*, 24; Mazuel, *L'Oeuvre Géographique*, 14.

154 Arabic بحر بلا ماء (Bahr Bila Ma'), 'Waterless Sea,' Arabic name for the Sahara Desert, generally used for the desert area to the west of Wadi al-Natrun; Johann L. Burckhardt, *Travels in Syria and the Holy Land* (London: John Murray, 1822), 461.

155 Hatiyat Maghra, with its homonymous lake, "Attyeh el-Moqarrah" in Jomard, *Voyage*, pl. I (map).

providence and in the speed of our march, we crossed the whole Bahr Bila Ma' and at sunset we reached the first waters of the Wadi al-Natrun. Here our scarce provisions finished.

'Bahr Bila Ma" in Arabic means 'sea without water': its width from shore to shore can be four hours' walk. It is completely filled with sand and the surface is scattered with a large quantity of petrified wood, which is more abundant on the slope. This place is believed to have once been open to Lake Maryut. Some of these petrifications are tree trunks measuring twelve feet and more in circumference, others are just branches measuring a few inches. There are petrified trees of many species, as is apparent from the different shape and larger or smaller size of the fibers, but since there is no cortex, one cannot identify them with certainty, except for the palm tree. There is quartz, flint, Egyptian gravel, and other materials that do not come from this place, but from the mountains of Egypt. I guess this lake was once fed by the inundation of the Nile.

At dawn on the 14th we set off, heading toward the Christian monasteries in Wadi al-Natrun. This valley lies parallel to the Bahr Bila Ma' and is divided from it by a hill running southeast to northwest. Its surface is covered with hardened natron, which makes walking very difficult for animals as much as for men. After an hour and a half in this valley we saw, almost in the middle of it and at a certain distance, a large square building looking like a castle.[156] Tormented by hunger, we accelerated and, exhausted, we finally reached it. I do not think there can be on earth a more horrendous position than that of this monastery. Built in the middle of a desert completely deprived of vegetation, there is no plant, no road, no trace of life. The Arabs call it Sidi Suryan and the monks St. Macarius.[157] It can be reached passing under an arch, whence, via a long and comfortable staircase, it is possible to have access to a drinkable water spring, used by the monks and by travelers as well. We rang a bell and the gate was immediately opened by a monk. Our first question was whether they had food for us, determined otherwise to go in search of it somewhere else. He answered he had nothing else but bread and onions, and invited us to follow him, ushering us to the kitchen. At the sight of bread, after the unbearable hunger that had tormented us, we abused it, not without damage. In fact, afterward we all more or less suffered colic pains, produced not only by the quantity we ate, but also by the fact it was roughly baked and made with a mixture of different flours, such as chickpeas and others that cause gas: but how to resist hunger?

This monastery offers absolutely nothing of interest. It could contain twenty monks, but at that time it had only three, two laymen, and a priest.[158] A small church with no paintings,

---

156 From the outside Deir Anba Bishoi, Deir Anba Maqar, and Deir al-Baramus have the same massive and solid appearance of a fort.
157 Deir al-Suryan (in antiquity, Deir Theotokos Anba Bishoi, different from Deir Anba Bishoi also in the Wadi al-Natrun) and Deir Anba Maqar are in fact two different monasteries in the Wadi al-Natrun, at a distance of twelve kilometers from each other. The name Saydi Suryan ('My Syriac Master') is also attested in Charles N.S. Sonnini de Manoncourt, *Travels in Upper and Lower Egypt* (London: John Stockdale, 1799), 364.
158 General Andréossy reckons eighteen monks; Antoine-François Andréossy, "Mémoire sur la vallée des lacs de Natroun," in *Description de l'Égypte, ou Recueil des Observations et des Recherches*, État Moderne I (Paris: Imprimerie Impériale, 1809), 291. In 1837, Lord Curzon finds two or three monks only, abbot included; Robert Curzon, *Visits to the Monasteries in the Levant* (London: John Murray, 1849), 82–84.

a library almost deprived of books, where we saw only a few Coptic manuscripts in very bad condition, and a garden in the middle, which provides the monks with a few legumes—this is, in summary, the description of this place. In a courtyard there is a large tree, which they call the stick of St. Euphemius.[159] They say that this saint, rebuking one of his disciples who was protesting about living in such inhospitable solitude with no vegetation of any sort, handed him his stick and ordered him to plant it deep. He prophesied it would become a beautiful tree. The stick in fact blossomed—the narrator told me—and was soon full of branches. This fact brought back to life the faith of the unenthusiastic disciple. This tree is a tamarisk.[160]

After two hours' rest we left to visit the libraries of the other monasteries, which are three.[161] We did not find anything interesting because a few months earlier, according to what the monks said, some Europeans had come and bought the best books. We thought a lot about who they could be, but we could not figure it out.

The monks who live in these monasteries are all Coptic Christians, dressed the Arab way. They are never molested because of their extreme poverty: in fact, they live on alms they collect daily at Tarrana.

We had already left when we were surprised by a very violent hurricane coming from the north. It raised clods of sand and stones that tormented us greatly. Then, heavy rain followed, with wind, lightning, and thunder, to the point that the camels gave their backs to the wind and lay down. No shout or hit of stick could force them to move until the storm ended. The sky was still full of thick clouds and we decided to take shelter under the ruins of an ancient monastery called al-Kassar, where we lit a fire, dried our clothes as much as we could, and spent the night.

Even though some authors speak of six different lakes in the Wadi al-Natrun, we could see only two: it is true that we did not have time to visit the area thoroughly, so I would not dare to challenge those writers. The waters of the lakes grow and decrease in reverse compared to the Nile flood and so follow the common laws of all lakes, having low waters in summer and high waters in winter. On the shores there are marsh canes, reeds, and other plants. Here the green of the vegetation contrasts beautifully with the white of the

---

159 In fact, St. Ephraim, possibly Ephraim al-Suryan, whose commemoration falls on 15 Abib (22 July); René Basset, "Le Synaxaire arabe jacobite, V, Les mois de Baounah, Abib, Mésoré et jours complémentaires," in *Patrologia Orientalis* XVII (Paris: Firmin-Didot, 1923): 655–59. This stick transformed into a tree is in the monastery of Deir al-Suryan.

160 Almost all travelers report on this miraculous tree, from Jean Coppin, French consul in Damietta, in 1638 to Andréossy during the Napoleonic Expedition. De Thévenot records the story told by the monks, whose sources are the *Acts of St. Ephraim* in Syriac and the *Life of Bishoi* in Arabic; Jean de Thévenot, *The Travels of Monsieur de Thevenot into the Levant* (London: H. Clark, 1687), 244. The story Ricci tells is another tree's, the so-called "Tree of Obedience" of St. John the Short, which appears in the *Apophthegmata Patrum*. Both trees were still living in the Wadi al-Natrun at least in the 1930s and the Tree of St. Ephraim until now. Cf. Otto F.A. Meinardus, *Monks and Monasteries of the Egyptian Deserts* (Cairo: American University in Cairo Press, 1992), 106; Hugh G. Evelyn-White and Walter Hauser, *The Monasteries of Wâdi 'n Natrûn*, part 2, *The History of the Monasteries of Nitria and of Scetis* (New York: The Metropolitan Museum of Art, 1932), 108, pls. V [a] and LXXIV [b].

161 From northwest to southeast: Deir al-Baramus, Deir al-Suryan, Deir Anba Bishoi, and Deir Abu Maqar.

salt crystals and the horrendous color of the sands. When the lakes are low, the Arabs come to collect crystallized natron that is deposited for the depth of one arm along the shores. Natron has many uses, especially for manufacturing. There is an abundance of aquatic birds and there is even a large number of boars, which rummage the soil and breed in peace because nobody hunts them down.

On the 15th we greatly accelerated our walk, pressed by the need of rest, in order to quickly arrive at Tarrana. In order not to allow the slowness of the camels to delay our march—being themselves very tired—we used a trick adopted by the Arabs in similar cases, which is to walk in front of the animal singing. The camels are greatly amused by singing and willingly accelerate their pace in order to reach the preceding man.

At three in the afternoon, we were surprised again by another hurricane, much milder though than the previous one because it had discharged its fury toward Alexandria. Despite it, we continued our journey and after an hour we finally saw Tarrana and the lovely banks of the Nile. At that view we immediately forgot all hardships and we greeted Egypt with a fusillade from our rifles.

At a short distance from Tarrana we met Mr. Kalinkut, a Greek who presides over the factories of nitre. We were forced to accept his hospitality, which he offered with the insistence of true friendship. We were kindly welcomed in his house and celebrated our return that evening with a nice and delicate dinner.

The following day Mr. Linant and I bid farewell to Mr. Drovetti and Mr. Frediani, and set off to Cairo, where we arrived on 17 April 1820. We dismounted at the house of Mr. Salt, English general consul, who could barely recognize us, so much were we deformed by fatigue and sun.

The unhealthy air, caused principally by saline exhalations and the large quantity of swamp waters, together with the pernicious nature of the drinkable water which powerfully affects the body, alongside the incertitude of routes and many other causes (that can be easily gathered reading the present report), make the journey to the Siwa Oasis the most dangerous a European could ever attempt in a desert. I would not suggest it to anyone unfamiliar with the weather, in order to avoid almost certain death.

Travel to Mount Sinai

Only four months after my return from the Siwa Oasis, I had the idea of undertaking a new journey to visit Mount Sinai, venerable monument of our faith. Mr. Linant, to whom I made the proposition, agreed with pleasure to accompany me and without further delay we gathered a sufficient number of camels, hired a dragoman, and set off from Cairo toward Suez on 1 September 1820. The Arabs who served us as cameleers and escort belonged to the Towara tribe, who, when going to Suez, prefer the route they call Darb al-Anqabiya,[162] which is shorter than the others.

---

162 Anqabiya is the name of a mountain and two wadis that run in a north–south direction a little to the east of Cairo. The track (darb) followed by Ricci runs between Darb al-Hagg, the pilgrimage route, and a more southern road along the mountains.

At a short distance from Cairo, to the left of the road, there is Birkat al-Hagg, a station for the pilgrims who every year accompany the carpet woven at Cairo and destined for Mecca.[163]

The day was very hot and the Fahrenheit thermometer marked 112 degrees in the shade. Toward the evening, the monotony of the desert was interrupted by the appearance of a large caravan coming from Suez with a load of coffee, ostrich feathers, ivory, gum, and other trade goods. After we saw the imposing convoy parading in front of us, we pitched our tents next to a *sant* tree,[164] the only one we had met during the whole day and that serves both as marker and station for travelers since it stands almost halfway to Suez.

On the 2nd we set off at dawn and crossed the bed of two very close streams, clustered with many *sant* trees. According to our guides, only one of the two streams carries water in winter, after the rains that ordinarily fall on the nearby mountains. Around midday we reached Agruda, where we took some rest. All the stretch of desert walked during the day is perfectly plain and uniform: the soil is sandy with small stones which make it more solid and help the pace of camels. There are also here and there some silica stones and pieces of petrified wood.

Agruda is a small castle with few lodges, where a *qaymaqam*[k] lives with a small garrison. We gave him a bottle of spirit in exchange for a vase of brackish water, the only available in that place. Because of the excessive heat suffered and possibly because of sunstroke, I suddenly felt exhausted and I fainted. Mr. Linant rubbed my temples and nostrils with brandy and made me drink little sips of water in order to refresh my mouth. He succeeded in this way to restore to me some vigor and after half an hour I fully recovered. This happened under the canopy of the castle, where the *qaymakam* spends the hottest hours of the day with his soldiers and receives the travelers who pass by daily, Agruda being the only station between Cairo and Suez. The castle has water tanks which are filled in winter with rainwater, but the rarity of rain is such in the desert that the water collected lasts for two or three months only. During the rest of the year the garrison is forced to drink brackish water, which is found in two or three wells excavated in the sand near the castle.

The discomfort I suffered delayed our departure and it was late at night when we reached Suez. At a short distance from the city there is a *saqya*[l] that provides water to the caravans: the Arab who acts as warden locks himself inside the wall[165] during the night for safety reasons and we had to pay him dearly to induce him to open up and get the necessary refreshment we all needed.

The distance between Cairo and Suez is around thirty hours on camel: reckoning three miles per hour, it makes ninety miles. We walked it in only twenty-five hours because we had excellent camels.

---

163   The black cloth, called *kiswa* or *burqu'* in Egyptian Arabic, which covers the stone of the Ka'ba at Mecca. From the thirteenth century to 1930 it was the duty of the sovereign of Egypt to provide the *kiswa* and send it to the Holy City with a lavish procession called *mahmal*. Birkat al-Hagg was a station on the way to Suez, now a suburb 17 kilometers northeast of Cairo; cf. Francis Arundale, *Illustrations of Jerusalem and Mount Sinai* (London: Henry Colburn, 1837), 4–5.

164   Arabic سنط (*sant*), 'acacia' or *Mimosa nilotica*, Giuseppe Gabrieli, *Ippolito Rosellini e il suo Giornale della Spedizione Letteraria Toscana in Egitto negli anni 1828–1829* (Rome: Reale Società Geografica Italiana, 1925), 27.

165   An inscription dated the building back to AD 1610; Burckhardt, *Travels in Syria*, 464–65.

Suez is a city and a port on the Red Sea and is built on the isthmus that bears the same name. The land is unproductive, which gives the landscape a very sad appearance. The sea surrounds the isthmus from all sides and ends with two small strips three miles deep into the desert. The strip from the side of Asia is in part occupied by a sandbar, visible during low tide. The city is defended from the southeast by long walls, which will soon be completely useless, being in ruin all along. The houses of Suez are in general badly built and have a very poor appearance. The biggest have usually two floors. The main traders of the city live on the side of the sea and their houses are the most comfortable and the most striking. The mosques are very beautiful, some even built of stone and with a certain degree of grandeur. Despite this, there is a huge difference between this and the other cities of Egypt. The small population of Suez is made up for the most part of Muhammadans and a few Greeks, but its bazaars, or markets, are well frequented by the other nations who come here for trade. This city is a storage point for the goods coming from the Indies; its main traffic is coffee.

Basic supplies are shipped to Suez from Cairo: meat in general is lacking and sometimes even bread, but fish is abundant and makes the main resource of the inhabitants, who also trade in it. Water is always more or less brackish, wherever it is taken from: the best comes from Bi'r al-Nab', four miles distant,[166] and from Ayun Musa, or 'Fountains of Moses,' by means of a boat assigned for its transport twice a day. Water is sold in the morning and evening in the public square; outside of these times it is difficult to find. A goatskin, called *gharba*[167] by the Arabs and that can contain around a thousand pounds of water, costs one Cairo piaster. For this reason, the inhabitants consider water supply as the most burdensome of their expenses. The poor, who can only buy enough water for them to drink, are forced to wash their clothes in the sea. When we visited the city, a new spring of drinkable water had just been discovered, but it had such a low flow that it could barely supply the *kashif* and a few other families.

In case of siege, the safety of Suez would rely uniquely on the courage of the defenders to openly attack the enemy. If the defense should be prolonged, even by a few days, the lack of water would force the city to surrender unconditionally.

The inhabitants, and principally the poor, enjoy greatly the refreshment offered by watermelons from Burullus (the province of Egypt in the area of Damietta), which are shipped in numbers, and by grapes from Mount Sinai.

Ma'allim Hayl, English agent in Suez,[168] to whom we were recommended, hosted us in a *wakala*[m] by the sea. On the second day, we went to visit the *kashif*, an amiable man, much

---

166 Cf. Arundale, *Illustrations of Jerusalem*, 12, who places this well five hours to the northeast; William G. Browne, *Nouveau voyage dans la Haute et la Basse Égypte, en Syrie et au Darfour où aucun Européen n'avait pénétré* (Paris: Dentu, 1800), 263, places it directly to the north, while Burckhardt, more precisely, "two hours distant from Suez, in the hills on the eastern side of the gulf," Burckhardt, *Travels in Syria*, 466. The well was probably on the long road flanking the Bay of Suez, now disappeared because incorporated into the canal, not far from the ruins of ancient Arsinoë/Cleopatris.

167 Arabic قربة *(qurba)*.

168 Very likely the same English agent mentioned by Burckhardt, *Travels in Syria*, 469, in charge of attending the ships coming from Bombay and shipping their load to Great Britain. He was also viceconsul; Louis Maurice Adolphe Linant de Bellefonds to William John Bankes, 15 April 1821, HJ 1/139, Deposit/Bankes of Kingston Lacy and Corfe Castle, Dorset History Centre, Dorchester.

interested in the good of the populace and extremely kind to all foreigners. He welcomed us affectionately and presented us with coffee and pipe. Informed about the aim of our journey, he not only granted at a moderate price all the provisions we needed, but also recommended as guide a shaykh called Salah, of the Towara tribe, and assisted us greatly during the whole of our stay in the city.

The air of Suez is unhealthy because of the brackish and swampy land that surrounds the city and causes, especially during the summer, high fevers and typhus. The inhabitants delude themselves that these diseases can be prevented by drinking spirits, and there is not in all Egypt a city where the abuse of alcohol is so excessive. The sea is deep, with fewer rocks on the west side than on the opposite one, where the sandbars are exposed during low tide and are scattered with an incredible quantity of shellfish.

At our arrival, ten large tradeships were anchored one mile from the city and a large number of small ships were by the shore, a few steps from the houses.

Suez is the starting point of a large convoy of ships trading with the Indies: it is necessary that all of them are ready when the regular winds start blowing. The ships that are not ready are forced to delay their departure to the following year.

The city is not defended by any fortress and there are only a few dismantled iron cannons on a sort of dock, which is gradually decaying.

The place where once the famous Arsinoë used to lie is near Suez, but all that is left are the ruins of a stone aqueduct, which, its direction suggests, used to carry water from Bi'r al-Nab'. Any other trace of the city has completely disappeared from the surface of the earth.

When I was in Cairo I heard talk of a Persian monument, seen and described by Mr. de Rozière, French chief engineer at the time of the Bonaparte expedition to Egypt. They said it was on the trail connecting Suez to al-Arish .[169] Since I was in the area, I became curious to see the monument for myself, but despite surveying on camelback all directions and asking many times of the locals, I could not succeed in finding it, nor collect more information.

Twelve days after our arrival at Suez we searched for shaykh Salah, who was to accompany us on the journey as a concession by the *kashif*. We heard with regret that he had left to escort a caravan directed to the sulfur mines, some days distant from Suez, and that he would then come back to guide us to Mount Sinai. The incertitude on the date of his return and the fear of being forced to stay too long in Suez in order to wait for him made us decide to leave without him, taking as escort a relative of the same shaykh called Iuclep.[170] On 13 September at dawn, we sent the camels to ford the east bay and we crossed it on boat. We then headed toward the southeast and reached at midday Ayun Musa ('Fountains of Moses') where, under the shadow of

---

169 al-Arish , on the Mediterranean coast. Ricci refers here to an essay in the *Description de l'Égypte*: François-Michel de Rozière, "Notice sur les ruines d'un monument persépolitain découvert dans l'isthme de Suez par M. de Rozière, ingénieur en chef des mines," in *Description de l'Égypte, Antiquités, Mémoires* (Paris: Imprimerie Impériale, 1809), 1:265–76. The monument was a little north of Suez, in the isthmus bed, and was made of granite blocks with Persian cuneiform inscriptions and reliefs. Cf. *Description de l'Égypte, Antiquités* 5, Pl. 29, [1]–[4].

170 The name does not sound Arabic at all. It is a faulty transcription by Ricci, who also transcribes the name of Shaykh Salah as "Izalek."

four majestic palm trees, we took our rest. These famous fountains are in fact many springs and wells, whose waters are quite brackish and ferruginous.[171] The Arabs believe they are salutary and they prefer them to those of Bi'r al-Nab': they experienced that the former restores health to the sick, while bathing in and drinking of the latter have a completely different effect. Except for one spring only, which is surrounded by stones, the others are always murky and muddy because the Arabs let the camels in. Therefore the travelers drink and make provision only at the former. Around the springs there are the ruins of many houses and walls, from which it is easy to guess that this place once used to be very populous. The abundance of waters, in fact, possibly attracted people to live by the springs, in a place where hot weather makes water the most precious element for human survival. Beside the sea, there are ruins of what looks like a dock.

Close to the springs I found a chameleon of a different species from those of Cairo: its color was dark grey, but when I took it in my hands it became upset and changed to black. I put it back on the ground and I covered it with a handkerchief. After fifteen minutes I uncovered it and I found it almost white. I guess that this animal is white in condition of absolute rest, dark grey when moving, and black when agitated and angry. The chameleons in Cairo are on the contrary light yellow and become dark yellow and then green when changing their mood from calm to movement and furor.

After a short rest in that swampy and unhealthy place, we continued our journey at a short distance from the sea. In the evening we pitched our tents in a sandy plain completely devoid of vegetation.

On the 14th we followed the same direction and traveled all day on a monotonous and desert terrain. We suffered the heat more than usual, to the point that we could hardly breathe.

On the 15th at two in the afternoon we met some small hills of sandstone and some palm trees, under whose shadow we took some rest because, despite the northwest wind that was strongly blowing, the sun's rays were unbearable. In the evening we reached Wadi Amura, where there is a well of brackish water that slightly smells of sulfur and has the same taste of water into which a red-hot iron has been dipped.

This was probably the place where, three days' march from the Red Sea, the Israelites had a stop, whining and murmuring against their leader for the bad quality of the water they were forced to drink.[172] In fact, down to Ras Muhammad, which is eight full days from Amura, there are no more brackish water wells, despite their proximity to the sea. From this place to Wadi Gharandal, where we arrived late at night, there is plenty of a kind of thorny bush, called by the Arabs *nabaq al-jebel*, which is the buckthorn.[173] The fruit is red and transparent, as big as a cherry, sweet and refreshing. Our guides ate a large quantity of it and we felt encouraged to do the same, without suffering any consequence.

---

171 Cf. Gaspard Monge, "Observations sur la fontaine de Moïse," in *Description de l'Égypte, État Moderne* (Paris: Imprimerie Impériale, 1809), 1:409–12.

172 Exodus 15:22–24.

173 Possibly *Rhamnus disperma* or *Ziziphus spina-christi*; Mahmoud A.K. Zahran and Arthur J. Willis, *The Vegetation of Egypt* (New York: Springer Publishing, 2009), 223, 241.

The Wadi Gharandal is quite long and during the winter gathers much water from the rains that fall in the nearby mountains, but in summer it is completely dry. From this very same stream many others flow to the northwest, all leading to the sea. The water of these streams is good and drinkable, but when closed in bottles, it exudes a light sulfur smell. From this I gathered that the nearby mountains contain this mineral.

On the banks of the Gharandal, shaded by thick bushes of tamarisk, and in the highest places around, there are the ruins of many walls and pottery shards scattered here and there. There is no doubt that this part of the desert was once inhabited.

On the 16th at dawn we moved the caravan and after two hours we reached a plain where the crew of an English ship, which wrecked some time ago,[174] was massacred and then buried by the Arabs in order to steal what little was left of the cargo and to seize freely whatever the sea would throw on the shore.[175] Around midday we saw again the shores of the Red Sea, which the mountains had until then kept hidden. At two, we camped at Hammam Fara'un ('Baths of Pharaoh'). All that the scripture says about the exodus of the chosen people guided by Moses, Pharaoh's persecution, and his death in the Red Sea by virtue of divine protection is perfectly known by the Arabs, who relate it to the travelers. From this memorable episode, the two grottoes in the slopes of the mountain got the name of Pharaoh's Baths. Inside, there are very hot waters, up to 156 degrees Fahrenheit. Whatever is the origin of the name, it is certain that craftmanship contributed in the past to make the springs accessible. They could even today be made more available, with little expense, to the benefit of the entire human race. These baths look from the outside like a cave, ten feet higher than the ground, accessible through two natural openings, cut with a certain regularity. One leads to the spring through a narrow and steep slope. With the escort of an Arab, I wanted to venture into the passage and I reached very close to the spring. As soon as one enters inside the cave he begins to sweat as in a Turkish (or steam) bath. It is impossible to resist the heat of the water if one attempts to dip in. The Arabs come here to treat many diseases and especially skin illnesses. They have the constancy to spend up to forty days inside that sort of *calidarium*, eating bread and dates and leaving only to rest in the tents which they pitch almost at the entrance of the cave. Under the cave, a spring gushes in different directions toward the sea, a quarter of a mile further on, without losing heat at all. The stones where the waters pass by are always hot and encrusted with white tartar, sometimes of a very brilliant green, especially when the sun shines. It seems to be a mixture of salt, sulfur, and vitriol: this is our opinion after we crushed a piece of tartar, but it is possible that an accurate analysis would disclose other elements that we could not detect.

We pitched our tents close to the sea, under the shadow of a few tamarisks, in order to be more comfortable in our observations, but the violence of the wind soon forced us to move under the mountain. At this point the sea is not deep: it might be three or four

---

174 "More ships have been wrecked in the Bay of Birket Faraoun than in any other part of the gulf of Tor," Burckhardt, *Travels in Syria*, 620. In a letter to Patrizio Rontani dated 1 October 1820, Ricci is more precise: "Around twenty years ago"; Sammarco, *Alessandro Ricci*, 156.

175 Probably near Ras Mal'ab.

leagues in width. The presence of many mountains directly on the sea generates fierce winds, which calm down at sunset and contribute to lowering the waters of the sea. The ships that come and go from the Indies do not dare to cross it unless it is calm, which happens, as I said, in the evening.

I would not be able to decide if this, rather than Ayun Musa, was the place where the Israelites crossed the Red Sea. Here, the three days' march and the waters changing from brackish to drinkable by the miraculous stick agree with the scriptures. On the contrary, at Hammam Fara'un there is a spring of pure water at a short distance from the sea. Here the width of the channel, albeit shallow, and the constant blowing of winds would make the crossing unlikely. On the other side, the tradition maintained by the Arabs of the extraordinary event makes me think that the miracle happened in this very place. Without venturing into too much speculation, I would limit myself to observe that, if we did not have the invincible witness of the holy pages to confirm the miraculous liberation of the people of God, we would have the same tradition preserved by the Arabs. This, too, cannot be doubtful, because it has been passed from father to son up to the present generation.[176]

On the 17th we set off again and at a short distance we met on the left a mountain of medium height made of layers of porous rock, perfectly red. I collected some fragments which I still possess and that I believed to be pure iron oxide. In fact, the nearby soil, which we crossed for the distance of more than a mile, was covered by very fine iron powder, similar to the one we still use and buy in Europe. We then entered into a valley so narrow and deep that in certain points the sun's rays could barely enter. On the rocks there grows a sort of caper, much larger than ours. Its zest, green at the beginning, becomes bright red when the fruit is perfectly ripe. The pulp is yellow, full of little seeds, and has a sweet and spicy taste at the same time. The Arabs ate straight of it, but we knew by experience that this fruit acts as a powerful laxative to whoever is not used to it. After almost an hour's march in this dark and winding valley, we entered a second one, much more pleasant, flanked by low mountains and many tamarisks and palm trees. We then met a mountain chain, which we climbed via a comfortable sandy slope. One would think that this path was cut by men, so precisely carved are the rocks on the two sides. Atop the mountain the sea is again visible. Through a similarly easy descent, we reached Jebel al-Kabrit, or sulfur mine, where we camped. Muhammad Ali had recently sent some Europeans to visit it, intending to reopen the quarry. I do not know the results of their mission, but if the underground veins are not more abundant and compact than the ones on the surface, which we found very thin and mixed with sandstone, it is unlikely this project would bring the satisfactory results the viceroy had possibly hoped for.

From Hammam Fara'un to Jebel al-Kabrit, the mountains often change color, but all have a metal appearance and it seems they contain several metals, especially iron and sulfur.

During the night, Mr. Linant, my fellow traveler, was attacked by a fierce fever. It continued for many days and was eventually defeated by the constant use of quinine,

---

176 Ricci seems unaware that the Exodus is also narrated in the Quran.

which I always carry with me. This unfortunate incident forced us to remain three entire days at Jebel al-Kabrit and thence to proceed almost always during the night, to avoid the burning rays of the sun. During our stay there I walked all the surrounding mountains, which have a volcanic look. This and the absolute lack of any kind of vegetation make the region even gloomier.

On 20 September, toward the evening, we abandoned the sulfur mines and after five hours of very slow march, in order not to fatigue the invalid, we pitched the tents in a valley surrounded on all sides by high mountains. We set off before dawn to reach al-Maghara early in the morning: here, close to a rock protruding into Wadi Sidri, we camped under the shadow of many *sant* trees. I provided Mr. Linant with all good treatments the circumstances allowed and then went to visit the nearby mountain called Mukattab,[177] which is the 'written' mountain. For a good stretch of its surface one can see a large number of roughly carved inscriptions in Greek, Arabic, and mainly other characters unknown to me. I copied the best preserved and the clearest, which can be seen on plate 36, from no. 3 to no. 19. All these inscriptions are placed without order. This, together with the many languages used, makes me think that they are simple memories left by the Christians on their pilgrimage to Mount Sinai at the time of the early church. In fact, many of the inscriptions bear a cross on top. Similar inscriptions are to be found all around the peninsula and on many parts of Mount Horeb itself. I am convinced of this, more so because the road of al-Maghara is by all means the most comfortable to make the pilgrimage.

On the 22nd I visited al-Maghara, a few steps away from our camp, so called because of the many caves one can see. In fact, *maghara* in Arabic means 'excavated hole' or 'excavation.'[178] The mountain is made of sandstone layers in perpendicular veins and with irregular directions. On the surface there are caves that go many feet deep inside the mountain. I could not verify their depth since they are almost all filled with debris and stones, carried by the heavy rains. Two very narrow paths, enlarged here and there by human hands, lead to the top of the mountain, where more caves are to be found, some almost inaccessible. Nevertheless, I could visit them all, but with extreme fatigue and not without peril. The main caves are four and the largest two have pillars to uphold the roof, as in our stone quarries. I could easily get in crawling on all fours. The way these caves were excavated and the mineral fragments that are still around, all of this, to sum up, makes me believe that they used to be ancient copper mines. They were later abandoned either because of scarcity of metal or for other reasons, which is useless as much

---

177 Wadi Mukattab has important Roman, Byzantine, and Nabataean graffiti carved on the rocks and dating from the second century BC; Said Gohary and Jocelyn Gohary, "Report on Cultural Heritage Sites in South Sinai," http://st-katherine.net/en/downloads/Cultural%20Heritage%20Sites.pdf [12]; Burckhardt, *Travels in Syria*, 620–21.

178 The famous ancient Egyptian turquoise and copper mines, exploited since the Early Dynastic period. Exploitation restarted at the end of the nineteenth century AD, but the indiscriminate use of dynamite caused the complete destruction of the ancient mines; Alan H. Gardiner, Thomas E. Peet, and Jaroslav Černý, *The Inscriptions of Sinai*, 1 (London: Egypt Exploration Society, 1952), 22.

as impossible to determine. At the entrance of almost all the caves there are hieroglyphic rock stelae: some bear a date, which possibly indicates the year they were opened. Plate 37, nos. 1, 2, 7, 8. It is very unfortunate that some of these rock stelae are so damaged as to make copying them impossible, for this kind of inscription must be, in my opinion, very interesting. No. 2 of Plate 38 is an offering table in bas-relief that contains the name of the offerer and the date of the offering. Of the same kind are inscriptions nos. 4 and 5 of plate 39. No. 3 of this plate, a stunning bas-relief, is also quite important since it bears a name and many emblems. These rock stelae can be found not only in the caves, but in many parts of the mountain. I copied part of them and Mr. Linant did the rest on our way back. The style of hieroglyphs is not always the same and while some subjects are strikingly refined, others are only roughly sketched. It is therefore possible that they were carved in different periods and maybe at a whim or as a pastime by workers, such as for example no. 3 of plate 37. This idea is not so improbable, because in all the places where Egyptians built great monuments, such as Biban al-Muluk, Abu Simbel, and Philae, the nearby rocks are everywhere covered in endless hieroglyphs, roughly carved inscriptions, and many weird, meaningless figures.

As for the better-style sculptures that are at the entrance of the quarries, representing a foreign man being slaughtered by an Egyptian, I think they could be memories of battles that were fought close to the mines between the Egyptians and other peoples. It is possible that continuous aggressions by the nearby peoples forced the Egyptians to abandon these mines. Plates 38, no. 1, and 39, nos. 1 and 2, represent some of these battles. In the two figures in no. 1, the subject is almost identical: the facial features and the dress of the foreign man look very much like those carved on the side of the gate at Abu Simbel, which I copied in my *Travel to Nubia*, plate 18, no. 2. They are believed by some to be Hebrews and by others the Shepherds.[179] Even though I am unable to solve the problem, I think that they could really be Hebrews, who lived closer than any other nation to the mines. It is noteworthy that in the second of the two figures in no. 1 [plate 39], the Egyptian seems to sacrifice the foreigner to the ibis-headed god Thoth. As for sculpture no. 2, it also must relate to a fact of the same nature, since the Egyptian represented here is armed with a knife as in the other two bas-reliefs.

Beside the aforementioned hieroglyphic inscriptions, there are in the mountains some polished stones with holes, or dots, gathered in groups. See plate 37, no. 9. Would these be by any chance numeric records or some other kind of unknown, less common encrypted writing?

Halfway from Mukattab to al-Maghara there is a large granite rock on which there is a hieroglyphic stela: Arabs who more frequently attend this valley say that it bears the name of a city that used to be in this place a long time ago. I do not know how trustworthy this tradition is: I could not see in its environs any trace of houses or ruined walls, as is usual in all places where a city used to exist.

---

179   That is, the Hyksos.

Wadi Sidri, where we had camped, abounds with *sant* trees. They produce a gum and for this reason it is absolutely forbidden to cut them, under the fine of twenty piasters and a goat. There is also a spring of excellent water and it is inhabited by many Bedouin families. We bought a goat from one of them.

On the evening of the 23rd, we left this place and, walking through many valleys, always flanked by high mountains, we reached before dawn Wadi Firan, homeland to shaykh Salah. This is the same man that the *kashif* of Suez intended for our escort and who, now back from his previous mission, showed great satisfaction to meet us here. He received us in a frank and friendly way. A lamb was immediately slaughtered upon our arrival and as soon as we dismounted from the camels, he offered us coffee, to be drunk in his company. This is the most certain mark of friendship that can be received by Bedouins, because he who eats or drinks with them will be safe, even if he is an enemy or a prisoner: he and all his belongings become sacred and untouchable. A huge rice pilaf, eggs, and the lamb roasted on charcoal were part of our lunch. We spent a pleasant half an hour with our host, seated under a canopy made of six palm-wood pillars, with our legs crossed and surrounded by our caravan guides, who were looking forward to taking our place after we finished. We were offered sour milk to drink, but we preferred fresh water as more suitable for our habits and our body.

Salah is the son of a shaykh by the same name, who had helped General Kléber at the time of the Napoleonic expedition and had received a saber, which he still kept in the family as a memory of the famous invasion. He is the head of the Towara tribe. Because on this trip we took as guides some Arabs of his own tribe, this obliged him more than anything else to take care of us by all means. He was dressed like all the other men of his tribe except for the turban, which was of colored cashmere, while the others bear it of white wool only. He also had a long red dress, which he uses for particular occasions with another shawl as belt, and yellow slippers. This is, in general, the dress of all tribe chiefs.

His camel is famous because of its beauty and its incredible speed. He told us that he refused very large sums of money for it, having as a rule that a good mount is the most necessary thing for a man of war living in the desert.

This valley is inhabited by around thirty families, almost all relatives of the shaykh. He stations here while the season is cool and then, when the heat comes, moves around with his tribe.

When we were alone with him we offered him a cup of spirit, which he drank with pleasure, but not before he had made sure nobody could see him.

His family, composed of his wife, two female slaves, and two children, was always hidden from us.

The village is a day's walk from the sea, through a route all along the valley adorned with palms and tamarisks. The high mountains around it are partly of granite and partly of sandstone. On the slope toward the valley there are many well-cultivated orchards, which produce abundant grapes, pears, pomegranates, apples, and other fruits that along with dates are yearly traded by the locals in Cairo. Tobacco is also cultivated and used by the Towara and other tribes: they chew it mixed with some natron. It is the custom of all Arabs to hang on their saddle a small bag of tobacco, which they put in their mouths between lips and gums to excite salivation. In this way they prevent thirst and keep their teeth clean, which also happens because of the simplicity of their food.

The dress of the Towara is almost the same as that of any other tribe: a filthy white cotton turban and a black tunic with large and long sleeves, called *zabut*, tied at the hips with a white wool belt, where they stick a small curved knife or a long saber. In winter they also wear a wool cloak with black and white stripes. When cool, they walk barefoot and this is the reason they have hard and calloused feet, but, when the sun heats the sand, they wear a piece of leather sole tied up with little ropes. It often happens that they are seen wearing only one such and transfer it from foot to foot alternately.

Despite the shaykh keeping his women strictly hidden, the Arabs of his tribe are not so scrupulous and, since among them women do not use the veil as they do in Cairo, we could see the faces of many. They wear a black tunic similar to the one worn by men. They style their hair in small braids, gathered in groups on the forehead and decorated with colored glass ornaments. They put on their ears rings so large that the hand can easily pass through. They also use a necklace, which among the richest is a solid silver ring and among the poorest is made of false amber and colored glass beads. The same for bracelets. They also wear ankle bracelets made of iron or silver, according to their wealth, and in general the women of the rich distinguish themselves using more and heavier ornaments.

It is not easy to know with certainty the age of an Arab, rare being those who know how to write and it not being customary among them to keep track of birthdays. So, to say that one child is older than another, someone would say that the former mounts camels and the latter can only lead them to drink. A father would state that his son is six Ramadans old, instead of six years. And so, with other time references, one can tell the age of each of them, but always in an uncertain and doubtful way.

Bedouins are hospitable and do not sit for their meals without inviting foreigners, saying, "Bismillah,[180] sit with us." Refusal would be taken very ill, so everybody makes sure to accept and to eat with greed, to show appreciation for the food.

If a member of the tribe is ill, each of them makes it a duty to visit and suggest remedies he has found effective in similar cases. Desert plants provide them with remedies and one in particular, called *tamar*, is used in the treatment of many sicknesses. The ground leaves of this plant, reduced to a sort of poultice, are used to treat wounds and injuries, which heal immediately. Bedouins constantly refuse to use treatments found or suggested by people living in the territory of a different tribe because they have as a rule that the sick must be treated with medicines of his own tribe. A European physician, on the contrary, can easily drive away this opinion, and the Arabs blindly submit to

---

180 Arabic باسم الله *(bismillah)*, 'In the name of God.'

whatsoever prescription is given. This is not because they trust the medical principles we use, but because they think that Europeans have talismans suggesting the most suitable remedy. When they suffer from headache, they tighten around the head two rounds of rope or, more commonly, a strip of coarse leather soaked with a mysterious substance, which they keep secret. It never fails.

This valley was in ancient times populated,[181] especially by Christians. There are still the ruins of many houses and monasteries, the largest of which, completely destroyed, is in the middle of the valley, on a small hill. This building was of solid construction. The walls, still standing, are one-third made of large squared blocks of stone and the rest of bricks, which still keep their bright red color as if they have just come out of the kiln.[182] The gardens, which were annexed to the monastery and of which there are still some remains, were defended by strong fences and not a few houses are surrounded by a stair leading to the upper floor, almost two arms' length higher than the ground level. Tombs were built in the highest places of the surrounding mountains and were made of four stone walls assembled with mortar, five to six feet long, over two feet wide, and were covered by large slabs of stone after the burial. In some of the tombs there were still bones, as white as snow. At a lower level in the same mountains there were caves, now used as storerooms, but I would not know how they were used in ancient times.

At a short distance from the tombs there is a granite mountain, the highest in the valley, on top of which there is a building, believed by the Arabs to be a windmill; so, in fact, they call it.[183] They state that the devil has been living there for centuries and for this reason nobody dares to get close. When I announced my decision to visit it, the Arabs tried to discourage me and they were really astonished when, after two hours, they saw me coming back safe and

---

181 A bishop of Pharan (Greek for Firan), called Netra or Nektarios, is mentioned already at the end of the fourth or beginning of the fifth century (*Apophthegmata Patrum*, PG 65, col. 312). The *Piacenza Anonymous* around AD 550–70 reckons eighty (or eight hundred; the manuscript tradition is ambiguous) soldiers with their families (*Antonini Placentini Itinerarium*, 40); cf. René-Georges Coquin, "Pharan," in *The Coptic Encyclopedia*, vol. 6, 1952–53, http://ccdl.libraries.claremont.edu/cdm/singleitem/collection/cce/id/1573/rec/1; Bernard Flusin, "Ermitages et monastères: Le monachism au mont Sinaï à la période protobyzantine," in *Le Sinaï durant l'antiquité et le moyen âge: 4000 ans d'histoire pour un désert. Actes du colloque "Sinai" qui s'est tenu à l'Unesco du 19 au 21 septembre 1997*, ed. Charles Bonnet and Dominique Valbelle (Paris: Errance, 1998), 134, 137; Daniel F. Caner, ed., *History and Hagiography from the Late Antique Sinai* (Liverpool: Liverpool University Press, 2010), 260, note 40. Archaeological excavations were undertaken in the 1990s by Peter Grossmann; cf. Peter Grossmann, "Report on the Season in Firan–Sinai (February–March 1992)," *Byzantinische Zeitschrift* 89 (1996): 11–36, and Peter Grossmann, "Wadi Fayran/Sinai: Report on the Seasons in March and April 1985 and 1986 with an Appendix on the Church at Mount Sinai," in *Annales du Service des Antiquités de l'Égypte* 75 (1999–2000): 153–65.

182 From the fourth–fifth to the sixth century, Firan was the seat of the archbishop of Sinai. The site was abandoned during the seventh century for the monastery of St. Catherine, which was a safer place. Firan was a fortified city and hosted a large basilical cathedral and two more churches; Peter Grossmann, Michael Jones, and Yiannis Meimaris, "Report on the Season in Firan–Sinaï (February–March 1995), *Byzantinische Zeitschrift* 91 (1998): 345, 347.

183 Jebel Tahuna, literally 'Mountain of the Mill,' Gohary and Gohary, "Report on Cultural Heritage Sites," [10].

sound. After I reached the peak with extreme fatigue, I found that the so-called windmill is nothing other than a Christian church.[184] See plate 40, no. 10. The columns are made of sandstone, the arches of bricks, and the walls of large stone blocks joined with very strong mortar. On the opposite side of the same mountain there are the remains of another church, smaller than this, but built with the same architecture. Beside it there are the ruins of a very large monastery and of an isolated chapel. Many ruined houses are all around these buildings. It is likely that the fame of some miracle worked by Moses in this valley moved the early Christians to leave a memory here by erecting these holy buildings. At a short distance there is Wadi Aliyat, crossing which one can finally climb Mount Horeb. Pilgrims usually prefer this road to go up Mount Sinai, and then come down by the side of the monastery. From the inscriptions carved on the rocks of this valley, similar to those of Mukattab, one can guess that in ancient times also pilgrims used the same road. Two of these inscriptions are on plate 36, nos. 26 and 27. This valley, once property of the monks, is now controlled by shaykh Salah.

Since Mr. Linant started to feel better, I wanted to try to walk during the day. Therefore, on the morning of 27 September, I had the caravan set off. We traveled until midday among the mountains of granite and other stones, all bare of vegetation, except for a few palm trees here and there. A cave served us as shelter in which to spend three of the hottest hours and in three more hours we reached the second gardens of Sinai. Here, we slept beside a spring of excellent water, to which we paid a visit more than once during the night. The vegetation here is similar to that of Firan: the same trees grow abundantly and the grapes are even better because the vines propagate along the veins in the rock, which protect them from the excessive heat and make the fruit more spicy and tasty.

On the following day, 28 September, after six hours of march, we reached the monastery. The adjacent garden, placed in the middle of bare cliffs, arouses wonder and pleasure at the same time, and the contrast with nature could not be more beautiful. Raising the sight from the bright and varied green, high mountains of red and black granite appear behind the monastery. Imperceptibly expanding, they form a background of endless desert.

Once we arrived under the monastery, which from the outside looks like a castle, we met with many Arabs: monks were lowering provisions for them from the top of the walls with long ropes.

As soon as we announced ourselves as Christians asking for hospitality, they lowered a rope made in a way to easily carry heavy weights. By the means of it, one after the other, Mr. Linant and I, with the dragoman and a servant, were introduced inside the monastery. Our Arabs camped at a distance with the others.

---

184 According to the tradition, on the spot where Moses watched the battle of the Israelites led by Joshua against Amalek (Ex. 17:8–16). The church (called "Church C") seems to be mentioned already in Egeria, *Peregrinatio,* PD Y 15, and was later converted into a mosque; Peter Grossmann, "Early Christian Ruins in Wadi Fayran (Sinai): An Archaeological Survey," *Annales du Service des Antiquités de l'Égypte* 70 (1985): 78–80; Uzi Dahari, Rivka Calderon, Yael Gorin-Rosen, William D. Cooke, and Orit Shamir, *Monastic Settlements in South Sinai in the Byzantine Period: The Archaeological Remains* (Jerusalem: Israel Antiquities Authority, 2000), 184–85; Caner, *History and Hagiography,* 216n33.

We were received very warmly by the monks and lodged in the best quarters: they immediately brought us some excellent bread, fresh fruit, cheese with spirit and wine, and a bottle of very fresh water. The wine, made by the monks with the grapes of their garden, is not very good because they do not know how to make it. It is, anyway, too little to suffice their annual consumption, but they keep a good provision in their cells coming from the outside through relations and money. They share it willingly with the visitors, who usually pay for it generously.

The monastery is built in such a narrow spot in the valley that while a part of the building rests on the southeast side of Mount Sinai, the other leaves only a tiny passage between the monastery itself and the opposite mountain.

The four high walls of the monastery are built with large stones connected with mortar and have buttresses at each side, so that the building looks more like a fortress than a convent. One cannot enter but through a window on the south side, more than thirty feet high. The only entrance gate is always closed with large granite blocks, permanently walled, and this sort of defense is never demolished, except for the visit of the bishop or to let in the donkey that turns the grindstone of the mill. This happens very rarely, in fact; the one we found inside was almost thirty years old.[185] Everything else is let in through the same window. The rope is activated by a wheel, supervised by two laymen under the orders of the doorkeeper, which in the monastery is a very important office. Part of this building was restored during the French expedition by the orders of General Kléber. By means of stairs cut in the inner part of the walls, it is possible to make the complete tour of the monastery and run to its defense in case of danger. The corners overlooking the desert have two small pieces of artillery.[186] From the observatory of the monastery, one can see at a glance all the buildings inside its enclosure, which as a whole looks like a little castle. The inner distribution of the monastery is badly planned: there is a large number of rooms, but no regularity. The part intended for the pilgrims is separated from the rest by means of a courtyard and is accessible through a different staircase. On the door which leads to the quarters of the monks, I read inscription no. 12 on plate 40. Each monk has two rooms, or cells, one used for study and the other for his rest, and a piece of land to cultivate in the inner courtyard of the monastery, where there are cypresses, herbs, and flowers.

The quarters of the bishop, which gather all imaginable comforts, are always empty.[187] There is a chapel annexed to celebrate the liturgy in case he feels indisposed or for any

---

185   It is still called the Patriarchal Gate. Burckhardt states that since 1760 no archbishop had resided in the monastery and that the gate had been sealed since 1709; Burckhardt, *Travels in Syria*, 549, 570.

186   A present from General Kléber but never used, except to scare the Bedouins; Burckhardt, *Travels in Syria*, 556.

187   The archbishop of Sinai, Pharan, and Raithou, formally dependent on the Greek patriarch of Jerusalem, was abbot of the monastery. Archbishop Constantius II (1804–59) resided at Constantinople at the time. He was later elected patriarch of Constantinople as Constantius I; Burckhardt, *Travels in Syria*, 549, 570; Adrian Marinescu, "The Hierarchs' Catalogue of Monastery St. Catherine in Mount Sinai," *Études byzantines et post-byzantines* 4 (2001): 288, http://www.orththeol.uni-muenchen.de/personen/professoren/marinescu/publ-marinescu.pdf

other reason he wishes to do it privately. The hall of these quarters is decorated with different paintings. Among them are the original plan of the monastery and a view of the convent and of Mount Sinai. Amid the paintings there are some that are quite old, in Greek style, and many portraits of the bishops. The portrait of the current one was made by a skilled artist and the color in particular is beautiful and vivid.[188]

There is a specific large room in the monastery where the workshops of all the most useful crafts, including the armory, are gathered. The tools themselves were made in the monastery and the different crafts are practiced by monks.

In case of attack by the Arabs, the monks can seek refuge in the vast basements of the monastery, which they normally use to store their provisions. In one of these I copied an inscription, which I placed on plate 40, no. 13. There are twenty-four chapels, all more or less decorated, where liturgy is celebrated during the year according to the respective feasts.

The main church is nowadays called St. Catherine's, even though in origin it was dedicated to the Transfiguration. It is a rectangle 200 feet long and 100 feet wide. The roof is supported by two rows of granite columns, which the monks—I know not why—have painted in white. The dome overlooking the main altar is intact and in the same condition as when built by order of Emperor Justinian, with all the rest of the monastery. It has never needed restoration and bears the representation of his portrait, that of Empress Theodora, and the Transfiguration.[189] The church, in general, is rich in marbles and carvings, and also inlays of hard oriental woods and ivory, all work of the monks. Most admirable is a pulpit in the same style and decorated with mother of pearl: the colors are so well distributed and produce such a beautiful effect that the best artist could not have done better. There are many lamps made of gold and silver, most being offerings from princes and other rich pilgrims. Altar drapery and vestments were mostly woven in the monastery itself, but some are presents from various notables. The value of all these objects is, as one can imagine, considerable. We were lucky enough to see the most magnificent of them during the feast of Saint Catherine, which happened to be during our stay and which was celebrated with much pomp. The roof of the church is covered with lead plates. The place where God appeared to Moses in the shape of a burning bush is, according to the monks, behind the main altar and is called *alyka*.[190] Entrance is only allowed barefoot, on the knees, and with special permission by the father superior, who rarely grants it. Every Saturday, a mass is celebrated on an altar erected by the entrance door.

---

188 The portraits of the archbishops are now kept in a large hall of the library building. Of the paintings Ricci saw in 1820, only one survives: a portrait of Archbishop Ananias (1661–71) in liturgical vestments. There is a portrait of Archbishop Constantius II, but it was painted after Ricci's visit.

189 The mosaic, a masterpiece of Byzantine art, is on the apse (not exactly a dome) and represents the Transfiguration of Christ between Elijah and Moses, with Peter, James, and John looking on with reverence. In the surrounding medallions, there are the apostles, the prophets, Deacon John, and Abbot Longinus. What Ricci claims to be portraits of Theodora and Justinian, possibly misled by the monks, are in fact images of St. John the Baptist and the Virgin Mary; Kurt Weitzmann, "The Mosaic in St. Catherine's Monastery on Mount Sinai," *Proceedings of the American Philosophical Society* 110, no. 6 (1966): 392, 403–404; same mistake in Burckhardt, *Travels in Syria*, 542.

190 Arabic العليقة (*al-aliqa*), 'bush'; Burckhardt, *Travels in Syria*, 542.

In the lower part of the church there is a much venerated place, because it is the burial site of many monks, slaughtered by the Arabs during an attack on the monastery a long time ago. A Greek inscription reminds visitors of the terrible and memorable massacre.[191]

The refectory can easily accommodate one hundred people, but strangers are rarely let in. There is a separate kitchen for them as well. On the entrance door of the monks' kitchen hangs a copper plate with an inscription: I started to copy it, but as two monks came suddenly in, I interrupted my work so as not to look indiscreet, and then never had the opportunity to finish. I placed on plate 40, no. 14 the part I was able to copy.

The library is large and rich in manuscripts in oriental languages, but generally little frequented.

It seems strange that in such a famed holy place there is a Muslim mosque, capable of holding a hundred and fifty people and guarded by two Arabs. These also serve the monks in their needs and in exchange they are fed by them. The history of the foundation of this mosque, as preserved by tradition, although unlikely, is as follows. They say that when Sultan Selim conquered Egypt, he was very friendly with a young Greek priest, who used to follow him everywhere. This priest fell sick in the vicinity of the monastery and the sultan had him moved there in order to be treated. He then left for Constantinople, where, not much later, the news reached him of the death of his friend. In the excess of his sorrow, he ordered the general destruction of all Christian monasteries. The monks were immediately informed by their friends about the barbaric decree and started to build a mosque inside the monastery. The most naive say it was built in only one night. This expedient, they say, saved the monastery, which was the only one to be spared.[192]

The monastery has two very deep wells; one is perennial and is called 'Well of Moses' because tradition says he was the first to drink of its water.[193] This is fresh and pure like few

---

191 It might be the inscription commemorating the forty martyrs of Raithou; Philip Mayerson, "An Inscription in the Monastery of St. Catherine and the Martyr Tradition in Sinai," *Dumbarton Oaks Papers* 30 (1976): 375–79; Caner, *History and Hagiography*, 51–63.

192 The legend recorded by Ricci has full confirmation in Burckhardt, *Travels in Syria*, 543, and it must represent the version offered by the monks at that period. The narration recalls one of the two traditional stories on the foundation of the mosque. A first story involves a certain Solomon, future abbot of St. Catherine, who, during the anti-Christian persecutions of the Fatimid caliphs, ordered the construction of the mosque to avoid the destruction of the monastery. A second story is recorded on a Quran holder in the monastery itself and dates the foundation of the mosque to the period of the prince Anushtakin al-Dizbiri (died 1042). A date between the eleventh and twelfth centuries is confirmed by the minbar of the mosque, which carries the date AH 500 (AD 1106): the object was a gift from the vizier al-Afdal, who served under al-Amir bi-Ahkam Allah (1101–30), but started his career under al-Hakim; Aziz S. Atiya, *The Monastery of St. Catherine in Mount Sinai* (Cairo: Misr S.A.E., 1950), 43, and especially Jean-Michel Mouton, "Les musulmans à Sainte-Catherine au Moyen Âge," in *Le Sinaï durant l'antiquité et le Moyen Âge: 4000 ans d'histoire pour un désert. Actes du colloque "Sinaï" qui s'est tenu à l'Unesco du 19 au 21 septembre 1997*, ed. Dominique Valbelle and Charles Bonnet (Paris: Errance, 1998), 178–79. Contrary to what is believed, the mosque was not built anew, but occupied an original sixth-century building; George H. Forsyth, "The Monastery of St. Catherine at Mount Sinai: The Church and Fortress of Justinian," *Dumbarton Oaks Papers* 22 (1968): 7. Sultan Selim I reigned between 1512 and 1520.

193 Cf. Exodus 2:15–22.

others: it flows underground from Mount Sinai, called by the Arabs Jebel Musa, which is 'Mountain of Moses.'

In the monastery there is one bell only and it is never struck except on occasions of great solemnity. I asked the reason and I was told that, since the monastery is on infidel soil, caution presses not to show off in order to avoid any pretence for aggression by the Arabs. When the monks are called to prayers, to study, to the refectory, or to any other daily occupation, they replace the ring of the bell by hitting with a wooden hammer a large oval slab of red granite, hanging by a rope. It makes a peculiar sound, which can be heard everywhere inside the monastery.[194]

The monks pointed out a tower where a patriarch of Constantinople was confined for life. They do not say the reason, though.[195]

Through a little stair I descended into a long subterranean corridor, closed at both ends by iron gates, whose keys are deposited every evening in the cell of the abbot. Through the corridor one can access the garden of the monastery, where the monks walk during the hours devoted to relaxation. The garden is quite large and surrounded by high walls, but they are less strong than those of the monastery itself. It abounds with exquisite fruits and vegetables of all sorts, while fountains supplied with water from Jebel Musa generously provide for the cultivation.

The two Arabs delegated to guard the mosque can, if they want, sleep inside the monastery and they have a small tower for themselves. This is closed with an iron gate, above which there is the inscription on plate 40, no. 15. They say this tower was built by orders of St. Helena, mother of Constantine. Nearby there is the monks' cemetery.

In the old times, this monastery was populated by more than three hundred cenobites. We found thirty-one, and only five of them were priests. This lack of proportion should not be surprising, since only the laymen perform in the monastery the jobs of baker, gardener, gunsmith, shoemaker, distiller, candlemaker, cook, etc.

Fifty Bedouin families, most of them living around the monastery, daily receive food from the monks. Other nomadic tribes believe that they can claim the same right and every now and then come and ask for it in large numbers.[196]

The products of all the orchards cultivated by the monks or by the Arabs salaried for this purpose—comprised of the so-called second gardens, six hours distant from the

---

194 It is called *semantron* or *semanterion* (Gr. σήμαντρον, σημαντήριον) and in the oriental tradition was the means to call for prayers before the introduction of bells in the eleventh century. It is generally made of wood or metal and it is possible that Ricci is mistaken as to the material, even though Burckhardt, too, records a granite semantron; Burckhardt, *Travels in Syria*, 544.

195 Burckhardt, *Travels in Syria*, 544, states that the tower was built forty to fifty years before his visit (1816), so between 1766 and 1776. The patriarchs who finished their reign in this period are Meletius II (1769), Theodosius II (1773), and Samuel I Chatzeres (1774). Fr. Justin, monastery librarian, pointed out to me a partly collapsed building on the east wall, traditionally called "Patriarch's Apartment."

196 Felix Fabri in 1483 estimates between eighty and a hundred Bedouins fed daily by the monastery; Mouton, "Les musulmans," 181 and note 32. Burckhardt mentions thirty to forty people every two days; Burckhardt, *Travels in Syria*, 554.

monastery—are not enough to sustain the monastery and even less the ceaseless distribution of food to the Bedouins. For this purpose, every fifteen days a caravan of ten to twelve camels leaves Cairo with all sort of provisions for the monastery.

My companion Mr. Linant was attacked by a fever as soon as we reached the monastery and could not, for this reason, be overly strained by long, fatiguing trips: I therefore visited Mount Sinai alone.

The Greeks divide it into two parts: Sinai and Horeb. The lower part of the mountain is assigned to the former, while they call the upper part Horeb, up to the peak. I ascended along a staircase that leaves from the walls of the monastery to the north side[197] and has, as they say, three thousand steps. It has been neglected and nowadays it looks like blocks of granite placed so as best to ease the climb. After half an hour of hard ascent there is a cave which houses a spring of fresh water: this is the one that supplies the Well of Moses through a subterranean duct, as I mentioned before. Here, many pilgrims wrote their names and there are many other inscriptions on the rocks, similar to those of Mukattab. After another half an hour, on the left there is a small chapel with a side room, called the House of Prophet Elisha;[198] plate 40, no. 2. After that, I reached a sort of rock-cut cell, supported by an arch of pink granite, where, as I was told by a layman who was my guide, in ancient times a monk used to live. This monk also used to give all pilgrims who wanted to visit the peak of Mount Sinai a pass, later verified by another monk living in a similar cell fifteen minutes uphill. At the same distance there is another chapel, dedicated to the Prophet Elijah;[199] plate 40, no. 3. It is absolutely without decoration except for a side chapel with some paintings. There used to be a small garden, now completely neglected, in the middle of which, beside a natural water reservoir, there is a cypress of considerable height. From this point onward is precisely Mount Horeb, and in the old times pilgrims could not proceed except barefoot and on their knees. At the distance of a few steps in the direction of the peak there is a human-like footprint, left, according to the Arabs, by Muhammad on his visit to Mount Sinai,[200] and according to the monks by a pilgrim saint whose name they do not remember. From this point, one does not climb directly, but has to bypass many hills, which make up Horeb. This is the reason the spot where Moses received the Law cannot be seen from any part of Mount Sinai. On the highest of these hills, which can be considered the peak of Mount Horeb, there is a large rock of beautiful pink granite, on top of which there is a flat semicircular stone. Here, they say, was the exact spot where the Almighty stood when he gave Moses the Tablets of the Law; plate 40, no. 5. No. 4 of the same plate is a church with a perimeter of seventy feet, almost destroyed by the Arabs. At a distance of a few steps and

---

197 In fact, from the south side.

198 The Chapel of Our Lady of the Oikonomos (also called Oikonomissa). Prophet Elisha is the second dedicatee, together with Prophet Elijah of another chapel, mentioned later. "Chapel," and not "House," because according to the Bible Elisha did not live on Mount Sinai.

199 Cf. 1 Kings 19:4–18. It is the Chapel of Elijah and Elisha.

200 Ricci seems to confuse two different traditions: the first regarding the footprint of Prophet Aaron, which is in fact to the northwest of the monastery; the second regarding the footprint of the she-camel of Prophet Muhammad.

in a lower position, there is an arch, which they say marks the spot where Moses, prostrated in front of the Presence, received the Law from God (no. 6, same plate). By the arch there are the remains of another chapel (no. 7, same plate), accessible via seven steps and which was destroyed like the other by the Arabs.[201] In relation to these destructions they say that a long time ago for two consecutive years it failed to rain. This caused high mortality among men and cattle as well. The Arabs then resorted to the monks, asking them to make use of the 'Book of Moses,' which they believed to be in the monastery, to beseech the gift of rain from God. The monks insisted they did not have such a book, but the Arabs became enraged, climbed Horeb, and destroyed the two chapels. The monks then decided to pray in front of them with a book in their hands. After two days, rain fell so heavily that it destroyed tents and huts, and drowned cattle and even men. The Arabs were even more furious than before, believing they were betrayed by the monks. They went back in large numbers to the monastery and threatened the monks with a general massacre. Peace was restored only after the monks threw money and food from the walls. I report this story exactly as it was told and later confirmed by the monks themselves, with the warning that only a remote tradition guarantees its authenticity.[202]

From the southeast, I passed to Mount St. Catherine, which is of black granite, much higher than Horeb and more difficult to climb. Before reaching its summit I met three chapels,[203] plate 40, nos. 8 to 11. Next to each chapel there used to be in the past a garden, but nothing is left now except some bushes, which produce a red fruit similar to our azaroles. In a cell next to the first chapel (no. 11), I copied the inscription no. 2 of plate 36. It

---

201 In antiquity there were at least two churches on the top of the mountain: one built by Julian Saba in 363 and another erected by Justinian and dedicated to the Theotokos (Eutychius, *Annales*, PG 111, col. 1071). The destruction happened between the eighth and the tenth centuries, while a new church was built only in 1934, reusing the scattered blocks. The measurements reported by Ricci definitely describe a much smaller church (3.5 × 7 meters) than the Justinian basilica (11 × 25 meters); Uzi Dahari, "Les constructions de Justinien au Gebel Mousa," in *Le Sinaï durant l'antiquité et le Moyen Âge: 4000 ans d'histoire pour un désert. Actes du colloque "Sinaï" qui s'est tenu à l'Unesco du 19 au 21 septembre 1997*, ed. Dominique Valbelle and Charles Bonnet (Paris: Errance, 1998), 151–55. One of the two ruins in fact could be the small Fatimid mosque, built by the same prince Anushtakin (d. 1042); Gohary and Gohary, "Report," [5]; Sami Salah Abd al-Malik, "Les mosquées du Sinaï au Moyen Âge," in *Le Sinaï durant l'antiquité et le Moyen Âge: 4000 ans d'histoire pour un désert. Actes du colloque "Sinaï" qui s'est tenu à l'Unesco du 19 au 21 septembre 1997*, ed. Dominique Valbelle and Charles Bonnet (Paris: Errance, 1998), 171, 173–74; Mouton, "Les musulmans," 181; Arundale, *Illustrations of Jerusalem*, 32. Burckhardt (Burckhardt, *Travels in Syria*, 566, 568) describes both the mosque and the semi-destroyed chapel, recording a recent but partial repair made by a Bedouin shaykh called Salah.

202 Without mentioning the destruction of the chapel, Burckhardt records the same tradition regarding the Book of Moses, the alleged power of the monks to control the rains, and the disastrous inundation that had occurred a few years earlier; Burckhardt, *Travels in Syria*, 567–68. The incident is narrated also by Minutoli, who knew it directly from Ricci. Minutoli interprets the Book of Moses as the Torah; Minutoli, *Reise*, 140. Fr. Justin, the monastery librarian, suggested to me that this vicissitude may have originated from the existence, in the Orthodox *Proseuchologion* (Book of Prayers), of a specific prayer to ask of God the gift of rain.

203 In fact, the series of chapels here described by Ricci are on Jebel Safsafa, to the northwest of Jebel Musa, while Jebel Katrina is to the southwest.

commemorates the piety of a devout man called Gregory of Mount Sinai who, for many years, every day used to climb the mountain with a censer, returning back to the monastery every evening. He then wished to be buried in this chapel.[204] When I reached the peak of the mountain after much effort, I saw a small church in ruin, which can also be seen from the nearby valleys. It is dedicated to St. Catherine, because her body was found in this place. From this spot one can overlook an immense part of desert, partly flat, partly mountains. All the sharp and bizarre, extremely blackened mountains inspire terror and the region looks as if devastated by volcanoes. Many travelers who were lucky enough to visit during clear and sunny days could see from this spot the two branches of the Red Sea, the Suez and the Aqaba gulfs. I did not have this pleasure because that day the atmosphere was gloomy and misty. Since there was nothing else left that attracted my attention, I speedily descended in order to have enough time to visit the beautiful garden on its south slope. I found it well cultivated with fruits and olive trees: it is called the Garden of the Martyrs[205] and there is a small hermitage with enough space for three people. The Arab warden who also cultivates the land lives there with his family, while the monks do not come except for short vacations. This mountain is the most fertile for gardens, pasturage, and balsamic herbs.

The stone where Moses made the water gush in order to quench the thirst of the Israelites[206] is, as the monks say, in the valley below, called Arba'in.[207] Here, almost at the level of the plain, there is a large isolated rock of irregular form, twelve feet high and resting only on a small part, so that it looks like hanging in balance. It bears many holes, from where they say the water gushed in twenty spurts. The holes are on the three sides of the rock in a line, ten to twelve inches long, four inches deep, and two or three inches wide.

Without doubting the miracle, it is permitted to question the identification of this rock with the one on which Moses worked his wonder. It is also not clear why he would be forced to do it, in order to calm down the rioting and thirsty people, in a place so rich in springs of pure water. One must think that either the tradition is faulty or that by another miracle the rock was carried to Mount Sinai.

Walking back to the monastery, I observed three more gardens cultivated by the Arabs for the monks and I met several Bedouin families, camped with tents in the nearby valleys. They showed me the footprints of a camel on a large slab of stone, stating it was impressed by the camel of Muhammad.[208] At a short distance from the monastery, I was shown a

---

204 The monks were forbidden to sleep on the mountain. It was tradition to cense the top in the evening and return back to the monastery to recite the prayers before dawn; Dahari, "Les constructions," 152. Gregory of Mount Sinai is a saint who lived in the thirteenth century; Joseph J. Hobbs, *Mount Sinai* (Austin: University of Texas Press, 1995), 119–20.

205 Probably the Monastery of the Forty Martyrs (Deir al-Arba'in), which in fact is to the north, between Jebel Musa and Jebel Katrina.

206 Cf. Exodus 17:1–7.

207 Wadi al-Arba'in, the 'Valley of the Forty [Martyrs].' The rock of Moses (Hajar Musa), venerated by Christians and Muslims alike, is halfway into the wadi. A chapel dedicated to the Nativity of the Virgin Mary was built later.

208 Arabic مطب للناقة *(matabb al-naqa)*, 'footprint of the she-camel,' is in fact almost on the top of Horeb. This Muslim tradition, possibly invented by the monks to make the place more venerable to the Muslims, is a medieval legend; Mouton, "Les musulmans," 178.

stone with different holes where they say a monk had found a rich cache of gold. When I entered the monastery, the last rays of the sun were shining.

During our stay in the monastery, I went many times to visit the Bedouins living around Mount Sinai, whose lifestyle is the same as all nomadic Arabs. Their tents are usually supported by seven or nine sticks, three of which are higher than the others, while the one in the middle is the tallest of all. The fabric which is superimposed is just a rough blanket, completely black, sometimes striped black and white, woven by the women with the wool of their own lambs and goats. The latter's wool is more esteemed than the other because it is more consistent and long-lasting. Some are content with a cloth of wool, stretched on four or six sticks, or on nearby trees, where there are some, and here they live as if they were under an ordinary tent. A mat serves at the same time as chair, table, and bed. One or two vases for the coffee, some others to cook food, a goatskin or two to keep water, butter, some wooden cups, and other small objects make all of their furniture. The monastery dispenses bread and coffee daily, while the Bedouin women offer in exchange legumes, fruit,[209] and other products of their gardens, which are introduced into the monastery through a narrow opening in the garden wall. This window is sometimes used to talk when long meetings with the Arabs are needed. The Bedouin families regularly fed by the monks are sedentary and live in the vicinity of Mount Sinai. It seems they renounced their nomadic life and can be considered as dependent on the monastery and employed in its service. In fact, they cultivate all the land not included within the monastery wall, down to the so-called second gardens; they harvest the products, and then give an account to the monks.

On the gate of the monastery there is an inscription, which I copied on plate 36, no. 1.[210]

It is now more than a hundred years that this holy place has not been visited by the bishop. He would need to leave from Constantinople, where he resides, and this journey would cost him an immense fortune because, beside the essential expense for his retinue and his luggage, which is already huge, custom forces him to feed all the Arabs that come to the monastery during his presence. Even though this reason justifies the extreme rarity of the bishop's visits to the monastery, such neglect is the main cause of the progressive decrease in the number of monks. If the ancient zeal does not arise once more in the bishops, it is already foreseeable that it will not take much time before this venerable monument of the piety of the early Christians is completely abandoned.

---

209 The constant reference to fruit harvest in the gardens of Sinai is a novelty compared to other known sources. This absence had raised some suspicions in Rabinowitz: "Descriptions of deciduous fruit agriculture near the monastery of Saint Catharine are conspicuously absent from nineteenth-century accounts. Considering the abundance of these orchards in the last 60 or 70 years, this is intriguing," Dan Rabinowitz, "Themes in the Economy of the Bedouin of South Sinai in the Nineteenth and Twentieth Centuries," *International Journal of Middle East Studies* 17, no. 2 (1985): 217. On the other hand, Ricci fails to record the presence of a fundamental element of Bedouin economy: charcoal.

210 This is the monumental dedicatory inscription of Justinian; August F.J. Böckh, *Corpus Inscriptionum Graecarum* IV.2, part xi (Berlin: Officina Academica, 1857), 8634.

In the small mountains opposite Mount Sinai there are many burial places of pious men, all marked by a cypress.[211]

The west valley[212] is where, according to the scriptures, the Israelites camped. I was pointed out the place where they rebelled before God called their leader up to the mountain, where they raised the golden calf, and the Tablets were broken, and so on.[213]

The alleged miracles worked by Muhammad when he visited Mount Sinai contribute greatly to making the place worthy of respect by the Arabs. Otherwise, their harassment would be unbearable for monks and pilgrims alike, and travelers, too.[214]

A stay in Sinai could not be more fitting than in the three seasons when the air is fresh and pure, but winter must be very hard when it happens, as I was assured that snow covers the mountains.

On the origin of the monastery, they say that St. Helena, mother of Constantine, had a chapel built on the exact spot where God was believed to have appeared to Moses in the shape of a burning bush.[215] They say that, later, many faithful people, imitating the example of St. Helena, came to build chapels and houses. Because of the continuous aggressions of the Arabs, life was becoming impossible and they petitioned Emperor Justinian in order to build a monastery where they could peacefully perform divine worship and, if necessary, defend themselves. The plea was favorably received by the emperor and workers were immediately sent from Constantinople and Egypt to build a monastery on the top of Mount Horeb. The project was immediately halted for the absolute lack of water: the construction was therefore transferred to the slopes of Mount Sinai and was rapidly brought to an end. The church was dedicated to the Transfiguration. After a few years, a holy monk dreamed that the body of St. Catherine, martyred in Alexandria, had been moved by angels to the top of the highest mountain near the monastery. The monks went up in procession, found the bones of the saint, and moved them to their church, which was to be called, from that moment on, St. Catherine. The name is retained today and so too the mountain where the relics were found.

---

211 The tombs of shaykh Awad in Wadi Sulaf; shaykh Nabi Salah, shaykh Muhsin, and shaykh Harun in Wadi al-Shaykh.

212 Wadi Shu'ayb.

213 Cf. Exodus 32:1–35.

214 Monastic and Muslim traditions preserve the memory of a visit of the Prophet to Sinai. Nevertheless, there is no doubt that it is only a medieval legend. In the second year of the Hijri (AD 623), Muhammad, requested by the monks, is said to have granted safety to the monastery through a 'Letter of Protection.' The document, on which the Prophet imposed his hand, was taken by Selim I (1512–20) or by Sulayman the Lawgiver (1520–66) and stored in the Imperial Treasury at Constantinople. The document alleged to be the original is nevertheless false, and while the monastery keeps some sixteenth-century copies, the original seems to be lost; Mouton, "Les musulmans," 177.

215 It is believed that the journey of Empress Helena to Jerusalem took place around 327 and that the Chapel of the Burning Bush and the nearby tower were erected in 330. The place became the seat of the hegumen of Sinai, who gathered together at the weekends the monastic community, which was spread thinly in the desert, and who was responsible for hospitality toward pilgrims. According to Eutychius (*Annales*, PG 111, 1071–72), this was the nucleus of the monastery before the erection of the walls and of the *katholikon* by orders of Justinian in the sixth century.

When my travel companion, Mr. Linant, was perfectly recovered, we decided to resume our journey to Aqaba, in order to visit the ruins of Petra, ancient capital of the region. Nevertheless, it turned out to be impossible to find a single Arab who wanted to guide us there. Shaykh Mahmud, head of the Arabs who live in the desert between the monastery and Aqaba, to whom we also pleaded for guides, refused to comply, adducing as sole reason that Aqaba was a lair of Arabs who had fled from many tribes after commiting every kind of crime. He added that they lived only from murders and thefts and, although we were Christians, he did not want to expose us to certain death for a vile motive. All this was confirmed by the monks, and to validate their statement they showed us the names of French travelers, written on the walls of the guesthouse among many others, who were massacred there. We abandoned our project and we decided to go directly to al-Tor, where the monks have an agent, with the intention of finding an easier opportunity to reach the aforementioned ruins.

We left a good sum of money for the monastery and we also generously compensated the monks for the many attentions paid to us during our twenty-two days' stay among them. We then prepared to set off, with a letter from the abbott to the agent of al-Tor. We dismissed the escort of Iuclep and hired that of shaykh Mahmud. It must be noted that this change of escort is essential to whoever wants to travel in safety, because the tribes that one meets in the desert would hardly let their territories be crossed with camels and guides of a different tribe. It is a tacit agreement that is rigorously observed among the Bedouins. For this reason, our good Salah did not want to accompany us on this journey and we only obtained his promise, which he later kept, to join us on our way back from al-Tor.

On 19 October, as soon as a turbulent storm that had threatened us since dawn had resolved itself in a heavy shower, we set off and did not stop until we reached Wadi al-Shaykh. This is the burial place of a holy Turkish man who was caught by death after he visited Mount Sinai. Many Muslims before going to Mecca visit Sinai, because they hold Prophet Moses in high esteem. They sacrifice a lamb and invoke Moses and Muhammad to assist them to have a prosperous pilgrimage. Here we filled our goatskins at a spring of very fresh water and then went a bit further to spend the night under some trees in a garden property of the monks. From the monastery to that point the road is sandy, with scattered sandstone and limestone pieces and fragments of granite.

On the 20th, proceeding between high dark-colored granite mountains and heading south, we reached the end of Wadi al-Shaykh. This spot, for a stretch of an hour and a half, is full of tamarisk trees, but of a different kind from those we met in the desert before reaching Sinai. The bursar of the monastery made me try a certain substance, yellow and tasting like honey, which he said is called manna and is gathered in the spot where we were at that moment. I remembered the story and asked our guides about it. One of them told us that they knew the manna very well: it is produced by the tamarisk tree, but not every year, since it usually comes after abundant rainfalls, which are very rare. He added that this substance drips from the leaves and forms little globes on the ground: the Arabs pick them before the sun's rays destroy them, and close them in little leather bags.

Here we found many ruined houses and around midday we turned to our left, in order to refill our goatskins at a spring that flows on the slopes of a mountain. I collected a hard green stone, which I still have, from the many that had rolled down from the top. We continued heading south, then camped in a small valley with many *sant* trees, and spent the night.

On the following day, the 21st, we crossed a chain of granite mountains in four hours, through steep and almost impracticable paths, where the camels could barely pass without much effort. In the valley below, I collected thirty granite pieces of different colors and many talcum stones. The fragments of the latter, pulverized on the ground, produced a beautiful effect and sometimes it looked like we were walking on a terrain sprinkled with gold powder. This mountain chain is called by the Arabs Agrat Safha. We finally reached Wadi Hibran and felt encouraged when we learned from our guides that from that point to al-Tor there was only flat terrain. From Wadi al-Shaykh to here there is everywhere, even on top of the mountains, a large number of ruined houses, some looking recent.

Wadi Hibran, which runs in the middle of high granite mountains, is the most fertile of those we had so far crossed: the *sant* trees, the wild palms, and the reeds grow in abundance. There also are some rare tamarisk trees. The valley is watered by a spring of pure water, which runs for a long stretch and then gets lost in the sand, until it reappears further down to flow into the sea. Some time ago, there was a small pleasant village, but the houses, which were all made of palm wood, were turned to ashes in just one night when an accidental fire broke out. Fortunately, nobody perished. At the entrance of this valley, I observed on the rocks some inscriptions similar to those of Mukattab. See plate 36, nos. 20, 21, and 22. Once out of the valley, one can already see al-Tor, five hours in the distance. We arrived there on the 22nd at around nine in the morning.

This is a small town with a port on the Red Sea. It consists of around fifty houses scattered on the shore and made for the most part of corals and other shells mixed with mortar and shaped into large bricks. Around thirty Greek families and a few Arabs live here. Ma'allim Hayl of Suez,[216] a rich merchant established here as British agent, welcomed us in his house and did not spare any effort to make us eat the best fish of the port. Fish is abundant and forms the primary food source of the inhabitants.

Tide is very noticeable on the shore: shortly before midday the sea is at its highest. The shores are covered with all kinds of shells. In the vicinity there are wild palms and a few fruit trees, especially figs. The soil is not good for cultivation and the inhabitants sow wheat, but the harvest is usually poor. The air of al-Tor is unhealthy because of the dew deposited in the morning and in the evening. The inhabitants retire into their homes quite early and do not go out until the sun has dried off the humidity somewhat. They feed a few sheep and some goats, while donkeys are the only means of transportation. At a short distance to the south there are the ruins of a citadel (plate 40, no. 1), which is believed to have been founded by the Portuguese and which was destroyed by Sultan

---

216 Cf. p. 224.

Selim.[217] In a palm wood to the north, one hour distant from the city, there is a small monastery in the shape of a tower,[218] a dependency of the Monastery of Mount Sinai. Here resides an agent, whose task is to gather the products of the land possessed by the monastery around there. Nobody can enter except with a rope like at Mount Sinai. In the nearby garden there is a spring of warm mineral water, which mainly contains sulfur and iron. Here one could build comfortable baths, while daily experience proves that they would be very useful. We visited this monastery showing the agent the letter given us by the superior of Mount Sinai, but since we did not find anything interesting we stayed only one hour.

During our short stay at Tor I would have liked to form a collection of shells, but I could only collect a few on the beach because it was not the right season. Anyway, the most beautiful shells are on the opposite shore, carried by the waves in winter, when a strong northeast wind blows. In spring, the Arabs travel to the opposite side and collect the shells that are amassed on the shore. They wait for the summer to go and collect them from the seabed, when the water is very low, which usually happens at full moon. It takes them seven hours to cross the channel and land opposite al-Tor, at the slopes of a high black mountain, which they call Zaytun, or 'Mountain of the Oil,' a name which derives from the petroleum, commonly referred to as 'stone oil,' which is collected there.

On 24 October, guided by a local, we almost reached Ras Muhammad, which is the southern point of the Sinai peninsula. We proceeded along the coast and did not find any trace of vegetation or house. Coming back, we passed by a mountain all covered in sand where a peculiar phenomenon happens, but not new to me since I had observed it before at Abu Simbel. This is a light detonation that gradually grows in intensity and that imitates the sound of thunder. The Arabs call this noise, and the mountain where it comes from, Naqus,[219] which means 'bell.' They also tell many absurd stories not worth relating here. I suppose that the roar of the sea waves follows the wind and hits the mountain, which

---

217 A square fort, eight kilometers south of al-Tor, in the area of Ras Raya. Ricci names once again Sultan Selim I. The mention of the Portuguese origin of the fort is a very curious example of mnemohistory and relates to the military campaign undertaken in the Red Sea by Alfonso de Albuquerque in 1513. The Portguese did not penetrate into the Red Sea to Sinai, limiting themselves to a naval siege of Aden and an attack on Karaman Island; Malyn D.D. Newitt, *A History of Portuguese Overseas Expansion, 1400–1668* (New York: Routledge, 2005), 87–88. According to Caner, *History and Hagiography*, 33n5, the fort was built by Emperor Anastasius I and then converted into a monastery. On the archaeological excavation of the Japanese Mission at Ras Raya cf. Mutsuo Kawatoko, "Archaeological Survey in the Raya/al-Tur area, South Sinai," *Al-'Usur al-Wusta: The Bulletin of Middle East Medievalists* 16 (2004): 26–30.

218 A *kathisma*, a smaller monastery, in a palm oasis called Hammam Musa, 3.5 kilometers to the north of al-Tor, where a warm water spring flows.

219 Arabic جبل الناقوس *(jebel al-naqus)*, 'mountain of the bell,' a few kilometers to the north of al-Tor. The phenomenon of the so-called 'booming sand' seems to be generated by the wind and the wavelength of moving sand; Nathalie M. Vriend, Melany L. Hunt, Robert W. Clayton, Christopher E. Brennen, Catherine S. Brantley, and Angel Ruiz-Angulo, "Solving the Mystery of Booming Sand Dunes," *Geophysical Research Letters* 34 (2007), doi: 10.1029/2007GL030276; Frank Kühnemann, "Physics of the Sand" (Presentation, Physics Department, German University in Cairo, 3 March 2008), http://physics.guc.edu.eg/pdfs/BoomingSand.pdf. Described also in Frederick Henniker, *Notes during a Visit to Egypt, Nubia, the Oasis, Mount Sinai, and Jerusalem* (London: John Murray, 1823), 214.

emanates a bang, sometimes weak and sometimes strong, according to the nature of the rock. It is also possible that the sand falling into cavities beneath produces this noise, like at Abu Simbel.

On 26 October, we left al-Tor, unable to persuade the Arabs to take us to Aqaba. Following a northeast route, we headed toward Wadi Hibran, in order to reach Firan. At sunset we entered the valley and camped for the night. On our way we found a sack of dates beside the track and our Arabs ran to seize it. From some pieces of wood placed on the sack, they recognized that it belonged to a friendly tribe and did not touch it. They told us that in cases when a camel falls sick or dies in the desert and his owner does not have the means to take its load, he leaves it there with the marker of his tribe, in order to come back and retrieve it after a few days. He is sure to find it because the Arabs are very scrupulous about this matter.

Heading in the same northeast direction, we set off early on the 27th and, while passing through a narrow passage in the valley in order to reach a spring of water not far off, we were caught by an earthquake that lasted around six seconds. We observed the high rocks leaning out above us and we were terrified: the Arabs increased our fear by telling us that earthquakes are not rare there and that a few years ago in a spot not far from where we were a strong quake had plucked up and rolled down enormous rocks.[220] Fearing that the earthquake would come again, we speedily abandoned the dangerous gorge. Once we reached Wadi Talaty al-Naghab, having on our left the road to Mount Sinai, we camped for the night.

On the 28th, around midday, we met Iuclep and dismissed the escort that had been with us since we left al-Tor. With him we reached Wadi Firan, but we did not delay our journey in order to sleep at Mukattab, where we actually arrived late at night. When we took our leave from shaykh Salah, he forced us to accept as a sign of his friendship a domesticated gazelle, which used to pasture with the lambs and come back in the evening. This was a hindrance for us, but we were careful not to refuse the gift and thereby upset our friend. We therefore took the pretty animal with us. We had to drag it by force for four hours, but finally it fled away and went back to its previous shelter, so we were informed some time later in Cairo by the same Salah.

We left Mukattab on the 29th and after eleven hours of fast march on a regular and plain terrain we reached the slopes of a mountain called Serabit al-Khadim,[221] which we intended to visit. This exploration was particularly hazardous, as the Arabs of the tribe that controls the territory are extremely jealous of it because of the ruins that attract travelers to visit and search for treasures. We thought it wise to behave with much caution so as not to expose ourselves to any fight, especially because the Arabs of Salah, who were serving as our escort,

---

220 In fact, through the Red Sea there is a rift that moves by two centimeters every year, causing small earthquakes; Ministry of State for Environmental Affairs, South Sinai Governorate, *South Sinai Environment and Development Profile* (Cairo: n.d. [before 2003]), www.eeaa.gov.eg/english/reports/seam/e1_12.pdf.

221 Porter and Moss, *Topographical Bibliography* 7:345–66. An ancient Egyptian mining site with a sanctuary dedicated to Hathor "Lady of the Turquoise," built during the Twelfth Dynasty and with additions down to the Ramesside period; Dominique Valbelle and Charles Bonnet, *Le sanctuaire d'Hathor maîtresse de la turquoise: Sérabit el-Khadim au Moyen Empire* (Paris: Picard, 1996).

showed much aversion to following us. We ordered the caravan to hide in a bend of the valley, with the strict order to stay vigilant and inform us in case of aggression. At midnight, Mr. Linant and I, with our servant and the dragoman, furnished with a few provisions and well equipped with weapons, set off on a difficult track toward the summit of the mountain, where we arrived after little more than an hour. Here we hid for the rest of the night in a cave almost closed by a large granite rock and, to tell the truth, we could not have found a better shelter. As soon as dawn appeared we started to survey the place. The summit of this mountain is a large plain with isolated hills here and there, which make it picturesque. There are many monuments, the main one being an Egyptian temple. Although it was much ruined, Mr. Linant was able to draw a plan. It has many rooms and is quite different from the usual architecture of other Egyptian temples.

This building looks to have been restored many times with stones coming from other monuments and many blocks have new inscriptions placed on old ones that were erased, as one can see on plate 41, no. 1, which is part of the façade wall of one of the rooms. The style of sculpture makes me think that this temple is very old, but I do not dare to give a decisive opinion on the subject. The rooms are almost all ruined. In one of them we found a fragment of bas-relief with three kneeling figures, in another the trunk of a statue made of a stone similar to granite, which when hit resounds like metal. There was also in the same room a fragment of a small black granite monkey. Digging between the ruins I found pieces of glazed pottery of very bright colors and many shards of painted pottery, which also abounds around the temple.

Two enclosure walls used to surround the temple, twenty-five feet one from the other. In the first I observed many stelae of different sizes, round-topped. Some of them are possibly in the original position in which they were erected, since their bottom is buried more than three feet under the ground. This is the case of the one I copied on plate 42. Many other stelae were removed by the Arabs. Some of them are a total of eleven feet tall and five wide; see plate 43. The two drawings on plate 44 and those marked no. 1, 2, and 3 on plate 45 are also fragments of stelae. All these stelae are interesting for the date some bear and for the style, which could not be better. It is possible that they are religious memorials consecrated to different gods and more specifically to the goddess Isis, also called Hathor, to whom most of the offerings are directed and to whom the sanctuary itself seems to be dedicated.

In many places I observed caves carved in the rock, around which there are many rock inscriptions. I copied some of them on plate 41, nos. 2, 3, and 4, as well as no. 4 of plate 45. The aforementioned fragment no. 2 represents a row of directors of works, a guess I make from their attitude, which is similar in many bas-reliefs I observed in other monuments, and particularly in a scene copied in a cave at Shaykh 'Ibada, showing the transportation of a colossal statue, as I mentioned before in my *Travel to Nubia* (see plate 1).

The style of this temple and of its sculptures is similar to that of al-Maghara, which makes me think that the construction of this temple and the opening of the copper mines there happened at the same time. It is even probable that the mineral extracted was then smelted in the workshops of Serabit al-Khadim. This latter place holds a position very defendable in cases of aggression from nearby peoples. In fact, scattered in many places around the temple and even on the slopes of the mountain, there are piles of burnt materials with traces of melted metal in little globes. Some of them are nothing other than pure copper and were collected by me in the second enclosure of the temple, where it seems they worked the mineral. In the same area I found fragments of real turquoise mixed with sandstone. After our return to Cairo, I donated the biggest and most beautiful piece to the pasha, in order to encourage him to search for the valuable cave that should be nearby. This stone, when treated with acids, does not melt, but gains a brighter color. In fact, the acid acts only on the matrix, which, as I said, is sandstone.

At the distance of half an hour from the temple, on the top of the mountain, there is a steep and high rock overlooking a pool, which perhaps was a water tank used by the workshop. Here there is a beautiful hieroglyphic inscription, which I copied (see plate 46). The subject must surely be interesting, because there is a name, a date, and many numbers.

On 4 November, two armed Arabs appeared: they asked with an awkward attitude permission to enter the cave that we used as shelter, but we refused. They stayed for some time in silence studying us, then became more confident and offered to guide us to a distant place where, according to them, there was a treasure, on the only condition that we would divide it with them. We pretended to accept their proposal, which was possibly an excuse to plot something against us, and we dismissed them with good manners, promising to wait for them in the same spot at sunset. Their mysterious behavior aroused suspicions in us: we did not believe what they said and, since we had already visited around the temple and finished the drawings of the most interesting subjects, as soon as they disappeared we rejoined our caravan. On our way down to the plain, we found many other fragments of turquoise. In less than forty-five minutes we reached the plain and without hesitation we moved the camp. We reasonably feared that the Arabs would go back to the cave as we agreed and, disappointed at not finding us, would chase us in larger numbers. To tell the truth, at the end of such a happy journey it would have been a real shame. The high speed of our camels freed us from any danger and after three hours of fast march we camped again.

The following morning we set off early and, meandering through the mountains, we entered an immense sandy plain, closed to the right by a long chain of limestone mountains. Our guides told us that the chain starts at Suez and ends at Aqaba and is known under the name of Egicherfi.[222] Late that night, we reached Gharandal, whence in less than two days, along the same road we had followed on our way to the monastery, we reached Suez. Here we rested two days.

While we were getting ready for our journey to Cairo, we were told that at the time of Bonaparte's expedition, a French soldier mounted on a camel covered the distance in sixteen hours. This was enough to arouse in Mr. Linant the idea of doing the same. He proposed that I should try the enterprise with him and I agreed. Then we left the caravan. In little more than six hours we were already halfway. Here I started having spasmodic pains in the lower abdomen, so acute that I could not breathe, and even though I was wearing a strong

---

222   "Te" or "Errahkney" in Henniker, *Notes*, 246.

belt, I could not stand the violent movements of the camel. I dismounted and lay down on the ground: a small goatskin of water, which I had taken the precaution of carrying with me, was of great relief. The large quantity I drank possibly freed me from an intestinal inflammation. Mr. Linant, who also was in pain, had the strength to proceed and reached Cairo in thirteen hours, so red in the face that everybody was amazed at how he could have resisted the strain. As for me, I rested half an hour and when the pain calmed down a little, I mounted the camel again and in fourteen hours and a half I reached Cairo, without suffering any further inconvenience. The same was not true for Mr. Linant, who was attacked by dysentery which affected him for the entire next four months. There is no less comfortable ride than that of a camel, especially at a fast trot and at a gallop. The Arabs never expose themselves to long runs without the precaution of strongly girding their lower abdomen either with large strips of leather or with a rope, in order to prevent dysentery, which is the first effect of the extreme agitation of the bowels.

Our caravan also reached Cairo after two days, on 9 November. Our dragoman died shortly after of typhoid and our European servant, who also suffered the same sickness, was lucky enough to survive.

Travel to Sennar

The campaign against Sennar, which was prepared in Egypt for a long time and to which I referred in my *Travel to Nubia*, was by then already ongoing, progressing rapidly and successfully under the supreme command of Isma'il Pasha, son of Muhammad Ali, viceroy of Egypt. The latter wanted to make sure of the good result of this enterprise by sending his other son, Ibrahim Pasha, to cooperate in the execution of his plans. Following the decision of the viceroy, Ibrahim set off on 10 June 1821 with an expedition force of 150[223] infantry and horsemen to join the main army and arrange with his brother the subsequent operations.

The departure of Ibrahim to Sennar aroused in me the desire to follow him, in order to visit the region. But to succeed in this, it was necessary to obtain permission from the viceroy to cross the Second Cataract. It was very difficult at the time to do so, but my insistence and that of Mr. Linant, who also joined me in this journey, plus the unrelenting attentions of Mr. Salt, British consul general, overcame all obstacles and not only were we allowed to follow Ibrahim, but we were also granted a letter of recommendation for him. We therefore rented a small boat with four sailors and a *rais*, and bid farewell to our friends, who in vain had tried to dissuade us from undertaking such a long and dangerous journey. We boarded on 15 June 1821 and sailed at around two in the afternoon, at the exact moment when the water of the Nile started rising.[224]

---

223 Perhaps to be amended to 1,500. Nevertheless, this is not a copying mistake because Georges Douin, who could read directly from Ricci's original manuscript, reports the same number in his citation; Georges Douin, *Histoire du Soudan Égyptien*, vol. 1, *La pénétration, 1820–22* (Cairo: Société Royale de Géographie d'Égypte, 1944), 182.

224 Giovanni Finati was also part of the group in the role of janissary and dragoman, and it is strange that Ricci does not mention him.

In the circumstances we preferred to dress like the *kashif*s on their journeys, wearing the most comfortable of all outfits. It is a simple blue high-necked shirt with wide sleeves, a pair of Barbary shoes, a white turban, and a saber. We were often greeted as *kashif*s in the many villages we passed through on our journey. We were also cautious enough to take with us other kinds of clothes, to wear according to the circumstances.

The northwest wind blew constantly during the whole night and until nine in the morning of the 16th, when we reached Kafr al-Girza. Here the wind ceased completely and we had to wait for six hours, after which, the wind having returned, we shortly arrived at Maidum, where we slept not far from the pyramid. Around midnight, we saw a large group of people getting close to the boat in very deep silence. I guess they were the inhabitants, attracted by curiosity, but since we were ignorant of their intentions and feared they were thieves, we used the oars to move to a nearby island where we camped safely.

At midday, dense clouds started to move toward Abyssinia—a thing that happens regularly every year at the time of the inundation. This made us hopeful of continuing our journey with a propitious wind, and in fact we took advantage of the blow and sailed off. After three hours, the wind having completely ceased, we had to resort to the poles in order to proceed. These poles are like the vertical oars used by our boatmen to move upstream in rivers. The Arabs immerse in water the larger part, which is covered in iron, and adapt the thinner part to their chest, then they push with all their body weight to the extent that all their veins swell and it seems like their eyes are about to pop out of their foreheads. It is necessary to proceed this way not only when there is no wind, but also when the stream is too strong to be overcome by the use of the rope only. This is pulled from the banks by many men, as happens among us. Our crew maneuvered this way for six continuous hours, always singing, according to the habit of the Egyptians, who always sing when at work. It is surprising how those men could persist for so long, considering that it was a very hot day— up to 110 degrees Fahrenheit—and they were fasting because of Ramadan. It is known that during this month, which corresponds to our Lent, they are not allowed to eat, drink, or smoke from dawn to sunset.

At around three in the afternoon, we met Mr. Le Lorrain coming back from Dendera. He had on board the famous zodiac to which I referred earlier.[225]

Close to Beni Suef, where we arrived in the evening, the river is so narrow and shallow that when the waters are low a loaded *ma'ash*[n] cannot proceed unless unloaded first.

On the 18th we docked at Biba, a small and poor town, where we found so little food that in order to get some butter we had to walk one hour into the desert where some Bedouin families were camped. This day we suffered strong heat: we measured the temperature of some wool cloth with a thermometer and it marked 115 degrees Fahrenheit. The wind had almost ceased around sunset. Nevertheless our sailors were working hard to secure the boat: beside dropping the two small anchors, they also tied it to the dock with two thick ropes. We did not understand all these precautions, but the sailors, used to Nile navigation,

---

225   Cf. *Travel to Nubia*, 170.

observing the atmosphere, which was extremely foggy, guessed that some strong winds were approaching. In fact, as soon as the boat was secured, a strong whirlwind from the northeast turned the air fiery red, loaded with very fine sand. This storm lasted at the same intensity for two full hours and then all of a sudden ceased. Such havoc more often occurs in autumn and spring.

The next day we continued our journey and reached Jebel al-Tayr, which means 'Mountain of the Birds,' so called for the wondrous number of birds nested here. It is a limestone mountain and from a distance its appearance is very gloomy. On its summit there is a monastery, a dependent of that of Sinai.[226] The monks who live here do not pay any tax and live on alms which they gather from the boats passing by the cliffs. They go down to the river with some difficulty and lower from the cliffs a leather bag hanging from a rope: all travelers of whatsoever religion put some coins in.

After we passed the village of Minya, we reached, on the 21st, al-Rairamun, where Mr. Brine, about whom I have already spoken,[227] offered us every sort of refreshment and good treatment. He informed us that Ibrahim Pasha was at Asyut, where he intended to go himself to pay homage. Taking advantage of our passage, he wanted to make this small journey in our company. We left the following day and reached Manfalut in the evening, but we continued to Asyut, where he landed.

It was our intention not to introduce ourselves to Ibrahim until we reached Sennar: if we were to do so before, no doubt he would invite us to follow him and perhaps we would be unable to refuse. If we were forced to follow the army, we would have to give up all the observations and research we had in mind to do. As a consequence, when Mr. Brine landed in Asyut, we continued our journey and passed Sohag, Akhmim, Girga (cities where many Christians live), and other places. On the 29th we were in sight of Qena, sailing with great caution to avoid the sandbanks that can be found in this part of the river and that are very dangerous, especially when the waters are low.

Three cannon shots fired in the city announced the end of Ramadan:[228] this was a signal of joy for our crew and all came to greet us saying: "Kulla sena enta taib!"[229] which corresponds to our Easter greetings. We presented them with coffee and a lamb, but they did not eat it immediately, apologizing that at that solemn moment it would not be acceptable for the Prophet to accept the present of a Christian.

Despite the rising Nile, the water here was so low that in order to land at Qena we had to move into a smaller boat. We found the entire population celebrating the feast: men and boys were jumping from a rock overlooking the Nile, surrounded by members of the populace of both genders, cheering with shouts and unrestrained laughter, and clapping at the

---

226 The monastery, called in Arabic Deir al-Adhra ('Monastery of the Virgin'), belongs in fact to the Coptic Orthodox Church.

227 Cf. *Travel to Nubia*, 168.

228 In the first days of the month of Shawwal, the end of the Ramadan fast is celebrated with a feast called in Arabic Eid al-Sughayyar or Eid al-Fitr.

229 Arabic كل سنة و انت طيب (*kull sana wa inta tayib*), a common expression of good wishes in Egyptian Arabic meaning 'Every year [may] you be well.'

most skilled. The house of the government contractor, to whom we were recommended, was full of street women, very abundant in this town. They gathered there to receive their baksheesh,[230] or gift, which was usually due on such a solemn occasion. These contractors are established in most of the second- and third-rank cities and, by paying yearly to the government a determined amount of money, they acquire the exclusive right to trade and sell spirits, and to tax the street women. This tax depends entirely on their will, and since these speculators are usually unscrupulous otherwise, they relieve the weight of the contribution with an annual present, which they distribute on the occasion of the *bairam*.[231] Among those women there was the famous Julbeas, the Egyptian Phryne, an extraordinarily beautiful Arab woman, as smart as she was attractive, with whom many *kashif*s had spent all of their money.[232] All the coffeeshops were full of people and only with much effort and by paying a large sum could we get some watermelons and kebab. This is lamb meat cut into pieces, put on a stick, and slowly barbecued: it is very spicy, especially because of the large amount of pepper they use to flavor it.

We left the following day and sailed to the bend of Qamula, which, because of the strong current, the Arabs pass using ropes. The *rais* and the rest of the crew were pulling two ropes, but one broke. We were on board and then thought of opening the foresail. With this maneuver we overcame easily the difficulty of the passage and docked shortly after at Qurna. We found a *kashif* with thirty soldiers camped beside the grand *gimez*, or sycamore.[233] He had come to town to collect the annual capitation from the inhabitants. When we arrived they were carrying out a verdict on a wretch who had refused to pay the tax and was sentenced to a hundred lashes of the whip on the soles of his feet. The whip they use is made of hippopotamus skin. This punishment is undoubtedly very cruel, especially because it is repeated every day until the tax is paid, either by the person sentenced or by somebody else. It is nevertheless clear that tax collectors have none but this very violent means to get the money, and it often happens that some people would rather experience the painful punishment than pay what is due. In the whole world, perhaps, there is not a nation as greedy as this: instead of using the money to procure the comforts of life, the Arabs bury it, unbeknownst to their families, and it is not rare that entire fortunes get lost this way. At Qurna, for example, most of the inhabitants live in the tombs and few own houses, which are in any event cheap to build, being all of mud. Yet this village should be rich from the immense amount of money that has flowed through it since the French occupation, when excavations started. Since then, Messrs. Salt, Drovetti, General Minutoli, Lord Belmore, and many others before and after have spent enormous sums, and all the antiquities have been paid

---

230 Arabic بكشش *(baksheesh)*, today refers more commonly to 'tips.'
231 Turkish word of Persian origin meaning 'feast.'
232 Turkish *gül beyaz*, 'white rose'; Gian Battista Brocchi, *Giornale delle osservazioni fatte ne' viaggi in Egitto, nella Siria e nella Nubia 2* (Bassano: A. Roberti, 1841), 354.
233 Arabic شجر جميز, *(shagarat gimmiz)*, 'sycamore.' A geographical landmark mentioned by many travelers of the time. The core of the village of Qurna with its anchorage was close to the Temple of the Millions of Years of Seti I; Nigel Strudwick and John Taylor, *The Theban Necropolis: Past, Present and Future* (London: The British Museum Press, 2003), fig. 127.

for at a very dear price. Nevertheless, the inhabitants still live in the ancient tombs and eat as before, nor have they improved their clothes; what has become of all the money? The natural greed of this nation and the fear of seeing their wealth seized by the government agents are, in my opinion, the only causes of its disappearance.

We stayed in Qurna until 6 July because I wanted to see once again the tomb at Biban al-Muluk . . . oh, how much different I found it from when I made my drawings! One of those storms that, though rarely, happen in the Theban mountains had so raged this year that the flood entered the tomb and knocked down part of the walls and the pillars, and destroyed many paintings. The ancient Egyptians, in order to avoid the consequences of such disasters, dug at the entrance of the tomb a very deep shaft which Mr. Belzoni, quite unwisely, filled up. For this reason and to give the waters a different direction, a large rampart was built on the side of the mountain where the tomb begins: this wall and its destination, known to the Arabs of Qurna, were in fact pointed out to Belzoni, who then decided to dig there.[234]

I took advantage of our stay and made two drawings I had already made during my first visit to Thebes and that were left to Belzoni. These drawings are the subject of plates 47 and 48. The first is a superb bas-relief existing in the aforementioned tomb, representing the goddess Hathor welcoming the deceased monarch, whom Mr. Champollion recognized to be Pharaoh Usirei-Akenkheres I. This sculpture is definitely one of the finest as to style, beauty, and liveliness of its colors. The second drawing, which I also made in the same tomb, is the copy of a bas-relief which, fortunately, is unfinished: I say fortunately because without it we would not know what the method followed by the Egyptians to carve their sculptures was. The method is, in fact, clearly shown in this drawing: first of all, once the composition and the number of figures were clear in the mind of the artist, he traced red lines at the level of the head, knees, and feet; he then tracked in red the shape of the bodies and the hieroglyphs. This first sketch was later corrected with light black lines, in order to retouch the outline of the figures and the details. Finally, the chief artist refined the drawing by tracing heavy black lines, with a frankness of style that is surprising today. The figures were eventually chiseled out. Even though in other monuments there are similar examples of unfinished sculptures, there is not one as clear as this, which also proves false the opinion that Egyptian sculptures were traced from templates.

Qurna and the other villages built on the ruins of the ancient Thebes are full of scorpions and serpents, but there are very skilled men, according to the inhabitants, who are experts at enchanting and disinfesting them. One of those, called Abd al-Mina, wanted at all costs to initiate me into his secrets in exchange for a few piasters. He posited as the only condition

---

234 This seems to agree with the recent theory of Beatrix Gessler-Löhr, "Who Discovered 'Belzoni's Tomb'? A Glimpse behind the Scenes of Early Exploration and the Antiquities Trade," in *Talking along the Nile: Ippolito Rosellini, Travellers and Scholars of the Nineteenth Century in Egypt. Proceedings of the International Conference Held on the Occasion of the Presentation of Progetto Rosellini, Pisa, June 14–16, 2012*, ed. Marilina Betrò and Gianluca Miniaci (Pisa: Pisa University Press, 2013), 101–24.

that I would swear not to practice his teachings in any house against the *Harts al-Beit*,[235] which is the 'guardian of the house.' This is a serpent the Nubians let peacefully live in their houses; its death would be regarded as a bad omen for the owners. If the enchanter had limited his conditions to this, I would probably have accepted, but he also wanted to force me to drink a cup of water in which he had immersed scorpions and serpent heads, a thing I absolutely refused to do. Anyway, besides the absurdity of such things, it is certain that in Nubia they know a plant, which is quite common in the deserts of Africa, the sharp smell of which annoys serpents and prevents their attacks on whoever carries it.

We left Qurna on the 6th and, without stopping at Luxor, we sailed through the bend of Armant. On the 8th, we spent the night at Isna. Here, a regiment of cavalry was camped, about to leave for Dongola to enter the service of the Egyptian commanders as an auxiliary force. The mountains we met up to this point are generally made of limestone, but a little beyond Isna they change and become sandstone.

On the 9th we reached the wall that is not far from Eileithyia,[236] but which is not the same as the one I previously described. This is made of stone while the other is of very large mud bricks. Mr. Bankes copied here, on his first trip to Nubia, a Greek inscription which is visible only when the waters of the Nile are low.

On the 10th we arrived at Edfu and the following day at Jebel al-Silsila, which is the 'Mountain of the Chain,' so called for an ancient tradition that, in case of emergency, navigation on the Nile could be prevented by the means of a large chain stretching from one bank to the other and secured to the rocks. In one of the caves excavated in the mountain I copied the bas-relief which is on plate 49. I am not able to explain its meaning.

Early on the 12th, we docked at Kom Ombo. Here there are the remains of two temples. No. 1 of plate 50 is a bas-relief copied from the outer wall of the pylon of the largest of the two temples and represents a woman offering lotus flowers and animals. The tray she carries on her right hand, bearing different heads of animals and other offerings, is surmounted by a row of cypress-looking trees. The lotus plants at her feet look like they are inside a vase of water which is marked, as usual in Egyptian representations, with small lines, sometimes straight and sometimes wavy. What is special about this bas-relief is that, while women serving as priestesses are usually represented naked and with a beard in the lowest register of monuments, this one is on the contrary dressed and without beard, even though she is undoubtedly a priestess. Nos. 2 and 3 of the same plate are very beautiful symbolic friezes, carved on the molding of the same temple. As for the ruins of the smaller temple, these are so exposed to the stream of the Nile that they decrease by the day and their complete destruction will occur after not much time.[237]

On the 13th, in three hours we reached Aswan and after midday we passed the island of Elephantine, where we bought a large and long papyrus in Greek and Coptic, containing

---

235 Arabic حارس البيت *(haras al-bayt)*, 'guardian of the house.'
236 al-Kab; Porter and Moss, *Topographical Bibliography* 5:171–75.
237 Ricci is here probably referring to the *mammisi* of Ptolemy VIII Euergetes II, the western side of which was in fact wiped away by the flood of the Nile; Porter and Moss, *Topographical Bibliography* 6:198–200.

part of the last book of the *Iliad*. This valuable relic was found by a woman of the island, sealed inside a pottery vase in the side of a cave. We handed it over to Mr. Bankes and it is now part of his beautiful collection of Egyptian antiquities.[238] In the evening, we went back to Aswan.

Hamid Agha, an Albanian, was at the time governor of the city, subject to the *kashif* of Minya, a man as rough and haughty with travelers as Hamid was officious and polite. We went to pay him homage, but we were little satisfied with his welcome. We also visited Hassan Agha, at the time retired, and we told him about our project to go to Sennar via land, if we could find camels and guides. He answered politely that he had no influence any more, but that nevertheless he would try to help us.

We went to set the price with the *rais* of the *shillal*, or 'cataract,' for the rent of a boat we needed to ship the pedestal of Philae to Cairo. This is interesting because of a long Greek inscription. The obelisk now in the possession of Mr. Bankes used to stand on this pedestal. When the gentleman left Egypt, he had asked us to take care of this shipment. Through Hassan Agha we easily reached a deal and he himself assured us he would oversee the loading.

Philae is four miles distant from Aswan, or Syene, and is easily reached by a comfortable road, which can be shortened by sailing on the Nile and docking near the cataract. On the land road there is a granite mountain with some Muslim tombs beside which there are others with Greek and Kufic inscriptions. The closeness of these burials belonging to different religions caused the locals to come up with a story of a war between the saints of the different religions. In this story, as it can easily be argued, the Muslim saints triumphed. A mile away from these tombs begins a large wall of mud bricks. It is called Hayt al-Aguz and goes as far as Philae, crossing a sandy plain among the many rocks.

In the following days we visited again the island of Elephantine, which is almost oval and not very big. On the island there are some mountains of granite of different colors, small woods of palm and *sant* trees, and beautiful plains. These are cultivated with industry and such a symmetry that a European who would like to spend some time in Egypt could not choose, in my opinion, a more pleasant and delightful place. The locals are not many and look of a very meek temperament: in fact, they warmly welcome the foreigner. They walk around naked until they reach puberty, except the females who wear a sort of short skirt made of very thin leather strips. The adults of both genders wear a long white or blue shirt, with very wide sleeves. They also anoint their hair with palm oil and their skin is so dark that it is almost black.

In ancient times there were many buildings on this island, but now all is in ruin, as can be seen in the general plan of the island on plate 51, no. 1, made after the great French work, which I put here only as a key to my drawings. No. 2 on the same plate is the plan of the

---

238 William J. Bankes, *Narrative of the Life and Adventures of Giovanni Finati, Translated from the Italian and Edited by W. John Bankes* (London: John Murray, 1830), 2:357–58. This is p. Lond. Lit. 28 ('Bankes Homer'), dating back to the second century AD and carrying Book XXIV of the *Iliad*.

small temple; no. 3 the plan of the large temple; and no. 4 the Nilometer with its inscriptions. The marks of the old measurements are perfectly preserved.

The drawings I made on this island are scattered on different plates, which I will explain in the following paragraphs as per their numbering.

Plate 52, no. 1. Exterior of the portico, east side, where there is the access to the temple, marked (1) in the plan. One cannot imagine anything more elegant in Egyptian architecture than the two beautiful columns supporting the molding or more precise than the bas-relief of the decoration. No. 2 is the frieze of the outer wall of the corresponding portico, from the west.

Plate 53. Exterior of the portico, north side, marked (2) in the plan, restored in some parts with what remains of the hieroglyphic inscription on the south side of the same portico.

Plate 54. Outer part of the sanctuary, under the portico, to the east, marked (3). The bas-reliefs and the hieroglyphs are of the most beautiful execution. It is possible that this temple was dedicated to Amun, who is represented on both sides of the entrance gate in the act of welcoming the hero, or a king, possibly the same one who built this temple.

Plate 55, no. 1. Sculptures in very elegant bas-relief, existing on the outer part of the sanctuary, north side, marked (4). In the first register Amun and the goddess Tpé impose their hands on the head of the hero, which possibly means that he has the favor of the two gods. The goddess has in her left hand a very peculiar symbolic stick, like the ornament hanging from the same arm. In the two following registers there are offering scenes, and in the fourth the hero is introduced to the god of procreation along with four tied oxen, perhaps to symbolize that he protected and encouraged agriculture during his life. No. 2 is a sculpture on the opposite side of the sanctuary, to the south, marked (5), in which there is a double image of the god Amun pouring on the hero from two vases an infinite number of symbolic keys: the meaning of this scene is that the hero was admitted to enjoy immortality and all the advantages of divine life. Nos. 3 and 4 are also from the same part of the sanctuary, only to show the many different symbolic sticks in the hands of the goddesses. The last one, which is no. 4, is the most peculiar. In no. 5 there are bas-reliefs of the outer side of two pillars in the portico, to the west, marked (6) in the plan, which are no less perfect and elegant than the other scultpures.

Plate 56. Bas-relief inside the sanctuary, south wall, marked (7). The subject of this sculpture is also related to the hero or king, who here, too, is represented on one side while making offerings and libations and on the other between the goddess Nut and Amun, who is warmly welcoming him. The sacred bark is different from the others I have seen and copied before. The beauty of this sculpture and the mastery of the shapes are impressive.

Plate 57. Nos. 1 and 2 are bas-reliefs existing on the wall marked (a) of the small temple. Only half of its plan was done, because the rest no longer exists. The execution is good, but I am not able to explain its meaning, although it seems there is a deputation of priests heading toward some hero in order to appease him with gifts and prayers and to obtain peace, celebrated later by women playing the sistrum.

We were camped on the island by a sycamore tree, which, according to the locals, can make women fertile. For this reason, the young brides of Aswan come with great devotion to collect some of the leaves, which they burn on charcoal while addressing fervent prayers, which are usually fulfilled.

When we finished the drawings at Elephantine we went back to Aswan and took up residence in a small house in the countryside, from where the view of the old ruined city, built on a granite mountain, had a beautiful effect as it looked like many little towers. Its extent must have been considerable and the surrounding walls were very strong.

The new city is built in a much lower position; it is for the most part inhabited by the descendants of a Bosnian colony established by the orders of Sultan Selim after the conquest of Egypt.[239] The people of Aswan are very proud of their morals and especially praise the modesty and honesty of their women: they are so rigorous about this that if any of them is convicted of adultery, she is immediately and without any other trial thrown into the Nile. They get their main revenue from dates and the few gardens that they cultivate produce excellent grapes. They mix the dough of their bread with a bit of chickpea flour, which gives it a particular taste.

Near the city there are the caves where the ancient Egyptians used to quarry granite. Here still lies on the ground a large obelisk, broken in two halves.[240] From its examination I could understand that, in order to separate from the rock even the largest blocks, they used almost the same techniques we use nowadays in our quarries. After taking the measures of the block they intended to cut, they carved holes two inches deep on the same line, at a little distance one from the other, in order to insert wedges, which were then all hit at the same time. Traces of these holes, which can be seen for the whole length of the obelisk and exactly correspond to the marks left on the rock, seem to validate my opinion. What is most surprising is that the cutting and polishing of hard stones was at the time carried out with copper tools only; it is inconceivable how they could obtain such perfect results, unless the Egyptians knew how to give their tools a tempering unknown to us.

On the evening of 21 July, Ibrahim Pasha arrived in Aswan with some boats of his retinue. He came from Asyut, where he had stayed to settle some financial matters, and intended to proceed immediately on his journey. While the crews were busy trying to make the boats pass the cataract, the beautiful *canjiah* of the pasha was carried away by the current, hit the rocks, broke up, and sank; the *rais* died in the accident. The departure was immediately suspended in order to retrieve the objects from the *canjiah* and especially a large sum of money. The following morning, the best swimmers of the country dived in the Nile and soon everything was recovered except for a few small objects of little value. The day after, the body of the *rais* was found in the vicinity of Aswan, on the banks of the Nile: the pasha ordered that he be buried and donated 200 rupees to those who found him. On the 24th he sailed again. A regiment of cavalry, which had come from Cairo on the previous day, had already set off.

---

239 Bosnian garrisons were stationed at Aswan, Ibrim, and Sai by Özdemir Pasha around 1550, during the reign of Sulayman the Lawgiver (1520–66); Peter M. Holt, *A Modern History of the Sudan, from the Funj Sultanate to the Present Day* (London: Weidenfeld and Nicolson, 1961), 24.

240 Porter and Moss, *Topographical Bibliography* 5:224.

In the following days we attended the circumcision of a son of Hassan Agha, celebrated with much pomp and immense participation of the people. We then started to think about our departure to Sennar. Even though renting a boat to the Second Cataract was more comfortable and safer for us, we preferred to travel by land as the best way to achieve the goals we had fixed for this journey. We were nevertheless afraid of not finding camels at Wadi Halfa because the army of Ibrahim had requisitioned them all. We then turned to Hassan Agha, who proved to have a favorable inclination toward us. In fact, he offered to provide all the camels we needed at the price of twenty Spanish dollars each until Dongola, promising also to oblige the son of a shaykh to guide us there for our greater safety. It was an exorbitant price: before accepting the deal, we wanted to ascertain if the *kashif* of Minya, despite his roughness, was fairer. In fact, when he listened to our request, he said that at the moment he only had forty camels at his disposal, but that we were free to take ten of them and a dromedary, which he would rent, trappings included, at the price of eight Spanish dollars each, settling the payment at Dongola. We did not hesitate to accept the deal and we understood that, despite his most flattering appearance, Hassan Agha was a much more venal person than the rough and haughty *kashif* of Minya. I must observe that the latter changed his attitude toward us after the free assistance I gave to many of his sick soldiers and to him, too, setting him free from an intermittent fever that had tormented him for almost a month.

We finally collected all that we needed for the journey and on the 15th of August we left Aswan, walking on the east bank of the Nile. Without entering Birbe, which is the last village of Egypt beyond Philae,[241] we crossed Saqyat al-Jamal, the border between the districts of Wadi Halfa and Dabod, and we began to climb the *agaba*, or 'mountain,'[242] at Wadi Shillal. In the evening, we camped at Shamat al-Wah, where we found a small caravan of forty camels carrying young slaves of both genders.

On the 16th we reached Siali, a village on the banks of the Nile. On the 17th we went along the river as far as the mountain of Kalabsha and afterward we spent the hottest hours under the shadow of some palm trees. We crossed the mountain in the evening and descended again to the Nile at a spot called Wadi Rahma: here we found another caravan of two hundred camels, coming from Berber, where it had delivered flour for the army.

The mountain of Kalabsha is very high and hieroglyphs can be observed here and there roughly carved on the rock. It is mainly made of sandstone, but from the side of the Nile it progressively changes into black granite, similar to charcoal, where hit by the sun's rays. In some spots there are hollow pebbles, similar to those of Abu Simbel, of which I spoke in my *Travel to Nubia*, but in small quantity. Along the banks of the Nile there are short walls, built in antiquity to support the soil carried forth by the inundation, but now for the most part in ruins.

On the 18th we traversed two sandy plains, called Abu Hor and al-Shaykh, crossed by two dry wadis. Here, for the first time after we left Aswan, we saw some houses, badly built,

241 Gazirat al-Birbi, in fact, is the Arabic name of Philae Island.
242 Arabic العقبة (*al-aqaba*), 'mountain.'

and surrounded by small fields of *dhura*, a cereal correponding to our sorghum, even though it has a larger and milkier grain.[243] Not far from this village there are the ruins of a small temple with some hieroglyphic stelae.[244] One hour after midday we reached Dandur[245] and, after resting some time in a tomb, we crossed a second mountain. This was of difficult access, with a few very narrow tracks overlooking its frightful cliffs. If a camel were to fall down, it would be impossible to save it. As soon as we descended, we observed the ruins of an ancient city, probably of Saracen origin. We reached Gerf at night. This is a large village, not far from the Nile, in the midst of good and extensive cultivated fields. At the beginning the locals refused to feed the camels, but after we threatened to let them loose in the fields, they acceded to our request.

The 19th was a very hot and windless day. We crossed a sandy plain strewn with small sandstones, detached from the rocks that here and there emerge in this part of the desert. We passed through Wadi Kushtamna and camped at Quban, not far from Allaqi, which is a station for caravans coming from Berber, al-Demer, and Darfur. Here we found a small regiment of cavalry, directed to Cairo with dispatches from Ibrahim Pasha. Shortly before setting off, we saw another black man with white spots on his skin, for the same reason I have already mentioned.[246]

At Seyala, the inhabitants spontaneously gave us provisions to refresh the entire caravan: this is one of the main villages in the district of Allaqi and is made up of only a few houses. It is noticeable that in Nubia two houses together, and sometimes even only one, is called a village. The miserable inhabitants of this part of the country between Shillal and Allaqi, who were already damaged by the passage of the Egyptian army, had to suffer another terrible plague: many swarms of grasshoppers came to destroy all that had survived military devastation.

On my first Nubian trip with Mr. Bankes, I encountered near Kalabsha a passage of these insects; it lasted two days. They cross Egypt two or three times yearly and if strong winds do not push them toward the sea or the mountains, woe to the place where they land! They fly not far from the ground in very large groups, to the extent that the passage of one of them lasts two or more hours and creates the effect of a cloud between the earth and the sun. During the night they land on the vegetation: fires, cries, shouts, and the noise of tools clapped together do not scare them and, once they leave, the place where they spent the night is unrecognizable because of the sudden change from green to dry. They vary in color and size, some being green and others grey with spots. They are long, up to four inches. Their flight does not differ much from that of small birds, just more uniform and plain; they can fly for a long time without rest. In some places, people eat them, but this is small reward compared to the huge damage they cause.

---

243 Arabic ذرة *(dhura)*, *Sorghum vulgare*.
244 Likely the Greco-Roman temple of Abu Hor East, later destroyed; Porter and Moss, *Topographical Bibliography* 7:39–40.
245 Porter and Moss, *Topographical Bibliography* 7:27–33.
246 Cf. *Travel to Nubia*, 189.

On the 20th at around ten, we reached a small village in front of Shayma Amalika, on the opposite bank of the river, and we spent the night in Wadi al-Sebu'a. Among the districts south of Aswan, this is the one where the cultivation is more extensive and the inhabitants richer, as a consequence of the commerce with Berber.

On the 21st, after two hours of march, we lost sight of the cultivated land and entered a desert made up of small hills of sandstone, of a dark color. We passed the village of Shaturma and started climbing the mountain chain that crosses Wadi al-Sebu'a, as high and steep as the Theban cliffs. The difficult road forced us to unburden the camels, putting some of the load onto those that we were riding. I saw a small path along the bank of the Nile and left the caravan to follow it. I found it badly made and very slippery; nevertheless it must have been quite a busy road in the past, as some hieroglyphs carved on the rocks prove.[247] This path cuts the road short by two hours and it presumably used to be wider and more comfortable than now.

On the 22nd, the road we followed was also narrow and fatiguing, and we were forced again to take the same precaution as the previous day in order to avoid any accident to the camels. Our first stop that day was at Korosko, a small village beyond which the cultivated land stretches two miles into the desert. The villages are here larger, more populated, and built more like in Egypt. Always walking under the shadow of thick palm woods, we camped in the evening at Diwan, in front of Amada. We left early on the 23rd and arrived at Derr in a short period of time. This city is built with regularity and has more than two hundred houses: it is the capital of Nubia. Most of its inhabitants are of Bosnian origin, like those of Aswan, who came to populate it by the orders of Selim.[248]

Not far from the city there is an immense sycamore tree, under the shadow of which two hundred people can comfortably stand: the inhabitants take special care of it. The cultivation of palms is their main occupation, because not only it is their main source of food, but also they trade in it, sending the saplings to Egypt or selling them to the merchants of Cairo, who come and buy them by the thousands. The government annually earns a levy of twenty paras on each tree, whether fully grown or just a sapling.

All the stretch of country we had crossed from Aswan to Sebu'a takes the name of Wadi Qenus: the Arabs who live here, known under this generic name, are divided into different tribes, each one named after the place they live in. The Ababda[249] occupy all the mountains between the Nile and the Red Sea, from Quseir to Derr, and many of them also live in the cities on the banks of the river and work as caravan guides. Their origin is—so it is

---

247 Perhaps the remains of the rock stela of Amenemhat I; Porter and Moss, *Topographical Bibliography* 7:84.

248 On the memory of an involvement of Selim I in Nubia, the following lines by Holt are particularly enlightening: "The connection of Selim I with these exploits is entirely fictitious. . . . The ascription of events of Süleyman's reign to that of his predecessors is in line with an Egyptian mythopoeic tendency, during the Ottoman period, to enhance the deeds and person of Selim. As the overthrower of the old-established Mamluk sultanate, and the only Ottoman ruler to visit Egypt before the nineteenth century, Selim occupied a prominent place in popular imagination," Peter M. Holt, "Sultan Selim I and the Sudan," *Journal of African History* 8 (1967): 22.

249 Ababda, tribe of the Beja that settled around Aswan, between the Nile and the Red Sea.

believed—different from that of other nomadic Arabs, and the most common opinion in Egypt is that they descend from the Shepherds who took over the country in antiquity. Anyway, they are divided into different tribes, like the other Bedouins, and share the same habits, but, even though they are in contact with the Bisharin,[250] who are undoubtedly the most barbarian and bloodthirsty of the Arabs, their temper is much different: in general they are human, hospitable, and very receptive, so that among all, they are the most likely to be readily civilized.

The temple of Derr[251] is not far from the city and it is half free-standing and half rock-cut; the plan is quite irregular. The sculpture style seems to date back to the most remote antiquity. On the left wall of the main hall there is a bas-relief with a bark carried by many men, preceded by another man announcing the offering:[252] the god Horus follows immediately and then the hero comes, carried amid tree branches.[253] On the opposite wall, the same subject is repeated with little difference.[254] In the vicinity of the temple there are the ruins of a small old building, consisting of five pillars and an unfinished gate, all without hieroglyphs.[255]

On the 24th we left Derr. The mountain between here and Ibrim is full of square caves, almost all of the same dimension, and it is not easy to guess if in the past they served as tombs or houses: I incline toward the latter explanation because of some square holes, regularly cut in the exterior, above the entrance door, close to one another and on the same line. It seems they served to house sticks holding curtains to protect against the sun. On the four inner walls of the most interesting[256] of these caves there are sculptures in bas-relief with mythological scenes, as shown on plate 58. The style is the same as the temple of Abu Simbel.

We spent the hottest hours of the day at Qatta, a small village, and by the evening we reached Ibrim. All the country from Korosko to Ibrim is carefully cultivated and in some parts even better than in Egypt. The cliffs in front of Ibrim are very steep and perfectly perpendicular to the Nile, which waters their slopes. At half height there are a number of very elegant rock-cut caves;[257] some are inaccessible, unless one abseils from the top of the rocks. It is difficult to understand why the ancient Egyptians planned and carried out such works in such an inaccessible place; it is possible that in the past there used to be a more accessible way, which has collapsed with time.

---

250 Bisharin, one of the most important Beja tribes, also occupying the desert between the Nile and the Red Sea; Shinnie, *Linant de Bellefonds*, 28.
251 Temple dedicated by Ramesses II to Re-Horakhty; Porter and Moss, *Topographical Bibliography* 7:84–90.
252 Porter and Moss, *Topographical Bibliography* 7:87 (11).
253 Porter and Moss, *Topographical Bibliography* 7:87 (13).
254 Porter and Moss, *Topographical Bibliography* 7:87 (16).
255 Unidentified building.
256 The temple of Ellesiya, built by Thutmose III; Porter and Moss, *Topographical Bibliography* 7:90–91.
257 Rock-cut shrines of the viceroys of Kush during the Eighteenth to Nineteenth Dynasties near Ibrim; Porter and Moss, *Topographical Bibliography* 7:92–93; Ricardo A. Caminos, *The Shrines and Rock-Inscriptions of Ibrim* (London: Egypt Exploration Society, 1968).

On the 25th, in four hours we crossed the mountain of Ibrim; on its slope there are still the ruins of the city and the castle which bears the same name. There are also the ruins of a very large Greek church.[258] After the destruction of the city, the inhabitants moved to the plain and now occupy the nearby villages. They also are of Bosnian origin. Their temperament is bold; they dress like the Egyptians and disdain to be identified as Nubians. Passing through Wadi al-Bustan, where there is much cultivated land, we reached the village of Tushka, which marks the border of the valley of Ibrim; we camped here. In this place the mountain chain becomes wider and the isolated peaks take weird and picturesque shapes.

On the 26th we saw for the first time the *sultan ter*, which is the 'king of birds,' so called in Nubia because of the beauty of its feathers.[259] This bird is as big as a pigeon and has a large head surmounted by a bright red tuft. Its black beak is curved and its coat is blue, fading to white at the ends of its wings, whose main feathers, like those of the tail, are red. The breast and the area under the wings are white, the legs are black.

From Tushka we reached Farriq and then Arminna,[260] where on the nearby rocks there are some hieroglyphic and Arabic inscriptions, but of an irregular and imperfect craftsmanship.

On the 27th, we passed by Abu Simbel: the caravan headed toward the *agaba*, or mountain, of Farriq, and I followed the Nile along a narrow track on the banks, which is usually submerged during the inundation. At Mashakit,[261] which is the first village after Arminna, the mountains are less steep. We then reached Endekana;[262] its territory is rich in palm trees. I examined the burials near the village and observed that the Nubians adorn them with palm branches, putting some wooden cups on the top, which they fill from time to time with water. Around midday I reached Dandur, a small town, where I waited for the caravan which I saw descending the mountain. Here, too, I observed rock-cut caves, with square holes in the outside, similar to those of Derr: this confirms my opinion that the grottoes were home to the locals.

In most of this district, the Nubians sleep in the open air in order to avoid contact with the *dud*,[263] also called *harda*,[264] a small worm that annoys the sleepers and eats their clothes. The beds they sleep in are three arms'-length raised from the ground and made of mats hanging from four or six poles. One of the poles has notches, to allow the person to climb up. They also hang another mat on the top of the bed, in order to protect the sleeper from the sun. The women also spend part of the day on these beds, in order to scare the birds which invade the sown fields and damage the crops.

---

258 Fred Aldsworth, *Qasr Ibrim: The Cathedral Church* (London: Egypt Exploration Society, 2010).

259 Ar. سلطان طائر , 'sultan bird,' a species I was not able to identify.

260 In fact, Arminna is to the north of Farriq, where there are graffiti and rock-carved hieroglyphs; Porter and Moss, *Topographical Bibliography* 7:119.

261 "Massaquette" in Linant. Champollion calls the site "Maschakit" (Jean-François Champollion, *Notice descriptive* [Paris: Firmin Didot, 1844–89], 1:79), while Rosellini has "Masciahit" (Ippolito Rosellini, *Monumenti dell'Egitto e della Nubia: Monumenti del Culto* [Pisa: Niccolò Capurro, 1844], 2). This is Jebel al-Shams.

262 Possibly Adindan.

263 Arabic دودة (*duda*), 'worm.'

264 Arabic ارضة (ardha), 'termite.'

From Dandur, we arrived opposite Faras Island in less than two hours and then spent the night at Serra, a small village. Here, despite the strong heat we had suffered during the day, we were much annoyed by the cold, caused by a thick fog that vanished only at dawn.

On the 28th, we met two Arabs coming from Dongola: they assured us that Ibrahim Pasha was very close and was heading back with a large retinue. This was very bad news for us, but in the end nothing happened. At six in the afternoon, we reached Wadi Halfa: loud noises and continuous shouts that we heard coming from the village made us decide to camp at some distance, in order to avoid any possible inconvenience. We inquired about the noise and they told us it came from a group of people gathered around a fire, dancing and singing to heal a sick young man. A very bizarre method, but practiced generally in the whole of Arabia. We asked those people why they were performing their ceremonies around the fire, despite the season and the weather being very hot: they answered that it was necessary to chase away the evil spirits from the sick man and that for the same reason they were shouting and clapping their hands.

From Aswan to Wadi Halfa, the navigation on the Nile is very difficult because of many sandbanks which are formed here and there during winter, when strong winds blow from the northeast and cause a lot of sand to fall into the river from the nearby western mountains. Because it collects all the falling sand, the riverbed protects the small amount of cultivated land on the east bank, which for this reason is generally more populated.

The Second Cataract looks very romantic because of the incredible quantity of rocks of various shapes and sizes, all of a bright black color and scattered in the river and along the banks: the mountain from the east side ends here, only to rise again a few miles upstream.

When a boat arrives to pass through the cataract, it is necessary at first to unload it. In proportion to its size, they tie two or more ropes that are pulled by a large number of men walking on the banks and in the river. With huge effort they win against the current and are able to move the boat beyond the falls, where they keep on pulling for some distance. It sometimes happens that a boat on the edge of the cataract is suddenly pulled back by the current, dragging the men at the ropes. These people are used to such accidents: they just swim back to the banks and in larger numbers pull the boat again until it passes the falls. Sometimes the boat is pulled back by the current with such violence that it cannot be steered, hits the rocks, and sinks, as actually happened at Aswan to the *canjiah* of Ibrahim Pasha. There are no better swimmers than the Arabs of this district, who jump with much courage into the middle of the strongest current, avoid the rocks with incredible ability, and even cross the river from bank to bank if necessary.

The descent of the cataract is much easier and it is only necessary to steer the boat adeptly in order to avoid the rocks, maneuvering with the helm and slowing down the boat with the ropes.

After we showed the viceroy's firman, which authorized us to pass the cataract, to the agha in charge[265] we continued our journey on the 29th and in four hours we met in succession

---

265 Mustafa Agha; Shinnie, *Linant de Bellefonds*, 2.

three more falls, four large islands, and two ruined fortifications.[266] The first of these fortifications is very big: it begins at the slope of the mountain and ends directly on the banks of the Nile. A sort of blockhouse is still visible in the middle, solidly built with bricks. The outer walls are made of large blocks of granite assembled with mortar. The second, of similar construction, was built on a hill at some distance from the river.

We finally reached Amka, a small village of few houses, where by the orders of Ibrahim there was recently established a storehouse for army provisions and uniforms. This was under the surveillance of an agha with a few soldiers. The house of this commander is on the top of a hill; it dominates the whole valley and has a stunning view of the cataract.

On the 30th, we passed many small islands, mainly cultivated, and Gemai, a small village, where the bed of the Nile is so narrow that one could easily throw a stone from one bank to the other. For this reason, the stream acquires more strength here. In fact, it is precisely in this place that the Second Cataract begins, while a short distance away there are no more rocks, the river becomes wider, and the waters have a more uniform and calm flow. We then entered the Wadi Mershed. The first village we met was made up of only five miserable huts, hidden among the granite rocks. There are two *saqya*s close to Sitt Hagga, another village, where the main occupation is weaving cotton cloth. Their loom is similar to that of the ancient Egyptians, a depiction of which I copied at Qurna and can be seen on plate 7. The Muslims hold this village in great veneration because it was home to a very charitable female saint and the inhabitants prove to be as charitable, to follow her example. The rocks are here at some distance from the banks and are no longer of granite, but of sandstone. The sands as well take a bright red color and are clearer than before. After we crossed the mountain Esep, which slopes gently toward the Nile at the entrance of the Wadi Saras, we met Mugufini Island, oblong in shape and housing the ruins of two churches. We then passed by Kagnarti Island, which means 'donkey back' because of its shape, and, finally, we reached another village that marks the border of the Wadi Saras. Here we spent the night.

On the morning of the 31st, while the caravan was heading to the mountain, I kept following the banks of the Nile, as was my custom, and reached shortly afterward a small village, made up of only eight reed huts. Because all men able to carry a weapon were forcibly recruited into the Egyptian army, I found the village inhabited by only a few old men, children, and women. The latter were busy at their looms. I walked on and passed Uronarti, the longest and highest of all the islands south of Wadi Halfa to this point, which hosts many modern ruins. Not far from it there is another island called Costarhen, or 'of the henna,' because this plant grows abundantly. The Egyptian women extract from it the red color that they use to dye their nails and their fingertips. Shortly after, I reached

---

266 "There are many ancient sites along this stretch of the river. Meinarti, Kisinarti, Dorginarti, Abkanarti and Dabanarti are all islands on which there are ruins. Dorginarti and Dabanarti have the remains of Egyptian Middle Kingdom forts on them; the others have Christian churches and other buildings, most of which are now in a very ruinous state," Shinnie, *Linant de Bellefonds*, 3; Andriolo and Curto, *Catalogo*, 9–12.

Contra Semene,[267] almost at the same time as the caravan. Here, there is a temple built on a hill and buried under the sand for two-thirds of its height. It must have been an elegant construction, but was then abandoned and converted into a tomb, which can be argued by all its doors being shut with large rocks. The plan of this temple is on plate 59, no. 1. It was surrounded by a large enclosure wall, which can be seen at no. 2, where letter (a) marks the arrangement of the temple rooms: the entrance was to the east. On the outer façade, I could still read some hieroglyphs, which I copied in the same plate, no. 3. In the left part there is an ibis-headed Thoth in front of the god Amun; he seems to make a mathematical reckoning.[268] The irregular line that interrupts this drawing marks the level of the sands. On the rocks beside the road leading from Contra Semene to the temple there are badly carved hieroglyphs, much corroded by time.[269] Consecutive falls create here a considerable cataract, after which the bed of the Nile is full of very sharp scattered rocks. These look very bright because of the quantity of mica and talc they are covered in, and which make a very beautiful effect when hit by the sun's rays.

The drawings of the temple kept us there for two days; we then left on 2 September, heading to the mountain al-Banat ('the girls').[270] After one hour and a half, we descended back to the Nile at the Island of the Sun;[271] we then entered the Wadi Attiri and, crossing another mountain called Duweishat, we reached the tomb of a shaykh, in front of which there are the ruins of two churches.

On the 3rd, we passed by the villages of Burma, Izbit,[272] and Narvi, and then observed the beautiful Slave Island[273] and two more islands called Turmukki and Atara, by which there are three small falls easily crossable by just sailing with a favorable wind. We then met the Jebel Alimula, in the shape of a pyramid, and, marching fast, we reached by late evening the borders of Sukkot.

All the country from Wadi Halfa to Sukkot takes the generic name of Wadi Haggar, or 'valley of the stones,' so called as a reference to its great barrenness: the many valleys that are part of it are filled with granite rocks and only a few are flat land, cultivated with much effort by this miserable population, which is forced to use the *saqya*s because of the steep river banks. There are no palm trees here, which in other places supply for many needs.

Before Abdin Bey[274] took control of Dongola, *saqya*s used to pay an annual levy of eight thalers each: this levy, already heavy, was then raised to twelve thalers. The misery of the

---

267 Semna East (Kumma). There is a temple dedicated to Khnum and built by Thutmose II, Thutmose III, and Amenhotep II; Porter and Moss, *Topographical Bibliography* 7:152–55.
268 Porter and Moss, *Topographical Bibliography* 7:152 (7).
269 Porter and Moss, *Topographical Bibliography* 7:155–56.
270 Or perhaps Batn al-Hajar, 'belly of the stones'?
271 Mashamarti; Shinnie, *Linant de Bellefonds*, 8.
272 Arabic عزبة ('izba), 'villa,' 'manor,' 'domain,' a common name in toponyms, usually coupled with a second name, but perhaps here a corrupt version of the toponym (Khawr) Kisbitta.
273 Perhaps Ambikol.
274 "Abidin Bey el-Arna'ut was an Albanian officer, and one of Mohammed Ali's friends. He was appointed second in command of Ismail Pasha's army. He distinguished himself in the fighting, especially at Korti, and when the army moved on to Sennar, he was left to govern the country between Halfa and Merowe," Shinnie, *Linant de Bellefonds*, 13.

population, which rose in proportion, had them so much discouraged that most sowed just enough land for their bare survival. *Dhura, dukhn,*[275] a few lupins, and pumpkins are the only products of this wadi: senna grows, too, but little profit is earned by the inhabitants, its trade being extremely scarce and almost insignificant.

When the inhabitants of the islands want to reach the mainland, they make up for the lack of boats by riding, both men and women, a large trunk, the length of six arms, carrying their clothes on their heads and using their hands as oars. It is not rare to see three or four people crossing the Nile this way on the same trunk, guided by a man swimming.

The many remains of churches and Christian monasteries mixed with Muslim burials which can be observed in this part of Nubia make me think that these places were alternately inhabited by anchorites of the two religions. When abandoned by both, the buildings fell into ruin, as also happened to many fortresses and castles that used to flourish here in the past and are now nothing but ruins.

On 4 September, we continued our journey, keeping at a distance from the Nile in order to avoid the sand mounds that clutter its banks for a stretch of road. After we crossed Jebel Ukma, we went back to the river, opposite the ruins of a monastery built on the west bank. From this place, two mountains can be seen at a distance, looking very much like pyramids. Only by getting closer can one find out their real nature. For more than two hours' march, the banks of the Nile are occupied on both sides by buildings, all more or less ruined, remains of churches and monasteries. The most remarkable of these ruins is close to the village of Akasha: it is a vast fort, with large walls flanked by buttresses. The entrance gate is to the north and, from what is left of the building, it looks like a monastery. Its size makes it the largest in the area. The nearby land used to be cultivated, but is nowadays mainly covered in sand: the *sant* and acacia trees are abundant and there also are some palms, but in very small numbers.

The village of Akasha is made up of only ten straw houses, built with such solidity and industry as to be able to efficiently provide shelter from bad weather. At a short distance, there is Kulb Island and the entrance to the district of Kulb. In the area there is plenty of a very bitter rock salt. At this point of the valley, the bed of the Nile widens, the mountains recede, the sands are less abundant, and the first palm plantations appear: these changes in the landscape are only on the east side, while on the other bank the desert continues for a large stretch of land.

On the 5th, in two hours we crossed another mountain and when we descended back to the Nile we found ourselves before a large plain, well cultivated and shaded here and there by thick woods of palms. The mountains were far in the distance and there were only small isolated rocks, almost all on the same line, as if they were placed to mark the road. After we passed two villages and a small cataract, we reached Sarkamatto in the Wadi Dal, almost at the slopes of a mountain called Meme, after which three more mountains follow at a short distance. We finally slept at Mograkka, a notable village in the middle of a palm wood.

---

275 Arabic دخن (*dukhn*), 'millet,' *Pennisetum glaucum* (L. 1753); Shinnie, *Linant de Bellefonds*, 57.

On the 6th, we reached Firka,[276] which marks the border between the territory of Mograkka and Sai. It is in front of a large island, where there are the ruins of modern buildings.[277] In little more than four hours we reached Amara. Hamid Kashif, who had so badly received us on our first trip to Nubia, was forced to join the army of Ibrahim Pasha against Sennar.

The road from Amara to Sai Island is shaded by palms and covered with fragments of quartz stone. The cultivation of the palm tree increases as one approaches the Kingdom of Dongola.

From Wadi Halfa to Sukkot, there is not an island longer than Sai: it takes at least five hours to cross it from edge to edge. In contrast, it is quite narrow in width and it takes only half an hour to cross it. Except for a granite mountain, not very high, which is in the middle of the island, I can say that Sai is flat. The land is well cultivated along the banks and beautiful plantations of palm and *sant* trees border it all along its length, making a pleasant and delightful sight for travelers. There are ruins of buildings by the river. The banks are frequented by crocodiles: this is the reason why the inhabitants generally land on the south edge when they need to go to the island.

Without losing sight of this green and pleasant place for a long stretch of road, we continued our journey. After we crossed a very steep mountain, we reached Shaykh, a village[278] famous for the tomb of a Muslim saint, which is believed to be miraculous. Not far from it we found an enclosure wall of around three hundred square feet with eight round buttresses. The walls are four feet wide and built in such a way that they look covered with tiles, with fragments of stone mixed with mortar so that it seems all in one piece. Inside this wall there were once houses, now completely ruined. It is possible that this was an ancient military outpost: in fact, there are no traces of churches or burials. Shortly after, we entered Wadi Hamid, before which Sai Island ends and another island begins, completely flat and cultivated. Here we observed a gathering of burials, some marked with an outline of round stones, possibly the tombs of the heads of the nearby villages. In contrast, the tombs of the populace are simply marked with two stones, one at the head and one at the feet.

Early on 7 September, we entered Wadi Abudiya, whence in four hours we reached Iraw, the border of the province of Sukkot with that of Mahas. The villages are from here on built with more regularity: houses are part mud brick and part straw, according to the wealth of the owners. It is general use in Nubia to put jars along frequented roads for the benefit of travelers. Here, this healthy custom is more than anywhere else observed, a man being paid solely to keep them always filled. There are many *saqya*s and the land is cultivated with wheat, *dhura*, pumpkins, beans, and other legumes. Male and female inhabitants walk barefoot and wear nothing but a strip of cloth around their hips to cover their private parts:

---

276 Firka is in fact to the north of Mograkka.
277 A fort dating back to the sixteenth–eighteenth century; Shinnie, *Linant de Bellefonds*, 14.
278 Probably Qubbat Shaykh Idris and the ruins a little to the south of Koyikka. It is a monumental six-story tomb with a dome; Martin Fitzenreiter, "Geschichte, Religion und Denkmäler der islamischen Zeit im Nordsudan," *Mitteilungen der Sudanarchäologischen Gesellschaft zu Berlin* 10 (2000): 88, fig. 3.

generally women arrange the whole strip to cover their breasts as well. They do not veil their faces like the women of Egypt and have waists much more curved than those, due to the habit they have of carrying around their babies on their hips, while the Egyptians keep them on their shoulders. They arrange their hair like the Ababda and habitually anoint the body with palm oil. The color of their skin is almost black, but they retain, with little alteration, European features. Here, too, like in Wadi Haggar, the inhabitants sleep in the open air in suspended beds. The women, who for the same reason spend part of the day on them, move from time to time long ropes that go from one edge of the sown fields to the other. There are rags hanging from the ropes, in order to scare the birds.

From Iraw we went to Wawa in half an hour: here there is a populated island and on the west bank the ruins of the temple of Soleb. After Wawa there is Irun[279] and then Ager, one of the largest villages of Mahas, located at a short distance from a Christian monastery, completely ruined.[280]

On the 8th, after two hours' journey, we reached Dangul, a small village with the ruins of an enclosure wall of three hundred square meters and whose walls are built with mud: inside the enclosure there is no sign of any building.[281] These ruins are located atop a high granite rock, watered at its slopes by the Nile. Wadi Abu Sari, where we entered shortly after, is interrupted from time to time by low hills and the entire bed of the river is occupied by two middle-sized islands, both inhabited, located one after the other with little space between. We then entered Wadi al-Nuat:[282] the Nile, which flows amid small black granite rocks covered in vegetation, a huge quantity of birds, a *saqya* located at the entrance of the wadi beside four tall and majestic palms, and the cultivated lands nearby, well, all these things produce a beautiful effect and make this pleasant valley really interesting. Beyond an island all of granite and without vegetation of any sort there is the village of Kidimmula, where we slept. Soon after sunset, the sky was filled with very bright colored clouds: the inhabitants told us that it was a clear sign that the day after would be a very hot day, which, in fact, it happened to be.

On the 9th, we entered the district of Dalqu and for a long stretch of road we found the Nile cluttered with a large number of uninhabited, still green, small islands. After the ruins of a city, of which nothing is left but heaps of stones and mud bricks, we met another four islands, all flat and well cultivated: they are named Aglash, Beibegh, Bajboj, and Artimiri. The village named Kaibar is in front of the latter, on the west bank, and the fields around

---

279   Unidentified toponym, but present also in Linant's description, as discussed by Margaret Shinnie: "There is some mystery here, as Irau is some five miles north of Sulb; and it seems unlikely that the temple would be visible at that distance. (Waddington and Hanbury took about 2½ hours to reach Sulb from Irau), he may have seen Sedeinga and thought it Sulb, but it seems more likely that it was not at Irau that he stopped but further south in the neighbourhood of Wawa," Shinnie, *Linant de Bellefonds*, 14. Rather than a mistake, as proposed by Shinnie, I would suggest this is a different place, possibly a very small settlement, because when Ricci mentions Irun he is perfectly aware of Iraw.

280   Perhaps Koya.

281   The citadel of Tinari; Shinnie, *Linant de Bellefonds*, 15.

282   Unidentified toponym: the description of the landscape seems to fit the district of Gurgud.

it are well cultivated and rich in palms. At Kokka, one of the usual military storehouses was established. From this point in three hours we reached Sabu, a large and well cultivated village. Here, for the first time since we left Aswan, we saw pigeons. We spent the night at Fareig, another village oddly built with groups of five to six houses scattered here and there among the palms. Its area is so large that it takes two hours to cross it all. Here we saw the first beautiful Dongolawi horses, much esteemed in Egypt.

Early on the 10th, we reached Jeddi, located on the slopes of a limestone hill. We subsequently met the ruins of a city, facing Korta Island, and, shortly after, the villages of Melegab, Masida, Gumara, and Kor,[283] whence for a short stretch of road the plain is replaced by rocks and granite blocks similar to those of the Second Cataract. In the Nile there are many scattered small islands, which make the current stronger. On the opposite side there must be a cataract—I assume this from the loud noise of the water.

I was almost always traveling by foot, crossing the villages and the woods, in order to assemble an ornithological collection. I unintentionally happened to scare the inhabitants of Kor by shooting at a little bird at the entrance of their village. Some of them were gathered at the shaykh's to celebrate his birthday and, hearing the noise of the shot, came out extremely scared. They soon calmed down when I assured them that I was not a soldier but a physician, and then they invited me cheerfully into the house of the shaykh. He saw me recharging my rifle with fine ammunition, about which he had some experience, and proved himself eager to have some: I pleased him, sharing with him what I had in my leather bag. He wanted me to stay at his banquet, but I was in a hurry to rejoin the caravan and had to leave. Then I proceeded to Semele, where, all together, we spent the night.

On the 11th, at around ten in the morning, we reached the borders of Mahas with the Kingdom of Dongola, marked by two rows of large granite blocks one on top of the other, looking like the artificial cliffs built around maritime fortifications in order to break the force of the waves. In front of Tombos Island, almost in the middle of the road, there are two large blocks of pink granite bearing bas-relief figures and a hieroglyphic stela.[284] I copied half of it, the rest being completely corroded; plate 60. On another granite block located beside it, there is the drawing of a small temple and, a little further on toward the desert, there is a colossal statue lying on the ground. It is of black granite, but unfinished, and eleven feet long. In the many quarries of the area in front of Badin Island there are many unfinished sculptures and for more than twenty minutes along the road there are pottery shards and bricks: it is possible that here there used to be a city or at least a workshop area for sculptors, who from these beautiful quarries sent their works to Soleb, Argo, Barkal, and Meroe.

Before proceeding with the narration of our journey, I would like to treat some topics related to the Kingdom of Mahas, now reduced to a province, since I said but few things when I announced our entrance into its territory. Houses here are mostly made of straw, either round in the shape of a Chinese pavilion or humpbacked, like common huts. Many

---

283 Perhaps Kur or Akur, both islands.
284 Stela dating to the second regnal year of Thutmose I. The colossus, mentioned later, is variably identified as Taharqa or Tanutamun; Porter and Moss, *Topographical Bibliography* 7:174–75.

are built with straw painted in white and black stripes; from a distance they look varied and charming. Every group of four to five houses is surrounded by a fence or a palm-tree wooden palisade, which defends it from the attack of wild animals during the night. I have already said that the inhabitants' complexion is almost black and that they have European features, but their countenance is grim, their gaze sinister, and from their appearance one can judge their heart. They always brought provisions for the caravan, that is true, but they never did it joyfully or in the familiar ways typical of a good soul, and they never smiled. They claim to descend from the Quraysh, the tribe to which Muhammad belonged.[285] Before the passage of the Egyptian army, by which this people was so oppressed and subjugated, no caravan could enter its territory without being completely looted or at least mistreated. If sometimes they spared the life of caravan members, they did it as compensation for allowing themselves to be robbed. Their antisocial behavior reached the point that they chased away beggars from other tribes, a thing unheard of among Muslims. They were under a chief whose title was *malak*,[286] but they are now directly under the governor of Dongola. For this reason, they have fallen into an extreme depression and the severity with which they are treated has somehow tamed their ferocity. Comparing this people with many other tribes among which I traveled, I am convinced that the place strongly influences the character of the inhabitants: I observed that, in general, those who live in the plains are good and hospitable, while, on the contrary, proud and nasty are those who live in the mountains and in wild regions, as most of Mahas province is. In this region there grows in abundance a plant called *ergel*, which replaces senna[287] and has the same effects when taken, and, moreover, when applied on wounds as a poultice it heals them very quickly. This plant or, better, bush, is usually as tall as the myrtle, with the same leaves but a bit larger and of a lighter green. The colocynth also grows in the plains, but in small quantity. There are goats, sheep, cows, and many gazelles. For short trips, the locals ride donkeys. There are also many beetles.

The Kingdom, or dominion, of Dongola seems at its entrance the continuation of that of Mahas, but imperceptibly the desert becomes broader on both sides of the Nile as one approaches the capital. The banks of the river are also covered with *sant* trees. The first island of the province is Tombos, then there is Badin. In front of the latter, we camped for the night. As soon as we pitched our tents, the Ababda, our guides, wanted to celebrate the memory of a battle which was fought there in the past, resulting in the victory of their tribe: to this effect, they slaughtered a lamb and ate the whole liver raw and still steaming. Then

---

285 Banu Quraysh. It is in fact another mythopoeic phenomenon: "This Arabization is sometimes limited to the statement of an Arabic ancestry, preferably related to the family of the Prophet. Thus between the 2nd and the 6th cataract many groups of sedentary 'Arabs' relate (except the Shaiqiya of the region of Merowe) to the ancestor Ibrahim Ga'al, himself a descendant of Abbas, uncle of the Prophet. They are consequently called Ga'alin (or Jalin) or Abbasid," Robert Cornevin, *Histoire de l'Afrique*, vol. 2, *L'Afrique précoloniale du tournant du XVIe au tournant du XXe siècle* (Paris: Payot, 1966), 258.

286 Arabic ملك *(malak),* 'king.'

287 A species of small bushes of the family of the *Fabaceae* (Mill. 1754), from which a laxative was produced.

they cut the meat and divided it among them to eat it barbecued the next day. They also ate the bone marrow raw, spread on bread baked on the spot.

On the 12th, right after our departure, we observed at a certan distance from the Nile, deep into the desert, some large buildings which looked like pyramids. We left the caravan, Mr. Linant and I, in order to explore them.[288] The most distant is one hour of speedy dromedary march from the Nile. It has a hundred-foot circumference and is fabricated with large mud bricks, of a bluish color, to the point that they look made of pure clay.[289] The entrance is on the south and on the west side there is a horizontal opening, not very large, left open when they built the pyramid. A second square opening can be observed almost at half height, by which we could penetrate inside: there, we saw two large slabs of sandstone, possibly used as tombstones, as far as we could judge from their dimensions. There were also a pink granite pedestal, on top of which there were carved some parallel lines, the upper torso of a small statue, and the fragments of an alabaster vase scattered on the ground. In general, this pyramid is so damaged that it seems about to collapse. At a certain distance there are some other burials, which I could recognize from the disposition of the stones all around, as I described before. The other pyramid is much closer to the Nile and it is better preserved:[290] its entrance is on the west and it is eight feet wide. On the walls there are the remains of very hard mortar with which they were plastered. A few steps from the entrance, we turned to the left and then back to the right and entered a very large room, with two more annexes. These rooms were completely empty and we did not find any trace of hieroglyphs. In the outer part, looking north, there is an opening that seems to have previously been used to penetrate inside the pyramid. This construction possibly has a circumference of 120 feet: the mud bricks used are similar to those of the other pyramid, but here there are also some baked bricks. Many unburied human bones are scattered around on the sand, possibly belonging to other burials uncovered little by little by the blowing winds.

The caravan had the order to wait for us at the village of Hannak; we reached it quite late and then spent the night at the same place.

On 13 September, after two hours' march, we found ourselves in front of Argo Island, which is the largest in the part of the Nile Valley we had thus far traveled. On this island we saw large and thick palm woods and beautiful cultivations. From this point on, there are no mountains; they are replaced by immense desert plains of sand, interrupted now and then by long rows of doum trees. The island is not always visible because the banks of the Nile are sometimes quite high.

---

288 This is the site of Kerma. Linant is a bit more precise and writes: "Since the morning I had seen two things a bit elevated in the plain and with the telescope they looked like rocks or some earthen ruins" (Shinnie, *Linant de Bellefonds*, 20); he then visits with his guide. On the following day, he goes back to the site in the company of Ricci in order to visit the easternmost ruin, likely Deffufa K. II.

289 This should be Deffufa K. I, dating back to the age of Senwosret I: rather than a pyramid tomb, the site is a fortified military and administrative settlement; Porter and Moss, *Topographical Bibliography* 7:175–76.

290 Probably Deffufa K. II, dating back to a period between the Twelfth and the Eighteenth Dynasty; Porter and Moss, *Topographical Bibliography* 7:176.

At around eleven in the morning, we were surprised by the most beautiful mirage we had ever seen in Egypt: until one in the afternoon, when the illusion vanished away, it seemed we were surrounded everywhere by water. This phenomenon, about which many others have written profusely, happens in plain and sandy places, almost always in the hottest hours of the day. In six more hours, we reached the village of Mugazzi,[291] still in sight of Argo Island. We passed it completely only on the following day, the 14th, before reaching Maragha, or New Dongola, capital of the kingdom of the same name, before which we stopped at midday sharp. Here, we had the moving sight of a corpse devoured by hyenas, which had probably disinterred it in the previous night. By the black turban, which distinguishes Copts and Jews from Muslims, and which we could see in shreds on the ground, we understood the corpse belonged to someone of these two religions in the service of Isma'il Pasha, recently buried here.

We fired our weapons twice to announce our arrival and call for a boat to come and take us to the capital. In fact, not much later, a *canjiah* arrived, carrying the effendi[292] of Abdin Bey. He informed us that the bey himself knew about our arrival and that we had at our disposal the apartments of Abd al-Rahman Bey,[293] head of the Mamluks, who had taken refuge here. Before embarking, we dismissed our camels and paid the agreed sum, giving extra for the guides and the *kabir* who, happy about our generosity, prepared to set off again.

We arrived in the city and were taken to the aforementioned house; after a while we were treated to an excellent lunch in the company of the effendi, who then left us free to rest as much as we wanted. The following morning he paid another visit and informed us about the imminent return of Abdin Bey, who had accompanied Ibrahim Pasha for a stretch of river. In fact, at dawn on the 16th, four gunfire shots announced his return. At about ten, we went to pay him a visit and we were kindly received with all possible attentions, as much as a European could have offered. In the same day, two Arabs sent to Darfur brought the news that Defterdar Bey, governor of Asyut, had conquered Kordofan, a region eighteen to twenty days from Dongola. In the evening, the bey sent to our house three beautiful horses, lavishly harnessed, with the invitation to make free use of them. He pushed his kindness toward us to the point of sending us every day, from his kitchen, food prepared as much as possible according to European taste. Many times we had lunch in his company and then took coffee in his pavilion, discussing more than anything else the way to prevent dysentery and intermittent fevers, which attack the inhabitants after the rainy season. Unfortunately, I could leave him but a few remedies for his own personal use.

Dongola is the place where, after the loss of Egypt, the few Mamluks who survived their destruction took refuge. Gathered together, there were eight hundred of them, including the slaves they had trained in the use of weapons. They did not find another safe place and chose this country as their last asylum. They did not want to mix with the locals and therefore built their own houses along the river, but these were soon destroyed by an inundation

---

291 Perhaps Magassir.
292 Émile Effendi, a slave of Abdin Kashif, born in Albania of an Abyssinian slave; Shinnie, *Linant de Bellefonds*, 25–26.
293 Abd al-Rahman Bey, head of the Mamluks who survived the massacre of 1811 and took refuge at Ibrim and Dongola.

of the Nile. They built new houses a bit farther from the river, but these too were wiped out, so they then decided to build them on the same level as the city. To keep some distinction, they built them at a certain distance from the houses of the natives. After some time, when they exhausted the money they had, they were content to receive a part of the harvest, which they still had to pay for in cash. This encouraged agriculture and pushed the natives to sow more land. The caravans passing by were forced to pay a tribute. In this way, they kept living for some time, governing themselves according to their own laws. It seems that this revenue was not enough and in the end they became as miserable as the natives. Nevertheless, they always refused to submit to the viceroy of Egypt, who more than once offered them his pardon. When the Egyptian army arrived, they did not fight, for the misery, as often happens, had divided them into parties: Abd al-Rahman Bey, determined to die rather than bow, gathered his own men and set off to Darfur in order to organize a coalition with those tribes and mount resistance to the Egyptian army. He did not succeed and decided to cross the great desert, heading toward Tunis or Tripoli. Even though Abd al-Rahman is not mentioned specifically by Major Denham,[294] he was definitely among the beys met by him in a small village close to Murzuk. The ones who stayed in Dongola threw themselves at the feet of Isma'il Pasha, begging for pardon and obtaining it. Some, who had intermarried with the natives, preferred to stay; others were sent to Egypt and later obtained positions according to their abilities. Thus disappeared forever what was left of those formidable men, who had much troubled the viceroy of Egypt before he could manage to subdue them. Their ferocity could not be tempered by the most woesome misery, in which most of them deluded themselves for a long time that the genius and the warlike ardor of Abd al-Rahman Bey would finally restore to them possession of their lost domains.

The houses of the inhabitants are generally made of straw, except those of the notables, which are made of mud: the city is placed in an open, but low and swampy, area. Air is therefore unhealthy and, after the fall rains, many intermittent fevers spread. The situation is further worsened by the proximity of a large forest of *oshur* trees,[295] which, whenever pierced or cut, ooze in abundance a sort of poisonous milk, dangerous for the eyes. I suffered the effects myself because, unaware of the pernicious qualities of this milk, I inadvertently rubbed my eyes with my dirty hands. I suffered an inflammation that, had I not treated it quickly with the appropriate remedies, would have degenerated into true ophthalmia. The inhabitants do not use this tree for their fire, but rather to build huts used as stables. The largest trunks are used to fabricate one-piece saddles, which have a raised part in the front and a large and high headboard which they use as a support while fighting. It is usual among the Arabs to ride with very short stirrups; standing and

---

294 Ricci is here referring to Dixon Denham, Hugh Clapperton, and Walter Oudnay, *Narrative of Travels and Discoveries in Northern and Central Africa in the Years 1822, 1823 and 1824* (Boston: Cummings, Hilliard & Co.), published in 1826.

295 *Calotropis procera* (Aiton). In Sudan its milk was used to induce abortion; Ahmed Abdel Halim, "Native Medicine and Ways of Treatment in the Northern Sudan," *Sudan Notes and Records 22* (1939): 42.

leaning on the headboard, they act as if standing on the ground. These saddles are covered in goatskin and when used by the wealthy are decorated with silver sheets, polished to perfection.

From this point of Africa southward the difference of temperature between the day and the night is perceptible and is the primary cause of dysentery. The symptoms become more serious as one approaches the equator: right after sunset the air becomes humid and heavy. This variation influences the spirit as well as the body, and one becomes restless and develops a great propensity for sleep. For this reason, the inhabitants are generally lazy and of an emaciated and weak constitution. Their temper is very sweet and I can say from experience that they become easily familiar with strangers, whom they help willingly in all that they can. All their clothes are a sort of cotton blanket in which they wrap themselves. The hair is collected in small braids like the Ababda and they anoint their body with castor oil, a plant that grows in abundance in their territory. They sow *dhura* rather than *dukhn* and, by order of Abdin Bey, other crops were introduced, such as wheat, pumpkins, watermelons, and many vegetables. They have a wonderful breed of horses, very tall, of the darkest bay, with a white oblong spot on their head and white spots on their legs. They do not shoe them; nevertheless their hoof resists, being very hard. Their cattle have very long horns, curved forward, while cows are attractive for the variety of the spots on their coat. Sheep have a very large and heavy tail and the lambs are excellent, their meat being almost preferable to that of calves.

When the Mamluks settled in Dongola, they attracted from different places many women, who were abandoned when they fled: Abdin Bey exiled them all to keep good order among his troops.

It is presumable that under the Egyptian government this city will gradually expand. Following the example of the bey, who had a large house built for himself, many of the main traders had already substituted their straw huts with large mudbrick houses, much more comfortable and roomy. Instead of the blanket, they now wear a long tunic, usually blue, as generally used in Arabia.

Two *malak*s, or heads of the nearby villages, came on the 21st to compliment the bey: one of them was escorted by two almost-naked soldiers, armed with a long spear and a shield. Their hair is shaped in the form of a wig and they spend much time in crinkling and anointing it with tallow. In fact, this hair style—especially on half-naked men—gives them such a silly appearance that, if one is not used to it, it is difficult to suppress laughter at first sight. The *malak* wore a long white cotton tunic, high-necked, over which he had a white cloak. On his head he had a white silk bonnet decorated in arabesques, with two horn bands loose over the ears, hanging below the chin. A red silk band was an ornament to the bonnet, too.

The other *malak* and his retinue were on horseback. His clothes were more or less the same as the former, just with different colors: the cloak was red and the bonnet made of yellow silk, more richly embroidered: the bands were raised and they looked like horns. I would not find a better comparison to describe them with than the rays of light with which the head of Moses is usually represented.[296] In ancient Egyptian paintings there are scenes of kings wearing clothes and especially a bonnet very much like these *malak*s.

After eight days in Dongola, we left on 22 September, quite late because of a heavy shower that lasted until ten. The bey gave us a good boat, where he had stored many provisions for free. The crew was made up of only four people, *rais* included: such was the limit for boats of that size. We set off at around eleven; the beginning of our journey was made more pleasant by the beauty of the Nile banks, shadowed by an infinite number of *sant* trees covered in fragrant yellow flowers, some of which had fallen on the flat green ground around, embellishing its surface. The day was cloudy until the evening and four times we heard, at a distance, roaring thunder. Our first stop was the small Arti Island, which is flat and well populated.

On the 23rd, with a good north wind, in less than two hours we reached Abd al-Rahman Island, which is beautiful, but completely deserted. Facing this island, to the west, there is a village called Kajatti, with many *saqya*s, used to irrigate the land because the banks of the Nile are quite high here. Around the village there are also many wild palm trees. At a distance of half an hour there is Khanag,[297] another village to the west, made up of a few houses, part in mud and part in straw, in front of Sahaba Island. On the same line, to the east, there are the ruins of an ancient city, not large, but protected by strong and wide stone walls. The surface occupied by these ruins does not exceed six hundred steps.[298] The gate was to the south and from what remains it seems that the side looking over the Nile was more fortified. In the vicinity there are many pyramid-shaped tombs built on three levels. Among the ruins we found a shameplant,[299] as tall as a man, with very little leaves: on just touching the tip of one of them, all the foliage retracted and stayed almost hanging; the Arabs call this plant *geseban*. Proceeding in our journey, shortly after, we met Suruma Island and Darar Island, both inhabited. The village of Sahaba is a little distant to the west and, from this point on, in three more hours of navigation we reached Teiti, another village located beside the ruins of a city, which the Arabs call Derr. From these ruins Abdin Bey had bricks removed to build his own palace at Dongola. For a long stretch of road beyond Derr, the west bank is better cultivated than the eastern and the bed of the Nile is perceptibly narrower.

---

296 A cap characteristic of royal dignity, called *tagia* or *taqiyya umm qarnayn*, already attested in Christian Nubia and very rare right after Ricci's visit; Holt, *A Modern History of the Sudan*, 31. "It was made of cotton cloth and the ends were stuffed with raw cotton to form horns. The tagia of Mek Nimr of Shendi (the last Jaalin Mek) was made from the skin of a leopard (nimr)," Arthur E. Robinson, "Some Notes on the Regalia of the Fung Sultans of Sennar," *Journal of the Royal African Society* 30, no. 121 (1931): 367–68.

297 Khanag is actually to the north of Kajatti and far to the north of Sahaba Island.

298 Qasr Wad Nimayri, dating back to the end of the eighteenth century; Shinnie, *Linant de Belle-fonds*, 29; "High earth (mud-brick) walls can be seen, remains of a fortress that I judged Muslim work; some fragments of ancient columns are here remarkable," Frédéric Cailliaud, *Voyage à Méroé, au Fleuve Blanc, au-delà de Fâzoql dans le midi du royaume de Sennâr, à Syouah et dans cinq autres oasis: fait dans les années 1819, 1820, 1821 et 1822: accompagné de Cartes géographiques, de Planches représentant les monuments de ces contrées, avec des détails relatifs à l'état moderne et à l'histoire naturelle* (Paris: Imprimerie Royale, 1826), 2:12.

299 *Mimosa pudica* (L. 1753).

On 24 September, in one hour, we reached Urbi, a quite large and populous village on the west bank. After this, on the same side, in the middle of a vast, well-cultivated plain and at a distance from the river, there is Sori, whence we reached Khandaq in three hours.[300] This is the capital of the district called by the same name, where there are the ruins of a large city, with a fort close to the Nile banks. The lower half of its walls is built with beautiful regular stone and the rest with bricks. At the four corners there are buttresses with loopholes: those built on the desert side are more solid. The city gate is to the south and that of the fort to the east. Inside the fort there are two long and wide hallways, whose high ceilings are supported by doum-palm beams placed on columns of the same wood. In many of the buildings inside the fort, the door lintel is made of one piece of sandstone decorated with a meander motif; in other buildings it is made of wood with the same decoration. Next to the fort gate there is a large black granite vase three feet high and one and a half feet wide, with a line of hieroglyphs around the rim, though almost illegible. The houses of the city were solidly built with stone and mortar, the roads were large and regular. At a short distance there is a pyramidal tomb, which is nevertheless a much more recent construction. Even though this was the most sizable ruined city we had ever encountered, nobody could tell us its name. Defterdar Bey had established there a military depot and at that time a large regiment was stationed to ensure communications with Kordofan, since a road leads there directly from this city. In two more hours we reached Goled, a small village built on the ruins of an ancient walled city; the walls still had battlements made of sun-dried bricks. An Arab seated on the threshold of a house was playing a lyre interestingly crafted: half of a pumpkin, covered with the skin of a reptile called by the Arabs *waran* (which is the Nile lizard), made up the sounding board. At its sides there were two sticks, one arm long, connected at their edges by another stick. The lyre had five gut strings, but since they were all almost of the same thickness, the note variations were rather imperceptible.

On the 25th, one hour after sunrise, we were at the island of Nawi, meaning 'of the magicians,' administered by a *kashif*[301] called "Devouring Magician." Our crew told us wonderful and incredible things about this island: they guaranteed in the first place that its inhabitants have human form during the day and change into crocodiles at night, and that shortly before they had eaten the brother of *malak* Sha'us,[302] who had landed on the island while going to Dongola to visit his mother. They also said that luckily Isma'il Pasha defeated the magicians and that some of them drowned in the Nile, while others took refuge in the mountains and went back to the plains after the Egyptians left. Our crew said all this nonsense with great seriousness and proved to be particularly anxious to pass this dangerous island. They absolutely refused to land, even though we offered them some money. All these stories possibly originate from the large number of crocodiles that frequent the island and that perhaps make it particularly dangerous. Maybe the savageness of its inhabitants contributes to its bad reputation, too. In the village of Fergi, on the west bank, only half

300   Khandaq, "Andak" in Linant. A Christian fort reused and restored by the Funj.
301   Linant calls him shaykh Naseramshamto; Shinnie, *Linant de Bellefonds*, 31.
302   Sha'us of Adlanib.

an hour from this island, we found a piece of pink granite column lying on the ground; there were no traces of hieroglyphs, though. In the evening, we reached Tongol, or Dongola al-Ajuza[303] ('Old Dongola'), built to the east on a slope of sandstone rock, at average height and partly covered in sand. This city was large and well built. In the midst of its ruins one can still see the remains of columns, some of them entirely preserved.[304] On the desertward side, in an elevated place, there is a castle built during the reign of the caliphs. It has a square plan and it is partly cut into the rock. The gate is to the west and in each of the four sides there is a large window. In the middle of the castle there is a mosque, the dome of which is supported by four columns of black granite: I noticed some tiny Coptic inscriptions and a stone with an Arabic inscription. Here, too, there was a garrison, under the command of Abdin Bey, stationed in order to hold in subjection the Arabs Kababish, who live in this desert.

On the 26th we sailed only four hours, always against wind, and we reached Tangasi in the evening. The desert is flat and sandy on both sides of the Nile, and the many islands are covered with woods, for the most part inhabited by hordes of Bedouins, who dwell in huts built deep in the forest and live on milk and *dhura* bread.

Tangasi is a very large island, for the most part wooded, with many *saqya*s and villages. Here, too, on a low hill there are the ruins of an ancient city, with a ruined mosque where there is still standing a pink granite column, six feet tall and with a circumference of only one foot. At a certain distance from the ruins there are two tombs, built in the shape of a pyramid, with a square base and round toward the top.[305]

On the 27th, the headwind kept blowing and we could only land at Ari, to the west: this is a village in the district of Masne, where some sandy hills interrupt the uniformity of the Nile banks. We observed in many places that when the east bank is cultivated, the west bank is deserted, and vice versa. The Ababda and the Bisharin of the mountain take their cattle to the islands of this district during the Nile flood; at this time they also sell their butter. They go back to their usual abode when the waters pull back.

On the 28th we reached quite early the ruins of Keret,[306] to the west: these are a few mud houses and a brick enclosure wall. We then passed the village of Karmakoi and the island of Girra. At four in the afternoon, we stopped at Abker, to the east, in order to visit the ruins of a fort, half an hour distant and built on a hill dominating the desert. The walls of this fortress are very solid and in part cut in the same rock it stands on. On the other side, they are made of mud mixed with Nile algae and cattle excrement; nevertheless they

---

303 Arabic عجوزة *(ajuza)*, feminine 'old.'

304 Porter and Moss, *Topographical Bibliography* 7:193. Similarly Cailliaud: "Eight hundred steps toward the north 44° west of the mosque, we notice two small gray granite columns, originally from a Christian church: they are three meters thirty-five centimeters tall; one of the two is reversed: the bad style of these columns and a fragment of capital decorated with a Greek cross qualify them as Coptic work," Cailliaud, *Voyage à Méroé*, 2:24.

305 Mounds probably dating back to the late Meroitic period; Porter and Moss, *Topographical Bibliography* 7:193.

306 According to Margaret Shinnie this could be Gabriya, where Linant describes the ruins of a monastery, even though there is a toponym Keret eight kilometers southeast of Gabriya.

are very strong. In the middle of the fort there is still a large squared water reservoir, which is now completely useless because it is filled with stones. At some distance to the north there are a large number of tombs, disproportionate to the size of the small fortress: one must think that nearby there used to be some villages, now lost.

On the 29th, after we passed Goshabarti Island, we met another island called Qanatti where we had to use the ropes in order to overcome the strong current produced by the bend of the Nile toward the northeast. The river bends again and imperceptibly changes to a southeast direction until Mugrat Island, where it turns back to the north. In the evening we landed at the southern edge of Qanatti Island and, among a large quantity of ruins, we saw the remains of six pink granite columns of very bad style. An enormous crocodile, eighteen to twenty feet long, was standing on the bank, but as soon as it saw the boat approaching it threw itself into the Nile, producing a noise like a large rock falling into the water. Shortly after sunset, we enjoyed the sight of a meteor, light blue and very brilliant: it stretched from the southeast to the northwest and lasted for almost five minutes, after which it disappeared gradually in the same span of time, first losing its splendor and then decreasing in volume, until it completely disappeared. Mr. Linant judged it to be of the same nature as the aurora borealis.

On the 30th we met the ruins of a fortress,[307] the most recent of all we had seen until then. It was perfectly square, with round buttresses at the corners and a large number of loopholes. The outer walls, still standing, are made of large stones up to two-thirds of their height; the rest is of bricks. The isolated rock hill where it stands is surrounded on its slope by another brick wall. At a distance, in the plain, there are the ruins of some houses, among which still stands a black granite column in two pieces; a cross is carved on its capital. In the middle of the fort there is a large rock-cut water reservoir, of oval shape and very deep. In a burial enclosure, next to the aforementioned ruins, there are two tombs surmounted by large square stelae of very beautiful white marble, but without any inscription or carving. Before reaching the village of Mansurkoti, the impetuosity of the stream and the violence of the wind put us in real danger because the river at this point is full of rocks. In fact, we hit several; nevertheless, we overcame this dangerous spot without accident. Passing by the two islands of Gigernarti and Husaynarti, both large and populous, we reached Hetani,[308] a small village on the right bank of the Nile, almost facing Husayn Island. The Shaiqiya[309] used to own, some time ago, some mud buildings in this village and at Ambikul, too, which was their meeting point when they wanted to go looting and lay waste to the nearby districts. The Mamluks of Dongola, disturbed by their incursions, seized those buildings during an attack, but were afterward driven out by the Shaiqiya themselves, who decided to tear them down in order to avoid new attempts at invasion. This is why they now lie in ruin.

---

307 The fort of Diffar.
308 Hetani, a site now lost; Shinnie, *Linant de Bellefonds*, 38.
309 "Shaiqiya Tribe. Arabic is their language, and they claim Arab descent. They were, and are, renowned as warriors, and made a brave fight against the army of Muhammad Ali," Shinnie, *Linant de Bellefonds*, 27.

On October 1st, the stream being very violent and knowing we were soon about to meet small cataracts and many rocks, we decided to take on board more men in order to pull the boat when needed. We struggled to find only eleven because, when they see boats on the Nile, they all flee to the mountains. After the passage of the Egyptian army, the inhabitants of all villages on the banks of or near to the Nile were forced by Isma'il Pasha to serve the boats for free. Since many cruel officers would beat them up after a long day of work, the poor villagers tried to hide and avoid ill treatment. As for us, every time we were forced to use their services, we made sure to treat them mildly, feeding them and even giving them little presents. In this circumstance, when the women saw that we were taking their men, they ran toward us crying bitterly, pleading we would not mistreat them or take them to war. We could only succeed in calming them down with much effort, assuring them that if they were to do their duty we would send them back by night. Despite our promise, we were forced to retain the men until Ambikul. Had we not done this, we would have been in trouble, since there is no other village until that place. We arrived on the 2nd at around eight in the morning. Here Omar Kashif, who was in charge, gave us fresh men and we could dismiss the others. Right outside this village there is Debesh Island, which we passed at around ten. At midday, we reached Korti. A high mountain[310] marks here the border between the Kingdom of Dongola and the Kingdom of the Shaiqiya, more precisely marked in the middle of the mountain by an enormous rock. At sunset we stopped at a small village on the slopes of the same mountain. As we arrived, a large number of women came to the banks of the river, carrying on their heads vases of milk, which they asked to exchange for wheat or *dhura*, complaining that for many months they had not eaten bread. The scarcity of our own provisions did not allow us to give them any; nevertheless we handed over a few measures of cereals to cheer them up.

The Kingdom of the Shaiqiya has a large population which used to live off robbery and was extremely jealous of its freedom. It is divided into two districts: Merowe and Hannakab, ruled by two *malak*s, or little kings, both independent. Although always at war with each other, they would quickly ally against any common enemy. The conquest of this kingdom was extremely important for Isma'il Pasha in order not to have such a fiery enemy left at his back and to recruit soldiers for his army. He wanted to acertain whether he could reach his goal by avoiding bloodshed. Therefore, when he reached Korti, he sent an ambassador to the two *malak*s, Sha'us and Sibayr,[311] to invite them to submit voluntarily by acknowledging the sovereignty of Muhammad Ali. From the proud negative answer he easily realized he would meet resistance. In fact, those ferocious peoples, driven by their astrologers or necro-mancers,[312] who promised to make them invulnerable if they would fight for their common

---

310   Perhaps Jebel Kulmakol.
311   Sha'us of Adlanib and Sibayr of Hannakab, W. Nicholls, *The Shaikiya: An Account of the Shaikiya Tribes and of the History of Dongola Province from the XIVth to the XIXth Century* (Dublin: Hodges, Figgis & Co., 1913), 30.
312   *Fiki*s, "rural holy men specializing in spells and magic potions," Andrew J. McGregor, *A Military History of Modern Egypt: From the Ottoman Conquest to the Ramadan War* (Westport: Praeger Security International, 2006), 72.

independence, came boldly to the battle,[313] armed only with spears and shields and very few firearms. They fought with fury until they were overwhelmed by the number and the superiority of the equipment of their enemy, in particular by the canister shot—an utterly new thing for them—and fled the battlefield, leaving many of their warriors wounded on the ground.[314] Among the prisoners was the daughter of one of the two *malak*s. She was brought to the presence of the pasha, but despite being very beautiful, he respected her and sent her back to her father with a good escort of men, after he had changed her silver ornaments into many more golden jewels. When the *malak* saw her coming, he coldly asked her if she was still a virgin: when she replied affirmatively, he wanted to assure himself. He was then convinced of the pasha's virtue and he let him know that from his side he would try all means to reach a peace deal, not willing at all to make war against the person who respected his daughter.[315] Despite all his efforts, he nevertheless could not win over the obstinacy of the magicians. A few days later, four thousand Shaiqiya, most on horseback, assaulted the Egyptian camp, but were again repulsed with great loss and took refuge on Mount Daiqa. Here they were attacked by the pasha and were completely annihilated in a horrible massacre.[316] The few who survived the manslaughter fled to the desert. After this last defeat, they became disenchanted with the deception of their magicians and refused to believe them and fight again. The losses among the Egyptians were few compared to those of their enemies, and it must have happened that the Shaiqiya, trusting the spells of the magicians, advanced despite their wounds until they died: many bodies covered with amulets were found on the battlefield bearing four or five shots in the chest.

On 3 October, we passed Mount Daiqa, where, as I said, the last battle of the Shaiqiya was fought and their complete defeat took place. We could still see on its slopes the unburied bones, leftovers of the hyenas which for a long time afterward found something to satiate themselves here. Hunger forced some of those who had sought refuge in the desert to come back to these places impregnated with their own blood. They were so exhausted that they resembled walking ghosts. War had, here more than anywhere else, left horrible marks: *saqya*s destroyed, villages burnt and deserted, and abandoned fields. All these were baleful memories, feeding the pain and the fear of the few people who had come back to live here. Every time they saw a boat, they fled away, leaving behind even the cows employed at the *saqya*s. After his victory, Isma'il Pasha had given precise orders to his soldiers to avoid destruction, but he could not restrain the ardor of his men, who, despite the strictest punishments, indulged in every kind of excess. The pasha wanted to give a bit of peace to those

---

313 The battle of Korti was fought on 4 November 1820; Cailliaud, *Voyage à Méroé*, 2:54–58; McGregor, *A Military History*, 71–72.

314 In fact, in the battle of Korti the Turco-Egyptian army did not make use of artillery, which did not make it to the battlefield in time for the fight; McGregor, *A Military History*, 72.

315 The episode is narrated firsthand in Waddington and Hanbury, *Journal*, 96 and with more details in Cailliaud, *Voyage à Méroé*, 2:64–65. The princess's name was Safiya.

316 Battle of Jebel Daiqa, 2 or 4 December 1820; McGregor, *A Military History*, 72; Osbert G.S. Crawford, *The Fung Kingdom of Sennar* (Gloucester: John Bellows, 1951), 264; Arthur E. Robinson, "The Conquest of the Sudan by the Wali of Egypt, Muhammad Ali Pasha, 1820–1824," *Journal of the Royal African Society* 25, no. 97 (1925): 53.

miserable populations and therefore deployed a small detachment of soldiers in each village, so that at the passage of the troops the villagers would not be harassed and could go back to their farming.

When we reached Usli Island, inhabited by only a few families, we found one busy loading on a *ramus* its house and few pieces of furniture (a mat, two empty pumpkins, and three ram skins) in order to move to Dongola and search for a better life. It should not be any surprise that the natives can easily move their houses from one place to another because since these are made of straw and divided into many small square mats, they are easy to disassemble and equally easy to assemble. After this island, there is Messawi Island and then the village of Bakhit, on the left bank of the Nile. Here, there are the ruins of an enclosure wall of around three hundred square meters, built on an elevation called Hileila by the natives: it is made of large stone blocks outside and bricks inside. Every side has two small gates, each of them defended by a round buttress. There is no reason to believe that inside the walls there used to be houses, and only a few irregular stones are scattered on the ground, plus some holes looking like tombs, out of use since the Arabs now bury their dead in the nearby mountain.[317]

Although from Fareig, toward the border of the Kingdom of Mahas, one can already see the famous horse incorrectly called Dongolawi, this beautiful breed belongs to the Kingdom of the Shaiqiya. At the time of our passage, they had become very rare because some of them were requisitioned by the Egyptian army and the fleeing natives took with them nearly all the rest.

On 4 October, we could barely gather ten men, and then set off, but after one hour five of them fled away: we ordered our crew to chase them and only with great effort were they able to catch them and bring them back to the boat. At around nine, Malak Sibayr, the one who ruled over Hannakab, passing on land by the boat, asked to be received on board. We did not hesitate to oblige him so as not to lose a good opportunity to talk to a man so renowned in those lands. He ordered his twelve accompanying slaves to assist with the ropes of the boat and then sat with us. His emaciated appearance and the disheartenment into which he had fallen were proof of how sensitive he was about his defeat. We treated him to pipe and coffee. He expressed the desire to have one of our spirit cups and we presented him with one at once, accompanied by a bottle of our wine, which he promptly accepted. We started talking about the war he had fought and he confirmed what I already said, adding that the spells of the white men were stronger than their own, and particularly the canister, which he believed a product of magic; without it, he added, he believed it impossible to beat the Shaiqiya, fighters brave enough to conquer even Cairo. He informed us that after the last battle Sha'us, scared, fled away, but as for him, he sincerely submitted, persuaded that Isma'il Pasha was a virtuous man by the generosity with which he had sent back untouched his virgin daughter, although she was a beautiful girl. He also said that he made the right choice because the pasha let him keep his belongings,

---

317 The fort of Bakhit, probably dating back to Christian Nubia. The mudbrick walls mark the remains of a church; Shinnie, *Linant de Bellefonds*, 41.

gave him many presents, and exempted him from all taxes; in the common disgrace, he said, he was lucky. In the meanwhile, we reached Hannakab, place of his residence, where he wanted to land. He expressed clear signs of friendship and when he was on the banks he assured us that we would see him very soon in Sennar, where he was called by Isma'il to command a battalion.

At Hannakab, the banks of the Nile are very high and there is no other place where the *saqya*s are so numerous: when we passed, only a few of these machines were restored. We stopped shortly after sunset and during the night we suffered an impetuous whirlwind, which luckily did not last long.

On the 5th, the wind was favorable and we could make sail, saving the trouble of searching for men. In one hour we reached al-Zuma in front of Abu Rannat Island, beyond which we met another island called Tedukol, a small, flat, and well-cultivated island. At Tulbenab, another island two hours farther on from the latter, a woman rules according to old traditions: this oddity prompted us to stop and visit the lady who was reigning at the time. She was in her forties and proved to be very amiable and hospitable toward us, offering us with goodwill all the help that was in her hands. Her husband had recently died and had not enjoyed any sort of authority on the island. After half an hour, we embarked again, but soon after passing this island the wind ceased completely and we could not reach Tangasi before two in the afternoon. This is the capital of the district of Merowe, ancient seat of *malak* Sha'us. Sulayman Kashif was in charge, by order of the pasha, with a large detachment of Egyptian soldiers in defense of the newly established military depots. He was getting ready to set off to Dongola and we only had time to greet him: we found him quite unhappy about his task, assuring us that he would have preferred to command animals rather than this race of men, to whom severity and kindness were the same thing.[318] There is no other place among those we visited where women prostitute themselves more brazenly: they used to come spontaneously to our boat and offer their good graces in exchange for some wheat or ornaments of colored glass. They would even lower their sights to please our crew, had we not immediately left the village to set ourselves free from their importunity and spend the night two miles distant.

On the 6th, we made sail early in the morning with a propitious northeast wind and shortly after we met the ruins of a small village, known under the name of Detti, not far from which, in a fortified place[319] facing Kandif Island, there are the houses of Malak Sha'us. In the most distinguished of these there still lived his women. Around nine, we reached Jebel Barkal, or, better, the closest spot to it from the Nile, since this mountain is three miles distant on the right bank of the river. Without stopping, we proceeded to Bellel, where there is a high cataract with a very strong current, which cannot be overcome without

---

318 Probably the same Sulayman Kashif met in 1829 by Lord Prudhoe as governor of Sennar. The attitude is exactly the same: "The Cachief said it was only a country for desperate men," Algernon Percy (Baron Prudhoe, Duke of Northumberland), "Extracts from Private Memoranda Kept by Lord Prudhoe on a Journey from Cairo to Sennar, in 1829, Describing the Peninsula of Sennar," *Journal of the Royal Geographical Society of London* 5 (1835): 51.
319 Merowe East.

risk and a large number of men, as the Egyptian army did before us. Since we lacked the means to pass it and, anyway, we intended to stay in the area in order to record the many and interesting ruins, we doubled back to the small village of Nuri and dismissed our boat, intending to continue our journey by land. Once we finished these operations, we headed toward Jebel Barkal, also called by the natives Jebel Dahab[320] or 'Mountain of Gold,' in the belief that it must hide treasures. It is possible that some gold pieces were found among the ruins and thus originated this belief. Anyway, the Shaiqiya were so jealous of these alleged treasures that, before being suppressed by the Egyptians, they never tolerated a foreigner to approach the ruins, not even at a distance.

To the northeast of this mountain there are some pyramids: the farthest are also the better preserved, and they are eight in number.[321] Plate 61, no. 1. The first pyramid, marked (a), has a circumference of thirty-four feet and three inches, and thirty-six steps from the base to the top; it does not have a shrine[o] and is much ruined. The second (b)[322] is thirty-eight square feet and has forty steps; it is surmounted by a globe and is well preserved, except for the shrine, which is partly ruined. The third (c)[323] is thirty-four square feet and has forty-one steps: above the entrance door, almost at the top of the pyramid, there is a square opening, but we could not guess its use. No. 1 of plate 62 is the plan of this pyramid and its shrine, and no. 2 is a sketch of its elevation. No. 1 of plate 63 represents a relief on the left wall of the shrine and no. 1 of Plate 64 is the drawing of the back wall, in front of the entrance door.

The fifth pyramid (e)[324] is thirty-eight square feet and has seventy-nine steps, but is in large part ruined: the shrine is, however, perfectly preserved. No. 2 of plate 64 is a drawing of the inner part of it leading to the pyramid. No. 1 of plate 65 and no. 5 of Plate 66 are bas-reliefs carved on the side wall of the same.

The sixth pyramid (f)[325] is almost completely ruined, but its shrine is intact and it retains all its colors. No. 2 of plate 63 is a colored bas-relief existing on the left wall of this shrine, well-finished work, but not of the good Egyptian style. The ceiling is painted with vine motifs, with hanging grapes still retaining vivid colors. Digging inside this shrine, we found a fragment of statue representing three seated figures, almost completely corroded.

The other two pyramids (g, h)[326] are completely destroyed and what is left is just enough to recognize the foundations.

---

320 Arabic دهب (dahab), 'gold.'
321 The so-called North Group; Porter and Moss, *Topographical Bibliography* 7:204–207.
322 Pyramid No. 2, belonging to an unidentified king; Porter and Moss, *Topographical Bibliography* 7:205.
323 Pyramid No. 3, built for an unidentified queen; Porter and Moss, *Topographical Bibliography* 7:205.
324 Pyramid No. 5, built for an unidentified prince; Porter and Moss, *Topographical Bibliography* 7:206. The fourth pyramid (d) is not mentioned.
325 Pyramid No. 6, built for Queen Nawdamak; Porter and Moss, *Topographical Bibliography* 7:208.
326 Pyramid No. 7 (unidentified king) or No. 8 (unidentified queen); Porter and Moss, *Topographical Bibliography* 7:207.

Many of these monuments have at the four edges a thin square frame, which in some becomes round at two-thirds of the height; this ornament is in some cases also observed around the base, but here it is always square.

The pyramids to the southeast of the mountain are many more. In the first (a), which was almost completely ruined, we found a few inches under the ground a cavity large enough to house a body, where in fact we found many very white bones.

The second (b) is almost nonexistent, being at that time already reduced to a pile of stones.

The third (c) is twenty feet and six inches square at the base and twenty-six steps, without shrine. The frame of this pyramid does not continue to the top as in the other pyramids, but stops at three-quarters of its height. See plate 62, no. 3.

The fourth (d),[327] which seems to have been the main one, was ninety-four square feet at the base, which is measurable on one of the sides. This is still intact from the base up to the seventeenth step: all the rest is lost.

All the other pyramids, which are eleven in number, are so degraded that only from the shape of their base can one judge that once they were pyramids.

The material used to build all these monuments is for the most part sandstone, cut in two-square-foot blocks, smoothed out to perfection only on the outer face and well laid with strong mortar.

From pyramid (e) of No. 1 to pyramid (c) of No. 2 there are 900 feet; from the latter to the bigger one, marked (d), there are 254 more feet, and from this point to the first rock-cut building I measured 1,497 feet. In this last stretch there are many Muslim tombs.

On the slopes of Jebel Barkal there are many rock-cut buildings: the plan of the first is no. 4 of plate 62, but both the hieroglyphs and the reliefs are entirely corroded by time.[328] From this first excavation to the second, which is much bigger and is marked no. 5 in the same plate, there are forty-seven feet:[329] the back of the walls of this temple used to be of a very bright blue and the bas-relief figures were also painted, but now are extremely damaged. On the inner sides of the door leading to the sanctuary, there are two carved gods, portrayed almost in the same attitude, surmounted by hieroglyphs looking the same on both sides: this makes me think that the the two figures represent one and the same god;[330] see plate 66, no. 1. The style of these sculptures is ancient and robust. The decoration of the Typhonium of this temple was carved in bas-relief on white background, but everything is now in very bad shape. From one of the pillars of this hall I drew a bas-relief representing Typhon;[331] see same plate, no. 2. In the second portico of this temple (plate 62, no. 5, letter

---

327 This should be Pyramid No. 11, built for an unidentified king; Porter and Moss, *Topographical Bibliography* 7:207.

328 Possibly the small rock temple of Amun B 200, erected by Taharqa; Porter and Moss, *Topographical Bibliography* 7:208.

329 The large rock temple of Mut B 300, called 'Typhonium' by early travelers because they identified the dwarf god Bes with Typhon. It was built by Taharqa on the site of a temple probably erected by Ramesses II; Porter and Moss, *Topographical Bibliography* 7:208–11.

330 Porter and Moss, *Topographical Bibliography* 7:211, (9)–(10): Onuris and Nefertem.

331 A Bes-pillar; Porter and Moss, *Topographical Bibliography* 7:211.

'e'), the rock-cut part ends and the free-standing begins: here there used to be six columns, three of them are still standing now. No. 3 of plate 66 is the drawing of one of the columns. In the first portico ('f') there are ten columns. The eight side-columns have three lines of hieroglyphs, the other two closer to the entrance of the propylaeum are in the shape of two Typhons facing each other, erected on a square base without hieroglyphs. This propylaeum was rather big and built with large stone blocks. In front of the same propylaeum there were four very large columns, which are now destroyed; only the base survives among the ruins.

Beyond this monument there were some grottoes cut in the mountain (plate 61, no. 3, letter 'c'), probably tombs, which are now completely empty and bear no sign of hieroglyphs or stelae. In the spot marked 'd' in the same plate and number there was a monument now destroyed: there are two pink granite lions still standing, a beautiful work.[332] The hieroglyphs carved on their base, or rather pedestal, are on plate 63, nos. 3, 4, and 5. Fragments of small columns also remain from this monument, while its ruins cover a considerable area up to the mountain. In the spot marked 'e' there are the remains of a wall built with large stones, but I could not judge the nature of the ruins surrounding this place. At a short distance, in the spots marked 'f' and 'g' on the same plate 61, there were two other monuments,[333] partly rock-cut and partly free-standing. The free-standing part was almost completely destroyed by the fall of an enormous granite block, which detached from the mountain and still dominated the ruins. The plans of these two monuments are on plate 67, nos. 1 and 2. The first was of beautiful style: in front of the propylaeum there were two orders of columns. Part of this propylaeum is completely destroyed, while in the other part, which is also poorly preserved, there is a bas-relief of a hero holding the hair of a large number of men—probably his enemies—similar to those depicted in the same conquered attitude in the temples of Abu Simbel and al-Maghara, while with his right hand he threatens them holding a sort of club.[334] Lying on the ground, there is a life-size black granite statue, representing a seated sphinx with lion head: the hieroglyphs carved on the back side of the chair are copied on plate 63, no. 8. In the inner rooms of this temple there are reliefs with priestesses and a large number of women differently decorated, most of which have a narrow collar of a beautiful blue. No. 4 of plate 66 is taken from one of these rooms; among many other things, the delicacy and the precision of the carving are particularly worthy of admiration.

The second temple (g) is in a far worse condition than the previous one, to the point that it was impossible for me to draw anything there.

---

332 Shinnie, *Linant de Bellefonds*, 49–50. The building, now destroyed, was B 1100; Porter and Moss, *Topographical Bibliography* 7:211–12. These are the lions of Amenhotep III originally from Soleb and then moved to Britain by Lord Prudhoe in 1835; British Museum, "Red granite lion of Amenhotep III," http://www.britishmuseum.org/research/collection_online/collection_object_details.aspx?objectId=117626&partId=1&searchText=granite+head+amenhotep+III&page=1

333 Possibly temple B 600 ('enthronement pavilion' on the site of a building erected by Thutmose IV) and B 700 (temple of Osiris–Dedwen); Porter and Moss, *Topographical Bibliography* 7:213–15. Cf. also a drawing by Linant published in Miles F. Laming Macadam, "Gleanings from the Bankes Mss.," *Journal of Egyptian Archaeology* 32 (1946): pl. X.

334 Porter and Moss, *Topographical Bibliography* 7:214.

The ruins 'h,' far from the mountain, are the remains of a temple in large part destroyed.[335] In the spot marked 'a' there is a pedestal: nos. 6 and 7 of plate 63 are the plan and the elevation of it. It bears a bas-relief with eleven prisoners, three of them kings; all of them are tied by the neck with a long rope, held at the two ends by two vultures. The two figures carved on the first step of the pedestal are also prisoners, whose broken bow can be seen at their feet; plate 65, nos. 2 and 3. It is possible that they used to slaughter victims on this pedestal or altar because, beside the reliefs related to sacrifices, I observed that its upper surface is dark red sandstone. The color does not seem to be natural and does not correspond to the color of all the many other sandstone blocks among the ruins, which are white. I assume that this diversity comes from the blood shed on it and absorbed by the stone. It is known that the ancient Egyptians used to cut off the hands or phalluses of their prisoners, a custom that can be clearly seen in many reliefs and especially in those of Madinat Habu. Given the above, it is possible that the pedestal that I am describing was used for this barbarous ceremony: the prisoners carved on it with a bandage in their hands, which possibly was used to cover their eyes at the moment the amputation was carried out, seem to validate my opinion.

The great temple (k)[336] was of considerable extent, but is now extremely damaged; see the plan at plate 67, no. 4. In the sanctuary (a) there is an altar of black and white granite of superb quality: the bas-reliefs on it are perfectly carved, like the best works of Thebes. Plate 68 shows the drawings of the four faces of this altar in their current condition: no. 1 shows the side facing the entrance; the two lateral sides are nos. 1 and 2 of plate 69.

In room 'b' there is a much damaged pedestal of the same kind of granite, probably destined to be the base for some statues, as a few little square holes on its surface seem to indicate.[337] Details are to be found on the same plate, nos. 3 and 4.

In the first portico there were two orders of columns, with a pedestal in the middle (c).

Of the many beautiful columns that once adorned this temple, only one is intact (d). Excavating at its base, we found the body of a black granite hawk, four feet high: a very fine product of craftsmanship, but unfortunately headless. We searched for the head, but we could not find it among the ruins.[338]

In the second portico there are still remains of bas-reliefs with men and horses. From the many fragments scattered on the ground, we found out that in three of the porticoes in this temple the decorative theme was warfare.

A hundred feet from the first propylon there is a pile of ruins, but it is impossible to distinguish to what kind of building they belonged; ninety-four feet further on there is a pedestal and 295 feet from it there is a column, all aligned with the right side of the propylon.

---

335 Perhaps temple B 800 (temple of Kashta or Piye, reconstructed by Aramatelqo) or B 900 (temple of Piye, reconstructed by Harsiotef); Porter and Moss, *Topographical Bibliography* 7:212–13.
336 Building B 500, the Great Temple of Amun, erected in the Eighteenth or Nineteenth Dynasty, bearing the names of Ramesses II, Piye, and Natakamani; Porter and Moss, *Topographical Bibliography* 7:215–21.
337 Perhaps relief (47), Porter and Moss, *Topographical Bibliography* 7:220.
338 The statue was part of a pair erected by Amenhotep III at Soleb and now split between Berlin and Boston museums; Porter and Moss, *Topographical Bibliography* 7:219 (34), (35). The statue seen by Ricci and Linant is in Berlin (inv. 1622) and represents Horus of Sopet.

In the spot marked 'o' (plate 61, no. 3) there are a large number of grottoes, where we found vases similar to those of Saqqara, used there to bury ibis mummies. In the spot 'p' there are the remains of many small columns lying on the ground. Finally, letter 'q' marks the remains of a vast colonnade and a fragment of lintel. The capitals of the columns—some of them still intact—were of perfect craftsmanship, but mixed style.

From the spot marked 'r' to the Nile, for a vast area in all directions, we walked among piles of bricks and pottery shards, a certain sign that here there used to be a vast city, now replaced by the *oshur* and *sant* trees, grown to a considerable height among the ruins. The English traveler Hanbury, who visited before us, thinks these could be the remains of famous Napata.[339]

The ruins of Nuri, half an hour away on the left bank of the Nile, are only pyramids: one of them is intact, seven are damaged, and twenty-one completely destroyed. They are of different sizes and all are built around the biggest, which can be seen at plate 70.

All these drawings kept us there until October 17th: that day we hired camels and guides at the village of Gerif, on the right bank of the Nile, and then spent the night at Kassinger.

On the 18th, we passed by Gerf al-Handil, we crossed Mount Kulgelli, and proceeded to Umm Mereikh, where we were welcomed by the natives with all demonstrations of the most unselfish hospitality, a rare thing among the Shaiqiya.

On the 19th, we met Uli Island and Saffi Island, both mountainous and populated. The village of Argub, which lies a little farther, is completely ruined and deserted: opposite it, on the left bank, there is Ghalia, a village, and between the two there is Tetami Island, which is beautiful and well cultivated. On a granite rock at a short distance we observed the remains of an enclosure, two hundred feet square, with the ruins of some houses in the middle. We then passed al-Haggar Island, Faras, and the village of Shababit, where we observed beautiful cultivations of *dukhn*. The inhabitants, thinking that we were soldiers, all fled and a poor old lady, who was left alone in the village, presented us with some fresh onions, which we had not seen for a while.

Some long and wide granite dikes, which from the banks of the Nile go deep into the desert, produce here a very singular effect. Proceeding across these rocks we reached Rasuff, homeland and seat of Omar Kashif, whose jurisdiction once extended to Aqaba Boni. His house is in the center of the village and is round, in the shape of a Chinese pavilion. Although made of straw, it is very elegant and built with such mastery that rain cannot leak in.

On the 20th, we observed on our way a cataract four feet high: this is the most considerable of all the kingdom of the Shaiqiya after the one at Bellel. The village of Boni, where we took some rest, is regularly built and the houses, all square, are made of straw painted in black, red, and yellow stripes, so well distributed as to produce a beautiful effect. Amri Island, at a little distance from the village, has some ruins, which look like the remains of a modern, unimportant fortress. In this place, the Nile is full of small islands, very close to

---

339 Hanbury visited shortly before Ricci and believed he had discovered the ruins of Meroe on this spot. This appears quite clearly in the correspondence between Salt and Bankes in the months after the discovery (D/BKL HJ 1/159). Ricci is here quoting the corrected opinion expressed by Hanbury in his 1822 publication, an opinion he had changed after Linant and Cailliaud discovered the real ruins of Meroe; Waddington and Hanbury, *Journal of a Visit*, 185.

each other. Its banks are so high that for some stretches they hide the view of the river, but all of a sudden they become low again, and the Nile appears larger and more majestic, with the plain behind it. In the evening we reached Geni.

On the 21st, after two hours of march, we lost sight of the beautiful and pleasant plain, and the landscape was replaced by a chain of granite mountains, the curved lines of which are followed by the Nile. This chain is known under the name of Aqaba Boni: we began to climb it at eight and we crossed it in three hours. It was not because of its height that it took us all that time, but rather for the difficulties in climbing it. We then spent the hottest hours at the village of Boni and from three to six in the afternoon we crossed a second mountain called Salmiya. We finally spent the night in the village that bears the same name, built on its slopes.

On the 22nd, we crossed Mount Us and at ten we were at the border between the Shaiqiya and the Kingdom of Berber, where the rule of Abdin Bey ends.

Until the Shaiqiya were ruled by their own kings, they were the plague of caravans, which were forced to enter the desert in order to avoid their attacks. In this way, they exposed themselves to the most cruel discomforts, and especially hunger and thirst. It was not uncommon that a caravan would lose some men and many camels during this journey. The savagery of these people was such that when there was no occasion to exert it against foreigners, they turned their weapons against each other, more out of pure bloodthirstiness than for any plausible reason of mutual discontent. Attacked, as I mentioned, in their refuges by the Mamluks, whom they could resist, it was the fate of the Egyptian army to subdue them. If, as is presumable, force and law will civilize them a bit and quench this ardent thirst for blood of theirs, their descendants will bless this adventurous catastrophe, by which at the price of their own blood and freedom they will find themselves regenerated. With this philanthropic project in mind, the pasha already called part of the inhabitants of Dongola to settle in this territory in order to repopulate it with a better race.

The country of the Shaiqiya is in part mountainous and the air is good and salubrious. Its inhabitants are healthy, robust, and good-looking. In general, they are very thin and tall, more than the average. Their color is not uniform because some of them are completely black and some others are of a reddish color, tending to black. This variety comes from mixing with other peoples. Their facial features are completely European and they have not got any characteristic of the black race. Women are comely and devoted to prostitution: they wear glass ornaments, but are very sophisticated in the way they style their hair, which they divide in small braids and wrap around the head in many different ways to the point that in some there is a perfect resemblance to ancient Egyptian wigs. Men also divide their hair in braids, but then leave them loose on their shoulders. Their houses are made of straw because it is more resistant to the rain than mud. In any case, they do not know how to fabricate bricks. These people skillfully maneuver their horses and have a breed of greyhound smaller than ours, which they use to hunt gazelles.

After we crossed the borders of the Shaiqiya, the first district of Berber is Wadi Hamra, administered by a *kashif* dependent from the capital. As soon as we entered the district, the caravan was forced to head toward the mountains because there is no road large enough on the banks of the Nile. As for me, I wanted to follow on foot. The first thing I saw was an enclosure with a perimeter of two hundred meters, built on a granite rock. In the wall overlooking the desert there were many loopholes, similar to those in our fortresses. In the middle of the fence there was an isolated rock and a brick tower on it. There are no traces of houses and the only thing I could see were many pottery shards scattered on the ground. It is certain that this station was in the past very strong. Here the mountains end, the sandy desert reappears, and at the village of Shirri, which is the first of the district, the Nile broadens; its waters flow more slowly and I did not hear any more the dull noise, similar to thunder, produced by the cataracts in the aforementioned mountains.

While I was hunting for birds and medicinal herbs along the banks of the river, something unusual, which moved for a moment at the top of a high and thick tree, drew my attention. I stared and I saw a dark tangle, like the nest of a large bird of prey. I wanted to make sure of its nature, so I walked around the tree: its immobility persuaded me I was right. I wanted to examine it closely, so I placed a bullet in my rifle to try to make it fall, but while I was aiming, I heard: "Fi ardak, ya sidi!" ('Master, have mercy!'). At the same time I saw the tangle breaking up and a young woman appeared. I invited her to come down: she dropped the cloth that she had wrapped herself in and she descended from the branches of the tree despite its many thorns. With incredible agility she jumped down. I thanked the Heavens that forbade I should commit an involuntary murder and, persuaded that the poor creature was deadly scared, I reassured her: she kissed me on my forehead, in a sign of respect as it is general custom among the Arabs, and she put herself under my protection. She was a girl thirteen to fourteen years old, good-looking, made even more charming by the odd situation she was in. I asked her why she hid in the tree and she replied that as soon as she saw me from afar, she sought refuge to protect herself from any possible offense, thinking I was an Egyptian soldier. I asked her to point me the way back to my caravan and she fulfilled my request without fear, guiding me along a small path. In a short time we reached my companions; I presented her with a blue glass necklace and a piaster, and then bid her goodbye. After a short rest under the shade of some wild palms, at a certain distance from the Nile, we set off again and reached in the evening Abu Rumayla, a small village close to a cataract. Here we spent the night.

Our camel drivers were engaged to serve us until the borders of the Shaiqiya, where we hoped to replace them, but since we could not find new camels on entering the Kingdom of Berber, because a battalion had requisitioned them all, we could not dismiss them and we forced them to go on. This set them in a bad mood and they became restless: we had to constantly keep an eye on them and at the same time be generous with promises. Nevertheless, during the night the *kabir*, or chief driver, fled. I then remembered the discomforts I suffered during my first Nubian trip with Mr. Bankes, when all the camel drivers fled.[340] We then became very wary, and in order to prevent the others from following the example of their chief we finally reached an agreement that they would serve us for two more days.

---

340 Cf. *Travel to Nubia*, 179.

On the 23rd, at a short distance from the village of al-Kab, we met the ruins of two forts; one of these, of modern construction, was the residence of a *kashif*. The other one, older, is surrounded by a double wall, twelve feet wide, with strong buttresses at its four corners. The many sand hills that in this spot interrupt the banks of the Nile forced us to go half a league deep into the desert in order to continue our journey more comfortably. At sunset we found ourselves not far from the river, without knowing where to spend the night or refresh our camels. The noise of barking dogs, which we heard toward the Nile late in the evening, made us head in that direction in the hope of finding a house, but one hour later, when we reached the banks of the river, we realized that houses and *saqya*s were on the opposite side. We then had to unload the hungry camels and watch them all night, ignoring the complaints and imprecations of the guides, who were protesting against proceeding any further.

On the 24th, after long discussions, we convinced them to set off. This state of acute discontent could not last long and we would have found ourselves, maybe the very same day, in particularly serious distress if a group of empty boats had not appeared shortly afterward by chance. They were going up the Nile after taking to Abu Rumayla a caravan of slaves from Sennar and on their way to Cairo to be drilled as soldiers there. We called one of these boats to the shore in order to bargain and the *rais* approached promptly. We easily agreed that he would take us to Berber, but he did not want to embark us on the spot in order to allow all the other boats to pass before him. We agreed that we would proceed by land to the village of Kulli al-Kabir,[341] on the border between Wadi Hamra and Wadi al-Mugrat, where the *rais* wanted to spend the night in order to set off the day after, early in the morning. We trusted his promise and continued our journey until, in three hours, we reached the place agreed. The boat appeared an hour later, the *rais* having delayed the departure in order to avoid sharing part of his profit with a Maghrebi officer[342] who was in charge of the inspection of all boats and who was on board of one of them. We dismissed the camel drivers, rightly restless, and we boarded our boat, spending the night on it.

On the 25th, taking advantage of the favorable wind that had been blowing since the morning, we made sail. At around seven, the wind ceased and we were forced to stop to search for men. In that spot, the right bank of the Nile is not suited to travel with the help of the ropes because it is frequently interrupted by sand hills, so we had to move to the left bank, which is flat. At midday, we encountered Aar Island, small and deserted, and at four we reached the village of Askut, where the commander in charge of the district lives. Here we slept.

On the 26th, we set off with sixteen men at the rope and this way we passed many small cataracts amid a strong current: at this point the Nile is very narrow and full of rocks. We

---

341 Perhaps Kihayli.
342 A *shawish*, 'sergeant,' in the service of the pasha. "It turned out that this man was from Zante and under British protection, and that he had long time served on British vessels; he showed me his passport and we found that he had been on the same boat with the doctor," Shinnie, *Linant de Bellefonds*, 63. We have no information on other travels made by Ricci by ship, while he states that the ship that took him to Egypt was flying the Egyptian flag.

passed by Mount Murum,[343] which overlooks the Nile, and then moved back to the right bank of the river, which here becomes level and low again. The cultivated land extends deep into the desert and is subjected to inundations. The first village we met in this area is Angebal, then the small island of Tanta follows, to the north of which there are the ruins of a modern fortress. Further on there is another small village of few houses, where we were forced to stop because the men at the rope were exhausted. Some of them even abandoned us on the way.

On the 27th at nine, we crossed a cataract three feet high. A large rope pulled by fifteen men broke all of a sudden: all the men fell and the boat, left to its fate, moved back with violence and hit the rocks a couple of times: we used long canes to take it back to the bank. To avoid the rope breaking again, we used two and this way we passed the cataract. Around midday we encountered another and it took us two hours to pass it. At three we stopped at the village of Zaraf Mugrat to caulk the boat, which because of the hits was leaking in many parts. We continued our journey and before reaching the small village of al-Shillal in order to spend the night, we met two other cataracts, smaller than the previous ones and easy to cross.

On the 28th, we had to go three miles deep into the desert to find fresh men. When, around midday, we gathered fourteen, we set off again. We passed a first cataract near Kendi Island and then we met a second, three feet and half high. It is called Absabat: here, some of the boats transporting the Egyptian army had sunk. We passed it easily and we reached Serandi and then the large island of Mugrat, which has many villages. From this point it took us seven more days to arrive at Berber, capital of the kingdom of the same name. During this stretch of time we visited the islands of Mugrat, Bedi, Karmel, Argat, and many others, all more or less populated. Karmel was the residence of Mahmud Kashif, commander of the Kingdom of Rabatab, which extends from the borders of the Shaiqiya to the village of Muse, on Argat Island: from here it takes three days of forced dromedary march to reach the Red Sea.

The Kingdom of Rabatab, which is today part of Berber, was in the past ruled by a *malak*, who had his residence at Bezem, then considered the capital of the kingdom. This is divided into three districts, which are Dar al-Hamra, Mugrat, and Dar al-Egli. In the first there are forty islands, in the second twenty, and in the third sixty. The description of each and every one would be too monotonous. All this territory is inhabited in large part by the Arabs who invaded it during the caliphate of Omar. Since then, many other tribes have moved here, including the Ababda, who are easy to recognize by their long curly hair styled like a wig. The banks of the river we passed during these last days are for the most part shaded by a kind of thorny tree, with a large trunk and covered up to the top by a kind of ivy, which the Arabs feed to their camels. It is in fact very nutritious and fattening. There are also other kinds of plants, and besides the *sant* tree with yellow flowers, there are others which blossom in red; these are very fragrant and host large numbers of hummingbirds, which feed on their flowers. The quantity of these small birds is impressive. There are also other birds with

---

343   Or Hurum.

beautiful and colorful feathers and which sing pleasantly. Two other *sant* tree varieties grow along Mugrat Island: one carries leaves similar to the *Mimosa nilotica* and produces a fruit like our pomegranate, the peel of which is used by the natives to tan leather. The second variety produces a flower similar to the European mignonette. Its very nice fragrance can be perceived at a distance.

The impatience of the *rais* of our boat, who was in a hurry to proceed farther to al-Demer after leaving us at Berber, prevented us from measuring Mugrat Island, so we could not ascertain whether it is longer than Argo Island; certainly it is much wider. Mugrat has a semicircular shape and when the boat reaches half of its extension, where the Nile is wider and deeper, it offers the perspective of an amphitheater: the multitude of villages makes it even more interesting and picturesque.

On Hadadia Island, the inhabitants wear a cap of palm leaves of the same shape and size of those that can be seen on the heads of some prisoners carved on the walls of the temple of Abu Simbel: these are doubtless descendants of the ancient populations subjugated and dispersed by the Egyptian pharaohs. I am confirmed in this idea by the words of an Arab who told me, while I was examining his hat, that in Hadadia no foreign tribe had ever settled.

The skin color of the inhabitants of these various districts is like dark copper, their height is more than the average, and their bodies are handsome and well proportioned: there are no overweight people and their agility is surprising. They rub their entire body two or three times a day with castor oil and mutton fat. This helps maintain the elasticity of their muscles: they can jump from a considerable height, land with great stability, and run quickly without stopping. Their women, who can compete in beauty with those of the Shaiqiya, are also very genteel and devoted to prostitution.

During the last days we traveled sometimes sailing and sometimes with the help of ropes and canes. In fact, we met many cataracts, some of them very dangerous. Thanks to the strict orders of Isma'il Pasha, all the villagers came voluntarily to work at the boat, with the exception of the people of Abu Hamad, absolutely savage, and whom the Egyptian army could not subjugate because at its passing they had all fled to the mountains. In fact, we too found the village deserted. Their neighbors told us that these savages are Ga'alin: they descend from the first Arabs who abandoned paganism to accept the Muhammadan religion preached by the Prophet. For this reason, they call themselves nobles of the Banu Quraysh tribe, which is the tribe of Muhammad himself. There is not a more fanatic people than they, nor a more fierce enemy of Christianity. In this place there is plenty of a kind of skylark, which in very large groups alight on the seeds. For this reason they are feared as much as the grasshoppers: if it were not for the scarecrows and the cries they use to chase them away, they would cause considerable damage to crops. Even though Mr. Cailliaud in his travel marks only five large cataracts, all the passages I have described here should be considered as many small cataracts, which can be easily crossed without the ropes when the waters are high.

The closer we got to Berber, the more different was the way of building houses: most were built of Nile mud mixed with finely minced straw. When dried in the sun, the mud becomes very solid. Instead of a roof, they have a terrace with parapets made in the same fashion and with a drainage system. I examined how they build the terraces because I could not persuade myself that they could effectively shield the house from moisture. Tree branches, especially *sant* tree, are arranged crosswise on the walls of the house. On top of them they place some more in the opposite direction, forming a sort of mesh with very small intervals between the branches. The empty spaces are filled with packs of straw, so that the surface is leveled up. The whole surface of the roof also leans toward one side. Then they add very thin branches and level the surface with Nile mud. On top of this they add a layer of cow dung, and, when all this is dried out, they cover it with a mixture of mud and straw and then raise the parapets all around. These houses have one room only, are quite low, and are square in shape. On the terrace, which can be reached by a ladder, the inhabitants leave milk to ferment. The huts for the cattle are beside the house and are made of straw only.

At Albell, a village not far from Berber, we saw for the first time the river-horse, also called hippopotamus. The enormous size of this amphibious creature is really frightening: its head is as big as three horse heads. It has short legs with five nails, except the hind legs which have only four. The jaw has many teeth. Four of them stick out two palms'-length; two of these are straight, while the other two are like boar fangs. It has a sort of white star on the front, which continues in a stripe of the same color down to the nostrils. This animal spends its day in water or on the islands, and comes out at night to eat in the cultivated fields. The damage it inflicts is enormous, because in order to feed itself it devastates the cultivation to the point that the inhabitants consider lost the crop of a field where a hippopotamus has passed only once. It sometimes happens that this animal attacks the boats passing on the Nile, especially during the mating season, when they double their ferocity. They fight each other with incredible fury. I gathered all this information from shaykh Mustafa, commander of the district, who also wanted to persuade me that hippopotamus meat is excellent. He added that the inhabitants prepare a large banquet whenever they manage to kill one.

On the morning of the 5th at ten, we entered Berber, capital of the eponymous kingdom. This is a very large city, built in the middle of a sandy plain on the east bank of the river, half an hour from the Nile. Almost all its houses are square, built with mud bricks and plastered on the outside with Nile mud. On the walls there are many handprints made as a decoration on the wet mud. Most of the houses have a large courtyard at the entrance, surrounded by a high protective wall. In it, ladders lead to the upper rooms, usually three: one serves the family, the second is for guests, and the third is used as a storage place for provisions and trade goods. The rooms are large and have one window only, generally overlooking the back. Houses have one floor only and a terrace on top, similar to the ones I already described. Doors are locked, as in Egypt, by the means of a wooden key. Roads are very wide but irregular because of the courtyards of the houses, which sometimes are longer than others. There are large squares and two *wakala*s, or slave barracks, for both genders. The surroundings of Berber are sterile and its population is not in proportion to the extent of the city: there are no more than 2,500 souls here. Isma'il Pasha appointed Ahmad Bey as governor. Before our arrival he had led the garrison against a horde of Bisharin scorching the territory of Berber.

The inhabitants of this kingdom differ little in color and shape from those of Rabatab and are, like them, healthy and robust. All their furniture consists of a few water pots and other measuring vases, some goatskins, and some mats fabricated locally from tastefully intertwined, different colored strips, which are highly regarded and sought after even in Cairo. They also have *angaribs*[344] made of cow skin, which from time to time they perfume with sandalwood and therefore have a nice fragrance: these are used as seats during the days and as beds at night. The richest wear a wide-sleeved shirt, which is the ordinary dress of the Arabs, and a sort of white vest with a red hem, down to the knee. The populace walks around almost naked, girding the waist with a piece of cloth and wearing another one on their head to protect themselves from the sun. Except for the wealthy, who buy leather shoes from Cairo, all the others adapt to their feet shapeless pieces of cow leather, tied with strips, and a sole made of palm-tree leaves to protect themselves from the hot sand. In general they all dye their eyebrows with kohl, which can be found in large quantities in the mountains toward the Red Sea. They habitually anoint their body with mutton fat, sometimes mixed with sesame, which has a very strong smell. The wealthy are more refined in this, using an ointment made of fat, musk, and sandalwood, and they use it especially when they visit their women.

Berber is full of street women, most being freed slaves lacking all means of subsistence. Some of them are employed in the preparation of *busa*, a fermented drink made of *dhura* and similar to beer: depending on the degree of fermentation, this drink bears the name of *busa* or that of *umm bulbul*, which means 'mother of the nightingale,' a name that probably refers to the cheerfulness and elation which it brings to whoever drinks it.

Berber is a trade center and its inhabitants prefer this occupation rather than agriculture, in which they engage just for their subsistence. They sow along the banks of the Nile and on the nearby islands, which they reach with the *ramus*. This work is exclusively done by the slaves, with every family owning a number in proportion to its wealth. The ordinary price of a young slave, capable of sustaining heavy labor, is forty thalers. There are two weekly markets which are attended by the inhabitants of the nearby region, coming with their asses loaded with *dhura*, *dukhn*, tobacco, onions, and other agricultural products. Bargaining is done through exchange rather than with money.

We stayed in Berber until 8 November;[345] then, having obtained from the bey's *kasnadar*[346] permission to use the same boat as far as al-Demer, we continued our journey. One hour after our departure we saw a battalion of Maghrebi soldiers camped on the west bank: here, the bed of the Nile is noticeably wider and on both sides it is flat and well cultivated. A little after Sulaymaniya,[347] we began to distinguish the waters of the Nile from those of the Atbara,

---

344 *Angarib*, "a low-lying wooden bed strung with cattle hide," Melissa Parker, "Rethinking Female Circumcision," *Africa: Journal of the International African Institute* 65, no. 4 (1995): 509.

345 There is no correspondence with Linant's diary, where the departure from Berber is marked under the date of 5 November and the arrival at al-Demer the same evening "two hours before sunset," Shinnie, *Linant de Bellefonds*, 72.

346 A title not different from agha.

347 Sulaymaniya is far north of Berber: Ricci must be mistaken and in fact Linant calls the place "Sallama"; Shinnie, *Linant de Bellefonds*, 72. There is a place called al-Salama twenty kilometers south of Berber.

which are clearer. At one in the afternoon we reached the confluence of the two rivers, which is thirteen to fourteen miles from Berber. The Atbara is not deep and its sources arise in the country of the Bisharin; its banks are so high that it has never happened that the river has flooded the nearby regions. A very thick palm-tree wood overshades the left bank, close to the Nile. In the river bed there are two huge *sant* trees, which during the rainy season, when the waters occupy the full river bed, must produce a beautiful effect. Hordes of Ga'alin, living near Berber and scattered in many places down to Sennar, also live by this river, but they do not move too far from the Nile so as not to risk being left without water, since during the summer the Atbara dries out. This river is the border between Berber and al-Demer, where we arrived at three in the afternoon.

Al-Demer, a city in the district of Shendi, is built on the plain at around one hour from the right bank of the Nile. It is far smaller than Berber, but the houses are better built and many are made of baked bricks and are two stories tall. Streets are narrow but regular. There is a nice mosque in the main city square, in the shadow of sycamore trees. Nearby there are many schools where children of both genders are taught to read the Quran. The population is for the most part made up of Arabs of the Mediaidin tribe and their main occupation is trade. The vast plains of al-Demer are well cultivated and there is a large number of *saqya*s.

In al-Demer there live many men called *yakaki*, believed to be very skilled in writing talismans. For this reason, the city is respected by all the neighboring peoples, including the Bisharin, who refrain from any kind of aggression toward its territory, believing that the *yakaki* with their magic can make them die of thirst when in the desert.

Al-Demer trades with Dongola and Shendi the most. There is a great market, called *suq*, which is held once a month, and other markets are held weekly, scheduled in order not to fall on the same days of those of Berber. Here the natives produce beautiful mats and cotton fabrics, which, along with cereals, make the most considerable branch of the city's trade.

Opposite al-Demer, on the other bank of the river, there is an abandoned village which they reach on floating tree trunks used as rafts, to sow the fertile land around it and to harvest in the appropriate season.

Since our boat had to remain available for the *kashif* at al-Demer, we were forced to stay and search for camels, but we could barely find three, enough for only one of us. This was because camels are very scarce here; the locals use donkeys almost exclusively, and the few camels around were requisitioned by the army. We then agreed that Mr. Linant would use the camels and I would stay and reach him at Shendi as soon as I could find camels. As a consequence of this agreement, the following morning we separated.[348]

Shortly after the departure of Mr. Linant, the commander of al-Demer came back from Atbara, a city thirty miles distant from the Nile, on the banks of the river to which it gave the name. I immediately went to visit him to see if he could help me in finding camels, but he told me that it would be a difficult task. He instead suggested I should wait for some boat not belonging to the government, the passage of which was not an infrequent sight at

---

348 Ricci fails to mention here his quarrel with Linant, the real cause of their separation. Compare Sammarco, *Alessandro Ricci*, 18–19; Bankes, *Narrative*, 382–83.

al-Demer. In fact, three days afterward one boat heading to Sennar passed by and I agreed with the *rais* on the price of my journey. I left al-Demer on 14th November after I spent a very cold night in the boat: this was the first time since I left Cairo that I used a blanket. We sailed for almost the whole day and we reached in the evening a village called Aliyab, which marks the border between the district of al-Demer and that of Shendi.

On the 15th, at a short distance from the east bank of the Nile, we met a mountain chain. Immediately beyond this there is the village of Iebayl, where the bed of the river begins to widen and gradually becomes so deep that its water looks like that of the sea for its beautiful blue color and the many waves. The rocking provoked by the waves caused a Greek who was on board, also heading to Sennar, to feel sick.

On our way I killed a white ibis. This bird, so famous for the veneration in which it was held by the ancient Egyptians, is as tall as a stork; when strutting to look around, it can be two feet tall. Its head and the long neck are almost bare and covered by a thin black fluff. The beak is also black and curved exactly as shown in hieroglyphs. Its feathers are pure white and have some black at the extremity of the wings and the tail, which is very short. The legs are black and very long, with four toes, all provided with strong claws, especially the rear ones. It lives in humid areas, but spends most of its time in the cultivated fields, where it hunts insects. This instinct is maybe the real reason for the cult the ancient Egyptians offered to it, doubtlessly grateful for the good it did to agriculture, freeing the seeds from parasites. I kept the skin of my ibis with me, but I lost it with many other objects during my hasty return from Sennar.

During this day we met some sandbanks, then we passed a village where there are salterns supplying the whole country from Berber to Sennar. Beyond it, we found ourselves in the middle of vast plains that extend on both sides of the Nile for an immense distance. During the right season, many wandering Arab tribes bring their flocks here, taking advantage of the generous pasture. In the evening we reached Shendi.

This city is the capital of the district by the same name and it is built to the east at about twenty minutes from the Nile. It is divided into different neighborhoods separated by public squares. There are around a thousand houses, all built with mud bricks. The internal architecture is quite similar to the houses of Berber; most of them also have a terrace on the roof. Streets are regular. Its population amounts to about five to six thousand souls and is composed of a mixture of Arabs of different tribes, especially Ga'alin. Many traders from Sennar, Kordofan, Darfur, and Dongola have settled here as well. Trade is considerable and consists mainly of tobacco, tamarind, sandalwood from the Indies, elephant tusks, Arabic gum, ostrich feathers, cotton cloths, sugar, white wool blankets with a red edging, all kinds of cereals, colored glass ornaments, Egyptian shoes, and many other things. The sale of all these products is made in specific public squares on Thursdays and Saturdays, which are the main market days. Not only do inhabitants from the region convene here, but also people from Berber and al-Demer. Besides these two markets, there are daily markets for provisions, such as *dhura* bread, a large quantity of onions, and sour and fresh milk brought by nearby Bedouin women. In a square far from the center, ox, cow, mutton, goat, and camel meat is sold, all at a very dear price except the camel, which is less sought after and therefore costs less. The trade of slaves is very extensive in Shendi, and traders, even the richest, readily yield one or more slaves at the price of a thaler per day, so that they still have a revenue stream in this infamous traffic. When they manage to sell a woman to white men, their price is lower because if the woman becomes pregnant, they sell the son as an Abyssinian mulatto, which is the most sought-after race because they are very meek and more able to bear fatigue than any other people.

Overlooking the main square, where the great market is held, there are many square rooms on the same alignment, built of mud and covered with mats. They are used to store trade goods for sale in order to protect them from the bad weather and the sunlight. On the other side there are the workshops of locksmiths, mat makers, and saddlers, the only crafts practiced in this city.

The land is cultivated by slaves, like at Berber. Cattle provide a large amount of meat and, through their excrement, an alternative to firewood, which is lacking here like in Egypt.

The dress of the natives is not much different from that used in the nearby districts, except that most wear large hats made of elegantly intertwined palm leaves. Men are generally armed with knives a palm long, whose blade is sharp on both sides. They carry the knife tied with a small rope on their forearm.

Here, too, there are brothels where *dhura* spirit is fabricated and sold, but if the morals are not better than at Berber, at least they are more discreet, and one does not see in public scenes of debauchery that usually surprise and disgust Europeans, accustomed as we are to the decency that reigns among us.

I heard many times about sewn women, called by the Arabs *hajat*, but I had never been able to gather sufficient and correct information on the matter. My short stay at Shendi gave me the chance to fully satisfy my curiosity, thanks to a slave merchant who had thirty sewn women in his *wakala*, all girls between ten and thirteen years old. He told me that the operation is performed on those wretches when they are three to four years old: they cut a small portion of the labia majora, thus producing an artificial wound, and then they sew them together, with the effect that, after they heal, there is but a very small hole for the drainage of urine. Sometimes, instead of the cut, they pass hot iron on the intimate parts of the child, along the extremity of the labia. This produces the same effect: when healing, the labia join together and they adhere so much that it looks as if they were never separated. When these girls are sold and their masters want to use them, it is necessary to cut above and below the narrow hole that was left open, and this is a very painful operation. This refinement of barbarity, devised by greed, has no other object than to sell these violated victims at a higher price, being in no doubt about their virginity.

The old *malak* of Shendi, like those of Berber, al-Demer, and other places where they used to rule despotically, were allowed to live in their palaces, but exert no power of any sort after Isma'il Pasha appointed beys as governors in every conquered region. They treat these old chiefs with distinction, in order to more easily consolidate Egyptian control.

On the evening of the 17th, Mr. Linant arrived at Shendi, but, since the same difficulties we had met at al-Demer were still in place, we mutually agreed to continue, he by land, and

I by water, especially since I agreed with the *rais* of my boat for transport to Sennar.[349] As a consequence, he left on the 18th and I made sail on the 19th at dawn and then spent the night at Ban Naqa, a city on the east bank of the Nile. Nearby there is an isolated mountain, the slopes of which end directly in the Nile, thus making the bed of the river significantly narrower. The inhabitants of Ban Naqa assured me that in the desert, at a day's-walk distance toward the south, there are large ruins and many pyramids.[350] I would have loved to go and make some drawings, but the *rais* of the boat refused to stay because he wanted to take advantage of the favorable wind. I decided to go and see them on my way back—something that did not happen, though.

On the 20th, early in the morning, we made sail, but the wind ceased all of a sudden and we barely reached the village of al-Quz, on the border of the district of Shendi with Halfaya. This is marked by a large rock directly on the bank, called by the Arabs Hagar al-Asad, 'rock of the lion,' because of its shape, somehow recalling this animal. The small stretch of river we sailed during the day is scattered with many islands, all flat, populous, and very close to one another.

On the 21st, after two hours' sailing, the wind ceased again and we stopped by a small island, where I observed with admiration an immense sycamore tree whose empty trunk could comfortably host twenty people. It is divided into eight branches of extraordinary size, extending fifteen feet from the trunk in the shape of a star. The resulting shadow on the ground has a circumference of more than a hundred feet. The joint of the eight branches in the middle of the trunk produces a sort of platform, where the inhabitants of the island lie, up to thirty people at a time, to get some fresh air during the hottest hours of the day. Who could reckon the age of such a huge tree? A light gust of wind having risen shortly afterward, we tried to continue, but it did not last long and we were forced again to land alongside Marnat Island. The place is covered by a thick forest and there is a large quantity of guinea fowls: I killed a couple and their excellent meat was an appreciated solace for my stomach, to which such delicate foods were by then a rarity.

On this island I also saw a two-foot-long reptile, called by the Arabs *waran*, which is the true lizard of the Nile. Its shape is similar to the crocodile, from which it differs in the movement of the jaws and in the color of the scales, which are of a variegated green and yellow, very bright, especially when hit by the sun's rays.

Few families live on this small, pleasant island: their huts are made of Nile mud and covered with a dome of *dhura* straw. Each family possesses four or five huts, all adjacent to each other, connected inside by small doors. As soon as the inhabitants saw the boat approaching, they came offering bread and fresh milk. I went deep inside the island with them and when I reached their village I found some of them suffering from intermittent fevers, a common sickness in these places during the autumn. I felt for them and I told

---

349 Linant states that he met Ricci again at Shendi under two different dates: 13 November in the Paris version of his diary (Sammarco, *Alessandro Ricci*, 13) and 11 November in the Kingston Lacy version (Shinnie, *Linant de Bellefonds*, 77). The date of his arrival according to Ricci is 17 November. The meeting is cold and the two travelers are not able to settle their dispute.
350 The Meroitic sites of Musawwarat and Naqa, later visited and documented by Linant.

them I was a physician. I took on board with me a venerable old man and gave him a good quantity of my cinchona, giving him instructions on how to take it. The man came back shortly after, accompanied by two others and a woman, and tried to persuade me by all means to stay on the island, promising to make me their chief and give me their daughters as spouses. This peculiar proposal was offered with such insistence and sincerity that I could only refuse under the promise that I would stay with them after coming back from Sennar. This is what the survival instinct can do to men: the mere hope in the success of my remedy was enough for them to choose me as their chief.

On the 22nd, at a short distance from Marnat, we met two other parallel islands, which divide the Nile into three branches: we preferred to sail in the middle, wider and deeper than the two others. Beyond these islands the mountain chain of Qerri begins, running from east to west deep into the desert. The Nile flows between these mountains and it is forced to follow their windings; sometimes it even seems to disappear. This is possibly the origin of the belief, held in antiquity, that the Nile passed through a mountain. This mountain chain is made of reddish limestone and from the middle to the top is completely devoid of vegetation. The stream is very strong among these rocks and the river bed is so narrow that from bank to bank there is but a gunshot. Here, too, there are huts and a few trees on the slopes of the mountains, but we did not see anybody. After two hours' sailing, the Nile gradually becomes wider; there are some islands, mostly flat and occupied by very thick *sant* forests. Finally, there are two isolated mountains, one opposite the other on the two banks of the Nile, beyond which the stream is less impetuous, the mountain chain ends, and the Nile bed becomes extraordinarily wide: both banks are very low and the horrid and steep rocks are substituted by immense plains. In the evening we stopped at Gimaab. This village is not far from Qerri, a city built on a small hill, whence in seven days one can reach Korti, crossing the Bayuda desert, where the Kababish,[351] fierce and bloody men, live.

On the 23rd, we observed six hippopotamuses enjoying the sun on a flat isolated rock protruding into the Nile from the west side. As soon as our boat appeared they jumped into the Nile, making a scary roar. We sailed along the coast of a woody island and in the evening we reached Halfaya. This city is not far from the east bank of the Nile and much smaller than Shendi. Here, too, the houses are built of mud bricks and are one story high with a roof terrace. The customs are the same as at Shendi and the same mix of Arabic races makes up its population. We delayed our departure to take advantage of the market on the following day and buy provisions: as for me, I had to pay thirty-five piasters for a pair of shoes that in Cairo I would have paid only three piasters for.

Among the Egyptians in the garrison of Halfaya there were two Italians who were serving under Ibrahim Pasha. They assured me that the previous day an Arab with dispatches

---

351 "The Kababish, the largest and wealthiest of the camel-owning tribes, are mainly nomadic, and the country inhabited by them extends from the Sahara in the north to Kordofan in the south, from the Darfur border in the west, to the Wadi Muqaddam in the east," Shinnie, *Linant de Bellefonds*, 103.

for the army covered the distance between Cairo and Halfaya with a very fast dromedary in only twenty-three days. This city completely lacks wells and the inhabitants have to get water from the Nile.

On the 24th, at around eleven in the morning, we left Halfaya and shortly after we reached the confluence of the Nile with the White River (Bahr al-Abyad), so called for the clear color of its water, to which the inhabitants attribute medical properties. Its stream flows southwest to northeast until it connects with the Blue River, then it goes north. All the land between the White River and the Blue River is called Sennar Island, even though it is actually a peninsula. With the gift of a bottle of spirit, I obtained the agreement of the *rais* that the boat would enter the White River for one hour; I wanted to see its banks. During this time I observed two dried torrents. Presumably they get filled during the rainy season and discharge into the river. Some banks of sand were occupied by crocodiles and the country seemed an impenetrable forest. Two men, who appeared on the west bank and whom I questioned, assured me that the forests are populated by lions, tigers, panthers, elephants, and other wild animals to the point that nobody ever dared to penetrate inside. After this very short exploration of the White Nile, we went back and entered again the Blue River. We stopped beyond a small village on the east bank, next to a *sant* forest, in order to spend the night. Here I took advantage of the remaining light of the day to land and enter the woods through a small path that I found by chance. A few minutes were enough to cross the forest in all its width: on this bank the trees do not extend far from the banks. On the other side, I found a well-cultivated plain, with different trees scattered here and there and, at a short distance, some villages, all on the same line.

On the 25th, we passed three villages in a row, all built on hills overlooking the Nile and made up of a few round straw huts with an incredibly low door. We stopped at the last of these villages and the inhabitants came to the boat, inviting us to spend the night in their huts. The kindness of their invitation persuaded me to accept and, following two of them, I entered the largest hut, where my hosts immediately roasted some mutton fat on embers, which with *dhura* bread and milk formed our dinner. I asked them why they do not eat lean meat and they answered that it is their custom to feed it to the dogs looking after their cattle. After this frugal meal, a young female of the family took a lyre, similar to the one I have already described, and started to sing in very corrupted Arabic a love song, while three girls, dressed only with a skirt similar to the one in use at Elephantine, represented the subject of the song with their gestures and movements. When this entertainment was over, I lay on my *angarib*, as did my hosts, falling into a quiet sleep. At dawn, I greeted them and left some trinkets for the women of the family, then I went back to the boat and we immediately made sail.

The wind abandoned us shortly afterward and we were forced to take some men for rope service. The slowness of the journey invited me to follow the boat by land, walking now along the bank, now at a certain distance in order to avoid the thorny bushes that occupy it. Huge flocks of waterfowl covered the Nile, while other kinds of birds were flying over the trees. Here, for the first time since I left Cairo, I saw a monkey. The agility of this animal is really surprising: it can jump from tree to tree, even over large distances, and then hang from the branches by its tail. It seems they very much enjoy this position. The most common trees are of different species: the *sant* trees, which are usually very tall and widely branching, are here small and do not exceed a height of four arms; their leaves are small, too, and the thorns very pointy, attached to the branches with a round base, in the shape of a pear. There is also the so-called *adele* tree, similar to the doum, but much higher and with larger leaves. It produces its fruits in bunches, like grapes, but as large as an apple, green at the beginning and then red when ripe. There are also tamarinds, whose young branches have a delicious sour taste. Finally, there are here and there some wild palms, which do not produce any fruit, and other plants. On this day we did not meet any village and we stopped in the evening alongside the bank, choosing a place without forest, to avoid being visited during the night by wild animals.

On the 27th, we resumed our journey and after four hours' sailing, the Nile moved toward the northeast. Its stream increased rapidly to the point that it was necessary to use canes to direct the boat and overcome the current. This goes back to normal when the river resumes its original direction. In the evening we reached Arbaji,[352] a large city once ruled by a *malak* depending from Sennar and now the residence of an agha with an Egyptian garrison.

On the 28th, a little beyond Arbaji, we found the bed of the Nile considerably narrower and very shallow. It was some days since we had seen *saqya*s along the banks and the nearby land was not cultivated because of the forest and the large number of wild animals, so that the country on both sides of the Nile was completely deserted. We reached a small village at around three in the afternoon and we had a stop: among the few huts there was one distinguished by means of three ostrich eggs strung on a stick on top of it: it belonged to the chief. I went toward the hut and I was received very warmly. The house was divided into two rooms and in one of them I found a young lady lying on an *angarib*, who the *malak* told me was his wife. She was attacked by severe ophthalmia and I assured the man that by using a medicine I would leave him, she would quickly recover. I went back to the boat and made a preparation of zinc and liquid laudanum, a remedy that in similar cases I found very effective. I then went back to the chief and gave him the medicine: I cannot express how grateful the man was. Since he had noticed that I was looking with curiosity at a lyre and a horse harness, he absolutely wanted to give them to me and without uttering an extra word he put the saddle on his shoulders, grabbed the lyre with his hand, and moved toward the boat, where I followed him. At that moment a caravan of traders was passing by, heading toward Sennar; the men wore hats of palm leaves woven with much elegance.

On the 29th, we continued toward Sennar, and on the 30th, two hours after midday, we passed this city without stopping, heading to Ibrahim Pasha's camp, which we were told was two hours farther to the south. Favored by the wind, we reached it at sunset.

---

352 Ricci digests here many days of navigation (24–29 November) in a few topographical indications: the distance between Halfaya and Sennar is in fact around 380 kilometers. The place is marked under the name of Harbagi (Arbaji) in the map of Lord Prudhoe, between Khartoum and Sennar; Percy, "Extracts," [38b].

When he was informed of my arrival, the pasha called me to his tent, whence four European doctors were coming out after he had consulted them on the sickness he had been suffering for a month. Isma'il Pasha, his brother, was in his company and both of them forced me to take a seat and offered me coffee, a thing that Turks do toward people of distinction and friends who enjoy great confidence. "Your arrival," Ibrahim told me, "pleases me for two reasons: the first, because I am sick, and then because my first physician, Mr. Scotto, whom you know very well, is dying, victim of the abuse of spirits. The other doctors in the camp, I have no doubt they are experts, but I do not trust them. Let's then go together to visit my chief physician and see if there is any hope we can save him from death. Otherwise, knowing how much Mr. Salt, English consul, esteems you, I propose that you take the place of Mr. Scotto, becoming my chief physician." After he said that, he steadfastly stood up and went toward the tent of the sick man, where I followed. We found Scotto in agony and at around three in the following morning he passed away. The doctors told me that his sickness was a nervous fever so violent that on the second day he lost the ability to speak and could not get better with any of the usual remedies of the art. It lasted for five days and the day before my arrival he had lost all his strength.[353] As he entered the tent, Ibrahim called to the dying man in a loud voice, but when he saw the man did not give any sign of life, he immediately went out.

The following morning, he made me call on him and mourned the departure of Mr. Scotto, who had served him for fourteen years. Then he told me, "Here I am in your hands." During the night, I thought a lot about the proposition of the pasha and, since I was not willing to give up my travels, I had decided not to accept it. I tried under many pretexts to disengage myself, assuring him that I would assist and cure him until he was perfectly healed. After that, I would ask him to let me continue my travels. "Well," he said, "so let it be," and he wanted to immediately give me details of his sickness, which I discuss in a separate memoir.[354]

As a Christian, I had it in my heart to provide a decent burial for the deceased chief physician, as far as it was possible among Turks, and taking advantage of my familiarity with the pasha, I asked his permission, and obtained it. I gathered all the Christians of the camp and went with them to the tent of the deceased: I had him washed, dressed, and placed on a litter carried by four Copts. We then left the camp. The procession was headed by the physicians of the army and many other Copts, who in a low voice and in their language

---

353   If Scotto was an older man, paralysis could be simply caused by a stroke. According to Cailliaud, he died victim of an "inflammatory fever," as did dozens of people during those days in the camp of Ibrahim Pasha: "Mr. Ricci, Italian, has arrived with Ibrahim Pasha. He was charged with the task of drawing the sculptures of the ancient monuments for Mr. Bankes, English traveler. Mr. Ricci, who had some knowledge of medicine, abandoned the main goal of his journey and preferred to replace the first physician of Ibrahim: he would not leave this prince during the whole campaign," Cailliaud, *Voyage à Méroé*, 2:325–26.

354   The medical memoir occupies pages 282–303 of the original manuscript of the *Travels* and was published in 1928; Angelo Sammarco and Ernesto Verrucci Bey, *Il contributo degli italiani ai progressi scientifici e pratici della medicina in Egitto sotto il regno di Mohammed Ali* (Cairo: Société Royale de Géographie d'Égypte, 1928).

were praying according to the circumstance. Some Turkish officers, friends of the deceased, followed with respectful demeanor. A group of wild palm trees, twenty minutes distant from the camp, seemed the most suitable place to bury him. I had a very deep grave dug, so that wild animals would not disinter him, and had him lowered inside. Each one of us threw a handful of soil and the Turkish officers followed us. The *shawish* of the pasha finished by filling the grave and marked it with two large stones.

The camp of Ibrahim Pasha was, as I said, two hours south of Sennar, on a hill by the Nile overlooking a vast plain with some sycamore trees. We could see in the distance the city of Sennar and some villages to the south, breaking the monotony of the desert. The soldiers domesticated many gazelles, which roamed around the camp at their pleasure.

The pasha was eager to proceed in his enterprise, but sickness prevented him from moving because he wanted to recover before traveling further. In order to take advantage of this delay, I asked Ibrahim permission to go and visit the city. He not only granted my request, but also wanted me to mount one of his horses and gave me an escort of two *shawish*. Before reaching Sennar, in a spot very close to the city, I passed through a field covered with bones and corpses of unburied animals, whose putrefaction emitted such an unbearable stench that I could hardly bear it. With such lack of care from the inhabitants on a matter of the greatest importance for public health, it is not surprising that they are subject to epidemic fevers, which kill as many as dysentery.

Sennar, capital of the province by the same name, is built on an elevated place to the west of the Nile, safe from inundations. Before the arrival of the Egyptian army, there was a first-rank *malak*,[355] whose rule extended to Werkat. Isma'il Pasha made it his residence and left to the *malak* a shadow of sovereignty, about which—sincerely or for political reasons—he seemed happy. The city occupies a large area, but the population does not exceed 15,000 inhabitants. The main buildings are only two: a mosque and the old palace of the kings, four floors high (the upper two have collapsed and the rest threatens to fall as well). Isma'il occupied the house of the *malak*, which is the largest in the city and built with bricks. Many houses are made of mudbrick, and most have terraces on the roof. The rest are made of straw. There are large squares and the streets are sufficiently wide, but irregular because irregular is also the way they build their houses. In one of these squares there are, lying on the ground, six cannons of various calibers, with the coat of arms of the House of Austria, carried by the English to Abyssinia and then transported to Sennar 150 years ago.[356] Despite all inquiries to know more about the history of these guns, I could not find anything.

---

355 In fact, a sultan rather than a king. At the time the ruling sultan was Badi VI Ibn Tabl (1805–21); Robinson, "The Conquest of the Sudan [Part I]," 58.

356 Cf. George B. English, *A Narrative of the Expedition to Dongola and Sennaar, under the Command of His Excellence Ismael Pasha, Undertaken by Orders of His Highness Mehemmed Ali Pasha, Viceroy of Egypt* (London: John Murray, 1822), 170–71. Arthur E. Robinson provides this explanation for them ending up in Sennar: "Probably part of the spoil taken by the army of Baadi Abu Sheluk (under the command of the Darfurian prince, Qamis) from King Yasus of Abyssinia, in 1744 (1157 A.H.)," Robinson, "The Conquest of the Sudan by the Wali of Egypt, Muhammad Ali Pasha, 1820–1824. Part II," *Journal of the Royal African Society* 25, no. 98 (1926): 165.

While going back to the camp, I met one of the physicians of Isma'il Pasha, who informed me that Mr. Frediani, the same Frediani I made the journey with in the company of Mr. Drovetti and Mr. Linant to the Temple of Jupiter-Amun, had became a madman shortly after he arrived in Sennar with the Egyptian army. I wanted to see him and I found him locked in a subterranean room, in chains and closely guarded. I must confess that this sight moved me to tears: he was kneeling in the middle of the room, wearing a long blue robe with a leather belt; hanging from his neck there was a rosary with a large cross. He had his arms crossed on his chest in the act of praying: pale, exhausted, dripping with sweat, his eyes fixed on a small window through which light filtered into the room. I called him by his name many times, I reminded him of various circumstances of our journey to Siwa, but nothing shook him. His warden assured me that the wretch spent his days and nights in this way, while during some moments of apparent calm he mentioned a friend in Cairo and then, crying that he was a great sinner, fell back into his furious ravings. Despairing of his recovery, Isma'il Pasha wanted to send him back to Cairo before proceeding to Fazogli, but I observed that in his condition he could not bear the discomforts of such a long journey and would die on the way. Then the pasha decided to leave him at Sennar, where shortly after he miserably ended his days.

When I arrived back at the camp in the same evening, I went to visit Ibrahim Pasha and he told me that Isma'il, his brother, had lost almost a third of his soldiers in one year to dysentery, while the various methods tried by the physicians had saved only a few of them and that he himself, with so many fatal examples in front of his eyes, feared for his life. I tried to encourage him and, as for the soldiers, I suggested he give the order that each soldier should keep his lower abdomen wrapped with a wool or flannel cloth. In fact, I believe that the great difference in temperature between the day and the night is the primary cause of dysentery. This order was promulgated in the camp during the following day and the success corresponded to my expectations, because dysentery attacks became rarer among the troops.

In the meanwhile, the favor I enjoyed with the pasha encouraged me to plan an expedition to the sources of the White River, a project whose execution would finally remove every doubt about their mysterious location.[357] I thought, and I still believe it, that the Nile properly begins at the northern point of the island of Sennar, where the waters of the White River and the waters of the Blue River join together. To be called discoverer of the sources of the Nile, it is not enough to find those of the Azraq,[358] as Bruce[359] did, but it is necessary

---

357 The same idea had already been expressed by Bankes in 1821, when he was back in Britain; Usick, *Adventures in Egypt and Nubia*, 151. As trustee of the African Association, Bankes was to give Linant the task of making a first attempt in 1825. The Frenchman in fact complied in a journey that lasted from 1826 to 1827; Marcel Kurz and Pascale Linant de Bellefonds, "Linant de Bellefonds: Travels in Egypt, Sudan and Arabia Petraea (1818–1828)," in *Travellers in Egypt*, ed. Paul Starkey and Janet Starkey (London and New York: Tauris Parke, 2001), 66.

358 Arabic أزرق (*azraq*), 'blue'; and the following Arabic أبيض (*abyad*), 'white.'

359 James Bruce (1730–94) arrived in Egypt in 1768 with the purpose of finding the sources of the Nile. In 1770, leaving from Ethiopia, he saw the sources of the Blue Nile and tracked its flow back down to Sennar, where he was imprisoned by Sultan Isma'il (r. 1768–76). Eventually in 1772 he arrived at Aswan and the following year was back in Europe.

to see also those of the Abyad. This was my project and there had never been before a more advantageous occasion to undertake it: with the escort of troops and the means that the two Egyptian generals had at their disposal, success could not be but total. The main problem was to make Ibrahim Pasha like the idea. I was waiting for a suitable moment to make my proposition, when he himself gave me the occasion, bringing up the discussion on my decision to continue my travels. "Where do you intend to travel, after my health is restored?" "Toward the sources of the White River," I answered without hesitation to this question of the pasha. "But," Ibrahim added, "how do you want to penetrate further with no escort, few provisions, exposed to a thousand perils?" "I know," I replied, "that the enterprise is very difficult, but I have decided and I want to try it at any cost. But if you would like to be part of my project, all difficulties would be overcome and, independently from the result, which is doubtless, your name, already great for many glorious deeds, would acquire further celebrity." I then explained in detail my project and I added that such an interesting discovery—so many times attempted and for which many travelers before had sacrified their lives in vain—would grant him the admiration and the gratitude of all Europe. The pasha's own pride could not resist such a flattering prospect and we decided on the spot to continue until Werkat, last province of the Kingdom of Sennar, eight days to the south of Sennar city. There he would grant me all the necessary: food, beasts of burden, and an escort of enough soldiers to defend ourselves from the attacks of the idolatrous, savage, and almost wild hordes that live along the banks of the White River, some of whom are even believed by the inhabitants of Sennar to be cannibals. Ibrahim Pasha himself, after capturing as many slaves as possible, would join us with his army to go together to Darfur. I intended to communicate this common project involving the pasha to Mr. Linant, who would not much delay joining us, being sure that he would be more than happy.

In the meanwhile, the sickness of the pasha became less alarming and within a few days he could hopefully resume the march. I took advantage of the delay to take tours of the city and the surrounding areas. The following are the results of my observations.

The heat of Sennar is so unbearable that during the day one breathes with difficulty. It starts in January and ends at the close of April. Then, abundant rains come and last for three full months. After this period, the backwaters infect the atmosphere and cause great mortality among men and animals. The main sicknesses reigning during this period are intermittent fevers and dysentery. The country is beautiful during the rains, but when the sun begins to burn, everything changes appearance and the most lavish green is succeeded by a general aridity. The soil is fertile and the harvest includes *dhura*, *dukhn*, and a small and dark kind of rice. *Bamya* and *mulukhiya*[p] also grow, and a large quantity of onions, too. In the city, as much as in the surroundings, there are many gardens dedicated exclusively to the cultivation of lemons, which are small, green, and full of excellent sour juice. With a bit more work, one could harvest in Sennar a large quantity of legumes and other vegetables that are now unknown here.

The inhabitants are in general tall and slim, but robust; their skin is black and they have long curly hair. The whole population is divided into three classes: traders, warriors, and the populace. There are also slaves, available at a very low price: they are employed to cultivate the land. Merchants, some of whom are very rich even though they outwardly appear miserable, trade with the caravans passing by Sennar from the Red Sea and Darfur. Trade consists of slaves, gold dust, elephant tusks, all kind of spices, ostrich feathers, tamarind, gum, and more. Here, as well, people bury their money, as in many parts of Nubia, and generally of Arabia.

Warriors do not have any other weapons apart from a very long spear and a shield made of elephant, hippopotamus, or giraffe skin: some of the shields are round, some oval, all large enough to protect the whole body. They march on foot and on dromedary, which they can maneuver with great skill. Sennar warriors are very brave and once they start the fight they rarely flee.

The third class, the populace, is busy with different crafts: they fabricate a large quantity of cotton cloth, which is the main export of Sennar; beautiful mats, as valuable as those of al-Demer; saddles; and more. This class also takes up arms in case of emergency.

The luxurious and rich clothing of the *malak* is in great contrast with what the rest of the population wears. Except traders, who wear a blue tunic, all men and women use a single piece of cloth around their waist and are otherwise completely naked. They generally walk barefoot, but some of them, and especially the most distinguished women, put a piece of leather under their feet in the guise of a sandal and they tie it to the leg with small laces.

The ordinary food of the population is *dukhn*, but the rich eat *dhura* bread with butter and honey. After the harvest, cereals are stored in large and deep pits to preserve them from parasites, which would turn them to dust.

The natives are Muslim, but fanatically so. They are generally devoted to laziness and the most revolting libertinism is the foremost consequence of this natural inclination of theirs. Street women are abundant, but are not native to the country and come from many other places: this is why their skin color is different from that of the locals. In fact, there are also local prostitutes.

In the first days of December, an epidemic spread among the horses in the camp. With the others, many horses personally belonging to Ibrahim Pasha died, most of them Nedj horses, which are bred in Mecca and Derri. These animals are tall, beautiful, and almost all used as saddle animals: they endure fatigue and can travel thirty to forty miles a day, even for several days in a row if, before setting off, they can drink a lot. The loss of these horses much displeased the pasha, and even though the army veterinarians tried all means to save them, all was in vain. The first sign of the sickness was a shiver in the nostrils, which imperceptibly spread to the rest of the body: the horse opened its mouth and raised its lips, showing the teeth, and in less than two hours fell, completely overwhelmed, passing away just a few moments later. Fortunately, the deadly epidemic lasted only for a short period of time because they were immediately moved to another place.[360]

---

360 It seems to be a poisoning syndrome: perhaps the horses had eaten poisonous plants (of the type containing strychnine) or drunk water contaminated by a certain type of algae.

One morning some Arabs presented Ibrahim with a young giraffe captured in the kingdom and domesticated. It was ten feet tall in the front and much shorter in the rear. Because the rear legs of this animal are almost half the size of the front legs, it cannot lower its head to the ground, and when it wants to drink it must kneel or spread its legs. For this reason it eats tree leaves, which it can reach by stretching its neck. The Arabs who brought it used to cut branches and offer them at the right height, so it could eat comfortably. Its jaw is toothless, like the camel, and it has very thin legs and two small nails per leg. This animal was designated by the pasha as a present for the Grand Seigneur.[361]

Ibrahim was increasingly eager to advance and there was no day in which he did not discuss with me the planned expedition. On my side, I wanted to delay his departure, first of all because he had only improved, but not fully recovered, from dysentery; secondly, because his extreme weakness made me fear a relapse. All my arguments did not succeed and on December 12th the order for the march was finally given.

On the 13th at dawn, the army moved by land and Ibrahim, with three officers and me, boarded an eighteen-oar *canjiah*, with a chosen crew and good musicians to entertain the pasha. Twenty-five Mamluks of his retinue boarded another *canjiah* and at around ten in the morning three cannon shots were the signal for the departure. The banks of the Nile were high, shadowed on both sides by a thick forest populated by monkeys, and it happened that often a wild animal was spotted in the open. One hour after midday, we reached a village on Abu Sherif Island, whose inhabitants came in crowds to pay their homage to the pasha. Toward sunset, a huge elephant approached the river to drink: the Mamluks asked and obtained permission to hunt it. They landed at a place where the animal could not see them and got across the wood to around thirty feet from it: while it was drinking, they discharged their rifles, each loaded with two bullets. The enraged animal emitted a frightening roar and ran toward the place whence the shots had come. All the Mamluks managed to board the *canjiah*, with the exception of two, who were frightened and got lost in the woods. One of the two remaining men was quickly reached by the fierce animal, which opened its path by destroying whatever was in its way: he hit the thigh of the Mamluk with its tusk, then grabbed him with its trunk and threw him in the air. Then it ran away and disappeared into the forest. When the other Mamluks realized that two of them were missing, they went back and found one unharmed: from him they found out what had happened and ran to the place where the other wretch had fallen. He was lying in the middle of thorny bushes and did not give any sign of life. They carried him in their arms and brought him back to the *canjiah*, where, by order of the pasha, I immediately went to visit him. A profuse phlebotomy made him regain consciousness. The muscles of the thigh were torn down to the bone and his face was in such bad shape because of the thorns that he was barely recognizable. He also had a fracture of the metacarpus. Nevertheless, I was fortunate enough to save him and after his recovery he had no handicap of any sort.[q]

---

361 This giraffe, captured in Sennar and sent to the Ottoman sultan in 1824, was portrayed by Linant; Usick, *Adventures in Egypt and Nubia*, 186. At the time, the reigning sultan was Mahmud II (1808–39).

On 14 December, after three hours' sail, we reached the village of al-Raraba, where the army, which was following us by land, was camped. Here Ibrahim ordered his tent to be pitched to receive reports and meet with the *malak*s of Sennar and Fazogli, who had already been summoned for the purpose. Ibrahim wanted to find a possible way to push the heathen tribes nearby to submit voluntarily, without further bloodshed. The two *malak*s arrived on the same day: the one of Sennar at around eleven in the morning, and the other toward the evening. Unfortunately, they could not or did not want to find a way to second the pasha or to personally engage in the task of negotiating with the enemies. Despite the inner annoyance that was readable on his face, the pasha dismissed them with kindness and apparent friendliness. The *malak* of Sennar[362] did not wear the cap that is the usual distinction of his dignity and his hair was braided. He was wearing a long tunic made of cloth of the Indies, embroidered in gold and open on his chest, while at his waist he had a superb cashmere shawl[363] and very tight long pants made of scarlet cloth. His shoes were made of yellow morocco and a long saber richly decorated in gold was hanging from his side. His brother stayed at a certain distance from the pasha's tent, in command of ten soldiers—the escort of the *malak*—and was much more simply dressed than he. The other *malak*, that of Fazogli, was dressed quite similarly, but wore a hat lavishly decorated with gold fringes and two long appendages floating on the shoulders. They were both perfectly black and the latter had two perpendicular scars on each cheek, one inch long, according to the customs of these nations. They make two to four scars at the distance of three lines one from the other and they consider it a sign of beauty.

Immediately after our arrival at al-Raraba, Ibrahim ordered a detachment of a hundred soldiers to leave and open up with fire a path in the middle of the thick thorny forest of short *sant* trees in order for the army to advance more comfortably and less harassed by wild animals, which every now and then used to approach the camp.

On the 15th, we kept sailing, with the aim of advancing as far as the depth of the river allowed it. The wind was favorable and we passed the village of Abda without stopping.[364] At around midday we arrived at Seru.[365] The woods around this village have many baobab

---

362 Sultan Badi VI.

363 This was also a sign of royal dignity: "A silken *emma* (scarf, handkerchief or shawl), from which the turban is made. These silken shawls were made specially in Syria and exported from there to all parts of the Mediterranean and Red Sea," Robinson, "Some Notes," 372. The sword, too, was a symbol of the sultan's power.

364 Apparently Abdin, near Umm Durraba, but this site is north of al-Raraba; Carl Flemming, *Nordöstliches Afrika: Entworfen und gezeichnet von F. Handtke*. Lithographie [map]. 1:5,450,000. Glogau: Druck und Verlag von C. Flemming, 1855.

365 "Sirvi" in Linant, "Siraywa" according to Shinnie, *Linant de Bellefonds*, 97. Siraywa is nevertheless 210 kilometers from al-Raraba, a distance too long to be covered in only half a day's sailing, unless Ricci is once again mistaken. The place is apparently the same as the one marked "Seirrou" in John Arrowsmith, *Nubia and Abyssinia* [map], 1:3,860,000 (London: Arrowsmith, 1832), "Seru" in Flemming, *Nordöstliches Afrika*, "Seyrou" in F.A. Garnier, *Afrique Orientale, comprenant l'Égypte, l'Abyssinie, et partie du Takrour Oriental. Extrémité orientale de la cote d'Afrique, d'après la carte de M. le commt. Guillain. Atlas sphéroïdal & universel de géographie dressé par F.A. Garnier*, géographe [map], 1:8.000,000 (Paris: Veuve Jules Renouard Éditeur, 1860).

trees, which the natives call *ufa*. When he saw four trees of extraordinary size, under which there were ten huts, Ibrahim wanted to land in my company in order to measure them: we found that the largest two had a circumference of 102 and 94 feet respectively. The cortex was carved with many marks, but none of the villagers could tell us about their age: we were only informed that the last four were made on their wedding day by four generations of chiefs belonging to the same family. The fruit of this tree looks like a coconut: the pulp is juicy and it tastes sweet and sour at the same time. The natives have great veneration for this tree and they do not cut it for any reason. They also usually choose places where it grows to build their huts.

Beyond Seru, the Nile was not navigable any more for our *canjiah*, so we had to proceed by land. I was persuaded that the movements of the dromedary would be detrimental to the pasha and I tried to convince him to go back, as I had already done before, but he absolutely wanted to proceed. While he gave me one of his best dromedaries, he mounted one which had cost him eight thousand Spanish dollars. This animal had a trot so mild as to be almost imperceptible: these dromedaries are trained when they are young, forcing them to trot with a stretched neck and low head. After a very short march, we made camp and the army reached us a few hours later.

On the 16th, the pasha sent thirty more men on horse to precede us and cut the thorny branches with axes; this was in addition to the detachment that was clearing the path with fire. So thick was the forest that without these precautions we could not advance. Shortly after our departure, we started to walk on the ashes of the fire, which had spread and in some parts was still burning. We were often disturbed by the smoke, according to the direction of the wind.

The pasha's health was deteriorating and we were forced to stop many times. In the meanwhile, the vanguard of Isma'il Pasha reached us at the village of al-Rumayla and continued its march to Zeis, a little further than Ghess, where we arrived late in the evening. Two hours later Isma'il arrived, too.

Before arriving at Zeis, we found that the forest was less thick; moving finally away from the banks of the Nile we could continue more comfortably, among rare examples of a kind of *sant* tree, five to six feet high, which oozes a gum and on which nests a small silkworm. I found some cocoons and I broke many, finding very fine white silk inside. If the country was more populated and the inhabitants were to employ themselves in this business, they would easily harvest a large quantity of silk, as soft and shiny as the Persian, with which it shares a lot of similarities.

On the 17th, the march of the two armies was very slow for one hour because they had to cross a plain covered with wild oats so high and thick that camels and horses stumbled. At around two in the afternoon, we reached a place called Fil, which means 'elephant,' where there is a large block of red granite, twelve square feet in size.[366] Because of the noise that the soldiers made while camping, many night birds flew out of its numerous cracks.

---

366 So says Ricci, although the measurement does not seem to fit the context.

There was still a long stretch of road to reach Werkat and we had to leave very early on the 18th. We crossed some small woods of *sant* trees, then large plains and *dhura* fields. At around nine we arrived at a small hill, on top of which there were some ruins, but so destroyed that it was impossible to understand what kind they were. After a short break, we proceeded to a village called Hasiheisa, made up of a small number of huts and whose few inhabitants had all fled. An old man in his fifties was caught by a group of soldiers while entering the nearby forest and was brought to the presence of the pasha. He refused for a long time to answer the many questions, until he finally overcame his shock and fell to the feet of the pasha, crying and saying in corrupted Arabic that the village was inhabited by the Kababish, that they all were related to each other, but that he did not know where they had gone. This man was covered in sheepskin, tied around his neck and hips, with the furry side on the outside. He had very white beard and hair, and his finger- and toenails were extremely long. The pasha ordered him to be given some biscuit: the man looked around astonished and hesitated a long time thinking whether he should eat it or not. In the end, after smelling it many times, he started to gnaw it. Ibrahim ordered him to be released and he walked slowly toward the village, where he was followed by some of us. A mat and two carved half pumpkins were all the furniture left in the abandoned huts. In one of them I found two wrappings of thick paper, blackened by smoke and written on both sides: I did not understand the content, so I showed them to the Muhurdar Effendi, keeper of the seals of the pasha, and he told me that they were fragments of the Quran.

At five in the afternoon, we reached Werkat, capital of the province known by the same name, part of the Kingdom of Sennar, where there are four villages. The detachment that preceded us had arrived the day before. The chiefs of the two closest villages were waiting with the army to pay homage to the pasha, and when they were admitted to the audience, they openly declared that there could be no illusion of defeating the pagans without bloodshed. They added that they had tried many times to convert them to the true faith and to civilize them. Anyway, they said, their subjection was an easy task, since they had little or no defense, and to fight against them was like gazelle hunting. Muhammad Ali was well informed of this when he decided to send this expedition: in fact, after the occupation of these provinces, his armies have never lacked recruits, whom beys specifically charged with the task gather annually in the numbers they want, due to the mere presence of the garrisons and no opposition of any sort from the miserable populations.

On the 19th, the army of Isma'il set off at dawn to advance into Fazogli, passing by Mount Iabi, inhabited by pagans. Mr. Cailliaud was part of the expedition, entrusted by Isma'il Pasha to explore the golden mines of Fazogli. On the other hand, Ibrahim's army could not move because the long march of the previous day worsened his condition during the night and a colonic inflammation kept us at Werkat for many days. This unfortunate combination did not destroy my hope of executing my plan, wishing to stay in this place until the health of the pasha was completely restored. I would be joined by Mr. Linant as well, who by orders of Ibrahim Pasha was to be provided with all that he needed and escorted to our camp. His delay was caused by an attack of intermittent fever, which forced him to proceed slowly; this I knew when I met him on my way back.

The different phases of the sickness of the prince until our arrival in Egypt are described in detail in the memoir that I wrote; therefore I will not discuss them here except for the aspects that are relevant to the narration.

The villages of Werkat are built on the slopes of three high granite mountains, covered with many kinds of trees such as the acacia, the doum, the tamarind, and the *ufa*. There are also springs of very pure water. Each village is made up of forty to fifty houses, or straw huts, round and built randomly, without regularity, so that in the distance they look more like military encampments rather than villages proper. The inhabitants are all soldiers and are armed with a long spear and a shield. They constantly fight the pagans and then they sell them in the markets of Sennar. They possess a few sheep and goats and hens: they keep the latter to provide eggs and the former for wool and milk. They rarely kill them, and when this happens they keep the fat for themselves and take the meat a certain distance away from the village to feed the lions, which are abundant in the mountains. This trick, according to them, is very useful to keep them away from the village. One morning, accompanied by two villagers, I wanted to climb the highest of the three aforementioned mountains, whence with a powerful telescope I could see the mountain chain of Rank, maybe six days to the southwest of Werkat. I asked my guides the name and the distance of the isolated mountains in front of us, so that I could place them on my map.

Sennar as seen from the top of this mountain looks like a vast plain, often interrupted by granite mountains, sometimes close to each other, sometimes distant. Everywhere there are houses, partly on the slopes of the mountains, partly underneath. Very thick impenetrable forests cover both banks of the Nile and deep into Sennar Island. My guides told me that nobody would dare to enter the woods, where it is impossible to open a passage and where wild animals of all kinds are hidden.

The excessive heat accelerates the development of the natives to the point that at the age of nine females are ready to get married. On the other hand, the exhalations from stagnating water make the air unhealthy. Because of this, they rarely reach old age.

At Werkat and in other parts of Sennar the inhabitants rest their head on a sort of stand, made of one piece of very hard wood, half a foot high and with a large base. This piece of furniture, which is very uncomfortable to whoever is not used to it, is very important to them. They always have many of them in their huts and it is the first thing they offer to their guests, because they use it also to rest their arm when seated. The use of these headrests is very old. I have two of them in my collection: one is modern and the other was found in a tomb of Qurna.

Before leaving Werkat, I wanted to have a quick look at Sen, the last village of this province. I took the precaution of being escorted by four well-armed soldiers in order to prevent any incident. It took us almost two hours of fast dromedary march to get there. At the halfway point we met a lion, which was relaxed, lying at a short distance from us. When we appeared he stood and stared at us without moving. The dromedaries, which greatly fear lions, became almost frenzied and it took us much effort to hold them. In the meanwhile, we prepared our weapons, in order to shoot at it in case it attacked us. We deviated from the main road and resumed our journey, always ready for defense. When the lion saw us going away, it lay back on the ground. It is possible that it did not attack us because it was not hungry, although our guides believed it was because of the fever: as we do in Europe, the Arabs too think that this animal is periodically prone to it. On this occasion I could observe the difference between the free lion and the imprisoned: the vivacity of the glance and the movements of the former are not in any way comparable to those of the latter, which, being forced to receive its food from human hands, becomes sad and seems to pity the loss of its original freedom.

Sen marks the border between the subdued, Muslim man and the free, pagan man. I went up a hill and I could see many of the mountains inhabited by those nations against which the expedition was mainly directed. The closest mountain is around three hours' walk from Sen; the others are toward the south and the southeast. My guides assured me that those savages are in continuous war against each other, with mutual ambushes. The only purpose of such hostility is to capture prisoners and sell them to the *jalaba*,[367] that is, the heads of the caravans, in exchange for *dhura*. Sometimes the *jalaba* capture the slaves directly themselves, suddenly attacking the first they meet, thus saving on the price of the transaction. The inhabitants of Sennar consider them heathen, but they could not tell me what their religion was and it is possible that they do not have any. The mountains that are their shelter are far from each other and create separate communities, which are, as I said, in continuous hostility. Those wretches always live holed up in their huts and do not go out but to sow and harvest the *dhura* or make provision of water, the only needs they have. They are naked and only have a small stick as weapon.

The *jalaba* divide the slaves of both genders into three groups: in the first there are children up to ten years, in the second up to fifteen, and all the rest are in the third group. The price of those wretches is cheapest in Sennar and amounts to eight to twelve thalers at most, according to age and gender. Those who have already had smallpox are the most expensive: the mother is always sold with her suckling son, as mares are in Europe. The operation of sewing the young female slaves is done in Sennar. Slaves call their masters indiscriminately *abuya*, which means 'father,' or *sidi*, which means 'master.' After the market, many caravans leave Sennar heading to Cairo and the journey takes a lot of time, considering that the adult slaves are forced to walk all the way. There are barbarous masters who beat them when they are very tired or tie them to the tails of the camels, in order to force them to go on.

---

367 "The *jallaba*, i.e. dealers in Sudanese merchandise, and in particular slave dealers, were known for generations to be 'dark-skinned people from the districts of the Oases, Aswan, and Ibrim,'" so Gabriel Baer, "Slavery in Nineteenth Century Egypt," 427, quoting the seventeenth-century Turkish traveler Çelebi. "In earlier times the accepted term was *khawaja*, a word that carried connotations of pale complexion and foreign origin. By the nineteenth century a more common term for private merchant was *jallab*, which might well mean 'foreigner' in some contexts, but which did not imply non-Sudanic origin. During the nineteenth century the *jalaba* of the Nile Valley joined private traders of Mediterranean origin as agents in the conduct of the foreign trade of the western sultanates," Lidwien Kapteijns and Jay Spaulding, "Precolonial Trade between States in the Eastern Sudan, ca. 1700–ca. 1900," *African Economic History* 11 (1982): 39.

During the journey their food is *dhura* mixed with butter. Every day, fat is distributed for them to anoint their bodies. Many hardships make the caravan lose up to half of its slaves before reaching Cairo, and this is the reason why a slave in Sennar is worth ten thalers and in Egypt ninety. Incredible also are the obscenities that some *jalaba* commit on young slaves of both genders and there is no excess to which these brutal masters do not indulge in order to satiate their unrestrained lust. Let us be consoled by the hope that the united efforts of all civilized nations will finally succeed in completely abolishing such an inhumane and shameful traffic.[368]

When I arrived back at the camp, I found the pasha's health noticeably worsened. Firmly believing that the cause of his sickness was the climate, I persuaded myself that the only way to save his life was to go back. On 24 December, when his health slightly improved, he gave his orders to the generals, who were remaining with the army, and sent a Mamluk with a good escort to his brother Isma'il to inform him of what was going on. He then lay on a bed suspended between two camels, which I had arranged for him, and we set off. After four hours we stopped at al-Qarabin.

I would in vain try to express the sorrow I felt to be forced to abandon an enterprise that many favorable circumstances contributed to result in certain success. We would certainly have raised a monument at the sources of the Nile, mentioning our names and the date of the discovery. But the responsibility I had accepted was so big as to silence in me all other thoughts and I resigned myself to my fate, and I devoted myself to the treatment of the sick man.

On the 26th, we reached Zeis, where we met Mr. Linant, who was unaware of our coming and intended to join us at Werkat. His regret was not less than my own when I told him that the planned expedition could not be done any more. Since his recovery also proceeded very slowly, he decided to go back to Sennar and from there to visit the ruins of Meroe.[369]

The *canjiah* of Ibrahim Pasha, which could only with great effort go up from Seru to Zeis, took us back to Sennar, where we arrived in the evening of 28 December. We were accompanied by only three officers and a few Mamluks, while the rest of the pasha's retinue stayed with the army. I also abandoned my ornithological collection, an assortment of seeds, and many other objects acquired during my journey or received from the pasha as a present, such as clothes, agricultural tools, musical instruments, and furniture. Although Ibrahim Pasha gave the strictest orders to readily ship everything to Cairo, I lost all of them, so that in this aspect, too, I was very unlucky.

On 11 January 1822 we reached Berber and on the 16th Shendi,[370] where we changed the *canjiah* for a *dahabiya*, in order to make our journey faster. This is a much smaller and far

---

368 The slave trade was abolished by the British Parliament in 1807. (Slavery itself was not abolished until 1833.) Spain and Portugal followed in 1817, the Netherlands and France in 1818. The Ottoman Empire would abolish the African trade of slaves in 1847 and slavery in 1882.

369 The ruins of Meroe, modern Bagrawiya, were visited by Linant on his way back to Cairo. This was the ultimate goal of the travel funded by Bankes.

370 This is Ricci's mistake in the original Italian. The dates should be reversed, since Shendi is to the south of Berber.

faster boat. Its only cabin was so small that the pasha's bed could barely fit in. I was forced with my other travel companions to adapt to the lack of space and for two nights we slept in a very uncomfortable situation. We left Shendi on the same 16 January at five in the afternoon and, traveling day and night, we passed without ropes the cataracts of al-Humar and Gabalab. I watched with admiration the pilot, who was able to skillfully avoid all the rocks. This fast and dangerous rush brought us to Agaba, or the mountain of Abu Hamad, on the 18th late in the evening, and the following day the Mamluks of the retinue arrived, too. Here, the *rais* of the *dahabiya* remarked to Ibrahim that continuing the journey with such a small boat would be very unwise because the bed of the Nile to the north was occupied by many rocks and there was a great risk of sinking, especially at night. On the other hand, even if the boat was bigger (and this could be done by just waiting for the pasha's boat that was left at Shendi), the journey to Cairo would be very long, and Ibrahim, who was getting better by the day, was extremely impatient to arrive. To satisfy his impatience there was no other means but to take the land route, heading to Sebu'a through the desert. The discomforts of this road made me tremble for him; nevertheless this was the road the pasha chose.[371] The chiefs of the two closest villages were summoned to gather information and we were assured that from that point we could reach Sebu'a in only nine days, through a desert that had only one source of drinkable water halfway. The journey was, in addition, extremely dangerous for the presence of the Bisharin, who always wander in this part of the desert. Despite this information, Ibrahim persisted in his decision and kept the two chiefs to serve us as guides, with the threat to cut off their heads if they deceived us. The *rais* of the *dahabiya* was ordered to set off to Cairo with most of the pasha's belongings and we also got ready to leave.

I was very concerned about how to make this journey the least stressful as possible for Ibrahim, but eventually I thought of a sort of stretcher placed between two dromedaries, where he could lie comfortably. On 20 January, with the stock of forty large containers of Nile water, each of them with the capacity of two barrels, a sufficient reserve of biscuit, and a little rice, we set off: we were fifteen people in all. A very cold north wind, blowing in our face, was very disturbing for us and the camels. It also made us feel very cold, especially considering the usual climate of the place in which we were. At around midday, we took a break, sheltering behind a hill, and after a while we resumed the march, reaching al-Farut at sunset. The stretch of desert we traveled was sandy, but we also met some limestone hills and a few thorny plants, which the camels fed on.

On the 21st, the same wind blew even stronger and we felt colder than during the previous day. We passed through two chains of high mountains and saw on the ground a human skull and some animal bones, probably dead of thirst. Crows were constantly following us, as usually happens with caravans crossing the desert. At night we could hear hyenas and jackals howling. In the evening, we camped on the slopes of Jabal Kerri Berar, a very high mountain. My fur stretched on the ground in the pasha's tent served at the same time as my bed and my blanket.

---

371 The linear distance is 370 kilometers: the land route connects Abu Hamad with Wadi al-Sebu'a.

On the 22nd, still hindered by the same wind, we arrived at the plain called Abu Siha.

On the 23rd, the cold was unbearable. Toward the evening, we inspected the water containers and we found that little water was left, not because we drank a lot of it, since the cold prevented us from thirst, but for the lack of discipline in the distribution and for the neglect of the servants, who had given large quantities to the camels. Despite this, we were encouraged by what the guides had said and, since we were almost halfway, the pasha ordered we should proceed during the night till we should reach al-Murra,[372] where the spring described by the two shaykhs lies. We therefore walked for four more hours after sunset, by the light of many torches, and finally reached al-Murra. What a surprise when we found that instead of the drinkable fresh water that we hoped could fill our goatskins, we found bitter water. The guides apologized, saying that the spring of fresh water was dry—which was true, indeed—and that this was something unusual. Nevertheless they believed we could drink of the other water without risk. The pasha did not allow it and ordered the water to be tested on a camel. This died swollen before dawn. The pasha, choleric and impetuous by nature, became furious and threatened to cut the heads off the guides. The poor shaykhs fell at his feet, begging for mercy, swearing that they had always found water in this place and that if by chance the spring was dry, it was not their fault. At the same time, they implored the pasha to accelerate the march, giving an uncertain hope of finding water after another two days' march.

On the 24th, we were left with one water bag and a half: I took five bottles for the use of the pasha and myself for the remaining five days of the journey and the rest was left for the caravan, with an officer in charge of supervising the distribution. This measure was the cause of the loss of a Mamluk, who, urged by thirst and not scared by the death of the dromedary, absolutely wanted to drink from the water of al-Murra before setting off. He was attacked by fierce colic pains, followed by dysentery, and after two days he died. The pasha had a grave made for him so as not to abandon his body to the desert animals, and the tomb was marked with two large stones, according to the general use. From the deadly effects it produced we believed that the bitter water of al-Murra, filtering through some dike of arsenic, carried some particles of this poison.

In the meantime the fear of dying of thirst made us all adopt a strict diet. As for me, I used to go through the day with only three pieces of biscuit and in the evening drink my half bottle of water. The pasha did the same and in this circumstance showed the greatest firmness.

During this day, in which the cold was no less intense than on the previous, we reached at one in the afternoon a narrow valley called Dila, which is accessed by a narrow passage between three mountains, in the shape of a gate. In this valley there are many doum trees and some low thorny bushes, at the time dried out. Spring reigned here and we could warm up a little. The exit of this valley is similar to its entrance and is marked by two other mountains,

---

372 Probably the modern Murrat; "Mour-had" in Adrien H. Brue, *Carte détaillée en deux feuilles de l'Afrique et des iles qui en dépendent (partie septentrionale) par A. Brue, Géographe du Roi: Abyssinie et pays des Gallas* [map], 1:15,000,000 (Paris: Brue, 1828). It is "Moor-had" in Arrowsmith, *Nubia and Abyssinia* (which specifies "Brackish water"), "el Mora" in Flemming, *Nordöstliches Afrika*, and "el-Morrat" in Garnier, *Afrique Orientale*.

so close one to the other that there is enough space only for two camels at a time. The valley goes from right to left and it is likely the bed of a stream, one of those that have their origin in the Red Sea mountains and carry water only during the rainy season. On our way, the two guides, who were afraid for their life after the pasha had threatened them, approached me to ask me to intercede for their forgiveness. I was completely surprised when one of the two men revealed himself to be the same Ababda shaykh who had kindly received me when I was forced to give up my journey to Berenike, because of the rudeness and arrogance of Belzoni, and was heading back to Thebes without provisions and extremely tired by my rapid ride.[373] I remembered his help and was happy that I had a chance to pay him back, so I acted in their favor with the pasha and I obtained his pardon for them. My host hugged me with all the effusion of his heart when I told him the news and in his happiness made me many offers, promising to send me his famous horse as a gift, but I refused everything, satisfied with being able to show my gratitude to a virtuous man in such an important thing for him, which is his own life. It might be worth mentioning here that among Turkish princes the physician has the right to ask for similar pardons, which are usually granted. In the evening we stopped at Talata Gindi.[374]

On the 25th, the cold was so sharp that I was afraid the water would freeze in the bottles. Nothing happened during the day and we camped at sunset on the slopes of Mount al-Hil, where we saw a prodigious quantity of camel bones. In order to avoid thirst we resorted to talking as little as possible, besides eating less.

On the 26th, the Mamluk I wrote about died.

On the 27th, we started to be overwhelmed by hunger and thirst, and most of the people in our retinue were so exhausted and disheartened that they did not have enough strength to proceed. The pasha was encouraging everybody, but after all that we suffered, the idea of spending another full day, and maybe half of another, without water was extremely painful for us. In this extreme situation, divine providence was looking over us: in the evening the Ababda shaykh, who had sharp sight, as is general in all the Arabs of the desert, saw at a distance something moving, but none of us was able to recognize what it was. The pasha instantly ordered the two shaykhs to hurry ahead in order to verify it and, despite being weaker than the others because they were given only enough water to wet their mouths, they set off in that direction. In the meanwhile, human voice, which seemed banned in the camp for two days, resounded again and everybody expressed his point of view on the nature of the object seen. Finally cruel uncertainty disappeared with the return of the shaykh who first had discovered it. He came accompanied by two dromedaries loaded with food and water, and two full water bags were emptied on the spot. The caravan proceeded happily to Wadi al-Sebu'a, where we spent the night.[375]

The almost miraculous apparition of water was due to the foresight of the viceroy, who, after the arrival of dispatches from Sennar with the news of the dangerous condition of Ibrahim Pasha and of his return to Cairo, believing it possible that in order to speed up

---

373 Cf. *Travel to Nubia*, 172–73.
374 Possibly Tilat al-Sufar.
375 Wadi al-Sebu'a is a different toponym from Sebu'a, which they would reach the following day.

we would take the desert road, ordered his physicians[376] to leave immediately and travel day and night until they met Ibrahim. He also simultaneously ordered Muhammad Bey,[377] governor of Aswan, to send dromedaries loaded with food and water every day from Sebu'a, with instructions to come back only late at night if they had not met us. This order, sent by a very fast dromedary, had arrived three days before in Aswan: the governor immediately moved to Sebu'a to oversee the execution of the orders. The water that saved our lives was in fact the water sent on the same morning from Sebu'a. The dromedary that had carried it was immediately sent back to the city in order to inform the governor of our imminent arrival, bearing the news of the good health of Ibrahim. In the evening, we celebrated our salvation: happiness was on the faces of everybody, and while just two hours before we had all considered ourselves doomed to die in the desert, the certainty of being safe, and the sweet refreshment that providence had sent us, restored our strength and gave us a delectable and peaceful sleep.

On the 28th, after nine hours' journey among the gorges of high mountains, saluted every now and then by cheers and discharges of musketry by the soldiers following Muhammad Bey, who had advanced to meet the pasha, we reached Sebu'a. Here, I must point out the incredible speed with which news spread, because, although it seems impossible, on the 26th, word had spread in Sebu'a that the pasha had died and that his embalmed body, placed in a coffin, was being transported across the desert to Aswan. Considering, on one hand, the speed of our march, to the extent that nobody could have preceded us, and also that there was certainly no shorter road than the one we took, I could not understand how such news could have spread. If the governor Muhammad Bey had not assured us of it, I would not have believed it.

The litter that I had built for the pasha at Jebel Abu Hamad and that the people mistook for a coffin was the innocent cause of an insurrection at Shendi, where news of the alleged death of the pasha had also quickly spread. Mr. Linant, who had moved there, was very nearly a victim of it: he was forced to hide for many days until an expeditionary force quelled the insurrection.

Even though during this journey we suffered a lot from the cold, this was also of providential assistance because we felt less thirsty. If the north wind that constantly blew during those days had ceased and the atmosphere had consequently become hotter, it is certain that the scarce quantity of water that was left on the 24th would not have been enough, and that many of us would have died miserably in the desert.

On the 29th, we boarded a *canjiah* and at midday we arrived at Aswan, where, during the night, the physicians of the viceroy had also arrived. We moved into the house of Muhammad Bey. Here, Ibrahim, seeing a portrait of Napoleon and hearing of his death on the island of St. Helena,[378] observed it carefully, assigning to every physical characteristic an intellectual

---

376 Among them undoubtedly the chief physician Yanni Botsaris, brother of the infamous Demetrios, physician of Isma'il Pasha with whom he would share a tragic death at Shendi in October 1822; Mohamed Rifaat Pasha, *The Awakening of Modern Egypt* (Cairo: The Palm Press, 2005), 31.

377 Muhammad Bey Lazughlu, director of the new military school established by the viceroy at Aswan, where the black slaves were trained to be soldiers. He is the same man who in 1822 destroyed the temples of Elephantine.

378 On 5 May 1821. The news reached Egypt around July, when Ibrahim had already set off to Sennar.

attribute, and exclaimed: "O, such a fate! A Muslim is nevertheless forced to worship a Christian!" The following day, he wanted to inspect a battalion of black soldiers recently instructed and organized in the European fashion by Colonel Sève, now Sulayman Bey,[379] and, considering the short time that they took to learn the new maneuvers they executed, he was particularly satisfied. Aswan is the place intended by the viceroy for the organization of the black troops and they were already building large barracks, while the military storehouses were full of uniforms and weapons.

In the meanwhile, the doctors of the viceroy took responsibility for the treatment of the pasha, more as a formality than anything else, because he had recovered from dysentery and was only a little weak, something easy to cure with military treatments.

While we remained in Aswan, Ibrahim wanted me to have meals with him, and from these occasions I happened to find out about the exceptional addiction of Muhammad Bey to spirits: during the dessert, which consists of sweets and jams according to the Turkish custom, this man usually drinks a large gilded silver cup, which can contain a pound and a half of liquid, full of spirit. The pasha assured me that he drinks up to three every day, without any consequence to his lucidity. It is customary among the Turks not to allow those who eat with the great and good to drink during the meal, but only at dessert. The pasha dispensed me from this uncomfortable prohibition, not so much for being a European, but because I was his treating physician.

On 4 February 1822, we left Aswan and, with a bit of headwind, we reached Cairo on the 9th,[380] where I was decorated with fur and saber, and received a monetary reward and four magnificent horses. The viceroy welcomed me with the utmost distinction and, even though I was no longer Ibrahim's personal physician, he consulted me many times on the treatment method adopted by the chief physician. This method was, essentially, the same I had suggested in our first meeting at Aswan.

After two months of necessary rest, I decided to go back to Europe, but before my departure I wanted to travel to the pyramids of Giza, where I could not stay longer when I left Cairo for Thebes. I would have been sorry to leave Egypt without having copied the interesting representations of the ancient arts and crafts of the Egyptians which can be found in many tombs around the pyramids. Since these are only three hours from Cairo, I could comfortably go there many times.[381]

---

379 'Colonel' Sève (the actual military rank is disputed) had served in the French army at Trafalgar and Waterloo. After the fall of Napoleon in 1820, on his way to Persia, where he intended to pursue a military career, he stopped in Egypt and entered the service of Muhammad Ali. He introduced the drilling of soldiers according to the European model and occupied a military rank inferior only to Ibrahim Pasha; Khaled Fahmy, *All the Pasha's Men: Mehmet Ali, His Army and the Making of Modern Egypt* (Cairo: American University in Cairo Press, 2002), 80.

380 The date does not coincide with other sources of the period: the general consul of the Two Sicilies records 7 February (Sammarco, *Alessandro Ricci*, 12), while Drovetti writes: "Ibrahim Bacha . . . est arrivé au Caire le 6 de ce mois," Driault, *La formation*, 238.

381 The long list of plates is here omitted and the reader is referred to chapter 7 for more details. An odd theory on the purpose of the pyramids, according to which these were built to fence off the desert sand, is also omitted here.

Around the middle of November I finished my drawings at Giza, to which I dedicated myself, with interruptions, after my return from Sennar. Since I did not want to further postpone my departure to Europe, I bid farewell to Mr. Salt and my other acquaintances and, on the 28th, I embarked for Livorno, where I arrived on 24 December 1822. Here, during my quarantine, I heard with sorrow the news of the death of Governor Spannocchi,[382] to whom I intended to offer some small gifts. Since I did not have any other reason to stay in the city, as soon as my quarantine finished I moved to Florence, where, using the notes that I had carefully taken during my journeys, I was able to compile the present account.

Notes

[a] *canja*.[383] A long, thin, and light boat, with three lateen sails, twelve to twenty-two oars, which are used when there is no wind or just to speed up navigation.

[b] See Filangieri Legis, *Note giustificative de' fatti*, No. 31[384] and *Suida* quoted there.

[c] To tell the truth, to my utmost regret, I later saw, in some modern books where the drawings of the tomb of Biban al-Muluk are mentioned, that these are cited as the work of Belzoni, while all the travelers who were at the time crossing Egypt know that these drawings are my work, and Messrs. Salt, Bankes, Huyot, and Beechey can testify to it.

[d] *kabir*.[385] It means properly 'great,' 'powerful,' but in this and similar cases it means 'chief,' 'guide,' 'head,' referring to the authority exerted over the other men serving a caravan.

[e] *jalaba*. Generic name for all trade caravans.

[f] *narghile*.[386] Pipe placed on a metal or pottery bottle, with large base, full of water, which also has an opening to insert a long pipe in order to smoke. The smoke of tobacco, attracted by the inhaling of the smoker, passes through the water and enters the mouth purified and fresh: in its passage it makes a sound similar to boiling liquid. Nevertheless, if this way of smoking satisfies taste, on the other hand it is very dangerous for health, because of the continuous effort made by the lungs in order to attract the smoke. This is possibly the main cause of asthma and catarrh, which affect the Turks in advanced age and kill them.

[g] *Barabra*. Arabs living between the First and the Second Cataracts, in harsh and desert places, but always close to the Nile.

[h] Anyone who has traveled in the desert would not find this particularly miraculous since it often happens that crows follow the caravans to feed on the waste, such as excrement and corpses, when animals die on the way.

---

382 On 20 October 1822 at Livorno; Luigi Zangheri, *Feste e apparati nella Toscana dei Lorena, 1737–1859* (Florence: L.S. Olshki, 1996), 215.

383 Tr. *canjiah*; Gabrieli, *Ippolito Rosellini*, 10–11.

384 A reference to the book of Gaetano Filangieri, *La scienza della legislazione*, Naples 1780–1785, and to the Byzantine lexicon *Suida*.

385 Arabic كبير (*kabir*).

386 Farsi *nargil*, Turkish *nargile*, Arabic شيشة،نرجيلة (*shisha, nargila*).

[i] *ramus*.[387] The Arabs call indiscriminately by this name anything that is not a boat, but is able to carry men and their belongings on water.

[j] *kabar*.[388] A sort of veil that hangs from the forehead to the feet, covering the face, with two holes for the eyes.

[k] *qaymaqam*. It roughly corresponds to what we call 'guard commander.' Even a private can hold this title, when responsible for a military position.

[l] *saqya*.[389] Hydraulic machinery that looks a lot like what we use to draw water from wells and water our vegetables in orchards.

[m] *wakala*.[390] A large building divided into quarters, which can be inhabited by many families.

[n] *ma'ash*.[391] This is what the largest boats that sail on the Nile are called.

[o] The shrine annexed to these pyramids serves as an entrance, always being adherent to the pyramid walls, so that, in order to enter the pyramid, one has to pass through the shrine. Nevertheless, some do have a separate entrance.

[p] *Bamya. Hibiscus bamia*[392]—Targioni, *Decadi*.[393] *Mulukhiya. Chorchorus Ulitorius Linnei*.[394]

[q] This Mamluk is the same who, sent by Ibrahim Pasha with many others to Europe in order to learn the language, now lives in the city of Prato in Tuscany, where I went to meet him shortly after his arrival.

---

387 "Ramus, it's a boat or raft made with reeds and dry gourds tied together, and sometimes pieces of wood that the Nubians put under their belly to cross the Nile more easily," Shinnie, *Linant de Bellefonds*, 13.

388 "A cloak of black silk called *habarah*," Lady Herbert, quoted in Deborah Manley and Sarah Abdel-Hakim, *Traveling through Egypt: From 450 B.C. to the Twentieth Century* (Cairo: American University in Cairo Press, 2004), 57.

389 Arabic ساقية (*saqya*), a water wheel.

390 "Early in the nineteenth century there was in Cairo a special *wakala* (caravanserai) for the slave-trade, called *wakalat al-jallaba*, which was described as follows: 'It has nothing remarkable but its decay and great dirt; the two genders are separated in small bad rooms, which have great analogy with our prisons, while others are divided into groups and left in the great court of the *wakala*, often on the trade goods of their masters,'" Baer, "Slavery in Nineteenth Century Egypt," 429.

391 Arabic مركب المعاش (*markab al-ma'ash*); cf. Gabrieli, *Ippolito Rosellini*, 10n3.

392 *Abelmoschus esculentus Moench* (also *Hibiscus esculentus* L.); Arabic بامية (*bamya*).

393 Ottaviano Targioni Tozzetti (1755–1826) was a Tuscan physician and botanist, author of various books on botany such as *Lezioni di agricoltura specialmente toscana* (1802–1804), *Istituzioni botaniche* (1802), *Observationum botanicarum* (1808–10), and *Dizionario botanico italiano* (1809). From 1802 he was professor of botany at Pisa University.

394 Ar. ملوخية (*mulukhiya*), *Corchorus l.*

Plates

Plate 1. Transportation of a colossus, from a tomb in Deir al-Barsha.

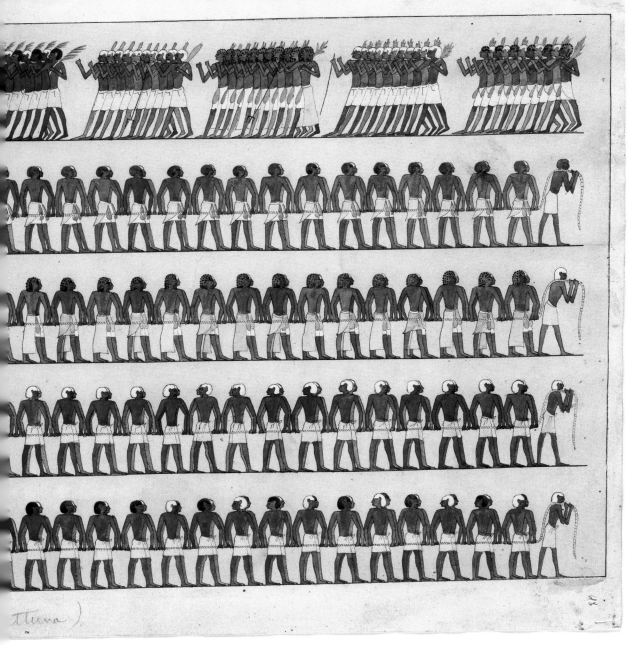

ttena)

Plate 2. Reliefs and column, from the portico of the temple of Thoth at Ashmunayn.

324

Plate 3.
1. Plan of the temple at Kanays.
2. Seti I offering Maat.
3. Dedicatory inscription of Seti I.

Plate 4. Gods with animal heads, from the tomb of Ramesses III.

Plate 5. God in a naos, from the tomb of Ramesses III.

Plate 6. Neferhotep and Parennefer honored by Horemheb

1

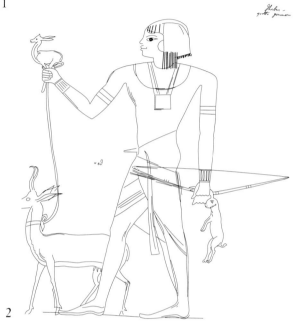

2

Tavola VII
Gournack
Incisione a basso rilievo.

3

Tavola VII
Gournack
Incisione a basso rilievo.

4

Plate 7.
1. Net makers and weaver, from the tomb of Khety at Beni Hasan.
2. A hunter with his game, from a Theban tomb.
3. A woman holding a sistrum and lotus flowers.
4. Personified *djed*-pillar, from TT 183.

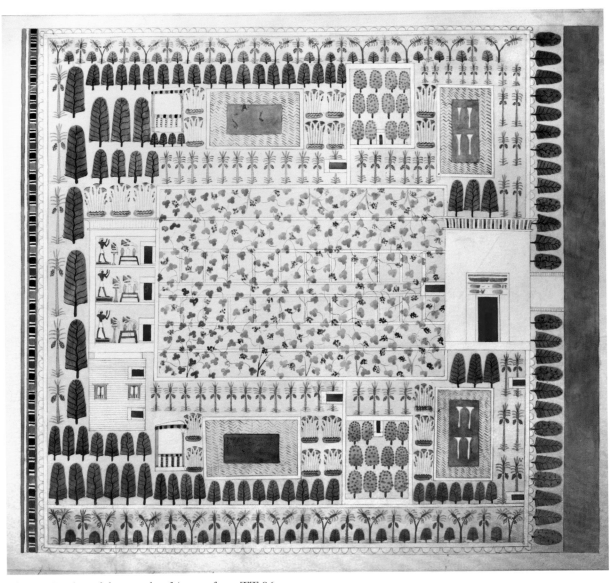

Plate 8. Garden of the temple of Amun, from TT 96.

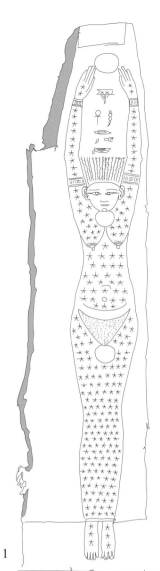

1

2

Plate 9.
1. Wooden coffin lid with stretched figure of Nut.
2. Wooden stela of the chantress of Montu Nestjerenmaat, from Salt's collection.
4. List of offerings from Luxor.

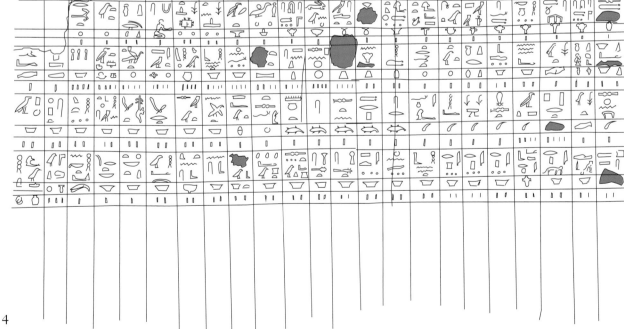

4

Basso rilievo in una Camera del Tempio
di Lugsor.

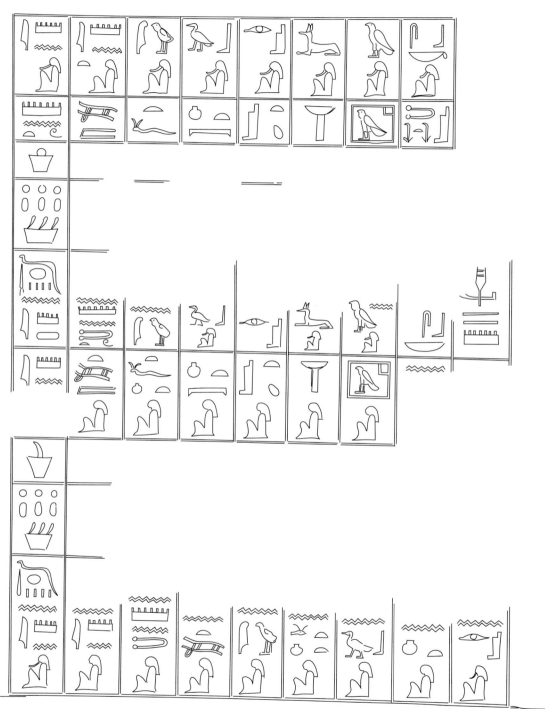

Plate 10.
1. Relief with names of gods and offering list, from Luxor.
2. King wearing an elaborate crown, from Luxor.
3. Relief with the *kas* of child Amenhotep III, from Luxor.
4. *Rekhyt* bird, from Luxor.
5. Ibis.

2

4

5

3

333

Plate 11. Reliefs from the temple of Khnum at Semna East

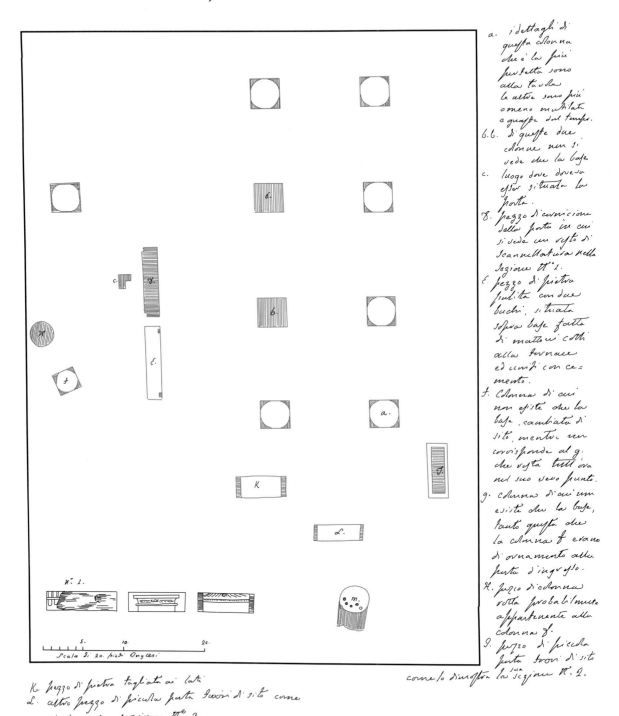

Plate 12. Plan of the Meroitic temple at Amara.

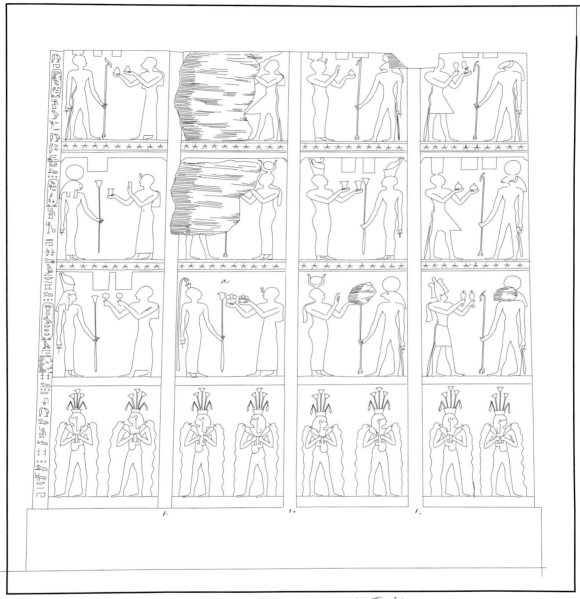

Tavola XI.   *Amara.*

Amara. Dettagli della Colonna marcata a. nel piano generale del Tempio;

1. Linee di Geroglifici che confusati dal tempo che è impossibile copiarli.

Plate 13. Column from the Meroitic temple at Amara.

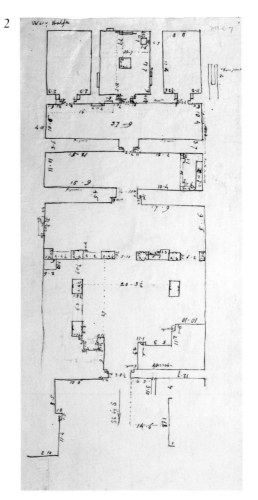

338

Plate 14.
1. Plan of the temple of Horus at Buhen.
2. Plan of the temple of Isis at Buhen.
3. Stela of General Montuhotep, from Buhen.
4. Plan of ruins at Buhen.
5. Plan of ruins at Buhen.
6. Plan of ruins at Buhen.
7 and 8. Plan of two rock-niches on Faras Island.

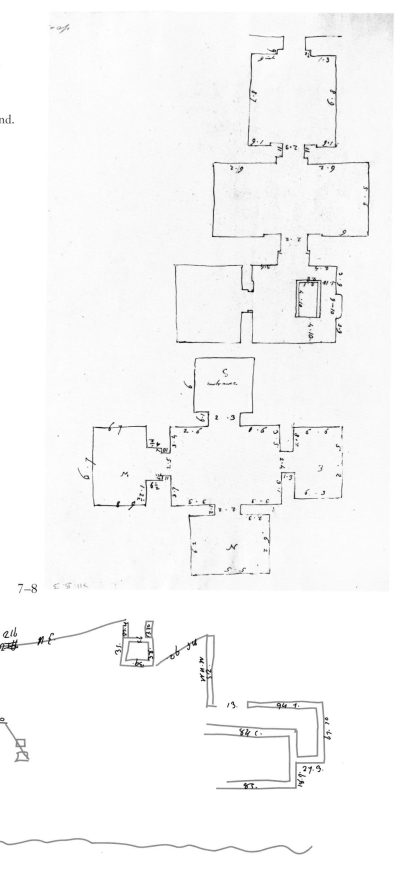

7–8

4–5–6

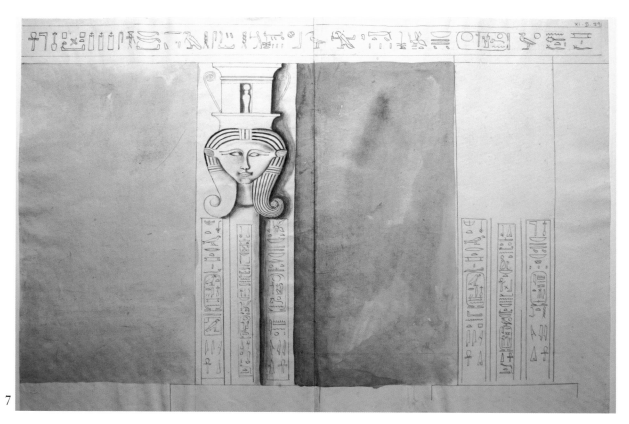

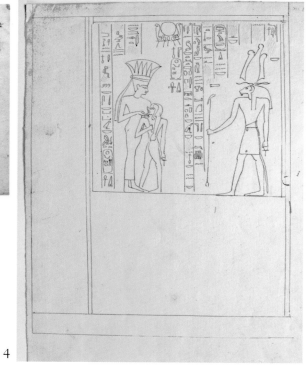

Plate 15.
1. Rock-stela of Hor, from Jebel al-Shams.
4. Anuket suckling the young pharaoh, from the rock-temple at Jebel Adda.
7. Hathor-head pillar, from the Small Temple at Abu Simbel.

Plate 16.
1 and 2. Osiris pillar, from the Large Temple at Abu Simbel.

1

2

342

4

3

Plate 17.
1. Reliefs of Ramesses II, from the Large Temple at Abu Simbel.
2. Ramesses II offering in front of Amun-Re, from the Large Temple at Abu Simbel.
3. Ramesses II in front of deified self, from the Large Temple at Abu Simbel.
4. Ramesses II offering to Thoth, from the Large Temple at Abu Simbel.

1a

1b

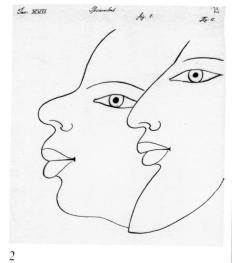

2

3

Plate 18.
1. Ramesses II offering prisoners, from the Large Temple at Abu Simbel.
2. Nubian and Hittite prisoners, from the Large Temple at Abu Simbel.
3. Feather-bearing prince, from the Large Temple at Abu Simbel.

Plate 19.
1. Ramesses II offering to Horus.
2. Ramesses II welcomed by Amun-Re, from the Large Temple at Abu Simbel.

Plate 20. Ramesses II offering lettuce,
from the Large Temple at Abu Simbel.

1

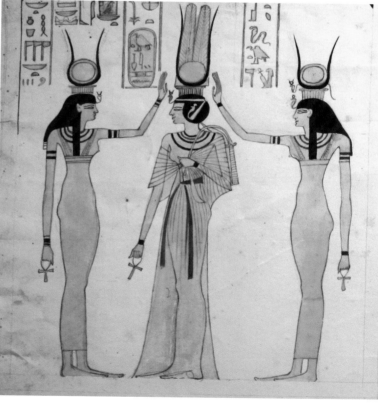

2

Plate 21.
1. Queen Nefertari playing the sistrum, from the Small Temple at Abu Simbel.
2. Queen Nefertari crowned by Hathor and Isis, from the Small Temple at Abu Simbel.

Ihsambul Piccolo Tempio.

Plate 22. Ramesses II and Nefertari offering to Taweret, from the Small Temple at Abu Simbel.

Plate 24. Ramesses II censing the bark of Amun-Re, from the temple of Wadi al-Sebu'a.

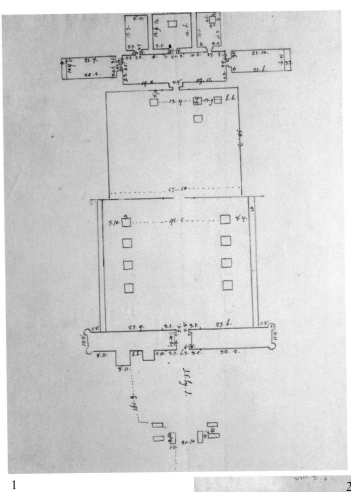

1

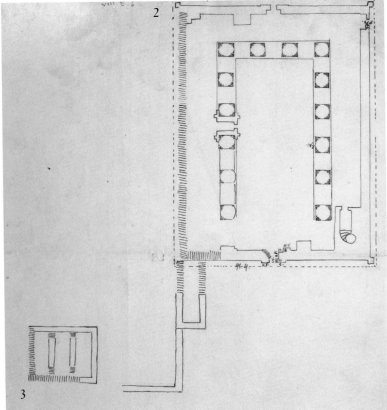

2

3

350

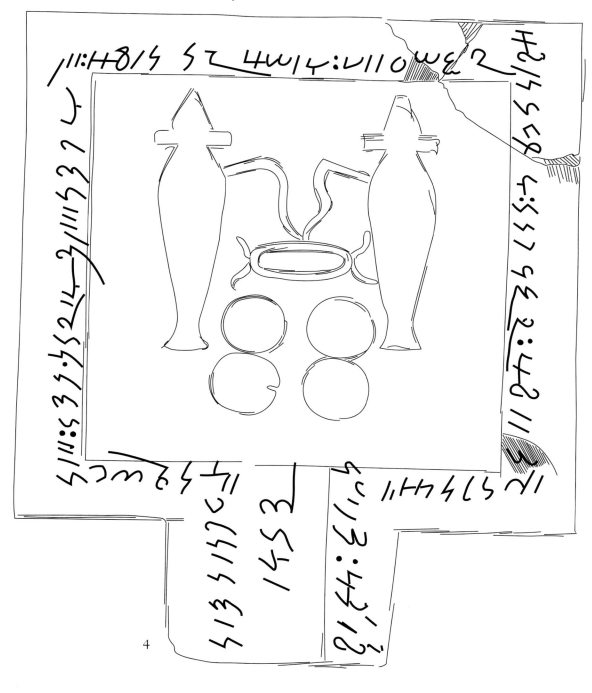

offrande maharaqa

4

Plate 23.
1. Plan of the temple of Wadi al-Sebuʿa.
2. Plan of the temple of Serapis at Maharraqa.
3. Plan of the small temple at Maharraqa.
4. Meroitic offering table from Maharraqa.

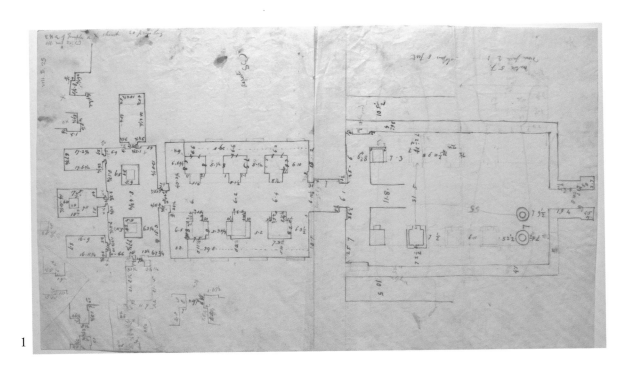

1

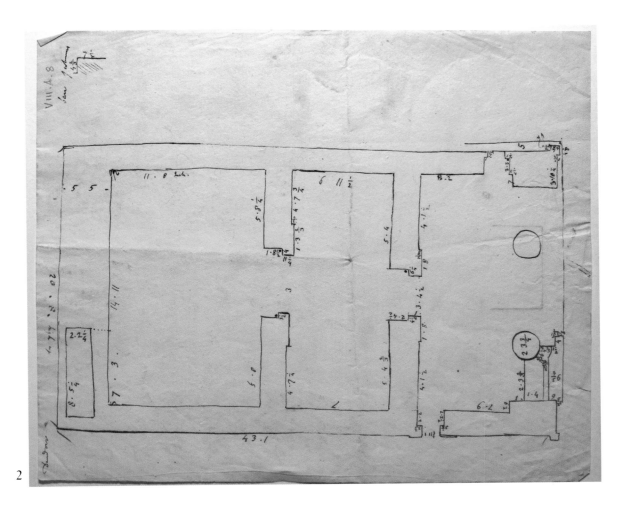

2

352

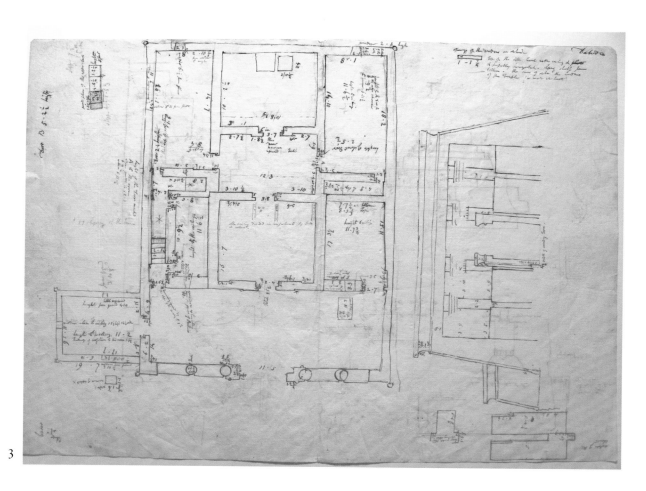

3

Plate 25.
1. Plan of the temple of Ptah at Gerf Hussein.
2. Plan of the temple of Peteisi and Padihor at Dandur.
3. Plan and front view of the temple of Isis at Dabod.

Plate 26.
4. Relief with the *abaton* of Osiris, from Philae.

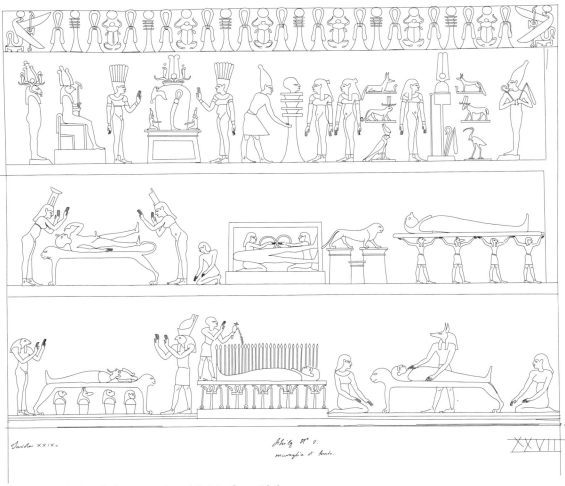

Plate 28. Relief with the mysteries of Osiris, from Philae.

354

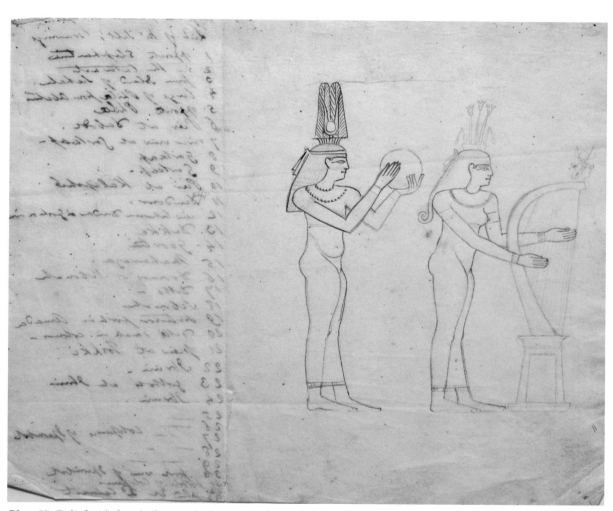

Plate 27. Relief with female figures playing music, from Philae.

Tav. XXXII.

Philæ n° 4.
parte dritta entrando on li quea alla porta.

XXVII

Plate 29. Relief with the mysteries of Osiris, from Philae.

356

Plate 33.
1. Frieze of the doorway of the temple of Amun at Siwa.
8. View of the necropolis of Abu al-Awaf, east of Siwa.
9. View of a funerary chapel at Abu al-Awaf, east of Siwa.

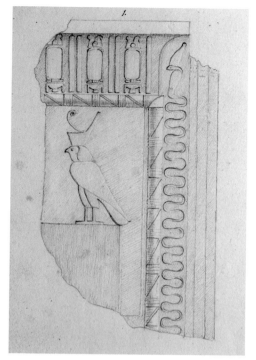

1

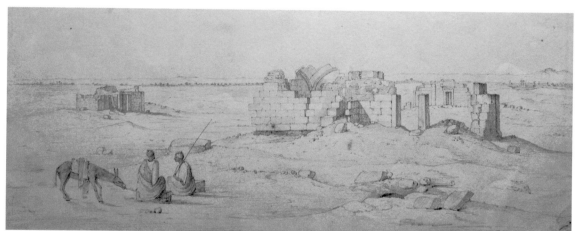

8

9

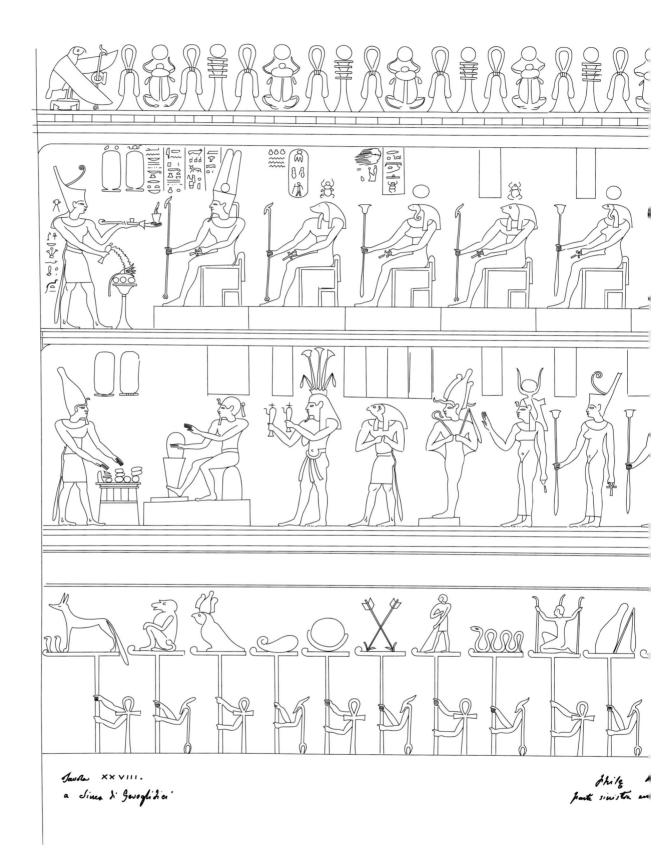

Tavola XXVIII.
a linea di Geroglifici

Phile
parte sinistra

Plate 30. Relief with the mysteries of Osiris, from Philae.

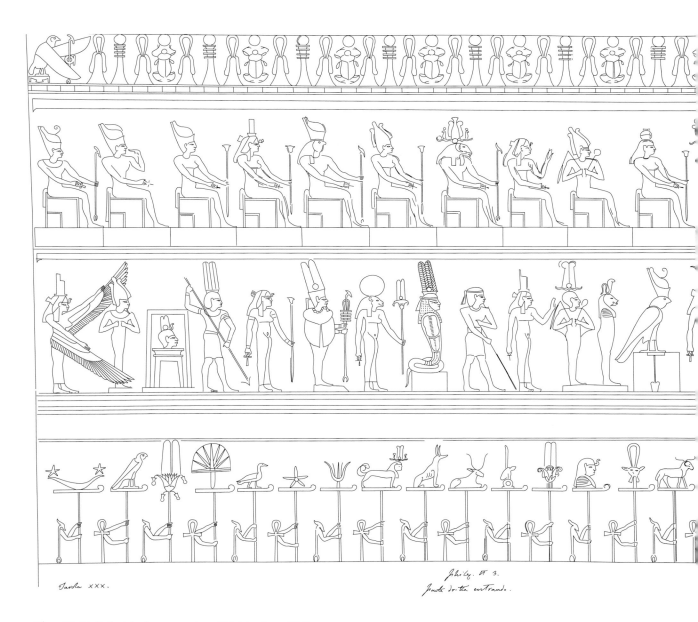

Tavola XXX.

Philae. IV 3.
Parte destra entrando.

Plate 31. Relief with the mysteries of Osiris, from Philae.

Tav. XXIX. Nº 2.

Tav. XXX. Nº 3.

Tav. XXVIII. Nº 1.

Tav. XXXII. Nº 4.

a. pianta della Camera.
b. piccolo muricciolo alto mezzo piedi, e largo. b. polli.

Philij seguito del Nº 3.

Tavola XXXI.

questa è la fine della tavola 30 è va unita precisamente
alla riga di fondo. marcata a. , e ciò perchè questa muraglia
e quasi mezzo braccio più lunga dell'altra. Io l'hò fatta netta più lunga come comparisci dalla scala qui aumesta per culevarve che due
correggersi restringendo le figure

Scala di 3 piedi Inglesi

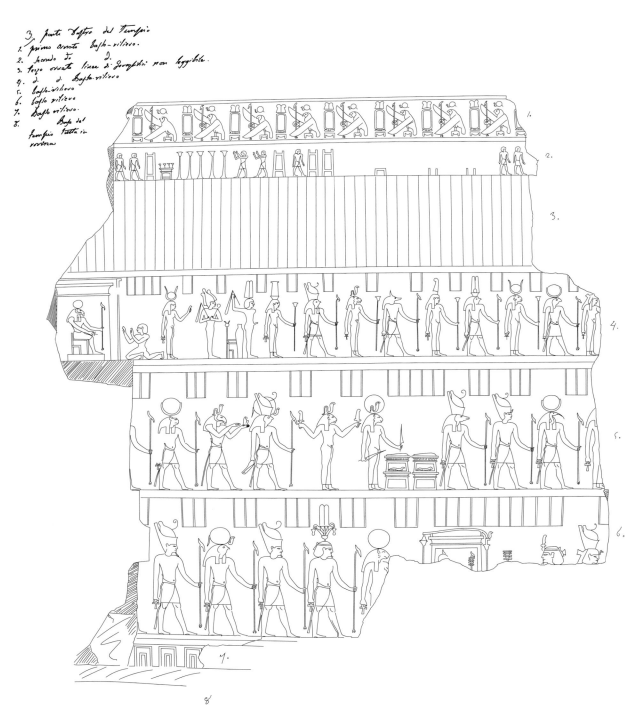

Plate 34. Reliefs on the west wall of the temple of Amun at Siwa.

362

1

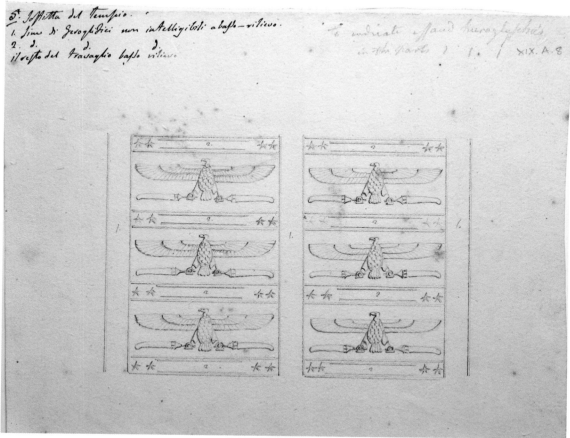

3

Plate 35.
1. King offering to Amun-Re and Mut, from the temple of Amun at Siwa.
3. Ceiling of the temple of Amun at Siwa.

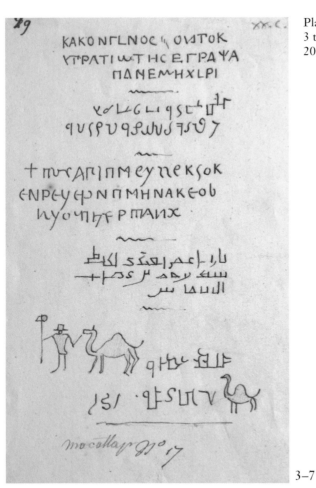

3–7

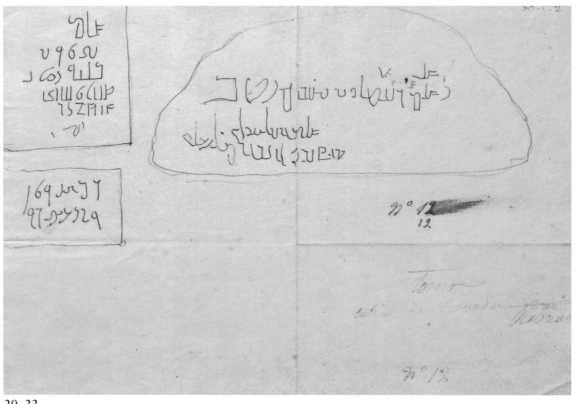

20–22

Plate 36.
3 to 7. Nabataean inscriptions from Wadi Mukattab.
20 to 22. Nabataean inscriptions from Wadi Hibran.

Plate 37.
3. Graffito of Sabi, Inspector of Administrators, from al-Maghara.

1

2

Mayara

Serabit el-Hadim

Plate 38.
1. Rock-stela of Niuserre, from al-Maghara.
2. Stela of Ameny, Great Overseer of the Cabinet of the Treasury, from al-Maghara.
7. Rock-stela of Dedusobek-Renefseneb, from al-Maghara.
8. Stela from al-Maghara.

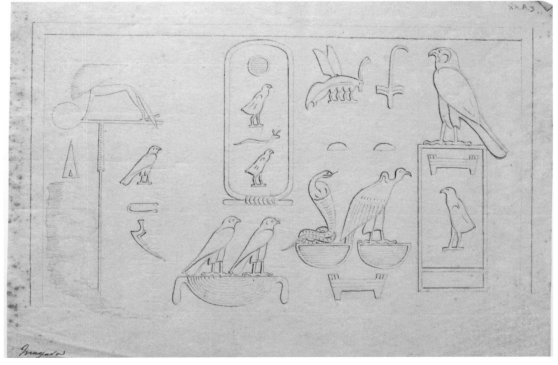

7

8   Mariette

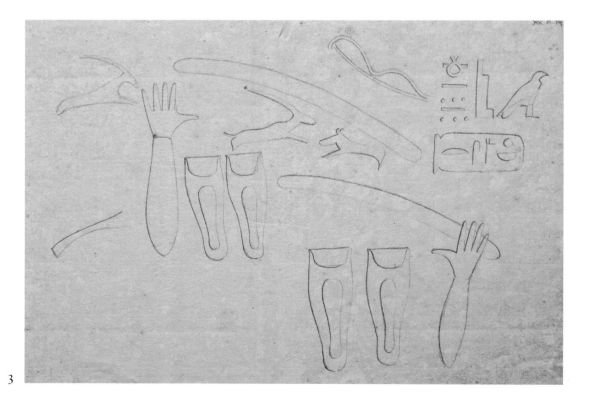

Plate 39.
1. Rock-stela of Khufu smiting an enemy in front of Thoth, from al-Maghara.
2. Rock-stela of Sanakht, from al-Maghara.
3. Graffiti of emblems, from al-Maghara.
4. Inscription of Khuy, Servant of the Great House, and Nabataean inscription from al-Maghara.
5. Stela of Senaaib, Overseer of Treasure, from al-Maghara.

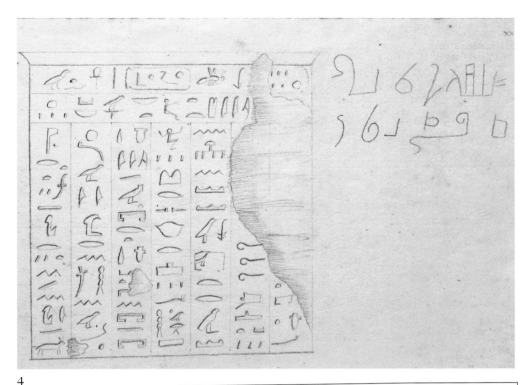

4

5   Serabit el Khadim

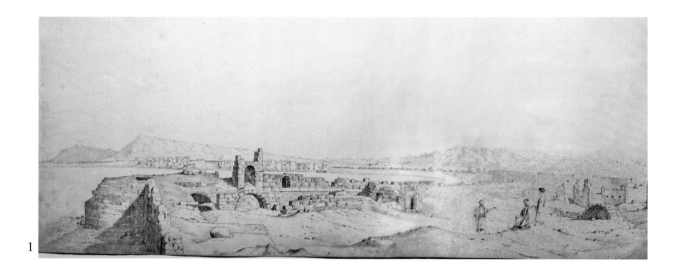

1

10

Plate 40.
1. View of Ras Raya fortress.
10. Ruins of monastic settlements in Wadi Firan.

Plate 42. A king in front of Hathor and Ptah, on a stela from Serabit al-Khadim.

1

Plate 41.
1. Seti II with high officers, from Serabit al-Khadim.
3 and 4.
a. Rock-stela with Thutmose III in front of Hathor and Hatshepsut in front of Sopdu, from al-Maghara.

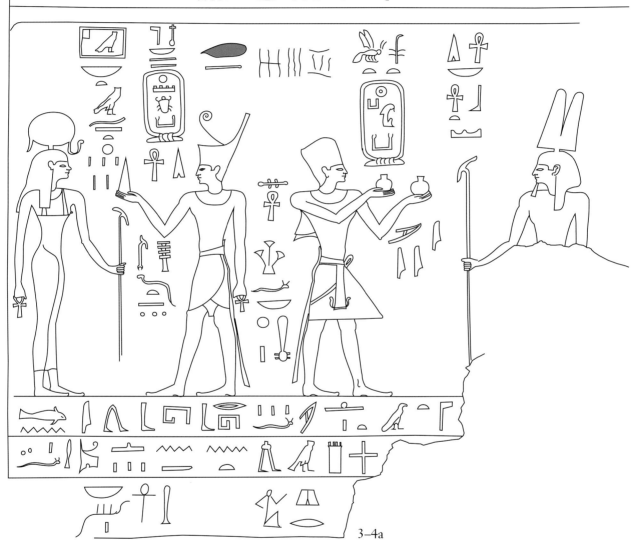

3–4a

3–4b

Plate 41.
3 and 4.
b. Rock-stela of Thutmose IV in front of Hathor, from Serabit al-Khadim.
c. Rock-stela of Saneferet, Overseer of the Cabinet, Overseer of Lower Egypt, and of General Iuki, with Amenemhat III in front of Hathor, from Serabit al-Khadim.

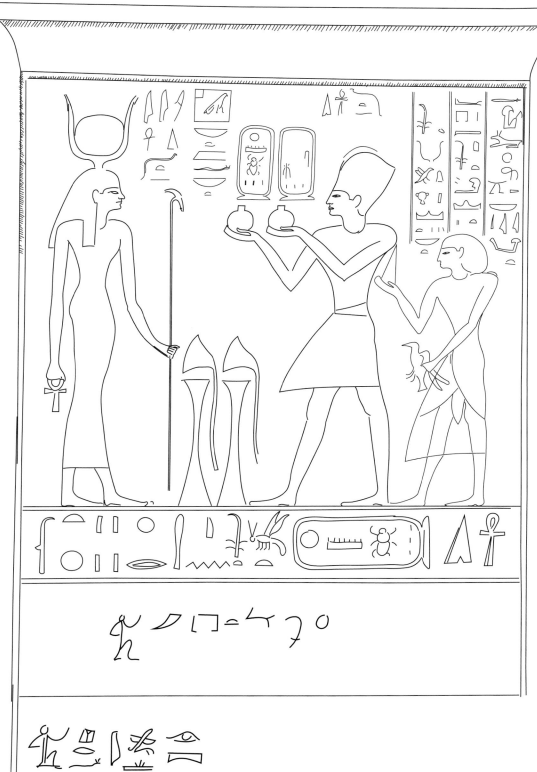

3–4c

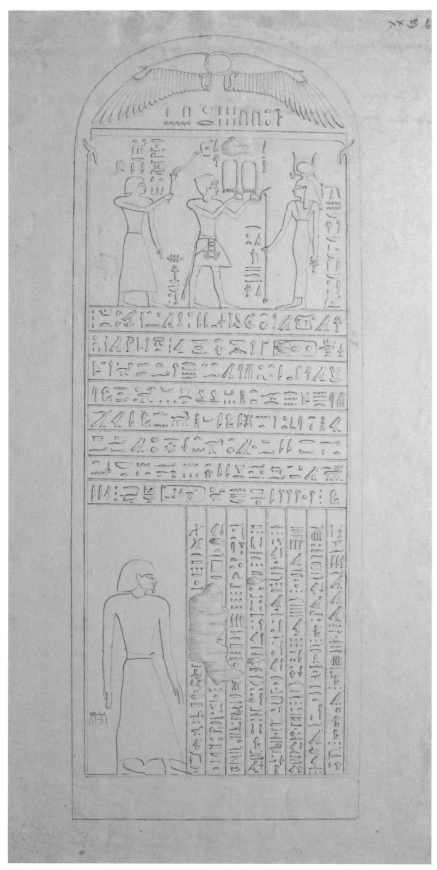

Plate 43. Thutmose III in front of Hathor, on a stela from Serabit al-Khadim.

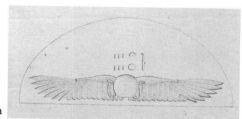

1a

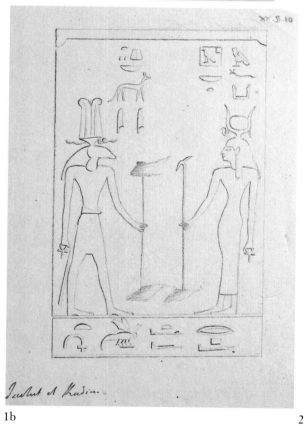

1b

2

Plate 44.
1. Khentekhtai in front of Hathor, on a stela from Serabit al-Khadim.
2. Amenemhat IV offering to Khentekhtai and Seneferu offering to Sopdu, on a stela from Serabit al-Khadim.

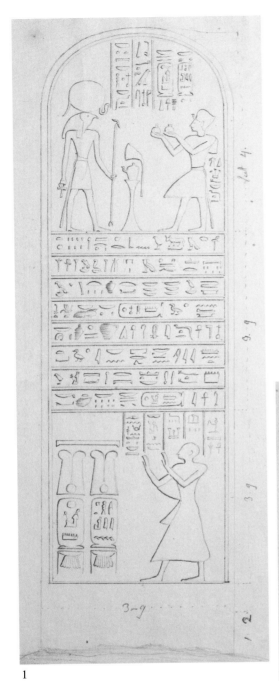

1

2

Plate 45.
1. Seti I in front of Re-Horakhty, on a stela from Serabit al-Khadim.
2. Stela of Saneferet, Overseer of the Cabinet, from Serabit el-Khadim.

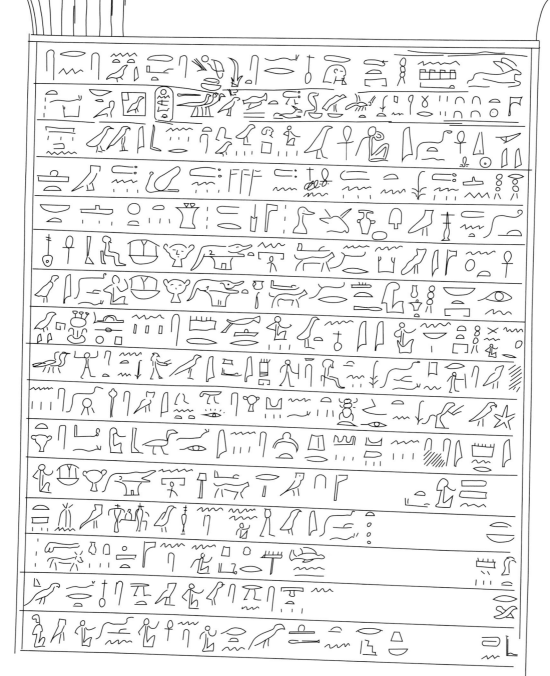

Plate 46.
Rock-stela of Sobekherheb, Overseer of the Cabinet of the Treasury, from Serabit al-Khadim.

Plate 47. Seti I welcomed by Hathor, on a relief from KV 17.

Plate 48. Seti I libating or censing in front of the gods, on a relief from KV 17.

Plate 49. Queen Nefertari playing the sistrum in front of Taweret, on a relief from Jebel al-Silsila.

Plate 50.
1. Goddess of the fields carrying offerings, on a relief from Kom Ombo.
2 and 3. Decorative detail of the cornice from Kom Ombo.

382

Plate 52.
1. East front of the bark shrine of Amenhotep III on Elephantine Island.
2. Inscription of the west front of the bark shrine of Amenhotep III on Elephantine Island.

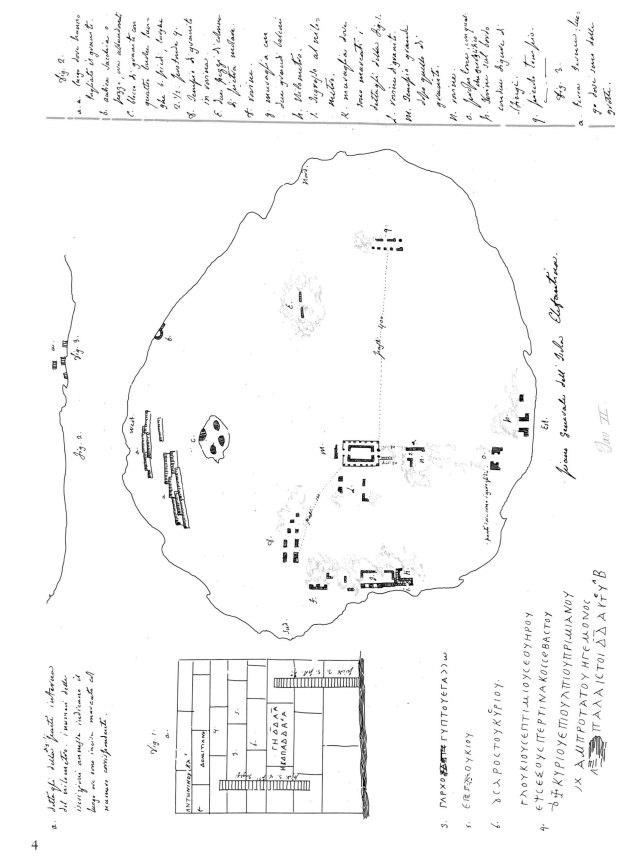

Piano del Tempio d'Elefantina

Dettagli della Fig. 1.

a.a. Scannellatura, che va sino ad una certa altezza dentro le colonne per uso credo io della porta.

B.B. Due muraglie fabbricate in altro tempo dopo la costruzione del Tempio.

C. pezzo di muraglia, che pare aver fatto servito di recinto al Tempio.

D.D. due pietre quadrate di granito

E. Continuazione di fabbricato in pietra calcarea di due piedi circa, e quadde gesografico.

F. altro fabbricato di mattoni secchi al sole in rovina.

g. principio di una muraglia in rovina, di cui non esistono che venti piedi = alla Distanza di 70 piedi vi sono altre rovine che dovevano a questa muraglia appartenere.

vest

Fig 1.

2

Fig. 2.
Piano del piccolo Tempio.

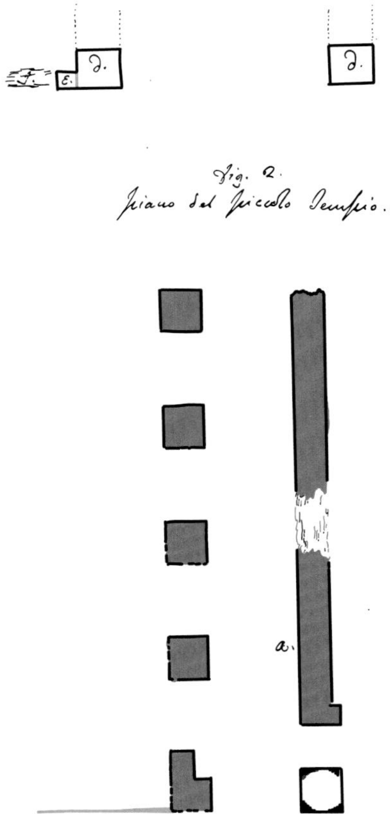

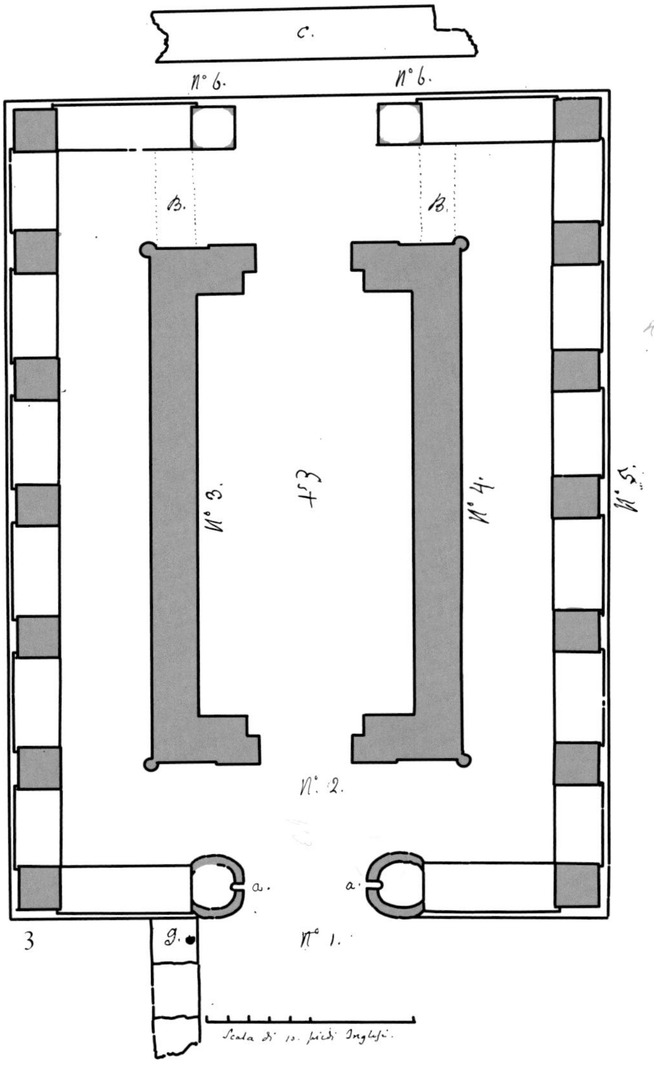

3

Plate 51.
1. Plan of the island of Elephantine.
2. Plan of the bark shrine of Ramesses II on Elephantine Island.
3. Plan of the bark shrine of Amenhotep III on Elephantine Island.
4. Nilometer of Elephantine with six Greek inscriptions.

a. in quest'ornamento si conservano ancora i colori verde rosso in mezzo al Blu

b. I geroglifici appartengono alla parte Sud

c.d. Pilastri ristorati con geroglifici del Sud.

E. Geroglifici del Sud.

f.f. Non è stato possibile ristorarli mancando interamente da ambe le parti

g. Il coltello in questo nome inciso sopra il globo e la tazza è stato fatto dopo.

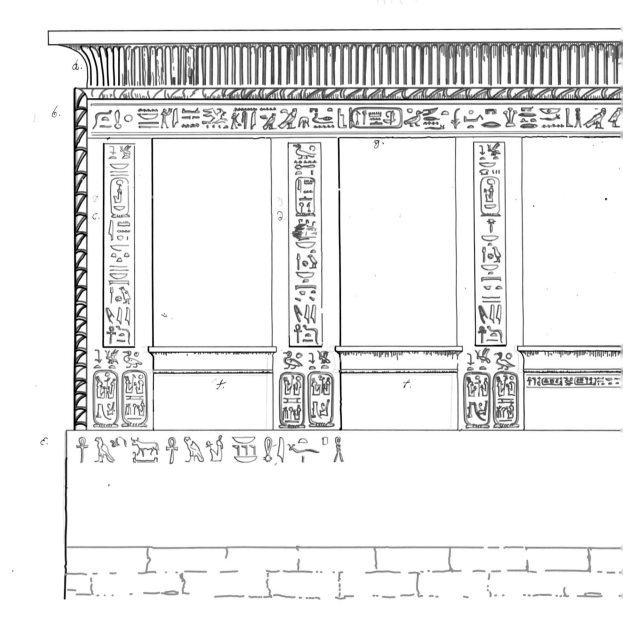

Plate 53. North front of the bark shrine of Amenhotep III on Elephantine Island.

cerno del portico: parte nord:

387

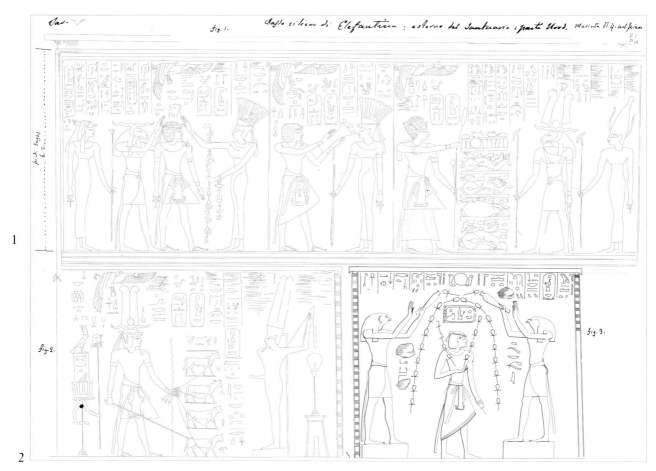

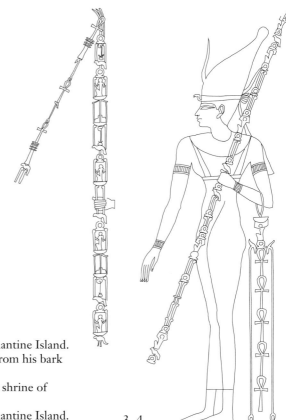

Plate 55.
1. Various reliefs of Amenhotep III from his bark shrine on Elephantine Island.
2. Amenhotep III purified by two hawk-headed gods, on a relief from his bark shrine on Elephantine Island.
3 and 4. Satet holding an elaborate staff, on a relief from the bark shrine of Amenhotep III on Elephantine Island.
5. Various reliefs of Amenhotep III from his bark shrine on Elephantine Island.

3–4

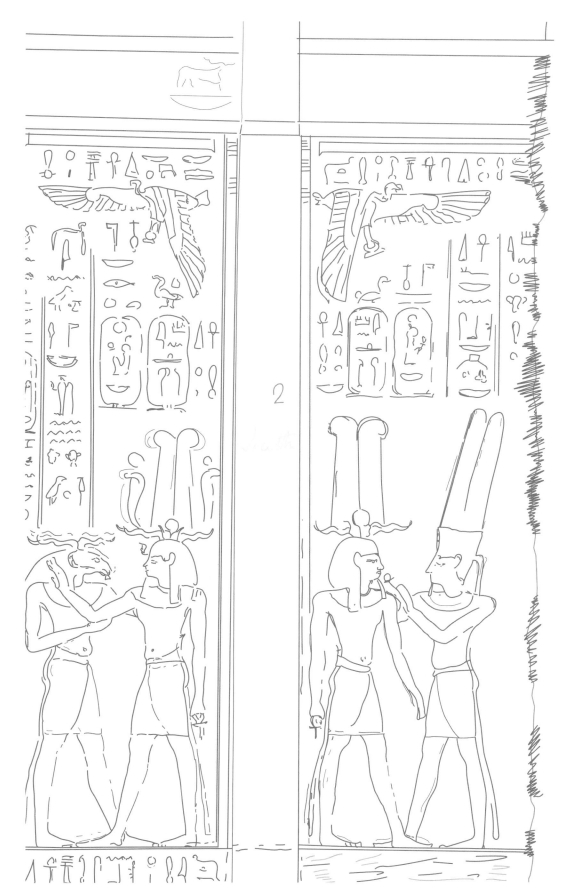

2

5

Plate 56. Various reliefs of Amenhotep III from his bark shrine on Elephantine Island.

s. piedi Inglesi.

Plate 57. Relief from the bark shrine of Ramesses II on Elephantine Island.

Plate 54. East front of the inner sanctuary, bark shrine of Amenhotep III on Elephantine Island.

Plate 58. Thutmose III on various reliefs, from the temple of Ellesiya.

Tavola XVII.   Piano del Tempio di Semne. Est.

a.   Colonna che sostiene l'architrave.
B.   Il Cornicione dell'architrave è travagliato
C.   lo stesso è sdrucito da questa parte.
d.d. Due piccole Camere con geroglifici coloriti
E.   qui doveva essere la porta d'ingresso:
     in seguito turata con grosse pietre.
ff. Due Colonne con base sepolta, e capitelli rotti.
g.g. Pilastri con geroglifici confusi dal tempio.
H.   le figure di questa camera sono incise
     a differenza delle altre che sono a basso
     rilievo delicato.
I.   In questa parte si vede un resto di cornice
     fuor di sito, chi sa se apparteneva al
     tempio. Per dei la parte esterna, fino quella d'ingresso,
     è formata di grosse pietre rozze ancora.

H.   vi ci è stata messa una pietra per chiudere la porta.
L.L. due stipiti mezzo consumati.
M.   pezzo di pietra fuor di sito.

     I Cornicioni, le porte ed i pilastri erano
     incisione a basso rilievo.

Fig. 1.

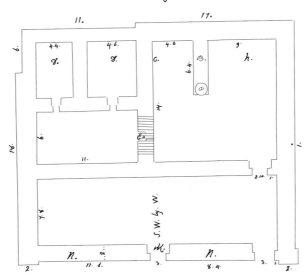

S. W. by W.

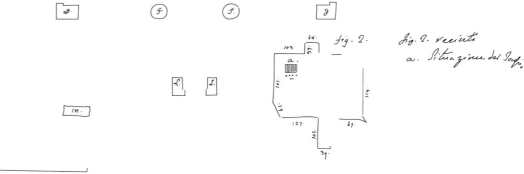

Fig. 2.   Fig. 2. veduto
a. Situazione del Sas...

Scala di 10. piedi Inglesi.

1–2

Semene Est.
dettagli facciata esterna marcata N. nel piano.

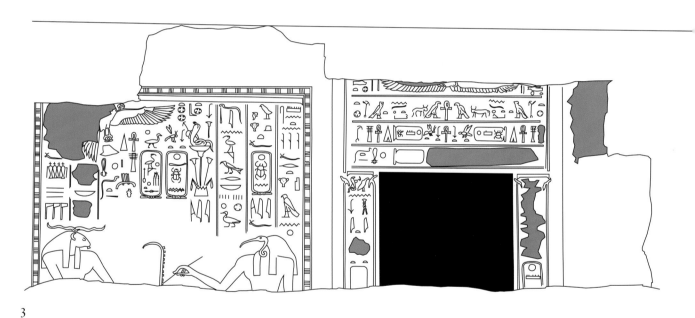

3

Plate 59.
1 and 2. Plan of the temple of Khnum at Semna East.
3. Khnum and Thoth, on a relief from the temple at Semna East.

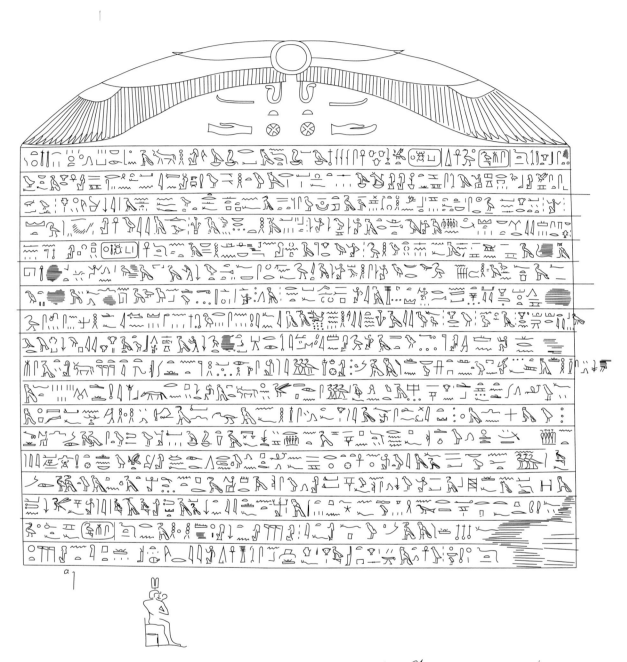

ai confini di *Congola* *Nuova* *una* *rocca* di faccia all' Isola *Tummy*   incisione
a. deve *essere* della larghezza *dote* marcata a.

Plate 60. Rock-stela of Thutmose I at Tombos.

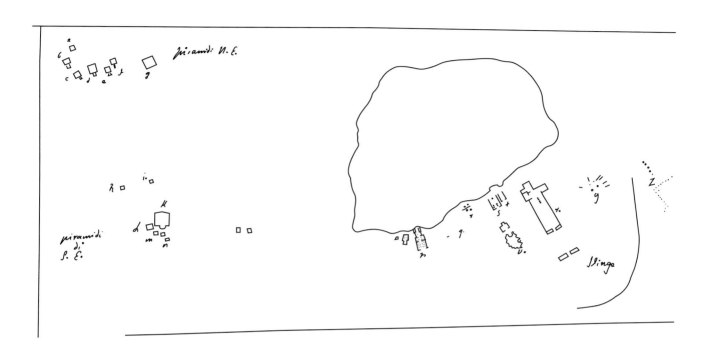

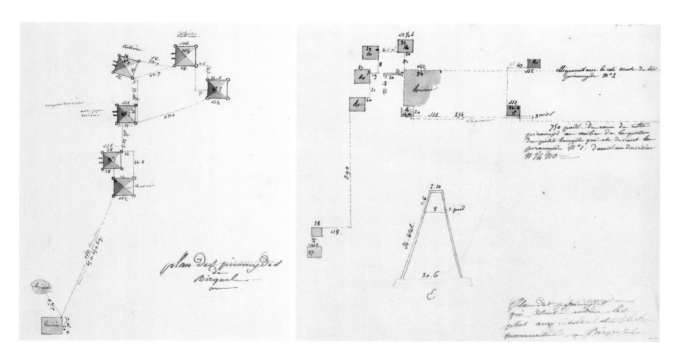

Plate 61.
1. General plan of the site of Jebel Barkal.

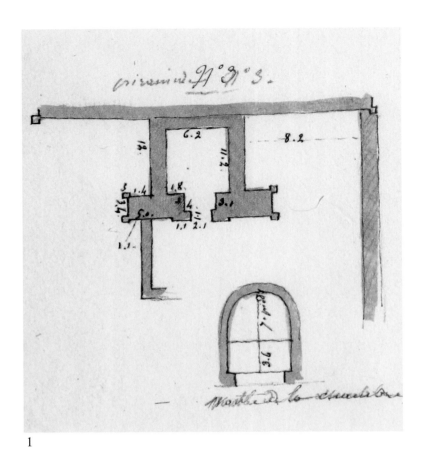

1

2

Plate 62.
1. Plan of pyramid No. 3 at Jebel Barkal.
2. Front view of pyramid No. 3 at Jebel Barkal.
4. Plan of Temple of Hathor, Tefnut, and unknown goddess at Jebel Barkal.
5. Plan of Temple of Mut of Napata at Jebel Barkal.

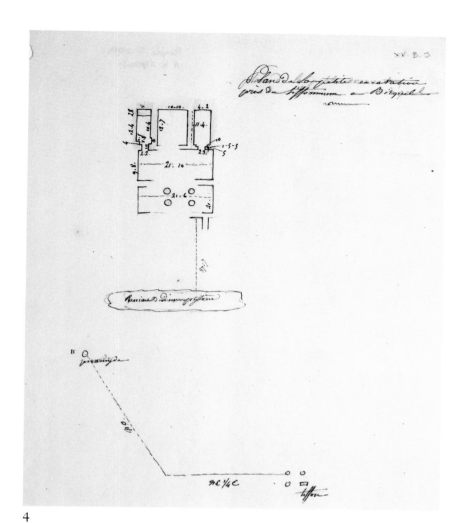

4

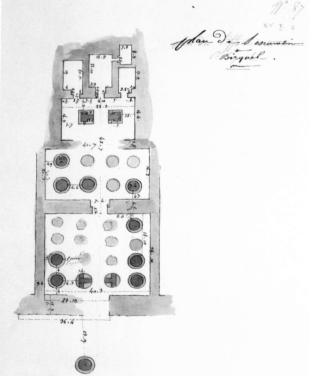

5

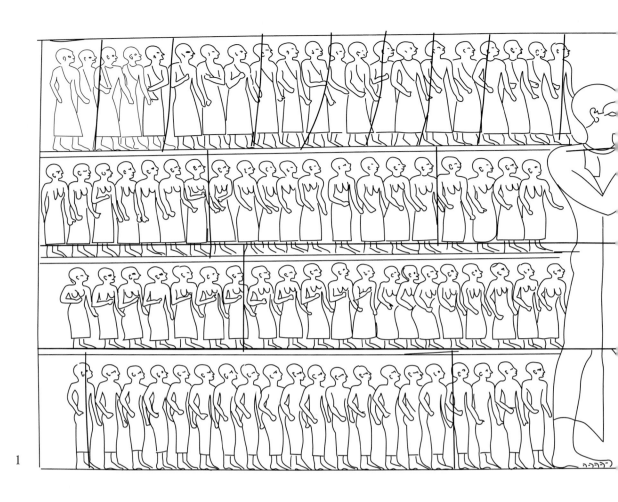

1

Plate 63.
1. Reliefs from the chapel of pyramid No. 3 at Jebel Barkal.
2. Prince Yetaretey in front of Queen Nawdamak, from the chapel of pyramid No. 6 at Jebel Barkal.

K at x in N°6 plan B

M

Berchel

Geroglifici dietro la sedia della Statua detta Berchel

Ai piedi del leone.

Linea di Geroglifici intorno al piedistallo del leone × consumati

Leone sotto

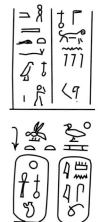

3–5

Plate 63.
3 to 5. Inscriptions on the pedestal of the "Prudhoe lions."

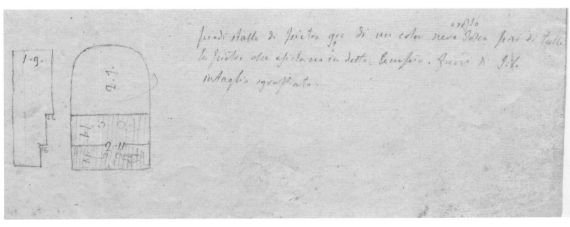

Plate 63.
6 and 7. Upper and side view of a granite pedestal from Jebel Barkal.

Tempietto N.º 3. muraglia di fondo.

1

Plate 64.
1. False door from the chapel of pyramid No. 3 at Jebel Barkal.
2. False door from the chapel of pyramid No. 5 at Jebel Barkal.

Tempietto П. 1.
Muraglia di fondo basso rilievo
ᵃ tutto questo basso rilievo si alza 4. pollici dalla Muraglia.

2

Plate 65.
1. Prince with censer in front of a seated king, on a relief in the chapel of pyramid No. 5 at Jebel Barkal.
2 and 3. Granite pedestal with tied prisoners held by a vulture, from Jebel Barkal.

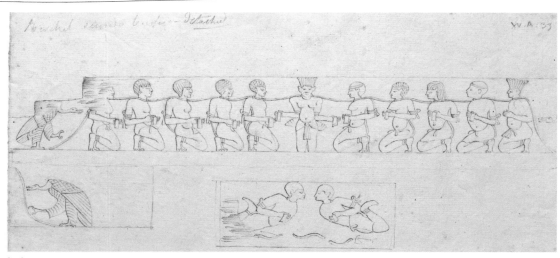

2–3

1

Plate 66.
1. Onuris and Nefertem, on a relief from temple B 300 at Jebel Barkal.
2. Bes-pillars in temple B 300 at Jebel Barkal.

pilastro allo *Sinistra* entrando : 2 : di dietro del Pilone   pilastro alla *Dritta* entrando

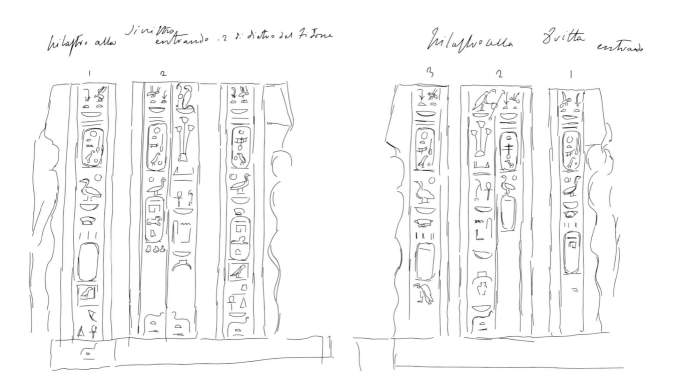

2

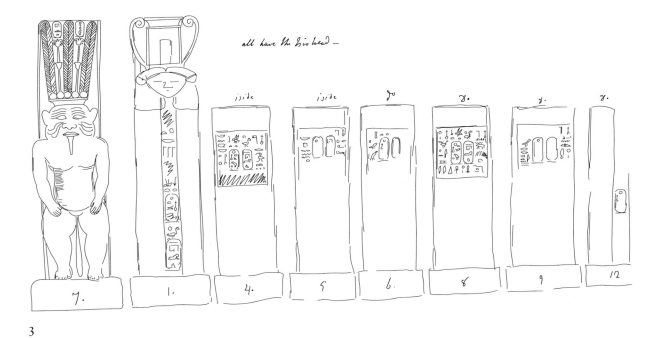

Pihone e Colonne der portico — Barchel Scavazione (Refer to plan B)

all have the Isis head —

iside   iside   Io.   X.   X.   X.

3

7.   1.   4.   5.   6.   8.   9.   12.

Plate 66.
3. Column of the second hall of temple B 300 at Jebel Barkal.
4. Royal princesses of Atlanersa, on a relief from the pylon of temple B 700 at Jebel Barkal.
5. Prince censing a seated king, on a relief from the chapel of pyramid No. 5 at Jebel Barkal.

410

4

5

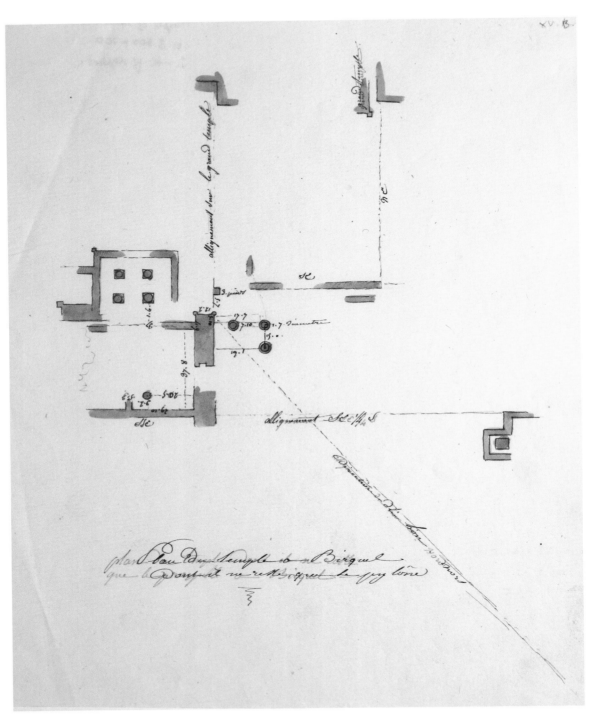

1–2

Plate 67.
1. Plan of temple B 600 at Jebel Barkal.
2. Plan of temple B 700 at Jebel Barkal.
4. Plan of temple B 500 at Jebel Barkal.

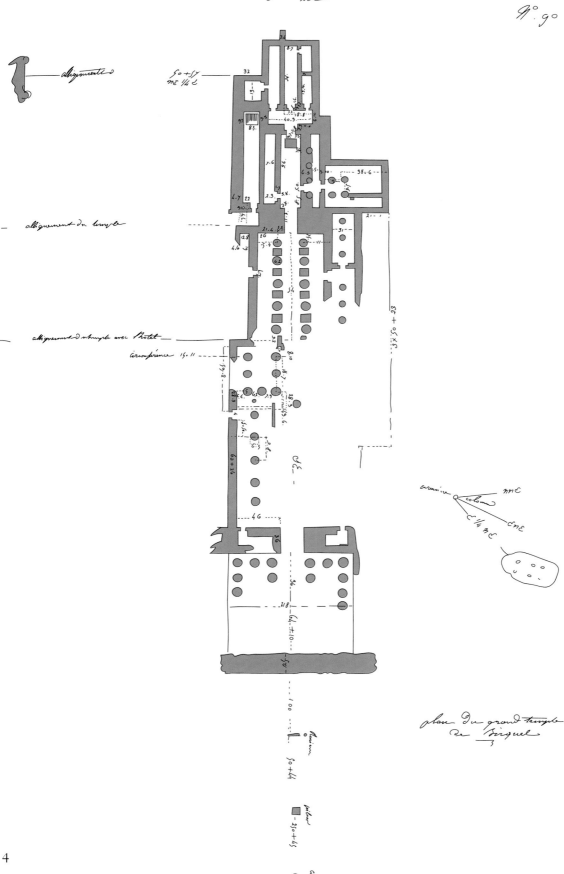

plan du grand temple a Birguel

4

413

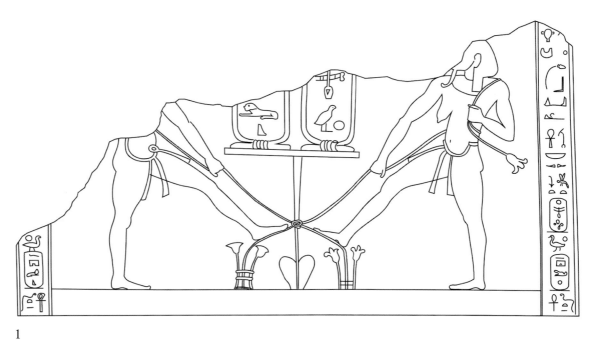

1

Plate 68.
1 and 2. Granite altar with Nile geniuses performing the *sema-tawi*, from Jebel Barkal.

2

415

Plate 69.
1 and 2. Granite altar with four images of Taharqa upholding the sky, from Jebel Barkal.
3 and 4. Black granite pedestal with figures of Taharqa upholding the sky, from Jebel Barkal.

416

3–4

417

Plate 70.
View of the necropolis of Nuri, with the pyramid of Taharqa.

1

4

Plate 71.
1. Bucolic scene, from the mastaba of Iymery at Giza.
4. Harvest scene, from the mastaba of Iymery at Giza.
7. Fishing scene, from the mastaba of Khafre-ankh at Giza.

7

2

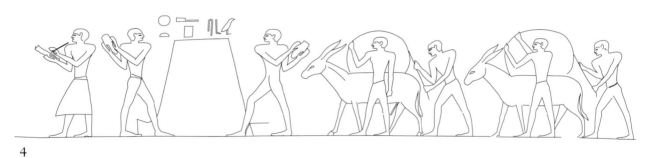

4

Plate 72.
2. Scribe registering the harvest and punishment of a thief, from the mastaba of Iymery at Giza.
4. Donkeys carrying goods to a warehouse, two men unloading, and a scribe recording, from the mastaba of Iymery at Giza.
5. Scribes, two men carrying geese, and a man pulling a bull, from the mastaba of Iymery at Giza.
6. Three offering-bearers and a man driving three bulls from, the mastaba of Iymery at Giza.
8. Three seated scribes, from the mastaba of Khafre-ankh at Giza.

5

6

8

423

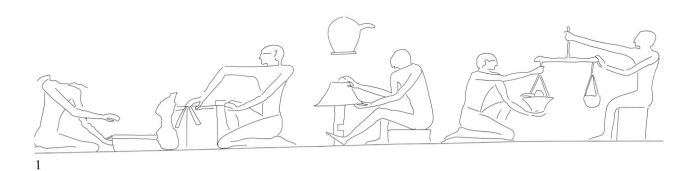

1

10

Plate 73.
1. Fabrication of metal vases, on a scene from the mastaba of Nebemakhet at Giza.
10. Baking and spit-roasting a duck, on a scene from the mastaba of Iymery at Giza.

Plate 74.
1 to 5. Various crafts, on a scene from the mastaba of Iymery at Giza.

Plate 75.
1. A sailing boat, on a scene from the tomb of Ramesses III.

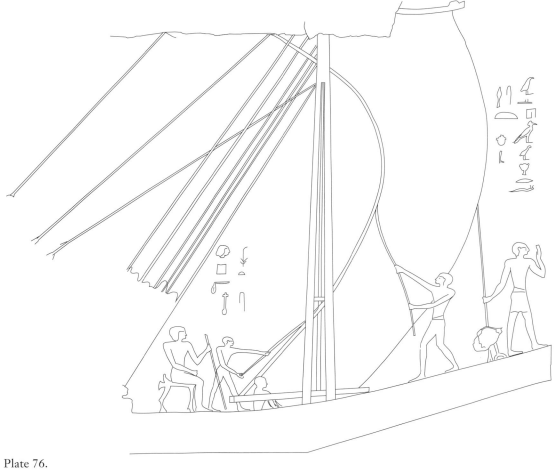

Plate 76.
5. Sailing boat, on a relief from the mastaba of Seshemnefer at Giza.

426

1

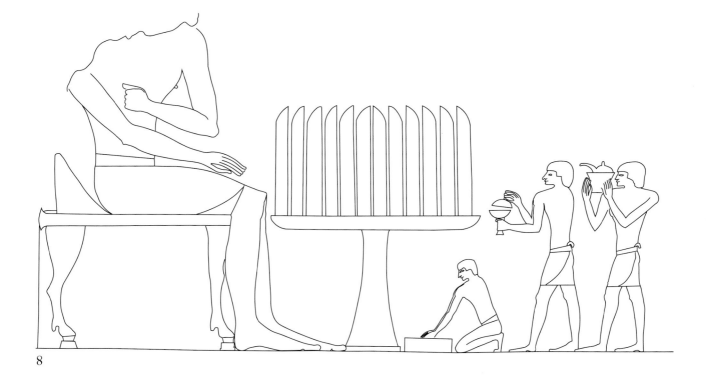

8

Plate 77.
1. Sailing boat, on a relief from the mastaba of Seshemnefer at Giza.
8. Offering scene, from an unidentified mastaba at Giza.

1–2

3

Plate 78.
1 and 2. Iymery carried on a palanquin, on a scene from his mastaba at Giza.
3. Offering-bearers ascending the ramp toward the statue of the deceased, on a scene from the mastaba of Debhen at Giza.

428

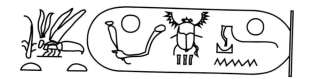

Plate 79. Royal cartouches from Giza, Heliopolis, and Luxor.

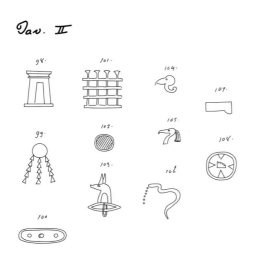

Ipsambul.
1. 2. 3. 4. 5. 6 7. 8. 9. 10. 11.
12. 13. 14. 15. 16. 17. 18. 20.
22.

el Kalabsci
19. 23. 24. 25. 26. 27. 28.
29. 30. 31. 32. 33. 34. 35.
36. 37. 38. 39. 40. 81. 82.
83.

Dendur.
21.

Phile
41. 42. 43. 44. 45. 46. 47.
48. 49. . 51. 52. 53. 54.
55. 56.

Luqxor
57. 84. 85. 86. 87. 88. 89.
90. 91. 92. 93. 94. 95.

amada
58. 59. 60. 61. 62. 63.

Semene
64. 65. 66. 67. 68. 69. 70.
71. 72. 73. 74. 75. 76. 77.
78. 79. 80.

Sacchi
96. 97. 98. 99. 100. 101. 102.
103. 104. 105. 106. 107. 108.

Plate 87. Selection of hieroglyphs from different inscriptions.

430

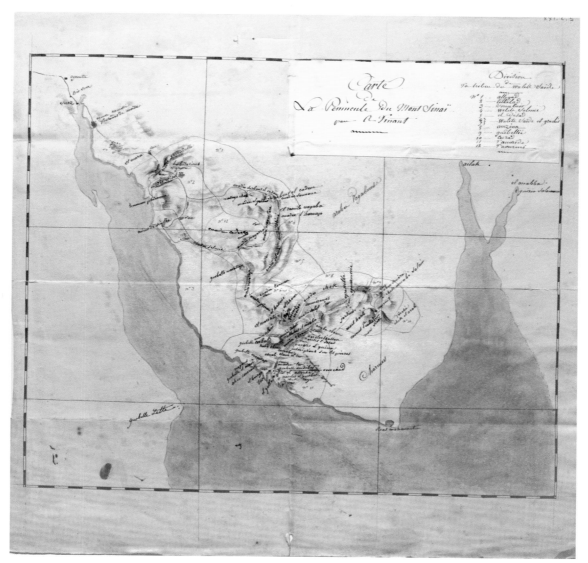

Plate 89. Map of the travel to Sinai.

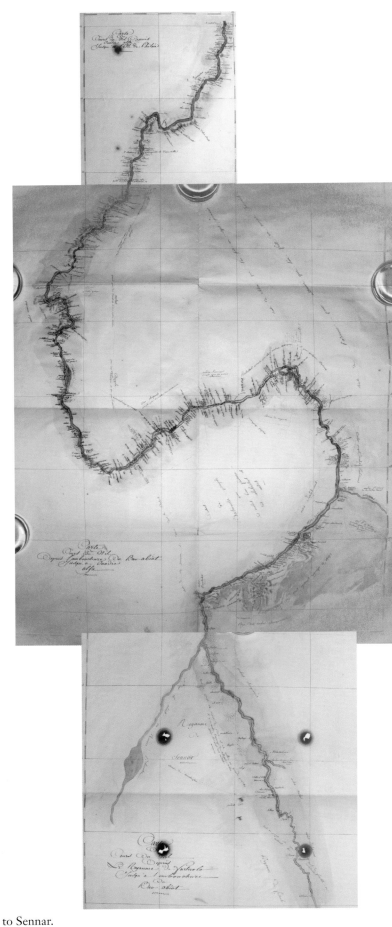

Plate 90. Map of the travel to Sennar.

Bibliography

Archival Material

Archivio dell'Opera del Duomo, Florence, Italy

Archivio del Museo Egizio, Florence, Italy

Archivio di Stato, Florence, Italy

Archivio di Stato, Siena, Italy

Archivio Storico delle Gallerie Fiorentine, Florence, Italy

Biblioteca Comunale, Siena, Italy

Biblioteca Universitaria, Pisa, Italy

Bibliothèque Centrale des Musées Nationaux, Paris, France

Bristol City Museum & Art Galleries, Bristol, United Kingdom

British Museum, Department of Ancient Egypt and Sudan, Archive, London, United Kingdom

Dar al-Watha'iq al-Qawmiya (National Archives of Egypt), Cairo, Egypt

Dorset History Centre, Dorchester, United Kingdom

Geheimes Staatsarchiv Preußischer Kulturbesitz, Berlin, Germany

Kingston Lacy House, Wimborne Minster, United Kingdom

Staatliche Kunstsammlungen zu Dresden, Dresden, Germany

Secondary Sources

Abd Allah, Mahmud M. "Siwan Customs." *Harvard African Studies* 1 (1917): 1–28.

Abdel Halim, Ahmed. "Native Medicine and Ways of Treatment in the Northern Sudan." *Sudan Notes and Records* 22 (1939): 27–48.

Adalian, Rouben. "The Armenian Colony of Egypt during the Reign of Muhammad Ali, 1805–1848." *Armenian Review* 33, no. 2 (1980): 115–44.

Adams, William Y. "J.L. Burckhardt, Ethnographer." *Ethnohistory* 20, no. 3 (1973): 213–28.

Aldsworth, Fred. *Qasr Ibrim: The Cathedral Church*. London: Egypt Exploration Society, 2010.

Andréossy, Antoine-François. "Mémoire sur la vallée des lacs de Natroun." In *Description de l'Égypte, ou Recueil des Observations et des Recherches*, État Moderne I, 279–98. Paris: Imprimerie Impériale, 1809.

Andriolo, Donatella, and Silvio Curto. *Catalogo delle chiese della Nubia*. Turin: Accademia delle Scienze, 2000.

Apophthegmata Patrum. In Jacques Paul Migne, *Patrologiae cursus completus, seu bibliotheca universalis, integra, uniformis, commoda, oeconomica, omnium Sanctorum Patrum, Doctorum Scriptorumque Ecclesiasticorum*. Series Graeca Prior, PG 65. Paris: Imprimerie Catholique, 1864.

Arrowsmith, John. *Nubia and Abyssinia* [map]. 1:3,860,000. London: Arrowsmith, 1832.

Arundale, Francis. *Illustrations of Jerusalem and Mount Sinai*. London: Henry Colburn, 1837.

Atiya, Aziz S. *The Monastery of St. Catherine in Mount Sinai*. Cairo: Misr S.A.E., 1950.

Baer, Gabriel. "Slavery in Nineteenth Century Egypt." *The Journal of African History* 8 (1967): 417–41.

Baines, John, and Jaromír Málek. *Atlas of Ancient Egypt*. Oxford: Andromeda, 1995.

Balboni, Luigi Antonio. *Gl'italiani nella civiltà egiziana del sec. XIX*. Alexandria: Stabilimento Tipo-Litografico V. Penasson, 1906.

Bankes, William J. *Narrative of the Life and Adventures of Giovanni Finati, Translated from the Italian and Edited by W. John Bankes*. London: John Murray, 1830.

Barrois, Georges A. "The Mines of Sinai." *The Harvard Theological Review* 25 (1932): 101–21.

Basset, René. "Le Synaxaire arabe jacobite. V. Les mois de Baounah, Abib, Mésoré et jours complémentaires." In *Patrologia Orientalis* XVII, 655–59. Paris: Firmin-Didot, 1923.

Beaucour, Fernand, Ynes Laissus, and Chantal Orgozo. *The Discovery of Egypt*. Paris: Flammarion, 1990.

Belzoni, Giovanni Battista. *Narrative of the Operations and Recent Discoveries within Pyramids, Temples, Tombs and Excavations in Egypt and Nubia; and of a Journey to the Coast of the Red Sea, in search of the Ancient Berenice; and another to the Oasis of Jupiter Ammon*. London: John Murray, 1820.

Benvenuti, Gino, and Gianfranco Benvenuti. *Vita di Ippolito Rosellini, padre dell'Egittologia italiana*. Pisa: Giardini, 1987.

Betrò, Maria Carmela. "Con Ippolito Rosellini, lungo il Nilo, a Tebe e oltre." In *La Piramide e la Torre: Duecento anni di archeologia egiziana*, edited by Edda Bresciani, 71–127. Pisa: Cassa di Risparmio di Pisa, 2000.

———, ed. *Ippolito Rosellini and the Dawn of Egyptology: Original Drawings and Manuscripts of the Franco-Tuscan Expedition to Egypt (1828–29) from the Biblioteca Universitaria di Pisa*. London: Golden House Publications, 2010.

———. *Lungo il Nilo: Ippolito Rosellini e la Spedizione Franco-Toscana in Egitto (1828–1829)*. Florence: Giunti, 2010.

Bierbrier, Morris L. "The Salt Watercolours." *Göttinger Miszellen* 61 (1983): 9–12.

Böckh, August F.J. *Corpus Inscriptionum Graecarum* IV.2, part xi. Berlin: Officina Academica, 1857.

Bonotto, Giovanni C. *Egitto magico: Monili e amuleti del deserto e delle oasi*. Turin: Celid, 2007.

Bosworth, Clifford E. "Al-Jabarti and the Frankish Archaeologists." *International Journal of Middle East Studies* 8, no. 2 (1977): 229–36.

Bovot, Jean-Luc. "La reconstruction de la tombe de Sennefer." In *La peinture égyptienne ancienne: Un monde de signes à préserver. Actes du Colloque International de Bruxelles, avril 1994*, edited by Roland Tefnin, 105–10. Brussels: Brepols, 1997.

Bresciani, Edda. "De Jean-François Champollion à Angelica, le 6 décembre 1827: la lettre retrouvée. Un nouveau portrait de Champollion à Pise." *Bulletin de la Société Française d'Égyptologie* 119 (1990): 15–24.

———. "I Lorena e l'Egitto svelato." In *Sovrani nel Giardino d'Europa: Pisa e i Lorena*, edited by Romano Paolo Coppini and Alessandro Tosi, 161–74. Pisa: Pacini Editore, 2008.

———. "Il richiamo della piramide: J.-F. Champollion e I. Rosellini in Egitto." In *La Piramide e la Torre: Duecento anni di archeologia egiziana*, edited by Edda Bresciani, 15–69. Pisa: Cassa di Risparmio di Pisa, 2000.

British Museum. "Red granite lion of Amenhotep III." http://www.britishmuseum.org/research/collection_online/collection_object_details.aspx?objectId=117626&partId=1&searchText=granite+head+amenhotep+III&page=1

Brocchi, Gian Battista. *Giornale delle osservazioni fatte ne' viaggi in Egitto, nella Siria e nella Nubia* 2. Bassano: A. Roberti, 1841.

Browne, William G. *Nouveau voyage dans la Haute et la Basse Égypte, en Syrie et au Darfour où aucun Européen n'avait pénétré*. Paris: Dentu, 1800.

Brue, Adrien H. *Carte détaillée en deux feuilles de l'Afrique et des iles qui en dépendent (partie septentrionale) par A. Brue, Géographe du Roi: Abyssinie et pays des Gallas* [map]. 1:15,000,000. Paris: Brue, 1828.

Burckhardt, Johann L. *Travels in Syria and the Holy Land*. London: John Murray, 1822.

Cailliaud, Frédéric. *Voyage à l'oasis de Thèbes et dans les déserts situés à l'orient et à l'occident de la Thébaide fait pendant les années 1815, 1816, 1817 et 1818*. Paris: Imprimerie Royale, 1821–62.

———. *Voyage à Méroé, au Fleuve Blanc, au-delà de Fâzoql dans le midi du royaume de Sennâr, à Syouah et dans cinq autres oasis: fait dans les années 1819, 1820, 1821 et 1822: accompagné de Cartes géographiques, de Planches représentant les monuments de ces contrées, avec des détails relatifs à l'état moderne et à l'histoire naturelle*. Paris: Imprimerie Royale, 1826.

Caminos, Ricardo A. *The Shrines and Rock-Inscriptions of Ibrim*. London: Egypt Exploration Society, 1968.

Caner, Daniel F., ed. *History and Hagiography from the Late Antique Sinai*. Liverpool: Liverpool University Press, 2010.

Cauville, Sylvie. *Le Zodiaque d'Osiris*. Leuven: Peeters, 1997.

Champollion, Jean-François. *Lettre à M. Dacier relative à l'alphabet des hiéroglyphes phonétiques*. Paris: Firmin Didot, 1822.

———. *Lettres à M. le Duc de Blacas d'Aulps*. Paris: Firmin Didot, 1826.

———. *Lettres écrites d'Égypte et de Nubie, en 1828 et 1829*. Paris: Firmin Didot, 1833.

———. *Monuments de l'Égypte et de la Nubie*. Paris: Firmin Didot, 1835–45.

———. *Notice descriptive*. Paris: Firmin Didot, 1844–89.

Clayton, Peter. *The Rediscovery of Ancient Egypt: Artists and Travellers in the Nineteenth Century*. London: Thames and Hudson, 1984.

Cline, Walter B. *Notes of the People of Siwah and el Garah in the Libyan Desert*. Menasha: G. Banta Pub. Co., 1936.

Coquin, René-Georges. "Pharan." In *The Coptic Encyclopedia*, vol. 6, http://ccdl.libraries.claremont.edu/cdm/singleitem/collection/cce/id/1573/rec/1

Cornevin, Robert. *Histoire de l'Afrique*. Vol. 2, *L'Afrique précoloniale du tournant du XVIe au tournant du XXe siècle*. Paris: Payot, 1966.

Coutelle, Jean-Marie-Joseph. "Observations sur la topographie de la presqu'île du Sinaï, les moeurs, les usages, l'industrie, le commerce et la population des habitans." In *Description de l'Égypte*, État Moderne, II.1, 278–304. Paris: Imprimerie Impériale, 1813.

Crawford, Osbert G.S. *The Fung Kingdom of Sennar*. Gloucester: John Bellows, 1951.

Curto, Silvio, and Laura Donatelli, eds. *Bernardino Drovetti Epistolario*. Milan: Cisalpino Goliardica, 1985.

Curzon, Robert. *Visits to the Monasteries in the Levant*. London: John Murray, 1849.

Dahari, Uzi. "Les constructions de Justinien au Gebel Mousa." In *Le Sinaï durant l'antiquité et le Moyen Âge: 4000 ans d'histoire pour un désert. Actes du colloque "Sinaï" qui s'est tenu à l'Unesco du 19 au 21 septembre 1997*, edited by Dominique Valbelle and Charles Bonnet, 151–56. Paris: Errance, 1998.

Dahari, Uzi, Rivka Calderon, Yael Gorin-Rosen, William D. Cooke, and Orit Shamir. *Monastic Settlements in South Sinai in the Byzantine Period: The Archaeological Remains*. Jerusalem: Israel Antiquities Authority, 2000.

Daris, Sergio. *Giuseppe Nizzoli: Un impiegato consolare austriaco nel levante agli albori dell'Egittologia*. Naples: Graus Editore, 2005.

D'Athanasi, Giovanni. *A Brief Account of the Researches and Discoveries in Upper Egypt, Made under the Direction of Henry Salt Esq*. London: John Hearne, 1836.

Dawson, Warren R., Morris L. Bierbrier, and Eric P. Uphill. *Who Was Who in Egyptology*. London: Egypt Exploration Society, 1995.

Denham, Dixon, Hugh Clapperton, and Walter Oudnay. *Narrative of Travels and Discoveries in Northern and Central Africa in the Years 1822, 1823 and 1824*. Boston: Cummings, Hilliard & Co., 1826.

Denon, Dominique Vivant. *Voyage dans la Basse et Haute-Égypte pendant les campagnes du général Bonaparte*. Paris: P. Didot, 1802.

de Rozière, François-Michel. "Notice sur les ruines d'un monument persépolitain découvert dans l'isthme de Suez par M. de Rozière, ingénieur en chef des mines." In *Description de l'Égypte, Antiquités, Mémoires*, 1:265–76. Paris: Imprimerie Impériale, 1809.

Description de l'Égypte, ou Recueil des observations et des recherches qui ont été faites en Égypte pendant l'expédition de l'armée française. Paris: Imprimerie Impériale, 1809–22.

Desroches-Noblecourt, Christiane, Sergio Donadoni, and Gamal Moukhtar. *Le speos d'el-Lessiya*. Cairo: Centre de Documentation et d'Étude sur l'Ancienne Égypte, 1968.

Desroches-Noblecourt, Christiane, and Charles Kuentz. *Le petit temple d'Abou Simbel "Nofretari pour qui se lève le Dieu-Soleil."* Cairo: Ministry of Culture, Centre de Documentation et d'Étude sur l'Ancienne Égypte, 1968.

de Thévenot, Jean. *The Travels of Monsieur de Thevenot into the Levant*. London: H. Clark, 1687.

Devilliers, Édouard. "Description des antiquités situées dans l'Isthme de Suez par M. Devilliers ingénieur en chef des ponts et chaussées." In *Description de l'Égypte, Antiquités, Déscriptions*, 2:8–10. Paris: Imprimerie Impériale, 1818.

Douin, Georges. *Histoire du Soudan Égyptien*. Vol. 1, *La pénétration, 1820–22*. Cairo: Société Royale de Géographie d'Égypte, 1944.

Driault, Édouard. *La formation de l'empire de Mohamed Aly de l'Arabie au Soudan (1814–1823): correspondance des consuls de France en Égypte*. Cairo: Société Royale de Géographie d'Égypte, 1927.

Elsner, Gudrun. *Ägyptische Altertümer der Skulpturensammlung: Ausstellung im Albertinum zu Dresden, 30. Juli 1993–24. Juli 1994*. Dresden: Staatliche Kunstsammlungen, 1993.

English, George B. *A Narrative of the Expedition to Dongola and Sennaar, under the Command of His Excellence Ismael Pasha, Undertaken by Orders of His Highness Mehemmed Ali Pasha, Viceroy of Egypt*. London: John Murray, 1822.

Evelyn-White, Hugh G., and Walter Hauser. *The Monasteries of Wâdi 'n Natrûn*. Part 2, *The History of the Monasteries of Nitria and of Scetis*. New York: The Metropolitan Museum of Art, 1932.

Fahmy, Khaled. *All the Pasha's Men: Mehmet Ali, His Army and the Making of Modern Egypt*. Cairo: American University in Cairo Press, 2002.

———. "The Era of Muhammad 'Ali Pasha, 1805–1848." In *The Cambridge History of Egypt*, vol. 2, *Modern Egypt from 1517 to the End of the Twentieth Century*, edited by Martin W. Daly, 139–79. Cambridge: Cambridge University Press, 1998.

Fakhry, Ahmed. *Siwa Oasis: Its History and Antiquities*. Cairo: Government Press, 1944.

Fasano Guarini, Elena, Giuseppe Petralia, and Paolo Pezzino. *Storia della Toscana*. Vol. 2, *Dal Settecento ad oggi*. Rome–Bari: Laterza, 2004.

Finkelstein, Israel, and Asher Ovadiah. "Byzantine Monastic Remains in the Southern Sinai." *Dumbarton Oaks Papers* 39 (1985): 39–75, 77–79.

Fisher, Marjorie M., Peter Lacovara, Salima Ikram, and Sue D'Auria. *Ancient Nubia: African Kingdoms on the Nile*. Cairo: American University in Cairo Press, 2012.

Fitzenreiter, Martin. "Geschichte, Religion und Denkmäler der islamischen Zeit im Nordsudan." *Mitteilungen der Sudanarchäologischen Gesellschaft zu Berlin* 10 (2000): 84–111.

Flemming, Carl. *Nordöstliches Afrika: Entworfen und gezeichnet von F. Handtke*. Lithographie [map]. 1:5,450,000. Glogau: Druck und Verlag von C. Flemming, 1855.

Flusin, Bernard. "Ermitages et monastères: Le monachism au mont Sinaï à la période proto-byzantine." In *Le Sinaï durant l'antiquité et le Moyen Âge: 4000 ans d'histoire pour un désert. Actes du colloque "Sinai" qui s'est tenu à l'Unesco du 19 au 21 septembre 1997*, edited by Dominique Valbelle and Charles Bonnet, 133–38. Paris: Errance, 1998.

Forsskål, Peter, and Carsten Niebuhr. *Flora Aegyptiaco-Arabica sive descriptiones plantarum, quas per Aegyptum inferiorem et Arabiam felicem detexit, illustravit Petrus Forskål*. Copenhagen: Möller, 1775.

Forsyth, George H. "The Monastery of St. Catherine at Mount Sinai: The Church and Fortress of Justinian." *Dumbarton Oaks Papers* 22 (1968): 1–19.

Forti Messina, Annalucia. "Studenti e laureati in medicina a Pavia nell'Ottocento pre-unitario." *Mélanges de l'École Française de Rome, Moyen-Age, Temps modernes* 97, no. 1 (1985): 489–530.

Frasca, Francesco. "La vittoria della Royal Navy nella battaglia d'Abukir." *Informazioni della Difesa* 2 (2003): 49–58.

Fuller, John. *Narrative of a Tour through Some Parts of the Turkish Empire*. London: Richard Taylor, 1829.

Gabrieli, Giuseppe. *Ippolito Rosellini e il suo Giornale della Spedizione Letteraria Toscana in Egitto negli anni 1828–1829*. Rome: Reale Società Geografica Italiana, 1925.

Gardiner, Alan H., Thomas E. Peet, and Jaroslav Černý. *The Inscriptions of Sinai* 1. London: Egypt Exploration Society, 1952.

Garnier, F.A. *Afrique Orientale, comprenant l'Égypte, l'Abyssinie, et partie du Takrour Oriental. Extrémité orientale de la cote d'Afrique, d'après la carte de M. le commt. Guillain. Atlas sphéroïdal & universel de géographie dressé par F.A. Garnier, géographe* [map]. 1 :8.000,000. Paris: Veuve Jules Renouard Éditeur, 1860.

Gessler-Löhr, Beatrix. "Who Discovered 'Belzoni's Tomb'? A Glimpse behind the Scenes of Early Exploration and the Antiquities Trade." In *Talking along the Nile: Ippolito Rosellini, Travellers and Scholars of the Nineteenth Century in Egypt. Proceedings of the International Conference Held on the Occasion of the Presentation of Progetto Rosellini, Pisa, June 14–16, 2012*, edited by Marilina Betrò and Gianluca Miniaci, 101–24. Pisa: Pisa University Press, 2013.

Giles, Sue. "The Belzoni Collection of Paintings of the Tomb of Sety I in the Collections of Bristol Museums, Galleries & Archives." In *L'Egitto in Età Ramesside: Atti del Convegno, Chianciano Terme, 17–18 Dicembre 2009*, edited by Daniela Picchi, 19–26. Cinisello Balsamo: Silvana Editoriale, 2011.

Gohary, Said, and Jocelyn Gohary. "Report on Cultural Heritage Sites in South Sinai." http://st-katherine.net/en/downloads/Cultural%20Heritage%20Sites.pdf

Grossmann, Peter. "Early Christian Ruins in Wadi Fayran (Sinai): An Archaeological Survey." *Annales du Service des Antiquités de l'Égypte* 70 (1985): 75–81.

———. "Excavations in Firan–Sinai (February 1998)." *Annales du Service des Antiquités de l'Égypte* 76 (2001): 135–41.

———. "Report on the Season in Firan–Sinai (February–March 1992)." *Byzantinische Zeitschrift* 89 (1996): 11–36.

———. "Wadi Fayran/Sinai: Report on the Seasons in March and April 1985 and 1986 with an Appendix on the Church at Mount Sinai." *Annales du Service des Antiquités de l'Égypte* 75 (1999–2000): 153–65.

Grossmann, Peter, Michael Jones, and Yiannis Meimaris. "Report on the Season in Firan–Sinaï (February–March 1995)." *Byzantinische Zeitschrift* 91 (1998): 345–53.

Guidotti, Maria Cristina. "A proposito di Deir el Medina prima della scoperta: un pezzo della collezione Ricci nel Museo Egizio di Firenze." In *L'Egitto fuori dell'Egitto: Dalla riscoperta all'egittologia. Atti del Convegno Internazionale, Bologna 26–29 marzo*, edited by Cristiana Morigi Govi, Silvio Curto, and Sergio Pernigotti, 209–19. Bologna: CLUEB, 1991.

———. "Dall'Egitto a Firenze via Pisa." In *La Piramide e la Torre: Duecento anni di archeologia egiziana*, edited by Edda Bresciani, 129–63. Pisa: Cassa di Risparmio di Pisa, 2000.

Hall, Henry R. "Letters to Sir William Gell from Henry Salt, [Sir] J.G. Wilkinson, and Baron von Bunsen." *Journal of Egyptian Archaeology* 2 (1915): 133–67.

Halls, John J. *The Life and Correspondence of Henry Salt Esq. FRS*. London: Richard Bentley, 1834.

Hari, Robert. *La tombe thébaine du père divin Neferhotep (TT50)*. Geneva: Éditions de Belles-Lettres, 1985.

Henniker, Frederick. *Notes during a Visit to Egypt, Nubia, the Oasis, Mount Sinai, and Jerusalem*. London: John Murray, 1823.

Hill, Richard L. *A Biographical Dictionary of the Anglo-Egyptian Sudan*. Oxford: Clarendon Press, 1951.

Hobbs, Joseph J. *Mount Sinai*. Austin: University of Texas Press, 1995.

Holt, Peter M. *A Modern History of the Sudan, from the Funj Sultanate to the Present Day*. London: Weidenfeld and Nicolson, 1961.

———. "Sultan Selim I and the Sudan." *Journal of African History* 8 (1967): 19–23.

Hunter, Robert. *Egypt under the Khedives, 1805–1879: From Household Government to Modern Bureaucracy*. Pittsburgh, PA: University of Pittsburgh Press, 1984.

Irby, Charles L., and James Mangles. *Travels in Egypt and Nubia, Syria, and Asia Minor; during the years 1817 & 1818*. London: T. White and Co. Printers, 1823.

Jomard, Edme-François. *Voyage à l'Oasis de Syouah, rédigé et publié par M. Jomard*. Paris: De Rignoux, 1823.

Kapteijns, Lidwien, and Jay Spaulding. "Precolonial Trade between States in the Eastern Sudan, ca. 1700–ca. 1900." *African Economic History* 11 (1982): 29–62.

Kawatoko, Mutsuo. "Archaeological Survey in the Raya/al-Tur Area, South Sinai." *Al-'Usur al-Wusta: The Bulletin of Middle East Medievalists* 16 (2004): 26–30.

Keimer, Ludwig. "Glanures II: Les deux Botzaris." *Cahiers d'histoire égyptienne* 7, no. 3 (1955): 196–203.

Kramp, Mario. "Ägypten für Entschlossene: Die abenteuerliche Expedition des Kölners Franz Christian Gau 1818/1819." In *Ägypten, Nubien und die Cyrenaika: Die imaginäre Reise des Norbert Bittner (1786–1851)*, edited by Lisa Schwarzmeier, Ernst Czerny, and Mario Kramp, 33–46. Ruhpolding: Verlag Franz Philipp Rutzen, 2012.

Kuhlmann, Klaus P. *Das Ammoneion: Archäologie, Geschichte und Kultpraxis des Orakels von Siwa.* Mainz am Rhein: Von Zabern, 1988.

Kühnemann, Frank. "Physics of the Sand." Presentation, Physics Department, German University in Cairo, 3 March 2008. http://physics.guc.edu.eg/pdfs/BoomingSand.pdf

Kurz, Marcel. "Un homme d'action dans l'Égypte du XIXe siècle." In *Voyage aux mines d'or du Pharaon*, edited by Marcel Kurz, 17–101. Saint Clément de Rivière: Fata Morgana, 2002.

Kurz, Marcel, and Pascale Linant de Bellefonds. "Linant de Bellefonds: Travels in Egypt, Sudan and Arabia Petraea (1818–1828)." In *Travellers in Egypt*, edited by Paul Starkey and Janet Starkey, 61–69. London and New York: Tauris Parke, 2001.

Laming Macadam, Miles F. "Gleanings from the Bankes Mss." *Journal of Egyptian Archaeology* 32 (1946): 57–64.

Leclant, Jean. "De l'égyptophilie à l'égyptologie: érudits, voyageurs, collectionneurs et mécènes." *Comptes-rendus des séances de l'année—Académie des inscriptions et belles-lettres* 4 (1985): 630–47.

Lee, Lorna, and Stephen Quirke. "Painting Materials." In *Ancient Egyptian Materials and Technology*, edited by Paul T. Nicholson and Ian Shaw, 104–20. Cambridge: Cambridge University Press, 2000.

Lepsius, Karl Richard. *Denkmäler aus Aegypten und Aethiopien nach den Zeichnungen der von Seiner Majestät dem Koenige von Preussen, Friedrich Wilhelm IV., nach diesen Ländern gesendeten, und in den Jahren 1842–1845 ausgeführten wissenschaftlichen Expedition auf Befehl Seiner Majestät.* Berlin: Nicolaische Buchhandlung, 1849–59.

Letronne, Jean-Antoine. *Recueil des inscriptions grecques et latines de l'Égypte* 2. Paris: Imprimerie Royale, 1848.

Lucas, Alfred. *Ancient Egyptian Materials and Industries.* London: Edward Arnold & Co., 2003.

Manley, Deborah, and Sahar Abdel-Hakim. *Traveling through Egypt: From 450 B.C. to the Twentieth Century.* Cairo: American University in Cairo Press, 2004.

Manley, Deborah, and Peta Rée. *Henry Salt: Artist, Traveller, Diplomat, Egyptologist.* London: Libri, 2001.

Marchetti, Francesco. "Alessandro Ricci da Siena e la sua collezione a Dresda." MA thesis, University of Pisa, 2004.

Marinescu, Adrian. "The Hierarchs' Catalogue of Monastery St. Catherine in Mount Sinai." *Études byzantines et post-byzantines* 4 (2001): 267–89. http://www.orththeol.uni-muenchen. de/personen/professoren/marinescu/publ-marinescu.pdf

Marro, Giovanni. *Il corpo epistolare di Bernardino Drovetti ordinato ed illustrato*. Rome: Reale Società di Geografia d'Egitto, 1940.

Mayerson, Philip. "An Inscription in the Monastery of St. Catherine and the Martyr Tradition in Sinai." *Dumbarton Oaks Papers* 30 (1976): 375–79.

Mazuel, Jean. *L'Oeuvre Géographique de Linant de Bellefonds: Étude de Géographie Historique*. Cairo: Société Royale de Géographie d'Égypte, 1937.

McGregor, Andrew J. *A Military History of Modern Egypt: From the Ottoman Conquest to the Ramadan War*. Westport: Praeger Security International, 2006.

Meinardus, Otto F.A. *Monks and Monasteries of the Egyptian Deserts*. Cairo: American University in Cairo Press, 1992.

Menconi, Gasparo. *Notizie compendiate di Egitto di Gasparo Menconi di Lucca*. Lucca: Benedini e Rocchi, 1820.

Mengin, Félix. *Histoire de l'Égypte sous le gouvernement de Mohammed-Aly: ou, Récit des événemens politiques et militaires qui ont eu lieu depuis le départ des Français jusqu'en 1823*. Paris: A. Bertrand, 1823.

Ministry of State for Environmental Affairs, South Sinai Governorate. *South Sinai Environment and Development Profile*. Cairo: n.d. (before 2003). www.eeaa.gov.eg/english/reports/seam/e1_12.pdf

Minutoli, Johann H.K.M. von. *Reise zum Tempel des Jupiter Ammon in der Libyschen Wüste und nach Ober-Aegypten in den Jahren 1820 und 1821, nach den Tagebüchern Sr. Excellenz herausgegeben und mit Beilagen begleitet von Dr. E.H. Toelken*. Berlin: Rücker, 1824.

Monge, Gaspard. "Observations sur la fontaine de Moïse." In *Description de l'Égypte, État Moderne*, 1:409–12. Paris: Imprimerie Impériale, 1809.

Mouton, Jean-Michel. "Les musulmans à Sainte-Catherine au Moyen Âge." In *Le Sinaï durant l'antiquité et le Moyen Âge: 4000 ans d'histoire pour un désert. Actes du colloque "Sinaï" qui s'est tenu à l'Unesco du 19 au 21 septembre 1997*, edited by Dominique Valbelle and Charles Bonnet, 177–82. Paris: Errance, 1998.

Murray, George W. *Sons of Ishmael: A Study of the Egyptian Bedouin*. Cairo: Farid Atiya Press, 2012 [original edition London: Routledge, 1935].

National Trust Collections. "Stele. National Trust Inventory Number 1257709." http://www.nationaltrustcollections.org.uk/object/1257709

Newberry, Percy E. *El-Bersha, Part I (The tomb of Tehuti-hetep)*. London: Egypt Exploration Fund, 1895.

Newitt, Malyn D.D. *A History of Portuguese Overseas Expansion, 1400–1668*. New York: Routledge, 2005.

Nicholls, W. *The Shaikiya: An Account of the Shaikiya Tribes and of the History of Dongola Province from the XIVth to the XIXth Century*. Dublin: Hodges, Figgis & Co., 1913.

Pamminger, Peter. "Amun und Luxor: Der Widder und das Kultbild." *Beiträge zur Sudanforschung* 5 (1992): 93–138.

Parker, Melissa. "Rethinking Female Circumcision." *Africa: Journal of the International African Institute* 65, no. 4 (1995): 506–23.

Parkinson, Richard B., and Patricia Usick. "The History of the Nebamun Wall Paintings: An Archival Investigation." In *The Nebamun Wall Paintings: Conservation, Scientific Analysis and Display at the British Museum*, edited by Andrew Middleton and Ken Uprichard, 5–15. London: Archetype Publications, 2008.

Pearce, Susan M. "Giovanni Battista Belzoni's Exhibition of the Reconstructed Tomb of Pharaoh Seti I in 1821." *Journal of the History of Collections* 12, no. 1 (2000): 109–25.

Percy, Algernon (Baron Prudhoe, Duke of Northumberland). "Extracts from Private Memoranda Kept by Lord Prudhoe on a Journey from Cairo to Sennar, in 1829, Describing the Peninsula of Sennar." *Journal of the Royal Geographical Society of London* 5 (1835): 38–58.

Pinon, Pierre. "L'Orient de Jean Nicolas Huyot: le voyage en Asie-Mineure, en Égypte et en Grèce (1817–1821)." *Revue du monde musulman et de la Méditerranée* 73–74 (1994): 35–55.

Pococke, Richard. *A Description of the East and Some Other Countries*. Part 1, *Observations on Egypt*. London: W. Boyer, 1743.

Porter, Bertha, and Rosalind L.B. Moss. *Topographical Bibliography of Ancient Egyptian Hieroglyphic Texts, Reliefs, and Paintings*. Vol. 1, *The Theban Necropolis*. Part 1, *Private Tombs*. Oxford: Clarendon Press, 1960.

———. *Topographical Bibliography of Ancient Egyptian Hieroglyphic Texts, Reliefs, and Paintings*. Vol. 1, *The Theban Necropolis*, Part 2, *Royal Tombs and Smaller Cemeteries*. Oxford: Griffith Institute, Ashmolean Museum, 1999.

———. *Topographical Bibliography of Ancient Egyptian Hieroglyphic Texts, Reliefs, and Paintings*. Vol. 2, *Theban Temples*. Oxford: Clarendon Press, 1972.

———. *Topographical Bibliography of Ancient Egyptian Hieroglyphic Texts, Reliefs, and Paintings*. Vol. 3, *Memphis*. Part 1, *Abû Rawash to Abûṣîr*. Oxford: Clarendon Press, 1974.

———. *Topographical Bibliography of Ancient Egyptian Hieroglyphic Texts, Reliefs, and Paintings*. Vol. 4, *Lower and Middle Egypt*. Oxford: Oxford University Press, 1934.

———. *Topographical Bibliography of Ancient Egyptian Hieroglyphic Texts, Reliefs, and Paintings*. Vol. 5, *Upper Egypt: Sites*. Oxford: Griffith Institute, Ashmolean Museum, 1962.

———. *Topographical Bibliography of Ancient Egyptian Hieroglyphic Texts, Reliefs, and Paintings*. Vol. 6, *Upper Egypt: Chief Temples*. Oxford: Griffith Institute, Ashmolean Museum, 1991.

———. *Topographical Bibliography of Ancient Egyptian Hieroglyphic Texts, Reliefs, and Paintings*. Vol. 7, *Nubia, the Deserts, and Outside Egypt*. Oxford: Griffith Institute, Ashmolean Museum, 1995.

Rabinowitz, Dan. "Themes in the Economy of the Bedouin of South Sinai in the Nineteenth and Twentieth Centuries." *International Journal of Middle East Studies* 17, no. 2 (1985): 211–28.

Reid, Donald Malcolm. *Whose Pharaohs? Archaeology, Museums, and Egyptian National Identity from Napoleon to World War I*. Berkeley and Los Angeles: University of California Press, 1997.

Rifaat Pasha, Mohamed. *The Awakening of Modern Egypt*. Cairo: The Palm Press, 2005.

Robinson, Arthur E. "The Conquest of the Sudan by the Wali of Egypt, Muhammad Ali Pasha, 1820–1824." [Part I.] *Journal of the Royal African Society* 25, no. 97 (1925): 47–58.

———. "The Conquest of the Sudan by the Wali of Egypt, Muhammad Ali Pasha, 1820–1824. Part II." *Journal of the Royal African Society* 25, no. 98 (1926): 164–82.

———. "Some Notes on the Regalia of the Fung Sultans of Sennar." *Journal of the Royal African Society* 30, no. 121 (1931): 361–76.

Rosati, Gloria. "Alessandro Ricci." In *Il Nilo sui Lungarni: Ippolito Rosellini, egittologo dell'Ottocento*, edited by Maria Cristina Guidotti, 39–42. Pisa: Nistri-Lischi and Pacini Editori, 1982.

Rosellini, Ippolito. *Monumenti dell'Egitto e della Nubia: Monumenti Civili*. Pisa: Niccolò Capurro, 1832–36.

———. *Monumenti dell'Egitto e della Nubia: Monumenti del Culto*. Pisa: Niccolò Capurro, 1844.

———. *Monumenti dell'Egitto e della Nubia: Monumenti Storici*. Pisa: Niccolò Capurro, 1832–41.

Salah Abd al-Malik, Sami. "Les mosquées du Sinaï au Moyen Âge." In *Le Sinaï durant l'antiquité et le Moyen Âge: 4000 ans d'histoire pour un désert. Actes du colloque "Sinaï" qui s'est tenu à l'Unesco du 19 au 21 septembre 1997*, edited by Dominique Valbelle and Charles Bonnet, 171–76. Paris: Errance, 1998.

Saltini, Guglielmo Enrico. *Giuseppe Angelelli pittore toscano, ricordo biografico*. Florence: F. Bencini, 1866.

Salvoldi, Daniele. "Alessandro Ricci's Travel Account: Story and Content of His Journal Lost and Found." *Egitto e Vicino Oriente* 32 (2009): 113–19.

———. *Catalogue of William John Bankes (1786–1855): Egyptian Drawings*. Dorchester: Dorset History Centre, 2011. https://www.dorsetforyou.gov.uk/libraries-history-culture/dorset-history-centre/dorset-history-centre.aspx

———. "The Catalogue of William John Bankes' Egyptian Portfolio (1815–1822)." *Bulletin of the Association for the Study of Travel in Egypt and the Near East* 51 (2012): 20.

———. "New Sources on the Life and Death of Domenico Enegildo Frediani (1783–1823), Traveller and Poet in Egypt and the Sudan." *Göttinger Miszellen* 233 (2012): 51–67.

———. "Per una stima in termini di valuta contemporanea delle spese sostenute dai pionieri dell'Egittologia britannica." In *Sotto l'ala di Thot: Un contributo alla diffusione della cultura dell'antico Egitto*, edited by Gilberto Modonesi, 93–104. Milan: Museo di Storia Naturale, 2012.

———. "Representations of Copts in Early Nineteenth-century Italian Travel Accounts." In *Studies in Coptic Culture: Transmission and Interaction*, edited by Mariam Ayad, 117–41. Cairo: The American University in Cairo Press, 2016.

———. "Ricci, Belzoni, Salt and the Works in the Valley of the Kings: New Light from the Ricci Travel Account." In *L'Egitto in Età Ramesside: Atti del Convegno, Chianciano Terme, 17–18 Dicembre 2009*, edited by Daniela Picchi, 33–41. Cinisello Balsamo: Silvana Editoriale, 2011.

———. "A Treasure House of Egyptology: The Catalogue of William John Bankes' Egyptian Portfolio (1815–1822)." *National Trust Arts, Buildings, Collections Bulletin* (Summer 2012): 11–12.

Salvoldi, Daniele, and Simon Delvaux. "The Lost Chapels of Elephantine: Preliminary Results of a Reconstruction Study through Archival Documents." In *Proceedings of the XI International Congress of Egyptologists, Florence, Italy, 23–30 August 2015*, edited by Gloria Rosati and Maria Cristina Guidotti, 552–58. Oxford: Archaeopress, 2017.

Sammarco, Angelo. "Alessandro Ricci da Siena e il suo giornale dei viaggi recentemente scoperto." *Bulletin de la Société Royale de Géographie d'Égype* 17 (1929): 293–326.

———. *Alessandro Ricci e il suo giornale dei viaggi*. Vol. 2. *Documenti inediti o rari*. Cairo: Société Royale de Géographie d'Égypte, 1930.

———. "Ippolito Rosellini e Alessandro Ricci da Siena." In *Studi in Memoria di Ippolito Rosellini nel primo centenario della morte*, edited by Evaristo Breccia, 107–16. Pisa: V. Lischi, 1949.

Sammarco, Angelo, and Ernesto Verrucci Bey. *Il contributo degli italiani ai progressi scientifici e pratici della medicina in Egitto sotto il regno di Mohammed Ali*. Cairo: Société Royale de Géographie d'Égypte, 1928.

Sanacore, Massimo. *Francesco Spannocchi governatore di Livorno tra Sette e Ottocento*. Livorno: Debatte, 2007.

Savary de Brèves, François. *Relation des voyages de Monsieur de Brèves, tant en Grèce, Terre Saincte et Aegypte qu'aux royaumes de Tunis et Arger, ensemble un traicté faict l'an 1604 entre le roy Henry le Grand et l'empereur des Turcs, et trois discours dudit sieur, le tout recueilly par le S.D.C.* [Jacques Du Castel]. Paris: N. Gasse, 1628.

Schulenburg-Minutoli, Wolfradine A.L. *Mes souvenirs d'Égypte*. Paris: Nepveu, 1826.

Shinnie, Margaret. *Linant de Bellefonds, Journal d'un Voyage à Meroe dans les années 1821–1822*. Khartoum: Antiquities Service Occasional Papers, 1958.

Silvano, Flora. *La Collezione Picozzi*. Pisa: ETS, 1996.

———. "Memorie d'Egitto a Pisa." In *La Piramide e la Torre: Duecento anni di archeologia egiziana*, edited by Edda Bresciani, 165–207. Pisa: Cassa di Risparmio di Pisa, 2000.

Silva White, Arthur. *From Sphinx to Oracle: Through the Libyan Desert to the Oasis of Jupiter Ammon*. London: Hurst and Blackett, 1899.

Silvera, Alain. "The First Egyptian Student Mission to France under Muhammad Ali." *Middle Eastern Studies* 16 (1980): 1–22.

Sonnini de Manoncourt, Charles N.S. *Travels in Upper and Lower Egypt*. London: John Stockdale, 1799.

Spaulding, Jay. "The Government of Sinnar." *The International Journal of African Historical Studies* 6 (1973): 19–35.

Stanley, C.V.B. "The Oasis of Siwa." *Journal of the Royal African Society* 11, no. 43 (1912): 290–324.

Steindorff, Georg. "Ein ägyptisches Grab in Siwa." *Zeitschrift für Ägyptische Sprache und Altertumskunde* 61 (1926): 94–98.

Stone, Michael E. "Sinai Armenian Inscriptions." *The Biblical Archaeologist* 45 (1982): 27–31.

Strudwick, Nigel, and John Taylor. *The Theban Necropolis: Past, Present and Future.* London: The British Museum Press, 2003.

Taylor, John H. *Death and the Afterlife in Ancient Egypt.* London: The British Museum Press, 2001.

———. *Egyptian Coffins.* Princes Risborough: Shire Publications Ltd., 1989.

Thompson, Jason. *Sir Gardner Wilkinson and His Circle.* Austin: University of Texas Press, 1992.

Toledano, Ehud R. "The Imperial Eunuchs of Istanbul: From Africa to the Heart of Islam." *Middle Eastern Studies* 20, no. 3 (1984): 379–90.

Usick, Patricia. *Adventures in Egypt and Nubia: The Travels of William John Bankes (1786–1855).* London: The British Museum Press, 2002.

———. "Berth under the Highest Stars: Henry William Beechey in Egypt 1816–1819." In *Egypt through the Eyes of Travellers*, edited by Paul G. Starkey and Nadia El Kholy, 13–24. Cambridge: ASTENE, 2002.

———. "The Egyptian Drawings of Alessandro Ricci in Florence: A List of Drawings from a Portfolio in the Museo Egizio di Firenze." *Göttinger Miszellen* 162 (1998): 73–92.

———. "The First Excavation of Wadi Halfa (Buhen)." In *Studies on Ancient Egypt in Honour of H.S. Smith*, edited by Anthony Leahy and John Tait, 331–36. London: Egypt Exploration Society, 1999.

———. "Not the Travel Journal of Alessandro Ricci." In *Studies in Egyptian Antiquities: A Tribute to T.G.H. James*, edited by Vivian W. Davies, 115–21. London: The British Museum Press, 1999.

Valbelle, Dominique, and Charles Bonnet. *Le sanctuaire d'Hathor maîtresse de la turquoise: Sérabit el-Khadim au Moyen Empire.* Paris: Picard, 1996.

Vercoutter, Jean. "Journal d'un voyage en Basse Nubie de Linant de Bellefonds." *Bulletin de la Société Française d'Égyptologie* 37–38 (1963): 39–64.

———. "Journal d'un voyage en Basse Nubie de Linant de Bellefonds (suite)." *Bulletin de la Société Française d'Égyptologie* 41 (1964): 23–32.

Verdery, Richard N. "The Publications of the Bulaq Press under Muhammad 'Ali of Egypt." *Journal of the American Oriental Society* 91 (1971): 129–32.

Verrucci Bey, Ernesto, and Angelo Sammarco. *Il contributo degl'Italiani ai progressi scientifici e pratici della medicina in Egitto sotto il regno di Mohammed Ali: Ricerche e documenti inediti a cura di E. Verrucci Bey e A. Sammarco.* Cairo: Tip. A. Lencioni & Co., 1928.

Vriend, Nathalie M., Melany L. Hunt, Robert W. Clayton, Christopher E. Brennen, Catherine S. Brantley, and Angel Ruiz-Angulo. "Solving the Mystery of Booming Sand Dunes." *Geophysical Research Letters* 34 (2007). doi: 10.1029/2007GL030276

Waddington, George, and Barnard Hanbury. *Journal of a Visit to Some Parts of Ethiopia.* London: John Murray, 1822.

Weber, Felicitas. "Der Totenbuchpapyrus des Anch-ef-en-Amun aus Dresden (Aeg. 775)." MA thesis, Rheinische Friedrich-Wilhelms-Universität Bonn, 2012.

Weigall, Rachel. *Correspondence of Lord Burghersh Afterwards Eleventh Earl of Westmorland, 1808–1840*. London: John Murray, 1912.

Weill, Raymond. *Recueil des inscriptions égyptiennes du Sinaï*. Paris: Société nouvelle de librairie et d'édition, 1904.

Weitzmann, Kurt. "The Mosaic in St. Catherine's Monastery on Mount Sinai." *Proceedings of the American Philosophical Society* 110, no. 6 (1966): 392–405.

Zahran, Mahmoud A.K., and Arthur J. Willis. *The Vegetation of Egypt*. New York: Springer Publishing, 2009.

Zangheri, Luigi. *Feste e apparati nella Toscana dei Lorena, 1737–1859*. Florence: L.S. Olshki, 1996.

Zatterin, Marco. *Il gigante del Nilo: Storia e avventure del Grande Belzoni*. Bologna: Il Mulino, 2008.

Ziegler, Christiane, Hervé Champollion, and Diane Harlé. *L'Égypte de Jean-François Champollion: Lettres et journaux de voyage (1828–1829)*. Paris: Jean-Paul Mangès, 1989.

Index

Henniker, Sir Frederick 32

Hermopolitan Ogdoad depictions 101, *192*, **358–59**

hieroglyphs: color of *189*, 189n98; copying of 8, 26, 35, 47, 58, 75; decipherment of 7–8, 16, 52, *185*; Ricci's talent in copying 15, 23, 24. *See also* inscriptions, hieroglyphic

homosexuality 31

Hor, stela of 92, *182*, **340**

Horeb, Mount *237–38*

Horus, temple of 90–91, *180*, **338**

Horus depictions 89, 95, 99, 120, *173*, *191*, *260*, **333, 346, 354, 393**

hot springs 33, *225–26*

houses and furnishings: *angaribs* (beds) *293*, 293n344; at Berber *291–93*; headrests 66, *310*; *mashrabiya* (balcony) *164*, 164n6. *See also* customs and practices

hunting depictions 86, 128, *172*, **329**. *See also* fishing depictions

hunting observations *181–82*

Huyot, Jean-Nicolas 26, 52, *173*, 173n38

Hyde, John 15, 27, 32, 33, *174*, 174n40, *175*

Hyksos (Shepherds) *228*

Ibrahim Pasha: in Aswan *256*; character of *314*, *316–17*; in command of support expedition 39, *248*, 248n223; and Franco-Tuscan Expedition 56; health of 45, 46–47, *309–10*, *312*; and intrigues at court 48–49; on return journey from Sennar 46–47, *317–18*; with Ricci taken as physician *301–302*, *303–304*; in search of Nile source *306–309*; visit to Italy by 5. *See also* Sennar military expedition

Ibrim *260–61*

illnesses *see* sicknesses

inscriptions, GREEK: at Abu Simbel *185*, 185n76; at Elephantine 117, *254–55*, **384**; at Jebel al-Dakrur 102–103; at Sinai 106–107; at St. Catherine's Monastery 34, 106, 111–12, *235*, 235n191, *240*, 240n210

———, HIEROGLYPHIC: in cartouches 137, **429**; at Elephantine 117–18, *255*, **383**; at Giza 130–31, **423**; at al-Hammam 103, *194*; at Jebel Barkal 123, *284*, **402**; at Kanays 84; at al-Maghara 107–10, *228*, **365–67, 369**; at Serabit al-Khadim 35, 112–15, *246*, *247*, **374–77, 378**; in Sinai 32; in tomb of Ramesses III 85, **326**; at Tombos **396**; at Umm al-Ubayda *214*; from various sources 137, **430**; at Wadi Hibran *243*

———, NABATAEAN 109, **364, 369**

———, VARIOUS *190*; at al-Hammam 103, *194*; in Sinai 106–107; at Wadi Aliyat *232*; at Wadi Mukattab 33, *227*, 227n177

Isis, temples of: at Buhen 91, *181*, **338**; at Dabod 99, *190*, **353**; at Philae 99–101, *191–92*,

354–56, **358–61**; at Qurta 98, *188–89*

Isis depictions 96, 99, 100–101, *191–92*, **346–47, 354, 356**

Isma *280*

Isma'il Pasha: abuse of natives by 49, *278*, *291*; in command of military expedition 38–39; conquest of Dar al-Shaiqiya by *278–81*; in Dongola *272*; governors appointed by *292*, *296*; in Sennar *301*, *302*, *303*; south of Sennar *308*, *309*; storied defeat of magicians by *275*. *See also* Sennar military expedition

Iuclep (guide in Sinai) *223*, 223n170

Iusas depictions 94–95, *184*, **344**

jalaba (trade caravan) *see* caravans

Jebel Adda 92, *182*, **340**

Jebel al-Dakrur 102–103, *202*, 202n127

Jebel al-Kabrit *226–27*

Jebel al-Mawta 102, *201–202*, 201n123

Jebel al-Shams ("Mashaket") 92, *182*, **340**

Jebel al-Tayr 37–38, *250*, 250n226

Jebel Barkal 42, 121–27, *281–86*, **397–417**; chapels at 122–25, *282*, 319n[o], **398, 400–406, 411**; pedestals at 124, *284*, **402–403, 407**; pyramids at 121–24, *282–83*, **398**; site plan of 121, *284*, *286*, 286n339, **397**; temples at 122–27, *283–85*, 283nn328–331, 284nn333–334, **399, 408–17**

Jebel Musa 110–11

Jebel Naqus 35

Jebel Safsafa 106, 111, *238–39*, 238n203, 239n204

Jebel Silsila 116, **381**

Jebel Tahuna 34, *231–32*, 232n184

jewelry: in Dresden Collection 64; in Siwa *210*, 210nn142–143; of Towara tribe *230*

Jomard, Edme-François 29–30, 31

judgment of the dead 124, **406**

Jupiter-Amun, Temple of (Umm al-Ubayda) 103–106, *213–15*, **357, 362–63**. *See also* Siwa Expedition

Justinian, Emperor *234*, 234n189, *241*, 241n215

al-Kab *176*, 176n50, *253*

Kababish tribe 298n351

kabir (caravan head) *318n[d]*

Kalabsha *189–90*, 189n97, *257*

Kanays 84, *170*, **325**

kashif 27, 28, *251*

Kerma *270*, 270n288

Khamisa *204*, 204n132

Khanag *274*, 274n297

Khandaq *275*, 275n300

Khentekhtai depictions 114, **377**

Khety, tomb of 86, *172*, **329**

Khnum, temples of 89–90, 120, *175*, *263–64*, **334–35, 394–95**